D0093248

Yesterdays

Popular Song In America

Yesterdays

Popular Song In America

CHARLES HAMM

W·W·NORTON & COMPANY
NEW YORK   LONDON

Since this page cannot legibly accommodate all the copyright notices, the Copyright Acknowledgments pages, beginning on page 504, constitute an extension of the copyright page.

Copyright © 1979 by W. W. Norton & Company, Inc.
Published simultaneously in Canada by George J. McLeod Limited,
Toronto. Printed in the United States of America.
All Rights Reserved
First Edition

Library of Congress Cataloging in Publication Data
Hamm, Charles E
Yesterdays.
Bibliography: p.
Includes index.
1. Music, Popular (Songs, etc.)—United States—History
and criticism. I. Title. II. Title: Popular
song in America.
ML3561.P6H35   784   79-12953
ISBN 0-393-01257-3

1 2 3 4 5 6 7 8 9 0

84.5
4182y

This book is dedicated to Frances, Richard, Howard, George, Noble, Alice, Margie, Vernon, Snuffie, Walter, June, Ward, Helen, Gilbert, Doug, Jadwiga, David, Bruce, Ron, Bill, Ruth, Royal, Gerard, Trixie, Chris, Ben, Laurel, Charles, Thelma, Stuart, Farwell, Ellsworth, Paul, Dennis, Mao, Marilyse, and all the others—forgotten or never known—with whom I have listened to America's popular songs over the decades.

190508

Contents

List of Illustrations   ix

Acknowledgments   xiii

Introduction   xvii

1. "Listen, Listen to the Voice of Love"; *or, British Concert and Stage
   Music in Early America*   1
2. "The Wounded Hussar"; *or, The First Songs Written in America*   26
3. "Erin, the Tear and the Smile in Thine Eyes"; *or, Thomas Moore's
   Irish Melodies in America*   42
4. "Hear Me, Norma"; *or, Bel Canto Comes to America—Italian Opera
   as Popular Song*   62
5. "The Minstrel's Return'd from the War"; *or, The First American
   Songwriters*   89
6. "Jim Crow"; *or, The Music of the Early American Minstrel Show*   109
7. "If I Were a Voice"; *or, The Hutchinson Family and Popular Song As
   Political and Social Protest*   141
8. "Come Back to Erin"; *or, More Gems from the British Isles*   162

9. "When the Swallows Homeward Fly"; *or, German Song in Nineteenth-Century America* 187

10. "Old Folks at Home"; *or, The Songs of Stephen Foster* 201

11. "All Quiet Along the Potomac"; *or, Songs of the Civil War* 228

12. "The Old Home Ain't What It Used to Be"; *or, American Song in the Postwar Years* 253

13. "After the Ball"; *or, The Birth of Tin Pan Alley* 284

14. "It's Only a Paper Moon"; *or, the Golden Years of Tin Pan Alley* 326

15. "Rock Around the Clock"; *or, the Rise of Rock 'n' Roll* 391

16. "Sympathy for the Devil"; *or, The Age of Rock* 425

Epilogue. The Seventies and Beyond 465

Appendix 1. The Most Popular Songs in America Printed before 1800 479

Appendix 2. The Most Popular Songs in America, 1801–1825 481

Appendix 3. Stephen Foster's List of Royalties Received for Various of His Songs, to 1857 483

Appendix 4. The Top-Selling Foreign Songs in America in 1870 485

Appendix 5. Top Forty: The Most Often Recorded Songs in America, 1900–1950 487

Appendix 6. *Variety* Magazine's Golden 100 Tin Pan Alley Songs, 1918–1935 489

Appendix 7. The Top Songs on "Your Hit Parade," 1935–1958 493

Bibliography 495

Copyright Acknowledgments 504

Index 507

List of Illustrations

Vauxhall Gardens	4
Thomas Arne	7
First page: "Blink oer the burn my Laddie dear"	15
Charles Dibdin	22
Benjamin Carr	28
First page: "The Little Sailor Boy"	29
James Hewitt	33
Alexander Reinagle	36
Title page: Moore's *Irish Melodies*	45
Thomas Moore	48
Maria Malibran	64
Manuel Garcia	65
Montresor and Pedrotti in *Il pirata* by Bellini	66
The Italian Opera House, 1833	67
Palmo's Opera House, 1844	68
Scene from Rossini/Lacy *Cinderella*	71
Sheet music cover: "Once a King there chanced to be"	73

Francis Hopkinson   90
First page: "Mary's Tears"   97
John Hill Hewitt   102
Charles Mathews in *Monsieur Tonson*, 1822   113
Playbill, 1821   115
Thomas Dartmouth Rice   119
Sheet music cover: "Sich a Getting Up Stairs"   119
A performance of *Jim Crow* at the American Theatre in 1833   122
Sheet music cover: "Zip Coon"   125
Cover of *The Celebrated Negro Melodies* . . . , 1843   128
Sheet music cover: "Dandy Jim from Caroline"   129
Illustration used on early printings of many Stephen Foster songs   132
The Aeolian Vocalists, 1841   143
Sheet music cover: "Get Off the Track"   151
Hutchinson Family Quartet, 1846   152
Sheet music cover: "The Song of the Shirt"   155
John Braham   163
First page: "Home Sweet Home"   166
John Howard Payne   168
Samuel Lover   174
Henry Russell   177
Sheet music cover: "Woodman! Spare That Tree!"   181
The Germania Musical Society, 1850   191
Franz Abt   196
Stephen Collins Foster   202
Sheet music cover: "Music of the Great Southern Sable Harmonists   209
Sheet music cover: "Old Folks at Home"   213
Sheet music cover: "Jeanie with the Light Brown Hair"   218
Sheet music cover: "Tramp, Tramp, Tramp"   233
Illustration for "John Brown's Body"   235
Sheet music cover: "Tenting on the Old Camp Ground"   237
Torchlight rally at High Rock, 1863   238
Sheet music cover: "I Wish I Was in Dixie's Land"   241
Sheet music cover: "Bonnie Blue Flag"   243
Illustration for "All Quiet Along the Potomac"   246
Sheet music cover: "Grand-Father's Clock"   257
Septimus Winner   259
Sheet music cover: "I'll Take You Home Again, Kathleen"   263
Will S. Hays   266
Sheet music cover: "The Old Home ain't what it used to be"   271
The Fisk Jubilee Singers, 1873   272

James A. Bland	274
Sheet music cover for James Bland songs	275
Harrigan and Hart in "The Mulligan Guard"	280
Sheet music cover: "After the Ball"	286
Tony Pastor's Opera House, 1881	288
Sheet music cover: "In the Good Old Summer Time"	295
Charles K. Harris	298
Sheet music cover: "Break the News to Mother"	301
Paul Dresser	303
Sheet music cover: "My Gal Sal"	304
Sheet music cover: "A Bird in a Gilded Cage"	311
George M. Cohan on the cover of "Give My Regards to Broadway"	314
Sheet music cover: "Over There"	315
Sheet music cover: "Bill Bailey, Won't You Please Come Home?"	320
Sheet music cover: "Sweet Adeline"	324
Irving Berlin, Ed Wynn, and Sam H. Harris, 1917	330
Sheet music cover: "Alexander's Ragtime Band"	331
Bing Crosby in Holiday Inn, 1942	335
Jerome Kern on the set of Caribbean Holiday, 1950	342
Sheet music cover: "Can't Help Lovin' Dat Man"	344
George Gershwin	347
Al Jolson singing "Swanee"	348
Fred and Adele Astaire in Lady, Be Good!	349
"Begin the Beguine" from Jubilee	353
Sheet music cover: "People Will Say We're in Love"	354
Harold Arlen	356
Vernon and Irene Castle	380
Vincent Lopez and his Pennsylvania Hotel Orchestra	381
Frank Sinatra and Tommy Dorsey	386
Bing Crosby, the Andrews Sisters, and Irving Berlin	388
Bill Haley and the Comets	393
Chuck Berry	395
Elvis Presley	398
Presley at a recording session	405
"Fats" Domino	409
The Everly Brothers	410
Frankie Avalon	413
The Beatles recording for EMI	418
The Beatles in concert	422
Burl Ives	427
Harry Belafonte	429

The Kingston Trio   430
Bob Dylan and Joan Baez   432
The Byrds   437
Jefferson Airplane   441
The Beatles costumed for *Sgt. Pepper* . . .   444
Mick Jagger and the Rolling Stones   446
Bob Dylan   447
Simon and Garfunkel   449
Scene from the rock opera *Tommy*   450
Janis Joplin   452
Woodstock, August 16, 1969   454
Ray Charles   459
Diana Ross and the Supremes, backed by the Temptations   461
Smokey Robinson   461
Marvin Gaye   461
Neil Diamond   467
Elton John   468
James Taylor   468
Billy Joel   468
Bruce Springsteen   468
Willie Nelson   470
Stevie Wonder   471
Earth, Wind, and Fire   471
Barbra Streisand   473

Acknowledgments

Though I had wanted to write this book for a good part of my life, the impetus for starting it was a conversation with Claire Brook at a cocktail party in Philadelphia. She has been my editor, advisor, and consultant at every stage; the book would not have come about without her.

Dale Cockrell gave invaluable assistance in the final stages, in reading the typescript, offering most valuable suggestions and even more concrete assistance, and talking about the subject whenever I wanted or needed an ear. He also did most of the thankless work of putting footnotes, bibliography, and music examples in final shape.

Richard Jackson at the Lincoln Center branch of the New York Public Library was always helpful, as were others at the many libraries I visited in my decades-long examination of sheet music.

"At last we have found it!" exclaimed we, some nights since, at the conclusion of the performance by the Cheney Family, in Niblo's saloon. . . . This, said we in our heart, is the true method which must become popular in the United States—which must supplant the stale, second-hand, foreign method, with its flourishes, its ridiculous sentimentality, its anti-republican spirit, and its syncophantic influence, tainting the young taste of the republic.

—Walt Whitman, *Broadway Journal*, Volume II, November 29, 1845

I cannot sing the old songs I sung long years ago,
For heart and voice would fail me, and foolish tears would flow;
　For bygone hours come o'er my heart,
　With each familiar strain,
I cannot sing the old songs, or dream those dreams again.

　　　　　　　　　　　　　　　　　　　—Claribel

Make songs for the poor, and you plant roses among the weeds.

　　　　　　　　　　　　　　　　　　—Ned Harrigan

As soon as the tubes warmed up, the music of stringed instruments sounded, and then the low passionate voice of Obukhova flowed into the quiet room:

"No, it's not you whom I love so passionately,
Not for me the radiance of your beauty. . . ."

It had to be that song—as though on purpose! Nerzhin fumbled for the knob, trying to turn off the set without being observed. . . . Only when the song came to an end did Nerzhin increase the volume. But the next one was no better:

"You will forget me quickly. . . ."

When that song was over, the fateful mysterious voice came back once more, returning to the same open wound:

"When you say farewell to me,
Tie my shawl around me tight."

Obukhova kept on singing, tormenting the heart:

"All is unpleasant, all is repulsive,
I keep on suffering for him. . . ."

Ah, there was no law of probability involved! It was simply that all songs—a thousand years ago, a hundred years ago, or three hundred years in the future—were, and would be, about one and the same thing. Parting requires songs; when you meet, there are better things to do!

　　　　　　　—Aleksandr I. Solzhenitsyn, *The First Circle*

I believe my music can make the blind see, the lame walk, the deaf and dumb hear and talk. . . . it regenerates the heart and makes the liver quiver, the bladder splatter, the knees freeze.

　　　　　　—Little Richard (Penniman), *The Rolling Stone Interviews*

Introduction

Popular song in America has a continuous, unbroken, and coherent history of some two hundred years. The thesis of this book is that any single chapter of this history, most certainly including the recent ones, is best understood in the context of the entire story.

I define *popular song* as a piece of music that is

written for, and most often performed by, a single voice or a small group of singers, accompanied by either a single chord-playing instrument or some sort of band, ensemble, or small orchestra;

usually first performed and popularized in some form of secular stage entertainment, and afterward consumed (performed or listened to) in the home;

composed and marketed with the goal of financial gain;

designed to be performed by and listened to by persons of limited musical training and ability; and

produced and disseminated in physical form—as sheet music in its early history, and in various forms of mechanical reproduction in the twentieth century.

This definition was arrived at after the fact, after I had grasped that popular song had a character and history distinct from that of any other kind of music. The definition embraces the songs of such figures as James Hook, Oliver Shaw, John Hill Hewitt, Henry Russell, Thomas Moore, Dan Emmett, Stephen Foster, Septimus Winner, Charles K. Harris, James Bland, Harry von Tilzer, Paul Dresser, George M. Cohan, Irving Berlin, Jerome Kern, Cole Porter, George Gershwin, Chuck Berry, Bob Dylan, Paul Simon, the Beatles, Elton John, the Rolling Stones, Dolly Parton, Patti Smith, and Bruce Springsteen. It excludes the music of William Billings, which is for vocal ensemble; Child ballads and other traditional Anglo-American songs, which were transmitted in oral tradition; the band music of John Philip Sousa and the ragtime music of Scott Joplin and others, which is instrumental; all church music, even that for solo voice; most jazz, which is instrumental.

The exclusion of these and other kinds of music from this book—except as they exert direct influence on popular song—does not imply that they are less interesting or important than the music dealt with here, merely that they are something different. Many of them are in need of comprehensive histories, which do not confuse different bodies of music and thereby obscure the uniqueness of each.

The first problem in dealing with popular song in a historical way is the sheer quantity of material. Many thousands of songs, by dozens and often hundreds of songwriters, were written in each of the many periods comprising the history of the genre. It is a sheer impossibility to examine more than a tiny fraction of this music; and depending on how a selection is made, quite different pictures of the various eras may emerge.

This problem is not unique to popular song; scholars dealing with the sixteenth-century madrigal or the eighteenth-century symphony, to cite only two examples, must confront equally unmanageable masses of music and must develop a philosophy and a method for deciding which pieces to consider and which to leave alone.

In such situations, musicologists often resort to the concept of natural attrition and selectivity, the somewhat Darwinian theory that over a span of time the best compositions will be recognized as such by audiences, performers, critics, and other composers. Thus a scholar concerned with the string quartet of the late eighteenth and early nineteenth centuries may begin with pieces by Haydn, Mozart, and Beethoven, because everyone now knows that these were the best of their time. Even if his concern is with other composers, he will prepare himself with a thorough knowledge of the masterpieces of the literature. It is not always clear at what precise point, or by whom, these judgments were made; but few scholars or critics have challenged them for many generations.

An alternate method assumes influence as the critical factor. The history of Western music is seen as always moving, always progressing, marching forward through a succession of musical styles, each replacing an earlier style only to be replaced itself by yet another. Beethoven is seen as a central figure because so many of his innovations were taken over by successors and younger contemporaries whose pieces shaped the musical style of the later nineteenth century. Scholars then feel justified in examining the compositions of certain of Beethoven's predecessors and older contemporaries whose music had some impact on Beethoven, whether or not their music is now thought to be of the highest quality.

Some writers have let chance settle the question of selectivity, studying certain compositions and composers merely because they happened to be easily available. Still others have chosen on the basis of personal preference and taste.

Though each of these methods has some usefulness in a study of popular song, none seems an appropriate basis for the construction of a comprehensive history. I have chosen to let the subject define the method: for each era, I have attempted to identify those songs demonstrably the *most* popular, the ones listened to, bought, and performed by the largest number of Americans. These songs have then formed the skeleton for my history.

Different methods have been necessary to identify the most popular songs of the various periods of the two-hundred-year history.

A basic tool for the period up to 1800 has been *A Bibliography of Early Secular American Music*. First compiled by Oscar Sonneck (chief of the Division of Music at the Library of Congress in Washington from 1902 to 1917) and published in 1905, then revised and enlarged by William Treat Upton in 1945, it is essentially a union catalog of all items of secular music—including popular songs—preserved in those American libraries with the most important collections of American items. It is thus a random sampling of a fraction of the sheet music published in this country for this era. Assuming that this fraction is a fair reflection of the whole, I have tabulated the songs represented by the largest number of preserved copies and the most different editions, given this list as Appendix 1, and based the first several chapters on these results.

Precisely the same procedure has been possible for the period 1801–25 because of the existence of another monumental work in the bibliography of early music in America: Richard J. Wolfe's *Secular Music in America, 1801–1825*, published by the New York Public Library in 1964. A list of the most popular songs from this era is given as Appendix 2 of the present book, and again I have used tabulations from this work as the basis for deciding which songs to examine and discuss.

No such bibliographical tools are available for the period from 1825 to the end of the Civil War. I have drawn on a variety of sources for my discussions of this period, one of the most critical in the entire history of song in America. Most important was a catalog of a representative collection of sheet music from this period, done in the style of the Sonneck/Upton and Wolfe bibliographies, which I prepared with a group of students during a seminar at the University of Illinois in 1967. Also, over the last decade I have visited and used many of the largest and most important collections of American sheet music—at the New York Public Library, the American Antiquarian Society in Worcester, the Newberry

Library in Chicago (the Driscoll Collection of sheet music), Brown University, and the University of Michigan. The collection at the American Antiquarian Society has been particularly useful, since it is grouped alphabetically by composer, facilitating judgments as to which songwriters produced and published the most songs. The smaller but quite selective collections at the University of Virginia and Dartmouth College were also often helpful because of the way they have been cataloged.

Also useful were my own lists of the contents of many dozens of song anthologies, from the *American Musical Miscellany* of 1798 through *Heart Songs* of 1909. Most of these collections represent attempts to bring together the most popular songs of the decades preceding their publication, and the presence of a given song in a series of such anthologies is almost always an indication of great popularity. Happily, songs identified in this fashion are almost without exception those already on the lists compiled from Sonneck/Upton, Wolfe, and my seminar.

A particularly interesting and useful item is a list drawn up by Stephen Foster in 1857 of royalties received on each of his songs brought out by his two chief publishers, Firth, Pond & Co. of New York and F. D. Benteen in Baltimore. One of the few items giving specific figures of this sort, it is reproduced as Appendix 3.

For the last four decades of the nineteenth century, scattered data can be found to establish at least a starting point in the identification of the most successful songs—occasional advertisements by publishers mentioning sales figures for some of their songs, comments and claims by composers, biographers, and critics. Such information, where available, may be found at appropriate points in Chapters 12 and 13. Anthologies are quite useful for this period also, particularly those brought out by major publishers such as Oliver Ditson of Boston; their collections *The Silver Chord*, *The Silver Wreath*, and *Wreath of Gems* surely contain the most popular items from the Ditson catalog.

Another key item is the *Complete Catalogue of Sheet Music and Musical Works* published by the Board of Music Trade in 1870. A union catalog of every item of music then in print, by twenty of the leading music publishers of the day, it is an invaluable checklist and is particularly useful in determining which European songs were most popular in America. Since there was no effective international copyright law, any song published abroad could be brought out by any American publisher, and once again I have assumed that those songs printed by the largest number of publishers here must have been the most successful and popular items. Appendix 4 lists these.

With the centralization of the popular music industry in New York at the end of the nineteenth century, even more data are available. Early Tin Pan Alley publishers wanted the world to know of their successes; with a bit of work, one can compile a list of songs known or alleged to have sold a million or more copies and of others that approached that magic mark. It is enough to base a study of popularity for this period on sheet music sales alone, since the phonograph disc and cylinder were not yet a means of dissemination rivaling the sale of sheet music.

Curiously, one of the most difficult periods for obtaining factual data on sales of sheet music is the era of the maturity of the Tin Pan Alley style, the age of Irving Berlin, George Gershwin, Jerome Kern, Cole Porter, and friends. Everyone knows today who the great songwriters were, and which of their songs were the best; but these judgments are not necessarily based on hard facts. *Variety* magazine offered a list of the Golden 100 songs of Tin Pan Alley some years back (reproduced as Appendix 6 of the present book), but did not volunteer information as to how the list had been drawn up. Some figures are available, for some of the early songs of Irving Berlin, for instance; a search through *Variety* and *Billboard* magazines yielded bits of information; but there seems to be no way to draw up a statistically sound list of the top forty or one hundred songs for the period between the two world wars of the twentieth century.

In an attempt to get some basis for evaluation, I turned to Roger D. Kinkle's *Complete Encyclopedia of Popular Music and Jazz, 1900–1950*, a massive, four-volume compilation of data of various sorts, including lists of songs for each year and of "representative recordings" both by year and by performer. Kinkle's data were compiled in no systematic way; but it is the largest collection of song titles and recordings for the period, and thus represents some sampling of the published and recorded songs of the era. Appendix 5 is a listing of the Top Forty songs based on a simple count of the number of times each is listed anywhere in the four volumes; it makes an interesting contrast with *Variety*'s Golden 100 songs of the same period.

"Your Hit Parade," a network broadcast of the most popular songs of the week as determined by the advertising agency of Batton, Barton, Durstine, and Osborn—through a survey of various music shops in different parts of America—was first on the air on July 20, 1935. It switched to television in 1950, where it persisted until June 7, 1958. Though some concern was expressed from time to time over the method of selection, the choice of songs generally corresponds with those determined in other ways to have been the most popular—and the fact of their appearance on "Your Hit Parade" meant that they were heard by millions of Americans. John R. Williams's *This Was "Your Hit Parade"* lists the songs played on every show and summarizes the number of appearances of each; it is the best guide of popularity for the last two decades of Tin Pan Alley.

In 1940, *Billboard* magazine began publishing weekly charts of the best-selling phonograph records of popular music, based on data obtained from retail outlets and from radio stations. At first only the ten top discs were listed, but gradually the number increased to the present one hundred. A similar chart of top-selling LP albums was begun in 1945, with the five most popular LPs; the number is now two hundred. Charts of country-western and rhythm-and-blues records were begun in 1949. Since the dissemination of popular song has taken place primarily through the phonograph record since 1955, these charts are indispensable for the eras of rock 'n' roll and rock, and allow for much more precision in identifying the most popular repertory than for any earlier period.

Several recent bibliographical works facilitate a grasp of the information contained in the weekly *Billboard* charts. *Top Pop Records, 1955–1972*, compiled and edited by Joel Whitburn, lists all 45-rpm singles appearing on the charts between November 2, 1955—when the number of charted discs first increased to one hundred—and December 30, 1972, indicating how many weeks each record was in the top one hundred, and the highest position it reached. Subsequent volumes in the series treat LP albums, country-western music, "pop" records from 1940 to 1955, and rhythm-and-blues recordings in a similar manner. Also, *Rock Almanac*, compiled and edited by Charlie Gillett and Stephen Nugent, gives comparative listings of the Top Twenty single discs and LP albums of the 1950s, '60s, and '70s.

These, then, are the tools and the methods I have used to determine which were the most popular songs in America for each period of the two-hundred-year history of the genre. After obtaining copies of each song discussed or even mentioned in the present book, I've listened to each, by playing through it at the piano, sometimes by having friends sing it, or by listening to recordings, when available. While much of the historical and bibliographical material is taken from other sources, the comments on songs—individually or collectively—and judgments on their quality are completely my own.

I have let this history shape itself. Chapter divisions correspond to stylistic changes in the popular-song repertory. Mention of general historical, social, and cultural events in the course of American history has been made only as such things are relevant to the story being told here. I hope the history of popular song will be of interest and even relevance to historians of other aspects of American history and culture; the chances of this happening would be increased, I believe, if my history proceeds along its own course rather than following already charted paths.

The proportions of this book reflect my desire to give full coverage to each phase of the two-hundred-year history of popular song in America. My first instinct was to devote relatively more space to the most recent eras, since so much material is readily available, and the songs are best known and remembered today. But as I learned more about the earlier songwriters, their times, and their product, I began to see that each era had its unique points of interest and relevance, its own songs of quality and appeal. If the balance has therefore swung a bit the other way, this results from my realization that the earlier portions of the history have been little understood in the twentieth century.

It would be impossible, and irresponsible, for a history covering so much ground and material to avoid generalizations. I believe these have been made on the basis of a knowledge of the material under discussion, and only when a more detailed explanation of a specific subject would be inappropriate in a book of the dimensions of this one.

Yesterdays

Popular Song In America

ONE

"Listen, Listen to the Voice of Love";
OR,
British Concert and Stage Music in Early America

POPULAR SONG, as defined in the introduction to this book, had its important beginnings in America only after the Revolution.

There is scattered evidence of solo secular song in the late colonial period. Educated, cultivated men such as Thomas Jefferson are known to have owned song collections printed in England, and to have performed from them in their own homes; songs were often included on concerts, and were performed in operas and as interpolations in spoken dramas. But none of this music was printed on this side of the Atlantic before the 1770s, and the only publications concerned with this repertory were a number of songsters (collections of texts, without music) such as *The American Mock-Bird* (1760) and *The American Cock Robin* (1764).[1] The publication of music in the colonies was confined to collections of psalms, hymns, spiritual songs, and anthems, by British composers and such American musical pioneers as William Billings.

The first secular songs published in America appeared as insertions in journals. "The Hill Tops. A new hunting song," for instance, was printed in the April 1774 issue of *The Royal American Magazine* (Boston), and "General

1. Irving Lowens, *A Bibliography of Songsters Printed in America before 1821* (Worcester, Massachusetts: American Antiquarian Society, 1976). The single trace of published secular music for

Wolfe," a poem "Set to music by a gentleman of this country" appeared in the March 1775 issue of *The Pennsylvania Magazine* (Philadelphia). This practice was continued in the late 1780s and early 1790s in such journals as *The Boston Magazine*, *The Columbia Magazine*, *The Universal Asylum*, and particularly *The Massachusetts Magazine* (Boston).

Francis Hopkinson's *Seven Songs for the Harpsichord* was brought out in Philadelphia in 1788 by J. Dobson, and *A Collection of Favourite Songs, Arranged for the voice and pianoforte by A. Reinagle* followed the next year. These were the first separate publications of solo secular songs in America, and Reinagle's collection in particular was a landmark in the history of song in this country: its four volumes contained some sixty songs by British composers, and a dozen of these were also printed and sold as single pieces of sheet music. Within a year or two, numerous publishers in various American cities and towns were issuing sheet music in a similar format, with the melody and its text occupying the top line and a figured bass (the bass line of the song, fitted with figures to indicate what chords were intended), the lower. It was part of the job of the accompanist to realize these chords at the keyboard, with appropriate figurations for the right hand.

There were at least two reasons why the publication of secular songs did not begin in the new country until the very end of the 1780s.

On the first Wednesday in March of 1789, the Constitution of the United States of America became the law of the land, having been ratified by the requisite nine states. Article I, Section 8 of the Constitution and the Fifth Amendment laid the legal foundation for the first national copyright act, passed in 1790, protecting books and similar materials (including printed music) for fourteen years, with the possibility of renewal for another fourteen.

Also in 1789, the ban on theatrical activities in force since the war was lifted. The Continental Congress had declared in Philadelphia on October 16, 1778, that since "frequenting Play Houses and theatrical entertainments, has a fatal tendency to divert the minds of people from a due attention to the means necessary for the defence of their country and preservation of their liberties," all such events would be banned. This ban had been a severe limitation on secular music in America, making it impossible for songs to be brought to the attention of potential customers through public performances, as was the custom in England at this time.

But with copyright protection and secular performances again possible in 1789, active music publishers sprang up in all major American cities and some

---

solo voice with keyboard accompaniment before the 1770s is a note in *Rivington's New York Gazette* for October of 1763 announcing the publication of

> *Clio and Euterpe*, a collection of celebrated songs and cantatas, set to musick by the most approved masters. With a thorough bass for the harpsichord . . . containing near 600 airs.

But no copies have been recovered, and it may well have been a "ghost" title, an announcement of a publication contemplated but never realized.

smaller towns.[2] They brought out many hundreds of songs, offered for sale at their own stores and also at retail outlets up and down the Atlantic seaboard.

A look at a list of the forty most successful of these songs sold in America in the 1790s (see Appendix 1) leads to three immediate conclusions: (1) the songs are all by English composers, by foreign composers active in London, or by English-born or English-trained musicians who had come to America; (2) the most widely represented composer is a certain James Hook, with ten songs out of the forty; (3); the songs were mostly written for one or another of the various pleasure gardens of London, or for ballad or comic operas.

Thus the story of popular song in America must begin in the pleasure gardens and theaters of London.

Londoners were in the habit of frequenting garden areas in and near the city in the seventeenth century. As early as the 1660s Samuel Pepys wrote of going to Spring Gardens for the waters and for walks. The British came to these privately owned gardens to enjoy the arbors, hedges, fruit trees, and the birds, particularly the nightingales, found there in such profusion. Addison wrote of a visit in the spring of 1712:

> We were now arrived at Spring Garden, which is exquisitely pleasant at this time of year. When I considered the fragrancy of the walks and bowers, with the choirs of birds that sung upon the trees, and the loose tribe of people that walked under their shades, I could not but look upon the place as a kind of Mahometan Paradise.[3]

By the third and fourth decades of the eighteenth century, the number of gardens had multiplied greatly. There were gardens connected with mineral springs, small tea gardens, and quite large ones. The season lasted from the first spell of good weather in the spring through September. The larger gardens often numbered "people of rank" among their customers, but anyone was admitted who had the price of admission (usually a shilling) and would conduct himself properly. There were hundreds of customers on good days, often thousands at the larger gardens. There were merchants, aldermen, apprentices, sempstresses, small shopkeepers. There were also pickpockets, purse snatchers, prostitutes, and "rogues and galants," as well as guards and patrols to protect respectable customers from these latter types. In addition to the natural beauty of these spots and the diversion offered by observing other patrons, there was food and beverage, as well as fireworks and other spectacles on special days.

Music was offered as early as the turn of the century; there is mention of

2. Philadelphia—B. and J. Carr, G. Willig, Dunlap & Claypoole; New York—B. Carr, G. Gilfert, J. Hewitt, J. and M. Paff; Boston—W. P. Blake, P. A. von Hagen, Thomas and Andres; Baltimore—J. Carr, R. Shaw; Worcester—Isaiah Thomas.

3. Warwick Wroth, *The London Pleasure Gardens of the Eighteenth Century* (London: Macmillan, 1896), p. 289.

The Vauxhall Gardens. A contemporary engraving showing the Great Walk and The Orchestra.

concerts at The Wells of Lambeth in 1697 and at Hampstead in 1701. When Mr. Jonathan Tyers purchased Vauxhall in 1728, he made extensive additions, including an orchestra building and an organ; the reopening on June 7, 1732, featured a grand "Ridotto al fresco," and for many years patrons were treated to a concert beginning in late afternoon and lasting until about nine o'clock at night.

The size of the orchestra at Vauxhall was increased in 1745 and Thomas Arne (1710–78) was hired as composer, to help implement Tyers's decision to have vocal music play a more prominent role. Arne's first Vauxhall songs, composed for the first concert of the new season and sung throughout most of the summer, were performed by his wife, Cecilia, daughter of the organist Charles Young, and by a favorite tenor of the day, Thomas Lowe.[4] The innovation of featuring vocal music on concerts became an immediate tradition. Other popular singers were featured at Vauxhall—Reinhold, Miss Stevenson, Mrs. Vincent, the tenor Vernon, Miss Brent.

A typical evening at Vauxhall began with a promenade, perhaps along the Great Walk (some nine hundred feet of gravel path bordered by magnificent elms), the South Walk (with three triumphal arches and a painting of the ruins of Palmyra), Lover's Walk, the Wilderness, or Rural Downs. Somewhere along the way, the strollers could pause to admire the famous statue of Handel executed by Roubillac, displayed at various locations after its unveiling in 1738. As dusk fell,

4. Eighteen of these were published later that year, with the title *Lyric Harmony; Consisting of Eighteen entire new Ballads . . . As performed at Vaux Hall Gardens. . . .* A second volume of *Lyric Harmony* was published the following year, 1746, and sets of songs sung and popularized at Vauxhall and other gardens followed almost every year.

several thousand lamps would be lighted, and the audience would collect in and around The Orchestra, which had supper-boxes and pavilions decorated with copies of scenes from Hogarth, other scenes from popular pastoral comedies, and still other paintings and tapestries representing rural scenes. The concert usually consisted of sixteen numbers, songs alternating with sonatas, overtures, and, inevitably, an organ concerto. Dinner, of chicken (very small ones), ham or beef (sliced extremely thin), and wines, could be taken during or after the concert. A last stroll, to listen to the nightingales, often concluded the evening.

Other large gardens followed Vauxhall's lead in making songs a prominent part of their concerts. Daniel Gough, who took over the management of Marylebone in 1737, recruited a band of the better players from the Opera and various theaters and offered nightly concerts of airs, concertos, and overtures. Even more ambitious works were sometimes offered, such as a performance of Pergolesi's *La serva padrona*, as adapted for the English stage by Stefano Storace, in 1758. Thomas Lowe became proprietor of Marylebone in 1763, featuring himself as principal singer. A formidable group of musicians was assembled under his leadership: the singers Mrs. Vincent, Mrs. Lampe, Nan Catley, Mrs. Forbes, Miss Brent; a good orchestra under the direction of Thomas Pinto; a talented young organist named James Hook. These were the best musicians London had to offer, and their performances of songs and instrumental pieces by Handel, Boyce, Arnold, Arne, and other popular composers of the day wrested the musical leadership of the gardens away from Vauxhall. By the 1770s, performances of such musical-stage works as Storace's *The Coquet*, Hook's *The Divorce* and *Il dilettante*, and even Handel's *Acis and Galatea* had become part of Marylebone's musical offerings.

Ranelagh also offered impressive musical programs. Charles Beard, who had sung in some of Handel's operas in London, was the principal singer for almost two decades, Charles Dibdin was a sometimes "singer of ballads," and Mozart played his own works there on harpsichord and organ when he came to London at age six.

The songs written for performance in the pleasure gardens by Arne and his contemporaries aimed to be appropriate to the rural, rustic environment, and also appropriate for the mood of the persons who had come there for perambulation, relaxation, refreshment, and flirtation. Most of them have rustic settings and are concerned with some sort of amorous adventure. The tradition of the pastoral drama was drawn on heavily, as can be seen from the names of the characters involved in the miniature dramas and vignettes sketched in the poetry: Cloe, Strephon, Mira, Mirtilla, Aminta, Delia, Celia, and Hebe. The following typical texts are drawn from Arne's first two collections:

Did you see e'er a Shepherd, ye Nymphs, pass this way,
Crown'd with Myrtles, and all the gay verdure of May?
'Tis my Strephon, O bring him once more to my Eyes,
From his Lucy in search of new Pleasure he flies.

In another vein:

> As Cloe came into the Room t'other Day,
> I peevish began, where so long cou'd you Stay?
> In your Life-time You never regarded your Hour:
> You promis'd at Two; and (pray look Child) 'tis Four. . . .
> Lord Bless me, said She; let a Body but speak,
> Here's an ugly hard Rose-bud fall'n into my Neck;
> It has hurt me, and pext me to such a degree—
> See here; for you never believe me, pray see,
> On the left side my Breast what a mark it has made,
> So saying, her Bosom she careless display'd.

The swains were often desolate:

> Behold the sweet Flow'rs around with all the bright Beauties they wear
> Yet none on the Plain can be found so lovely as Celia is fair.
> Ye Warblers come raise your sweet Throats, no longer in silence remain
> O lend a fond Lover your Notes, to soften my Celia's disdain.

as were sometimes their female counterparts:

> A Maiden's soft wailing I now shall recite,
> Whom Jealousy robb'd of each rural delight;
> Such strains never came from the Linnet's sweet Throat,
> Nor sings the gay Gold Finch so charming a note.
>
> At Dusk of the Ev'ning poor *Phillis* forlorn,
> With Love unreturn'd and hard Labour now worn,
> First lean'd on her Rake then with heart breaking Sighs,
> She vented her Grief from her Lips and her Eyes.

But, more often, there were simple appreciations of feminine beauty and charm:

> Fair is the Swan, the Ermine white, and fair the Lilly of the Vale,
> The Moon resplendent Queen of Night, and Snows that drive before the
>   Gale.
> In fairness there the rest excell,
> But fairer is my Isabel.

invitations to shared pleasure:

> Rosalind Oh! come and see
>   what Pleasures are in store for Thee;
> The Flow'rs in all their sweets appear,
>   the Fields their gayest Beauties wear;

The joyfull Birds in ev'ry Grove
   now warble out their Songs of Love,
For thee they sing and Roses bloom,
   and Colin Thee invites to come.

and more explicit amorous adventures, some ending with a moral:

When Hobbinol entreated Doll, within the Grove to enter,
She hung her head, and blushing said, she was afraid to venture.

His fond Request, he eager prest,
And swore no harm he meant her,
By Honour sway'd, be not dismay'd,
But kindly with me venture,

Doubt still possest, the Damsel's breast,
Till Virtue, Counsel lent her,
Hast, hast, he cry'd, be made a Bride,
And after you may venture.

Thomas Arne (1710–78). Caricature from an original sketch by F. Bartolozzi.

and some not:

> Young Damon perceiving Mirtilla pass by,
>   Like lightning to kiss her he flew,
> But she with a Struggle, and Frown made reply,
>   I vow I'll cry out if you do.
>
> For shou'd my Mamma, who is in the next Room,
>   But hear you, she'll cause you to rue,
> She'll forbid you the House, then do not presume,
>   I vow I'll cry out if you do. . . .
>
> The Youth by resistance, was still more inflaim'd,
>   And kisses he stole not a few,
> This rudeness forbear Sir, she softly reply'd,
>   I vow I'll cry out if you do.
>
> Then Damon resolv'd, his last Efforts to strike,
>   And soon made the Damsel come to,
> She sigh'd and reply'd, you may take what you like,
>   I vow I'll cry out if you do.

In some Vauxhall songs, classical names are replaced by vernacular ones, and the miniature dramas take place among modern-day rustics, often in Scotland:

> With tunefull Pipe and merry Glee,
> Young Jockey won my heart,
> A bonnier Lad you ne'er cou'd see,
> All beauty without art. . . .
>
> Young Jemmy courts with artfull song,
> But vain is A his love,
> My Jockey blith has lov'd me long,
> To him I'll constant prove.
>   —anon., "He Stole my Heart away," as
>   sung by Miss Thornton at Vauxhall

Arne's style of composition was conditioned by the musical environment in which he matured. London, in the second half of the eighteenth century, was a musically unique city. Handel was still the overriding figure, and his music—the oratorios, suites, organ concertos, even some of his operas—was familiar to all Londoners of the day with any interest in music. Purcell was still remembered. But Londoners were susceptible to new music as well. J. C. Bach and Abel brought a new continental style to England in the 1760s; Mozart came there as a child, and his music remained after he left; Haydn was well known and widely played even before he made his famous visits to the city. It was this acceptance of both old and new music, the blend of late Baroque, rococo, and early Classical styles, that lent the music of Arne and his contemporaries a distinct quality that could be called the "London style."

Arne's songs are tonal, diatonic in melody and harmony, and they rarely stray beyond the most common chords of the major keys, going no further harmonically than an occasional secondary dominant. Texts are set mostly in syllabic fashion, with occasional melodic flourishes.

The following typical passage will serve to illustrate the style.

THOMAS ARNE, "KINDNESS AND A GRACEFUL AIR PREFERRED TO BEAUTY"

As familiar as this style may seem to us today, a contemporary of Arne saw it as new in its day:

> It is not difficult, however, to fix the era of a change in our vocal Music, which seems to have remained stationary for near half a century. It was begun by the compositions and instructions of Dr. Arne, who endeavoured to refine our melody and singing, more from Italian than English models.[5]

Arne's vocal style is also heavily indebted to "mock-Scottish" elements popular in England at the time. Though there is no evidence of actual borrowing from Scotch folk melodies, some of his songs are labeled "Scots" airs, and these as well as other songs of his make pervasive use of a short first note followed by a longer second one—a reversal of usual Italian and German rhythmic patterns.

5. Charles Burney, A General History of Music from the Earliest Ages to the Present Period (1789), 2 vols. (London: By the Author, 1782–89; repr. New York: Dover Publications, 1957), 2:1017.

THOMAS ARNE, "PHILOSOPHY NO REMEDY FOR LOVE"

Long had_ I_ borne_ of_ love_ the_ pain and long in_

si - lence drag'd his chain

This "Scottish snap" permeates instrumental music of the time as well.

Critics and historians of the present century have been condescending of Arne's Vauxhall songs. "For something over ten years Arne submitted to the comparative drudgery of mass-providing musical entertainment for the theatres and pleasure gardens," writes one. "This . . . activity was perhaps unfortunate for Arne's artistic development in view of the temptation to mass-produce to a facile melodic formula. . . . And certainly the lyrics that he was called upon to set, with their procession of lovesick swains pursuing archly simpering maidens, can hardly have been inspiring."[6] Another writes, "The average Vauxhall song seems to our ears sufficiently thin and trivial."[7]

But his contemporaries had a somewhat different view. Charles Burney, who could be critical and even caustic in the face of what he took to be inferior music, often expressed admiration for Arne's songs: "[Arne] . . . furnished Vauxhall and the whole kingdome with such songs as had improved and polished our national taste."[8] And an anonymous critic wrote in *The Harmonicon*, early in the nineteenth century:

> There was in Arne's compositions a natural ease and elegance, a flow of melody which stole upon the senses, and a fullness and variety in the harmony which satisfied, without surprising the auditor by any new, affected or extraneous modulation. . . . *He apparently aimed at pleasing, and he has fully succeeded*. [Italics mine]

We have come, at the very beginning of this book, to a matter lying at the heart of the subject of popular song. Arne was paid to perform a specific musical task—to write songs for a certain audience. This audience consisted of those Londoners who chose to pay an admission fee to one of the pleasure gardens, an audience made up of a mixture of professions, with varying musical backgrounds, an audience in which "the humours of every class of the community [could] be watched with . . . interest or amusement."[9] Arne, an experienced and

6. Herbage, pp. 90–91.
7. Wroth, p. 304.
8. Burney, 2:1015.
9. Wroth, p. 292.

thoroughly professional composer, succeeded in writing music that did just what it was intended to do. He understood that such music must have immediate accessibility, that it would be judged on first hearing. Thus he did not fill his songs with complex and difficult passages that would interest and challenge other composers and professional musicians, though he was capable of doing so. He wrote strophic songs, so listeners would hear the same music three, four, five, or even more times at a song's first hearing. His songs had simple internal structures, so listeners would hear the chief melodic phrase two or three times within each strophe. They often concluded with a refrain line that was catchy or easily memorable. By the time an audience had heard one of his songs for the first time, they might not be able to sing it from memory, but at the very least they would have some memory of it, could recognize it if they heard it again, and by the end of the song very likely could sing the refrain line at the end of each stanza with the performer.

The deceptive simplicity of Arne's songs set them apart from the more florid, ornate songs and arias in the Italian style, and it was recognized that this new song style required a style of singing different from that heard at the Italian Opera. Arne's wife, the first featured Vauxhall singer, had such a vocal style; in the words of a contemporary observer,

> Mrs. Arne was deliciously captivating. She knew nothing in singing or in nature but sweetness and simplicity. She sung exquisitely, as a bird does, her notes conveying involuntary pleasure and undefinable delight.[10]

The tenor Vernon, who came to Vauxhall a few years later and was a great favorite for many years, was apparently the first in what was to become a great line of popular singers who infuriated critics because of inferior vocal equipment and technique, but who pleased audiences with style and manner:

> Vernon . . . had no voice, without which quality it is difficult to suppose a singer at all, and it is impossible that he could have arrived to any degree of reputation had he not been favoured by nature with strong conception, quick sensibility, and a correct taste.[11]

Just as these songs proved to be attractive and appealing to the thousands of Londoners who flocked to hear them in performance at the pleasure gardens, they also proved to be popular items in printed form. Musically literate Britons purchased them, to play and sing in their homes. Published by the thousands, individual songs and sets of songs became a commercial mainstay for a number of British publishers in the second half of the eighteenth century. Their sale was sufficiently brisk to attract unscrupulous competitors; Parke tells of a printer who brought out "pirated" editions of songs, which "were sold at so low a price as

10. Charles Dibdin, A *Complete History of the English Stage*, 5 vols. (London: By the Author, [1800]), 5:367.
11. Ibid., 5:365.

fourpence each; and the demand for them was so great, that I have seen the doors besieged by a crowd of purchasers from morning till night."[12]

Pleasure garden songs, along with those from ballad opera (see pp. 17–20), were the first musical products to be aimed at a wider spectrum of the British people than had previously been involved with listening to and performing notated music.

We have discussed Arne because of the critical role he played in the formation of this genre of song, not because of his popularity in America. Publication of pleasure garden songs came to America only after the Revolution, some half-century after the establishment of this tradition in London. By this time—the late 1780s and the 1790s—Arne's songs had been superseded in popularity by those of a second generation of songwriters. Thus none of Arne's early Vauxhall songs and only a handful of his later ones were printed in America, and the most talented and popular British song composer by this time was James Hook.

This amazingly prolific man, born in Norwich in 1746, was a musical prodigy, playing keyboard instruments at four, performing in public at six, and composing a ballad opera at eight. He supported himself as a musician from age eleven, as an organist, teacher, and copyist. He went to London around 1763, soon finding employment at one of the small tea gardens, the White Conduit House, where he "daily entertained visitors with his executions on the organ." Appointed organist at Marylebone Gardens in 1769, he attracted a large following with his playing and his compositions, and by the time he assumed the musical direction at Vauxhall in 1774, he was recognized as the leading composer of songs and "light" instrumental music. In addition to his position at Vauxhall, which he held for almost half a century (until 1820), he was organist at St. John's (Horseleydown) and a widely sought-after private teacher, earning the large sum (for the day) of about six hundred pounds annually from this latter activity.

Hook's reputation as a composer was built on his songs, which he turned out in amazing quantity. His Opus 1, prophetically, was A Collection of New English Songs, published c. 1767. A Collection of Songs Sung at Vauxhall and Marylebone Gardens, a set of six volumes, was published in 1768–69, and similar volumes were published each year until 1804, for the next thirty-six years. In all, he wrote some twenty-five hundred songs. Of these, approximately 260 were published in America in the late eighteenth century and the first two decades of the nineteenth, and at least 100 more were sold here in British editions.[13]

Vauxhall soon wrested musical leadership of the pleasure gardens back from

12. W. T. Parke, Musical Memoirs; Comprising an Account of the General State of Music in England, from the First Commemoration of Handel, in 1784, to the Year 1830, 2 vols. (London: Henry Colburn and Richard Bentley, 1830), 2:138.

13. Oscar George Theodore Sonneck, A Bibliography of Early Secular American Music (18th Century), revised and enlarged by William Treat Upton (Washington: The Library of Congress, 1905; rev. ed., 1945); Richard J. Wolfe, Secular Music in America, 1801–1825; A Bibliography, 3 vols. (New York: The New York Public Library, 1964).

Marylebone, and this leadership remained unchallenged until the last entertainment was held there in 1859. Marylebone Gardens closed at the end of the season of 1776 and never successfully reopened; musical entertainment at Ranelagh never again reached its peak of the 1760s. Vauxhall was able to hire the best singers of the day—the tenors Vernon and the great Charles Incledon, who first sang there in 1786 at the age of twenty-two; Mrs. Weichsell and Mrs. Wrighton, in the 1770s and 1780s; then a new generation of Charles Dignum, Mr. Darley, Mrs. Bland, and their best contemporaries. There were musical innovations: catches and glees were first sung in 1775, and a band of drums, fifes, horns, and clarionets "perambulated" the Garden after the formal concert. Hook was an excellent organist, and his nightly organ concerto was a high point of each concert.

During Hook's tenure, Vauxhall prospered as never before. The Gardens were illuminated and decorated by tens of thousands of lamps. A large "saloon" was erected for dancing, which often followed the evening concerts. Fireworks were introduced in the last decade of the eighteenth century. Parke describes the birthday of the Prince of Wales, August 12, 1799:

> . . . a gala was given, which had never been equalled at that fashionable place of entertainment. On that occasion the gardens were illuminated by twenty thousand lamps of various colors, formed into devices; and in the saloon and several parts of the gardens, finely executed transparencies were exhibited. In the well-selected concert, the vocal and instrumental performers exerted themselves with the happiest effect; and the display of fireworks was both novel and splendid. The company on that night amounted to twelve thousand persons; and the supping was so general, that amongst the refreshments consumed were one hundred dozen of chickens, and a hundred and forty dozen bottles of port wine.[14]

But the character of Vauxhall began to change near the end of Hook's tenure, with more emphasis on spectacle and mass entertainment. Mme. Saqui of Paris was engaged in 1816 to perform a nightly act of balance and daring, walking 250 feet up an inclined rope to a height of sixty feet, then descending in a shower of fireworks. In 1833 the management lowered the price of admission and was rewarded on the first night of reduced admission (August 2) with a crowd of 27,000 persons. Interest in music lessened steadily, and with the exception of the period of Henry Bishop's brief tenure as composer and musical director from 1830 to 1832, when performances of complete comic operas were mounted, little of musical significance took place at Vauxhall from Hook's retirement in 1820 until the Gardens closed in 1859.

Hook's songs represent the peak of pleasure garden songs, in quality as well as in their more obvious quantity. Most of their texts are similar to those of Arne

14. Parke, 1:276–77.

and his contemporaries, ranging from pastoral laments, so appropriate to Vauxhall's setting:

> The Woodlark is heard thro' the Grove, the Linnet the Lark and the
>   Thrush,
> The Blackbird and sweet cooing Dove, with Music enchant ev'ry Bush,
> Yet vain the delights of the Spring, how vain bloom the Flow'rets so gay,
> The Birds tho' melodious they sing, delight not while Damon's away.
>   —Hook, "Pastoral"

to hunting songs, often with echo phrases:

> Hark Eccho, sweet Eccho, repeats the loud strain,
> The shouting and hooting of chaste Dian's Train,
>   (the shouting and hooting of chaste Dian's Train)
> Aurora smiles sweetly and comes on apace,
>   (Aurora smiles sweetly and comes on apace)
> The hounds and the horns calls us forth to the Chace.
>   (the hounds and the horns calls us forth to the Chace.)
>   —Hook, "Hark Eccho Sweet Eccho"

to mock-Scottish ballads:

> Where, where shall I seek the lovely swain, that woo'd me on the Banks of
> Tweed,
> Where, where hear the soft and tender strain, he play'd upon his Oaten
> Reed,
> O sweetly cou'd the shepherd play, the bonny boy that won me soon,
> For Sandy stole my heart away, while playing by the silver Moon.
>   —Hook, "The Silver Moon"

to simple appreciation of feminine beauty and love:

> Hush ev'ry breeze, let nothing move,
> My Delia sings and sings of love,
> Around the winning Graces wait,
> And calm contentment guards thy seat.
>   —Hook, "Noon," Sonnet II from *The
>   Hours of Love*

Hook's musical style is similar to that of Arne. There is the same balance of declamatory, songlike, syllabic setting with graceful flourishes at phrase endings and on expressive words. There are the same pervasive strophic forms, the same use of refrain lines at the ends of strophes. But even more than in Arne's songs, the various stylistic elements making up the "London" song style

"Blink oer the burn my Laddie dear," from *A Second Collection of Songs* by Mr. Hook. London: Preston, 1788.

have merged. The Italian, Handelian, Purcellian, pre-Classical, mock-Scottish elements are integrated into melodies of exquisite shape, in which no seams show. Such a melody as the following is a graceful, characteristic, totally integrated, distinctive, and completely successful tune that explains Hook's enormous success and popularity.

JAMES HOOK, "LISTEN, LISTEN TO THE VOICE OF LOVE"

O lis-ten, lis-ten to the voice_ of _ love, He calls_ my_

Daph - ne _ to _ the _ Grove, The prim - rose_ sweet_ be -

decks_ the _ fields._ The tune - ful birds_ in - vite_ to _ rove._

Even though the subject matter of his songs is the same as that of Arne and his contemporaries, there is sometimes a subtle but profound difference. Some of Hook's songs are concerned with recognizable human beings rather than stylized shepherds and shepherdesses and stereotypical Scottish lads and lassies. Many of his songs are expressions of dramatic or emotional situations not unlike those his listeners might have encountered in their own lives. Whether this is so because he set texts of more intensity than did earlier composers, or because his musical settings are more direct, his songs sometimes have an emotional thrust missing in those of Arne, where the listener is always one step removed from the affection of the text. One would never take a song by Arne to be relative in any way to "real" life. But such a song by Hook as "The Tear"

> My heart from my bosom wou'd fly, and wander oh wander afar,
> Reflection bedews my sad eye, for Henry is gone to the war.
> O, ye winds! to my Henry bear, one drop let it fall on his breast,
> The tear, as a pearl he will wear, and I in remembrance be bless'd.

touches on a situation encountered by listeners who had experienced separation from a loved one. Thus the song deals with sentiment not as an abstraction, one-dimensional and isolated from real expression and feeling, but with a situation and a resulting emotion that is human, that can be responded to at the first-person level. And Hook's setting of the text—a steady, drumlike accompaniment underlining the voice as an insistent reminder that Henry has "gone to the war"; brief, delicate roulades on critical words; and unexpected chords in sequence on the phrase "the tear as a pearl he will wear"—gives the song a kind of immediacy not found in earlier pieces.

Thus the character of the pleasure garden song had changed, ever so slightly, by the time the genre was transplanted to America, and audiences in the new Republic were offered some songs that dealt rather directly with human situations and emotions, that pointed ahead to the expressive content of nineteenth-century song rather than back to the dying tradition of pastoral drama.

Many of the first songs printed in America were written as airs in ballad and comic operas.

Opera in England in the first part of the eighteenth century had been dominated by Italian composers and singers, until the appearance of John Gay's *The Beggar's Opera*, first performed at Lincoln's Inn Fields on January 29, 1728. The impact of this momentous work is perhaps best conveyed by Charles Dibdin, writing from the vantage point of the century to which it belonged:

> This piece . . . was performed sixty-three nights, the first season, and repeated the following season with the same extraordinary success. It was performed thirty or forty times at most of the principal towns in the kingdom; at Bath and Bristol it was repeated fifty nights. The ladies carried about the favourite songs in fans, and handkerchiefs, and houses were furnished with them in screens. . . . this piece has so much of what Swift calls "not wit, nor humour, but something better than either"; as the songs are most charmingly written; as the fair purposes of honest satire are triumphantly accomplished; and, lastly, as we owe to this lucky hit the ballad opera, which has so eligibly served the cause of the drama, of poetry, and of music; I know not to whom the stage in any one instance has had more obligations than in this to Gay. [15]

The Beggar's Opera can best be seen today in the sense in which it was offered and understood at the time of its premiere: as a statement against the domination of the British stage by foreign performers singing in a foreign tongue, and as a testament to the talents and vitality of British writers and stage performers. The Beggar says to the audience, in the Introduction, "I hope I may be forgiven, that I have not made my Opera throughout unnatural, like those in vogue."

The stage was populated with thieves, prostitutes, pickpockets, crooked lawyers, and the like, rather than the kings and princesses of contemporary Italian opera; the dialogue was in English, spoken English, rather than recitative sung in Italian; the airs in Gay's work were simple, strophic songs—many of them already familiar to the audience because their tunes were borrowed from street ballads and songs—in contrast to the florid, bravura, highly embellished arias of Italian opera; the singers were all English, and the men practiced the "manly art of singing" rather than "modulating through all the meanderings of *falsetto*" in the style of the castrati of Italian opera. [16] The result of all this was a piece of musical theater readily accessible to a much larger audience than that which patronized Italian opera.

The unprecedented success of *The Beggar's Opera* spawned successors and imitators. Gay's *Polly*, advertised as "The Second Part of the Beggar's Opera,"

15. Dibdin, 5:32–33, 35.
16. Ibid., 5:365.

followed the next year, 1729; the next five years saw over a hundred ballad operas—by Henry Fielding, Robert Drury, and many others—on the stage in London, elsewhere in England, and in Scotland and Ireland. There were ballad operas on historical, patriotic, and classical subjects; there were nautical and village and court settings; there were pastorales, political farces, comedies of amorous intrigue; there were Irish, Scottish, and eventually American works.

The tunes used in ballad operas were drawn from a body of oral-tradition English songs. In the mid-nineteenth century, William Chappell reconstructed much of this repertory,[17] from a variety of sources: sixteenth- and seventeenth-century English keyboard pieces built on popular tunes; collections of country dances from the same era; instruction books by John Playford and others using familiar tunes for pedagogical purposes; and such song collections of the day as *Wit and Mirth: or Pills to Purge Melancholy.* But the number of familiar oral-tradition tunes was apparently quite small by Gay's time, small enough to be depleted after several decades of ballad operas.

Though ballad opera had run its course after several decades, *The Beggar's Opera* and its successors proved to be an important turning point in the history of the English stage, establishing that native musical-dramatic works could be successful, and that native singing actors and actresses were quite capable of challenging the Italians who had ruled the British stage for many years. As Dibdin put it,

> When the *Beggar's Opera* begat so many musical pieces, the theatre gave such a tone of simplicity to English music, that not only celebrated singers began to be known, but those who had before conceived it indispensibly necessary to be musicians professionally, in order to attain reputation as singers, were astonished to find that a good voice, a correct ear, a little feeling, and an unaffected utterance embraced the whole mystery.[18]

English comic opera of the second half of the eighteenth century was built on the reforms and successes of ballad opera, so much so that the dividing line between ballad and comic opera is not always perfectly clear. Plots are often similar; both have spoken dialogue leading to dramatic situations suitable for songs or airs. The difference is that songs in comic operas were written by the composer of the work, rather than being adapted from songs already in circulation. Even this distinction did not always hold, though, since many comic operas have songs by several composers, or songs from one work were interpolated into another, so that the distinction between a "folk" song and a newly composed air was not always clear to audiences of the day—or to scholars of today.

Such operas engaged the talents of England's leading composers during the

17. William Chappell, *The Ballad Literature and Popular Music of the Olden Times; a History of the Ancient Songs, Ballads, and of the Dance Tunes of England, with Numerous Anecdotes and Entire Ballads; also a Short Account of the Minstrels*, with an Introduction by Frederick W. Sternfeld, 2 vols. (London: [n.p.], 1859; repr., New York: Dover Publications, 1965).

18. Dibdin, 5:362.

second half of the eighteenth century; the best of them held the stage for decades and were exported to other English-speaking countries.[19] They served as showcases for some of the most talented singers in the history of the English stage. These were "popular" operas, in the sense that they could be understood and enjoyed by listeners of modest or even no musical training and experience.

These were works which engaged the talents of England's best composers, which held the stage for decades and were exported to other English-speaking countries, and which served as showcases for some of the most talented singers with which England has ever been graced. It has been suggested that they were not "serious" operas, and this is perhaps the point. This was a time of "popular" opera, in the sense that these works were comprehensible and enjoyable to listeners of modest musical training and listening experience. They were, simply put, vernacular operas—in setting, plot, language, and musical style.

The airs written for these operas are strikingly similar to the pleasure garden songs discussed above. They are strophic, often with a refrain line; the setting is largely syllabic, with frequent modest melismas on key words and at phrase endings; the subject matter is usually similar. It would be difficult to distinguish the following air from a pleasure garden song, on the basis of musical or expressive means:

THOMAS ARNE, "THE ECHOING HORN," FROM *THOMAS AND SALLY*

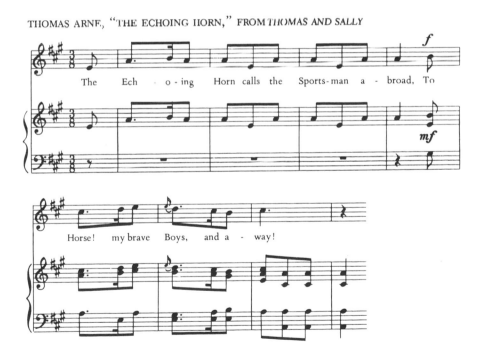

The Ech - o - ing Horn calls the Sports-man a - broad, To Horse! my brave Boys, and a - way!

19. Among the most successful were Thomas Arne, *Thomas and Sally* and *Love in a Village*; Stephen Storace, *No Song, No Supper* and *The Haunted Tower*; William Shield, *The Poor Soldier*, *The Woodman*, and *Rosina*; Thomas Linley, *The Duenna*; Charles Dibdin, *The Padlock* and *The Quaker*; William Reeve, *The Purse*; Samuel Arnold, *Inkle and Yarico* and *The Maid of the Mill*; James Hook and John Braham, *The English Fleet in 1342*.

As a matter of fact, performers (both singers and instrumentalists) moved freely from one genre to the other, and the same composers wrote for both. The music of both was brought out in sheet music form by the same publishers. Songs written for the pleasure gardens were sometimes interpolated into comic operas; favorite airs from popular operas were sometimes sung at Vauxhall and Ranelagh; songs from both were sung on concerts, in London and elsewhere in Britain.

Songs from the pleasure gardens and airs from comic operas together made up the first great era of popular song, which flourished in the British Isles in the second half of the eighteenth century.

"Being an English colony, our country naturally took England as a model in musical matters, whether they pertained to repertory, customs, or details of management."[20] Thus there were American pleasure gardens, in imitation of the famous London establishments and often named after them. The *South Carolina Gazette* ran a notice in July 1767 of concerts of vocal and instrumental music at "New Vauxhall" in Charleston; other gardens were opened in this city during the late years of the century, culminating with the opening in 1799 of "Vaux Hall Gardens, corner of Broad and Friend Streets . . . where every kind of accommodation and refreshment will be given to those who wish to spend an agreeable evening."[21] A certain Mr. Chambers, an opera singer lately returned from Europe, was engaged as principal singer, and in later concerts was assisted by Mr. and Mrs. Marshall, Miss Sully, and Mrs. Placide, wife of the proprietor. Typical of the songs listed on various programs were "Listen to the Voice of Love" (Hook), "Lovely Nan" (Dibdin), "Loose were her Tresses" (Giordani), and the vocal trio "Sigh No More, Ladies"—very much a Vauxhall repertory.

New York had pleasure gardens even earlier. Mr. John Jones opened a Ranelagh Garden there in 1765, announcing in the newspapers that his establishment "will be open'd on Thursday next (during the summer season) with a *Concert of Musick*, (if the weather will permit) and to begin precisely at six in the evening and will continue till nine." There were fireworks between the "acts" of the concert. Featured singers were Mr. Leonard, and later such popular singers as Mr. Wools and Miss Wainwright of the American Company theater troupe. The venture was successful, and New York's Ranelagh was open for four seasons, until Mr. Jones was forced by ill health to give up the venture. A curiously worded notice in the New York *Mercury* for June 30, 1766, describes the pleasures awaiting the visitor to Ranelagh:

> For Breakfasting, as well as the evening entertainment of Ladies and Gentlemen, are laid out, at a great expense, in a very genteel, pleasing manner, and judged (without exception) to be far the most rural retreat near the City.

20. Oscar George Theodore Sonneck, *Early Concert-Life in America* (1731–1800) (Leipzig: Breitkopf & Härtel, 1907), p. 324.
21. *City Gazette* (Charleston), June 19, 1799.

As an addition thereto, a compleat band of Musick is engaged, to perform every Monday and Thursday evenings, during the summer season.

A Vauxhall Garden was opened in the summer of 1765, by Mr. Samuel Francis, who advertised attractions including a "Group of magnificent WAX FIGURES, Ten in Number, rich and elegantly dressed," representing Publius Scipio with the king and princess of Carthage, and also "several masterly Pieces of Grotto-Work, and Flowers, composed of various Shells, etc."[22] Concerts featuring the singers Mr. Wools and Miss Hallam were offered on Monday, Wednesday, and Friday evenings. The following year, 1766, Mr. Edward Bardin opened his King's Arms Garden.

American pleasure gardens were a casualty of the war, but a new Vauxhall was in operation again, in even greater splendor, in the 1790s, with music, acrobatic feats, illumination with "upwards of five hundred glass Lamps," and a new generation of singers. The proprietor was Joseph Delacroix, a caterer and impresario who decorated his gardens at Great George Street with elegant taste and hired the best possible musicians, fifteen of them, for concerts of vocal and instrumental music on Tuesday, Thursday, and Saturday evenings. James Hewitt led the band, and songs were mostly from the English pleasure garden and comic opera repertory.

There was competition from a new Ranelagh Garden, opened by B. Isherwood near the Battery in 1798 and offering similar musical fare. The same summer, Joseph Corre opened his Columbia Garden, also near the Battery, with a "grand band" playing three times a week, J. C. Moller playing a newly built organ, and a stable of singers offering the usual repertory of Hook and his contemporaries. Mount Vernon Garden opened in 1800, with James Hewitt leading the band; such singers as Mr. and Mrs. Hodgkinson, Mr. Hallam, and Miss Brett; and a selection of songs that in the summer of 1800 alone included ten of the songs listed in Appendix 1 to this book as being most popular in America during the late eighteenth century.

Vauxhall and Mount Vernon Gardens continued their seasons into the early nineteenth century and were periodically challenged for leadership by new rivals. But the decade from 1795 to 1805 was the peak for the American pleasure garden, and it is no coincidence that this decade saw the first great period of song publication in America. With widespread public performances of songs by popular singers, and with these same songs coming off the presses of a growing number of American publishers, this decade marks the true beginning of the popular song industry in America.

Opera in eighteenth-century America was similarly patterned after that in Great Britain. The ballad opera *Flora; or, Hob in the Well* was performed in the Courthouse in Charleston, South Carolina, on February 18, 1735; New York saw several ballad operas, including *The Beggar's Opera*, during the winter of

---

22. George Clinton Densmore Odell, *Annals of the New York Stage*, 15 vols. (New York: Columbia University Press, 1927–49), 1:144.

Charles Dibdin (1745–1814), as Mungo in *The Padlock.* (Reproduced from *Dramatic Characters, or Different Portraits of the English Stage.* London, 1770.)

1750–51; and a company from New York offered several seasons of opera in Williamsburg in the 1750s. Hallam's London Company of Comedians came to America in late 1752, offering plays and ballad operas first in Williamsburg and then in New York. Renamed the American Company and later the Old American Company, it became the most active theatrical troupe in the colonies, offering such ballad and comic operas as *The Beggar's Opera, Thomas and Sally, Love in a Village,* and *The Padlock* up and down the Atlantic seaboard, in Maryland, Rhode Island, New York, Pennsylvania, and elsewhere, until political events forced it to leave the country in 1774.

Operatic performances resumed in the late 1780s. The old American Company established a regular "circuit" of seasons in Philadelphia, Baltimore, and New York, offering some fifty-three *different* operas in the period 1789–92.

The 1790s were dominated by two competing companies: the Old Americans, a largely new company established in 1792 and based in New York, first at the John Street Theatre; and a company in Philadelphia, established by Thomas Wignell in 1793 with Alexander Reinagle as musical director. The latter company was stocked with many of the best singers in England, including Miss Old-mixon from the Haymarket Theatre and Drury Lane and Miss Broadhurst from Covent Garden, and had a superb orchestra recruited from France and England. It was housed in the New Theatre on Chestnut Street, with a seating capacity of two thousand and reputedly the best and most modern theater in America.

The repertory of these two companies was modeled after that of the leading houses in London and was a perfect reflection of British taste. Both companies toured, and there were resident companies as well in Boston, Charleston, Providence, and several other cities. Contrary to popular belief today, Americans have not always regarded opera as an exotic, remote, difficult art form. During the first decades of the history of the United States, vernacular British opera was a stable item of entertainment, reaching Americans in almost all parts of the new country and received by them as a welcome and completely comprehensible part of their culture.

As in Great Britain, songs and airs written for the pleasure gardens and the operatic stage were frequently found on subscription and benefit concerts during the winter season. Songs shared programs with overtures, concertos, symphonies, and chamber works by Haydn, Pleyel, Stamitz, Abel, and other composers popular in London. Enough songs from concerts in New York are listed by title for us to identify the repertory: Hook's "Within a Mile of Edinburgh Town" and "Sweet Lillies of the Valley," Shield's "Amidst the Illusions" from *Hartford Bridge* and "How Can I Forget" from *Marian*, Arne's "Sweet Echo" from *Comus*, and Hewitt's "The Wish" are typical.

Charleston, Boston, Philadelphia, and other cities had similar concerts, with a similar repertory. Nor were such concerts confined to the larger cities. A program given in Portsmouth, New Hampshire, on August 3, 1796, featured a certain Mrs. Arnold singing Pleyel's "Henry's Cottage Maid," Shield's "The Heaving of the Lead" from *The Hartford Bridge*, Hook's "Listen to the Voice of Love," Reeve's "The Market Lass," and Relfe's "Mary's Dream, or Sandy's Ghost," the latter by "particular desire."[23]

Popular song in America, then, began with the repertory of the pleasure gardens and the opera houses. It was English music to the core: written by English composers for performance in England by English musicians; performed in America in pleasure gardens and opera houses modeled on those in England; sung by singers brought over from England. This was music in America, not American music.

The only American feature was choice of repertory. The hundreds of songs printed and sold in America were drawn from many thousands of songs brought out in Great Britain. And in this selection from among so many possibilities, something can be seen that points to the direction American song was to take when composers on this side of the Atlantic began writing their own songs.

British songs of this period tended in general to be light, humorous, funny, teasing, amusing, bawdy, suggestive, occasionally coarse. A small number, however, were of a different nature, serious and on rare occasions even tragic. And it was from this latter group, this minority, that most of the popular songs in America were drawn.

The most popular song in America before 1800, the song which appeared in the most editions and of which the largest number of copies have been preserved, is "The Galley Slave" from Reeve's opera, *The Purse; or, the Benevolent Tar*, to a libretto by James C. Cross. It was published in Philadelphia, New York, Boston, in at least eight different editions, the first in 1794. The three stanzas unfold the

23. Sonneck, *Early Concert-Life*, p. 319.

story of a slave ("Oh! think of my fate, once I freedom enjoy'd, . . . a captive, alas! on the sea. I was ta'en by the foe, 'twas the fiat of fate to tear me from her I adore"), who utters a final lament in the last stanza ("But despair wastes my spirits, my form feels decay") just before he "sigh'd and expir'd at the oar."

Hook's most popular pre-1800 song, "Lucy, or Selim's Complaint," is the lament of a love-struck youth, who explains:

> But since hard poverty's my lot
> No hope remains to wed with thee
> Thy beauties ne'er can grace my cot
> Oh! Lucy shed one tear for me.

"Henry's Cottage Maid," by Pleyel, is likewise the lament of an unfortunate lover:

> See from my cheek the colour flies,
> And love's sweet hope within me dies;
> For oh dear Henry thou'st betray'd,
> Thy love—with thy poor Cottage Maid.

Relfe's "Mary's Dream, or Sandy's Ghost" tells how Mary is visited in a dream by the apparition of Sandy, her lover, who had gone to sea, and tells her,

> O Mary dear, cold is my clay;
> It lies beneath a stormy sea,
> Far far from thee I sleep in death,
> So Mary weep no more for me.

Charles Dibdin wrote some 1500 songs, many of them sea songs of a robust, heroic, or comic character. He had a biting wit, a keen sense of satire. But his two most popular songs in America were "The Soldier's Adieu," a tender farewell song ("Adieu, adieu, my only wife, My honour calls me from thee, Remember thou'rt a soldier's wife, Those tears but ill become thee . . ."), and "Poor Tom Bowling," a requiem for a sailor dead at sea, written after the death of his brother Thomas:

> Here a sheer hulk lies poor Tom Bowling,
>   The darling of our crew,
> No more he'll hear the tempest howling,
>   For death has broach'd him too! . . .

> Thus Death, who kinds and tars dispatches,
>   In vain Tom's life has doff'd,
> For, though his body's under hatches,
>   His soul is gone aloft!

The titles of others give the clue to their expressive content: "Lullaby," "Since Then I'm Doom'd," "Alone by the Light of the Moon," "When Pensive I Thought," or "The Way Worn Traveller."

Thus, while the most popular songs in America were English, and were part of the song repertory of England, the selection of these particular songs gives the American repertory a quite different cast—more serious, less trivial, dealing mostly with love, separation from a loved one, death, and like sentiments. Perhaps Americans, so close to a desparate war, so concerned with shaping a new nation, were less attracted to light, comic, satiric, amusing songs. The process of selection gives the American repertory a distinct character.

These songs—written deliberately in a style that would appeal to a larger cross-section of the population than had traditionally been involved with notated music, marketed for profit—were the first popular songs according to my definition. The transplantation of this repertory to America at the end of the eighteenth century marks the first episode in the history of popular song in the United States.

190 508

TWO

"The Wounded Hussar";

OR,

The First Songs
Written in America

THE LIFTING of the ban on theatrical productions brought a wave of immigrant musicians to America in the late 1780s and the '90s, to help fill the orchestral pits and the stages for the operas and other musical entertainments that quickly followed. Among these new arrivals—most of whom came from Great Britain—were men who furnished the new country with most of the songs written on American soil during the three or four decades following the Revolution.

These musicians were perhaps the most versatile in the entire history of music in America. Specialization as we know it in the twentieth century simply did not exist then. Almost all had some proficiency on keyboard instruments, played at least one of the string instruments, and understood enough of the theory of music to be able to arrange and orchestrate pieces by other composers, if not to compose themselves. What was true in England was even more true in America. Musicians who came to the New World had to be ready and able to do almost anything, musically.

Few were of the first rank in England. There would have been little reason for a musician firmly established in London to leave one of the most active and sophisticated centers in Europe to come to a new country where musical culture was in a somewhat primitive state. Those who came to America were for the most part men willing to trade a life of being second best in an important musical center for a new career of being the best in a second-best musical country, or young men convinced they could rise to the top of their profession more rapidly in a country where competition was not so severe as in London.

Despite this, many of those who came to America in the 1790s possessed considerable talent, and often what they managed to produce in this country was not much below the level of what they had left behind in England.

Since they were versatile, complete musicians, many of them composed as an additional facet of their professional activity. They wrote music of the same sort composed in England—concertos, comic operas, keyboard sonatas, overtures, and songs—in a country beginning to develop almost imperceptibly a way of life and a culture which would eventually diverge from that of England.

Typical of these men was Benjamin Carr (1768/69–1831), who came to America in 1793 at the age of twenty-four.[1] He had been a student of Samuel Arnold and Charles Wesley in England, had some connection with the Ancient Concerts in London, and had published at least one song, "Poor Richard."

In America, he quickly involved himself in a wide range of musical activities. With his father Joseph Carr (1730–1819) and his brother Joseph (1780–1849), he established the music publishing firm of Carr & Company in Philadelphia in 1793. Once this business was established, his father went to Baltimore in 1794 to set up a similar publishing business, leaving the Philadelphia firm to Benjamin; soon there was a Carr publishing house in New York as well. Though he sold his New York store to James Hewitt in 1798 and gave up the Philadelphia business in 1800, he continued his publishing activities by selecting and arranging pieces for *The Musical Journal*, a serial publication of instrumental and vocal music begun in 1800.

Within a year of his arrival in America, Carr made his stage debut as a singer with the Old American Company, first in Philadelphia and then in New York in 1794 as one of the characters in a production of Thomas Arne's *Love in a Village*. He was a competent if not outstanding singer-actor:

> His deportment was correct, but timid, and he never acquired or deserved a reputation as an actor. His voice was mellow, and knowledge of music without the graces of action, made him more acceptable to the scientific than to the vulgar auditor.[2]

Lukewarm reception as a singer-actor was no serious matter to Carr, however; he had many more strings in his harp. He made himself generally useful to the Old American Company in the middle 1790s, adapting and arranging such stage works as Arnold's *The Children in the Wood* and Dibdin's *The Deserter* for American performance, and filling in as a keyboard player in the orchestra. He was active in concert management in New York and Philadelphia in the 1790s, was organ-

1. See Virginia Larkin Redway, "The Carrs, American Music Publishers," *The Musical Quarterly* 18 (1932): 150–77, for a discussion of the Carr family and its musical activity in America.
2. William Dunlap, *A History of the American Theatre* (New York: J. & J. Harper, 1832), p. 13.

Benjamin Carr
(1768/69–1831).

ist at St. Joseph's Church in Philadelphia, and in 1801 took over the direction of music at the Catholic church of St. Augustine in Philadelphia, a position he held until his death. He was one of the founders of the Musical Fund Society in Philadelphia, in 1820, and lived to see the opening of a handsome new concert hall for the programs of the society in 1824.

As a composer, he was active almost the entire period of his life in America. His *Federal Overture* of 1794, written for the opening night performance of the last Philadelphia season of the Old American Company (September 22, 1794), introduced the tune "Yankee Doodle," in what was probably the first printed appearance of this famous tune on this side of the Atlantic.[3] He arranged the music for a new ballad opera, *The Patriot, or Liberty Obtained*, performed early in 1796; no music from this piece has survived. Later that year he and the writer William Dunlap wrote an opera based on the story of William Tell, *The Archers, or The Mountaineers of Switzerland*, first performed on April 18, 1796, in New York by the Old American Company. This is one of the first operas written in America, and it is unfortunate that though the libretto survives in a number of copies, the music is lost, with the exception of two airs ("There Lived in Altdorf City Fair" and "Why, Huntress, Why") and an instrumental rondeau arranged by Carr from the opera's overture, "March of the Archers."

But he was most active as a song composer, publishing some sixty pieces during his lifetime. Several are arrangements of familiar tunes, such as "Auld Lang Syne" and "Down the Burn, Davy." Others were written to be interpolated

3. Irving Lowens, *Music and Musicians in Early America* (New York: W. W. Norton & Company, 1964), pp. 89–91.

into operas by other composers, a common practice of the day: "When Nights Were Cold" was introduced into a production of Samuel Arnold's *The Children in the Wood* by the Old American Company in 1794, "Ah How Hapless is the Maiden" (1800) was sung in Arnold's *The Spanish Barber,* and "Poor Mary" (c. 1800) was first heard in a production of *The Italian Monk.* But most of his songs were composed for stage or concert performance, written in the styles and forms favored by the English songwriters already discussed; and among these was the most successful song written in America before 1800, "The Little Sailor Boy,"

"The Little Sailor Boy" by Benjamin Carr. First page of the sheet music published in 1798.

advertised as "Sung at the theatres & other public places in Philadelphia, Baltimore, New York, &c. by Messrs. J. Darley, Williamson, Miss Broadhurst, Mrs. Hodgkinson & Mrs. Oldmixon" on the cover of the first edition (1798).

Like many songs written by Dibdin and his contemporaries, it is a sea song, a prayer for the safety of a loved one at sea. The text is by Mrs. Rowson:

> The sea was calm the sky serene
> And gently blew the eastern gale
> When ANNA seated on a rock
> Watch'd the LOVINA's less'ning sail
> To heav'n she thus her pray'r address'd
> Thou who cans't save or cans't destroy
> From each surrounding danger guard
> My much lov'd little Sailor boy.

The music to the song is an excellent example of how a songwriter attains "instant familiarity," i.e., makes the song familiar to the listener on some level at first hearing. The first phrase is made up of the simplest diatonic intervals, with melodic sequence making it even easier to grasp immediately:

The second phrase, beginning like the first, modulates to the dominant; but a simple sequence brings it immediately back to the tonic.

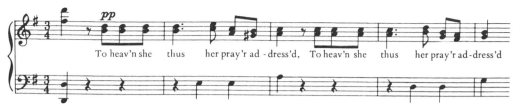

To heav'n she thus her pray'r ad-dress'd, To heav'n she thus her pray'r ad-dress'd

Following phrases are set as sequence pairs, also. The last line, a refrain line ending each of the three stanzas, is extended through textual repetition and melodic sequence.

My much lov'd lit - tle sail - or boy, My much lov'd lit - tle

sail - or boy, My sail - or boy, my sail - or boy, My

much lov'd lit - tle sail-or boy. *dim.* **pp**

Five of the eight lines of the poem are set to the same rhythmic pattern of three short notes leading to the first accented syllable, the fourth. Thus the song is immediately accessible. Not only are the musical elements simple to begin with, but the most important are repeated so many times that after a single hearing, a listener with any degree of musical comprehension is already familiar with them.

Although none of Carr's other songs approached the popularity of "The Little Sailor Boy," some enjoyed modest circulation. They were, for the most part, published in a single edition, by Carr himself, and there is no evidence that they gained wide popularity.

A somewhat more successful songwriter was James Hewitt (1770–1827), an exact contemporary of Beethoven's and another professional émigré from London. The son of a naval officer, he seemed well on his way to a career in the professional musical life of England, having been appointed leader of the orchestra at the court of George III when he was barely twenty. But he came to New York in 1792, possibly to escape memories of the death of his wife and infant son the previous year. Within a few months he and four other professional musicians offered a benefit concert to introduce themselves to their new country; one of the featured works was an *Overture in Nine Movements, Expressive of a Battle*, by Hewitt himself.

Hewitt quickly turned to opera, becoming leader of the orchestra of the Old American Company and in 1794 writing an opera himself, *Tammany, or, The Indian Chief*, to a libretto by Ann Julia Hatton. Produced for the first time on March 3, 1794, it thus predated Carr's first opera by two years. An announcement of the first performance states that "the overture and accompanyments [were] composed by Mr. Hewitt," suggesting that it was a ballad opera; but although two copies of the libretto survive, all trace of the music has been lost. The same is unfortunately true of his other opera, *The Patriot, or Liberty Asserted*, performed in New York on June 4 of the same year (1794). "Founded on the well-known story of William Tell, the Swiss patriot, who shot an apple from his son's head," this opera had "songs and overture by Mr. Hewitt"; but not a note of the music is extant.

Hewitt does not appear to have written stage works after 1794. He continued to conduct and compose, and soon became involved in the publishing and selling of music, buying Carr's New York business and eventually taking as a partner his son, John Hill Hewitt, who was to become an important song composer himself.

Hewitt's most popular song was "The Wounded Hussar," which he first published himself in 1800. It quickly became one of the best-selling items of sheet music, was brought out by other publishers in the first decades of the nineteenth century, and was published in such collections as *The Nightingale* (Portsmouth, 1804), *The Baltimore Musical Miscellany* (Baltimore, 1804–5), and *The Boston Musical Miscellany* (Boston, 1811). The text is still found in *Grigg's Southern and Western Songster* (Philadelphia, 1826, with new editions and reprints as late as 1846), one of the most popular songsters of the early nineteenth century.

The song is yet another treatment of the theme of separation and loss brought about by war. This time, the "girl left behind" actually wanders on the battlefield, after the fighting is over.

> Alone on the banks of the dark rolling Danube,
> Fair Adelaide hied when the battle was o'er,
> Oh whither she cried hast thou wander'd my lover
> Or where dost thou welter and bleed on the shore,

James Hewitt (1770–1827).

What Voice have I heard 'twas my Henry's that sigh'd,
All mournful she hast'ned nor wander'd she far,
When bleeding and low on the heath she descried
By the light of the Moon her poor wounded Hussar.

The ensuing two verses describe her attempts to console him; but "his faultering tongue scarce could murmur adieu," and he dies in her arms.

Like most songs of the time, "The Wounded Hussar" is strophic (three verses), completely diatonic, and written in a major key. There is a hint of a recapitulation of the first melodic phrase at the sixth line of the poem. Hearing the melody alone, without text, a listener of today would hardly imagine that this is music for such a melodramatic vignette. But it is always a mistake to approach the music of any given period with ears and aesthetic concepts of a different time. Hewitt's setting is quite expressive and even dramatic, within the stylistic bounds imposed on him by the period in which he lived. For example, in the following excerpt, large leaps in the melody, a wide range within a single short phrase, and even discreet dissonances serve to intensify the pathos of the text.

And such touches as the echoes of martial music which creep in from time to time serve to underline the dramatic situation.

when bleed - ing and low on the heath she des-cried by the

light— of the Moon her poor wound - ed Hus - sar by the

light of the Moon her poor wound-ed Hus-sar.

With repeated hearings of this song it is possible for us, even today, to begin to hear its expressiveness, and to understand why it was sung and listened to by Americans for over a quarter of a century.

Hewitt's next most successful song, "The Primrose Girl," likewise unfolds a pathetic tale, this time of "poor Kate," who roams the streets of London crying,

Come who'll buy— prim - ros - es, who'll buy— prim - ros - es,

who'll buy prim - ros - es, who'll— buy, who'll buy.

while dying inside, because "Friends and Parents I've none, I am look'd on with scorn, Ah! better for me that I ne'er had been born." First published by Hewitt in New York in 1794, to a text by Mrs. Pownall, it came out in five different editions before 1800, and was included in such anthologies as *Elegant Extracts* (Philadelphia, 1798) and *The American Musical Miscellany* (Northampton, 1798).

"The Primrose Girl" is one of a group of songs written at this time dealing with the same subject matter. The most popular of these in America was "Ellen, the Richmond Primrose Girl," a setting by Reginald Spofforth of a text by William Pearce, which was published here in at least six different editions in the 1790s. Ellen, in this forlorn saga, was doomed to roam the streets of "bow'ry Richmond" with her cry of "Primroses, Primroses, Primroses, two bundles a penny," while at home, "two Infant boys around her mother clung," orphaned when the father "died one stormy night, he lost his way, and never more beheld the day."

It is probably a distortion to view these as early examples of songs of social protest; composers of this time were more interested in using a melodramatic vignette to sell their songs than in taking a stand against conditions reducing humans to such a pitiful state. Nevertheless, such songs were straws in the wind; the subject matter of songs had moved, by the turn of the century, beyond the nymphs and shepherds and rustic country youths of the first wave of Vauxhall songs.

Hewitt was very much in the main current of popular song of the day, familiar with the repertory, responding to it, referring to it in his own songs, obviously expecting his listeners and performers to be familiar with it. Perhaps he did not develop a strongly personal style; various of his songs make musical reference to different styles. "How Happy Was My Humble Lot," for instance, has melodic and rhythmic patterns strongly reminiscent of the first section of the Baroque Italian overture, most widely popularized in England by Handel. But he was a professional musician and a skillful composer, and his best songs are not inferior in quality to those of his contemporaries who remained in England.

Probably the best composer in America at this time was Alexander Reinagle (1756–1809), born in Portsmouth, England, the son of an Austrian trumpet player who had emigrated to England. Young Reinagle was a student of Raynor Taylor in Edinburgh, had visited with C. P. E. Bach in Hamburg, and was a "member of the Society of Musicians in London" before coming to New York in 1786. A violinist and keyboard player, he had published six sonatas for violin and keyboard before leaving England. He quickly became involved in a variety of musical activities in America, publishing his *Selection of the Most Favorite Scots Tunes* in Philadelphia (1787), "with variations for the piano forte or harpsichord," and organizing a series of concerts in New York in 1788, performing at least one of his own keyboard sonatas. In or about 1789, he arranged and published four volumes of vocal and instrumental music under the title *A Collection of Favorite Songs*. These volumes are in the nature of an anthology, including favorite songs by Hook ("Bright Phebus," "The Tear"), Shield ("The Streamlet"), Arne ("The Soldier Tir'd," from his opera *Artaserse*), and J. C. Bach ("Ah Seek To Know").

Reinagle joined forces in the early 1790s with Thomas Wignell, who had resigned from the Old American Company in 1791 to organize a new theatrical company in Philadelphia. Wignell went to England to seek out new talent, returning in 1793 with no fewer than fifty-six recruits, and the following year the company offered Arnold's *The Castle of Andalusia* in the just-completed New Theatre in Philadelphia. One of Reinagle's functions was to make arrangements of such works as Kelly's *Blue Beard*, Dibdin's *The Lucky Escape*, and Shield's *Robin Hood*. This involved orchestrating these works (instrumental parts were never published at this time, and a new production of a stage work required a reorchestration), rearranging musical numbers, and often adding new songs to fit the taste of the members of the cast and the expected audience, as well as either writing a new overture or orchestrating the original one. Arnold's *The Mountaineers* as performed in Philadelphia in April of 1796, for instance, was advertised with "a new overture composed by R. Taylor. . . . The music of the songs, duets, glees, choruses by Dr. Arnold. The accompaniments by Mr. Reinagle."

Most of Reinagle's vocal music consisted of arrangements of pieces by other

Alexander Reinagle (1756–1809).

composers—songs in operas and such traditional songs as "Auld Robin Gray." His activity as an arranger often makes it difficult to determine just what role he played in the creation of certain songs. His most popular song, "I Have a Silent Sorrow Here," is a case in point. As first published in America, by the Carrs in Philadelphia and Baltimore in 1798–99, it is identified as being from Sheridan's opera *The Stranger*, first performed in New York on December 10, 1798. There is no mention of Reinagle, and the title says, "The air by the Duchess of Devonshire" (Georgiana Spencer Cavendish).[4] Two subsequent editions likewise attribute the song to the duchess, but an edition brought out by the Carrs in 1799 attributed the song to Reinagle. It is likely that his role was to supply an accompaniment for it for stage performance in New York, and it somehow became mistakenly attributed to him subsequently.

Of the songs bearing his name, the most successful appears to have been "Tantivy Hark Forward Huzza," identified as a "favorite Hunting Song Sung by Mrs. Iliff at Vauxhall." Brought out by J. Aitken in Philadelphia in 1789, it is a spirited, characteristic hunting song replete with echoes of hunting horns.

But this song too might not be Reinagle's. In none of the several editions is he identified as the composer, only as arranger.

Reinagle played an important role in the history of song in America by bringing out several of the earliest collections of stage and concert songs and by arranging and orchestrating songs in numerous operas presented on American stages in the 1790s. His role as a songwriter is murky, however.

4. Cavendish, who also wrote "Sweet Is the Vale" and the immensely popular "Charlie Is My Darling," was by no means the only successful female songwriter of the nineteenth century. Among many talented composers, the most influential was Claribel (Charlotte Alington Barnard), who wrote both words and music to some of the best songs of the mid-century. It was not until the first decades of Tin Pan Alley that women composers of popular song virtually disappeared from the scene, not to emerge again in significant numbers until the 1960s.

George K. Jackson, born in Oxford, England in 1745, came to America from a background of church and choral music and music pedagogy.[5] Granted a Mus. Doc. by St. Andrew's College in 1791, he came to America five years later, at the age of fifty, a mature and established musician.[6]

Unlike the other song composers discussed to this point, Jackson had nothing to do with the stage. He came first to Norfolk, in 1796, and in the following years can be traced in Alexandria, Baltimore, Elizabethtown, and Philadelphia. In 1800 he was advertising his "school of music" in Newark, and in 1801 he settled in New York, where his chief position was as organist and choir director at St. George's Chapel. In 1813 he moved to Boston, where he remained until his death in 1822. He became organist of the Handel and Haydn Society in Boston; in the last years of his life he befriended the young Lowell Mason and was instrumental in having the latter's first collection, the *Boston Handel and Haydn Society Collection of Church Music*, brought out in 1822.

Much of his musical activity falls outside the scope of this book. He wrote glees, cantatas, canons, and a great deal of church music. His best-known work today is his "Dirge for General Washington," written on the death of Washington in 1799; but the piece had little currency at the time. He brought out a collection of Masonic music around 1805, consisting of a series of canons for two to ten voices; his cantata "A Winter's Evening" was published posthumously in 1824. Jackson is perhaps best remembered as one of the musicians who impressed a taste for "proper" music on Boston early in the nineteenth century, establishing a climate that throughout most of the century resisted musical innovation and preferred "scientific" music—a term often synonymous with European music—to the effusions of more adventuresome American composers.

Despite all this, Jackson did write secular songs, particularly during his first years in America, and among them is a minor masterpiece, "One Kind Kiss," first published by the Carrs in 1796, the year of his arrival in America. The song is identified as "sung by Mrs. Hodgkinson," who had come over from England around 1792, made her American debut in a concert at Corre's Hotel in New York on January 25, 1793, and soon became one of the most popular singers in opera and concert. Brought out in several later editions in Boston and New York, anthologized in *Elegant Extracts for the German Flute or Violin* (Philadelphia, 1796) and *The Nightingale* (Portsmouth, 1804), in print throughout Jackson's lifetime (there was an edition as late as 1825), "One Kind Kiss" was among the most popular songs in America at the turn of the century.

It is a simple song of parting.

5. The best discussion of Jackson's musical life in America is found in H. Earle Johnson, *Musical Interludes in Boston, 1795–1830* (New York: Columbia University Press, 1943), pp. 201–20.

6. Some of his music may have preceded him; a "canzonett" by a composer identified only as "Jackson" was performed on a benefit concert for William Brown in Philadelphia in 1787, and George K. Jackson is known to have composed at least one vocal work called "Canzonet" before coming to America.

One kind kiss before we part,
Drop, drop a tear and bid adieu.
Tho' we sever my fond heart
'Till we meet shall pent for you.
One kind kiss before we part
Drop, drop a tear and bid adieu.

The song is the work of an accomplished and sensitive musician. With its arpeggiated accompaniment, a graceful melodic line with effective use of expressive appoggiaturas, and text repetition reflecting the unfolding melodic ideas, it is more reminiscent of Italian music than of English stage and concert songs.

Though other songs by Jackson were published in the last twenty-five years of his life ("The Fairies," for example, was first published c. 1800 and came out in a new edition after his death), none approached the popularity of his first "American" song.

Another excellent and versatile musician who was well established in England before coming to America was Raynor Taylor (1747–1825). Somewhat of a musical prodigy, he was accepted into the king's singing school as a member of the Chapel Royal; one of his contemporaries there was Samuel Arnold. Taylor became organist and music teacher at Chelmesford in Essex County, then was appointed musical director and composer at the Sadlers Wells theater at the age of eighteen. He was a prolific composer of music of many sorts—glees, anthems, songs, music for the stage, chamber and orchestral works. At some point he was in Edinburgh, where he was the teacher of Alexander Reinagle, and it may have been at his former student's urging that he came to America in 1792, at the age of forty-five. He was first in Baltimore, where he advertised himself as "music professor, organist and teacher of music in general, lately arrived from London." He was also organist at St. Anne's in Annapolis during his first year in America. After several years in the Baltimore region he moved to Philadelphia, where he was organist at St. Peters and at the Philadelphia Vauxhall Gardens, and where late in life he helped establish the Musical Fund Society.

Taylor continued to compose prolifically in America. He wrote overtures, keyboard music, songs for the stage, chamber music, and religious works. Recent performances of such works as his six sonatas for cello reveal him to be a composer of attractive lyric gifts with a firm command of compositional techniques.

Some three dozen of his songs were published in America in the decades surrounding the turn of the century. Yet, despite his skill as a composer, not one attained much popularity here. Almost all appeared in only one edition, published mostly by the Carrs, and none of the clues that a song had "caught on"— editions by other publishers, inclusion in anthologies and song collections, large numbers of copies still preserved in libraries and other collections—is present for any of his songs.

Soon after his arrival in America, Taylor, with the assistance of his pupil Miss Huntley ("late of the Theatre Royal Covent Gardens"), presented a series of "musical evenings," with "the whole of the music original and composed by Mr. Taylor." One of these was given in Annapolis on January 20, 1793, another in the same town on February 28 of the same year, others in and around Baltimore.

These productions, called "olios," consisted of a series of songs strung together with the thread of a plot, the whole preceded by an overture. Typical is the first to be done in Annapolis:

A breakfast scene, a month after marriage, a duet.
The Mock wife in a violent passion.
A Father's advice to his son-in-law.
Giles the countryman's grief for the loss of a scolding wife.
The Happy miller.
Dame Pliant's obediance to her husband.
The Obedient wife determined to have her own way, a duet.
New married couple reconciled, a duet.
Finale, All parties happy, a duet.

Some of Taylor's published songs can be identified as having been sung in these shows. "Amyntor, A Pastoral Song" was part of the first evening in Annapolis. The style is familiar: the text sketches a faithful shepherdess ("No other Swain my Mind shall tease, Without AMYNTOR what can please."), and the music is in a pastoral style long familiar to pleasure garden audiences in London. The cast of characters in his songs is familiar: Strephon, and Nancy of the Vale, and Phoebe, and Damon, and Jockey and Jenny, and Clora, and "Silvan, the shepherd swain." There are pastoral, amorous adventures, with texts carefully worded to be suggestive but not offensive, as in "The Lass of the Cot":

To the flower deck'd Altar of Hyman they went
Attended by Honor, by Health and Content;
To love & be lov'd is their conjugal Lot,
And both are quite happy altho' in a Cot.

Many of Taylor's songs were probably written before he came to America. They are the products of a good musician and a skilled composer; melodic lines are supple and graceful, the accompaniments are usually arpeggiated and more fully written out than those of many of his contemporaries. But the reasons for his lack of success as a song writer here are clear: he offered Americans a type of song harking back to the generation of Thomas Arne, now old-fashioned in music and text, in no way addressing itself to new moods and tastes in this country.

Styles in song change quickly. Taylor is an attractive and interesting figure to historians, but his songs held little interest for postwar Americans.

Despite the fact that almost all of the first generation of song writers in America were born and trained in Britain, there is a difference in the temper of songs written here in the decades surrounding the turn of the century and those written in England at the same time.

America had only recently experienced a difficult and divisive struggle for independence. The war was fought on American soil; many of the battles took place in and near centers of population. Large American cities had been occupied by the enemy. Casualties had been heavy, in relation to the size of the population. Americans had experienced separation from loved ones, death in battle, imprisonment. There was a powerful surge of patriotism before and during the war, and great pride in the heroic battle against great odds.

Thus it is hardly surprising that three of the first operas written in America—Hewitt's *The Patriot, or Liberty Asserted* (1794), and Benjamin Carr's *The Patriot, or Liberty Obtained* (1796) and *The Archers, or The Mountaineers of Switzerland* (1796)—were based on the story of the Swiss patriot William Tell.

Nor is it surprising that so many of the most popular songs written in America—Hewitt's "The Wounded Hussar," Carr's "The Little Sailor Boy," and others discussed or mentioned in this chapter—deal with the pain of separation from a loved one, or the tragedy of war or slavery.

It is difficult to identify specific musical characteristics differentiating the songs discussed in this chapter from those written in England at the same time. But there is a clear difference in subject matter and expression.

THREE

"Erin, the Tear and the Smile in Thine Eyes";

OR.

Thomas Moore's Irish Melodies in America

*Melancholy is the soul of music—all national airs
have a sadness in them: even those that seem gayest.*
—Thomas Moore, in preface to *Melodies, Songs,
Sacred Songs, and National Airs*

THE IRISH came early and often to America.

Though the most vivid popular memory is of the wholesale immigration of the 1840s, when the potato famine forced millions to flee Ireland, the Irish had been coming to the New World for several centuries, and their nature and character had been major factors in the shaping of the new republic.

As early as the first decades of the seventeenth century, they were flowing into the Atlantic colonies in great numbers, many brought as penniless passengers by sea captains who would sell them to planters for the cost of the transatlantic transportation. Irish Quakers were among the first settlers in Pennsylvania, and their enthusiastic reports on life in their new land encouraged many more of their countrymen to join them. Others came unwillingly, as prisoners, as when a hundred Irish Tories were sent to Virginia in 1653. By the end of the seventeenth century, they had come in such numbers to both Virginia and Maryland that various restrictions were put on further immigration of their countrymen.

Crop failures in 1716–17 in Ulster, in Northern Ireland, caused an exodus to the colonies, particularly Massachusetts and New Hampshire. The suppression of the Irish rebellion of 1798 brought another wave of political refugees, and another depressed period in Ireland in 1809–12 caused a new flood. Only four years later, in 1816, economic condiitons in America prompted still another wave of newcomers:

> . . . during the war (of 1812) many of the Eastern cities, New York in particular, had fallen behind in the construction of homes, warehouses, docks, stores and offices. Contractors needed masons, stonecutters, carpenters, woodworkers and hodcarriers, and they promised to pay in proportion to the need. Probably it was the assurance of jobs that induced so many Americans to provide prepaid passages; certainly the knowledge of these opportunities persuaded many of the immigrants to risk their last shilling as passage money. Most of the workmen were Irishmen.[1]

It was estimated that some thirty thousand immigrants came over in 1817, at least twenty thousand of them from the British Isles, the majority from Ireland.

By the first decades of the nineteenth century, hundreds of thousands of Irish had come to America, to all parts of the new country. Though they had come from various social and economic layers of Ireland, the majority of them had arrived poor, with skills only as laborers and farmers, and the majority of the American Irish at the turn of the nineteenth century were still laborers, small farmers, or tradesmen. Their popular image was of a rough, rowdy, hard-drinking people, who willingly became part of the new nation but at the same time retained an inordinate fondness for, and pride in, their home country.

Much of the unfavorable attitude was a reflection of the English view of the Irish as uncouth, troublesome, and somewhat cowardly, worthy of the suppression and oppression the British had traditionally heaped upon them. This view lingered well into the nineteenth century; a play written in 1812 by Alicia Sheridan LeFanu (1753–1817), *Sons of Erin; or, Modern Sentiment*, for production in London, has an "Advertisement" at the beginning of the published edition (Dublin, 1812) reading, in part:

> The principal object of the Author in the following Comedy, was to do away with any lingering prejudice that may still exist in England against the people of Ireland; thus she has endeavoured to effect, by drawing a character she believes to be new to the Stage, that of an *Irish Gentleman*, such as he now exists in society.

The Irish were also known as great singers and music lovers, bringing with them a rich store of oral-tradition music: ballads, other songs, dances of various sorts. A scattering of transcriptions or arrangements of Irish pieces was found among the earliest sheet music published in America, in the 1780s and 1790s.

There were individual songs and collections. "Had I a Heart" from Thomas

---

1. Marcus Lee Hansen, *The Atlantic Migration, 1607–1860; A History of the Continuing Settlement of the United States* (Cambridge: Harvard University Press, 1940), p. 84.

Linley's *The Duenna*, identified as the "Irish air of Gramachree," was sung in Philadelphia as early as 1789 and was printed in Book I of *Elegant Extracts*, published by J. Carr. In 1790, James Rivington printed and sold in New York *A New and Select Collection of the best English, Scots and Irish songs, catches, duets, and cantatas* . . . ; no copies are extant. "Coolun," a "celebrated Irish air," was printed in New York in 1798; "Drimendoo," a "much admir'd ancient Irish air," came out about 1800, as did "Thou dear Seducer of my Heart," a "favorite song, translated from the Irish." The *American Musical Miscellany* (1798) contained several pieces of Irish origin, such as "The Lasses of Dublin." And slightly later, James Hewitt compiled and published in New York in 1807, a collection:

> *The Music of Erin; being (a) Collection of Twelve Original Hibernian Melodies with English Words, imitated and translated from the works of the Ancient Irish Bards; with an Introductory Preface. Arranged for the Piano Forte and appropriate Symphonies.*

Many songsters printed before 1800 include texts of Irish songs.[2]

The texts of these songs portray the Irish as patriotic, proud, alcoholic, and earthy. The editor of *The American Songster*, mindful of this reputation, found it necessary to assure his readers that "Fair Americans may safely have recourse (to this collection), without the start of a blush upon their cheeks, or offending the most rigid virtue; . . . avoiding all manner of indecent songs and *double entendre*."

Far and away the most popular and important colleciton of Irish songs though—in America as well as England and other English-speaking countries— was the multivolume *Irish Melodies* brought out in Dublin and London by James and William Power. The first volume, appearing in 1808, contained twelve songs for one to four voices with keyboard accompaniment, traditional Irish melodies fitted with new texts by Thomas Moore (1779–1852), with "symphonies and accompaniments" by Sir John Stevenson (1761–1833). The two men collaborated on seven additional volumes; then Moore and Sir Henry Bishop (1786–1855) brought out two more, the last in 1834.

The *Irish Melodies* share the distinction with the songs of Stephen Foster of being the most popular, widely sung, best-loved, and most durable songs in the English language of the entire nineteenth century.[3] The songs became, quite

2. *The American Songster. Being a select collection of the most celebrated American, English, Scotch, and Irish songs*, printed in New York in 1788, contains texts for 227 songs, including the Irish "The Birks of Invermay," "Gramachree," "Balinamore Ora," and "Maggy Lawder." Part II of *The American Songster: or Federal museum of melody and wit* . . . (Warner and Hanna, Baltimore, 1799) has the texts of nineteen "Irish Patriotic Songs," including "Savourna Deilish," "Maggy Lauder," "Merrily Danc'd the Quaker," "Plankxty Connor," and "Derry Down." The apparent source for these was *Paddy's Resource. Being a select collection of original and modern patriotic songs. Compiled for the use of the people of Ireland* . . . , published in Dublin and reprinted by R. Wilson in New York in 1798, containing texts of thirty songs and the name of the tune to which each was to be sung.

3. The merest glance at the publication history of the *Irish Melodies* supports such an assertion. In England, Power's original edition had reached a fifteenth printing by 1843. Augener and Company of London brought out a new one-volume edition in 1859, a *People's Edition of Moore's Irish*

The title page of an edition of Moore's *Irish Melodies* published by Riches & Moore.

Melodies . . . with every one of the Melodies. . . . Novello, in London, brought out another one-volume collection of the *Melodies*, with "new symphonies and accompaniments for the pianoforte" by M. W. Balfe, and later in the century Boosey (also in London) published a competing one-volume edition with "the original airs restored and arranged for the voice (with pianoforte accompaniment)" by Charles Villiers Stanford.

By late 1808 or early 1809, G. E. Blake of Philadelphia offered an American edition of the first volume. There being no effective international copyright law at that time, Blake made up his own plates, duplicating the London-Dublin edition as closely as possible. Publication by Blake of each succeeding volume followed their appearance in London by less than a year.

simply, a cornerstone of English life and culture for the entire century; Dickens and Joyce refer to them constantly, fully expecting readers to be familiar with the set and with individual songs.

Their history in America is, if anything, even more remarkable. Individual songs appeared as sheet music, brought out by various publishers, and song anthologies began drawing heavily on the *Melodies* within a year of their first publication. *The Boston Musical Miscellany*, for instance, brought out by J. T. Buckingham in 1811, contains words and music for twelve songs from the first several volumes, and *The Minstrel* (Baltimore, P. Lucas, 1812) has eighteen of the *Melodies* among its hundred-odd songs. The songs reached large numbers of Americans so quickly that within a few years there were editions of the texts alone, in songsters and other pocket-sized books. The first of these may have been M. Carey's *Irish Melodies* (Philadelphia, 1815), with the texts of the seventy-two songs found in the first six volumes. Similar editions were brought out all over America—in New York, Salem, Boston, Hartford, Columbus (Ohio), Exeter, and elsewhere.

The *Melodies* quickly entered the mainstream of music in America, and stayed there throughout the nineteenth century. The *Complete Catalogue of Sheet Music and Musical Works* of 1870, a union catalog of twenty large music publishers making up the Board of Music Trade of the United States, lists some thirty-three of the *Irish Melodies* still in print, some by as many as fifteen different publishers. *Heart Songs*, an anthology of songs "Dear to the American People" brought out by the Chapple Publishing Company of Boston in 1909, a "Top Four Hundred" anthology of the nineteenth century, has five of Moore's *Irish Melodies*.

Perhaps nothing serves as well to demonstrate how these songs became familiar in America as recitation of some of their titles. " 'Tis the Last Rose of Summer" (tune: "The Groves of Blarney") has been the most peristently popular of the *Melodies*; the editor of the anthology *Songs That Never Die* (Boston, 1894) claimed that 1,500,000 copies had been sold in America alone during the nineteenth century. If true, this tune surely has the distinction of being the first to sell a million or more copies. Almost as popular were "Believe Me, If All Those Endearing Young Charms" (tune: "My Lodging Is on the Cold Ground") and "The Harp That Once Through Tara's Halls" (tune: "Gramachree"). "Love's Young Dream" (tune: "The Old Woman") and "Come, Rest in This Bosom" (tune: "Lough Sheeling") were in print throughout the nineteenth century in anthologies and separate sheet music editions, and "The Minstrel Boy" (tune: "The Moreen") has retained considerable popularity to the present day.

The *Irish Melodies* did not represent the first attempt to publish new arrangements of the treasures of traditional Irish melody. Edward Bunting, inspired by the music he heard at a meeting of "itinerant Performers on the Irish Harp" convened in Belfast on July 12, 1792, had brought out in 1796 *A General Collection of the Ancient Irish Music*, sixty-six traditional airs and two "jiggs," arranged and harmonized for piano, in proper late-eighteenth-century harmonic style complete with tempo and dynamic indications. The volume was published by W. Power and Company of Dublin, the same firm that was to publish the Moore-Stevenson collections.

Moore mentions Bunting's anthology in passing in the preface to the first volume of *Irish Melodies*. The debt was more substantial than Moore admitted: twenty of the first thirty-six *Melodies* appeared first in Bunting, whose collection was undoubtedly the source for Moore. But Bunting's collection had little circulation in the British Isles, and none whatsoever in America; it was Moore's wedding of his own superb poems to traditional tunes that gave the *Melodies* an appeal lacking in Bunting's wordless piano arrangements.

Moore's role in the creation of the *Irish Melodies* is widely misunderstood today; for most of the twentieth century, he has been remembered only as the author of the poems. But he did much more than set words to a melody. Writing to Power in April of 1824 to complain that proof for the title page of a new set of *Melodies* seemed to imply that he had no part in the creation of the music, he said:

> . . . the choice of the Air, the alterations in it (often so great as to make the Air almost my own), the suggestions of the Harmony and accompaniments, and, in short, all that gives character and originality to the Music proceeds from me.[4]

Earlier title pages crediting Stevenson with "Symphonies and Accompaniments" gave a more accurate picture, and it is unfortunate that modern bibliographical practice lists these songs under the name of Stevenson (and later Bishop), rather than Moore himself.

Moore thought of himself more as a musician than as a poet, and first conceived of many of his poems as songs, which he sang himself in public. He wrote in his diary: "I must try the reader's patience with some account of my beginnings in music—the only art for which, in my own opinion, I was born with a real natural love; my poetry, such as it is, having sprung out of my deep feelings for music."

He was already a successful songwriter and a singer of his own songs before the first number of *Irish Melodies* was in print. His "A Canadian Boat Song" ("Faintly as Tolls the Evening Chime"), first published in America in 1805, enjoyed great popularity; it is based on a tune Moore heard sung by oarsmen in Canada during his visit to North America in 1803–4. "Mary I Believe Thee True," though not one of the *Melodies*, has a tune that must have been drawn from Irish folk music, and may have been one of Moore's first attempts at the working method that proved so successful a few years later.

Nor were the *Irish Melodies* the only song collections by Moore. Two sets of

---

4. Thomas Moore, *Notes from the Letters of Thomas Moore to His Music Publisher, James Power, (the Publication of which were Suppressed in London), with an Introductory Letter from Thomas Crofton Croker* (New York: Redfield, [1854]), p. 111.

Sacred Songs (1816 and 1824) were a collaboration between Moore and Stevenson, of the same sort that had produced the *Melodies*; the six sets of *National Airs* were published between 1818 and 1828, the first in collaboration with Stevenson, the last five with Henry Bishop. These songs were created in the same way as the *Irish Melodies*: Moore fitted his own texts to modern transcriptions of melodies from many countries (Scotland, Portugal, Russia, India, Hungary, Italy), and his collaborator made the resulting songs musically respectable. These collections yielded such gems as "Oft in the Stilly Night," a Moore poem set to a Scottish tune, one of the most popular songs of the entire nineteenth century.

Moore sang the *Melodies* to his own arrangements, and though he was persuaded to allow "more scientific" accompaniments to appear in the printed versions, he was far from happy about it.

> It has always been a subject of some mortification to me, that my songs, as they are set, give such a very imperfect notion of the manner in which I wish them to be performed; and that most of the peculiarities of character, which I believe they possess as I sing them myself, is lost in the process they must undergo for publication; but the truth is, that not being sufficiently practised in the rules of composition to rely on the accuracy of my own harmonic arrangements, I am obliged to submit my rude sketches to the eyes of

BIRTHPLACE.　　　　　RESIDENCE.

Thomas Moore (1779–1852), his birthplace, and his residence, in an engraving by William Riches.

a professor, before they encounter the criticisms of the musical world; and, as it but too often happens that they are indebted for their originality to the violations of some established law, the hand that corrects their errors is almost sure to destroy their character, and the few little flowers they may boast are generally culled away with the weeds.[5]

After explaining the nature of some of his "mistakes"—such things as consecutive fifths—he proceeds to discuss another inhibition placed upon his songs as they appear in print, the restrictions of meter and strictly measured time:

> There is but one instruction I should venture to any persons desirous of doing justice to the character of these ballads, and that is, to attend as little as possible to the rhythm, or rime in singing them. The time, indeed, should *always* be made to wait upon the feeling, but particularly in this style of musical recitation, where the words ought to be as nearly *spoken* as is consistent with the swell and sweetness of intonation, and where a strict and mechanical observance of time completely destroys all those pauses, lingerings, and abruptness, which the expression of passion and tenderness requires. The truth of this remark needs but little enforcement to those who have ever heard a song of feeling and delicacy paced along in the unrelenting tramels of an orchestra.[6]

Moore's creative process, as outlined in these and other documents, was remarkably different from that of most poets of the nineteenth and twentieth centuries. In the *Irish Melodies* (and in other songs), he began with a melody, a traditional Irish melody, and wrote his poetical lines to fit this tune, which he would sometimes alter to accommodate the shape of the emerging poem. The resulting pieces were songs, not poems, and he insisted throughout his life that the *Irish Melodies* were incomplete as poems; he stated a "strong objection to this sort of divorce," being "well aware that my verses must lose even more than the *animae dimidium* in being detached from the beautiful airs to which it was their good fortune to be associated."

Moore was a poet, not an ethnomusicologist. The tunes serving as the basis for his muse came not from his own fieldwork, but from published and unpublished collections of tunes. The preface to the first volume concludes with a request for aid: "Power will be much obliged by the Communication of any Original Melodies which the Lovers of Irish Music may have the kindness to contribute to this work." Moore wrote to Power in May of 1818 to tell of a particularly useful response:

> I have got a most valuable correspondent and contributor for our future Melodies—a Mr. Croker, near Cork, who has just sent me thirty-four Airs,

5. Thomas Moore, *Melodies, Songs, Sacred Songs, and National Airs; Containing Several never before Published in America* (Exeter: J. & B. Williams, 1836), pp. iii–iv.
6. Ibid., p. v.

and a very pretty drawing of a celebrated spot in his neighbourhood. He promises me various traditions too, and sketches of the scenery connected with them. All which will be of the greatest service to us.[7]

Even though we hear Irish songs as familiar and simple in style today, they fell on ears in the late eighteenth and early nineteenth centuries as something quite different from other music. Writer after writer speaks of Irish airs as novel, wild, irregular, even barbaric. William Shield, of whom it was said that "certainly none of his contemporaries were so happy in giving accompaniments to the beautiful but wild melodies of Ireland,"[8] was set the task, in 1798, of harmonizing the "old Irish airs" of the comic opera *The Lad of the Hills* by O'Keefe:

These Shield had to harmonise and give accompaniments to, which, from the irregularity of the melodies, was a difficult task. . . . At that time Shield played at the opera, and having one evening two or three of them in his pocket, he jocasely asked Stamitz, the celebrated German composer, what sort of bass he would put to them? Stamitz, having looked at them attentively, replied,—"None—they won't bear harmony."[9]

And James Hewitt, in the preface to *The Music of Erin,* after speaking of the "singular and plaintive beauty," the "characteristic wildness and melting pathos of Irish music," goes on to say:

To the ear, which is alone made up to the delicacies of Italian music, or the Refinements of scientific composition, the following melodies will probably sound wildly inelegant, or barbarously simple; (they are offered) as "the native wood notes wild" of those, whose genius, unimproved by art, unrestrained by rule, only vibrated . . . to the genial beam of heaven's own light. . . . If the excellence of musical composition is to be estimated by the effect it produces on the human mind, by its power over the passions, or its influence over the heart, the Irish melodies, it must be allowed, graduate to a very high degree on the scale of musical excellence.[10]

We have here, for the first but not last time in the history of popular song in America, a confrontation between a tradition of composed, notated music—the music with which the two preceding chapters have been concerned—and music in oral tradition, with irregularities and complexities of rhythm and structure that confound the traditionally trained musician.

Certainly the translation of oral-tradition Irish music into conventional Western notation, in the *Irish Melodies* and in similar songs of the time, robbed

7. Moore, *Notes,* p. 65.
8. W. T. Parke, *Musical Memoirs; Comprising an Account of the General State of Music in England, from the First Commemoration of Handel, in 1784, to the Year 1830,* 2 vols. (London: Henry Colburn and Richard Bentley, 1830), 1:266.
9. Ibid., 1:266.
10. James Hewitt, *The Music of Erin* (New York: n.p., 1807), p. 2.

the tunes of much of their characteristic freedom, elasticity, and unfettered spirit. Certainly the imposition of traditional Western functional harmony on these tunes strips them of even more of their original character.

But Irish (and Scotch) music of the early nineteenth century, even when altered to be more palatable to musical taste shaped by the composed songs of Arne, Hook, Shield, Hewitt, and their peers, was received by performers and audiences as a refreshing change from the latter.

And Moore's poetry was also quite different from the texts that had been set by Arne, Hook, and their contemporaries. A first obvious difference is that Moore's poems are mostly written in the first person, describing situations and emotions from within, from the point of view of a person experiencing these emotions; the texts of the songs of the pleasure gardens, and even many songs from comic operas, deal with persons, events, even emotions as viewed from the outside, in the third person, objectively, from the point of view of an observer rather than a participant.

There is more to it than labeling Moore's songs personal and subjective, however. A dominant theme in his songs—and also in his letters, essays, and prefaces—is that Ireland had a glorious past, but was suffering through a dismal present. The most direct and eloquent exposition of this theme is in the suppressed preface to the second number of the *Irish Melodies:*

> Our history, for many centuries past, is creditable neither to our neighbours nor ourselves, and ought not to be read by any Irishman who wishes either to love England or to feel proud of Ireland. The loss of independence very early debased our character. . . . Hence it is that the annals of Ireland, through a long lapse of six hundred years, exhibit not one of those themes of national pride, from which poetry borrows her noblest inspiration, and *that* history which ought to be the richest garden of the Muse, yields nothing to her but weeds and cypress! In truth, the poet who would embellish his song with allusions to Irish names and events, must be content to seek them in those early periods when our character was yet unalloyed and original, before the impolitic craft of our conquerors had divided, weakened, and disgraced us.[11]

Again, even more directly:

> The language of sorrow, however, is, in general, best suited to our music, and with themes of this nature the poet may be amply supplied. There is not a page of our annals which cannot afford him a subject; and while the National Muse of other countries adorns her temple with trophies of the past, in Ireland, her altar, like the shrine of Pity at Athens, is to be known only by the tears that are shed upon it; "*Lacrymis altaria sudant*" (Statius. *Thebiad,* lib. 12).[12]

11. Moore, *Notes*, p. 2.
12. Ibid., p. 3.

But we would know of these sentiments from Moore's songs themselves. The very first set of *Irish Melodies* contains one of his most enduring songs, expressing his recurring theme so beautifully that the first line was taken as a title to one of the best biographies of Moore:

> The harp that once, thro' Tara's halls,
>   The soul of Music shed,
> Now hangs as mute on Tara's walls
>   As if that soul were fled:—
> So sleeps the pride of former days,
>   So glory's thrill is o'er:
> And hearts, that once beat high for praise,
>   Now feel the pulse no more!
>
> No more to chiefs and ladies bright
>   The harp of Tara swells;
> The chord, alone, that breaks at night,
>   Its tale of ruin tells:—
> Thus Freedom now so seldom wakes,
>   The only throb she gives
> Is when some heart indignant breaks,
>   To show that still she lives!

This theme, usually associated with the image of the harp as a symbol of ancient Ireland, runs through song after song, particularly in the earlier volumes:

> Dear Harp of my Country! in darkness I found thee,
>   The cold chain of Silence had hung o'er thee long, . . .
>
> I was but as the wind, passing heedlessly over,
>   And all the wild sweetness I waked was thy own.
> > (tune: "New Langolee")
>
> Sing, sweet Harp, oh sing to me
>   Some song of ancient days,
> Whose sounds, in this sad memory,
>   Long-buried dreams shall raise:— . . .
> > (tune: unknown)
>
> Weep on, weep on, your hour is past,
>   Your dreams of pride are o'er;
> The fatal chain is round you cast,
>   And you are men no more.
> > (tune: "Song of Sorrow")

Increasingly, in later songs, this same theme is personalized: now it is a person, rather than a country, overwhelmed with thoughts and dreams of a happier past. Perhaps there is no better expression of this theme than "Oft, in the Stilly Night"—from Moore's *National Airs*—a song identified in a note in the Ditson edition of 1893 as second in worldwide popularity only to "Home, Sweet Home":

> Oft, in the stilly night,
>   Ere Slumber's chain has bound me,
> Fond Memory brings the light
>   Of other days around me;
>   The smiles, the tears,
>   Of boyhood's years,
>   The words of love then spoken;
>   The eyes that shone,
>   Now dimmed and gone,
>   The cheerful hearts now broken!
> Thus, in the stilly night,
>   Ere Slumber's chain hath bound me,
> Sad Memory brings the light
>   Of other days around me.
>
> When I remember all
>   The friends, so linked together,
> I've seen around me fall,
>   Like leaves in wintry weather,
>   I feel like one,
>   Who treads alone
>   Some banquet-hall deserted,
>   Whose lights are fled,
>   Whose garland's dead
>   And all but he departed!
> Thus, in the stilly night,
>   Ere Slumber's chain has bound me,
> Sad Memory brings the light
>   Of other days around me.

This chord is struck again and again and again in the *Irish Melodies*:

> Oh! the days are gone, when Beauty bright
>   My Heart's chain wove;
> When my dream of life, from morn till night
>   Was love, still love.
> ("Love's Young Dream"; tune: "The Old Woman")

> Has Sorrow thy young days shaded,
>   As clouds o'er the morning fleet?
> Too fast have those young days faded
>   That, even in Sorrow, were sweet?

Does Time with his cold wing wither
   Each feeling that once was dear?—
Then, child of misfortune, come hither,
   I'll weep with thee, tear for tear.
(tune: "Sly Patrick")

She cried, "Oh Love! is this thy doom?
   Oh light of youth's resplendent day!
Must ye then lose your golden bloom,
   And thus, like sunshine, die away?"
("She Sung of Love"; tune: "The Munster Man")

Nostalgia became one of the dominant threads of literature in the nineteenth century. It would be simplistic to suggest that this theme was transmitted to America only by Moore's *Irish Melodies*; however, these songs had much greater currency in America than any other works treating the same theme. And certainly the post-Moore American songwriters, who dealt with this theme for a good half-century, took Moore as their model, rather than German poets or philosophers.

America was a young, expanding, vigorous nation, one with a brief but proud past, a collection of people with little as yet in the way of a shared background, a country where poor, oppressed, disadvantaged people from various countries were finding opportunities denied them elsewhere. It seems a strange stage to be filled with songs of nostalgia, particularly those contrasting a dismal present with a much better past. But the fact remains that songs treating precisely this theme were at the dead center of much of the American song literature for a good fifty years, beginning with Moore and going through the period of the Civil War. The point, I think, is that while Americans collectively had very little of a past, individually they had pasts as rich as those of any persons in any part of the world; and the common denominator linking these individual pasts was the fact that *all* Americans had left homes and homelands and friends and families, that all Americans—no matter how they might be prospering at the moment or how bright the future might appear—suffered from a sense of rootlessness. The theme of nostalgia was in fact one of the most appropriate ones for Americans.

Concerning the music of Irish song, Bunting, in the preface to his collection of 1796, advanced the claim that the tunes were from a "very distant period," from a time of "high antiquity." He believed that these oral-tradition tunes had been transmitted "with the utmost reverence," that they had been sung for centuries without the "slightest innovation," without "a single variation in any essential passage, or even in any note." He based these remarks on his observation that all the harpers assembled in Dublin in 1792 performed certain common pieces precisely the same way, though he was convinced that none had heard any of the other performers before this occasion.

Moore had a quite different idea: "It is certain that our finest airs are modern," he wrote in the preface to the third number of the *Irish Melodies*; "perhaps, we may look no further than the *last disgraceful century* for the origin of most of those wild and melancholy strains which were at once the offspring and solace of our own grief." A somewhat later collector and editor of Irish folk songs, Petrie, offered the observation that the collections of both Bunting and Moore contained a number of different tunes that appeared to be regional or personal variants of the same melody.

Today we can see that Irish songs in collections of the late eighteenth and early ninteenth centuries do not represent a homogeneous body of music of common origin. Some were undoubtedly of ancient origin, passed on in oral tradition for several centuries; some have since been identified as more recent pieces, composed by such musicians as the great blind Irish harper, singer, and composer Carolan (1670–1738); some are instrumental dances—jigs, reels, and the like; some, we now know, originated in countries other than Ireland and passed into Irish oral tradition at some undetermined point.

Many of them, including some that appear to be the most ancient, use a gapped or pentatonic (five-note) scale, lacking the fourth and seventh degrees of our modern major scale or admitting these tones only as ornamental, nonstructural notes. Examples abound in the *Irish Melodies*; the following are: samples:

"AS A BEAM O'ER THE FACE OF THE WATERS MAY GLOW"

"I'D MOURN THE HOPES THAT LEAVE ME"

Even closer relationships appear when tunes are grouped in "families," according to certain common characteristics. For instance, many Irish and Scottish tunes, based on or suggesting a pentatonic scale, leap to the upper octave early in the first phrase, descend to the dominant note, and come to rest at the end of the phrase on either the lower tonic or a note in this register fitting into the dominant chord. A simple example of this melodic family is " 'Tis the Last Rose of Summer," perhaps the most popular of all the *Irish Melodies:*

" 'TIS THE LAST ROSE OF SUMMER"

Another is the anonymous "Her Absence Will Not Alter Me," printed on pages 147–49 of the *American Musical Miscellany:*

"HER ABSENCE WILL NOT ALTER ME"

Equally straightforward is the familiar "Annie Laurie":

"ANNIE LAURIE"

Slightly more complex is Moore's "Oh! Blame Not the Bard," to the tune of "Kitty Tyrrell":

"OH! BLAME NOT THE BARD"

Relating songs by such later composers as Stephen Foster to this tune family can be a useful device in tracing stylistic roots of their style:

STEPHEN FOSTER, "OLD FOLKS AT HOME"

Moderato

Way down up-on de Swa-nee rib-ber, Far, far a-way,

This particular tune family is only one of several that may be identified among the *Irish Melodies,* any of which may be used to make the same points: the tunes in this collection are part of a wider body of oral-tradition melodies; and later songwriters often show their indebtedness to the *Melodies* by consciously or subconsciously devising "new" tunes that are related structurally to various of the melodies chosen by Moore.

Moore's *Irish Melodies* served to rally Irishmen everywhere to the cause of Irish independence. They also represented a giant step in restoring Irish pride in their country and their culture. Even more than this, they were taken by "common people" in various countries, particularly in America, as examples of the force and beauty of folk culture and expression, as opposed to the learned, classical art of the aristocracy that had been taken by critics and historians as the highest expression of Western culture.

Moore disassociated himself from such interpretations of his songs. Though he had briefly participated in the Irish uprising that occurred during his student days, he was quite content to reap the rewards of his success in comfort, even to the extent of living in England, first in London and then in the country. As early as in the preface to the third number of the *Melodies,* he took pains to define the audience he had in mind:

> There is no one who deprecates more sincerely than I do any appeal to the passions of an ignorant and angry multitude; but that it is not through that gross and inflammable region of society a work of this nature could ever have been intended to circulate; it looks much higher for its audience and readers; it is found upon the piano-fortes of the rich and the educated; of those who can afford to have their national zeal a little stimulated, without exciting much dread of the excesses into which it may hurry them; and of many, whose nerves may be now and then, alarmed with advantage, as much more is to be gained by their fears than could ever be expected from their justice. [13]

In America, his songs found their way to the "piano-fortes" and voices of tens of thousands of the "motley mixture" of "weak barbarians"—in Moore's own words—making up the new Republic. The *Irish Melodies* were the most popular songs in America in the second and third decades of the ninteenth cen-

13. Thomas Moore, *Irish Melodies, with the Original Prefatory Letter on Music; and a Supplement Containing a Selection from His Poetical Works,* 3rd complete American ed., from the 13th London ed. (New York: R. P. Bixby & Co., 1843), p. 4.

tury. They were instrumental in shaping indigenous popular music in America; every American songwriter in the half-century after 1810 was strongly affected by both melodies and texts of the *Irish Melodies*; and their commercial success was a factor in the developing music publishing business. The irony lies in Moore's open disdain for America and its characteristic cultural identity, already evident in the first years of the nineteenth century.

Seldom, if ever, did a foreigner visiting America in the early years of its independence react in such a negative, unsympathetic, and uncomprehending way to the new nation and its ways—particularly to those aspects of the new culture that made it unique. Tom Moore enjoyed the company of only a few people while here—several young women and a few cultured and educated gentlemen, particularly in Philadelphia. As for the other people he met here, he registered only dislike or disdain.

Moore first came to America in the early winter of 1803, stopping off in Virginia en route to Bermuda. His first impression of America was that it was "really a most comical place." "Nothing to be seen in the streets but dogs and negroes," he wrote to his mother on November 7, 1803, "and the few ladies that *pass for white* are to be sure the most unlovely pieces of crockery I ever set my eyes upon." After some months in Bermuda, he sailed to New York in early May of 1804, and he found this town no more to his liking than Norfolk had been: "Such a place! such people! barren and secluded as poor Bermuda is, I think it a paradise to any spot in America that I have seen. If there is less barrenness of *soil* here," he wrote on May 7, 1804, "there is more than enough barrenness in intellect, taste, and all in which *heart* is concerned."[14]

After a week, he sailed for Norfolk, intending to travel by land to Halifax and book passage from there for England. Inland America was even worse than the coastal cities; writing from Baltimore on June 13, 1804, after a coach trip from Norfolk, he told his mother:

> Every step I take not only *reconciles*, but *endears* to me, not only the excellencies but even the errors of Old England. Such a road as I have come! and in such a conveyance! The mail takes twelve passengers, which generally consist of squalling children, stinking negroes, and republicans smoking cigars! How often it has occurred to me that nothing can be more emblematic of the *government* of this country than its *stages*, filled with a motley mixture, all "hail fellow well met," driving through mud and filth, which *bespatters* them as they *raise* it, and risking an *upset* at every step. God comfort their capacities! as soon as I am away from them, both the stages and the government may have the same fate for what I care.[15]

Moore met President Jefferson and took an instant dislike to him. He took pleasure in passing on the rumor that the President had a black mistress, and

14. Thomas Moore, *Letters*, ed. Wilfred S. Dowden, 2 vols. (Oxford: Clarendon Press, 1964), 1:84.

15. Ibid., 1:86–87.

wrote a most unflattering description of his home: "the President's House, a very noble structure, is by no means suited to the philosophical humility of its present possessor, who inhabits but a corner of the mansion himself and abandons the rest to a stage of uncleanly desolation, which those who are not philosophers cannot look at without regret." In another place he writes of "that vulgarity of vice, that hostility to all the graces of life, which distinguishes the present demagogues of the United States and has become indeed . . . the characteristic of their countrymen."[16]

His violent dislike for America even found its way into his verse:

Oh! was a world so bright but born to grace
Its own half-organiz'd, half-minded race
Of weak barbarians, swarming o'er its breast,
Like vermin, bender'd on the lion's crest? . . .

Did heaven design thy lordly land to nurse
The motley dregs of every distant clime,
Each blast of anarchy and taint of crime,
Which Europe shakes from her perturbed sphere,
In full malignity to rankle here?

Though Moore was to temper his view of Americans and their culture in later years, he remains the most unwilling hero in the saga of the development of an indigenous popular song in America.

From the beginning of publication of sheet music in America, Scotch songs made up a small but hardy group, and in the first decades of the nineteenth century they combined with Irish songs to form a most significant segment of popular song.

There were, first, songs by some of the best English composers of stage and concert music written in "Scots style." James Hook's "Within a Mile of Edinburgh" was first brought out in America in 1795 and rapidly became one of the most familiar songs in the country; it appeared in the first large American song anthology, the *American Musical Miscellany* (Northampton, 1798) and in practically every anthology for the next century. Of all songs published in America before 1800, it enjoyed the longest life and the widest dissemination. Two other "Scots" songs by Hook were also widely published and sung, "The Caledonian Laddy" (published first by Benjamin Carr in 1794–95) and "Jem of Aberdeen," brought out in *The Musical Repertory* (Boston) in 1796–97 and widely reprinted by a number of publishers in the early nineteenth century.

These songs were written in the "Scotch" idiom so widely popular in England in the waning years of the eighteenth century, an idiom whose most obvi-

16. Ibid., 1:92.

ous features were the characteristic rhythmic pattern known as the "Scottish snap," a tendency toward pentatonic character in the melodic line, and skips to the upper octave at critical points in the melody.

ANON., "HE STOLE MY HEART AWAY"

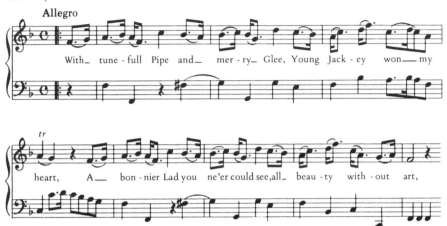

With_ tune-full Pipe and_ mer-ry_ Glee, Young Jack-ey won__ my

heart, A__ bon-nier Lad you ne'er could see, all_ beau-ty with-out art,

The year 1800 saw the appearance of perhaps the most popular Scotch song of all time in America, "The Blue Bell of Scotland." Different editions of the song came out in Philadelphia, Boston, and New York that year, and its popularity in the first decades of the nineteenth century was so great that it was the fourth most popular song of the period 1800–25, ranking behind only "Home, Sweet Home," Moore's "Come Rest in This Bosom," and "Life Let Us Cherish." An early edition brought out by P. A. von Hagen in Boston identifies it as having been "composed and sung by Mrs. Jordan at the Theatre Royal, Drury Lane," and it is often attributed to "Jordan" elsewhere, but it is likely that this lady, a celebrated Irish actress (Dorothy Bland Jordan) was responsible only for popularizing the song, not writing it.

It was not until the first years of the nineteenth century, several years after his death in 1796, that the songs of the greatest Scotch songwriter Robert Burns (1759–96) began appearing in America. Burns had made the acquaintance of James Johnson of Edinburgh in the 1780s, and the two men set out to compile a comprehensive collection of Scots songs. The first volume of the *Scots Musical Museum* appeared in 1787, with many others following in subsequent years. This collection is, in many ways, a predecessor of and companion to Moore's *Irish Melodies*. Burns's method of working was almost precisely the same as Moore's: he sought out folk songs, familiarized himself with a melody, then fitted a new text of his own creation to it, changing the tune if necessary for his poetical purposes. Burns's "poems" in these collections are just as much *songs* as were the *Irish Melodies*, and Burns felt—as did Moore—that the texts should not be separated from their melodies. His description of his creative process could have been written by Moore:

. . . untill I am compleat master of a tune, in my own singing (such as it is), I never compose for it. . . . My way is: I consider the poetic Sentiment, correspondent to my idea of when that is composed, which is generally the most difficult part of the business, I walk out, sit down now and then, look out for objects in Nature around me that are in unison or harmony with the cogitations of my fancy and workings of my bosom; humming every now and then the air with the verses I have framed; when I feel my Muse beginning to jade, I retire to the solitary fireside of my study, and there commit my effusions to paper.[17]

Burns, as a poet, was comparable to Moore—indeed, many critics rank him higher; his Scots songs occupy a role in the history of Scotland and its literature comparable to that of Moore's *Irish Melodies* in Ireland; several songs from the *Scots Musical Museum* ("Comin' thro the Rye," "Auld Lang Syne," "John Anderson My Jo") were fully as popular in America as any single one of Moore's songs. Yet the impact of Burns's songs on American life and culture was very small compared to that of the *Irish Melodies*.

There seem to be two reasons for this. First, the *Irish Melodies* were brought out—in London, Dublin, and America—in large, handsome, illustrated volumes; they were marketed, from the beginning, by successful, aggressive publishers and book dealers; the music was easy to read, because of the large format, and the accompaniments and "symphonies" by Stevenson and Bishop were fully realized, in modern style, not too difficult for amateur pianists but at the same time written so as to give full, idiomatic, rich, modern support for the voice. The *Scots Musical Museum*, on the other hand, was brought out by a regional publisher, in a small and visually unattractive format; it was not aggressively marketed in England or America;[18] and the musical arrangements by Stephen Clarke were done in a style rapidly becoming outdated—two lines of music were printed, the melody and the bass, and the accompanist was required to fill out the chords and devise appropriate figuration himself.

The second reason has to do with content. I suggested above that Moore's persistent theme of nostaliga, of longing for a lost home, childhood, and friends, struck a responsive chord among nineteenth-century Americans. Burns's subject matter was much more varied: there are patriotic and martial songs ("Scots What Hae wi' Wallace Bled"), songs of brave martyrs ("McPherson's Farewell"), simple love songs ("A Red, Red Rose"), songs of rustic love ("A Lammas Night"), songs celebrating historic battles and other events ("Bonnie Laddie, Highland Laddie"). The texts were in Scots dialect, which even then would have caused some problems with Americans of English or Irish descent. Any one of these songs was potentially attractive to numbers of Americans, but as a group there was no overriding, pervasive sentiment, save celebration of the Scotch folk.

17. Robert D. Thornton, ed., *The Tuneful Flame; Songs of Robert Burns as He Sang Them* (Lawrence, Kansas: University of Kansas Press, 1957), p. 4.
18. The single trace of the *Scots Musical Museum* in America before 1800 was a notice in a Philadelphia newspaper in January 1797 that a certain John Aitkin offered his edition of it for sale at his shop; no copy has been found.

FOUR

"Hear Me, Norma";

OR.

Bel Canto Comes to America— Italian Opera as Popular Song

LATE IN the second decade of the nineteenth century, a powerful new strain began flowing into the stream of popular song in America. It came from a new direction—from the Mediterranean, from Italy, the birthplace of opera and still the spiritual home of this complex musical-dramatic form. It was the first serious challenge to the English, Irish, and Scotch music that had dominated popular song to this point, and before this episode had ended, American song was changed and enriched.

Italian opera came to America by way of England, a country which had twice before yielded to the seductive strains of Italian melody. Neapolitan *opera seria* had swept over the musical life of London in the early eighteenth century. It first arrived during the lifetime of Henry Purcell, and in 1706 M. A. Bononcini's *Trionfo di Camilla, regina de' Velsci* was the sensation of the London theatrical season and paved the way for the arrival of a flood of singers, instrumentalists, and composers from Italy. One of these was Handel, whose *Rinaldo* in 1711 was the first of his thirty-six Italian operas produced in England. Addison, writing in *The Spectator* for March 21, 1711 (No. 18), complained that "we no longer understand the Language of our own stage," and that "our English Musick is quite rooted out."

English music reestablished itself with the success of *The Beggar's Opera* in 1728; its parody and ridicule of Italian opera, and the success of subsequent ballad and comic operas, swung English taste away from foreign opera. Italian opera was kept alive, barely, through scattered performances in small theaters, mostly for the benefit of a small band of hard-core aristocrats who had developed an insatiable taste for this foreign delicacy. Charles Burney could report by mid-century that "the opera, a tawdry, expensive, and meretricious lady, who had been accustomed to high keeping, was now reduced to a very humble state, and unable to support her former extravagance."[1]

Throughout the second half of the eighteenth century, English opera held the stage with ballad operas and comic operas of Arne, Arnold, Shield, Storace, Dibdin, and a host of lesser contemporaries. Almost imperceptibly, though, Italian opera reestablished itself. The talented composer Johann Christian Bach—the youngest son of Johann Sebastian—came to London in 1762, followed by the great singer Giovanni Manzoli in 1764 and the successful operatic composer Sacchini in 1772. A series of excellent productions of such fine Italian operas as Piccini's *La buona figliola* in 1766, Paisiello's *Il barbiere di Siviglia* in 1789, and Cimarosa's *Il matrimonio segreto* in 1794 built a new taste for Italian opera, which shared the stage with native works rather than competing with them.

The decades surrounding the turn of the century were again fallow years for Italian opera, marked by managerial squabbles, mediocre singing, and works by such minor composers as Nasolini, Paer, Radicati, and Guglielmi. The tide turned again with the first English production of Mozart's *La clemenza di Tito*, on May 27, 1806. This composer's major stage works gradually infiltrated the English stage: *Le nozze di Figaro* made its first appearance in 1813, *Don Giovanni* in 1817, *The Magic Flute* in 1819. These operas were so successful as to be made permanent repertory items.

With the first production in England of Rossini's *Il barbiere di Siviglia* in 1818, Italian opera soared to new heights of popularity. Mozart and Rossini proved to be an irresistible and irrepressible duo, with at least one new opera by the latter introduced every season—*L'italiana in Algeri* in 1819, *La Cenerentola* and *Tancredi* in 1820, *La gazza ladra* and *Il turco in Italia* in 1821. Rossini came to London in 1824, as musical director of the King's Theatre. The decade of the 1820s saw a peak in the popularity of these two composers, who were not supplanted in English esteem until the emergence of an even more popular Italian duo, Bellini and Donizetti.

America did not experience the first two waves of popularity of Italian opera in England. There was almost no musical theater here during the period of Handel's triumphs, and only occasional pieces by Cimarosa, Piccini, and Paisiello on concerts and recitals reflected the success of their operas in London. There were few singers and instrumentalists capable of handling such music on

1. Charles Burney, A *General History of Music from the Earliest Ages to the Present Period* (1789), 2 vols. (London: By the Author, 1782–89; repr., New York: Dover Publications, 1957), 2:827.

this side of the Atlantic, and no reason to believe that Americans would respond to such exotic musical fare. But the story was quite different in the 1820s.

November 29, 1825, is a historic date for the history of the American stage and the history of music in this country: it marked the first performance in America of Rossini's *Il barbiere di Siviglia* at the Park Theatre in New York. This was the first production in America of an opera in Italian, or for that matter in any foreign language, outside of New Orleans, where performance in French was customary.

The performance, fully costumed and staged, with an orchestra of twenty-five musicians, was mounted by an operatic troupe recently arrived from England. Heading the group was the Spanish baritone Manuel Garcia, fifty years

Maria Malibran (Signorina Garcia), one of the most celebrated singers of the century, who sang the role of Rosina in Rossini's *Barber of Seville* at the Park Theatre, November 20, 1825.

old at the time, who had sung with some success at the King's Theatre in London, and who was to become one of the great vocal pedagogues of the century. There were three other members of his family: his wife, the soprano Joaquina Sitchès Garcia; their son Manuel, a bass; and seventeen-year-old Maria, a daughter, who as Maria Malibran was to become one of the most celebrated singers of the century. The four other singers were the soprano Barbieri, the tenor Giovanni Crivelli, and the basses Felix Angrisani and Paolo Rosich.

This momentous event had been heralded in *The American* (New York) on November 16:

> Signor Garcia respectfully announces to the American public, that he has lately arrived in this country with an Italian troupe (among whom are some of the first artists of Europe), and has made arrangements with the Managers

of the New-York Theatre, to have the house on Tuesdays and Saturdays: on which nights the choicest Italian Operas will be performed, in a style which he flatters himself will give general satisfaction.[2]

Critical and public response was wildly enthusiastic. The *New York Evening Post* reported the very next day:

In what language shall we speak of an entertainment so novel in this country, but which has so long ranked as the most elegant and refined among the amusements of the higher classes of the old world? . . . Until it is seen, it will never be believed that a play can be conducted in recitative or singing and yet appear nearly as natural as the ordinary drama. . . . There were no less than six (singers) whom we would esteem in the ordinary comedy, performers of the first order, considered merely as actors and independently of their vocal powers.[3]

Il barbiere held the stage for the first five evenings, then was replaced on December 17 by an opera by Garcia himself, *L'amante astuto*. *Il barbiere* returned for several more performances—it was given twenty-three times during

Manuel Garcia sang the title role in Rossini's *Otello* on February 7, 1826, at the Park Theatre.

2. Quoted in George Clinton Densmore Odell, *Annals of the New York Stage*, 15 vols. (New York: Columbia University Press, 1927–49), 3:182.

3. Quoted in Julius Mattfeld, *A Hundred Years of Grand Opera in New York, 1825–1925* (New York: The New York Public Library, 1927), p. 14.

the season—then gave way to Rossini's *Tancredi*, featuring the cavatina "Di tanti palpiti" (already popular in America). Rossini's *Otello* was the next novelty, on February 7, 1826, then the same composer's *Il turco in Italia* on March 14 and Garcia's *La figlia dell'aria* on April 25.

A most interested observer of the season was Lorenzo da Ponte, librettist of Mozart's *Don Giovanni* and *Così fan tutte* and former court poet in Vienna, who had come to America in 1805 and had lived in New York since 1819, teaching Italian at Columbia College. Though an admirer of Rossini, da Ponte was disturbed that no other Italian composer was being offered to New York audiences. "A good chicken is certainly a delicious dish," he writes, "but when it was repeated many times in a banquet given by the Marchioness of Monferrato to the King of France, he asked her if nothing but chicken grew in that part of the world."[4] Accordingly, da Ponte approached Garcia with the suggestion that one of "his" operas be given, and the result was a historic performance of Mozart's *Don Giovanni* on May 23, 1826. The elder Garcia sang the title role, though he was a tenor, and Maria took the role of Zerlina. This was the first complete performance, in the original version, of any of Mozart's major operas in America.

When the long season ended on September 30, Garcia had given New York eighty performances of nine different operas. The troupe left for Mexico, for a successful season in Mexico City and a subsequent robbery of their profits by Mexican bandits. Maria stayed behind in New York with her new husband, a wealthy and elderly French merchant named Eugene Malibran; she soon left

Giovanni Montresor (Gualtiero) and Signora Pedrotti (Imogene) in Bellini's *Il pirata* performed at the Richmond Hill Theatre on December 5, 1832.

4. Lorenzo Da Ponte, *Memoirs of Lorenzo Da Ponte, Mozart's Librettist*, trans., with an Introduction and Notes by L. A. Sheppard (Boston: Houghton Mifflin, 1929), p. 367.

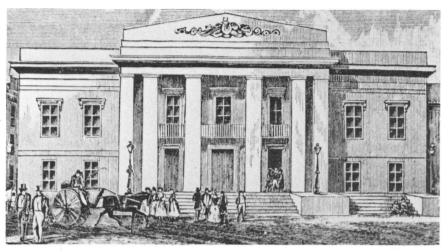

The Italian Opera House, at Church and Leonard Streets, was opened on November 18, 1833. The first theater built for opera in New York, it was subsequently renamed the National Theater.

him to pursue her career in Europe, where she achieved the stardom first predicted for her by New York critics.

Despite the artistic and financial success of the Garcia troupe in America, only scattered performances of Italian operas were given in the years following their departure. But da Ponte continually agitated for more, and a second season finally began at the Richmond Hill Theatre on October 6, 1832, with a performance of Rossini's *La Cenerentola*. Da Ponte was impresario and artistic director, stage and musical direction was entrusted to the tenor Giovanni Montresor, and a certain Signor Bagiloli led the twenty-piece orchestra. Subsequent works offered were Mercadante's *Elisa e Claudio*, Rossini's *L'italiana in Algeri*, and the first opera by Bellini, *Il pirata*. After a visit to Philadelphia early in 1833, the company resumed its New York season, but financial pressures forced the company to dissolve after some fifty-odd performances.

Undaunted, da Ponte was instrumental in raising some $150,000 for the construction of a new theater designed to house an Italian opera company. The Italian Opera House, at Church and Leonard Street, was opened on November 18, 1833, with the New York premier of yet another Rossini work, *La gazza ladra*. Da Ponte and Rivafinoli managed the company, Carlo Salvioni was musical director, and Luigia Bordogni the most popular singer. The first season saw some eighty performances—of Rossini's *La donna del lago, Matilde de Shabran, Eduardo e Cristina*, and the inevitable *Il barbiere*, Bellini's *La straniera*, and works by Cimarosa and Pacini, but it ended with a deficit of $29,275.09. A second season began on May 24, 1834; but the enterprise was doomed by poor management, squabbles among artists and financial backers, production costs that could not be met even with full houses, and a stable of singers of mediocre talent. The company was disbanded in May of 1835; the theater was sold and eventually renamed the National Theatre; and with the death of da Ponte in 1838 Italian opera in America lost its most persistent champion. Almost ten years went by before New York saw professional Italian opera on a continuing basis; the Havana Opera Company gave seasons in New York and Philadelphia in the summer and fall of 1843, offering works by Donizetti and Bellini, then Italian opera was offered at Palmo's Opera House in 1844–45 under the direction of Palmo and de Beguis. It was not until the 1850s that such operas were available on something approaching a permanent basis, at the Astor Place Opera House and the Academy of Music in New York.

Exterior of Palmo's Opera House, located at Chambers Street opposite City Hall Park. From an 1844 engraving by S. Hollyer.

Italian opera in America led such a checkered existence before 1850 because it did not have a sufficiently broad base of support. Despite the enthusiasm with which it was greeted in some circles, many Americans had reservations about it. For example, an anonymous writer in the *New York Literary Gazette and Phi Beta Kappa Repository* for December 17, 1825, summed up his impression of what must have been a first encounter with foreign opera:

> For ourselves (ignoramuses that we are!) we do not relish the music, because we do not understand the Italian. There are those, no doubt, who can, or pretend, to follow the composer through all his passages, even without a syllable of language; we have not so much skill, and never delight in vocal music without the words. There are some sweet English, Scotch, and Irish melodies which touch us deeply, and make us feel the poetic in-

fluence of music, and long after the strain has ceased, reverberate on the heart.[5]

From the beginning, Italian opera had appealed largely to America's "beautiful people." The *New York Mirror and Ladies' Literary Gazette* reported on December 3, 1825, "We were at a loss which to admire most, the powerful vocal talents of the operatic corps, or the galaxy of fashion and beauty that listened with admiration and applause," and *The American* wrote of the first-night audience for the first Garcia performance, "Never before within the walls of the Park Theatre has such an audience been assembled . . . the pit and boxes were filled to overflowing—the lower and second circle were occupied chiefly by elegant and well-dressed females." Walt Whitman, writing two decades later in the *Broadway Journal* (for November 29, 1845), spoke directly of the resentment many Americans felt of this foreign art form:

> As for us of America, we have long enough followed obedient and child-like in the track of the Old World. We have received her tenors and her buffos; her operatic troupes and her vocalists, of all grades and complexions; listened to and applauded the songs made for a different state of society— made, perhaps, by royal genius, but made to please royal ears likewise; and it is time that such listening and receiving should cease.

American opposition to Italian opera was perhaps best summed up by Philip Hone, a former mayor of New York who had been an important backer of the fund raising for the Italian Opera House, but had suffered a change of heart; he wrote in his diary for November 11, 1835:

> We want to understand the language; we cannot endure to sit by and see the performers splitting their sides with laughter, and we not take the joke; dissolved in "briny tears," and we not permitted to sympathize with them; or running each other through the body, and we devoid of the means of condemning or justifying the act. The other [reason] is the private boxes, so elegantly fitted up, which occupy the whole of the second tier. They cost six thousand dollars each, to be sure, and the use of them is all that the proprietors get for their money; but it forms a sort of aristocratical distinction. . . . These causes have prevented the success of the Italian opera, and I do not wonder at it.[6]

Recounting the successes and failures of these early Italian companies by no means indicates the full impact of Italian opera on America, nor is the conclusion that one is apt to draw from it—that Americans mostly rejected this music before 1850—a correct one. To the contrary, the music of Mozart, Rossini,

5. Quoted in Mattfeld, p. 15.
6. Quoted in ibid., p. 34.

Bellini, and Donizetti was received with such enthusiasm and affection that music in America was never the same again.

One must look elsewhere for the complete story.

Opposition to opera in a foreign tongue raged in England each time a new wave of Italian opera washed over the country. Henry Rowley Bishop, appointed musical director and composer at Covent Garden in 1810, found a way to solve the dilemma posed by works in which appealing music was cast in stage forms alien to British taste and tradition; he adapted foreign operas to the English stage, translating them into English, replacing recitative with spoken dialogue, and tailoring long and complex arias and ensembles to simpler and more symmetrical forms. His adaptions of operas by Mozart and Rossini have been roundly and unanimously condemned by music historians, but he did them for a purpose, he did them well, and he gave British (and American) audiences the chance to enjoy the incomparable music of these composers in stage works they could accept and understand.

Bishop's *The Libertine,* an adaption of Mozart's *Don Giovanni,* was first done at Covent Garden in 1817. This "new" work took less than a year to cross the Atlantic, being done at the Park Theatre in New York on November 7; it was the first of Mozart's operas to be performed on an American stage. Rossini's *The Barber of Seville* was given in Bishop's version at Covent Garden on October 12, 1818. Again the transatlantic crossing was rapid; *The Barber* was offered at the Park Theatre on May 3, 1819, with roles sung by T. Phillips, Spiller, Barnes, and Miss Leesugg—actor-singers known for their roles in English comic operas.

Bishop's *The Barber* was done at the Park every season from 1819 through 1824. Thus Garcia, in opening his 1825–26 season of Italian opera with *Il barbiere di Siviglia,* was offering a stage work already known to American audiences, albeit in an adaptation. Nor did the success of the Italian original drive Bishop's version off the stage. The Park Theatre gave *The Barber* on March 6 and 8 of 1826, in direct competition with Garcia, and after the Italians left for Mexico, it continued to be popular, with performances at the Park and several competing theaters through at least 1834. Thus the twenty-three performances of *Il barbiere* in Italian represent a mere fraction of the history of this opera in America.

Comparison of the history of another Italian opera in its original version and its "Englished" adaptation will put this matter in even better perspective.

Rossini's *La Cenerentola,* written in 1817, was first heard in America on June 27, 1826, in performance by the Garcias. Well received, it was repeated six times that season. As noted above, it was chosen by the Montresor company to open New York's second season of Italian opera, on October 6, 1832. It was a popular work during the two seasons of the ill-fated Italian Opera House, in 1833–35, and the celebrated singer Madam Alboni chose it for her New York debut at the Astor Place Opera House on December 27, 1851. After that, it disappeared from the American stage, for the remainder of the century.

But the success of this opera in its original version pales in comparison to its popularity in an English version by the Irishman Rophino Lacy. As *Cinderella; or, the Fairy-Queen and the Glass Slipper,* it was premiered at Covent Garden on April 13, 1830. Lacy retained the most popular portions of Rossini's music, but made "copious additions" of music from other operas by the same composer.

Once again, the work was on the American stage in less than a year after its London premier: *Cinderella* was given its first American performance on January 24, 1831, at the Park Theatre, with a cast of the best singers then in America, including Mrs. Austin, the darling of New York audiences,[7] in the title role. The work was an absolute sensation.

Mrs. Austin in the title role and John Jones (Felix) in Rophino Lacy's English version of Rossini's *Cinderella.*

Rossini's music made the most vivid impression on audiences and made *Cinderella* one of the most popular works of musical theater in the history of the American stage. There were fifty-old performances the first season alone, and the eightieth performance was celebrated at the Park on May 29, 1832. Mrs. Wood, the former Mary Ann Paton, made her American debut at the Park on September 9, 1833, in the role of Cinderella, with her husband singing the part of the Prince. The most celebrated female vocalist in all of England, Mrs. Wood had been prima donna at London's Covent Gardent and the Italian Opera, and had created the role of Cinderella in the London premier. She came to America in the prime of her career, and became the most popular singer here before Jenny Lind.

7. Mrs. Austin made her New York debut on January 2, 1828, as Rosetta in *Love in a Village,* and overnight supplanted Mrs. Knight as the reigning "queen of song" in America.

Cinderella quickly made its way to other cities. Its performance history in Philadelphia paralleled that in New York; it was the first opera presented in St. Louis (October 9, 1837). Its hardiness was little short of astonishing: adaptations were done at both the Broadway Theatre and Niblo's Garden in 1855; a libretto of a performance by the Richings English Opera Company in Philadelphia in 1867 agrees word for word with Lacy's original libretto of thirty-seven years earlier; Max Maretzek offered a *Cinderella* in a potpourri version containing much of the music from Lacy's adaptation at Booth's Theatre in New York as late as 1880. Less legitimate versions proliferated, also. Burlesque versions date from as early as 1842. Buckley's Serenaders did a series of burlesque operas in the Chinese Buildings in New York in 1853, with *Cinderella, Norma,* and *La sonnambula* as the core of their repertory; these were so well received that a new theater was built specifically for burlesque opera, opening on August 25, 1856. One of the most popular shows paired *Cinderella* with *Don John; or, a Ghost on a High Horse.* Circus and children's versions in the 1860s made use of some of the original music. Bryant's Minstrels offered *Cinderella in Black* on December 22, 1873.

I cite these scattered and quite incomplete references to the history of this work in America merely to establish the point that several generations of Americans became familiar with the music of *Cinderella* through stage productions at various levels of culture. And needless to say, parody and burlesque versions of a work are usually undertaken only if the piece is already familiar.

Publication, sale, and home consumption of this music in sheet music form accompanied its success on the stage. One song fashioned from the music of an opera by Mozart predated the popularity of his operas on the American stage. "Away with Melancholy," an adaptation and simplification of "Das klinget so herrlich" from *The Magic Flute*, was first published here by J. C. Moller in the late 1790s and proved to be one of the most popular items of sheet music in the first decades of the nineteenth century.

G. E. Blake in Philadelphia brought out *A Selection from the Vocal Compositions of Mozart, united to English Verse* in three volumes between 1815 and 1821, containing adaptations by David Thomson of twenty-two melodies from Mozart's operas. Bacon & Co. (also of Philadelphia) published *Select Airs from the celebrated Operas composed by Mozart* in three books, between 1819 and 1824. Most of the songs in the latter collection are from *Don Giovanni*, first performed in America in 1817.

Editions of single songs fashioned from Mozart's operas came out at the same time. The aria "Ah perdona al primo affetto" from *Don Giovanni* was especially popular, with such English texts as "Ah forgive this thoughtless error" and "Fare thee well!," the latter attributed to Lord Byron. The first English-text version of "La ci darem la mano" from *Don Giovanni* appeared in 1820, as "Now place your hand in mine, dear."

G. E. Blake's 1818 edition of the *scena* "Tu che accendi questo core—Di tanti palpiti" from Rossini's *Tancredi* is the earliest known publication of a piece by this composer in the United States. Though this opera was not seen on the

The decorative cover of the original sheet music for "Once a King there chanced to be" from Rossini's *Cinderella*.

American stage until 1825, the second part of the *scena*, "Di tanti palpiti," became a great favorite, sung in concert and interpolated into various operas. By 1820, it was available in a number of American editions, most of them with the English text "Here we meet too soon to part," and most of them arranged for voice and piano.

As published by Blake with "New Symphonies & Accompaniments for the

Piano Forte," the rather complex *scena* was simplified to a two-page strophic song in ABA form, not dissimilar at first glance to a song by Hook or Moore. What remains are Rossini's fluid, graceful melodic line, several passages of expressively florid writing (at ends of phrases and most notably just before the final cadence), an arpeggiated piano part that manages to suggest Rossini's typical accompaniments, and characteristic melodic turns that could have been written only by an Italian. Forced into a square Anglo-American formal structure, it strikes the ear as an Italian song with an English accent.

The success of the Rossini-Lacy *Cinderalla* on the American stage sparked a rash of publications of favorite songs from this opera. Most popular was "Once a King There Chanced to Be," based on the cavatina "Una voce poco fa," which Lacy borrowed from *Il barbiere di Siviglia.* Interestingly, the publisher Bourne in New York brought it out in two versions: one was a brief, two-page condensation containing only the principal melody, as sung by Cinderella, suitable for an amateur singer of modest musical endowments; the other was a six-page trio, a complex ensemble number.

A new era was ushered in on the night of November 13, 1835, when Bellini's *La sonnambula* was given its first American performance in English, at the Park Theatre. Mrs. Wood had her greatest success to date in the lead role of Amina. It was performed to the virtual exclusion of other operas for the remainder of the 1835–36 season at the Park, then was taken to other cities, where it was greeted with equal enthusiasm—particularly in Philadelphia. It was easily the most successful opera on the American stage since *Cinderella*, and it retained its popularity for more than a decade.

Publication in sheet music form of favorite sections soon followed its success on the stage. Adaptations varied from publisher to publisher, depending on the arranger; but all versions preserve the essential features of Bellini's music. The piano introduction and first phrase of "As I View These Scenes So Charming" is typical, with its arpeggiated accompaniment, melodic phrases beginning with an outline of the tonic chord and ending with graceful roulades, and the languishing appoggiaturas that gave this music such a new and distinctive sound.

mem - brance, my heart warm - ing of days long van - ish'd,

Though arias were frequently shortened into more compact and symmetrical song forms to conform with Anglo-American taste, there was no suppression of the vocal flourishes and fioritura passages that were such an important part of Bellini's style.

BELLINI, "AH! DON'T MINGLE"

Ah! don't min - gle,— one hu - man feel - ing, With these bliss - es,— o'er each sense steal - ing, While these trib - utes,— to me re - veal - ing, My El - vi - no faith-ful to his love. Ah! em -

brace me while thus for - giv - ing, Each a par - don,——— thus re - ceiv - ing,

From the extent of the demands made on the singer, one might question whether this music was intended for amateurs. But all evidence insists that it was indeed performed in the American parlor and that these operatic songs became part of the popular song repertory. They were printed and sold in the same form, by the same publishers, in quantities equal to and even greater than earlier successful songs. In numerous anthologies published later in the century, and in bound volumes of separate items of sheet music representing personal home collections, Bellini is found side by side with Thomas Moore, Henry Bishop, Henry Russell, the Hutchinsons, and Stephen Foster. There was not as yet a stylistic distinction between popular and classical music; popular music was simply whatever sold the most copies and was known to the most people, whether it be simple, strophic English song or an adaptation of music from Italian opera.

Furthermore, there is evidence that rather than being intimidated by the florid passages and embellishments of operatic music of the day, home singers delighted in it and embraced it. Copy after copy of sheet music known to have been in private possession has *additional* embellishments pencilled in. The British critic R. M. Bacon wrote in *The Musical Review* for March 30, 1839:

> The exuberance of florid execution has certainly grown into fashion in England since the powers of Billington were first displayed here. Catalani succeeded her, and confirmed the rage for *rifiorementi* amongst the females, whilst Braham gave the example to the men. Rossini's compositions have not only fixed the taste and the habit, but engendered a necessity for execution which makes the possession of facility absolutely indispensable. . . . Custom has created so ravenous an appetite for gracing, that all former composers, even Mozart himself, are decorated with the glistering passages borrowed from or appended to Rossini.

As has been already pointed out in this book, what was the case in England was also the case in America, to this moment in music history. Operatic songs were sung in the parlor, parlor songs were sung in recital and inserted into operas. Jenny Lind, the most popular singer of the entire nineteenth century, sang operatic arias and parlor songs such as "Home, Sweet Home" and "The Last Rose of Summer" side by side. The following vignette by Thomas W. Higginson dramatizes the way in which amateur and professional singers shared an identical repertory:

> I was once at a little musical party in New York, where several accomplished amateur singers were present, and with them the eminent professional, Adelaide Phillips. The amateurs were first called. Each chose some difficult operatic passage, and sang her best. When it came to the great singer's turn, instead of exhibiting her ability to eclipse these rivals on her own ground, she simply seated herself at the piano and sang "Kathleen Mavourneen," with such thrilling sweetness, that the young Irish girl who was setting the supper-table in the next room forgot her plates and teaspoons, threw herself into a chair, put her apron over her face, and sobbed as if her heart would break.[8]

The music of *La sonnambula* was not only sung, it was played and even danced to. Fiot, Meignen & Co. of Philadelphia published *Deux Quadrilles De Contredanses pour le Piano Forte, Composés & Arrangés sur des motifs de l'Opera de Bellini La Sonnambula* by Francis Johnson; dance figures are given for each of the simplified excerpts from the opera.

There was a veritable flood of arrangements of the music of *La sonnambula* that poured from the presses of American publishers in the years following its American premier. There were alternate ways to experience the music on stage, also. A dance-pantomime based on Bellini's music was done at the National Theatre in New York, in 1837. "Lo! som am de beauties," an "Ethiopian burlesque" of the opera, was first performed at Palmo's Opera House on February 24, 1845. By far the most popular of the many parody versions, though, was "The Roof Scrambler," a broad farce originally called "La Sonnambula Travestie" when it opened on April 17, 1837, at the National Theatre—the very building that had begun life as the Italian Opera House! This curious piece was the creation of the comedian William Mitchell, who had a bent for portraying female roles. Some idea of this enormously successful work can be gained from a review appearing in the *Spirit of the Times* for January 11, 1840:

> Would our readers "laugh and grow fat" let them drop into this house and see and hear the "Roof Scrambler." So happy a hit has not been made in many months in the way of fun. It is a travestie of "La Sonnambula," an opera almost too beautiful to be so used, but the wit is too genuine for us to condemn the attempt. MITCHELL plays *Amina*, under the English, if not more euphonious, name of *Molly Brown*. And how irresistible is the lovely *Molly*, whether in simpering gladness she engages in soft dalliance with her swain, *Swelvino*—whether upbraiding him for his ill-timed jealousy—whether scrambling over housetops, or descending by pump-handles and water-casks. . . . And then the musical charms of the "Roof Scrambler"—the glad voices which mingle in the swelling chorus to hail *Swelvino's* marriage: and the *silent* one which so eloquently describes to *Rodolpho* the mys-

8. *Franklin Square Song Collection, No. 2* (New York: Harper & Brother, 1884).

tery of the enchanted chamber! And in that grand *finale*, how mellifluously does *Molly Brown* glide from the exulting and rapturous burst of "Ah! do not mingle" into a fitting, a joyous double shuffle!⁹

These brief excursions have had the simple purpose of dramatizing the point that the music of Italian opera—in this case *La sonnambula*—was familiar to Americans in a wide variety of forms and at different cultural levels. And the success of *La sonnambula,* the near mania for this music, was a mere prelude to one of the central musical events of the entire nineteenth century, the arrival in America of Bellini's *Norma.*

Premiered in Milan at La Scala in 1831, it had its American premier in New Orleans in 1836; but its most important impact on American culture dates from its opening at the Chestnut Street Theatre in Philadelphia in 1840. The American composer, journalist, and critic William Henry Fry was largely responsible for this event; a passionate admirer of Italian opera, who was later to write two grand operas in the Italian style himself, Fry used his considerable influence in Philadelphia to bring the music he so much loved to his native city. Joseph Reese Fry, his brother, translated *Norma* into English for this occasion; unlike the adapters for the English stage, Henry Bishop and Rophino Lacy, Fry made only insignificant changes in the music. When Philadelphia publishers brought out favorite sections of the opera in sheet music form, immediately following its stage premier, they offered the music quite accurately, the only changes being those necessitated by a greater or lesser number of syllables in certain words and phrases in the English translation.

Norma came to New York soon after its Philadelphia success, opening at the Park Theatre on February 25, 1841. It quickly became a staple of the repertory, and no season passed without it for more than a decade. Oliver Ditson in Boston had brought out eight vocal selections from the opera, in a translation by Charles Jeffreys, in 1839, and it was this version that became best known.

The three excerpts with the greatest and most lasting success were "Hear Me, Norma" (the second-act duet "Mira, O Norma," sung by Adalgisa and Norma), "Where are Now the Hopes I Cherished" ("In mia man alfin tu sei"), and "Chaste Goddess" (Norma's celebrated florid aria from the first act, "Casta diva"). This is vintage Bellini, with ravishing melodic lines against arpeggiated chords:

Hear me, Nor - ma, in pit - y hear me, I would

9. Quoted in Odell, 4:403f.

fain dis-pel___ thy dark des - pair;___ At thy feet be-hold thy chil-dren

kneel - ing, Can___ a moth-er's heart___ re - ject their prayer?

expressive appoggiaturas, sometimes on almost every strong beat:

Where are now___ the hopes I cher - ish'd, Where the

joys that once___ were mine?___ Gone for - ev - er! all have

and gentle but breathtakingly florid, flexible, highly embellished melodic lines:

Norma was available to Americans in many other forms. The libretto, in Fry's translation, was published in Philadelphia by J. H. Gihon in 1841, hard on the heels of the first performance, and was picked up by publishers elsewhere; another widely issued translation was by J. R. Planche. There were the inevitable dances, marches, and sets of variations on favorite tunes for piano and for band. In the early 1840s, L. Meignen in Philadelphia issued *The tragic opera La Norma; complete, composed and arranged for the piano forte alone,* a thirty-nine page condensation, with all the favorite music. In those prephonograph days, the music of an opera could be heard only in stage performance, and piano arrangements of such pieces served the important function of making the music accessible to persons in their own homes. Somewhat later, the American Opera Publishing Company of Philadelphia issued George W. Tryon's *Norma. A Serious Opera in Three Acts,* containing the overture and "principal music." Publishing history was made in 1858 when Oliver Ditson in Boston brought out the complete *Norma,* in an excellent piano-vocal score, as the first of *Ditson's Standard Operas.* To my knowledge, this was the fist complete score of an Italian opera published in the United States.

Many other songs, some attaining considerable popularity, were based on tunes from *Norma,* but with the new texts. There is, for example, "Little Nell," a strophic song sketching the story of a homeless, freezing, dying young girl attempting to sell matches on the streets of an American city—a very close relative, obviously, of Hans Christian Andersen's *The Little Match Girl.* The music proves to be an adaptation of "Qual cor tradisti," the first section of the last-act finale of *Norma,* in which the heroine bids her lover Pellione farewell just before allowing herself to be consumed by the fire of a funeral pyre. Norma is a heroine in the classic sense, caught up in tragic circumstances but reacting with great dignity and majesty; her music for this scene becomes the vehicle for Little Nell to meet death in pathetic and highly sentimental poetry.

"The Hindoo Girl hath Decked her Shell," brought out between 1837 and 1839,[10] will serve as another example. The poetry, by a certain M. Lemon, recounts a Hindu tradition that a lighted candle or lamp placed upon a leaf and floated on water will either stay lighted or be extinguished, according to the

10. By Fiot, Meignen and Company in Philadelphia.

"truth or defection of absent lovers." An explanatory note on the title page states that "the Ganges is sometimes so thickly studded with them, that it seems . . . a Sea of Stars." The melody is taken from the concerted number in the first act of *Norma*, "Dell'aura tua profetica," with a piano introduction that has nothing to do with Bellini.

The mere titles of other songs based on tunes by Bellini tell us that the connection with the composer is merely a musical one: "The American Flag," "The Home of Youth," "Sunbeam of Summer" ("Duet, Poetry by Mrs. Hemans"), and the very popular "Katy Darling," with a lithograph of a young man kneeling before a tombstone engraved with the name of the tune.

Bellini's melodies were arranged as choruses and glees: *The Tyrolean Lyre: a Glee Book*[11] has "Hear Me, Norma" arranged as a duet and chorus; *The Academy Vocalist*[12] has a choral piece entitled "Bright Glowing Iris, arranged from Bellini"; *The Young Folk's Glee Book*[13] has an arrangement of "Katy Darling" for four voices. Instruction books for various instruments introduce the student to Italian opera while he is mastering his technique: *The Aeolian . . . six popular airs arranged for the Piano Forte, with Coleman's Aeolian Attachment*[14] opens with an arrangement of "Dell'aura tua profetica"; *The Guitar at Home*[15] offers the student two "airs" by Bellini in the first lessons; Stephen Foster's *The Social Orchestra*[16] contains arrangements for various combinations of instruments of eighteen pieces by Bellini and Donizetti and other operatic composers; Isaac B. Woodbury includes "Virgin Goddess" (="Casta diva") in his *The Cultivation of the Voice Without a Master*,[17] Jean-Baptiste-Laurent Arban's *Complete Celebrated Method for the Trumpet*, a pedagogical work widely used in America in the second half of the nineteenth century, has the trumpet student playing melodies from *Norma* ("Dell'aura tua profetica," "Deh! con te li prendi") as well as "Katy Darling" and airs from *La sonnambula, Beatrice di Tenda, La straniera, Romeo (Capuletti)*, and *I puritani*.

Nor was Bellini's popularity a passing fad. All eight songs first brought out by Ditson in 1838 were still in print in 1870, according to the *Complete Catalogue of Sheet Music and Musical Works*; one of them, "Hear Me, Norma," was still available through twelve of the twenty publishers represented in that catalog. "Katy Darling" was still in print in eleven editions.

Donizetti was no less popular in America than was Bellini. There was, first of all, *La Fille du regiment*, which had been premiered in Paris in 1840. Its first American performance was in New Orleans on March 6, 1843, and it was performed later that year in New York in French, by a troupe featuring the soprano Mademoiselle Calvé. The following summer it was presented for the first time in English, a more suitable language for Italian opera in America at this time; titled *Vivandiere; or, The Daughter of the Regiment*, it opened at Niblo's on June 5, 1844, and became as great a hit as had Bellini's two most successful "American"

11. Published by Oliver Ditson in Boston in 1847.
12. New York, 1852.
13. Oliver Ditson, Boston, 1854.
14. Wm. Oakes, Boston, 1845.
15. New York, Wm. Hall & Son, 1857.
16. New York, 1854.
17. New York, F. J. Huntington, 1853.

operas. Of the large number of excerpts from the opera published in the years following its arrival in America, "The Child of the Regiment" (sometimes titled "Ask Me Not Why," the first line of the text) became a great and lasting hit, rivaling the popularity of Bellini's most successful "songs." The most popular sheet music version had text translated by Charles Jefferys and music arranged by C. W. Glover as a simple, brief, strophic air. Its great success spawned the usual adaptations for chorus, piano variations, and various combinations of instruments.

Next came *Lucia di Lammermoor* (1835), done in New Orleans as early as 1841 but not staged in the East until Niblo assembled a collection of Italian singers to do it (in Italian) at his Garden on September 15, 1843. The first performance in English came on November 17, 1845, at the Park Theatre, and "I'll Pray for Thee," a simple strophic song adapted from the music of one of the favorite arias, became a best-selling item of sheet music.

And so it went with subsequent operas by Donizetti—popularization in America through stage performances, followed by the printing of various excerpts from the music, with one or two songs gaining considerable popularity. *Lucrezia Borgia* (1834) was first done in America in 1844 in New Orleans, then in New York at Palmo's Opera House on November 25 of the same year. "It Is Better to Laugh Than Be Sighing," one of two popular songs fashioned from this opera, is a fast patter song in compound meter, suggestive, when sung in English, of some of the better selections from Gilbert and Sullivan operettas—not surprising, since Italian opera was the cornerstone of their style.

"Make Me No Gaudy Chaplet," also from *Lucrezia*, epitomizes as well as any piece of this type the stylistic compromise between English-American and

Italian music: the vocal line is simple, flowing, graceful, with frequent small melismas and expressive leaps to remind the listener constantly of its Mediterranean ancestry; the accompaniment consists of simple, strummed chords, serving as a foundation for the melody but never calling attention to itself; and the square, symmetrical phrases and clear sectionalization make it orderly enough for the Anglo-American ear.

Not all Italian-style operas heard on English or American stages during this period were written by Italians. An important operatic composer of the day was the remarkable Irish singer and composer, Michael William Balfe (1808–70). The son of a dancing master, Balfe was playing the violin at the age of five and by age nine had made his public debut as violinist. With the death of his father in 1823, Balfe went to London, as violinist in the orchestra at Drury Lane, where he heard the operatic music of Mozart and Rossini for the first time. When his voice changed, Balfe aspired to sing operatic music. His first attempt, at Norwich in *Der Freischütz*, was a rather resounding failure, but it did bring him to the attention of a patron of means who arranged for him to go to Rome to observe and study Italian opera firsthand. In 1827 he was in Paris as principal baritone in the Italian Opera, making his debut as Figaro in Rossini's *Il barbiere*. Returning to Italy (Palermo) in 1829 as principal baritone, he wrote the first of several successful Italian operas, *I rivali di se stessi*, performed during carnival season of 1829–30.

Thus when he returned to England in 1833, it was as a successful singer and composer, thoroughly familiar with Italian opera, and friend of some of the giants of Italian opera: Rossini, Bordogni (his teacher), and Malibran, with whom he had sung at La Scala.

His first English opera, *The Siege of Rochelle*, enjoyed great success at Drury Lane in 1835. The next year he enticed Malibran to London to sing the principal role in *The Maid of Artois*; one of the songs from this work, "The Light of Other Days Is Faded," became the greatest hit of the season, and indeed was described by a contemporary as "the most popular song in England that our days have known."[18]

The success of these pieces paled in comparison to that of *The Bohemian Girl*, written to a libretto by Alfred Bunn and premiered in London on November 27, 1843. This opera was unquestionably the most successful and enduring musical stage work in English of the entire nineteenth century, before Gilbert and Sullivan. "Obviously the right of this opera to a place in history cannot be challenged. It represents hours out of all the private lives of England for over half a century."[19]

The Bohemian Girl made its American bow—at the Park Theatre in New York, of course—almost precisely a year after its London premier, on November 25, 1844. Mr. and Mrs. Seguin, who had sung the roles of Devilshoof and Arline at Drury Lane, created these same parts in America; Mrs. Seguin was

18. An unidentified quote in Maurice Willson Disher, *Victorian Song; from Dive to Drawing Room* (London: Phoenix House, 1955), p. 96.
   19. Ibid., p. 97.

particularly praised: "Her voice is a pure, flexible, melodious soprano, of rare modulation and exceeding sweetness. All her embellishments are in good taste," wrote the critic of the *Knickerbocker Magazine* for January 1845.

Success was instantaneous. By the close of the season, there had been twenty-two performances, and the Seguin troupe returned with the work in the spring and summer. Before 1845 was over, both the Bowery Theatre and the Albion had mounted their own productions of *The Bohemian Girl*, and the piece became one of the most popular operas of the entire century.

In America, as in England, its music took immediate and deep root. Two songs became extremely popular: "I Dreamt That I Dwelt in Marble Halls," sung by the soprano Arline at the beginning of the second act; and "Then You'll Remember Me," a third-act air sung by the tenor Thaddeus, a "prescribed Pole" (in the words of the libretto) who wins the heart of Arline, the Count's daughter. "I Dreamt . . . ." begins with a supple melody, against an arpeggiated accompaniment, which would have told us Balfe was saturated with the melodic style of Bellini-Donizetti school if we did not have that information already from his biography:

"Then You'll Remember Me" has a similar beginning, with expressive appoggiaturas on the first beats of the first two measures, and a particularly effective appoggiatura, approached by a leap, at the melodic climax of the first phrase:

The vocal climax of the entire song, coming shortly before the end on the highest pitch of the tune, is an effective use of the old Italian trick of dropping out the accompaniment to let the voice ring out alone on a sustained high note:

Balfe shows a superb mastery of Italian vocal writing. But no one should be fooled into thinking, despite all this, that the piece is by an Italian. The form is a simple, square, AABA design, with an exact repeat of the music for the second verse of the poem; and though phrase beginnings are Italianate, phrases do not end with the melting melismas that were almost a mannerism among the Italians. These two airs are superb examples of Italian melodic style modified by British conventions.

Maritana, with music by the Irishman William Vincent Wallace

(1812–65) to a libretto by Edward FitzBall, premiered at Drury Lane in 1845, enjoyed something approaching the success of *The Bohemian Girl*. Popular on the American stage, it furnished several hit songs: "Scenes That Are the Brightest," and "In Happy Moments." Wallace's music is as tinged with Italianisms as that of Balfe, though Wallace was never in Italy—he picked up the sound of Italian opera from his musical experiences in Dublin, where he played in the orchestra of the Dublin Theatre Royal as a young man.

The early 1850s in America saw the ascendancy of another Italian, Giuseppe Verdi. Songs were fashioned from many of his favorite melodies: "La donna è mobile" from *Rigoletto* (1851) became "Over the Summer Sea"; "Ah! I Have Sighed to Rest Me" was the English version of "Ah! che la morte" from *Il trovatore* (1853); *La traviata* yielded "Gaily Through Life I Wander," taken from the drinking song, "Libiamo," in the first act.

But the musical scene was changing in America: indigenous forms of musical theater had grown up, American-born composers of great talent had appeared. Popular support of opera, which had largely sustained it since the eighteenth century—through ballad opera and English comic opera to adapted versions of the great works of Rossini, Mozart, Bellini, and Donizetti—gradually eroded in the middle years of the nineteenth. Slowly but inexorably, opera became class entertainment, produced chiefly for the cultural and social aristocracy of America. Audiences of the sort that had been able to enjoy "Englished" versions of *Cinderella* and *Norma* and *The Child of the Regiment* were not able to cope with original-language productions of operas in the 1860s and 1870s. Nor were they expected to, because the audience for Italian, French, and German opera had become large and wealthy enough, at least in America's largest cities, to sustain the form. An occasional English version of an excerpt from a new opera enjoyed some success: the Bridal Chorus from Wagner's *Lohengrin* and his "Song to the Evening Star" from *Tannhäuser* were such exceptions. But popular music and opera had come to a parting of the ways, their paths never to converge again.

One point needs clarification. The notion of operatic music sung in the home may strike us as peculiar today. Operatic voices of the twentieth century would scarcely be at home in such an intimate environment. But operatic singing was a rather different thing in the early nineteenth century. The Italian style of singing in the first half of the nineteenth century was often called "bel canto"; the operas of Rossini, Bellini, and Donizetti were written for singers with flexible, agile voices, voices that could be both highly expressive and elaborately florid. Orchestral accompaniments were restrained: Wagner remarked that the Italians treated the orchestra like a great guitar. The statement is apt; the most expressive and florid passages are usually accompanied by strings, playing softly arpeggiated or strummed chords. A guitar (or a nineteenth-century piano) is a perfectly acceptable substitute. An aria from *Norma* or *Lucia*, sung by a clear, light, flexible voice, with piano or guitar accompaniment, can sound ravishing—much more so than the same aria sung by an "operatic" singer capable of filling a large, twentieth-century opera house, and accustomed to singing *against* an orchestra, as is necessary in most operas of the late nineteenth and the twentieth centuries. Bel canto was an intimate style, quite at home in an intimate setting. Chopin, after all, was inspired by it, and imitated it—in some of his smallest and most delicate piano pieces.

The music of Rossini, Bellini, and Donizetti filled the air of nineteenth-century America. Walt Whitman came to love it, and a case has been made that it was a major stylistic influence on his poetical style.[20] When Abraham Lincoln was inaugurated in 1861, a band played arrangements of music from *Rigoletto*. Later chapters will show that songwriters were numbered among those Americans who listened to Italian opera, and what went in their ears came out through their pens.

20. Robert D. Faner, *Walt Whitman and Opera* (Carbondale, Illinois: Southern Illinois University Press, 1972).

FIVE

"The Minstrel's Return'd from the War";

OR.

The First American Songwriters

FRANCIS HOPKINSON dedicated his *Seven Songs for the Harpsichord* to George Washington, writing in his preface:

> However small the Reputation may be that I shall derive from this Work, I cannot, I believe, be refused the Credit of being the first Native of the United States who has produced a Musical Composition.

This claim is much too extravagant: we now know that various compositions of several sorts by a number of composers born in America date from before these songs. Hopkinson does have a solid claim to musical immortality, however; had his dedication read "I cannot be refused the credit of being the first American to compose secular songs for voice and keyboard," there could be no dispute with the statement.

Hopkinson (1737–91) was a remarkable man of greatly varied accomplishments and skills. Born in Philadelphia and educated at the University of Pennsylvania—then called the College of Philadelphia—he became a lawyer, an inventor, a delegate to the Continental Congress, a writer and satirist, a poet, one of the signers of the Declaration of Independence, the first Secretary of the Navy of the new country, and a musician. His musical activity can be traced to his days at

Francis Hopkinson (1737–91).

the College, where he is known to have been a performer on the harpsichord. He was organist at Christ Church, instructing children of the congregation in the art of psalmody. In 1756–57 he was involved in a college production of *The Masque of Alfred the Great*, a stage work for which Thomas Arne had written songs and other music.

During his college days he copied out some one hundred songs for voice and bass, undoubtedly in order to improve his knowledge of the "science" of music. Hopkinson's manuscript is the largest collection of songs from this time in America and is a most useful document on several counts. None of the songs was published in America at this time, and one must assume that his sources were copies of printed music brought over from England; the collection gives us valuable information on American taste in English song in pre-Revolution days. It is very much a London repertory of mid-century. There are twenty-seven songs and airs by Thomas Arne and fifteen by Handel; there are Italian songs by Vinci and Palma, popular at the Italian Opera in London. J. Worgan, organist and composer at Vauxhall, is represented by five songs, and William Boyce by three. Other composers include Pergolesi, Purcell, J. C. Smith, Howard, Oswald, and other minor English composers of the day.

Six songs marked with the initials "F. H." are otherwise unknown and have been assumed to be the work of Hopkinson himself. Two are set to sacred texts; the other four are secular: "My Days Have Been So Wondrous Free," "The Garland," "Oh Come to Mason Borough's Grove," "With Pleasure I have Past My Days." The first has been almost universally hailed as the first American song, though the fact that it was the first copied is not conclusive proof that it was the first composed. Thomas Parnell wrote the poem for "My Days . . ."; the others are otherwise unknown and have been assumed to be products of Hopkinson's own pen.

These four songs have been widely printed, discussed, and performed in the present century, even before our U.S. Bicentennial celebration of 1976 focused so much attention on American music. They have been described as spontaneous creations, springing up in a climate conspicuously free of other songs even remotely resembling them. They are better understood, however, when viewed in a more accurate historical perspective: they are attractive imitations of the songs of Arne and his contemporaries, written in very much the same style as British songs for pleasure gardens and comic operas. Their melodic style is that of the London School of songwriting:

FRANCIS HOPKINSON, "MY DAYS HAVE BEEN SO WONDROUS FREE"

These first songs by Hopkinson were never published in his lifetime and remained unknown, except possibly to a few of his intimates. Had there been music publishers in the colonies in the 1760s, they might well have been published and given impetus to a budding school of American song. But they remained largely unheard until the twentieth century and therefore had no effect on the course of music in the colonies in the decades leading up to the Revolution. Hopkinson was clearly a man ahead of his time, writing songs when there was no native song literature. The fact that he apparently wrote no more songs for several decades would seem to be a commentary on the lack of urgency in this matter.

His *Seven Songs for the Harpsichord*[1] are a different matter. Published by J. Dobson in Philadelphia in 1788, the set actually contains eight songs, the last

---

1. Facsimile edition published by Harry Dichter (Philadelphia: Musical Americana, 1954).

apparently added after the title page and cover had been engraved. These are more substantial pieces, more reflective of the second generation of English writers of songs for pleasure gardens and the opera house. There are pastoral songs that would have fit perfectly at Vauxhall or Ranelagh:

> Enraptur's I gaze, when my Delia is by,
> And drink the sweet Poison of Love from her Eye . . .

There is a hunting song:

> O'er the hills far away, at the birth of the morn,
> I hear the full tone of the sweet sounding horn;
> The sportsmen with shoutings all hail the new day,
> And swift run the hounds o'er the hills far away.

There is a sea song, somewhat in the style of Dibdin:

> My love is gone to sea,
> Whilst I his absence mourn,
> No joy shall smile on me,
> Until my love return.

Another pastoral song invokes the famed birds of the pleasure gardens:

> Beneath a weeping willow's shade, she sat and sang alone,
> Her Hand upon her Heart she laid and plaintive was her moan,
> The mock-bird sat upon a Bough and listen'd to her Lay,
> Then to the distant Hills he bore the dulcet notes away.

Musically as well, Hopkinson's indebtedness to Arne, Hook, and their contemporaries is transparent. His songs are strophic, often with a refrain line at the end of each verse, and the vocal writing shows the same reliance on a basically syllabic style lightened occasionally by brief melismas on critical words and at phrase endings:

FRANCIS HOPKINSON, "ENRAPTUR'D I GAZE"

Though there is no evidence that Hopkinson's songs were sung at pleasure gardens or interpolated into comic operas, he makes it clear that they were conceived for persons of modest musical talents. Writing to Thomas Jefferson on October 23, 1788, he said, "The best of them is that they are so easy that any Person who can play at all may perform them without much Trouble, & I have endeavour'd to make the Melodies pleasing to the untutored Ear,"[2] and the *Pennsylvania Packet* advertised them late in 1788 as "songs . . . composed in an easy, familiar style, intended for young Practicioners on the *Harpsichord* or *Forte-Piano.*"

Hopkinson also indicated on several occasions that his intent was to appeal to the sentiment rather than the intellect. Another letter to Jefferson, this one accompanying the gift of a copy of the songs, suggests that "the last Song, if play'd very slow, and sung with Expression, is forcibly pathetic—at least in my Fancy. . . . But the Imagination of an Author who composes from his Heart, rather than his Head, is always more heated than he can expect his Readers to be."[3] Jefferson's reply must have pleased the composer: ". . . while my elder daughter was playing it (i.e., the last song) on the harpsichord, I happened to look toward the fire, & saw the younger one all in tears. I asked her if she was sick? She said 'no'; but the tune was so mournful."[4]

Hopkinson's story is an appealing one, and modern audiences have found pleasure in performances of his songs. The fact remains, however, that these pieces by America's first songwriter had little impact on his contemporaries. Judging from the mere handful of surviving copies, the printing was a small one; there was no second edition, nor were any of the songs printed separately. None appear in any of the numerous song anthologies of the late-eighteenth and early nineteenth centuries. Hopkinson wrote in his dedication:

> If this Attempt should not be too severely treated, others may be encouraged to venture on a Path, yet untrodden in America, and the Arts in Succession will take root and flourish amongst us.

There is no evidence that Hopkinson's songs were "severely treated"; rather, they appear to have been largely ignored. Taken in the context of "American" music, they appear to have sprung up without precedent; but seen in the context of English song of the second half of the eighteenth century, they are very much in the tradition discussed in the first chapter of this book. They were not distinguished enough to hold up against the songs of Hook, Shield, Reeve, Dibdin, and the like, and it would be almost two generations before native songwriters would take important steps along the path leading to characteristic American song.

2. Library of Congress (Washington), *Jefferson Papers*, 43:7401–2.
3. Ibid., 45:7728.
4. Thomas Jefferson, *The Writings of Thomas Jefferson*, ed. Andrew A. Lipscomb, 20 vols. (Washington D.C.: Thomas Jefferson Memorial Association of the United States, 1903–4), 6:299.

Boston was the center of the first regional school of song composition in America. Musicians like William Selby (1738–98), organist and composer, had chafed under the postwar ban on theatrical performances, quite rightly seeing the situation as restrictive for secular music of all kinds. Selby took out an announcement in the *Boston Evening Post* for February 2, 1782, to propose a publication to be called *The New Minstrel*, a collection of secular pieces; he took the occasion to address himself to all "friends of music and the fine arts" on the question of the moment:

> The promptness of this young country in those sciences which were once thought peculiar only to riper age, has already brought upon her the eyes of the world.
>
> She has pushed her researches deep into philosophy and her statesmen and generals equalled those of the Roman name.
>
> And shall those arts which make her happy, be less courted than those arts which have made her great? Why may she not be "In song unequall'd as unmatch'd in war?"
>
> A cry has gone forth against all amusements which are but a step from Gothism—the raisers of such a cry being unacquainted with distinctions, and little considering that "indulgences are only vices when pursued at the expence of some virtue" and that they intrench upon *No virtue*, they are innocent, and have in every age been acknowledged such by almost all moralists.

Despite his eloquence, the theatrical ban continued in effect for another seven years and his collection never materialized.

Selby was one of several musicians of the Boston area involved in the first large-scale publication of secular songs after the ban was lifted, a series of forty-odd pieces appearing serially in *The Massachusetts Magazine* beginning in January of 1788 and continuing monthly until May, 1792.[5] Four of Selby's songs appeared, along with five by Hans Gram (born in Denmark, but long active in Boston's musical life), four by Samuel Holyoke (1762–1820, best known as a composer and compiler of sacred works), three by Elias Mann (1750–1825) of Worcester, three attributed to "Philo Musico" (who may have been Chauncey Langdon), and others by less well known musicians of Massachusetts. As many as three songs appeared in each monthly issue, but by the summer of 1791 the supply of local songs appeared to run dry, and songs by European writers such as Thomas Arne, William Shield, James Hook, and even Christoph Willibald Gluck were printed until the series was ended in mid-1792.

These songs were more important for what they said about the spirit of the new country and the desire of Americans to be creative in music, than for their musical quality. These songs, like those of Hopkinson, must be viewed in the

---

5. A complete list of these songs is published in H. Earle Johnson, *Musical Interludes in Boston, 1795–1830* (New York: Columbia University Press, 1943), p. 261.

historical and stylistic context of British songwriting of the late eighteenth century; and in this setting, they can be seen only as derivative and amateurish. The texts fit nicely into the several categories of pleasure garden songs: pastoral, amatory, rustic, and bucolic:

Shady groves and purling rills,
   Walks, where quiv'ring moonbeams play,
Skreen the worldsick breast from ills,
   Lull the cares of noisy day.
          ("The Rural Retreat," William Selby)

How gloomy are the fields and plains,
How joyless all the languid swains;
No more the pipes or tabors sound,
Or nymphs dance on the verdant ground,
   For Daphne's dead and pleasure's gone,
   And silence reigns o'er mead and lawn.
          ("The Pensive Shepherd," words by
          J. Lathrop, music by S. Holyoke)

The music is similarly derivative of the style of Arne, Hook, and Shield, squarely within the stylistic bounds of the London school of songwriting already discussed. None of the songs was brought out as sheet music by commercial publishers; some ten were printed in the *American Musical Miscellany*, but none was otherwise anthologized. These comments are not intended to belittle this music, but merely to place it in proper perspective. Such a song as Selby's "The Lovely Lass" is far from the mature songs of Stephen Foster, but it and the other songs in this group represented a necessary first step toward distinctive American song.

July 5, 1817, is an important date in the history of American song. President James Monroe had chosen to celebrate the Fourth of July in Boston, and that city had elected to mark the occasion with a "Select Oratorio," a mammoth musical celebration mounted by the city's two finest musical organizations, the Handel and Haydn Society and the Philharmonic Society. The lengthy program opened with "President Monroe's March," especially composed for the event by one F. Granger, and continued with selections from such grand pieces as Haydn's *The Creation* and Handel's *Israel in Egypt*. Tucked in between these European masterworks were two songs by an American composer, Oliver Shaw (1779–1818) of Providence, Rhode Island: "Mary's Tears" and "All Things Bright and Fair Are Thine," both settings of poems from Thomas Moore's *Sacred Melodies*.

No such public honor had been paid to the songs of an American composer before, nor for that matter had a native songwriter produced pieces worthy of such distinction. Shaw wrote some seventy-odd songs during his creative lifetime, most of them printed by publishers in Providence, Boston, Philadelphia, Baltimore, and elsewhere. Some went through a number of editions and remained in print for some decades. A contemporary summed up his achievements:

> His songs were sung and his other musical compositions performed in every state and in every large town and city in the Union. . . . Gentlemen from Providence, who were occasionally in the Middle and Southern States, heard his music sung and played and applauded by ladies and gentlemen, who never heard the name of their author, but believed that they had the honor and happiness to learn and perform the most excellent and finished music of the first masters and doctors of Europe.[6]

This is an apt and accurate commentary, for even though Shaw was the first American-born songwriter to achieve widespread success, his musical training and compositional style were purely European.

Shaw's career as a musician and composer was exceptional, in that he became involved in music quite late in life. Born in Middleborough, Massachusetts in 1779, the son of a sea captain, he lost the sight of his right eye as a child, the result of a boyish prank, but sailed with his father to the West Indies despite this handicap. Tragedy struck again when, carrying out a solar sighting too soon after an attack of yellow fever, the sun's rays destroyed his other eye. He was plunged into a fit of deep despair:

> To his ardent and active spirit, the loss of his sight, at that time of life, and in the circumstances of his father's numerous and enterprising family, who were blessed with the privilege to sustain themselves by their own diligence and economy, his situation and prospects were inexpressibly afflictive.[7]

Having decided that the best hope for a young man with his affliction was the field of music, his family sent him off to Newport, Rhode Island, to study piano, organ, and "the science of music" with a certain Dr. Berkenhead, recently over from England. Progress was excellent, and he was sent on to Boston for advanced study with the most eminent musician of New England, Gottlieb Graupner. In a few years he was able to set himself up as a teacher of piano and organ in Dedham. It was here that he brought out his first publication, *A Favourite Selection of Music Adapted to the Piano Forte* (1806), which, despite the title, contained mostly songs for voice and keyboard, by Hook, Shield, and their contemporaries. Included also was a song of his own, his first to be published:

---

6. Thomas Williams, *A Discourse on the Life and Death of Oliver Shaw* (Boston: Charles C. P. Moody, 1851), p. 24.

7. Ibid., p. 7.

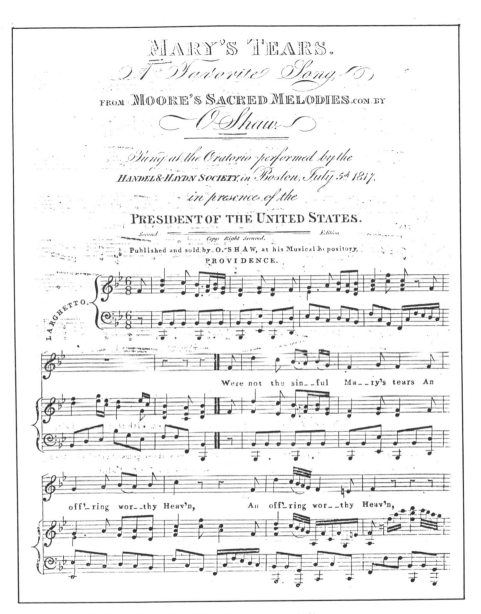

First page of "Mary's Tears" by Oliver Shaw (1779–1818).

"Address to a Tuft of Violets. A New Song—written by H. Mann—Music by O. Shaw."

In 1807 he moved to Providence, which was his home for the rest of his life. His first position was as organist of the First Congregational Society, and there was no want of private pupils. In addition, he soon began meeting weekly with certain citizens "for the purpose of improving them in the knowledge and practice of sacred music, and inculcating a more correct taste of it."[8] The group took out a charter as the Psallonian Society in 1815, grew to a size of more than 150 members, and for sixteen years offered concerts in Providence and surrounding towns of music by the "best and most approved European masters," mostly Handel, Haydn, Mozart, and Beethoven.

His first successful song, "Mary's Tears," was written in 1812, taken down note for note by one of his students from his playing and singing; it stayed in print for more than half a century. The opening phrase announces his indebtedness to Haydn and Handel; and his predilection for solid, diatonic, bottom-heavy sonorities reflects his fondness for the organ, his favorite instrument.

His most popular song, "There's Nothing True But Heaven," was written in 1816 and had gone into a sixth edition by 1829. One biographer comments that it "was repeated night after night by the Boston Handel and Haydn Society, and has been more widely circulated in this country than any other music of the kind."[9] Another contemporary makes the unsubstantiated claim that Shaw received $1,500 from this song alone.[10] Like "Mary's Tears," it is a setting of one of Thomas Moore's *Sacred Melodies*.[11]

Despite the handicap of blindness, Shaw was fully as versatile as were his European-born contemporaries. In addition to playing the organ, composing, and teaching, he also sang, traveling often to Boston to appear as soloist with the Handel and Haydn Society. He also sang during musical evenings held in his home in Providence, events that played an important role in the musical life there after the demise of the Psallonian Society in 1832. At least one of his children was a singer also; his song "Round the Wreaken"[12] is inscribed "as sung by Miss Mary Shaw at her father's Concerts." His Musical Repository was the leading music-publishing firm in Providence. And several men who were to play critical roles in the musical life of Boston were students of his: George Webb, who was to become president of the Boston Handel and Haydn Society, and Lowell Mason, who was to revolutionize music education in America.

Shaw continued to write songs until shortly before his death. A peak year was 1835, with some twenty songs bearing this date of publication; and "Home of My Soul" was written in 1846, less than two years before his death. But he never managed to match the success of his two most popular songs, "Mary's Tears" and "There's Nothing True But Heaven." The reasons for his decline will soon become obvious. His biographers said of him:

8. Frederic Denison, Albert A. Stanley, and Edward K. Glegen, eds., *Memorial of Oliver Shaw* (Providence: J. A. & R. A. Reid, 1884), p. 21.

9. Ibid., p. 24.

10. Williams, p. 25.

11. Which also served him for "All Things Fair and Bright are Thine" (1817), "As Down the Sunless Retreats of the Ocean" (1821), "Go, Let Me Weep," and "The Bird Let Loose" (1823), a duet.

12. Brought out by Oliver Ditson in Boston.

[God] selected and instructed Oliver Shaw to be the Teacher of a New School, and the Author of a New Era in the practice and science of music.[13]

We seem to see him walking the streets, led by a boy, or in the house of song and prayer preëminent for his devotion, his sightless eyes turned heavenward, as if he heard the heavenly music.[14]

If Shaw did indeed hear music from above, it was composed by Haydn, Mozart, Handel, and Beethoven. He was very much at the center of the New England Reformers of the time (who included Thomas Hastings, Timothy Flint, George Webb, and Lowell Mason) who had an unswerving conviction that the "true and scientific taste in music" was to be found only in the works of the great European Classical composers of the eighteenth and early nineteenth century, and that the only possible salvation for American composers was adulation and emulation of these men. Shaw's *Sacred Melodies*, published in 1818, contained three pieces by Haydn, two by Handel and Beethoven, one by Mozart, several by lesser Europeans—and none by an American.

The notion of the supremacy of the European style did have an effect on certain American composers who chose to write Classical music, and on several generations of New Englanders who were exposed as schoolchildren to the pedagogical methods and teaching materials developed by Lowell Mason and his school. But these ideas went unheeded by many thousands of other Americans whose chief musical enjoyment came from the songs they heard in the theaters, and from performing these songs at home. As early as the first decades of the nineteenth century, it was becoming clear that Americans liked novelty—songs in musical styles drawing on the various schools of national song brought to America by new immigrants. The aristocratic cultures of eighteenth-century Europe that had spawned and nourished the Classical style were of little or no concern to vast numbers of Americans who preferred the fresh and "wild" sounds of Irish and Scottish song, the cloying seductions of the new school of Italian opera, the exciting and amusing minstrel songs combining the neo-African sound of the banjo with Irish-Scottish melodies.

Oliver Shaw continued to write songs grounded in the symmetries and restrictions of the Classical style, into the 1820s and '30s, when popular song was moving in quite different directions. He clung to the patterns and gestures of a type of music that had run its course as a viable idiom for popular song, and his later songs were of interest only to a small and always decreasing circle of former students and admirers. He was the first American songwriter to face the reality, and suffer the consequences, of fickle taste in song.

13. Williams, p. 10.
14. Denison, et al., p. 26.

Nevertheless, his early songs caught the ears and hearts of his countrymen, and he was the first American-born songwriter whose compositions were accepted as the equal of those of European composers.

It is tempting to claim Charles Gilfert as an early American songwriter—a temptation I will not resist—though he was apparently born abroad. There are so few native-born composers in the first years of the nineteenth century that even a single addition to the list is welcome, and there are reasons for thinking of him as an American: he seems to have come here as a youth, thus some of his musical training is likely to have been in this country and all of his composition was done here; and no other country claims him, his birthplace remaining unknown. It is possible that he was related to George Gilfert, a music publisher who set up shop in New York in 1794.

Gilfert first turned up in New York around 1800, as a pianist. By 1805 he was in Charleston, South Carolina. Chiefly a man of the theater, he managed the Charleston Theatre from 1817 to 1825 and the Bowery Theatre in New York from 1826 to his death in 1829. Many of his songs were written for interpolation into stage works, and some were written for the singer Agnes Holman, whom he married in 1815. He was also a music publisher, the proprietor of the Musical Repository in Charleston—established in 1831—which brought out, among other items, a "Monthly Publication of Rondos, Airs with Variations, Waltzes, and Songs."

His most successful song was "Allen-A-Dale," first published in 1813 as one of several vocal works identified as being from "Rokeby." The English composer William Reeve wrote an opera at about this time entiled *Rokeby Castle*; it would appear that Gilfert was involved in an American performance of this piece, and followed the time-honored practice of inserting several of his own songs into the show, the others being "The Cypress Wreath," "To the Moon," and "A Weary Lot is Thine Fair Maid."

"Allen-A-Dale" became popular enough to be brought out by publishers in New York[15] and Philadelphia[16] and to find its way into various song anthologies and songsters of the time. As late as 1870, it was still listed in the catalog of a major publisher, Lee & Walker of Philadelphia. The five strophes spin out the tale of a lively, free-spirited, Robin Hood–like character who courts the daughter of a high-born family. He wins out:

> But loud, on the morrow, their wail and their cry!
> He had laugh'd on the lass with his bonny black eye;
> And she fled to the forest to hear a love tale,
> And the youth it was told by—was Allen-A-Dale!

The music is appropriately light-spirited, very much in the style of comic-pastoral airs from English operas of the time:

15. J. A. & W. Geib.
16. G. E. Blake and George Willig.

CHARLES GILFERT, "ALLEN-A-DALE"

Al - len - a - Dale has no fag - got for burn - ing,

Al - len - a - Dale has no fur-row for turn-ing,

Al - len - a - Dale has no fleece for the spin-ning, Yet

Al - len - a - Dale has red gold for the win-ning.

Most of Gilfert's other published songs were also written to be interpolated into such English operas as *Freedom Ho!*, *The Spanish Patriots*, and *The Virgin of the Sun*. His "The Horn of Chace" was introduced into the first New York performance of Weber's *Der Freischütz*, at the Park Theatre. Among songs written for his singer-wife were settings of four texts by Thomas Moore ("Love Thee Dearest!," "The Steersman's Song," "When E'er I See Those Smiling Eyes," and "The Wreath You Wove").

His published output consists of several dozen songs and a dozen or so piano pieces, mostly waltzes. It is the work of a good musician with a special flair for songwriting. Obviously composition was not Gilfert's chief concern; like so many musicians of the day, he was competent in various facets of musical activity. He furnished contemporary audiences with several handfuls of good songs, most of them written for the stage. He is as near a claim as America has to a writer of stage songs in the first decades of the history of the new country.

American popular song seemed to come of age, suddenly, with the appearance in 1825 of "The Minstrel's Return'd from the War" by John Hill Hewitt

John Hill Hewitt (1801–90).

(1801–90), son of the immigrant musician James Hewitt discussed earlier. The composer penciled the following comments on his autograph copy of the song, preserved in the Library of Congress in Washington:

> This song, as crude as it is, was one of my first musical efforts. It was composed in 1825 in the village of Greenville, S.C., now a city of 20,000 souls. When I returned to the North, I took this book with me to Boston. My brother James [Lang Hewitt] was a musical publisher. I gave him a copy to publish—he did it very reluctantly—did not think it worthy of a copyright. It was eagerly taken up by the public, and established my reputation as a ballad composer. It was sold all over the world—and my brother, not securing the right, told me that he missed making at least $10,000.

It probably would have been little consolation to James Hewitt to know he would be far from the last publisher to misjudge the potential appeal of a song!

The composer was not exaggerating the success of his song. Within a few years it had been brought out not only by the Hewitt firms in both Boston and New York, but also by many other publishers. Arrangements for guitar and voice soon appeared, as did piano variations on the tune. Its popularity continued for more than half a century: the *Board of Music Trade Catalogue* of 1870 lists five editions still in print.[17] It was, without any question, the single most popular song by an American composer before Stephen Foster. And, oddly, the failure of the Hewitts to secure copyright protection undoubtedly contributed to its success, since the numerous editions made it available in almost any store selling music, in any part of the country.

A look at the song itself sheds little light on the reasons for its enormous appeal. Though Hewitt was overly modest in calling it "crude," it is certainly a song of considerable simplicity, and its ancestry in the songs of Shield, Hook, and the older Hewitt is transparent. The three strophes outline the story of a minstrel who, having returned safely from battle, assures his lover that "the bugle shall part us, love, never." But the bugle signals another battle, he exchanges his guitar for a shield again, and the last stanza finds him dying on the battlefield.

The sentiment looks to the past, of course, to the songs of death in battle so popular in the decades immediately following the American Revolution. It is perhaps a mark of the intensity of feeling aroused by the events of that struggle that such a song could become so popular almost two generations after the end of hostilities. For a more specific model for the song, one need look no further than "The Wounded Hussar" by Hewitt's father, strikingly similar not only in plot and sentiment, but in musical style as well.

The first several phrases of "The Minstrel's Return'd" contain the chief musical material of the song. There is a marchlike piano introduction, suggesting trumpet fanfares, which persist into the first phrase of the vocal part. Then,

17. By Oliver Ditson & Co. in Boston, Lee & Walker in Philadelphia, William A. Pond & Co. in New York, George Willig & Co. in Baltimore, and D. P. Faulds in Louisville.

JOHN HILL HEWITT, "THE MINSTREL'S RETURN'D FROM THE WAR"

The Min - strel's re-turned from the war, With spir - its as buoy - ant as air; And thus on his tune - ful Gui - tar, He sings in the bow'r of his fair,

ing trumpet fanfares, which persist into the first phrase of the vocal part. Then, with mention of the hero's "tuneful guitar," the accompaniment suggests a serenade. The harmony never strays beyond the three principal chords of the major key. The last verse, with its tragic climax, is sung to precisely the same music as the first two stanzas, and thus it is left to the singer to bring about the darker mood at the climax of the story.

Hewitt's father, apparently determined that his son should follow a profession other than music, apprenticed him to a sign painter in Boston. The boy promptly ran away. Later the family secured an appointment for him at the Military Academy at West Point, where he was a classmate of men who were to play roles in the upcoming tragedy of the Civil War—Lee, Beauregard, Jackson, Polk, and Johnson. But Hewitt was mostly interested in pursuing private music instruction with the leader of the Army Band, a certain Willis, and when he was informed that his academic progress was not satisfactory enough to permit him to graduate with his class, he simply left and joined his family on a theatrical tour of the South. The venture came to an end in Augusta, Georgia, and young Hewitt stayed there as a music teacher, eventually working his way to South Carolina, where he studied law. After the death of his father in 1827, he settled in Baltimore, as a journalist—editing the *Minerva and Saturday Post* and then the *Baltimore Clipper*—a writer, a poet (his poem "The Song of the Wing" was awarded first prize, over Edgar Allan Poe's "The Coliseum," in a competition sponsored by a local journal) and a songwriter.

Hewitt's early songs showed continued stylistic dependence on English models. "O! Soon Return" (1829), "Farewell, Since We Must Part" (1829), and "The Soldier's Farewell" (1831), mine the expressive and stylistic strains of English stage and concert music of the turn of the century, and "Girls Beware" (1832) and "I'll Meet Thee, Love" (1833) show that he knew the lighter, comic-sentimental style of vintage Henry Bishop. The only echo of the success of "The Minstrel's Return'd" came with "The Mountain Bugle" (1833), which sold well enough to warrant a second edition in 1839 and was also brought out in an arrangement for guitar.

Later songs show that he was familiar with, and receptive to, the various bodies of national melody that became part of song in America in the three decades leading up to the Civil War. Indeed, his songs of the 1830s and '40s represent a sort of microcosm of song in America during this fertile period.

His ears were sensitive to the sounds of Italian opera sweeping over America in the early and mid-1830s. "They Told Me to Shun Him" (1834), "Ah! Fondly I Remember" (1837), and "Wilt Thou Think of Me?" (1836) tell us, with their arpeggiated accompaniments, expressive appoggiaturas, and supple melodic lines, that Hewitt had been listening to Rossini and Bellini.

The brief popularity of singing families from Switzerland and Austria, beginning in the late 1830s, inspired Hewitt to write "mountain" songs of his own: "Away to My Mountain Home Away" (1837), "My Own Native Mountains" (1841), and "The Alpine Horn" (1843), complete with yodel. Henry Russell's powerful and affecting singing of his own ballads inspired Hewitt to write "Fall of the Oak" (1841), a companion song to Russell's "Woodman Spare That Tree," and "Ho! For a Rover's Life" (1843), a "descriptive ballad" that captures the essence of the Englishman's songs so well that Russell sang it himself. Certain mock-folk, comic ballads of the Hutchinson Family seem to have been the inspiration for "Go and Ask My Mother" (1848), and Hewitt's "I Would Not Die At All" (1852) is a parody of Stephen Foster's "I Would Not Die in Spring Time."

JOHN HILL HEWITT, "WILT THOU THINK OF ME?"

A step in a different musical direction was taken with "Mary, Now the Seas Divide Us," published in 1840. The cover identifies the song as a "Southern refrain written and adopted by J. T. S. Sullivan, esq., with symphonies and Accompaniment by John Hill Hewitt." Its melody is of eloquent simplicity, suggesting by its pentatonic character that it may have been adapted from a tune in the Scotch-Irish-English oral tradition.

The harmonization is tasteful and expressive of the gentle, lamenting character of the tune and text:

>   Mary, now the seas divide us,
>   Dost thou think of me?

Who that e'er ador'd could chide us,
    Or my love for thee? . . .

Dost thou ere recall our parting
    On this lonely shore,
When the pearly tears were starting,
    Tears unknown before?

JOHN HILL HEWITT, "MARY, NOW THE SEAS DIVIDE US"

In this song, European influences have been so well absorbed that the piece, in character and in musical style, is recognizably and unequivocally American. Certainly Hewitt thought of himself as completely American; typical of his attitude is his reminiscence of a dinner party given by a wealthy planter in South Carolina, graced by music:

> There is something truly amazing to an American, I mean a democratic American, to sit for an hour or two listening to the caterwauling of a band of jabbering foreigners, who have clothed themselves with the title of prima donna, prima donna assoluta, tenore primo, primo basso profondo, et cetera, while attempting to give expression to our unpretending, yet with us, pleasing ballads.[18]

18. John Hill Hewitt, *Shadows on the Wall; or, Glimpses of the Past* (Baltimore: Turnbull Brothers, 1877), p. 96.

By the late 1840s, Hewitt was writing minstrel songs, many of them for a minstrel company resident in Baltimore calling itself "Kunkel's Nightingale Opera Troupe." Some of these are stridently antiabolitionist, and when the Civil War erupted in 1861, Hewitt cast his lot with the Confederacy. His minstrel and Civil War songs will be discussed later; it will suffice to mention here that his talent for songwriting in no way diminished during these later years, and in fact his "All Quiet Along the Potomac" of 1864, written when he was sixty-three years old, may be his best work.

His 300-odd songs are the product of an extremely skillful composer. He was a craftsman of the highest order, within the modest framework of the sort of music he chose to write. His accompaniments, for example, are idiomatic for the keyboard, richer than those of many of his contemporaries, easy to play, yet graceful to the ear. Many of his songs sound better today than those of some of his peers who achieved more popularity.

His most productive years were spent in and around Baltimore, and then further South; most of his songs were published in Baltimore, a large and musically active city. Yet it was somewhat culturally remote from other large Eastern cities, with closer ties to the upper South. Hewitt was somewhat of an outsider— geographically and politically—and it may well be that his songs were not as well known or as widely sung as they might have been had he lived and worked in a more cosmopolitan city such as New York or Boston.

Though none of the composers discussed here deserve to be ranked among the major songwriters of the nineteenth century, each contributed to the recognition of American composers as capable craftsmen—a necessary foundation for the emergence of Stephen Foster and other American writers who were equal to and even superior to foreign songwriters.

SIX

"Jim Crow";

OR.

The Music of the Early American Minstrel Show

We confess to a fondness for negro minstrelsy. There is something in the plaintive "Dearest Mae," in the affectionate "Lucy Neal," and in the melodious "Uncle Ned," that goes directly to the heart, and makes Italian trills seem tame. It is like Ossian's music of memory, "pleasant and mournful to the soul."
—Henry James, as quoted in *Dwight's Journal of Music*, July 24, 1852

STAGE IMPERSONATION of blacks by whites had its beginnings in America before the Revolution and built up to a crazy crescendo in the nineteenth century, reaching a peak in the middle years of that century, from which it declined only gradually. For several decades beginning in the 1840s, it was far and away the most popular stage entertainment in America, and many critics, including no less a notable than Charles Dickens, considered the minstrel show the most characteristic form of entertainment to be developed in this country and its greatest contribution to the nineteenth-century theater.

The present chapter will deal not so much with a history of the minstrel show—a history several times written by now[1]—as with an account of the music

1. Hans Nathan, *Dan Emmett and the Rise of Early Negro Minstrelsy* (Norman, Oklahoma: University of Oklahoma Press, 1962); Daily Paskman and Sigmund Spaeth, *"Gentlemen, Be*

performed during such shows, its musical character, its relationship to earlier and later popular song in America, and its dissemination in printed sheet music form into every part of America.

Black characters were sometimes found in English comic operas of the late eighteenth century, including some popular in America, and these characters were usually asked to speak and sing in what was to the English ear of the time a suitable dialect. The enormous popular success of *The Padlock* (1768), with music by Charles Dibdin, was due in no small part to the partly comic appeal of the black character Mungo, and when Dibdin in later years turned to the writing and performing of one-man entertainments at his Sans Souci Theatre, "negro" songs in dialect often appeared in his entertainments. For example, his *The Wags, or The Camp of Pleasure*, first performed in 1790, included "The Negro and his Banja":

> One negro wi my banjer,
>   Me from Jenny come,
>   Wid cunning yiei
>   Me savez spy
> De buckra world one hum,
> As troo a street a stranger
>   Me my banjer strum.

> My missy for one black dog about the house me kick,
> Him say my nassy tawny face enough to make him sick;
> But when my massa he go out, she then no longer rail,
> For first me let the captain in, and then me tell no tale.

"Poor Black Boy," a popular ballad from *The Prize* (1793), with music by Stephen Storace, is sung by a black character named Juba:

> Your care of money, ah care no more
> No tink if you be rich or poor
> No mind employ
> Me stay wid you or sorry no
> And where away my Massa go
> Go "Poor Black Boy."

> Me sigh with you when you be sad
> And when you merry much and glad
> Me share your joy
> For do my face be darky hue

Seated!": *A Parade of the Old-Time Minstrels* (New York: Doubleday, Doran, 1928); Robert C. Toll, *Blacking Up: The Minstrel Show in Nineteenth-Century America* (New York: Oxford University Press, 1974); Carl Wittke, *Tambo and Bones: A History of the American Stage* (Durham, North Carolina: Duke University Press, 1930).

There's still a faithful soul and true
In "Poor Black Boy."

There was no consistency to the dialect; within a song, there might be fluctuation from line to line between straight English and dialect; and some dialogue and songs by black characters make no attempt to capture dialect at all:

On Africa's wide plains where the lion now roaring,
With freedom stalks forth the vast desert exploring,
I was dragg'd from my hut and enchain'd as a slave,
In a dark floating dungeon upon the salt wave.
                    —"The Desponding Negro," from
                    The Evening Brush, music by Reeve

While British writers had some idea of the speech patterns of New World blacks, British composers had no idea whatsoever of the musical language of these people. Most songs sung by black characters flow along in a straightforward, unabashedly European style:

CHARLES DIBDIN, "YANKO DEAR"

Under the assumption that the music of nonliterate Africans or ex-Africans should be simpler than European music, a composer would occasionally write childishly simple music for a black character.

REEVE, "PAUL AND VIRGINIA"

There are a few instances where a composer goes even a step further. Storace's "Poor Black Boy" has a melody with strong suggestions of a Scottish tune, with its pentatonic scale and characteristic "Scottish snap" rhythmic pattern:

STEPHEN STORACE, "POOR BLACK BOY"

To Storace's ear, apparently, the melodic style of Scottish folk song represented an uncouth and primitive music, in comparison to the style of contemporary song and opera. When faced with the challenge of writing appropriate music for a character from another culture, a culture viewed even by those sympathetic to it as primitive and crude, he fell back on the only "primitive" style he knew, that of the folk song of a neighboring country—a country regarded by the British as inferior to their own, incidentally.

The first two decades of the nineteenth century saw further scattered examples of black characters introduced into English or American dramas, and a handful of songs similar to the ones just mentioned.

A serious investigation of the black American dialect and its utilization on stage for comic effect awaited the arrival in America of Charles Mathews, a celebrated English actor of the day. His American debut came in the fall of 1822, in Baltimore, and shortly thereafter he appeared on the New York stage for the first time, on November 7, at the Park Theatre. His fame was such that unprecedented crowds flocked to the Park to see and hear him in a succession of comic and tragic roles. Letters to his wife underline why he, and other famous actors and singers, were persuaded to come to America: his share of the receipts for his opening night in New York came to nearly $1800; his first eight nights at the Park brought him $10,962, "superior to anything I ever did out of London." Europeans tended to view America as a crude and comic place, but even at this early date, it had financial rewards to offer to the adventuresome performer.

Mathews's most popular appearances in London had been in a series of "At Homes," one-character entertainments dealing with some aspect of life in England or on the Continent. They were mixtures of monologues, anecdotes, jokes, songs, and the impersonation of various characters, drawn from his keen ear for various dialects and accents and his genius at reproducing these on stage. His first "At Home" in America was given at the Park on November 27, 1822; entitled "A Trip to Paris," it was made up of "Recitations, Stories, Anecdotes and Songs; as performed by him at the English Opera House, London, 40 nights in

The New York debut of Charles Mathews in Moncrieff's *Monsieur Tonson* took place at the Park Theatre on November 7, 1822. Miss Johnson played Madame Bellegarde. Watercolor by John Searles.

one season, with universal approbation & applause." These entertainments were well received during his several years in America, though he noted in a letter to his wife a problem with American theaters that has persisted to the present—they were often too large for entertainment that depended on subtleties: "[The theater] was too full to obtain the sort of silent attention that my 'Table-Talk' requires. The countenance and varieties of its expression were necessarily lost to a large proportion of the audience; and I therefore felt the want of powers to produce my usual effects."[2]

Mathews was not content to repeat entertainments already created in London; one reason for his trip to America was to gather new material, to hear and use new accents and dialects. From the day of his arrival in America, he listened with fascination to new speech patterns, which he painstakingly wrote down, phonetically. Of most interest was the speech of the black American. Mathews haunted theaters with black actors, streets most often frequented by blacks, and black churches. "I shall be rich in black fun," he wrote to his wife soon after his arrival in America. "I have studied their broken English carefully. It is pronounced the real thing, even by the Yankees."[3] He sent his wife, as a sample, a transcription from a sermon he had heard:

> My wordy bredren, it a no use to come to de mettumhouse to ear de most hellygunt orashions if a no put a de cent into de plate; de spiritable man cannot get a on widout de temporarilities; twelve 'postles must hab de candle to burn. You dress a self up in de fine blue a cot, and a bandalore breechum, and tink a look like a gemman, but no more like a gemmandan put a finger in a de fire, and take him out again, widout you put a de money in a de plate.[4]

Even more spectacular, for an Englishman, were performances of plays by Shakespeare by black troupes. One of the first of these was a production of *Richard III* in New York in August of 1821, at a spot known as the African Grove, an imitation of the English and American pleasure gardens run for the benefit of citizens of New York who wanted fresh air, refreshment, and entertainment on a summer evening and who, being black, were not admitted to the Vauxhall and Chatham Gardens. A critic for the *National Advocate* reported that several "fashionable songs" were interpolated into the drama, including "Eveleen's Bower," one of Moore's *Irish Melodies*! Mathews reported the following astonishing dialogue from a production of *Hamlet:* "To be or not to be, dat is him queston, whether him nobler in de mind to suffer or lift up him arms against one sea of hubble bubble and by opossum end'em."[5] The audience, having been reminded

2. George Clinton Densmore Odell, *Annals of the New York Stage*, 15 vols. (New York: Columbia University Press, 1927–49), 3:53.

3. Mrs. [Anne (Jackson)] Mathews, *Memoirs of Charles Mathews*, 4 vols. (London: R. Bentley, 1838–39), 3:390.

4. Ibid., 3:390–91.

5. Quoted in Nathan, p. 46.

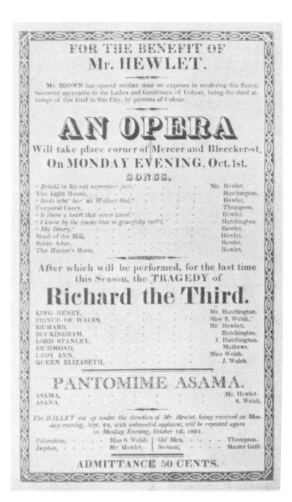

Playbill for an evening of mixed entertainment "by persons of Colour" on October 1, 1821.

of a song popular among them, clamored for and was given a performance of "Opossum Up a Gum-Tree":

Pos-sum up a Gum - Tree, Up he go, up he go,

Printed in England c. 1824, as a "South Carolinian Negro Air," the tune has some resemblance to the folk melody "The Lasses of Dublin." Like "Poor Black Boy" and other tunes from the early days of black theater, this song seems to indicate a link with Scotch-Irish melodic style.

Mathews incorporated his impressions of America and some of its people into an evening's entertainment, "All Well at Natchitoches"; one of the characters was a runaway slave named Agamemnon, a character allowing Mathews to

indulge in his "black fun" through a dialect new to his impersonations. He tried
out this new act in Philadelphia before leaving for home, but its greatest popularity was in England, where audiences were all too responsive to entertainment
that parodied and ridiculed life in America. Though some earlier "negro" songs
had dealt with slaves in sympathetic terms, Mathews showed no interest in the
human aspects of black life in America, but only in what he could extract for
humor and parody.

Stage impersonation of blacks continued in the American theater during the
1820s. A handful of songs associated with such impersonation began appearing
in print, no more than a trickle compared to the flood of Irish, English, and Italian music making up the musical mainstream. One of the earliest of these was
the "Bonja Song, a Favorite Negro Air."[6] The text, in a sort of dialect that could
have been written only by someone with little contact with the black American,
depicts him as an ignorant but carefree person:

> Me envy not de white men den
> Me poor, but me is gay,
> Me glad at heart, me happy when
> Me on my Bonja play.
>
> Me sing all day, me sleep all night,
> Me hab no care, my heart is light,
> Me tink not what to morrow bring
> Me happy so me sing.

The music is of the same sort encountered in the late eighteenth century, with
extreme simplicity of musical means intended to depict a simple person (or race):

ANON., "BONJA SONG"

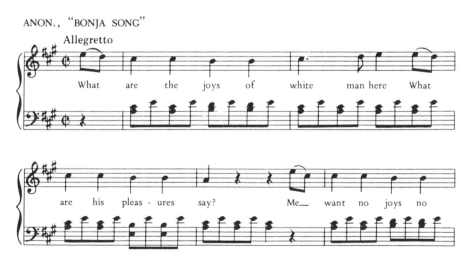

6. Brought out by J. A. & W. Geib in New York about 1820.

ills   me fear,   But   on   my   Bon - ja   play.

The melodic range is only a fifth; there are only two chords (tonic and dominant) in the entire piece. The words were attributed to the otherwise-unknown R. C. Dallas, in the *Portsmouth Weekly Magazine* of September 16, 1824; the music is anonymous and could have been conceived only by a shallow mind.

It is not known who first had the idea of using burnt cork to blacken the face of a white performer impersonating a black, but certainly George Washington Dixon was the first to establish a wide reputation as an entertainer in blackface. He was singing and clowning in blackface in Albany by 1827, and made his first New York appearance on July 19, 1828.[7] Two of the earliest "negro" songs to enjoy widespread popularity were featured in Dixon's stage acts in the late 1820s, and he claimed authorship for both: "Long Tail Blue," and "Coal Black Rose."

"Long Tail Blue" is a character sketch of an elegantly dressed urban black, who advises his audience, almost without dialect: "If you want to win the Ladie's hearts, I'll tell you what to do; Go to a tip top Tailor's shop, and buy a long tail blue." The front cover of the edition published in New York by Atwill has, in a lithograph by Endicott, a city black complete with elegant high hat, flared trousers, walking cane, eyeglasses on a chain, and of course his long-tail coat. "Coal Black Rose" deals with the other end of the spectrum of black society. The song is sung by Sambo, who is clearly an unlearned Southern black. He has come courting his Rosa:

> Lubly Rosa, Sambo cum,
> Don't you hear de Banjo—tum, tum, tum,
> Lubly Rosa, Sambo cum,
> Don't you hear de Banjo—tum, tum, tum,
>   Oh, Rose, de coal black Rose,
> I wish I may be cortch'd if I don't lub Rose,
>   Oh, Rose, de coal black Rose.

Everything goes well until the eighth stanza, when Sambo sees the whites of the eyes of his rival, Cuffee, gleaming in the corner of Rose's room; after a scuffle,

7. Odell, 3:354. New York's cultural role at this time may be judged from the fact that European performers and music by foreign composers were most often heard first in New York, then in other cities on the Atlantic seaboard and perhaps even later in inland cities and smaller towns. Native performers and music by Americans most often traveled this route in reverse, from small towns to medium-sized cities to Philadelphia and Baltimore and finally New York. This is an important cultural pattern at this time and later as well: indigenous American popular music—the Hutchinson Family, the minstrel show, Stephen Foster—came to New York only after it had been created and tested elsewhere. It was not until much later in the nineteenth century that New York became an originating point for popular music.

Sambo leaves, hot on the heels of Cuffee, his refrain line changed to "Oh, Rose, you blacka snake Rose!" The success of this song was so great that it was expanded into a three-character comic skit with music, called *Love in a Cloud*, which was presented for the first time as part of the bill at the Bowery Theatre in New York on September 24, 1829.

There are great similarities in the music of the two songs; both have simple melodies, with sequential, sing-song motives:

GEORGE WASHINGTON DIXON, "LONG TAIL BLUE"

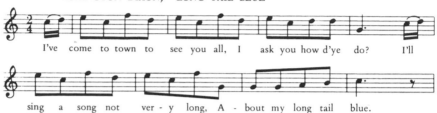

GEORGE WASHINGTON DIXON, "COAL BLACK ROSE"

It is curious that blacks were portrayed in such a simple musical style. The white authors of this early "minstrel" music obviously knew nothing of African or Afro-American music, which in rhythmic structures and patterns, and in melodic invention and embellishment, is among the more complex music of the world's people.

The late 1820s and early 1830s saw an increase in the number of white entertainers portraying black characters on stage, in dialogue, dance, and song. George Nichols, J. W. Sweeney, and Bob Farrell were among the most popular. But it was Thomas Dartmouth Rice (1808–60) who came up with an act that demonstrated just what potential there was in such entertainment. The story of "Jim Crow" has been told many times, but perhaps never so graphically as in the *Atlantic Monthly* in 1867. Some of the facts may be fuzzy, but the style is vintage, and inimitable. The author explains how Rice, born in New York City, an aspiring actor who had been a supernumerary at the Park Theatre before seeking more fame in provincial theaters, found himself in Cincinnati:

> Thus it was that, as he sauntered along one of the main thoroughfares of Cincinnati, his attention was suddenly arrested by a voice ringing clear and full above the noises of the street, and giving utterance, in an unmistakable dialect, to the refrain of a song to this effect:
>
> "Turn about an' wheel about an' do jis so,
> An' ebery time I turn about I jump Jim Crow."

Thomas   Dartmouth   Rice
(1808–60).

Struck by the peculiarities of the performance, so unique in style, matter, and "character" of delivery, the player listened on. Were not these the
elements—was the suggestion of the instant—which might admit of higher
than mere street or stableyard development? As a national or "race" illustration, behind the footlights, might not "Jim Crow" and a black face tickle the
fancy of pit and circle, as well as the "Sprig of Shillalah" and a red
nose? . . .

As his engagement at Cincinnati had nearly expired, Rice deemed it
expedient to postpone a public venture in the newly projected line until the
opening of a fresh engagement should grow out of the experiment. This en-

Sheet music cover for "Sich a
Getting Up Stairs" showing
T. D. Rice in blackface.

gagement had already been entered into; and accordingly, shortly after, . . .
he left for Pittsburg [sic].
        . . . There was a negro in attendance at Griffith's Hotel, on Wood
Street, named Cuff—an exquisit specimen of his sort—who won a precari-
ous subsistence by letting his open mouth as a mark for boys to pitch pennies into, at three paces, and by carrying the trunks of passengers from the
steamboats to the hotels. . . . Slight persuasion induced him to accompany
the actor to the theatre. . . . After the play Rice, having shaded his own
countenance to the "contraband" hue, ordered Cuff to disrobe, and proceeded to invest himself in the cast-off apparel. . . . Rice, habited in an old
coat forlornly dilapidated, with a pair of shoes composed equally of patches
and places for patches on his feet, and wearing a coarse straw hat in a melancholy condition of rent and collapse over a dense black wig of matted
moss, waddled into view. The extraordinary apparition produced an instant
effect. The crash of peanuts ceased in the pit. . . . The orchestra opened
with a short prelude, and to its accompaniment Rice began to sing, deliver-
ing the first line by way of introductory recitative:

"O, Jim Crow's come to town, as you all must know,
An' he wheel about, he turn about, he do jis so,
An' ebery time he wheel about he jump Jim Crow."

The effect was electric. Such a thunder of applause as followed was never heard before within the shell of the old theatre. With each succeeding couplet and refrain the uproar was renewed. . . .

Now it happened that Cuff, who meanwhile was crouching in *dishabille* under concealment of a projecting *flat* behind the performer, by some means received intelligence, at this point, of the near approach of a steamer to the Monongahela Wharf. . . . Driven to desperation, and forgetful in the emergency of every sense of propriety, Cuff, in ludicrous undress as he was, started from his place, rushed upon the stage, and laying his hand upon the performer's shoulder, called out excitedly: "Massa Rice, Massa Rice, gi' me nigga's hat—nigga's coat—nigga's shoes—gi' me nigga's t'ings! Massa Griffif wants 'im—STEAMBOAT'S COMIN'"!!

The incident was the touch, in the mirthful experience of that night, that passed endurance. Pit and circles were in one scene of such convulsive merriment that it was impossible to proceed in the performance.[8]

Thus was born "the first great international song hit of American popular music."[9] Rice "jumped Jim Crow" eastward, performing to wildly enthusiastic audiences in Louisville, Cincinnati, Philadelphia, Washington, Baltimore, and finally New York on November 12, 1832, at the Bowery. In 1836 he went to England, performing with great success in London and elsewhere; he was thus the first native-born American musician to carry across the Atlantic a type of music recognized abroad as characteristically American.

Audiences did not laugh with Jim Crow, they laughed at him, at his dialect and dress and even movements. If we are to believe the account of the first performance of the piece just quoted, the audience found Rice's portrayal of a black amusing, and equally amusing the real, live black who burst on the stage, confused and in an embarrassing state of undress. It should be noted that the caricature was devised and carried out by a native New Yorker, before an audience in a Northern city, and was described with obvious relish by a writer in a Northern journal *after the Civil War*.

Rice claims to have heard the music sung by a black. He may have been telling the truth. But the music is in no way remarkable and has no hint of any exotic element. It has been pointed out that the tune resembles both an Irish folk tune and an English stage song.[10] Blacks picked up the music of whites with ease and enthusiasm, and Rice could well have heard a black singing a tune derived from British folk or stage music. But it is equally likely that the story of the tune's

8. Robert P. Nevin, "Stephen C. Foster and Negro Minstrelsy," *Atlantic Monthly* 20 (November 1867). Later scholars have placed the first performance in Louisville.

9. Gilbert Chase, *America's Music: From the Pilgrims to the Present*, 2nd rev. ed. (New York: McGraw-Hill, 1966), p. 264.

10. Toll, p. 27.

A contemporary engraving of the American Theatre, Bowery, New York. The legend reads: "View of the Stage on the *fifty-seventh* night of Mᴿ T. D. RICE of Kentucky in his original and celebrated extravaganza of JIM CROW on which occasion every department of the house was thronged to an excess unprecedented in the records of theatrical attraction. New York 25ᵗʰ November 1833."

origin was invented to give authenticity to a white man's portrayal of a black. Any number of later minstrel tunes have similar stories of origin, always circulated by the "composer" or singer.

The tune is quite clumsy, sounding almost like a patchwork of several different melodies:

"JIM CROW"

Come lis-ten all you gals and boys, I'm just from Tuck-y-hoe; I'm
goin' to sing a lee-tle song, My name's Jim _ Crow. Weel a-bout and turn a-bout, And
do jis so; Eb - 'ry time I weel a-bout, I jump Jim Crow.

But Rice's act did not depend on a charming, appealing, or even memorable tune. His appearance, his movements, the grotesque dance he did between verses, and the text were what excited audiences. The song, as published by Atwill in New York, has no fewer than twenty-one verses, ranging from playful, punning boasting:

> I'm a rorer on de fiddle,
>   An down in ole Virginny;
> Dey say I play de skientific,
>   Like massa Pagganninny.

to crude burlesquing of black American habits:

> De way dey bake de hoe cake,
>   Virginny nebber tire;
> Dey put de doe upon de foot,
>   An stick im in de fire.

to crude attempts at satirical, topical humor. Rice was in the habit of extemporizing additional verses, making references to local persons and events. The tune was a vehicle for his verses, and an accompaniment to his posturing and dancing. Despite its fame, and the untold thousands of Americans who heard it sung on the stage by Rice, the melody did not catch on, was not a particularly successful item of sheet music, and, unlike many minstrel tunes, never took root in oral tradition.

Rice sang other songs. There was "Clar de Kitchen," with a spirited and impulsive tune and an apparently endless string of verses; Rice's claim of having written it was disputed by George Nichols, a contemporary entertainer. Rice also sang "Long Time Ago," one of the few songs of this genre with a hint of black musical practices: the song proceeds with alternation of a solo line and refrain, the "call and response" pattern so common to much African and Afro-American music:

"LONG TIME AGO"

go.   O   I   was   born____ down ole Var - gin - ee.   Long time   a - go.

go.   Long time   a - go.

go.   Long time   a - go.

The success of "Jim Crow" spawned many other similar acts featuring songs, dances, tunes, and comedy routines based on real or imagined aspects of black life and culture.

Bob Farrell, billed as "from the Southern Theatres" for an engagement at the Bowery Theatre in New York in 1834, was apparently the first to introduce the song "Zip Coon" on the stage, though George Washington Dixon probably sang it that year also. The tune, strongly reminiscent of an Irish or Scotch dance, has remained a favorite of country fiddlers, slightly changed and given the title "Turkey in the Straw." Zip Coon was another of the black dandies, judging from the lithograph on the cover of the edition brought out in 1834 by Hewitt in New York. The text varied from performer to performer and was a patchwork of unrelated verses ranging from vignettes of "negro" life to political commentary:

> O its old Suky blue skin, she is in lub wid me,
> I went the udder arter noon to take a dish ob tea,
> What do you tink now, Suky hab for supper,
> Why chicken foot an possum heel, widout any butter.

> I tell you what will happin den, now bery soon,
> De Nited States Bank will be blone to de moon,
> Dare General Jackson, will him lampoon,
> An de bery nex President, will be Zip Coon.

"Jim Along Josey" was written by Edward Harper, sung by him in the drama "The Free Nigger of New York,"[11] and sung by practically every blackface entertainer thereafter. Musically, it is another tune suggesting Irish or Scottish origin:

---

11. Edward LeRoy Rice, *Monarchs of Minstrelsy: From "Daddy" Rice to Date* (New York: Kenny Publishing Company, 1911), p. 24. "Jim Along Josey" was published in 1840 by Firth & Hall in New York.

Sheet music cover for "Zip Coon." The lithograph, by Endicott, reveals the essential attributes of this great dandy: the elaborate coiffeur, the ornamental jewelry, and the swallow-tailed jacket, which, according to tradition, was always blue.

EDWARD HARPER, "JIM ALONG JOSEY"

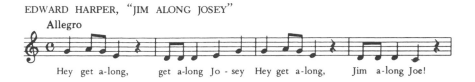

Hey get a-long, get a-long Jo-sey Hey get a-long, Jim a-long Joe!

"Old Tare River" was claimed by Joel W. Sweeney (1831–60), who is credited with introducing the five-string banjo and was a widely popular performer in America and then in the British Isles in the 1840s.

Billy Whitlock (1813–78) wrote "Miss Lucy Long," one of the first musical portraits of a black woman:

Oh! Miss Lucy's teeth is grinning,
    Just like an ear ob corn,
And her eyes dey look so winning
    Oh! would I'd ne'er been born.

The music in the first period of the minstrel song, then, was invariably a simple diatonic or even pentatonic tune harmonized with no more than two or three basic chords. The lyrics were in dialect, sketching several stereotyped black characters, reveling in the portrait of the American black as a simple-minded, grotesque creature apparently devoid of the finer human sentiments. It seems fair to say that the stage image of the black offered by these songs and their performers did nothing to create sympathy for the plight of the black slave, or even the black freedman. To the contrary, if these songs supported any side in the growing controversy over slavery, it was the one maintaining that the black race was inferior to the white, capable of only menial labor and deserving of ridicule.

Through the 1820s and '30s, blackface entertainers had shared the stage with other types of acts. Just as concerts of the time were mixtures of orchestral, chamber, vocal, and solo pieces, so evenings of theater offered mixtures of various sorts of entertainment. Dixon offered New York its first hearing of "Coal Black Rose" as part of an evening's fare that also included *William Tell*, and when he made his first appearance on the stage of the Park Theatre, "Coal Black Rose" was sandwiched between a new farce, *Brag Is a Good Dog, But Holdfast Is Better*, and no less a play than *Richard III*, with the famous Forrest in the title role. Daddy Rice's "Jim Crow" was first sung between the acts of *The Rifle*, an American farce, and its first New York performance was sandwiched between two serious plays, *The Hunchback* by Sheridan Knowles and *Catharine of Cleves*. Blackface singers, dancers, and comedians turned up in every form of entertainment of the day, including the circus.

It was not until early 1843, however, that the first more lengthy blackface entertainment involving a group of performers was given. On February 6, at the Bowery Amphitheatre in New York, occurred the historic

First Night of the novel, grotesque, original and surpassingly melodious ethiopian band, entitled the VIRGINIA MINSTRELS. Being an exclusively musical entertainment, combining the banjo, violin, bone castanetts, and tambourine; and entirely exempt from the vulgarities and other objectionable features, which have hitherto characterized negro extravaganzas.[12]

The Virginia Minstrels comprised four talented and experienced entertainers. William M. Whitlock, born in New York City in 1813, was a banjo player, singer, and dancer who had been so widely acclaimed that P. T. Barnum took him under his management in 1839. Frank Brower, born in 1823 in Baltimore, made his first professional performance in Philadelphia about 1838 and quickly established himself as one of the best blackface dancers of the time, though he also sang and played the bones. Dick Pelham, also a New Yorker, was born in 1815, and had built a considerable reputation, alone and with his younger brother, in "Negro Peculiarities, Dances, and Extravaganzas." And Daniel Decatur Emmett, born in Mount Verson, Ohio in 1815, had begun his musical career as a drummer and fifer in the United States Army, moved on to be a banjo player and blackface singer in various traveling circuses, and had come to New York in 1842 with his friend Brower as a blackface dancer, singer, and bone player. Whitlock described the genesis of the first minstrel show in *The New York Clipper* for May 19, 1878:

> One day I asked Old Dan Emmett, who was in New York at the time, to practice the fiddle and banjo with me at his boarding house in Cathcrine Street. We went down there, and when we had practiced two or three tunes, Frank Brower called in (by accident). He listened to our music, charmed to the soul. I told him to join us with the bones, which he did. Presently Dick Pelham came in (also by accident), and looked amazed. I asked him to procure a tambourine and make one of the party, and he went and got one. After practicing for a while, we went to the old resort of the circus crowd— the "Branch," in the Bowery—with our instruments, and in Bartlett's Billiard-room performed for the first time as the Virginia Minstrels.

Their first performance at the Bowery Amphitheatre was part of a circus evening; they played and sang as a group in a "Negro Concert" and also took part in several acts of the circus. On February 16 they performed at the Cornucopia, then went on to the Park Theatre, where they were part of the Olympic Circus from February 17 to March 1. In addition to their ensemble playing and singing, they presented mock lectures in black American dialect and the usual comic sketches. It was not until they went to Boston in early March that they were able to offer a full evening's entertainment alone. Their "Ethiopian Concert" at the Masonic Temple on March 7–8 was made up mostly of songs sung and played by the four—Emmett on violin, Whitlock on banjo, Brower on bones, and Pelham on tambourine, though there was almost certainly some switching of instruments by the versatile musicians. Included were "Old Dan Tucker," "Goin Ober de Mountain," "Old Tar (!) River," "Uncle Gabriel," "Boatman Dance," and

12. *New York Herald*, February 6, 1843.

Cover illustration of *The Celebrated Negro Melodies, as Sung by the Virginia Minstrels* (Boston, 1843). The artists are (left to right) Dick Pelham (tambourine), Dan Emmett (fiddle), Bill Whitlock (banjo), and Frank Brower (bones).

"Lucy Long," and the program ended with Emmett's singing of "Fine Old Colored Gemman," his parody of Henry Russell's well-known "Fine Old English Gentleman."

After more performances in and around Boston—a playbill from Brinley Hall in Worcester for March 20 announces that they will perform "songs, refrains, and ditties as sung by the southern slaves at all their merry meetings such as the gathering in of the cotton and sugar crops, corn huskings, slave weddings, and junketings"[13]—they returned briefly to New York. On April 21 they set sail for England.

Concerts at Liverpool and Manchester took them to London, where they offered a "Grand Ethiopian Concert" at the Adelphi Theatre on June 19. *The London Times* reviewed them favorably on June 26, commenting that "some of the aboriginal airs of the interior of Africa, modernized if not humanized in the slave states of the Union, and adapted to ears polite, have been introduced."

The troupe remained together only until July 14. Whitlock returned to America, Emmett and Brower performed together and with other musicians in England, Scotland, and Ireland before returning to America in September of 1844, and Pelham stayed on in England for the rest of his life.

13. Nathan, p. 120.

Sheet music cover for "Dandy Jim from Caroline," published in London in 1844.

Emmett returned to America to find that the genre of the minstrel show had proliferated beyond belief. Almost every American city had at least one resident band of minstrels, and dozens of other blackface entertainers toured the smaller cities and towns, singly and in groups. But Emmett's talents as a banjo player, actor, dancer, and composer had not diminished, and he quickly reestablished himself. For some years he was a star performer in entertainments managed by Charles White, who operated at "White's New Ethiopian Opera House" in New York. After a period in the Midwest—Chicago and St. Paul, mostly—Emmett returned to New York to join Bryant's Minstrels, performing with them for a decade. He retired from the stage in the early 1870s, living in Chicago and then returning to his home town of Mount Vernon, where he died in 1904.

Emmett continued to compose until the 1860s. *Old Dan Emmet's* [sic] *Original Banjo Melodies* came out in two volumes, in 1843 and 1844. His early songs remained popular, and new ones included "Dandy Jim from Caroline" (published first in England in 1844), "Jordan Is a Hard Road to Travel" (Oliver Ditson & Co., 1853), and "Dixie's Land," written in 1859.

The origins of many of "his" songs are cloudy: some are also claimed by other composers, and some seem to have been known before he performed them and published them under his own name. They were undoubtedly drawn from traditional Anglo-American melodies stored in his memory, single tunes or several patched together; if any were original, they were patterned closely on the same tune tradition.[14] Some of his texts were likewise drawn from a common fund of traditional lyrics. Thus Emmett and other early minstrel performers were more adapters than composers.

Performances in this first period of the minstrel show generally had the melody sung by one of the troupe, with a fiddle playing along in unison, embellishing the tune and using the lower strings as a drone. One or more banjos played elaborated versions of the melody, or ostinato melodic figures resembling those often found accompanying a singer in African music. The sound has been described as follows:

> The volume of the minstrel band was quite lean, yet anything but delicate. The tones of the banjo died away quickly and therefore could not serve as a solid foundation in the ensemble. On top was the squeaky, carelessly tuned fiddle. Add the dry "ra, raka, taka, tak" of the bones and the tambourine's dull thumps and ceaseless jingling to the twang of the banjo and the flat tone of the fiddle, and the sound of the band is approximated: it was scratchy, tinkling, cackling, and humorously incongruous.[15]

It is not necessary to imagine the sound, however. Something that must surely be very close in sound to the music of early minstrel shows can be heard today in the

14. Nathan, in Chapter Twelve ("Early Minstrel Tunes") and Chapter Thirteen ("Early Banjo Tunes and American Syncopation"), draws many convincing parallels between several of Emmett's songs and specific pieces of English-Irish-Scotch folk and stage music.

15. Nathan, p. 128.

earliest recordings from the 1920s of "hillbilly" music from the South, which capture performances of fiddlers and banjoists playing dance music of the Anglo-American tradition, including some of the very tunes known to have been heard in minstrel shows.

The only challenge to the claim of the Virginia Minstrels that they were the first minstrel troupe came from E. P. Christy, a native of Philadelphia (b. 1815), who stated that he was giving minstrel shows in Albany, New York, in 1842, though the first documented performance of his group dates from May 1844, some months after the public performance and success of the Virginia Minstrels in New York. Be that as it may, Christy's Minstrels made an indelible mark on the history of the genre. The original group was made up of four performers: Christy himself, who sang and played the banjo; George Christy, a great dancer, actor, and bones player; Tom Vaughn, a banjoist; and Lansing Durand, a "jig dancer" of exceptional merit. After performing for several years in and around Albany and Buffalo, they came to New York in 1846, where on April 24 this "original and far-famed band of Ethiopian Minstrels" opened an engagement at Palmo's Opera House. By now two new performers had been added, R. M. Hooley (an Irishman who joined Christy in 1844, later to form his own troupe in Brooklyn) and W. Porter.

On October 4, 1847, Christy's Minstrels opened an engagement at Mechanic's Hall that was to run for almost a year and establish their reputation as the most popular, entertaining, and successful minstrel band to that point. The company now numbered seven, and they offered a full evening's entertainment, in three parts, that was a far cry from the several songs and dances that the Virginia Minstrels had squeezed between several plays or the acts of a circus a few short years before. There was now a "full band," which opened the entertainment with an overture, performed several marches and dances through the evening, and accompanied much of the singing and dancing. There were songs, a dozen or more, sung by various members of the cast: but with the exception of "Lucy Long," claimed by Billy Whitlock of the original Virginia Minstrels, they had all been written in the five years that had elapsed since the first minstrel show. Included were "Stop that Knocking," written in 1843 by A. F. Winnemore, "Mary Blane," "The Gal with the Blue Dress On," and two brand new songs by a young composer named Stephen Foster, "Louisiana Belle" and "Old Uncle Ned." But there was much more, too—a duet for bones and violin, a banjo duet, solos for violin and accordion, a glee ("Where Is the Spot that We Were Born On?"), a chorus from Bellini's *La sonnambula* sung by the entire company, and a burlesque lecture in black American dialect on the subject of phrenology.

The American stage has rarely seen anything to match the explosion of blackface minstrelsy in the decade following the appearance of the Virginia Minstrels and the Christy Minstrels. Most of the names of these earliest troupes reflected the supposed ethnic origin of the genre. There were the African Melo-

The illustration used on early printings of a number of Stephen Foster's songs published by C. Holt, Jr., New York, and Oliver Ditson, Boston.

dists, the Congo Minstrels, and the Congo Melodists; the Ethiopian Melodists, Harmonists, Serenaders, Minstrels; the Ethiopian Mountain Singers, and a group calling itself simply the Ethiopian Band; there was even a Juvenile Ethiopian Minstrel Company, composed of performers aged three to ten years. Regional appellations were popular, from the first Virginia Minstrels through the Virginia Serenaders, the Virginia Harmonists, the Kentucky Minstrels and the Southern Singers, and the New Orleans Serenaders. Names stressing the skin color of the performers were equally popular: the Sable Minstrels, Sable Brothers, Sable Serenaders. There were combinations: the Sable Sisters and Ethiopian

Minstrels, and the Ethiopian Operatic Brothers and Sable Sisters. There was the Gumbo Family. Some geographical names were merely convenient, not descriptive: the Metropolitan Minstrels, the New York Minstrels. The United States Ethiopian Minstrels of Brooklyn touched as many bases as possible. Some names are enigmatic, such as the Hungarian Ethiopian Minstrels, and a few were poetic, such as the Nightingale Opera Troupe.

Repertory was as varied as the names of groups. During the winter of 1845–46, the Ethiopian Serenaders alternated evenings of Ethiopian songs with programs of selections from *Norma, La sonnambula, Leonora,* and other popular operas; even their "black" programs included "I Dreamt I Dwelt in Kitchen Halls" and "The Lip Hung Down," parodies on two of the most popular airs of Balfe's *The Bohemian Girl.* Nelson Kneass and his Ethiopian Troupe offered "The Virginia Girl," a parody on Balfe's opera. A program for the New Orleans Serenaders for the evening of December 1, 1848, identifies the performers as "Signori Boni, Banjoni, Ole Bull, Viola, and Tamburini"; these gentlemen gave imitations of Jenny Lind, Grisi, and Mme. Bishop singing excerpts from various Italian operas. This group also performed such popular sentimental ballads as Linley's "Thou Art Gone from My Gaze." Ordways Aeolians, Boston's most popular resident group of the 1850s, was under the direction of Dr. John P. Ordway, a practicing physician and later a member of the state legislature. He not only managed the company, but also appeared as a singer of his own songs, accompanying himself on the piano. "Twinkling Stars Are Laughing, Love" (1855) is typical of his output; it has nothing to do with "Ethiopian" music, in music or text, and everything to do with popular sentimental balladry of the day:

JOHN P. ORDWAY, "TWINKLING STARS ARE LAUGHING, LOVE"

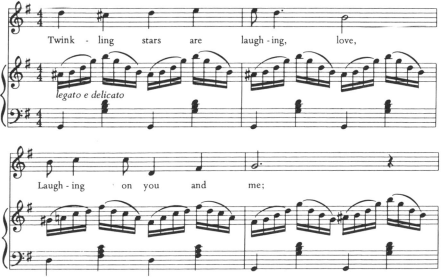

And some "minstrel" songs of this period, when looked at critically, have even less to do with the type of music generally associated with the minstrel show. "The Virginia Rose Bud" was published as a minstrel song by Oliver Ditson; written by F. H. Kavanaugh, a member of Palmo's Burlesque Opera Company in the 1840s, it offers a glimpse at the bizarre, hybrid product resulting from whites masquerading as blacks, parodying Italian opera. The story is tragic, of a child who has died; the lyrics fluctuate between more or less straight English and dialect:

> I had a rosebud in my garden growing,
> A plant I cherished with a father's care,
> When other darkies round that plant was hoeing,
> Its zefferessence seemed to fill the air.

The chorus, at the end of each stanza, is in dialect—and equally unequivocally in the musical dialect of Italian opera, Bellini to be specific:

F. H. KAVANAUGH, "THE VIRGINIA ROSE BUD"

The coda rushes through a Rossini-ish crescendo to a crashing climax, with the chorus singing "I hear dar hoofs upon de hill, I hear dem fainter, fainter still . . . Dey stole my child away." The whole thing is totally bizarre—and totally American.

New songs similar in style to the earliest minstrel songs by Dixon, Rice, and Emmett continued to appear. These may have been in the minstrel repertory in the earliest period and for one reason or another were not published until later, or they may have been newly created by minstrel performers of the '40s and '50s. One of the more popular of these was "Tom-Big-Bee River," a pentatonic tune attributed to Silas S. Steele, an obscure composer who may have had some connection with A. F. Winnemore and his Original Virginia Serenaders.

SILAS S. STEELE, "TOM-BIG-BEE RIVER"

Other songs of this earliest type were the anonymous "Jim Crack Corn," a somewhat similar tune arranged by H. T. Bryant and called "Balm of Gilead," a lovely Scottish tune arranged by J. B. Murphy into a minstrel song entitled "Nicodemus Johnson," and an anonymous song called "Piccayune Butler," with the following refrain:

"PICCAYUNE BUTLER"

Pic-cay-une But-ler com-in', com-in', Pic-cay-une But-ler come to town!

These songs and others like them surely represent tunes from English-Irish-Scotch traditional music transplanted to America; they became rare after the Civil War, but occasionally appeared even then, in such a song as "Shine On" by Luke Schoolcraft (b. 1847). An important new type of minstrel song was emerging in the 1840s, however. An early example is "Mary Blane." Written in the usual pseudo-black dialect, its tune is another of those simple, diatonic airs that sounds like so many other minstrel songs, but isn't:

"MARY BLANE"

I once did know a pret-ty gal, And took her for my

wife, She came from Loui-si - a-na, and I lik'd her as my life,

The text though, by Francis Germon of the Ethiopian Serenaders, is quite different from those of the earliest minstrel songs. It is a simple lament for Mary Blane, who "came from Louisiana, and I lik'd her as my life, We happy lib'd together, She nebber caused me pain," but who disappeared "one dark and dreary night." The last verse completes the vignette:

> I often asked for Mary Blane,
>   My Massa he did scold,
> And said you saucy nigger boy,
>   If you must know, she's sold.

And the chorus is heard now in its true context:

> Oh, farewell, farewell, poor Mary Blane,
>   One faithful heart will think of you,
> Farewell, farewell, poor Mary Blane,
>   If we ne'er meet again.

Suddenly, the minstrel song has taken on a new dimension. The singer (J. W. Raynor, born in Ireland) is not "delineating" some ridiculous, grotesque, marginally human creature, but is communicating grief over the loss of a loved one.

"Miss Lucy Neal," a "Favorite Ethiopian Song" by James Sanford, the

"Celebrated Negro Singer and Dancer" from Philadelphia who was one of the Original Virginia Serenaders, is another of the new type of minstrel song. Published in 1844,[16] the original version begins:

> I was born in Alabama,
>   My master's name was Meal
> He used to own a yallow gal,
>   Her name was Lucy Neale.

The story unfolded in the nine stanzas is again sympathetic and tragic. The singer-narrator tells how he fell in love with Lucy Neale, but how they were separated when "My massa he did sell me, because he thought I'd steal." Unable to find a way to get back to her, he hears news that "Miss Lucy she was taken sick, she eat too much corn meal; The Doctor he did gib her up . . ." The last stanza brings the tragedy to its conclusion:

> One day I got a letter,
>   And jet black was the seal
> It was de announcement ob de death
>   Of my poor Lucy Neale.

The lyrics slip in and out of dialect, but the narrator is a fully human, sympathetic character throughout. It may be reading too much into the situation to suggest that Sanford was a crusading humanitarian, using the minstrel song to drive home the point that blacks are indistinguishable in their emotions from any other person. He was probably interested only in the effectiveness of his song, and drew on a type of sentimental ballad popularized by such composers and singers as Henry Russell and the Hutchinsons, merely transplanting it to the minstrel show. But no matter what his motives, the fact remains that most of what people living in the North knew about blacks came from what they saw and heard at minstrel shows—widely held to be authentic depictions of black American life and character—and such sympathetic portrayals may well have been an important first step toward the widespread support of abolition.

The core of the minstrel repertory during the 1840s and '50s was this new type of "plantation song," with musical and poetical ties to sentimental balladry, and with gentler and more sympathetic treatment of black characters. Most popular were portraits of Southern slave women. We have a whole gallery of them, the prototype most probably being Sanford's "Miss Lucy Neal." Stephen Foster contributed a sizable collection, including "Melinda May" ("No snowdrop was ebber more fair, She smiles like de roses dat bloom round de stream, And sings like de bird in the air."), "Angelina Baker" ("Ebry time I met her she was smiling like de sun, But now I'm left to weep a tear cayse Angelina's gone"), and "Nelly Was a Lady." Cast in the same mold are James W. Porter's "Ella Ree" ("De

16. By A. Fiot (Philadelphia).

summer moon will rise and set, And de night birds thrill dar lay, And de possum and coon so softly step, Round de grave of Ella Ree"), "Dearest Mae," which may have been sung by the composer, L. V. H. Crosby, when his Boston Harmoneons performed at the White House for President Polk in 1846, and "Nancy Till," a favorite of White's Serenaders. Most popular of all was B. R. Hanby's "Darling Nelly Gray," a tragic tale of a female slave sold away from her home plantation in Kentucky ("The white man bound her with his chain, They have taken her to Georgia for to wear her life away, As she toils in the cotton and the cane") told by her lover, who pines away with a broken heart ("Hark! there's somebody knocking at the door, Oh! I hear the angels calling and I see my Nelly Gray.").

This new type of minstrel song also differed musically from its predecessors. At first glance its melodic style seems to resemble that of the earliest minstrel songs, with simple diatonic melodies sometimes suggesting pentatonic scales, and a similar simple statement of melodic sections with no trace of sequence or development of melodic material. But composers of the new plantation songs were well grounded in the harmonic practice of popular music of the day, and their melodies, stripped of their accompaniment, clearly imply more sophisticated harmonic, tonal chord progressions:

"DARLING NELLY GRAY"

Phrases, periods, and larger sections are regular, symmetrical, and balanced in melody and harmony. Also, these new songs are usually strophic with a choral refrain, most often written in four-part vocal harmony, following each stanza. This feature coincides with an increase in size of the usual minstrel troupe, and with the new practice of having the entire company join the soloist in the refrain after each verse.

These plantation songs were written for performance on the minstrel stage, but many of them became even more widely popular through sales of sheet music and performance in the home. The genre was so effective and appealing that many songwriters with no connection with black minstrelsy, and no desire to use texts in dialect, wrote songs of a similar nature. There was, for instance, H. S. Thompson's "Lilly Dale." [17] Thompson had nothing to do with the minstrel show; his text is in straightforward English with no trace of dialect; there is no mention in the text of slaves, or of the South. But Lilly Dale is a close relative of Nelly Gray and Ella Ree; the four verses record the tragic tale of her death ("Her cheeks that once glowed, with the rose-tint of health, By the hand of disease had turned pale, And the death damp was on the pure white brow, Of my poor lost Lilly Dale."); the chorus, in four parts, joins the narrator in lament ("Oh! Lilly, sweet Lilly, dear Lilly Dale, Now the wild rose blossoms o'er her little green grave, 'Neath the trees in the flow'ry vale.").

Cast in precisely the same mold are H. S Thompson's "Annie Lisle," "Nora O'Neal" by Will S. Hays ("Oh! why should I weep tears of sorrow? Or why does my hope lose its place? Won't I meet you, my darling, tomorrow, And smile on your beautiful face?"), and "The Hazel Dell" by George F. Root ("In the Hazel Dell my Nelly's sleeping, Nelly lov'd so long!"). There are Poulton's "Aura Lee," and "Listen to the Mocking Bird" by Alicia Hawthorne (= Septimus Winner) ("I'm dreaming now of Hally, sweet Hally . . . She's sleeping in the valley, And the mocking bird is singing where she lies."). And, for that matter, Stephen Foster's "Gentle Annie." There is not a black face in this collection of lovely and beloved ladies, but their tales and tunes would have been unimaginable without the plantation song of the minstrel stage.

But the gentle, lyric plantation song was to endure for scarcely more than a decade. In the years immediately preceding the Civil War, the minstrel song became strident, like almost every other form of literary and musical expression in America. Some troupes took one side of the intensifying debate over slavery, some the other. John Hill Hewitt, for instance, living in Baltimore and writing songs for a resident Baltimore minstrel troupe calling itself Kunkel's Nightingale Opera Troupe, had contented himself with producing typical plantation songs such as "Where the Sweet Magnolia Grows" (1848), with the refrain

Eulodie is dead and gone,
  I am left to sigh alone;
There's no joy in life for me,
  Parted from my Eulodie!

17. Published in 1852 by Oliver Ditson & Co. of Boston.

But the heightening of passions over the issue of slavery prompted him to turn out a very different type of song; "Aunt Harriet Becha Stow," written and performed the year after the appearance of *Uncle Tom's Cabin*, puts the following words in the mouth of a fugitive slave who has found his way to the North:

> I went to New York City a month or two ago,
>   A hunting for dat lady, Aunt Harriet Becha Stowe;
> I see'd de Abolitions, dey said she'd gone away,
>   Dey told me in de city it was no use to stay.
> She take away de dollars, and put 'em in her pocket,
>   She lai'd her hand upon it, and dar she safely lock it,
> Dey said if Massa come for me, den dey would quickly meet,
>   Dey'd make a lion of me, and gib m 'nuf to eat.
>
> Ole Massa's very kind, ole Missu's gentle too,
>   And much I love my Dinah in ole Virginny true;
> Now I'll go back and stay dar, and neber more will roam,
>   Lor bress de Southern Ladies, and my ole southern home!
> But don't come back Aunt Harriet, in England make a fuss,
>   Go talk against your County, put money in your puss;
> And when us happy niggers you pity in your prayer,
>   Oh! don't forget de *WHITE SLAVES* dat starvin ober dare!

The minstrel song, then, went through several stages of development in the period before the Civil War. Nor did its history end with that great conflict. To the contrary—minstrelsy enjoyed its peak popularity during the two decades after 1865, and new types of songs emerged, as will be recounted in a later chapter.

SEVEN

"If I Were a Voice";

OR,

The Hutchinson Family and Popular Song as Political and Social Protest

THE HISTORY of the Hutchinson Family is two stories in one.

The first has to do with the emergence, in the middle third of the nineteenth century, of American performers and composers of popular song fully comparable to Europeans.

The other concerns the use of popular song for purposes other than entertainment for the first time in America. The 1830s, '40s, and '50s were troubled, turbulent, dramatic, disturbing, memorable decades here; popular song, in becoming part of these events, took on a quite different character from what it had been before.

Both stories unfolded, simultaneously and dramatically, in the career of the Hutchinson Family.

The first—the coming of age of American performers and composers—is the easier to recount.

One Richard Hutchinson emigrated from England in 1634, settling in Salem Village in Massachusetts with his wife Alice and their four children. His descendants lived there until Elisha, of the sixth generation (born in 1751), moved to Milford, New Hampshire in 1799. Elisha's son Jesse, born in 1778, married Mary Leavitt, only fifteen at the time. The couple had sixteen children, of whom thirteen survived the rigors of birth and childhood.

It was a musical family from the beginning. The entire family sang in the choir of the Baptist Church in Milford, and three of the sons, Judson, John, and Asa, purchased instruments, practicing in the fields for fear their father would object to time spent away from chores. Judson and John also played in the town brass band on patriotic and political occasions. Thus their first musical exposure was to the hymns, psalms, and spiritual songs of an early-nineteenth-century small-town church, and to the marches and quicksteps of a local band.

On Thanksgiving Day, 1839, all thirteen children (the youngest, Abby, was only ten) gave a "concert" in the Milford Baptist Church. The program was made up of hymns, anthems, and glees from *The Social Choir*,[1] and of popular songs.

The Social Choir was a typical collection of the time, reflecting the various types of music popular in America in the fourth decade of the century. More than half of the selections had been adapted from opera or other forms of classical music: there were many choruses fashioned from operas by Mozart, Auber, Rossini, and Bellini; there were Scotch and Irish songs, including several of Moore's *Irish Melodies* arranged for chorus; Henry Bishop was there, and even Arne; and there was a scattering of pieces by Kingsley and several other obscure Americans.

The following year John Hutchinson heard a concert given in Lynn, Massachusetts, by the Rainer Family. Margaretta, Ellena, Lewis, and Semir, of the "tribe of Rainer," came to America in the fall of 1839, advertising themselves as the Tyrolese Minstrels and performing quartet arrangements of native songs in native costumes. They were a sensation in New York and equally popular in other parts of America. Within months their songs were being brought out by American publishers, and American family groups were being formed in imitation of them.

The Hutchinsons were one of these. John coached four of his brothers—Jesse, Joshua, Judson, and Asa—in as close an imitation of the Rainers as possible, and the five offered a public concert in Lynn, Massachusetts. After an unproductive trip to Boston resulting in no public performances, John, Judson, and Asa settled in Lynn, singing in the choir of the First Universalist Church, practicing, and building a repertory. In the fall of 1841, calling themselves the Aeolian Vocalists, the three performed in such towns as East Wilton, West Wilton, Wilton, and Wilton Centre, netting 6¼¢ from their first concert. But their most successful and well-received concert to date was back in Lynn, where they were joined by their baby sister Abby, eleven years old at the time. The four then traveled to Portsmouth, New Hampshire, and other "down-East" towns, gaining confidence and expanding their repertory.

Judson (born 1817) was the oldest of the quartet. "The eleventh child, the

1. Edited by George Kingsley of Boston and published by Crocker & Brewster in that city in 1835.

dear, confiding, generous, loving, humorous, gifted Judson"[2] had shown musical talent at a remarkably early age, family lore having it that he was heard to hum the melody of the hymn "Greenville" while playing on the nursery floor, before he could even walk. He saved money from selling vegetables to buy a fiddle, which he practiced until he was able to play two parts of a song on the in-

The Aeolian Vocalists—John, Judson, and Asa Hutchinson—at their first concert in East Wilton, Massachusetts, Fall, 1841.

strument and sing a third himself. Musically the most versatile of the group, he could move easily from a sentimental ballad, to a burlesque of Italian opera, to a comic dialect song of his own composition.

> Blending his sweet voice (for the age has not produced a sweeter one) with the exquisite touch of that violin which had become an element of his own soul, he was enabled to charm the admiring multitude who flocked in town and city to be fascinated by his exquisite strains.[3]

John (born 1821), "the bold, daring, ambitious, inflexible, gifted John,"[4] was the thirteenth child, four years younger than Judson. Several aspects of his character came out in an incident when he was no more than eight; as a student at a local singing school, he was dissatisfied with the slow pace of a tune given the scholars to sing, and took the lead in moving it along at a more spirited tempo, despite the indignation of the "professor." The spiritual leader of the quartet, his

2. Joshua [Hutchinson], *A Brief Narrative of the Hutchinson Family. Sixteen Sons and Daughters of the "Tribe of Jesse"* (Boston: Lee and Shepard, 1874), p. 35.

3. Ibid., p. 37.

4. Ibid., p. 42.

passions were to lead them into situations where the more cautious would not
have ventured.

Asa (born 1823), "genial, manly, companionable,"[5] showed an early interest in the bass line. His voice changed and deepened early, becoming "superla-
tively beautiful in the medium register, [and] equally so in the lower; so that he
could descend to the octave in C or double B flat with the most perfect accuracy
and ease."[6] Though younger than his two brothers, he was the steadying influence, the one to arrange programs and handle publicity and commercial spon-
sorship.

Abby (born 1829) was the youngest, the sixteenth child, "the innocent af-
fable, genial, loving, charming Abby, the household pet."[7]

> Blending with her genial nature a smiling face radiant with the joys of con-
> scious innocence, . . . she was truly the charm of the young Quartette, as
> from city to city, and from state to state, did they fly to minister to the grow-
> ing desire of a young nation . . .[8]

This was the cast of characters, the four Hutchinsons who, in 1842, bought
a carriage and set off on a concert tour against the wishes of their parents, reluc-
tant to see their baby daughter leave home.

They sang in such towns as Concord and Hanover, crossed the Connecticut
River to Vermont, sang their way westward across that state and into New York,
first to Saratoga and then as far as Albany. Their programs were a mixture of
solos by various members of the quartet and of songs arranged as vocal quartets.
John described them:

> Judson had a naturally high voice, a pure tenor. My voice was a baritone,
> though I sang falsetto easily, and Asa had a deep bass. Abby had an old-
> fashioned "counter" or contralto voice. The result was an effect like that of a
> male quartet, Abby's part being first tenor, Judson's second tenor, mine first
> and Asa's second bass, respectively. But we practised an interchange of parts
> as we sang, and the blending of the voices was so perfect that it seemed quite
> impossible for the audience to distinguish the several parts. . . . For many
> years we sang to the music of two violins and a violoncello. We sought to
> have Abby use a guitar, and she did to some extent. . . . In playing, Judson
> always kept the air, and I played second violin to him.[9]

They included in their programs more songs of the sort they now knew were
surefire audience pleasers. Henry Russell was a great favorite; they sang three of
his lengthy, melodramatic pieces ("The Maniac," "The Gambler's Wife," and

5. Ibid., p. 47.
6. Ibid., p. 49.
7. Ibid., p. 53.
8. Ibid., p. 54.
9. John Wallace Hutchinson, *Story of the Hutchinsons* (*Tribe of Jesse*), 2 vols. (Boston: Lee and
Shepard, 1896), 2:304–5, 294.

"Ship on Fire"). Lyman Heath, of Nashua, New Hampshire, furnished them with several equally melodramatic songs of his own composition—"The Snow Storm," "The Dying Child," and "The Grave of Bonaparte." Typical is his "The Snow Storm," to words by Seba Smith:

The cold wind swept the mountain's height,
    And pathless was the dreary wild,
And 'mid the cheerless hours of night,
    A mother wandered with her child.
        As through the drifted snow she press'd,
        The babe was sleeping on her breast.

At dawn a traveller passed by,
    And saw her 'neath a snowy veil;
The frost of death was in her eye,
    Her cheek was cold, and hard, and pale.
        He moved the robe from off the child;
        The babe looked up and sweetly smiled.

"The Vulture of the Alps," with music written by Judson to words "that we got out of an old school reader," was another melodramatic, narrative ballad, about a child snatched from the midst of his playmates by a ravenous vulture. Such strong fare was balanced by comic songs, like "Matrimonial Sweets" and "Cows in a Cornfield"; by such sentimental pieces as Lyman Heath's "The Cot Where We Were Born"; the Hutchinsons' own setting of George P. Morris's "My Mother's Bible"; and by Abby's rendition of Bernard Covert's Irish-sounding "Jamie's on the Stormy Sea."

They were befriended in Albany by a certain Luke Newland, who offered the valuable suggestions that they change their name from "The Aeolian Vocalists" to "The Hutchinson Family"; that they eliminate instrumental selections; and that they emphasize their regional background in programming and costume. He also persuaded a local publisher to bring out "The Vulture of the Alps," the first Hutchinson song to be printed.

With their new image and with new confidence, the Hutchinsons headed for Boston, the "Athens of America." Successful concerts in Pittsfield, Springfield, and Worcester along the way served to polish their new image and act, and they boldly engaged the Melodeon in Boston, where their concert made little money but was received with great enthusiasm by those who attended.

An important result of their first Boston engagement was the publication of four of their songs ("The Snow Storm," "Jamie's on the Stormy Sea," "The Grave of Bonaparte," and the temperance glee "King Alcohol") by Oliver Ditson, the most important music publisher in New England.

After singing in Boston again and making their first appearance in New York in the spring of 1843, the quartet launched their most ambitious tour to date, which took them to every major city on the East Coast. They sang for President Tyler at the White House, performed with the orchestra of the Philadelphia Musical Society, and met such famous people as Henry Wadsworth Longfellow and Daniel Webster. Firth, Hall, and Pond of New York brought out another dozen of their songs, and they returned home in the spring of 1844 with a profit of $4,750 over all expenses and a reputation as the most popular American singers of the day.

Their programs of 1843–44 were made up of the same sentimental and melodramatic fare that had brought them their first success. But gradually their own songs made up more and more of their repertory.

Easily their most popular song was "The Old Granite State." Jesse, who often traveled with the quartet as their manager, had fitted autobiographical words to the tune of a well-known Second Advent (Millerite) hymn, "The Old Church Yard":

> We have come from the mountains,
> We have come from the mountains,
> We have come from the mountains,
>   Of the old Granite State.
>   We're a band of brothers,
>   We're a band of brothers,
>   We're a band of brothers,
>   And we live among the hills.

Succeeding verses sketched more of their story: "We have left our aged parents . . . ," "We had ten other brothers . . . ," "We are all real Yankees . . . ," and so on. They sang the song for the first time in Lynn, between tours, with Jesse taking the words to each verse and the rest of the quartet singing the refrain. John's first thought had been that "the song seemed the essence of egotism to us, and we wondered that Jesse could have written it. We could not conceive that the public cared anything about the Hutchinson family names."[10] But audiences loved it, with its repetitious but rousing words and music. It soon became unthinkable for the Hutchinsons to close a concert with anything other than this song.

In the summer of 1845 the Hutchinsons were persuaded to go to England with the ex-slave Frederick Douglass. They first sang in Liverpool, on September 10, and were well received, but they were homesick and often uncomfortable with the language and customs, and conscious of the degree and depth of poverty. They gradually built an audience among the working class, and began singing at labor meetings. Their first London concert, on February 10, brought unfavorable reviews, and despite a friendship with Charles Dickens, they found London an unsympathetic place. Most of their eleventh-month stay in the British Isles was spent in smaller towns, singing for lower-class audiences, getting to know the conditions of life in a foreign country, talking and thinking about their

10. Ibid., 2:297–98.

own country and its own problems. They were invited to perform at Covent Garden, at the "annual complimentary concert to the talent of the kingdom," which began at six o'clock and lasted all night; they shared the stage with Braham, Henry Russell, Phillips, and "some Italians, Jews and Germans, who all sang and played very creditably." By the time they left for home, they had a large following in England, often singing to crowds of as many as six thousand people. Despite its tentative beginning, their stay in England had been a financial and artistic success.

The other part of the Hutchinsons' history and character was developing at the same time they were achieving such success as a popular singing group.

The Hutchinson boys had early contacts with alcohol and the human problems it could aggravate and initiate. John wrote:

> The drink habit was almost universal in our neighborhood and town. Old New England rum was the white-faced devil that tickled the palate of more or less of the careless individuals comprising the population. . . . Scenes of squalor characterized the drunkard's home, as they have from time immemorial—a lack of thrift, and total neglect; rags and old hats taking the place of the panes of glass that had been rudely dashed out; together with the sad countenances of wife, mother and half-child.[11]

There were neighbors and friends who suffered as a result of their addiction: the local musician, who gave violin lessons to Judson and John, but whose "love of the art and occupation were well-nigh sacrificed and bartered away for the pleasure of the dram-shop"; and a neighboring family, with a father who "when sober . . . was considered a most capable mechanic and expert blacksmith and pleasant companion," but whose fatal weakness for alcohol turned him into a "notorious sot" and led to "the family, one by one, [being] put out to be brought up by strangers."[12]

While living in Lynn in 1841, just before the first of their concert tours, the three Hutchinson brothers—then the Aeolian Vocalists—heard Hawkins, the "reformed drunkdard" who had come to the Boston area to inaugurate the Washington movement. They were so persuaded that they immediately took a temperance pledge and attended meetings for the cause, leading in the singing of such songs as "We Are All Washingtonians." Jesse was moved to fit temperance words of his own invention to the well-known tune "King Oliver," arranged as a trio for the Aeolian Vocalists; it was first sung at a great temperance rally in Salem, Massachusetts, held in the former Old Deacon Giles distillery, which had been converted into a temperance hall. The song, renamed "King Alcohol," became a great favorite on their commercial programs and was one of the four songs published by Oliver Ditson in 1843. With its lively, folkish character, and its lack of

11. Ibid., 1:28.
12. Ibid., 1:29.

"scientific" writing—parallel octaves and fifths abound, strange doublings are the rule—its sound is close to that of the hymns and anthems written by rural musicians in New England and later the South and West for use in singing schools:

HUTCHINSON FAMILY, "KING ALCOHOL"

Their devotion to a second great cause, the abolition of slavery, developed somewhat later. The Hutchinsons had grown up in a region remote from the institution of slavery. There they had known a freed slave—"Black as the ace of spaces, tall, well-proportioned, athletic, uneducated but witty . . ."—who was married to a white woman and had seven children, attractive and talented; but beyond remarking that the family "lived in comparative isolation," they seem to have given no thought to the matter. Their first direct encounter with slavery had come in Saratoga in the summer of 1842, during their first extended concert tour.

> 'Twas now we first observed our slave-holding neighbors, clothed in their wealth, displaying the elegance of their equipages, as they rolled in extravagance and splendor on the avenues, while we remembered this show as the product of the blood and sweat of the slave, who being forced could do no less than obey his master and submit to his fate.[13]

13. Ibid., 1:57.

In the meanwhile, brother Jesse had become acquainted with Frederick Douglass, who had "come panting up from the South with bloodhounds baying upon his tracks" and settled in Lynn. Jesse was soon involved in antislavery activities, and when the quartet returned from their first triumphant tour, he infected them with his ardor. There was shortly thereafter a dramatic incident: an escaped slave had found his way to Boston, pursued by his Southern owner, and had been arrested by local authorities. The only alternative to returning him to slavery was for a group of citizens to put up enough money to buy his freedom. Some fifty men, including several of the Hutchinsons, marched through the streets of Boston singing "Oh, liberate the bondman" to attract more supporters, then held a rally in Marlborough Chapel. During the rally,

> . . . a man came through the aisle of the chapel, and mounting the platform, shouted out to the crowd, "He's free! he's free!" I can never forget the expression of joy on the face of every citizen present.[14]

Four hundred dollars had been paid in ransom; the slave, George Latimer, was free. He settled in Lynn and was for years a fixture at antislavery rallies.

The Hutchinsons participated in their first large antislavery meeting at a state convention held in Faneuil Hall in Boston on January 25–27, 1843. "We were inspired with the greatness of the issue, finding our hearts in sympathy with those struggling and earnest people,"[15] wrote John. "We fully resolved to buckle on the armor, feeling proud to be engaged in such a great work for humanity." Their songs opened and closed each session, others were interspersed among the speeches and exhortations of Wendell Phillips, William Lloyd Garrison, Frederick Douglass, Edmund Quincy, and the like. Some notion of the temper of the sessions is conveyed by a motion offered by Garrison the last day, and adopted with ferocious enthusiasm: "*Resolved*, That the compact which exists between the North and the South is a covenant with death and an agreement with hell—involving both parties in atrocious criminality, and should be immediately annulled." The Hutchinson's role was eloquently described in the *Herald of Freedom*:

> The Hutchinsons were present throughout the meetings . . . and it was what they said, as well as how they said it, that sent anti-slavery like electricity to every heart. They made the vast multitudes toss and heave and *clamor* like the roaring ocean. Orpheus is said to have made the trees dance at his playing. The Hutchinsons made the thousands at Faneuil Hall spring to their feet simultaneously, "as if in a dance," and echo the anti-slavery appeal with a cheering that almost moved the old Revolutionists from their stations on the wall. On one occasion it was absolutely amazing and sublime. . . . Jesse had framed a series of stanzas on the spot, while Phillips was speaking, embodying the leading arguments, and enforcing them, as mere

14. Ibid., 1:71.
15. Ibid., 1:73.

oratory cannot, as music and poetry only can, and they poured them forth with amazing spirit, in one of the maddening Second Advent tunes. [NB: Jesse undoubtedly added stanzas to "The Old Granite State."] The vast multitude sprang to their feet, as one man, and at the close of the first strain gave vent to their enthusiasm in a thunder of unrestrained cheering. Three cheers, and three times three, and ever so many more—for they could not count—they sent out, full-hearted and full-toned, till the old roof rang again. . . . Oh, it was glorious! . . . I wish the whole city, and the entire country could have been there—even all the people. Slavery would have died of that music . . .[16]

Word of the Boston meeting spread rapidly, and in May 1843 they were invited to sing for an antislavery meeting in New York, sharing the stage with the Reverend Lyman Beecher. Immediately upon their return to New England, they sang at an antislavery rally in Concord, New Hampshire, then in similar rallies elsewhere in the area. The following summer they went to Boston again for an even larger Anti-Slavery Society meeting, at one point singing for some twenty thousand persons gathered on the Boston Common for a temperance meeting.

But commitment to social and political causes in their singing was by no means total at this point. This was the period of their most successful tours of the East, and their antislavery songs were reserved for appropriate rallies; Jesse's "The Bereaved Slave Mother," for example, never appeared on their public concerts. They were quite willing, in Washington and elsewhere, to omit certain "objectionable verses and parts of songs" so as not to antagonize paying audiences.

They soon became more militant. "Get Off the Track," an adaptation of "Old Dan Tucker" with words by Jesse, was so inflammatory that no publisher would bring it out. It was finally published,[17] with a lithographed cover depicting a railway coach labeled "Immediate Emancipation" flying banners of the two leading antislavery journals—*Herald of Freedom* and *American Standard*—being pulled across the country, illustrative of the song's text:

> Ho! the car emancipation,
> Rides majestic through our nation,
> Bearing on its train the story,
> LIBERTY! a nation's glory.
>   Roll it along! roll it along!
>   Roll it along! through the nation,
>   Freedom's car, Emancipation.

The effect of this song on antislavery audiences was electric. N. P. Rogers described a performance at an abolitionist rally in Boston, in the June 1844 issue of *Herald of Freedom*:

16. Ibid., 2:76–77.
17. By Henry Prentiss in Boston.

Their outburst at the convention, in Jesse's celebrated "Get off the track," is absolutely indescribable in any words that can be penned. . . . And when they came to the chorus-cry that gives name to the song—when they cried to the heedless pro-slavery multitude that were stupidly lingering on the track, and the engine "Liberator" coming hard upon them, under full steam and all speed, the Liberty Bell loud ringing, and they standing like deaf men right in its whirlwind path,—and the way they cried "Get off the track," in defiance of all time and rule, was magnificent and sublime. They forgot their harmony, and shouted one after another, or all in confused outcry, like an alarmed multitude of spectators, about to witness a terrible railroad catastrophe. . . . It was the cry of the people, into which their over-wrought and illimitable music had *degenerated* and it was glorious to witness them alighting down again from their wild flight into the current of song, like so many swans upon the river from which they had soared, a moment, wildly into the air. The multitude who have heard them will bear me witness that they transcended the very province of mere music—which is, after all, like eloquence or like poetry, but one of the subordinate departments of humanity.[18]

Warned by friends that they should avoid controversial songs on their next trip to New York, they responded that "As long as nothing was said, we could take our choice; but if we were told we must not sing a song that expressed our convictions, we then felt that, come victory or defeat, we must cry aloud and

The lithograph used on the sheet music cover of "Get Off the Track."

18. John Wallace Hutchinson, 1:117–18.

spare not";[19] accordingly, they programmed "Get Off the Track" at Palmo's Opera House on March 26, 1845. They were hissed, and objects were thrown at them. Rather than having an adverse effect on their popularity, the controversy attracted even more people to their programs, and five hundred were turned away from their last New York concert, at Niblo's Garden.

After their return from England, they were even less willing to continue singing one repertory for commercial concerts and another for antislavery rallies. They offered their New York audiences a new verse of "The Old

The Hutchinson Family Quartet in 1846.

Granite State" on their concerts in 1846, mentioning not only their position on slavery, but also their opposition to the war with Mexico:

> War and slavery perplex us
> And ere long will sorely vex us,
> Oh, we're paying dear for Texas,
>   In the war with Mexico.

The crowd in the Broadway Tabernacle had come for pleasure, not politics, and showed their displeasure by hissing and walking out. The mood of America had changed while they were in England: there was more tension, more polarization on the issue of slavery. In Philadelphia, three concerts were given, to mixed reaction and mixed reviews. The *Courier* wrote:

19. Ibid., 1:138.

It is really time that someone should tell these people, in a spirit of friendly candor, that they are not apostles and martyrs, entrusted with a "mission" to reform the world, but only a company of common song-singers, whose performances sound very pleasantly to the great mass of the people ignorant of real music.

A fourth concert, scheduled for the Musical Fund Hall—where they had sung with such success and acclaim only three years before—was canceled when the major insisted that "persons of color" be refused admission in order to prevent possible disorder. "Of course the Hutchinsons indignantly refused to exclude colored persons from their concerts," wrote the *Liberator*, "and consequently shook off the dust from their feet of this mobocratic city." Their way led through Manchester, Concord, Nashua, and Boston—cities where they had often sung, where they were virtually idolized—but they were hissed even here whenever they introduced "politics."

The following years saw an antislavery meeting in the Broadway Tabernacle, at which they were singing, broken up by a mob; cancelation of a scheduled concert in St. Louis, on their first trip to the West; and trouble even at the scene of their most glorious triumphs, Faneuil Hall in Boston, where a mob disrupted an antislavery meeting featuring the English abolitionist George Thompson.

There were troubles within the quartet as well. Abby married in 1849 and settled in New York with her husband, virtually giving up her singing. Judson, always moody, took to spiritualism and table rapping, and sometimes "freaked out" during concerts:

> . . . at Newburyport . . . he was impressed that it was his duty to do something for the poor of the town, [so he] proceeded to draw from his pockets handfuls of silver half-dollars, previously secured, which he threw into the broad aisle . . . Sometimes he would speak as if inspired . . . on the sinfulness of eating flesh, or wearing any garment that necessitated the killing of animals for its construction. Because of these theories he had discarded boots and shoes, clothing his feet in socks. His food was fruits, cereal and honey.[20]

Jesse, who had traveled with the quartet as manager and had written many of their best songs, suddenly deserted them for a rival quartet, the Alleghenians, who proceeded to sing pieces from the Hutchinsons' repertory. The Alleghenians traveled as far west as California, where Jesse became ill, dying in Cincinnati in 1853.

Despite these tragedies and traumas, the Hutchinsons persevered in their singing, in their championing of radical causes, and in the writing and performing of songs for these causes. Asa, Judson, and John made up the group now, with John's oldest son sometimes joining them. They joined a third great cru-

20. Ibid., 1:281–82.

sade—universal suffrage. They were present for a Women's Rights Convention in Akron, Ohio, in 1851; back East, they sometimes shared the platform with Lucy Stone, who dressed in bloomers and lectured on women's rights. A high point came in 1874, when John sang at the National Convention of Woman Suffrage Association, presided over by Susan B. Anthony.

Their songs were melodramatic but sympathetic to the plight of women in American society. There was Henry Russell's "The Gambler's Wife," and their own setting of Thomas Hood's "The Song of the Shirt":

> With fingers weary and worn,
>   With eye-lids heavy and red,
> A woman sat in unwomanly rags,
>   Plying her needle and thread.
>   Stitch, stitch, stitch,
>   In poverty, hunger and dirt,
>   And still with a voice of dolorous pitch,
>   She sang the song of the shirt.
>
> Work, work, work,
>   'Till the brain begins to swim;
> Work, work, work,
>   'Till the eyes are heavy and dim. . . .
> Oh, men with sisters dear,
>   Oh, men with mothers and wives,
> It is not linen you're wearing out,
>   But human creature's lives.

"Hannah's at the Window Binding Shoes" is an affecting *scena* of a woman sitting year after year at a window in a New England shoe factory, watching through a window for her husband, who will never return: "Old with watching, Hannah's at the window binding shoes. Twenty winters wear and tear the rugged shore she views; . . . Still her dim eyes silently chase the white sails o'er the sea; Hapless, faithful Hannah's at the window binding shoes."

This song, attributed to Asa B. Hutchinson, wasn't published until 1859. By this time the original Hutchinson Family quartet had disbanded and sang together again only on rare occasions. The last great tour of the three brothers (Asa, Judson, John) had taken place in 1855, characteristically in pursuit of still another cause. They set off for Kansas, after hearing a fiery speaker call for Free-Soil emigrants to Kansas to help insure that it not become a slave state. They were persuaded to give some concerts in the upper Mississippi Valley, after getting as far west as Illinois, and they fell in love with Minnesota, where they staked out a claim for land for a new town, Hutchinson. They returned to Massachusetts, rather than going further west, and for some years shuttled back and forth between New England and their new town, persuading families to settle there, trying to keep peace with the Indians.

Sheet music cover for "The Song of the Shirt," one of the Hutchinsons' songs championing the cause of universal suffrage.

By now each of the three brothers had his own growing family; eventually the family split into three groups. "The Tribe of Asa," made up of Asa, his wife, and their children Abby, Freddy, and "little Dennett," settled in Minnesota. They were so radical as to antagonize most audiences, even those in the North; at one point they joined forces with a trio of blacks, the Luca Brothers. Judson sang programs with his daughter Kate and enjoyed some success. He had shown signs of emotional instability for many years and finally hanged himself on January 11, 1859. Soon after this, Kate joined forces with Joshua (who had not been a member of the famous quartet) and Walter Kittredge, a New Hampshire singer and composer. John, who had often sung solo programs even while the original quartet was together, now formed his own family group, with his wife Fanny and two of their children, Henry and Viola.

There were important events and interesting music in the years after the original quartet ceased to exist. Both John and Asa campaigned enthusiastically for Lincoln in 1860; John, with Horace Greeley (then editor of the *Tribune* in New York), brought out *Hutchinson's Republican Songster for 1860,* and Asa brought out a Lincoln songster of his own. John's activities in helping to popularize several of the most famous Civil War songs will be noted in a subsequent chapter. Both John and Abby went to the South after the war, heard the singing of ex-slaves in Florida and elsewhere, visited Fisk University and heard its famous choir, and were among the first singers to perform arrangements of such spirituals as "My Jesus Says There's Room Enough" on the concert stage.

Despite all this, the peak of the Hutchinson Family's popularity and influence came in the period from 1841 to 1849, when the original quartet was together and their music and the way they presented it struck audiences and critics as new and fresh and very American.

It may well be that the Hutchinsons altered the course of American history, that their music hastened the confrontations and conflicts that led inexorably to the Civil War, that their songs fanned passions and created the sense of togetherness and resolve necessary to convert ideas and ideals into action, that their singing of "John Brown's Body" converted more people to the antislavery cause than all the speeches and sermons of the time.

There is no mistaking their sincerity, their deep and genuine concern for human misery. Their memoirs and writings are filled with vignettes of human suffering which they observed and tried to alleviate:

> . . . we observed a little old house the lower story of which had been destroyed, all except the cornerposts, by the winds and waves. I noticed smoke coming out of the chimney, although it seemed impossible such a structure could be inhabited. We went on, but not being satisfied, returned, and noticing a ladder, crawled up, and knocked on a door lying horizontally on the floor. A delicate woman, with a half-starved baby in her arms answered our summons. The woman was thinly-clad and almost frozen, for the tempest had washed nearly all her clothing away, and she was without means to get more. The next day, with Abby, we took them some clothing, and gave them money to move to a more secure dwelling. [21]

And there is no mistaking the fact that they made a deliberate choice, at a critical point in their career, to state their political and social views in public concerts, whatever the damage to their professional career.

21. Ibid., 1:132–33.

They sang at prisons, at poorhouses, at the smallest church that asked for them. They attended temperance and abolitionist rallies, when organizers had not known of their presence, and would stand in the audience at a critical point in the rally and give out with one of their "maddening" songs. They sang for the poor, the slaves, the freedmen, the Irish, women, Republicans, sailors. They were a voice crying out for freedom, peace, equality, temperance, devotion. They said it themselves, more eloquently than anyone else, in the song "If I Were a Voice," written by Judson, sung by Abby, quoted by John at the beginning of the chapter of his memoirs entitled "American Songs and their Interpretations":

> If I were a voice, a persuasive voice,
>   That could travel the wide world through,
> I would fly on the beams of the morning light
> And speak to men with a gentle might,
>   And tell them to be true.
> I would fly—I would fly o'er land and sea,
> Wherever a human heart might be,
> Telling a tale, or singing a song,
> In praise of the right, in blame of the wrong,
>   If I were a voice.

The Hutchinsons stressed their national origins from the beginning. A bit of doggerel verse (by Judson) was inserted on their early printed programs:

> When foreigners approach your shore,
> You welcome them with open doors,
> Now we have come, to seek our lot,
> Shall native talent be forgot?

Critics agreed that there was something very American about them, about the music they performed and the way they sang it, often equating "American" with simplicity. An early critic wrote:

> We like their music, because it is so simple and unadorned. It may not please those whose nice and critical taste love to hear music executed so that there is no music in it, but the people, the millions, appreciate their notes . . .[22]

And a critic in New York saw them as

> . . . genuine children of the rugged New Hampshire soil on which they were born. Endowed as they were by kindly Nature with sensitive musical

22. Quoted in Philip D. Jordan, *Singin' Yankees* (Minneapolis: The University of Minnesota Press, 1946), p. 158.

organizations and strong, simple characters, they brought into the atmosphere of the concert room a freshness and native sweetness of melody amd motive which won a way for them, at once, to the popular heart.[23]

A more specific comment was offered by a British writer for the *Birmingham Journal* of January 1846:

> After the *staccatos* and runs of Italianized vocalism, which are all very well in their own way, it is pleasant to hear music divested of its extraneous ornament and made subservient to the holy use of promoting good-will between man and man, and clothing the deep sympathy of the poet in the appropriate and winning garb of simple and unadorned harmony. How often have we longed for the quiet strain in which the untaught minstrel sung the airs which needed no ornament. . . . We never heard these themes attempted in the concert-room without dreading the coming embellishment, which drowns all appreciation of the sentiment of the song or the music, in surprise of the artist's mechanical skill.

They were not merely Americans—they were New Englanders. They avoided European songs (they rarely performed even such favorites as "Home! Sweet Home" or any of Moore's *Irish Melodies*) and songs associated with other parts of America, such as minstrel songs or the songs of Stephen Foster. Critics often chided them for their avoidance of familiar songs that would have made for more easy listening; the *Herald of Freedom* for December 9, 1842, for instance, said in the course of a generally favorable review:

> These Canary birds have been here again, charming the ear of our Northern winter with their woodnote melody. . . . The airs were modern, most or all of them; and though very sweet, were less interesting to me than if they had been songs I knew. If they had had some of the old songs intermingled, I think it would better please everybody—some of the Burns' "Bonny Doon" or "Highland Mary," for instance. Their woodland tone, their clear enunciation and their fine appreciation of the poetry, together with their perfect freedom from all affectation and stage grimace, would enable them to do justice to the great Scottish songster; and it would do the people good to hear them sing him.

But the Hutchinsons were American, not Scotch, and they had their own ideas about what would be good for their audiences.

From the beginning of their career, their programs were made up largely of pieces by composers from New England: Lyman Heath, Bernard Covert, Henry Russell (whom they considered a New Englander at least in spirit), and themselves. Increasingly, their own arrangements and compositions made up the larger part of their programs. John described their creative process:

23. Quoted in John Wallace Hutchinson, 2:303.

Whenever we found in the papers or had given to us anything effective or beautiful in the way of poetry, we would pin it up on a bedpost or side of the house, and start in on a tune, each one making up his own part. Judson usually took the air, and so in a sense became the composer of the tune. We have often made our songs and sung them in public without ever having seen a note. In this way we composed "The Good Old Days of Yore," "The Bridge of Sighs," and other well-known songs, which were really composed by "The Hutchinsons," it being impossible to say that either [sic] of the quartet was the actual composer.[24]

The origins of their style lie in the hymns and anthems of the New England churches—the religious music designed by Lowell Mason, George Webb, Thomas Hastings, and their contemporaries to elevate the morals and musical taste of literate Americans, contained in such collections as Mason's *Boston Handel & Haydn Society Collection of Sacred Music* and *Carmina Sacra*, Hastings's *Musica Sacra*, and William R. Bradbury's *The Jubilee*. The most widely sung pieces in such collections, the music the Hutchinsons—and millions of other American families—sang at home and in church, were simple, symmetrical, diatonic tunes harmonized with the most basic chords. This was the music that established the musical vocabulary and largely defined the musical taste and tolerance of most white, Protestant Americans in the North, East, and Midwest.

Their songs make use of diatonic, repetitious, regularly phrased melodies, supported by rather rudimentary chords. "Mrs. Lofty and I," a song that enjoyed much success as an item of sheet music and was often anthologized, is a fair sample of their style:

HUTCHINSON FAMILY, "MRS. LOFTY AND I"

24. John Wallace Hutchinson, 2:301.

coach-man, Than am I With my blue eyed, laugh-ing ba - by, Trund-ling by;

Several of their later songs, however, exhibit more musical sophistication. "The Song of the Shirt" is a rare instance from this period of a song in a minor key, and the insistent, incessant, arpeggiated accompaniment underlining the melancholy narrative creates an effect not unlike that of Schubert's "Gretchen am Spinnrad," a song the Hutchinsons most certainly did not know:

HUTCHINSON FAMILY, "THE SONG OF THE SHIRT"

With fin - gers wea-ry and worn, With eye - lids heav-y and red,

Later in the song, the rhythmic pattern of the accompaniment is broken by a series of dramatic, chromatic chords, underlining the climax of the poem:

HUTCHINSON FAMILY, "THE SONG OF THE SHIRT"

Oh God! that bread should be— so dear— And hu - man flesh so cheap.

and the song modulates to a distant key (B-flat minor), where it ends. The inspiration for this more adventuresome musical language is not difficult to trace: the accompaniment and harmonic style are reminiscent of the more dramatic songs of Henry Russell.

One of the loveliest of their songs, "If I Were a Voice," combines their usual melodic clarity and simplicity with somewhat more colorful chords:

HUTCHINSON FAMILY, "IF I WERE A VOICE"

No matter how appealing their story may be, the fact remains that they outlived their songs. Not one achieved enough lasting popularity to be included in the various retrospective song anthologies of the late nineteenth and early twentieth centuries.

Their songs, stripped of the emotional climate surrounding their composition and performance, have proved to be of less musical interest than those of certain of their contemporaries less involved in the great issues of this stirring time. The Hutchinsons' great contribution to American popular music was summed up by William Lloyd Garrison in a letter to Joshua, dated April 3, 1874: "Never before has the singing of ballads been made directly and purposely subservient to the freedom, welfare, happiness, and moral elevation of the people."

EIGHT

"Come Back to Erin";

OR,

More Gems from the British Isles

THE IMMENSE popularity of Italian song in America and the emergence of indigenous composers and styles by no means signaled the end of importation of songs from the British Isles. To the contrary, there was a steady stream of song from England and Ireland into America, from the first decades of the nineteenth century through the period of the Civil War and even afterward. Many of these songs took deep root in this country and became as important a part of American culture as those being created here.

Most of the songs published and sung in America in the late eighteenth century had been English products, and the first years of the new century saw no break in this pattern. A high point of the musical season of 1803–4 in London was the premier of an opera written by one of the most celebrated English singers of the day, John Braham, entitled *The English Fleet in 1342*, to a libretto by Dibdin. In the words of a contemporary observer, *"The English Fleet* encountered a violent storm of opposition during the first three nights; but . . . it was at length brought into safe and secure anchorage, where, with flying colours, it afterwards rode triumphant."[1] Its success was so great that an English publisher paid the

---

1. W. T. Parke, *Musical Memoirs: Comprising an Account of the General State of Music in England, from the First Commemoration of Handel, in 1784, to the Year 1830*, 2 vols. (London: Henry Colburn and Richard Bentley, 1830), 1:325.

John Braham (1777–1856).

composer the largest amount for the copyright to a musical work to that date, one thousand guineas.

Such success in England usually brought an opera to America in less than a year, but *The English Fleet* did not make such a voyage until 1819; an opera celebrating the armed might of England was not yet welcome on the American stage in the early years of the century.

This is not to say that the music of the opera remained unknown in America. Quite to the contrary; the duet "All's Well," sung in the original production by the two greatest English tenors of the day, Braham and Incledon, was published in America almost immediately and enjoyed great popularity here. As late as 1870, editions of it were still available through nine major American publishers.

Braham was a multitalented musician whose ability to pursue several careers in music simultaneously seems astonishing to later times, when specialization had become the rule. He was universally acclaimed as the greatest English singer of his generation. On the occasion of his debut on April 30, 1796, at London's Drury Lane Theatre in the opera *Mahmoud, or the Prince of Persia*, he was pronounced to have "a powerful and flexible tenor voice, a good shake and rapid execution."[2] Several years of study and performance abroad, in Paris, Italy, and Germany, sharpened his skills and matured his voice. When he returned to England in 1801, in the Reeve-Mazzinghi *Chains of the Heart*, he was found to have "astonishingly improved powers," though there was some consternation at the "profusion of embellishments he threw into even his most simple airs."[3] But the English soon adapted to his new style, and he became the most popular singer at Drury Lane and Covent Garden in both the Italian and English repertories. He was engaged at the Theatre Royal in Dublin, in 1809, on terms never before offered to a singer: two thousand guineas for fifteen nights.

Braham was no less successful as a composer of operas and songs. He furnished music for *The Americans, The Devil's Bridge, The Cabinet, Family Quarrels*, and other successful stage pieces of the first decades of the nineteenth century. His most enduring song was "The Death of Nelson."

The very factors that made the song such a success in England worked against it in America; it was too soon after the war for Americans to respond favorably to a song praising a British military leader, and the song remained almost unknown here. But three of his songs, in addition to "All's Well," were among the most popular songs in America early in the nineteenth century: "Is There a Heart That Never Lov'd" from *The Devil's Bridge* (1812), "Tho' Love is Warm Awhile" (1812), and "Beautiful Maid" (1802). They represent a happy blend of English and Italian traits, and are the products of an exquisitely musical nature.

2. Ibid., 1:319.
3. Ibid., 1:296.

JOHN BRAHAM, "IS THERE A HEART THAT NEVER LOV'D"

In 1840, at the age of sixty-eight, Braham came to America. Arriving in the fall, he gave his first recital at the Tabernacle in New York on the evening of October 28, singing a program made up largely of excerpts from operas and oratorios by Handel. Critics and audience were astonished; "he surpassed his fame—and surpassed all expectation," wrote the critic of the *Herald* the following day. "His pathos, sublimity, power, and wonderful execution cannot be described—he must be heard to be appreciated. He seemed to enjoy, at sixty [sic], all his great powers." Audiences flocked to hear him, evening after evening.

His fame had been established on the operatic stage, not in recital, and some Americans withheld judgment until his stage debut. This took place at the Park Theatre, on December 21, 1840, in *The Siege of Belgrade*, Stephen Storace's old favorite first performed in London a half-century before. Braham performed in six more operas in less than a fortnight, a staggering schedule for a singer in the prime of life, let alone one approaching the age of seventy: December 24, *The Devil's Bridge*; December 25, *Masaniello*; December 28, *The Cabinet*; January 4, *Der Freischütz*; January 5, *Artaxerxes*; January 7, *No Song, No Supper*.

But Braham survived, and went on to sing many dozens of other engagements—opera, oratorio, sacred concerts, recitals of ballads—before returning to England with enough Yankee dollars to sustain him for the rest of his life.

Braham was not a composer of great originality, and by the end of his life he was an anachronism, writing and singing music that had largely gone out of style. But he was a consummate musician who gave Americans a number of beautiful songs that helped pass the years until new styles emerged and American song began taking on a character of its own.

The most popular song of the entire century was "Home, Sweet Home," composed by the Englishman Henry Bishop to a text by the American poet John Howard Payne.

The song was written in 1823, as part of the opera *Clari; or, The Maid of Milan*, first performed in London at the Covent Garden Theatre on May 8. An observer of this historic event reported:

The first page of "Home Sweet Home" by Henry Bishop, as published by George Bacon of Philadelphia in 1823. This may well be the first American edition.

Miss M. Tree's song, "Sweet home," is a beautiful specimen of taste and simplicity. The melody is taken from one occurring in a German opera, and the effective accompaniments are composed by Bishop. This air, charmingly sung by Miss M. Tree, was honoured with universal applause and an encore. The music of this piece is altogether of a very superior description.[4]

The first American performance took place a half-year later, on November 12 at the Park Theatre. The honor of singing "Home, Sweet Home" on this occasion

4. Ibid., 2:183–84.

fell to a certain Miss Johnson. The New York *Mirror* of November 22 called the song "the most beautiful and tender we have ever heard . . . there was something in it inexpressibly tender," and said that the performance of Miss Johnson was ". . . inimitable. The deep feeling of her acting—the song—her emotion . . . as she listened to the echoing music that welcomed her home—we have *never* seen equalled. It was the truest, tenderest acting we have ever beheld."[5]

The success of the song was nothing short of phenomenal. An unsubstantiated claim has been made that it sold 100,000 copies in the first year of publication. In America, in the two years following its first appearance (1824–25), it was brought out in more different editions and sold more copies than any other song to that date.[6] So many publishers rushed it into print that it is impossible to pinpoint the first American edition. It appeared as a song with keyboard accompaniment, as sets of variations for the piano, and in arrangements for chorus, male chorus, children's chorus, band, and every conceivable instrument. It was interpolated in various operas other than *Clari*. It was sung by every famous female vocalist for many decades, including Malibran, Jenny Lind, and Adelina Patti, who sang it at the dedication of the Chicago Auditorium on December 9, 1889, and as late as 1911 at the Albert Hall in London. It was the favorite song of American soldiers on both sides during the Civil War. It endured, and continues to endure, the harshest sort of criticism ("Poetic justice has now taken its revenge, and one of the worst tunes [Bishop] ever wrote is cherished, possibly because of its utter misery."[7]). No one seems to have liked it but the millions of people who have sung it, played it, listened to it, and bought copies of it.

Several mysteries surround even so famous a song. As noted above, Parke, who was at the first performance, claims the tune was taken from a German opera; the first edition identifies it as a "Sicilian Air." Bishop himself was content to have it appear as an arrangement, not an original composition. Yet no model, German or Sicilian, has turned up in the century and a half since its creation, nor does the tune appear to be characteristic of songs of either nationality. A second mystery seems insoluble—the reasons for its unprecedented and protracted popularity. The absolute symmetry and squareness of form—AABBCB, each segment four measures in length—is relieved only in the C section, functioning as a bridge between the last two B sections. The vocal range is a mere octave, the supporting harmony restricted to the three basic chords of the major scale—tonic, dominant, and subdominant. Such simplicity lends the song a vaguely folklike quality (if one accepts the questionable notion that folk songs are simple).

But the secret of the popularity of "Home, Sweet Home" may lie less with the music than with the poem. Payne, born on June 9, 1791, in New York City, made his stage debut at the Park Theatre in 1809 and enjoyed some considerable

5. Quoted in Odell, 3:97.

6. Richard J. Wolfe, *Secular Music in America, 1801–1825; A Bibliography*, 3 vols. (New York: The New York Public Library, 1964), pp. 60–62.

7. Maurice Willson Disher, *Victorian Song; From Dive to Drawing Room* (London: Phoenix House, 1955), p. 85.

John Howard Payne (1791–1852).

success for many years. But he was a wanderer at heart and soon found himself in London and other European cities, writing poems and plays that rarely reached publication. He was in northern Africa, in Tunis, serving as United States Consul, when he died in 1852.

Payne's poem was written at a time when he was feeling the pain of separation from his home and homeland. Millions of people who had experienced similar longings, brought about by emigration, death, separation during war, or even voluntary exile, found reflections of their feelings in Payne's poem. Writers closer to the nineteenth century spoke to this very point.

> During one of these seasons [when Payne was in Paris] with its attendant dejection and despair, in that meanly furnished room, with the sounds of the happy, thoughtless crowds on the boulevard below welling up through the tiny casement, the opening words of the immortal song, "Mid Pleasures and Palaces," came to him as spontaneously as a sigh; and then and there he wrote the words that have since girdled the world. . . . [Later] Payne was wont to tell of a time when he stood on a Christmas Eve in a London street, penniless and hungry and cold, and heard with incredible feelings of loneliness "Home, Sweet Home" played in a rich man's parlor.[8]

> Certain of these songs of sentiment outlive those of more artistic composition simply because they touch the hearts of the people. Each and every word is understood because it has been written for them, and the music usually is simple enough to be readily grasped. America has produced much music of this kind, songs that will never die because they essentially vibrate in the home-life of the nation. Such a song is "Home, Sweet Home."[9]

Note the implication that "Home, Sweet Home" is an American song. This country has indeed felt more strongly about it than has England. The autograph manuscript is here;[10] the inscription on Payne's tombstone in Tunis spoke of "his" celebrated ballad, and when his body was brought back to American in 1883 for interment in Oak Hill Cemetery, the cortege included the president of the United States, his cabinet, and high-ranking individuals from the military and from private life. Newspapers throughout the country echoed the theme that Payne had finally come home.

Though Payne languished on the fringes of fame, Henry Bishop was accepted by his contemporaries as the most celebrated English musician of the time. Born in London in 1786, his first dramatic works were on the stage before he was twenty, and his first successful stage work, *The Circassian Bridge*, was performed at Drury Lane in 1809, when he was twenty-three. He was named composer-conductor at Covent Gardens as a consequence, a post he held for a decade. Dozens of stage works resulted from this engagement: original operas; collaborations with other composers; musical adaptations of Sir Walter Scott's novels (the first was *The Knight of Snowdoun*, based on *The Lady of the Lake*, in 1811); arrangements of older operas by Arne, Purcell, Arnold, Dibdin, and the like, usually with new pieces by Bishop himself interpolated into the new version; and his own adaptations of new foreign operas. In all, Bishop wrote or ar-

---

8. Henry Frederic Reddall, comp., *Songs That Never Die* (Philadelphia: J. H. Moore, [1894]), p. 149.

9. W. L. Hubbard, gen. ed., *The American History and Encyclopedia of Music*, 12 vols. (Toledo: Irving Squire, 1908): *History of American Music*, edited by W. L. Hubbard, p. 76.

10. In the Sibley Music Library of the Eastman School of Music in Rochester, New York.

ranged some one hundred stage works during his lifetime—and conducted most performances of all of them.

Bishop's songs had been known in America for a decade before "Home, Sweet Home." Several dozen had been performed and published here, most notably "Love Has Eyes," from the comic opera *The Farmer's Daughter*, first produced at Covent Garden Theatre in London on February 1, 1814. The libretto to the opera was by Charles Dibdin, son of the famous composer-singer of the turn of the century, and the music by no fewer than six composers. "Many hands make light work" was the wry comment of Parke,[11] but the opera was a huge success, with a high point being the singing of "Love Has Eyes" by the Scottish tenor John Sinclair. The first American performance was at the Park Theatre on September 26 of the same year, and American publishers in several cities rushed to bring out the hit song as a separate item of sheet music. The song is squarely in the Hook-Arnold-Dibdin mold—amatory, strophic, completely diatonic, with the text set syllabically, save for brief melodic flowerings at the ends of phrases.

HENRY BISHOP, "LOVE HAS EYES"

Among other pre–"Home, Sweet Home" songs by Bishop widely sung and printed in America were "Like the Gloom of Night Retiring"; "The Celebrated Echo Song" ("What Airy Sounds"); and "Tho' 'Tis but a Dream." The latter is from *Moore's National Melodies*, and it is probably wrong to attribute it to Bishop, since Moore undoubtedly chose the melody and fitted words to it, leaving Bishop to write the "symphonies" and accompaniments.

11. Parke, 2:96.

In his role as conductor and arranger, Bishop came to know, intimately, the music of most of the best composers of vocal music of the day, and many of the past also. For a composer of any but the most indomitable will and security in his own musical style, there is a danger in this, and it cannot be said that Bishop always escaped. His early songs are very much in the ballad-comic opera/pleasure-garden style of the late eighteenth century, true enough, and are easily recognizable as English. But various foreign elements creep into his style in the 1810s and '20s without being smoothly integrated, and certain songs by Bishop begin to sound quite unlike others. Some of his operatic songs and sacred solos begin to take on the sound and spirit of Handel and Haydn; some are harmonizations of Scottish or Irish tunes, others retain their English simplicity and squareness, and still others take on some of the grace of Italian melody.

The success of Bishop's most famous song encouraged publishers on both sides of the Atlantic to bring out even more of his vocal pieces, in the hopes that one or more would repeat the success. Thus even more songs by Bishop were published after 1823 than before. "Oh, No! We Never Mention Her!," with a text by Thomas Bayley, is a spritely folklike tune, quite attractive and memorable:

HENRY BISHOP, "OH! NO! WE NEVER MENTION HER!"

"Tell Me, My Heart," a song from late in Bishop's life, has the easy grace, the arpeggiated accompaniment, and the expressive appoggiaturas of Italian opera of the 1830s, without a strong personal touch that would stamp it as a song by Bishop:

HENRY BISHOP, "TELL ME, MY HEART"

The most successful song of Bishop's later years was "The Bloom is on the Rye," also called "My Pretty Jane," after the first line of Edward FitzBall's text. Written and first published in 1832, it was second in popularity only to "Home Sweet Home" among his songs. It is as close to a synthesis of several styles as Bishop was ever to come, combining the symmetry and simplicity of English song with some of the melodic grace and stylistic idiosyncrasies of Italian melody and an occasional rhythmic reference to Irish-Scottish song.

Bishop's career as a songwriter can be summed up easily: he wrote one great hit song, the most popular song of an entire century. But though he wrote many hundreds of other songs before and afterward, he never again managed to strike the chord in audiences and performers that was set in vibration by "Home, Sweet Home." Had he not written this song, he would receive only passing mention in this book, as a diligent composer who flooded the song market with his creations for several decades, but who never reached the heights of a Stephen Foster or even a Henry Russell.

Samuel Lover, born in Dublin in 1797, was the successor to Thomas Moore as the voice of Irish song in the opinion of many people, including Lover himself. In response to a letter from an admirer hailing him as an even greater songwriter than the author of the *Irish Melodies*, Lover gave his own opinions on a matter that was often on his mind:

I think there is more of the "touch of nature"—that quality to which Shake-speare attributes so much—in my writings than in his. I think also there is more feeling, and beyond all doubt I am much more *Irish:* . . . Moore was keenly alive to the *character* of a melody—hence, from those of his own land, which are so lovely, he selected judiciously the air suited to the spirit of his lay. Then, as the verses he wrote were meant to be sung (not merely read), with what consummate skill he has accommodated every word to be capable of the "linked sweetness long drawn out!"—*in this respect I think Moore MATCHLESS.* [12]

Born into a well-to-do family in Dublin—his father was a stockbroker—Lover, like so many creative artists, experienced a period of solitude as a child; his family sent him off to the country, at age twelve, away from the turmoil, clamor, and danger of Dublin at this tumultuous time.

By age seventeen, he had determined to devote himself to the arts; giving up his position in his father's firm, he concentrated on writing, painting, and music. His first writings appeared in the Dublin *Literary Gazette*, at about the time he was attracting attention as a gifted miniaturist and songwriter. The range of his talents and accomplishments is nothing short of astonishing: he wrote poems, songs, criticisms, plays, novels, and librettos (including two librettos for Balfe, one of them the popular *Il Paddy Whack in Italia*) and executed a portrait of Paganini, exhibited at the Royal Academy Exhibition in London, that es-tablished his fame as a painter. His first play, *Grania Uaile*, opened at the Theatre Royal in 1827; *Legends and Stories of Ireland* (1831), with his own illus-trations, stamped him as a sensitive and sympathetic observer of his own culture ("he wrote of a people, of their virtues and their foibles, their manners and cus-toms, their likes and their dislikes; and he did it without awakening their indigna-tion or wounding their susceptibilities"[13]). As a caricaturist for the Irish "Horn Book," he dealt in telling fashion with a national scandal, the tithe system im-posed by the British which forced the Catholics of Ireland to contribute to the support of the Established Church. In an unprecedented sequence, he wrote first a charming, narrative song, "Rory O'More," made it into a novel, *Rory O'More, a National Romance*, and then into a play, which ran for 109 nights at the Adelphi Theatre, starring the actor Tyrone Power. A charming and gregarious person, he moved easily in social and artistic circles in both Dublin and London.

Adversity, in the form of failing eyesight, merely nudged him in different directions. In March of 1844, at the Princess Theatre in London, he narrated Irish tales, read his own poems, and was joined by several other singers in selec-tions from his songs. These Irish Evenings were popular enough to persuade him to follow the footsteps of so many of his countrymen, to seek the American dollar. Landing in Boston in September of 1846, he chose to open his American

12. Quoted in James Jeffrey Roche, ed., *Rory O'More: A National Romance by Samuel Lover* (New York: The Athenaum Society, 1901), pp. xix–xx.
13. Ibid., p. viii.

Samuel Lover (1797–1868).

tour in New York, where American audiences first saw and heard him at the Stuyvesant Institute on the evening of October 6. He offered such evenings as "Paddy's Portfolio," "Outlaws and Exiles of Erin," "Paddy by Land and Sea," and "The Angel's Whisper." When he returned to New York the following year after traveling to other parts of the country (as far south as New Orleans and as far north and west as Lake Superior and Canada), he characteristically gave his audiences something new. His play *The Emigrant's Dream; or, the Land of Promise* opened on December 28, 1847, with Lover making his first dramatic appearance in America in the role of Phil Purcell, a "decayed farmer." A series of "farewell" appearances in New York extended his stay through the spring of 1848. He returned home to offer British audiences evenings of "American Impressions" and to continue his multifaceted activity until poor health forced him into retirement in 1864. He died on July 6, 1868, at the age of seventy-one, revered as one of the most famous and beloved Irishmen of his day.

Like Moore, he wrote the texts for his songs, some three hundred of them. There is an important difference, though: Lover wrote his own melodies, rather than adapting traditional Irish tunes. Lover's melodies often hint at the ancient melodic tradition of Irish song, with its modal-pentatonic character tracing back to a melodic, nonharmonic tradition:

SAMUEL LOVER, "THE ANGEL'S WHISPER"

A ba - by was sleep - ing, Its moth - er was weep - ing, For her hus - band was far — on the wild — rag - ing sea,

Others, founded more in the music of the nineteenth century, are still recogniz-able to our ears as Irish, through reference to jigs and other dances popular in Ireland in the nineteenth century:

SAMUEL LOVER, "RORY O'MORE"

Young Ro-ry O - Moore court-ed Kath-leen_ Bawn, He was bold as a hawk and she soft as the dawn, He wish'd in his heart pret - ty Kath-leen to please

Still others make little or no reference to traditional Irish music and are indistin-guishable from the songs of Bishop and other English composers of the day.

His songs rarely attempt to plumb depths of human emotion, but are rather cheerful and often sentimental vignettes of simple folk and their lives. Typical is "The Low-Back'd Car":

When first I saw sweet Peggy
'T was on a market day,

A low-back'd car she drove, and sat
   Upon a truss of hay;
But when that hay was blooming grass,
   And deck'd with flowers of spring,
     No flower was there
     That could compare
To the blooming girl I sing.

Nor did his poems on "American subjects" seem to capture much of the sound or sentiment of the New World; the first stanza of "The Flooded Hut of the Mississippi" is typical:

On the wide-rolling river, at eve, set the sun,
And the long-toiling day of the woodman was done,
And he flung down the axe that had fell'd the huge tree,
And his own little daughter he placed on his knee;
She look'd up, with smiles, at a dovecote o'erhead,
Where, circling around, flew the pigeons she fed,
And more fondly the sire clasp'd his child to his breast—
As he kiss'd her—and call's her the bird of *his* nest.

In retrospect, comparisons with Thomas Moore were premature and ill-founded. Lover was a fascinating and multitalented person, like so many of the men and women who wrote popular song in the nineteenth century. He furnished America with a handful of songs that were enjoyed for some decades— "Rory O'More," "The Angel's Whisper," "The Low-Back'd Car," "What Will You Do, Love?," "True Love Can Ne'er Forget." But his works had faded from the living repertory before the end of the century, and we can see him today as a gifted man whose songs floated along on the surface of popular style without reaching the depths of emotion or expression found in Moore, Bellini, the best of the minstrel composers, or Stephen Foster.

What man is ashamed of the tears that glisten in his eyes when he hears a familiar tune of long ago. . .[14]

Of all the songwriters of the British Isles of the first half of the nineteenth century, Henry Russell was easily the most popular and influential in America. Indeed, it is fair to say he was the most important writer of songs in America before Stephen Foster. Unlike the songwriters discussed to this point in the present chapter, he did not come to America as an established musician: his for-

14. Henry Russell, *Cheer! Boys, Cheer!: Memories of Men and Music* (London: J. Macqueen, 1895), p. 254.

Henry Russell (1812–1900).

mative years as a composer were spent here, his first successes as a songwriter and singer were on this side of the Atlantic, and there is some justification in viewing him as at least partly an "American" writer.

Born in Sheerness, Kent, of Jewish parents, on December 24, 1812, Russell recounts in his autobiography *Cheer! Boys, Cheer!* that he made his stage debut at the age of three and began piano lessons at six. His talents landed him starring roles in a children's opera company managed by Robert W. Elliston of Drury Lane Theatre, and Russell remembers that after a performance before George IV, the king took him on his knee and kissed him.

The first of the two great turning points of his career came when, at the age of ten, he met the great tragedian Edmund Kean:

"My dear boy," he said in his tragic way, "you will never become either a great actor or a great singer unless you learn to speak every word you utter distinctly and clearly. Unintelligibility and slovenliness in speech are the curse of the profession.[15]

When Russell's voice changed and he suddenly found himself a baritone, Italian opera was all the rage in London, and without hesitation he took off for Italy, arriving in Bologna in 1825. By his own account, he studied there with Rossini, and the two became great friends; he claims to have studied also with Bellini and to have known Donizetti and Balfe. Whatever the truth of the matter—and his writing had a tendency to become fanciful when he dealt with his early life—he was thoroughly familiar with the musical style of Italian opera, as a composer and as a singer.

Persuaded that musical opportunities for a young, unknown musician were greater in the New World than in London, Russell set sail for Toronto some time in the early 1830s. Having made no great impression in Canada, he accepted a call to Rochester, New York, as organist of the First Presbyterian Church; he soon was also a "professor of music" at the Rochester Academy of Music, and by 1835 had established himself as a leader in the musical circles of that city. It was here that the second dramatic turn of his career occurred: he heard the great orator Henry Clay. Moved not by the subject of Clay's oration, but by his magnetism and his ability to grip and move his audience, Russell wrote:

That speech of Henry Clay affected me to a singular extent. It may sound a strange statement, but I don't think I should be talking extravagantly, if I declare that the orator Henry Clay was the direct cause of my taking to the composition of descriptive songs.[16]

Excited and restless from hearing the great orator, Russell began work on a new vocal composition, "Wind of the Winter's Night, Whence Comest Thou?," that very evening:

All through the night I paced up and down my room arranging the music for the poem, and I remember that the notion uppermost in my mind was to infuse into my music the subtle charm, as it were, of the voice of Henry Clay.[17]

15. Ibid., p. 23.
16. Ibid., p. 61.
17. Ibid., pp. 61–62.

This setting of a "descriptive poem" by Charles Mackay, dedicated to the Rochester Academy of Sacred Music,[18] was apparently Russell's first printed song. The music changes tempo and meter frequently, in an attempt to match the changing moods of the poem. In concept and structure, the song resembles a *scena* from Italian opera, with a dramatic instrumental prelude moving to a quasi-recitation beginning, flowering into arioso and then to a more developed, ariosolike central section. The piano part is rich and virtuosic, the harmonies melodramatically chromatic, the voice part written for a fully developed operatic-type voice commanding a considerable range. The creative impulse may have come from Henry Clay, but the musical language is that of Italian opera.

Russell was completely unknown outside of Rochester when the song came out; in fact, the publisher thought it necessary to identify the song with another performer—"Sung with much applause by Mr. Brough"—to encourage potential buyers.

Armed with his new image of himself as the Henry Clay of vocal music, a voice described by critics as a light but pleasing baritone, a formidable technique at the keyboard, and an ever-growing collection of his own songs, Russell set out in 1836—at the age of twenty-four—to establish himself as a ballad singer. His first New York appearance was in October; after recitals elsewhere, he came back to New York in the spring of 1837, and by April of that year he was billed as "the popular ballad singer." Within a year, a contemporary writer could say:

> His fame was now fully established, and, devoting his whole attention to composition and singing, he traversed the States of America from extremity to extremity with a rapidity without parallel, singing at all places and at all times to multitudes that all but idolized him.[19]

Russell's songs were now coming off the American presses at such an amazing rate that one wonders how he found time to write them, given his busy schedule of performances. There were other songs in the mold of "Wind of the Winter's Night"—narrative, through-composed, dramatic pieces patterned after the solo *scena* of contemporary Italian opera.[20] The most popular work of this genre was "The Maniac" (1840), set to a text by Monk Lewis describing the plight of a man wrongly committed to an insane asylum who is being driven mad by the situation in which he finds himself.

Far more popular, and eventually more important for the development of

18. Published by Firth & Hall of New York in 1836.

19. *Musical Treasury* 4, p. 2; quoted in John Anthony Stephens, "Henry Russell in America: Chutzpah and Huzzah" (D.M.A. dissertation, University of Illinois at Urbana-Champaign, 1975), p. 14.

20. "The Mad Girl's Song" (1840), words by T. C. Grattan; "The Pilgrim's Address to the Deity" (1841), words by Henry J. Sharpe; "The Gambler's Wife" (1841), words by Dr. Crofts; "The Ship on Fire" (1842), words by Mackay; "The Dream of the Reveller" (1843), words by Mackay; "The Main Track; or A Leap for Life" (1844), words by George P. Morris.

indigenous American songs, were the simpler, strophic pieces making up the major part of his vocal recitals. Suitable for amateur singers and accompanists, they became the best-selling items of sheet music in this country before the songs of Stephen Foster.

Probably the most popular of these was "The Old Arm Chair" (1840), set to a text by Eliza Cook. The text—strophic and narrative—recites the saga of the narrator's favorite heirloom, an armchair:

> I've treasured it long as a holy prize,
> I've bedewed it with tears, and embalmed it with sighs;
> 'Tis bound by a thousand bands to my heart;
> Not a tie will break, not a link will start.
> Would you learn the spell—a mother sat there,
> And a sacred thing is that old armchair.

Succeeding verses recount the various stages of life at which the narrator saw his mother seated in her favorite chair, until finally, "I learnt how much the heart can bear, When I saw her die in that old arm chair."

The melody is simple, restricted in range, repetitious, designed to be sung by even the most modest amateur voice. Yet here too there is a constant undercurrent of the Italian style, in the arpeggiated accompaniment,

HENRY RUSSELL, "THE OLD ARM CHAIR"

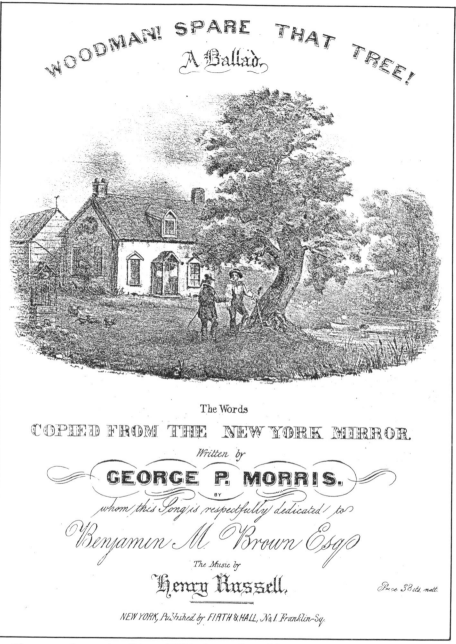

WOODMAN! SPARE THAT TREE!

A Ballad

The Words

COPIED FROM THE NEW YORK MIRROR.

Written by

GEORGE P. MORRIS.

BY

whom this Song is respectfully dedicated to

Benjamin M. Brown Esq

The Music by

Henry Russell.

Price 38 cts nett.

NEW YORK, Published by FIRTH & HALL, No 1. Franklin-Sq.

The cover of an early edition of "Woodman! Spare That Tree!"

in the chain of expressive appoggiaturas, in the graceful curve of the cadential figures, and in many other details of the writing.

Scarcely less popular was "Woodman, Spare That Tree" (1837), to words by the newspaperman George P. Morris, who supplied many texts for Russell and other songwriters. The melodramatic tale of a man who, seeing a woodman about to chop down a tree that sheltered him in his youth, persuades him to spare it, the song became a great favorite in the American parlor, was printed in numerous anthologies for the remainder of the century, and remained in print well into the twentieth century. But even this homely epic is offered in musical language that could easily be mistaken for that of Bellini:

HENRY RUSSELL, "WOODMAN, SPARE THAT TREE"

These two songs, and many others by Russell, echo one of the most persistent themes of the nineteenth century—nostalgia for youth, home, parents, old friends, lost innocence and happiness. It is the theme first sung—in the English language, at any rate—by Thomas Moore in his *Irish Melodies*; it persisted throughout the entire output of Stephen Foster and the songs of countless less gifted writers. The known external events of Henry Russell's life give no hint of unhappiness that would have driven him to escape into the past; his use of this theme seems to have been a matter of going along with trends of his time. Still other songs are of a livelier musical nature, melodically more suggestive of traditional English songs, such as "A Life on the Ocean Wave" (1838, the official song of the Royal Marines).

Russell became an immensely popular figure in America in the five years following his first New York recital of 1836. As early as 1838, the *Commercial Advertiser* (New York) commented in its issue of October 15 :

> His vocal exertions to please are always rewarded with a full attendance; and it is not surprising, for his voice and style are eminently qualified for general popularity.

His success was such that audiences would not tolerate other singers on the same program as Russell—this at a time when mixed concerts were the rule, and it was almost unheard of for a single performer to offer an entire program:

> Mr. Russell is the only singer we have ever known, who could sustain a concert alone. Madame Caradori Allen and all the other stars, have to introduce other voices to vary the scene and help keep up the interest. But if Mr. Russell introduces any other person, the audience soon grows impatient, and are glad to get rid of the interruption.[21]

Such success sparked criticism. J. S. Dwight, the self-proclaimed guardian of musical taste in Boston, pronounced him "a great charlatan." *The Musical Magazine* for April 11, 1840, claimed that "Mr. Russell's style of singing misleads to a false taste . . . his effects are not genuine effects of art . . . [they] bribe the untutored ear."

Such opinions were not shared by his contemporaries, who admired his songs and learned from them. As mentioned earlier, when the Hutchinson Family decided to embark on a professional career as a singing group, one of their first offerings was "The Maniac," which John sang with great effect for years; other Russell songs, such as "My Mother's Bible," were stable repertory numbers in the Hutchinsons' early years. John Hill Hewitt admired him, wrote a sketch of him in his autobiography, *Shadows on the Wall*, and composed a "descriptive ballad" for him, "Ho! For a Rover's Life" (1843). Stephen Foster heard him sing at least once (in Pittsburgh in 1843), was "inspired . . . to try great things himself" after that experience,[22] and wrote at least one song very much in Russell's style, "Farewell, Old Cottage."

Having established himself so firmly in America, Russell returned to his homeland to try his fortune there. His London debut was at the Hanover Square Rooms, on March 8, 1842. After a brief trip back to America, he returned once more to England, performing into the 1860s. He devoted himself increasingly to charitable causes, giving money and concerts for the benefit of the victims of the several famines in Ireland, the impoverished potters, the poor of the British Isles

---

21. *The Musical Review*, October 27, 1838.
22. Evelyn Foster Morneweck, *Chronicles of Stephen Foster's Family*, 2 vols. (Pittsburgh: University of Pittsburgh Press, 1944), 1:274.

who wished to emigrate to the United States, Canada, and Australia, temperance organizations, and the like.

Henry Russell's compositions marked a most important change of direction for song in America. He was trained as a classical performer and composer; he sang vocal compositions by Rossini, Donizetti, and Beethoven on his early programs; in addition to his solo vocal programs, he also sang in oratorios and other classical events; and he composed oratorios and cantatas. Yet he grasped early in his career—and he was perhaps the first musician to do so—that the audience for classical music was a limited one in America, but that there was a large and ever-increasing number of Americans who were literate, musically and otherwise, and who had an ear for music and a desire to hear and perform it. These people were, mostly, the first fruits of the move toward universal literacy that was so critical in American life of the nineteenth century. They came from classes with no history of exposure to classical music, nor to the culture that it represented.

In a very real sense, the concept of popular song may be said to have begun with Henry Russell—an English-born Jew who studied in Italy, first came to Canada, and then furnished Americans with songs in an Italian musical style, mostly to texts reflecting an Irish type of nostalgia. Of such ethnic mixtures was popular song in America born.

There were many others. Charles Edward Horn (1786–1849), for instance, the son of a German musician who settled in England in 1782, was a singer and songwriter who came to America in 1827 and involved himself in an incredible range of musical activities here, from singing opera and oratorio to organizing concerts, to conducting theatrical and sacred music, to organizing the Vocal Sacred Music Academy in New York, to publishing music himself. While in America he wrote songs, duets, glees, waltzes, sacred choruses, and arrangements of pieces by other composers. Several of his songs enjoyed some currency—"Cherry Ripe," for instance, written in 1825 to Herrick's famous lyric, and "I've Been Roaming" (1835)—but none survived him, probably because he clung to the musical styles of his youth and was eventually out of step with younger contemporary songwriters—and audiences.

A much more important songwriter, and indeed one of the most skilled and sensitive writers of the entire nineteenth century in Great Britain, was Charlotte Alington Barnard, who published songs and poetry under the name of "Claribel." Little is known of her life, save that she lived from 1830 to 1869, was married to C. C. Barnard, studied composition with a certain W. H. Holmes, and had instruction in voice from the famous singer Madame Parepa-Rosa (1836–74), who sang many of her pupil's songs in public for years. Claribel apparently married into a family of comfortable means and spent her life quietly composing and writing at home, with no contact with the world of professional musicians save through her voice teacher. Her songs are intensely personal, speaking most often of lost young love and of a present that is less golden than the past:

We sat by the river, you and I,
In that sweet summer time long ago.
So smoothly the water glided by,
Making music in its tranquil flow.

We threw two leaflets, you and I,
To the river as it wander'd on,
And one was rent and left to die,
And the other floated forward all alone.

And oh! we were sadden'd, you and I,
For we felt that our youth's golden dream,
Might fade and our lives be sever'd soon,
As the two leaves were parted in the stream. . . .

Strangers yet, after years of life together,
    After fair and stormy weather,
    After travel in far lands,
    After touch of wedded bands,
Why thus joined, why ever met?
If they must be strangers yet. . . .

One would guess that such songs were autobiographical, and that their success was due in large part to the intensity of expression, poetical and musical, that their creator brought to their writing.

Most popular in America were "I Cannot Sing the Old Songs," "Five O'Clock in the Morning," "Take Back the Heart," "Come Back to Erin," "Maggie's Secret," and "Won't You Tell Me Why, Robin," all brought out by a dozen or more publishers here and often anthologized in collections of the late nineteenth and early twentieth centuries. One would assume, from their style, that Claribel was familiar with much of the song literature of the day, for her songs often combine the clarity and symmetry of form of English song with accompanimental figures and the expressive dissonances of Italian opera and the chromatic coloring of German song.

CLARIBEL, "I CANNOT SING THE OLD SONGS"

can - not sing the old—— songs, Or dream those dreams a - gain.

Songs by these and other composers of the British Isles remained an important part of the musical culture of America into the period of the Civil War. Despite the emergence of indigenous popular song in America in the period covered by the present chapter, American audiences and composers continued to be receptive to songs from abroad, until the events of the Civil War period turned the attention of nearly everyone in America inward, to the events and problems of their own land.

NINE

"When the Swallows Homeward Fly";

OR.

German Song in Nineteenth-Century America

IN THE late 1830s one of Boston's leading music publishers, George P. Reed, issued the first of a series of songs called "*Gems of German Song;* From the Most Admired Compositions . . . . Adapted to English Words and arranged with an Accompaniment for the Piano Forte." A retrospective review speaks of this series as bringing about "the revelation of a new world of song to those who had only known English songs and ballads [and] sentimental love-strains with the most meagre common chord accompaniments."[1] The first seven "Gems," which appeared as a group, were:

No. 1	Last Greeting	Schubert
No. 2	Passing Bell	Schubert
No. 3	Amid this Greenwood Smiling	Thalberg
No. 4	All is Over	Weber
No. 5	Ave Maria	Schubert
No. 6	Grave Digger	Kalliwoda
No. 7	The Outlaw's Death	Muller

1. *Dwight's Journal of Music,* June 26, 1852, p. 52.

Songs by German composers, including some of those represented in Reed's series, had been printed in America before. But the appearance of the "Gems" coincided with a steady and growing stream of immigrants from German-speaking countries, and with a growing taste for German music of all sorts. The market for the series was modest at first, but expanding; within a decade, the number of "Gems" had passed sixty.[2] By mid-century German song was a popular genre, recognized as having its own musical characteristics.

A brief look at the early history of German-speaking immigrants will help set the stage for this new wave of national song into America.

On October 6, 1683, a group of Mennonites—mostly from Frankfurt am Main—arrived in America after a transatlantic trip on the ship *Concord*. They came to the New World because William Penn had visited their homeland in 1677 and converted many of them to Quakerism, and they quite naturally chose to settle in and near Philadelphia.

The pattern of mass emigration of religious groups and sects was repeated many times in the eighteenth century. In 1709, 13,000 persons fled from religious persecution in the Palatinate, stopping off first at London and then coming to America, where they settled in New York, Pennsylvania, and the Carolinas. Later, a similar group of Protestants left Salzburg because of persecution by Archbishop Leopold; most of them eventually made their way to America. Moravians, as the members of the Unitas Fratrum sect were called in America, established communities in Salem, North Carolina, and in Bethlehem, Ephrata, and other new communities in Pennsylvania. Other groups of religious refugees established communities in which not only their religion but also language, music, and general life-style were maintained in isolation from the predominant Anglo-American culture of their new land.

In addition to these religious groups, there was a steady stream of Germans, Austrians, and Swiss into America as individuals, family groups, and small neighborhoods. Many of these German-speaking immigrants became farmers; their native industry and determination to take full advantage of the opportunities of the New World made them successful settlers in Pennsylvania, Maryland, New York, and various parts of the upper South. Others, with more training and education, found a place for themselves and their trades and professions in cities and towns all along the Atlantic seaboard, particularly in Philadelphia, Baltimore, and New York.

In all, there were more than 200,000 German-speaking persons in the colonies when the Revolution broke out. Most of them joined in the struggle against the British and helped man the armies that brought about eventual victory.

There was harmony between this sizable ethnic minority and the English-

2. Firth & Hall (New York) reprinted the series, and other publishers began their own: Oliver Ditson & Co. (Boston) brought out *The Germania. New Vocal Gems from the German*, a series of seventy-odd songs by Eckert, Cherubini, Schubert, Lindblat, Gumpert, Meyerbeer, Mendelssohn, Kücken, Cramer, Abt, Niedermeyer, Voss, and Reichardt; Henry Tolman & Co., also of Boston, appropriated the title *Gems of German Song* for another series of some 150 songs by the same composers and their contemporaries.

Irish-Scotch majority dominating the culture and government of the new Republic. The religious communities were content to keep to themselves, and other people of German descent in rural and urban America quite willingly went along with the newly emerging patterns of American life. To the extent that they clung to their own language and culture, they restricted it to their own homes, churches, and social organizations. Their industry, thrift, ambition, and talent made them valuable and welcome citizens. There were occasional jokes about German-Americans, and their dialect and accented English were sometimes used in humorous songs and dramatic sketches on American stages. But they were, by and large, a peaceful and almost invisible strain of American life. When large numbers of them reached the West Coast in mid-century, they were as welcome there as they had been elsewhere; an article entitled "The Germans in California" sums up the American attitude toward them:

> They are almost universally republicans; nearly all become citizens; they learn English readily, and they adopt American manners and customs more readily than any other Europeans from the continent. . . . The German population is very orderly and industrious. There is probably no class among the people which has fewer representatives, in proportion, as offenders before the courts than the Germans, and they have very few or no gamblers among their number. There are some occupations, which they nearly monopolize; thus most of the dealers in cigars, musicians, and brewers in the city are German.[3]

Various musical organizations in America began to break away from programming patterns inherited from London, by sprinkling their programs with instrumental and vocal music of contemporary German composers. The Sacred Music Society of New York City performed Mendelssohn's *St. Paul* in 1838, only two years after its premier in Dusseldorf, and the same composer's *Elijah* was given a well-received performance by the Handel and Haydn Society of Boston in 1840. Beethoven's symphonies were played with increasing frequency in Boston, Philadelphia, New York, and Baltimore, by indigenous musical organizations made up mostly of English, American, and French musicians. Robert Schumann's *First Symphony* was given its first American performance by the Musical Fund Society of Boston in 1841, Spohr's oratorio *The Last Judgement* was done by the Boston Handel and Haydn Society in 1842, and the same year saw the establishment and first program of the New York Philharmonic Society, with pieces by Beethoven, Weber, Hummel, Mozart, and Kalliwoda. Only Rossini represented the non-Teutonic world.

Thus when George Reed began publishing German songs in the 1830s, it was not in response to demands from a large and visibly powerful ethnic group clamoring for pieces of native music, but rather a recognition of what many musicians were beginning to see as a powerful new direction in music, the domi-

3. *Dwight's Journal of Music*, July 2, 1853, pp. 101–2.

nation of all types of music by German composers. That Reed did not aim his *Gems of German Song* at the German community is obvious from the fact that the songs were brought out with English texts.

Political upheavals and famines in Germany in the 1830s and '40s brought an ever-increasing number of new immigrants. Many settled in the traditional "German" parts of America—Pennsylvania, Maryland, the Eastern cities. But many went further afield, to what is now the Midwest. Cincinnati's population jumped from 46,000 in 1840 to 115,000 in 1850; by mid-century, a good half of the city's population was newly arrived from Europe, and 30 percent of the inhabitants spoke German. St. Louis, Milwaukee, Louisville, and countless smaller towns also benefited from this sudden influx.

These new arrivals were not so inclined to melt into the mainstream of American life. They clung to their native language, and German culture, particularly music, became a much more visible part of the American scene. German singing societies were formed in Cincinnati in the early 1840s, and by 1849 the city was playing host to a regional *Sängerfest*, with participating groups coming from as far away as Louisville and Madison. A *Musikverein* was founded in Milwaukee in 1849, and New York had its own *Deutscher Liederkranz*, directed by a certain Dr. Ludwig, by 1847. By mid-century, New York, Philadelphia, and Baltimore had a dozen or more such organizations each, and there was talk of this movement spreading to New England.

Among the German immigrants of this period were a number of professional musicians. Matthias Keller (1813–75), a bandmaster and violinist, came to America in 1846 and was active in musical circles in Philadelphia, New York, and Boston for almost thirty years. Among his numerous compositions written in this country was the "American Hymn," judged the winning work in a post–Civil War competition for a new national anthem, and widely sung for decades until it was eventually supplanted by "The Star Spangled Banner." Julius Dyhrenfurth, a German-immigrant violinist, invited fellow German musicians to play in his home in Chicago; the group soon expanded, and became the Philharmonic Society of that city. German immigrants in Boston formed one of the first permanent chamber music groups in America, the Mendelssohn Quintette Club, which gave public performances in Boston and elsewhere for many years.

The most important German group for the history of music in America was the Germania Society, organized in Berlin in the mid-1840s by some twenty-five young musicians with a stated goal of performing music independent of patronage, under artistic conditions of the highest social and musical order. Finding Germany an unsympathetic environment, they went first to England, then to America in the fall of 1848, giving their first concert in New York. Before disbanding late in 1854, they gave more than 900 public performances in various parts of America. Their orchestra was of appropriate size for music of Mozart and Haydn, but too small for Beethoven and Schumann; so the group was often augmented by a dozen or more additional professional players from whatever city they performed in. Their first concerts were made up of the usual mixture of the

symphonic literature with lighter dance pieces, but American critics soon persuaded them to leave the latter repertory to other groups. The Beethoven symphonies formed the core of their repertory, and they were the first orchestra to
play these in many American cities; but they also performed pieces by such
modern masters as Schumann, Mendelssohn, Gade, Kalliwoda, and Spohr.
They gave the first American performance of Wagner's *Overture to Tannhäuser*,
a most difficult and advanced work for audiences of the time.

The Germania Musical Society, 1850.

Though they performed mostly in the cities of the East, they also gave
concerts in such cities as Buffalo, Rochester, St. Louis, Pittsburgh, Louisville,
Milwaukee, Minneapolis, and Cincinnati. They shared thirty-one concerts with
Jenny Lind, accompanying her and also playing several pieces of orchestral
music on each program, and they appeared with other great solo artists such as
Ole Bull, Strakosch, and Adelina Patti.

Their impact on music in America continued long after they disbanded in
1854. Becoming American citizens in a mass naturalization ceremony, they
dispersed to various parts of their new country, assuming a variety of roles. Carl
Lenschow, the first conductor of the Germanians, was so charmed with Baltimore that he settled there, married, and was leader of the local *Gesangverein* for
many years. Carl Bergmann, who succeeded him as leader of the orchestra,
became director of the New York Philharmonic Orchestra in 1855 and guided it
through the critical formative years with a firm hand, retiring from the post only
in 1876. Carl Zerrahn, principal flutist, settled in Boston; he was conductor of
the Boston Philharmonic from 1855 to 1863, directed and conducted the Harvard Musical Association for the period 1865–82, and conducted the prestigious
Boston Handel and Haydn Society from 1854 until his retirement in 1895; he also
found time to conduct the Worcester Festival and the Salem Oratorio Society.
Schultze (violin) settled in Syracuse, Brandt (manager) and Abner (trumpet)
went to Chicago, Albrecht (clarinet) and Sentz (percussion) chose Philadelphia.
Charles Stein (violin) and William Buchheister (viola) established the Boston

Music Store in Detroit, doing successful business there until 1880, while publishing compositions by themselves and other former Germanians.

When one adds to all this the fact that still other German musicians were instrumental in establishing music schools such as the Chicago Musical College and the Cincinnati Conservatory of Music, both founded in 1867, a picture of strong and increasing German domination of musical performance and teaching in America in the second half of the nineteenth century comes even more clearly into fucus.

No wonder, then, that George Reed's modest *Gems of German Song* flourished in the decades following its appearance, and became the model for similar—and more extensive—series by many other publishers.

The musical features distinguishing German song from English, Irish, Italian, and American vocal music of the mid-nineteenth century are already apparent in the first "Gem" in Reed's series, "Last Greeting" (also referred to by the first line of the text, "Adieu! 'Tis Love's Last Greeting"), attributed to Franz Schubert.

The piano has the first word, playing neither a mere rhythmic-harmonic pattern to set the key and establish the tempo nor a phrase or fragment of the vocal line to come, but rather a melodic phrase of its own:

"FRANZ SCHUBERT," "ADIEU! 'TIS LOVE'S LAST GREETING"

This material remains the almost exclusive property of the piano throughout, serving to frame the two verses.

The vocal part begins with melodic recitation, reiterating and revolving around a single note. Musical interest lies not in the melody, but in the working together of the voice and the accompaniment to underline and intensify the sense of the text:

"FRANZ SCHUBERT," "ADIEU! 'TIS LOVE'S LAST GREETING"

The song builds in intensity to the last eight measures, where, over a chromatically rising bass line quite reminiscent of "Der Wegweiser" in Schubert's cycle *Winterreise*, a climax is reached with the voice leaping up to its highest pitch:

"FRANZ SCHUBERT," "ADIEU! 'TIS LOVE'S LAST GREETING"

The last phrase of the vocal part, "For all eternity!," echoes the end of the piano introduction, and brings the voice and accompaniment together musically for the first and only time in the entire song.

It is a song of considerable but deceptive simplicity. There is no refrain line or chorus; the vocal part is almost recitative-like, syllabic throughout, and makes no more demands of range or technical agility than do the popular English and American ballads of the time. There is no trace of the floridity of Italian melody. But an effective performance demands a type of collaboration between singer and pianist not necessary in Irish, minstrel, and plantation songs. Simple though it may be, the song still demonstrates the characteristics of the German style: independence of the piano part, integration of voice and accompaniment, a certain amount of chromaticism, an unelaborated vocal line.

The song became widely popular, being brought out by a dozen or more publishers in various parts of the United States and widely anthologized in song collections of the late nineteenth and early twentieth centuries. It was the first "Schubert" song heard by thousands of Americans and remained one of the most popular of "his" songs for half a century. But, alas, the song is not by Schubert, but by one August Heinrich von Weyrauch. A setting of a poem by Karl Friedrich Gottlob Wetzel, it was first published in 1824 in Germany and probably found its way to America by way of a British edition, with a French translation of the poem by a certain Beranger.

A number of authentic songs by Schubert were published and sung in America at this time, though.[4] Most popular of all was "Serenade" ("Ständchen," from *Schwanengesang*), brought out by dozens of publishers in the United States and widely popular well into the twentieth century. Generations of Americans who never heard Schubert's symphonies or piano sonatas were acquainted with his style through this song as sung in American parlors, with its anonymously translated text beginning

Thro' the leaves the night-wind moving—
  Murmur low and sweet;
To thy chamber window roving,
  Love hath led my feet.

Silent prayers of blissful feeling,
  Link us, though apart;
On the breath of music stealing,
  To thy dreaming heart.

Musical ways have changed, and twentieth-century connoisseurs consider it a desecration for songs by Schubert to be sung in any language other than German. Yet it remains a historical fact that Americans first came to know his music through several dozen of his best songs published here in English translation in the mid-nineteenth century—a time when there was no distinction between "classical" and "popular" song. His songs were brought out by the same publishers who offered those of Moore, Bishop, Bellini, and Foster, purchased by amateur musicians who considered all these songs to be part of a single repertory,

---

4. Reed's first series of "Gems" included "Ave Maria" (Opus 52, no. 6) and "The Wanderer" ("Der Wanderer," Opus 4, no. 1), both in English translation. Henry Tolman's *Gems of German Song*, published slightly later in Boston with both German and English texts, had some twenty songs by Schubert, including "Fisher Maiden" ("Das Fischermädchen," from *Schwanengesang*), "Mignon Song" ("Lied der Mignon," Opus 62, no. 4), "Ye Faded Flowers" ("Trockne Blumen," from *Die schöne Müllerin*), and "Young Nun" ("Die junge Nonne," Opus 43, no. 1).

and performed in American homes by the same singers and accompanists who loved all this music. Who is to say that these people did not have sufficient musical background to comprehend these songs fully? Perhaps they understood them better than modern-day American audiences, who hear them sung in large concert halls in a language most of them do not understand.

Beethoven's "Adelaide" was widely popular in America, as were several songs apiece by Schumann, Loewe, Weber, and Spohr. Mendelssohn was a great favorite; the duet "I Would That My Love" ("Ich wollt' meine Leibe") was the most widely published of several dozen of his songs that obviously had great appeal for Americans. All these share similar musical characteristics: more elaborate and independent accompaniments than those found in other bodies of national song; strophic forms without refrain or chorus; a certain amount of chromaticism; and texts that share the popular sentiments of the Age of Romanticism without carrying them to the intense personal level often encountered in Irish and American songs.

The German composer whose songs were most widely published and sung in America in the nineteenth century, though, was Franz Abt, composer of more than 3,000 pieces, most of them for voice. Born in Eilenburg in 1819 and trained at the Thomasschule in Leipzig, Abt was involved for most of his life with amateur musical groups. Thrown on his own resources when his father died in 1837, he first made his living from writing and publishing piano arrangements and potpourris of familiar operatic airs, and also dances and other characteristic pieces for beginning and amateur pianists. Moving to Zurich in 1844, he began conducting student and town singing societies, writing part-songs for such groups, and organizing choral festivals. His first successful songs for voice and piano, including the widely popular "Wenn die Schwalben heimwärts zieh'n" (Opus 39, no. 1), date from this time. These diverse musical activities continued after his return to Germany in 1852; soon he was named "General-Gesangmeister" of one of Germany's largest choral festivals, the Bundes der Norddeutschen Liedertafeln. He came to America in 1872 as a participant in the World Peace Jubilee, organized by Patrick Gilmore, and stayed for some months to conduct in various cities, including Washington, where he was received at the White House by President Grant as a most distinguished visitor.

Abt's popularity in the United States began among the male singing societies established by German immigrants as a cultural link with their homeland. His part-songs were central to the repertory of such groups, and as German-Americans became more prosperous and could buy pianos for musical evenings at home, they quite naturally turned to the songs of the man who was already their favorite composer.

A look at several of Abt's most successful songs suggests reasons for their great popularity. Musical elements distinguishing German song from other national music are evident, but in modified form. There is chromaticism, but not enough to cause problems for untutored ears or for the fingers of amateur accompanists. There are moments when the piano part has some independence,

Franz Abt (1819–1885).

but never enough to make excessive technical demands. The songs are written for amateur performance by a man who spent his lifetime among nonprofessional musicians, a composer with a solid grasp of the needs, skills, and limitations of amateur but intent musicians.

"When the Swallows Homeward Fly," as well loved in America as in Europe, may consciously imitate certain elements of German folk song. The first phrases of the melody are simple and predominately diatonic:

FRANZ ABT, "WHEN THE SWALLOWS HOMEWARD FLY"

When the swal - lows home - ward fly, When the ros - es scat - ter'd

lie, When from nei - ther hill nor dale, Chants the sil - very night - in - gale;

The climax of the melody and the descent from it remind us how difficult it is to find a song from the mid-nineteenth century untouched by Italian influences; the last two phrases, with their languishing appoggiaturas and expressive melodic swoops, would be perfectly at home at the end of an arioso from an Italian opera.

FRANZ ABT, "WHEN THE SWALLOWS HOMEWARD FLY"

Can I, ah! can I e'er know re - pose, Can ___ I, ah!

can I e'er know re - pose.

"O Ye Tears!," a setting of a poem by Dr. Charles Mackay, was probably the most widely sung of all of Abt's songs in America and is more typical of his musical language. The piano has an expressive phrase at the beginning, with a touch of chromaticism at the approach to the cadence:

FRANZ ABT, "O YE TEARS!"

O ye tears! O ye tears!

The vocal line is characteristically semideclamatory, supported by repeated chords in the piano reminiscent of some of Robert Schumann's accompaniments, with chromatic elements here and there, and enough bits of melody to make the pianist feel part of a musical dialogue.

Abt's songs are often in triple meter, suggesting a waltz if in a fast tempo or a *Ländler* if slower:

FRANZ ABT, "EVENING SONG"
Rather slow

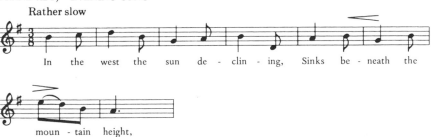

In the west the sun de - clin - ing, Sinks be - neath the
moun - tain height,

The waltz had been popular in America since the early nineteenth century, shortly after it had swept over Europe like wildfire. Thousands poured from American presses, written and arranged for every degree of technical competence—original waltzes by European and American composers, tunes from operas and instrumental works worked into piano pieces. But waltz rhythms rarely crossed over into popular song before mid-century. Such a waltz-song as Stephen Foster's "The Voices That Are Gone" is exceptional for an American composer. It remained for the Germans to demonstrate how effectively a song composer could utilize the musical characteristics of this popular dance.

Somewhat more demanding for both singer and accompanist are the songs of Friedrich Wilhelm Kücken. A musical twin to Abt, Kücken was born in 1810, was a choral director in both Switzerland and Germany, and composed hundreds of part-songs for male chorus and songs for voice and piano. In addition to his choral music and songs, he wrote chamber music and two successful operas, *Die Flucht nach der Schweiz* (1839) and *Der Prätendent* (1847). His musical horizons were thus more international and more oriented to instrumental music

than Abt's, as is evident in the following phrase from his song "Good Night,
Farewell" ("Gute Nacht"), in the texture of the piano writing:

FRIEDRICH KÜCKEN, "GOOD NIGHT, FAREWELL"

Songs in similar style by A. Reichardt, Gumbert, Moscheles, Lindblad, and
lesser contemporaries also enjoyed some success in America from mid-century
until they went out of fashion in the 1880s.

Though the songs of Kücken and his younger contemporaries were unmistakably German in style, they did not draw on the full harmonic, melodic, and
textual vocabulary of German chamber, orchestral, and operatic music of the
second half of the nineteenth century. Gradually, in Germany as elsewhere,
musical styles of Classical and popular music were diverging. The songs of
Schubert and Mendelssohn fit comfortably into the heterogeneous song repertory of the early part of the century; the songs of Brahms, Wagner, Liszt, and
Hugo Wolf never became part of popular culture. Wagner's "Bridal Chorus"
from *Lohengrin* and "To the Evening Star" from *Tannhäuser*, fitted with English
texts, enjoyed some currency in the British and American sheet music market,
but his later compositions moved in musical directions that made them unsuita-
ble for adaption as popular song. Critics of the time remarked on the growing

stylistic gap between serious and light music, without judging one type superior or inferior to the other. It remained for the twentieth century to take this step.

German song, then, enjoyed some vogue in America at mid-century, just at the time that the German population of the United States was swollen by new waves of immigrants. As a glance at Appendix 4 will show, songs by Schubert, Abt, and Kücken were among the European pieces most often published in America in the mid-nineteenth century. Their impact on American song was not as dramatic as that of English, Irish, or Italian music. Indigenous American song had blossomed a decade or so before German music established itself; once shaped, it was less susceptible to new musical influences.

Music from Central Europe, including some of the Germanic lands, did indeed play a decisive role in American song, but at a later time.

TEN

"Old Folks at Home";

OR,

The Songs of Stephen Foster

STEPHEN FOSTER was acclaimed during his lifetime as the best songwriter America had yet produced, a judgment that has prevailed since. Even writers and historians with little sensitivity for popular music acknowledge this evaluation, which is now firmly entrenched as historical fact, in all likelihood never to be challenged.

Despite such unanimity of praise, his precise role in the history of song in America has been consistently and often grossly misunderstood. In the more than a century since his death, writers and biographers have built a popular image of him that has rarely been questioned: that he

> had little or no training in music: "He was an untutored genius . . . ,"[1] "He accomplished that which many a better-trained musician has failed to do . . . .";[2]
> derived much of his musical material and inspiration from the music

1. *Grove's Dictionary of Music and Musicians*, 5th ed., ed. Eric Blom (New York: St. Martin's Press, 1955), 3:456.
2. John Tasker Howard, *Our American Music: Three Hundred Years of It* (New York: Thomas Y. Crowell, 1929), p. 184.

Stephen Collins Foster (1826–1864).

of slaves and other black Americans: "The peculiar negro flavor of many of his songs he acquired by attending negro camp meetings . . . ,"[3] "It is curious to observe the American white man . . . imitating and appropriating the melodic forms and tonal characteristics of the songs of the colored slaves . . . ,"[4] "By descent and temperament he was a Southerner, and this

3. W. S. B. Mathews, ed., *A Hundred Years of Music in America* (Chicago: G. L. Howe, 1889), p. 95.
4. Frédéric Louis Ritter, *Music in America* (New York: Charles Scribner's Sons, 1883), p. 437.

explains his keen sympathy with the sentiment and form of the songs and
music of the plantation . . .";[5]

was victimized by greedly publishers, who gave him a pittance for his
songs and grew wealthy from them, while he died in poverty.

Unfortunately, almost no one has looked at his songs from the perspective
of what popular song had been in America before and during his lifetime.[6] My
discussion of Foster will not deal with his biography, as such,[7] nor with the history of his songs after his death, but will place his work in the perspective of the
history of popular song in America before 1845.

Born in Pittsburgh on July 4, 1826—the fiftieth anniversary of the signing of
the Declaration of Independence—Stephen Foster was raised in an educated,
well-to-do family in which the arts were cultivated. Musical instruction was part
of the education of his older sisters, Charlotte Susanna (1809–29) and Henrietta
Angelica (1818–79). We know that there was a piano in the home for at least part
of the young Fosters' childhood. Charlotte played the piano and harp, and sang;
music was at the core of her short life. Letters by and about her mention her singing both at home and when she went off to Cincinnati, Louisville, and Bards-
town; and, if we are to trust the testimony of an eyewitness to her death, the family friend A. Hill Rowan, she sang literally on her deathbed:

> The night of the morning which she died, I sat up and was frequently in her
> room. . . . About an hour before day, when all were silent, she sang a song
> preserving with much melody and great accuracy, every note, but her voice
> was then so thickened than she did not articulate sufficiently plain for the
> words to be heard, or for the song to be recognized . . .[8]

Stephen was likewise drawn to music, early and strongly. His sister
Henrietta taught him chords on the guitar; he learned to play the flute and piano
and picked out melodies on these instruments as a young child. A letter from his
father in 1841 attests that "his leisure hours are all devoted to musick, for which
he possesses a strange talent."[9]

His brother Morrison tells us that he studied with Henry Kleber, probably
the most accomplished musician in Pittsburgh. Born in Germany in 1816,

5. *Grove's Dictionary of Music and Musicians; American Supplement, being the 6th Volume of
the Complete Work*, ed. Waldo Selden Pratt (New York: Macmillan, 1944), p. 117.

6. A recent book by William W. Austin, *Susanna, Jeanie, and The Old Folks at Home; The
Songs of Stephen C. Foster from His Time to Ours* (New York: Macmillan, 1975), is an important exception to this generalization; it examines Foster's songs, in detail, from the point of view of the most
important trends in American life and culture before, during, and after Foster's lifetime.

7. The standard biography, and still the most comprehensive study of Foster's life, is John
Tasker Howard, *Stephen Foster, America's Troubador* (New York: Thomas Y. Crowell, 1934).

8. Evelyn Foster Morneweck, *Chronicles of Stephen Foster's Family*, 2 vols. (Pittsburgh: University of Pittsburgh Press, 1944), 1:81.

9. Howard, *Stephen Foster*, p. 81.

Kleber came to Pittsburgh in 1830, became music instructor at Dr. Lacey's seminary for young ladies, established a piano and music store, performed as a tenor soloist and pianist, organized and directed a wind band, was an agent for the Steinway piano company, and composed popular dances.[10] Morrison wrote that during this time Stephen "studied deeply, and burned much midnight oil over the works of the masters, especially Mozart, Beethoven, and Weber. They were his delight, and he struggled for years and sounded the profoundest depths of musical science."[11]

Stephen Foster's first known song, "Open Thy Lattice, Love," was published in 1844,[12] and may have been written a year or so earlier. A brief song in two strophes, set to a text by the New York journalist George P. Morris, its musical ancestry may be traced to the stage and concert songs of the third generation of English writers, particularly Henry Bishop and Charles E. Horn. The simple, amatory, refined text, set in a placid 6/8 meter, is almost completely syllabic in Foster's setting; the four-measure piano prelude and postlude are static,

STEPHEN FOSTER, "OPEN THY LATTICE, LOVE"

10. Cf. Austin, pp. 22–23. Stephen published arrangements of three of his dances—"Pearl Polka," "Rainbow Schottisch," and "Coral Schottisch"—in his *Social Orchestra* (1854).

11. Howard, *Stephen Foster*, p. 108.

12. By George Willig (Philadelphia).

stuck on the tonic chord, and except for a brief modulation to the dominant at the end of the second phrase, the harmony is confined to the principal chords of the major scale; the accompaniment consists of simple strummed chords. It is a remarkably unremarkable song, one that would have been forgotten had it not been for the future career of its composer.

From various letters and other documents, we know that Charlotte Foster had known the songs of Bishop and such contemporaries and successors as Thomas Bayley ("I'd Be a Butterfly").[13] That Stephen himself knew songs by Lover, Glover, and Linley can be deduced from his inclusion of arrangements of some of their songs in his *Social Orchestra,* a collection of arrangements of vocal works and dances for various instruments. One need go no further than these for the models of "Open Thy Lattice, Love." And once the mold has been recognized, it can be seen that many of his other early songs are cast in the same image: "What Must a Fairy's Dream Be?" (1847), "Stay, Summer Breath" (1848), "Mary Loves the Flowers" (1850), "Once I Loved Thee, Mary Dear" (1851), "Molly, Do You Love Me?" (1850), "Willie My Brave" (1851), and "The Village Maiden" (1855). The stereotype persists, even in his later years: "Parthenia to Ingomar" (1859), "Jenny's Coming O'er the Green" (1860), "The Little Ballad Girl" (1860), "I Will Be True to Thee" (1862). Usually labeled "song" or "ballad," they are descendants of the songs written in the eighteenth century for Vauxhall and other pleasure gardens. They are usually dedicated to young women of Foster's acquaintance; the musical form is strophic, sometimes with a refrain line; they are most often in triple meter. Harmony is mostly diatonic, with an occasional touch of chromaticism.

Several of these songs rise above the mediocrity of most of the group, though. "Ah! May the Red Rose Live Alway" (1850) is one of his earliest songs to tap the profound lyricism that was to mark so much of his best work, though it had very little vogue during his lifetime. Superficially in the Bishop-Horn mold, the text (by Foster) evokes more than an echo of the deep nostalgia of Moore's *Irish Melodies,* specifically "The Last Rose of Summer":

Lulled be the dirges in the cypress bough,
   That tells of departed flowers!
Ah! that the butterfly's gilded wings
   Fluttered in evergreen bowers!
Sad is my heart for the blighted plants—
   Its pleasures are aye as brief—
They bloom at the young years joyful call,
   And fade with the autumn leaf.

and the tune begins to lose some of the squareness of English song:

13. Morneweck, 1:41.

STEPHEN FOSTER, "AH! MAY THE RED ROSE LIVE ALWAY"

Ah! may the red rose live al - way, To smile up-on earth and sky!___

Why should the beau-ti-ful ev-er weep? Why should the beau-ti-ful die?___

It is not surprising that these songs were relatively unsuccessful in the 1850s. Bishop had been popular in his day, but that day had passed, and with the exception of the perennial "Home, Sweet Home," his songs were rapidly dropping out of sight, replaced in popularity by works tapping newer and more vital musical styles—Italian opera and the minstrel song. These songs of Foster's were based on old and tired models, and if he had written in no other style, he would be forgotten now—deservedly so.

Foster's minstrel songs were his first truly successful pieces, the ones that established his fame in America and abroad and the first written in a style more distinctly his own.

According to Morrison, Stephen was involved with minstrel music for the first time at the age of nine, when he became a member of a neighborhood "Thesbian company" performing in a makeshift theater in a nearby carriage house:

He was regarded as a star performer, and was guaranteed a certain sum weekly. It was a very small amount, but it was sufficient to mark his superiority over the rest of the company. "Zip Coon," "Long-tailed Blue," "Coal-Black Rose," and "Jim Crow" were the only Ethiopian songs then known. His performance of these was so inimitable and true to nature that, child as he was, he was greeted with uproarious applause, and called back again and again every night the company gave an entertainment, which was three times a week.[14]

This would have been about 1835, some five years after George Washington Dixon began singing "Coal Black Rose" and "Long Tailed Blue" as part of his act, several years after "Daddy" Rice began "jumping Jim Crow" across the country, and some eight years before the first minstrel troupe was formed.

It was not until a decade later that Foster tried his hand at writing an "Ethiopian song" himself. About 1845, a group of young men calling themselves the Knights of the Square Table began meeting at his house in Pittsburgh twice a week to practice "songs in harmony" with piano, guitar, flute, and violin to support their voices. As Morrison remembers it:

> At that time, negro melodies were very popular. After we had sung over and over again all the songs then in favor, he proposed that he would try and make some for us himself. His first effort was called "The Louisiana Belle." A week after this he produced the famous song of "Old Uncle Ned."[15]

"Lou'siana Belle" was published several years later, in 1847.[16] The cover announced that the song was "Written for and Sung by Joseph Murphy of the Sable Harmonists," which is patently inaccurate, but a common tactic on the part of a publisher to link a song by an unknown composer to a well-known performer. Several other songs share the same history—written by Foster for his circle of friends in Pittsburgh and published later "as sung by" one of the minstrel troupes of the day. "Away Down South," "Uncle Ned," and "Susanna" were brought out late in 1848[17] as a set of "Songs of the Sable Harmonists"; "Old Uncle Ned" was brought out earlier in the year[18] as one of a series of sixteen songs titled "Music of the Great Southern Sable Harmonists; the best band of singers in the United States," with an elaborate lithographed cover portraying the six members of the company surrounded by junglelike floral designs.

"Oh! Susanna"[19] is identified by Morrison as one of the songs written by Stephen for his friends in Pittsburgh. This is Foster's first song to be associated with the Christy Minstrels; the cover of the first edition reads:

Music of the Original Christy Minstrels.
The Oldest Established Band in the United States,
As arranged and sung by them with distinguished success in all their concerts.

14. Howard, *Stephen Foster*, pp. 83–84.
15. Morneweck, 1:283.
16. By W. C. Peters in Cincinnati.
17. By Peters.
18. By W. E. Millet of New York.
19. Copyrighted by C. Holt in New York.

The florid lithographed cover announcing the "Music of the Great Southern Sable Harmonists" and featuring Foster's "Old Uncle Ned" and "Susanna."

It is one of sixteen songs by a number of composers in a variety of styles, including "Lucy Neal," "Dandy Broadway Swell," "Oh! Mr. Coon," and "Phantom Chorus, from Sonnambula."

Foster's contact with E. P. Christy had been exclusively by mail. The young composer had sent Christy manuscript copies of his songs, and—at least as of 1850—he had neither met Christy nor heard his "band."[20]

Foster's name does not appear on the first edition of "Oh! Susanna," but the success of several of his songs on the minstrel stage prompted Firth, Pond & Co. in New York to bring out a set of four of his new minstrel songs in 1850, with a cover featuring his name at the very top:

Foster's Ethiopian Melodies . . .
As Sung by the Christy Minstrels
    Nelly Was a Lady
    My Brudder Gum
    Dolcy Jones
    Nelly Bly

The same firm brought out a second set of four, later in 1850, advertising these as sung by both the Christy and Campbell minstrels: "Oh! Lemuel," "Dolly Day," "Gwine to Run All Night," and "Angelina Baker." "Oh! Lemuel" was advertised as an "Ethiopian Song," but the others in the series were called "Plantation Melodies," a new term that carried some considerable significance, as we shall see.

Thus, by 1850, Foster had published twelve minstrel songs, which quickly established themselves as staples in the minstrel show repertory, and their young composer, still in his mid-twenties, was recognized as one of the leading American composers of minstrel songs.

These early minstrel songs show their ancestry as clearly as did Foster's first songs in the English style. Melodies are diatonic, simple, restricted in range to an octave or less; pentatonic scales are often suggested or implied; tempos are usually brisk and dancelike. If the melodic character of the songs of "Daddy" Rice, Dan Emmett, George Washington Dixon, and their contemporaries was indeed shaped by English-Irish-Scotch folk music, this character echoes strongly through Foster's first minstrel songs. The texts, which he wrote himself, also echo themes of early minstrelsy. Written in heavy dialect, they portray the black as a simple, amusing, illiterate creature who spent his days laboring and his nights dancing and singing. There is, for example, "Brudder Gum,"

White folks, I'll sing for you,
    Nuffin else to do,
Spent my time pickin' on de banjo!
    Hay! Brudder Gum.

20. Morneweck, 1:377.

And "Lemuel":

> He makes de fiddle hum,
>   He makes de banjo tum,
> He rattles on de old jaw bone,
>   And beats upon de drum.

There are even crude caricatures of physical features of blacks:

> My lub she hab a very large mouf,
>   One corner in de norf, tudder corner in de souf,
> It am so long, it reach so far,
>   Trabble all around it on a railroad car.
>   —"Away Down Souf"

Even the most popular of these early songs, "Oh! Susanna," belongs to this tradition, with its nonsensical, prattling lines.

Despite their obvious indebtedness to earlier minstrel songs, these pieces by Foster contain unique, new features. There is, for example, the matter of the chorus. Many earlier minstrel songs had refrain lines, sung to the same music at the end of each verse. These were sometimes sung, in unison, by the entire troupe. Foster's very first minstrel songs have choruses in three- and four-part harmony. In fact, the most obvious difference between Foster's "English" songs and his "Ethiopian melodies" is that the latter invariably have choruses, the former never do.

Foster wrote choruses in four-part harmony in his first minstrel songs for his friends, who could read music and sing in parts. When he wrote other minstrel songs, knowing they would be sung by professional minstrel troupes, he continued writing choruses. A famous letter to Christy, written from Pittsburgh in June of 1851, implies that Foster was not certain how his songs would be done on the minstrel stage:

> Herewith, I sent you the m.s. according to agreement. [The song in question was "Oh! Boys Carry Me 'Long."] I am not certain that you use a piano in your band; but I have arranged an accompaniment for that instrument at a venture. If you have a tenor voice in the company that can sing up to "g" with ease (which is very probable) it will be better to sing the song in the key of "g." Thus you will not carry the bass voice quite so low. I hope you will preserve the harmony in the chorus just as I have written it, and practice the song well before you bring it out. It is especially necessary that the person who sings the verses should know all the words perfectly, as the least hesitation in the singing will damn any song—but this you of course know as well as myself. Remember it should be sung in a pathetic, not a comic style.[21]

21. Howard, *Stephen Foster*, pp. 186–87.

There is much naiveté in this letter, showing that even at this point in his career, Foster was out of touch with the realities of performance on the minstrel stage. There was a considerable difference between the way it would be performed in public—roughly, to the accompaniment of banjos and fiddles, in many cases in nonharmonic style—and the way it appeared in sheet music to be sung in American parlors—to a harmonic, piano (or guitar) accompaniment, with proper attention to the precise notes written down by the composer or arranger.

Several of Foster's early minstrel songs, usually called "Plantation Melodies," differ from those of his contemporaries in another important way—their texts begin to take a quite different view of the black American. "Old Uncle Ned," written no later than 1848, begins with a verse that is partly humorous, and certainly offensive to blacks today:

> There was an old Nigger, his name was Uncle Ned,
> He's dead long ago, long ago;
> He had no wool on de top ob his head,
> De place whar de wool ought to grow.

But there is a new spirit here; Uncle Ned emerges in the following verses as a gentle, kindly human being. The song is an elegy, the chorus concluding with:

> No more work for poor Old Ned,
> He is gone whar de good niggers go.

And the last verse suggests a black-white relationship never hinted at in earlier minstrel songs:

> When Old Ned die, Massa take it mighty bad,
> De tears run down like de rain,
> Old Missus turn pale and she look'd berry sad,
> Kase she nebber see Old Ned again.

"Nelly Was a Lady" goes the next step, of portraying profound human feelings among blacks in their relationship to one another;

> When I saw Nelly in de morning,
> Smile till she open'd up her eyes,
> Seem'd like de light ob day a dawning,
> Jist 'fore de sun begin to rise.
>
> Now I'm unhappy and I'm weeping,
> Can't tote de cotton-wood no more,
> Last night, while Nelly was a sleeping,
> Death came a knockin' at de door.

Nelly was a lady,
Last night she died,
Toll de bell for lubly Nell,
My dark Virginny bride.

Again a small step, from our perspective; but it was important in the consciousness-raising process necessary to bring whites to the point of regarding slavery as a crime and a sin.

Next came still another set of four minstrel songs. "Way Down in Ca-i-ro," "written and composed for James F. Taunt of the Empire Minstrels," is a brief and lively banjo song, as is "Ring de Banjo." "Oh! Boys, Carry Me 'Long" is a companion to "Old Uncle Ned," a song about an aged slave containing the first complaint (to my knowledge) in a minstrel song about the institution of slavery:

Der's no more trouble for me:
    I's guine to roam
    In a happy home,
Where all de niggas am free.

"Melinda May," a "beautiful Ethiopian Melody . . . As sung by the celebrated New Orleans Serenaders," breaks new ground in another way. An affectionate and lighthearted serenade, it is free from dialect except for the replacement of "th" with "d," and "v" by "b":

Lubly Melinda is bright as de beam,
    No snow-drop was ebber more fair,
She smiles like de roses dat bloom round de stream,
    And sings like de birds in de air.

The music is unlike that of any other minstrel song to this point. Its graceful melodic swoops and leaps, the appoggiaturas, the traces of chromaticism, the melodic embellishment—all are foreign to the minstrel style, but common to Italian opera:

STEPHEN FOSTER, "MELINDA MAY"

Foster's next five minstrel songs, written between 1851 and 1853, represent the peak of his inspiration in this genre. All five are identified on their covers as "Sung by Christy's Minstrels"; four of the five were and are among the most popular of all his songs:

"Old Folks at Home" (1851)
"Farewell, My Lilly Dear" (1851, "Plantation Melody")
"Massa's in de Cold Ground" (1852)
"My Old Kentucky Home, Good Night" (1853, "Plantation Melody")
"Old Dog Tray" (1853, "American Melody")

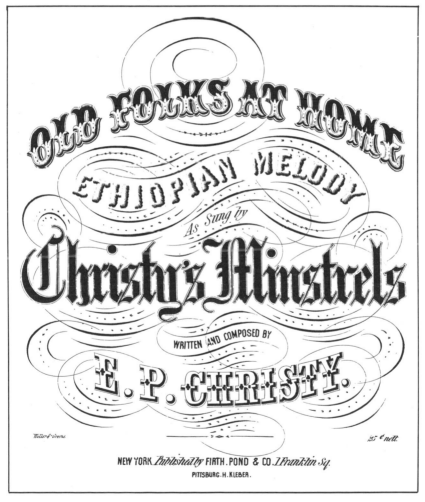

The sheet music cover for Stephen Foster's most popular song during his lifetime, "Old Folks at Home" (1851), nowhere mentions his name.

These are a far cry from the "nigger songs" of the early minstrel show. "Old Folks at Home," Foster's most popular song during his lifetime, still retains traces of dialect, but the text is a lament for lost home, friends, and youth, cutting across racial and ethnic lines and almost identical in substance (if not in style) to many of Moore's *Irish Melodies*.

> All de world am sad and dreary,
>   Eb'ry-where I roam,
> Oh! darkeys, how my heart grows weary,
>   Far from de old folks at home.

"Farewell, My Lilly Dear," a lament for a parted (but not lost) love, almost abandons dialect:

> The sun can never shine, love,
>   So bright for you and me,
> As when I worked beside you
>   In good old Tennessee.

"Massa's in de Cold Ground" may have fallen into disfavor in the mid-twentieth century because it is no longer compatible with contemporary political attitudes in its suggestion that slaves had strong sentimental attachments to their masters, but is again a sympathetic portrayal of a black. "My Old Kentucky Home" is almost completely free from dialect, and though the second and third verses identify the protagonist as a "darkey," the language is close to Moore:

> The day goes by, like a shadow o'er the heart,
> With sorrow where all was delight;

And the sentiment with which the song concludes—death as a welcome relief for the weary and troubled—was a universal nineteenth-century notion, much more general than slavery or the South or even America:

> A few more days for to tote the weary lead,
>   No matter, 'twill never be light,
> A few more days till we totter on the road
>   Then my old Kentucky Home, good-night!

The last song of this set, "Old Dog Tray," has no trace of dialect and makes no mention of slaves or the South; it is classified as a minstrel song only because it was printed as "Sung by Christy's Minstrels" and because it has a chorus.

These five songs mark a new stage in Foster's songwriting. Their content is a nonethnic one—nostalgia for lost youth, home, friends. They were written at a time when Foster faced severe personal problems. He had married Jane Mc-Dowell in 1850, and a daughter Marion was born in April of 1851. By early

1853, when he left for an extended stay in New York, there were rumors that he and his wife were separated. His song production dropped to its lowest point during this period; he published only four new songs in 1852, perhaps a reflection of internal upheavals. Also, America was beginning to experience the forces that were to tear it apart only a decade later. Foster, born and raised in the North, but in a section of the country geographically and culturally near the South, rarely expressed himself on social issues, but there is evidence that events of the early 1850s had a profound effect on him. *Uncle Tom's Cabin* had come out serially in 1851, and as a two-volume book in 1852. When it was first performed on the stage in Pittsburgh in 1853, a number of Foster's songs were interpolated into the production: "Old Folks at Home," "My Old Kentucky Home," and "Massa's in de Cold Ground," perhaps without his knowledge, though he raised no objections. Foster seriously considered abandoning the writing of "Ethiopian songs," but in a famous letter to Christy, dated May 25, 1852, he expressed a new attitude:

> . . . I find that by my efforts I have done a great deal to build up a taste for the Ethiopian songs among refined people by making the words suitable to their taste, instead of the trashy and really offensive words which belong to some songs of that order. Therefore I have concluded to reinstate my name on my songs and to pursue the Ethopian business without fear or shame . . .[22]

These songs are a first clue to what would prove to be Foster's reaction to both personal and national problems: to withdraw into nostalgia, to see the present as a poor substitute for the past.

This group of songs also represents the virtual end of Foster's career as a writer of minstrel songs. Having transformed the genre and made it expressive of sentiments far removed from those of the "nigger song," Foster wrote a mere handful of minstrel songs in the last decade of his life; "Ellen Bayne" (1854) and "The Glendy Burk" (1860) were the best of the lot, and neither rises above a rehashing of the melodic and textual formulae of some of his earlier songs.

Stephen Foster was of Irish extraction: his great-grandfather, Alexander Foster, emigrated from Londonderry, Ireland, in about 1728, settling in Pennsylvania. Stephen grew up in a family conscious of its heritage, in an emotional and cultural environment shaped in part by the poems, songs, and sentiments of Thomas Moore. An episode involving his older sister Charlotte will serve as a single illustration; Mrs. Foster recorded in her diary how the child, who played the piano and sang at an early age, was asked to perform for a gathering of family and friends. The child "lifted her soft blue eyes and looked sweetly" at the family friend who had asked her to perform, then "walked modestly" to the piano and played and sang one of Moore's *Sacred Melodies*. Her performance was "in a

22. Ibid., p. 196.

manner that touched the feelings and moved the hearts" of all present, prompting one of the gathering to ask that since "there is so much pathos in your song, do not leave the instrument until you have given us another."[23] Her repertory is known to have included such other songs by Moore as "Come Rest in This Bosom" and "Flow On, Thou Shining River."[24] Given this heritage and environment, Stephen Foster must have been familiar with Moore's songs in his childhood and adolescence.

The most relevant proof of Foster's acquaintance with Moore's songs, however, is to be found in his own music; many of his songs, including some of the best, show clear traces of an Irish ancestry.

As early a song as "The Spirit of My Song," written in 1850 to a text by Metta Victoria Fuller, has a first phrase outlining a pentatonic scale, as well as characteristic rhythmic patterns:

STEPHEN FOSTER, "THE SPIRIT OF MY SONG"

A pure example of Irish melody is "Sweetly She Sleeps, My Alice Fair," written in 1851 to a text by Charles G. Eastman. Again the opening phrase of the melody is pentatonic, and the tune is strongly reminiscent of several of Moore's *Irish Melodies*, among them "Has Sorrow Thy Young Days Shaded":

STEPHEN FOSTER, "SWEETLY SHE SLEEPS, MY ALICE FAIR"

23. Ibid., pp. 30–31.
24. Morneweck, 1:41.

Other songs by Foster showing strong resemblance to Irish tunes include:

"Mother, Thou'rt Faithful to Me" (1851)
"Maggie by My Side" (1853)
"Little Ella" (1853)
"Willie, We Have Missed You" (1854)
"I See Her Still in My Dreams" (1857)
"None Shall Weep a Tear for Me" (1860)

"Comrades, Fill No Glass for Me" (1855), which also bears a superficial resemblance to Irish melody, is one of Foster's most personal statements, his one direct mention in a song of something that was to plague him in the last years of his life—alcohol.

Oh! comrades, fill no glass for me
    To drown my soul in liquid flame,
For if I drank, the toast should be,
    To blighted fortune, health and fame.

This is no polemic against the evils of alcohol—it is a gentle complaint against outrageous fortune, and a statement that life, once so happy, has turned sour, leaving the poet with the remembrance of a happier past as his sole consolation. Foster echoes the same theme of nostalgia for lost friends, lost loves, lost hopes in song after song. There seems little doubt that his language as a poet was shaped in large part by that of Moore.

There are several ironies here. Foster, in allowing slaves human emotions, naturally granted them the most popular emotion of the day, nostalgia. Thus he wrote songs in which slaves sing of happy childhood and youth, the "old plantation," their "massa," and other aspects of slavery. Another irony is that the sentiments of Moore—the aristocratic poet who aimed his songs not at the "ignorant and angry multitudes" but rather "higher . . . the rich and educated"—should have been popularized in songs by Foster in which these sentiments were put in the mouths of persons who were very much a part of America's "ignorant and angry multitudes."

"Gentle Annie" (1856) demonstrates in another way how deep and persuasive was Foster's debt to Irish melody: it belongs to a tune family that includes several of Moore's *Irish Melodies* and various other Irish and Scottish songs (see pp. 55–57).

The most popular of all of Foster's "Irish Melodies" is "Jeanie with the Light Brown Hair," written in 1854. The melody is pentatonic throughout, except for two measures in the middle where a modulation to the dominant key takes place.

The sheet music cover for "Jeanie with the Light Brown Hair," published by Firth, Pond & Co. in 1854.

STEPHEN FOSTER, "JEANIE WITH THE LIGHT BROWN HAIR"

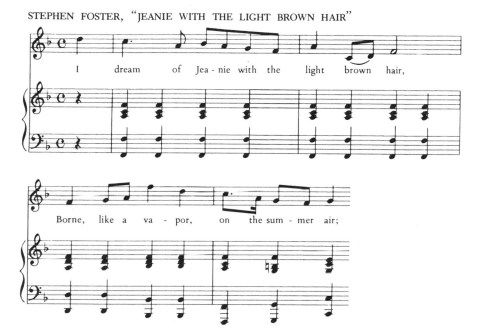

The text echoes many lines by Moore:

> I hear her melodies, like joys gone by,
> Sighing round my heart o'er the fond hopes that die: . . .
> Her smiles have vanished and her sweet songs flown,
> Flitting like the dreams that have cheered us and gone.

It is inconceivable that this song could have been written had there not been a Thomas Moore.

There is both external and internal evidence that Foster heard and absorbed the sounds of Italian opera that were sweeping over America during his childhood and early manhood. He was acquainted with Madame Eliza Ostinelli Biscaccianti, an operatic singer and granddaughter of James Hewitt, and attended a number of her concerts. Somewhat earlier, in 1843, he heard Henry Russell sing a program of his Italianate songs. His familiarity with at least the most popular "gems" from Italian opera is proved by his inclusion of a number of them in his *Social Orchestra* (1854).

Unmistakable echoes of Italian melody may be heard in as early a song as "The Voice of By-Gone Days" (1850); the arpeggiated accompaniment, graceful melodic curve, and almost obsessive use of appoggiatura are unlike anything in his English, Irish, or minstrel songs. The second phrase of this song makes unmistakable reference to Donizetti and Bellini, with its appoggiaturas, chromaticism, and melodic embellishment:

STEPHEN FOSTER, "THE VOICE OF BY-GONE DAYS"

Youth-ful fan-cy thee re-turns, Child-ish hope the bos-om burns,

Joy, that man-hood cold-ly spurns, Then flows in mem-ory's sweet re-frain.

"Farewell, Old Cottage" (1851) is Foster's tribute to Henry Russell; in both text and music, it is so reminiscent of Russell's more sentimental Italianate ballads that it approaches a parody, with even the lithograph reminding one of those decorating the covers of the older composer's more popular songs.

The duet "Wilt Thou Be Gone, Love?" reveals the full extent of Foster's familiarity with—and command of—the Italian style. If there were no other evidence connecting him with the music of Italian opera, this one song would be enough. From the first throbbing, beautifully sculptured opening phrases of this version of the Balcony Scene from *Romeo and Juliet*:

STEPHEN FOSTER, "WILT THOU BE GONE, LOVE?"

Wilt thou be gone, wilt thou be gone, love, gone, love, from me?

to the last, climactic, chromatic echo of the two voices:

the piece is an exercise in sensual, Italianate vocal writing. It is a well-crafted, beautiful duet, fully comparable to pieces by the leading Italian composers of the day. Familiarity with this song should dispel forever the notion that Foster wrote simple minstrel songs because he was incapable of writing any other kind of music.

Several other of his better songs are equally indebted to Italian opera.

"Come with Thy Sweet Voice Again" (1854) has a flowing melody against an arpeggiated accompaniment, which makes a point of the popular Italian device of a leap upward to a note out of the chord, with a downward resolution:

STEPHEN FOSTER, "COME WITH THY SWEET VOICE AGAIN"

Lulled —— in the lap of thy sighs, Let me dream,—— let me dream.

"Come Where My Love Lies Dreaming" (1855), written as a vocal quartet, has a fluid Italian melody, supported by repeated chords in the lower voices reminiscent of many of Rossini's ensemble numbers. "Linger in Blissful Repose" (1858) and "Beautiful Child of Song" (1860) are other successful songs of this type; they are all strophic, without a chorus, and in triple meter. The texts are almost all in the nature of a serenade.

Italian melody was so strongly imbedded in Foster's musical consciousness that it remained there to the end. One of his last songs, and one of the best, "Beautiful Dreamer" (1864), written perhaps in the last days of his life and published only after his death, has a flowing, gracefully sculptured Italianate melody set against an arpeggiated accompaniment, rising to climaxes on high notes near the ends of phrases.

Foster also knew some of the German songs just becoming popular in America. Firth, Pond & Co. of New York brought out, in 1851, "In the Eye Abides the Heart" by Franz Abt, as translated (from the original "In den Augen liegt das Herz") by Stephen Foster. There is no evidence that Foster knew German; he must have had help with the translation, possibly from his friend and teacher Henry Kleber, then refined and shaped the English text and fitted it to the music himself. *The Social Orchestra* contains an instrumental arrangement of another song by Abt, "When the Swallows Homeward Fly," and of dances by Kleber and Gung'l, who brought a German orchestra to America in the early 1850s. There is also an arrangement, one of the most elaborate in the entire collection, of "La Sérénade" by Schubert.

There are several obvious references to German style in Foster's songs; "Sadly to Mine Heart Appealing" (1858), for example, opens with a melodic and rhythmic pattern reminiscent of the opening of Schubert's "Serenade":

STEPHEN FOSTER, "SADLY TO MINE HEART APPEALING"

Sad-ly to mine heart ap-peal-ing. Sad-ly, sad-ly, well-a-day

Thus German song can be added to the various repertories known to Foster in his formative years as a songwriter.

As he matured as a composer, elements of various earlier song styles come together in the same piece.

There are what might be called his "white minstrel songs," for want of a better name. These begin with "Lily Ray" (1850), which stands squarely between his "English" songs and the minstrel songs. The melody is one of the simple, diatonic tunes so appropriate to the minstrel stage:

STEPHEN FOSTER, "LILY RAY"

While in their sun-ny bow'rs, Sweet birds re-joice,

Ming-ling with bud-ding flow'rs, Love's gen-tle voice,

But there is no chorus and no trace of dialect. "Laura Lee" and "Eulalie" are similar; both were written in 1851.

"Hard Times Come No More" (1855) is even more ambiguous. Melodically it belongs with such minstrel songs of that period as "My Old Kentucky Home," and there is a four-part chorus, a feature reserved for minstrel songs to this point in Foster's career. But there is no dialect, no mention of slavery or the South, and the song is identified on the cover as simply a "melody," with no mention of the minstrel stage. "Lula Is Gone" (1858) is similar, with a text linking it to an entire genre of minstrel songs dealing with the death of young women; it also has a chorus, but there is no hint that it was intended for minstrel performance.

"I Cannot Sing To-night" (1853) mixes Irish and Italian elements. The first phrase is one of the most blatantly Irish tunes Foster ever wrote:

STEPHEN FOSTER, "I CANNOT SING TO-NIGHT"

Later there are languishing appoggiaturas, word repetitions, and touches of chromaticism more reminiscent of the Italian style:

Yet the song makes complete musical sense, sounding quite simply like a song by Stephen Foster.

"Annie, My Own Love," also from 1853, likewise betrays a hybrid ancestry. The nature of the song is epitomized in the eight-measure piano introduction: the first phrase is pentatonic, somewhere between a minstrel song and an Irish melody; the accompaniment is arpeggiated, more in the style of Italian opera; and the last four measures, with their parallel thirds, appoggiaturas, and chromaticism, move much more into the world of Donizetti and Bellini. "Old Memories," a third song from 1853, likewise progresses from first phrases suggestive of a minstrel song to more Italianate ones.

Foster's early songs are patterned after one or another of the bodies of national song popular in America when he began composing. Later he integrated these into a personal style in which his own touch and taste as a melodist amalgamated all these elements—a style that was quickly accepted as uniquely American.

Born into an educated family of some means, Foster could have taken up some trade or profession that would have brought him a comfortable income, had he been so inclined. He was educated at a succession of private schools—Athens Academy, Tioga Point, Towanda Academy, Jefferson College. He was intelligent and did well enough in his studies, though he preferred to spend his time with music. In 1846 he went to Cincinnati to become a bookkeeper for his brother Dunning, a commission merchant. When Dunning went off to the Mexican War in the summer of 1847, Stephen was left to run the business himself. He was thus well launched on a business career by the time he was twenty-one.

He had published several songs with important publishers in the East, but the thought of making a living as a songwriter had probably never crossed his mind. No other American had ever done so. John Hill Hewitt, who had written the most successful song by an American composer, had been forced to support himself as a music publisher, journalist, and teacher. Even Henry Russell, the British composer-singer whose songs had been the best-selling items of sheet music in the history of American publishing up to 1840, had amassed his considerable income mostly from fees and box-office receipts for recitals and concerts, not from royalties on his songs.

But matters took an unexpected turn during the three years Foster was in Cincinnati. His first minstrel songs, particularly "Oh! Susanna," quickly achieved unprecedented popularity, being sung by minstrel troupes all over America and selling phenomenally well as sheet music. In 1849 he signed an agreement with Firth, Pond & Co. of New York bringing him two cents per copy for all new songs; at about the same time he signed a similar agreement with F. D. Benteen in Baltimore. These were unusual contracts for the time; the rights to most songs were bought outright, for a flat fee, with the composer relinquishing any further claim on earnings. In the following two years (1850 and 1851), Foster published fifteen songs with Benteen and fifteen with Firth, Pond & Co. One of the latter was "Old Folks at Home"; in the September 4, 1852, issue of *The Musical World and New York Musical Times*, Firth, Pond & Co. ran an advertisement claiming that this "most beautiful American melody" had already sold "nearly *Forty Thousand Copies.*" Two years later, another notice in *The Musical World* claimed that "Old Folks at Home" had sold more than 130,000 copies, "My Old Kentucky Home" some 90,000, "Massa's in the Cold Ground" 74,000, and a new song, "Old Dog Tray," 48,000 copies in only six months.

These figures may have been somewhat inflated, but the fact remains that Foster left his job in Cincinnati in 1850, went back to Pittsburgh, rented an office and became a full-time songwriter, making his living this way until his death fourteen years later.

It was not always a good or comfortable living. He did not realize as much money as he had hoped, and he had no talent for managing what he did have. The last decade of his life was filled with incidents that show he was only marginally successful in supporting himself and his family. By 1853, he was borrowing money from his brother Morrison, a practice that was to continue for the next decade; in 1856, a letter tells us that he owed his brother William the sum of $52.08, for five months' rent.

He also borrowed money from his chief publisher, Firth, Pond & Co. By 1853, at the peak of the success of his minstrel songs, he was drawing advances on his account. Though he signed a new contract that year, increasing his royalty on future songs to ten percent, he continued to draw more money than had accrued in royalties.

In 1857, he took a drastic step:[25] drawing up a list of all songs published with Firth, Pond & Co. to that date, he calculated that he had received $9,596.96 for them; in another column, he estimated future royalties on these songs, the total coming to $2,786.77. His publisher sent him $1,872.28, two-thirds of this amount, a sum amounting to $1,500.00 more than he was overdrawn at the time ($372.28). Thus Foster sold all future rights to thirty-six of his songs, including the most popular ones he had written, for less than $2,000.00. He did the same with his other publisher, F. D. Benteen; after calculating that his sixteen songs with that publisher had brought him $461.85 in royalties, he accepted $200.00 in 1857 as compensation for all future earnings on these, too. (Foster's figures are given in Appendix 3.)

Thus, in 1857, he wiped out his various debts and began afresh, with several thousand dollars in the bank. But he was overdrawn again by 1858, balancing his ledger this time by relinquishing all future income from his latest song, "I See Her Still in My Dreams." Within a year, he was overdrawn again by almost a thousand dollars, and by early 1860 he owed $1,479.95. Later in that year he signed over all financial rights on the sixteen songs published since the last settlement, in return for cancellation of a new debt of $1,396.64 and an additional $200.00 in cash.

His last years were even more difficult. His exclusive contract with Firth, Pond & Co. had expired; he was free to sell his new songs wherever he could get the most money. He wrote more songs in the last three years of his life than during any other period, but few achieved the popularity of his earlier songs—on which he had relinquished all financial claim. He often sold songs for a flat fee, in order to get quick cash. Some were still brought out by major publishers, but he also published in such places as *Clark's School Visitor* (a periodical for children of school age), the *Golden Harp* (a hymnbook for Sunday schools, published by Horace Waters in New York), and *The Athenaeum Collection* (another collection of Sunday school hymns).

These financial details establish that Foster did indeed support himself for almost fifteen years of his life as a professional songwriter. It has been estimated that he realized more than fifteen thousand dollars from his songwriting for the period 1850–60. As difficult as it is to relate these sums to financial conditions of the day, this amount was sufficient for Foster to survive, if nothing else, without other employment. And it is difficult to cast his publishers in the role of villains. Firth, Pond & Co. gave him a series of contracts paying royalties on each song,

25. Howard, *Stephen Foster*, pp. 266–71.

an unusual agreement for the time; he was allowed to draw advances of quite considerable sums of money; and he was given a sizable chunk of money on several occasions when he himself requested a flat sum in exchange for future royalties.

Truth is sometimes more flattering than fiction. To recognize Stephen Foster as a composer who

> was a professional songwriter, made it his business to be acquainted with the music of his contemporaries, and was a composer of skill and technique;
> had command of several national styles of song early in his career, and integrated aspects of each into a distinctive personal style during the most productive years of his career; and
> was the first American songwriter to support himself with his composition,

in no way diminishes his stature. To the contrary, such a portrait elevates him to his proper place high among the songwriters of the nineteenth century.

ELEVEN

"All Quiet Along the Potomac";

OR.

Songs of the Civil War[1]

THE CIVIL WAR of 1861–65 was the single most dramatic event in the entire history of the United States, with the possible exception of World War II. The fighting, the carnage, the brutal effects on soldier and civilian were unmatched by any other war in American history. In his preface to *Flawed Victory; a New Perspective on the Civil War*, James P. Shenton writes:

No event in American history had more devastating results than the Civil War. For four years the nation was wracked by a seemingly endless blood letting. When the guns finally fell silent in the spring of 1865, more than 630,000 Americans had died. Americans had inflicted upon one another more casualties than had ever been sustained in a previous, or subsequent, foreign war. [In comparison, some 606,000 Americans were killed in all other conflicts from the French and Indian Wars through Korea.] In the course of the struggle, a war of limited objectives had been translated into total war. The enemy was no longer armies but entire civilian populations. . . . When final defeat engulfed the South, its economy was in shambles; vast stretches of its territory were ruined; and its social institutions rooted in

1. Portions of this chapter were first published as liner notes for *Songs of the Civil War*, New World Records NW 202, 1976.

slavery had been smashed. . . . As one contemporary noted, the boundary between the two sections was drawn in blood.[2]

Such Northern states as Illinois and Connecticut sent almost fifteen percent of their population to fight in this war, and the percentage was even higher in most of the South. It was total war indeed, particularly in less populated areas, where such mobilization was severely felt: of 147 men of military age in one township, 117 were away at war; 111 of 250 eligible voters in a Wisconsin town volunteered early in the war.[3] Even today, more than a century later, a visit to towns in Virginia, Vermont, Mississippi, Maine, Georgia, with their statues of Confederate or Union soldiers and their cannon in town squares, their cemeteries with rows of graves still marked with flags, their memorials to men lost in the Civil War far outnumbering those from any other conflict, will suggest what this ferocious struggle meant in human terms.

Perhaps the most remarkable aspect of the war was the depth and intensity of feelings that were aroused—feelings that remained strong, and an important part of American life, for over three-quarters of a century. Emotions were strongest in the South, certainly at the beginning of the war, and it was this that enabled the Confederate states—outnumbered, inferior in arms and other military equipment, soon virtually cut off from supplies from outside—to prolong the struggle for four desperate years, when by all military and economic logic it should have ended in quick victory for the North. Although slavery was a crucial issue in the war, large areas of the South did not depend on slavery, and the majority of Rebel soldiers were from nonslaveholding families; but the entire region had a fierce conviction that states, towns, and individuals—not the federal government—should determine how their lives were to be led. This attitude was expressed with clarity and conviction in a letter that Charles C. Jones, Jr., a Georgian and an officer in the Confederate Army, wrote to his father early in the war:

> Surely we are passing through harsh times, and are beset with perils which humanity in its worst phases has not encountered for centuries. The Age of Gold has yielded to the Age of Iron; and the North furnishes an example of refined barbarity, moral degeneracy, religious impiety, soulless honor, and absolute degradation almost beyond belief. *Omnia vestigia retrorsum* ["all footsteps turn back upon themselves"]. . . . We can only make a proper use of those means which He has placed in our power, and with a firm reliance on the justice of our cause, and with earnest supplication of His aid who saves not by many nor by few, offer every resistance to the inroads of this inhuman enemy, and illustrate every virtue which pertains to a brave, God-

---

2. James P. Shenton, preface to William Barney, *Flawed Victory; A New Perspective on the Civil War* (New York: Praeger, 1975), p. vii.

3. E. D. Fite, *Social and Industrial Conditions During the Civil War.*

fearing people engaged in an awful struggle, against wonderful odds, for personal, civil, and religious freedom.[4]

The writer was not some provincial fanatic, but rather a successful lawyer, historian, and archaeologist, who held degrees from Princeton and the Harvard Law School.

The Civil War has left a heritage of music that reflects those times in the most vivid way. Indeed, this music was so intimately involved with events of the time that it became part of them.

In 1905, the Chapple Publishing Company of Boston announced plans to publish an anthology of "heart songs, dear to the American people." In response to an invitation to nominate songs for the volume, more than twenty thousand people sent copies of their favorite songs, with letters telling how these pieces had been "interwoven with the story of their own lives." In the words of the editor, Joe Mitchell Chapple:

> Songs that have entertained thousands from childhood to the grave and have voiced the pleasure and pain, the love and longing, the despair and delight, the sorrow and resignation, and the consolation of the plain people—who found in these an utterance for emotions which they felt but could not express—came in by the thousands. The yellow sheets of music bear evidence of constant use; in times of war and peace, victory and defeat, good and evil fortune, these sweet strains have blended with the coarser thread of human life and offered to the joyful or saddened soul a suggestion of uplift, sympathy and hope.[5]

Heart Songs, published in 1909, tells us not only which songs were most popular in nineteenth-century America but also how we felt about music then. It reminds us that emotions were expressed openly and, by today's taste, naively, and that music often served the function of intensifying verbal expression. Fully one-quarter of the songs in the volume were sung during the brief period of the Civil War.

These songs were concerned with the entire range of events of this momentous time. Antislavery songs helped arouse and unify the North—"John Brown's Body" (with a tune written, ironically, by William Steffe, a Richmonder) and "Kingdom Coming" by Henry Clay Work are but two examples. The great political rallying songs fanned the enthusiasm, fervor, and fanaticism of both North and South—Julia Ward Howe's "Battle Hymn of the Republic," Dan Emmett's "Dixie," George F. Root's "The Battle Cry of Freedom," Harry Macarthy's "The Bonnie Blue Flag." There were songs about heroes and political leaders—Jesse

4. Robert Manson Myers, *The Children of Pride; A True Story of Georgia and the Civil War* (New Haven, Connecticut: Yale University Press, 1972), p. 968.

5. Joe Mitchell Chapple, ed., *Heart Songs* (Boston: The Chapple Publishing Company, 1909), p. vi.

Hutchinson's "Lincoln and Liberty" and John W. Palmer's "Stonewall Jackson's Way." Almost every battle and campaign inspired songs, from J. Harry Hayward and Thomas D. Sullivan's "The Flag of Fort Sumter" to Henry Clay Work's "Marching Through Georgia." There were songs, many of them humorous, about conscription and the soldiers' life in camps, such as Work's "Grafted into the Army" and "Goober Peas" by a composer identifying himself as "P. Nutt, Esq." Some songs remind us that immigrants from various countries fought in the war—Work's "Corporal Schnapps," or the anonymous "Pat Murphy of the Irish Brigade." Others, like the anonymous "Treasury Rats," deal with political and financial corruption during the war.

They were sung in homes, North and South, but the war carried them elsewhere as well. Patriotic and political songs were sung at rallies, political gatherings, and mass meetings, and in no other war in American history has music played such an important role among the men involved in campaigns and battles. "I don't believe we can have an army without music," wrote General Robert E. Lee in 1864, and even the most casual browsing through Civil War literature leads quickly to mentions of music and what it meant to the men under arms.

Many of the soldiers carried songsters, pocket collections of the lyrics of favorite songs. The most popular of these among Southern troops were *Hopkins' New Orleans 5 Cent Song-Book, The Soldier Boy's Songster,* and *The Stonewall Jackson Song Book,* the latter published in at least eleven editions. Union soldiers carried *Beadle's Dime Songs for the War, The Camp Fire Songster, War Songs for Freedom,* or one of a dozen similar collections. The songsters were often retrospective, with words to songs popular before the war, which the publishers believed would be known to most of the men who bought these books. Thus songsters published early in the war contained texts for "Annie Laurie," "Yankee Doodle," "Auld Lang Syne," "Pop Goes the Weasel," Stephen Foster songs, prewar minstrel favorites, and the ubiquitous "Home, Sweet Home."

Fraternization of soldiers between battles was one curious phenomenon of this bloody war that extended to its music. In 1863 Lieutenant W. J. Kinchelos of the 49th Virginia Regiment wrote to his father of one such episode: "We are on one side of the Rappahannock, the enemy on the other. . . . Our boys will sing a Southern song, the Yankees will reply by singing the same tune to Yankee words." Another instance occurred when a Confederate soldier was "saved" by some of his more religious comrades, agreed to be baptized, and was taken to the bank of the Rapidan River, in northern Virginia, by some fifty troops for this purpose. Yankee soldiers appeared on the opposite bank to witness and to join in the singing of the hymn "There Is a Fountain Filled with Blood." Again, rival armies were camped within earshot of one another the night before the Battle of Murfreesboro. At one point the Northern band played "Yankee Doodle," and the Southern band responded with a patriotic Rebel tune; the two bands alternated this way for some time, then they played "Home, Sweet Home" together. The next morning the armies slaughtered one another by the thousands.

The texts and music of these songs were written by hundreds of Americans in all parts of the country and published in many cities. In the North, large numbers of war songs were brought out by such publishers as Oliver Ditson in Boston; John Church in Cincinnati; Firth, Pond & Co. in New York; H. Kleber and Brother in Pittsburgh; J. F. Gould in Philadelphia; W. F. Sherwin in Albany; Joseph P. Shaw in Rochester; and E. W. Billings in Providence.

The single most important publisher of the war years, though, was founded in Chicago in 1858 by E. T. Root and C. T. Cady. Three days after the beginning of the bombardment of Fort Sumter, the event precipitating the actual fighting, their first war song ("The First Gun is Fired! May God Protect the Right!") was off the press, and during the years of the conflict they published some eighty songs and piano pieces making direct reference to the war.

Root & Cady was fortunate to have the services of two of the most skilled and sensitive songwriters of the period, George Frederick Root (1820–95) and Henry Clay Work (1832–84), who between them wrote all the most popular pieces in the Root & Cady catalog during the war years. The figures given below for sales of each of these songs during the war years pertain to sheet music; these songs were also included in various anthologies, and appeared in arrangements for piano and guitar; their texts were included in various songsters; their total dissemination was even much greater than the figures suggest:[6]

"Kingdom Coming" (1862)	Work	75,000
"Battle Cry of Freedom" (1862)	Root	350,000
"Vacant Chair" (1863)	Root	100,000
"Just Before the Battle, Mother" (1864)	Root	100,000
"Tramp, Tramp, Tramp" (1865)	Root	150,000

When one adds to this list several other songs that sold nearly as well, such as Work's "Grafted into the Army" (1862), "Marching Through Georgia" (1865), and "Wake Nicodemus" (1864), and Root's "Brother, Tell Me of the Battle" (1864), the critical role played by this publishing firm during the war years comes even more sharply into focus.

Root, brother of one of the founders of the publishing house, was a native of Sheffield, Maine, who taught music in Boston (1839–44) and New York (1844–45) before going to Paris for a year of study. He fell first under the influence of Lowell Mason and his circle of "better music" disciples in and around Boston, and his early energy and activity was devoted to the study, teaching, and composition of music based firmly on European models. His transformation is best told in his own words:

6. Dena J. Epstein, *Music Publishing in Chicago before 1871: the Firm of Root & Cady, 1858–1871*, Detroit Studies in Music Bibliography, 14 (Detroit: Information Coordinators, 1969), p. 48.

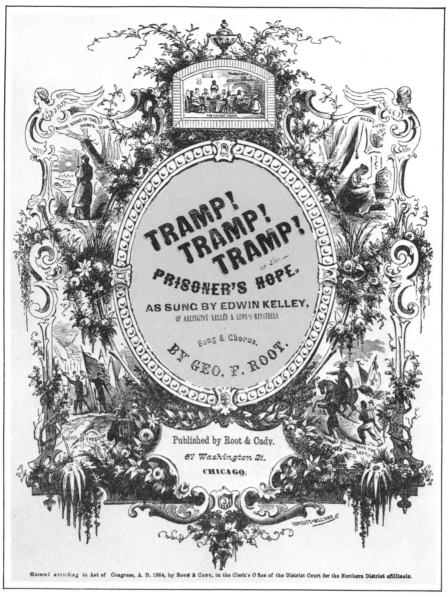

George F. Root's "Tramp, Tramp, Tramp" was one of the most popular songs of the Civil War years. This vivid lithograph was used by the publishing house of Root & Cady for the covers of many war songs.

I should be wasting my time in trying to supply the wants of a few people, who are already abundantly supplied by the best writers of Europe. . . .

I saw that mine must be the "people's song," still, I am ashamed to say, I shared the feeling that was around me in regard to that grade of music. When Stephen C. Foster's wonderful melodies (as I now see them) began to appear, and the famous Christy's Minstrels began to make them known, I "took a hand in" and wrote a few, but put "G, Friederich Wurzel" (the German for Root) to them instead of my own name. "Hazel Dell" (published in 1853 by William Hall & Son in New York) and "Rosalie, the Prairie Flower" (1855, by Russell & Richardson in Boston) were the best known. . . . It is easy to write *correctly* a simple song, but so to use the material of which such a song must be made that it will be received and live in the hearts of the people is quite another matter. . . . It was much easier to write when the resources were greater.[7]

Root, who had joined his brother in Chicago in 1859, gave the following account of the birth of "The Battle Cry of Freedom":

I heard of President Lincoln's second call for troops one afternoon while reclining on a lounge in my brother's house. Immediately a song started in my mind, words and music together:

"Yes, we'll rally round the flag, boys,
we'll rally once again.
Shouting the battle-cry of freedom."

I thought it out that afternoon, and wrote it the next morning at the store. The ink was hardly dry when the Lumbard brothers . . . came in for something to sing at a war meeting that was to be holden immediately in the court-house square just opposite. They went through the new song once, and then hastened to the steps of the court-house, followed by a crowd that had gathered, while the practice was going on. Then Jule's magnificent voice gave out the song, and Frank's trumpet tones led the refrain . . . and at the fourth verse a thousand voices were joining in the chorus. . . . [I am] thankful that if I could not shoulder a musket in defense of my country, I could serve her in this way.[8]

The song's effect on troops was so electric that some commanders ordered their soldiers to sing it while going into battle. In 1889, at a testimonial banquet honoring Root, J. W. Fifer—a former Union soldier—said:

The true and correct history of the war for the maintenance of the Union will place George F. Root's name alongside of our great generals. Only

7. George F. Root, *The Story of a Musical Life* (Cincinnati: John Church, 1891), pp. 83, 96–97.
8. Ibid., pp. 132–33.

The Second Battalion of the Massachusetts Infantry is immortalized in this lithograph by Copeland which was used to illustrate the song "John Brown's Body" in a collection entitled *The World's Best Music*, published in 1904.

those who were at the front, camping, marching, battling for the flag, can fully realize how often we were cheered, revived, and inspired by the songs of him who sent forth the "Battle Cry of Freedom."[9]

9. Quoted in *Songs of the Civil War*.

Henry Clay Work was even more prolific. Born in Middletown, Connecticut, he lived in Illinois as a child when his father moved to Quincy to assist runaway slaves escape to the North by the underground railway. The family returned east after the father was jailed for his activities and released only on the promise that he would leave the state. Henry returned to Illinois in 1855. He took a job in Chicago as a printer and wrote songs in his spare time. A self-taught composer, he had several songs performed and published before the war, including "We're Coming, Sister Mary," sung by Christy's Minstrels. The turning point in his career came in 1861, when he decided to bring one of his new songs, "Kingdom Coming," to the offices of Root & Cady. He was sent to George Root, who, after examining the composition, immediately offered him a job as a songwriter. Work wrote more than thirty war songs and continued to compose successful songs after the war as well.

Oliver Ditson in Boston brought out the definitive version of "The Battle Hymn of the Republic" in 1862 and "Tenting on the Old Camp Ground" in 1864, to rank second to Root & Cady in successful war songs. The story of the former song is complex. The tune is believed to have been written by William Steffe, a native of South Carolina, and was sung first to a camp-meeting text, "Say, Brothers, Will You Meet Us?"[10] After the execution of John Brown in December of 1859, following his capture of a government arsenal at Harper's Ferry for the purpose of obtaining arms for a possible slave uprising, new words were fitted to the tune: "John Brown's body lies a-mouldering in the grave/ his soul is marching on. . . ." Published in this version by several presses, with the text attributed to at least three different authors, it was popularized by a quartet made up of members of the Second Battalion of the Massachusetts Infantry and used as a marching song by the entire regiment as they marched down Broadway on July 24, 1861, on their way to the front in northern Virginia. Julia Ward Howe heard it while visiting friends in Washington, and in late 1861 she wrote new words to fit the tune, which were printed in the *New-York Daily Tribune* on January 14, 1862, and in the *Atlantic Monthly* the following month. Ditson published it with Mrs. Howe's five verses fitted to the original tune, with the "Glory, glory Hallelujah" refrain set for three-part chorus, and in a matter of days it was being sung in this form across the North, by troops, at patriotic rallies, and in the parlors of those left behind.

"Tenting on the Old Camp Ground" was by Walter Kittredge, born on October 8, 1832, in Reed's Ferry, New Hampshire, who worked later at a mill in Milford. Joining a group traveling to Concord to enlist *en masse*, Kittredge—who gave his occupation as "concert ballad singer"—was rejected by recruiters for "feebleness of constitution." Determined to contribute to the war in some way, he visited various army camps to sing patriotic and sentimental songs for the troops. He wrote "Tenting . . ." in 1862:

> His heart was fired with patriotism, but full of grief at leaving his home, and full of dread of war. In the middle of the night he awoke with the burden

10. Copyrighted in New York by G. S. Scofield in 1858.

The sheet music cover for the 1864 edition of "Tenting on the Old Camp Ground," published by Oliver Ditson.

still on his mind. He thought of the many dear boys already gone over to the unseen shore, killed in battle or dead from disease in the camps, of the unknown graves, of the sorrowful homes; of the weary waiting for the end of the cruel strife, and the sorrow in the camps, of the brave boys waiting for the coming battle, which might be their last. Suddenly the thoughts began to take form in his mind. He arose and began to write . . .[11]

He showed the song to John Hutchinson, who was at the time giving a series of torchlight rallies near his home at High Rock, Massachusetts, and the song immediately caught on with the thousands of persons who came there nightly. Ditson brought it out, and it soon became one of the most successful sheet music

11. John Wallace Hutchinson, *Story of the Hutchinsons (Tribe of Jesse)*, 2 vols. (Boston: Lee and Shepard, 1896), 1:417.

Torchlight rally at High Rock, Massachusetts, in 1863.

items of the day, selling ten thousand copies in the first two months and a hundred thousand by the time the war had ended. Its popularity continued unabated through the nineteenth century, largely because of its association with reunions and encampments of the Grand Army of the Republic, and in 1898 royalties were greater than in any previous year.

A third successful Ditson publication was Luther O. Emerson's setting of the text "We Are Coming, Father Abra'am." Like so many songs of the period, it was inspired by events of the times. The summer of 1862 was a dark time for the Union. After failing to capture Richmond with a frontal advance in the first year of the war, the Union army was taken by water to the mouth of the James River and advanced toward the Confederate capital from the east. But the Peninsular Campaign was no more successful than the attack from the north had been, and after a prolonged and discouraging battle the Northern forces once more withdrew to Washington. Casualties had been great, morale among troops and civilians was bad, and Lincoln, realizing that more force would be needed to continue the war and swing the balance in favor of the North, issued a call for 300,000 more troops.

An interested reader of Lincoln's call for volunteers was James Sloane Gibbons, a resident of New York. Born in Wilmington, Delaware, the son of a physician who was a Quaker and abolitionist, Gibbons himself had worked for the cause of abolition, becoming friendly with William Lloyd Garrison and other radical leaders. Realizing the need for support of Lincoln's call, he dashed off a patriotic poem and sent it to the New York *Evening Post*, which published it, anonymously, on July 16, 1862. The Boston *Daily Journal* printed it two days later, and the music publisher Oliver Ditson, recognizing its potential as a popular rallying song, clipped it out and sent it to Luther O. Emerson, a composer of popular gospel hymns, with a terse note. "Set these words instanter."

Emerson did the job quickly. By this time the poem—assumed to be by William Cullen Bryant, editor of the *Evening Post*—had been read at a war rally on Boston Commons and reprinted in other parts of the North.

The song sold well from the beginning, and soon other settings of the poem appeared, including those by the Hutchinsons, Stephen Foster, and Patrick Gilmore. By the end of 1862, some twenty different editions of different musical settings were available, and it has been estimated that two million copies of these were sold by the end of the war.

There is an ironic postscript to the story of this song. Far more people sang it than responded to its message: only ninety-one thousand men volunteered. As a result, the North was forced to resort to its first forced draft, in March 1863. This widely unpopular action led to demonstrations and riots in many cities. In New York a mob, knowing of Gibbons's activities, ransacked his house, destroying papers, books, and documents, and daubing the interior with tar to show what it thought of his championing of blacks. His wife and daughter were off nursing the wounded in army hospitals, and Gibbons himself escaped possible physical harm by mingling with the mob and thus evading identification.

Not all Civil War songs were patriotic and militaristic. Many of them, particularly those written in the latter years of the war, dealt with the human misery that became greater with each month of the struggle. Easily the most popular such song was "Weeping, Sad and Lonely; or, When This Cruel War Is Over," Henry Tucker's setting of a poem by Charles Carroll Sawyer.

The enormous success of this "tearjerker" puzzled critics, one of whom admitted his inability to come to terms with it:

> There is nothing in this sentimental song that enables one to read the riddle of its remarkable popularity during the Civil War. It has no poetic merit; its rhythm is commonplace, and the tune to which it was sung was of the flimsiest musical structure, without even a trick of melody to commend it. The thing was heard in every camp every day many times every day. Men chanted it on the march, and women sang it to piano accompaniment in all houses. A song which so strongly appealed to two great armies and to an entire people is worthy of a place in all collections of war poetry, even though criticism is baffled in an attempt to discover the reason of its popularity.[12]

Popular it certainly was. Sales approached a million copies after its publication in 1863 by Sawyer & Thompson in Brooklyn. Its popularity was as great in the South, where it appeared in four different editions, as in the North. It was said that certain generals forbade their troops to sing it, because it was so destructive of morale. The editor of *Singing Soldiers* wrote, "If any single song may be said to have expressed the emotions of millions in the 1860s, it was *Weeping, Sad and Lonely*."

Charles Carroll Sawyer (a native of Connecticut), who wrote the words, was more concerned with emotions generated by the war than with any political or military aspects of it. "He touched the hearts of all, regardless of loyalty," commented a contemporary; the cover of this song bears the dedication "Inscribed to Sorrowing Hearts at Home." The mere titles of some of Sawyer's other successful songs give the flavor of his creations: "Who Will Care for Mother Now?," "Mother Would Comfort Me," "I Dreamed My Boy was Home Again." As though to alleviate the black mood created by his greatest hit, Sawyer wrote his own "reply song," "Coming Home; or, The Cruel War Is Over."

Henry Tucker's music would seem singularly inappropriate for such a gloomy text: it is in major throughout, remarkably simple and straightforward in harmony and melodic structure. But somehow it fits the words perfectly, and once text and music have been heard together, the music heard alone creates the same sentiments as when the words are sung to it. Critics will probably always be baffled in attempts to analyze the success of a song like this, which uses precisely the same musical materials as countless songs that have failed to reach the hearts of listeners.

The South had two great patriotic rallying songs to counter the North's

12. Quoted in *Songs of the Civil War*.

"Battle Cry of Freedom" and "Battle Hymn of the Republic." The most enduring, of course, was "Dixie."

"I Wish I Was in Dixie's Land" was "Written and Composed expressly for
Bryant's Minstrels by Dan. D. Emmett," we are told on the cover of the first edition. [13] The composer's autograph copy, reproduced in facsimile in *The Confederate Veteran* of September, 1895, bears the title "Dixie's Land," identifies the

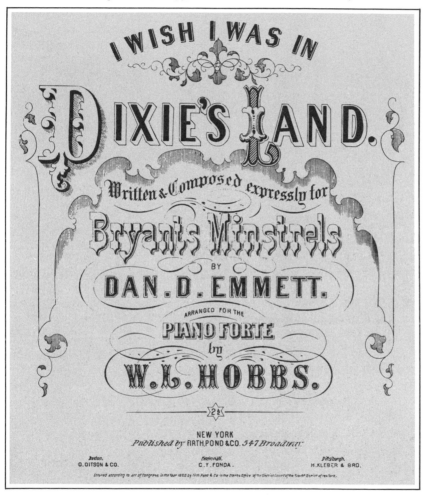

Sheet music cover for the first edition of "I Wish I Was in Dixie's Land" (1860).

piece as a "Walk 'Round," and is dated 1859. A letter from Emmett identifies the
autograph as "The original copy of 'Dixie,' made on that rainy Sunday in 1859."
Asked to write a new, lively piece early in 1859, he sat down one day in his room
and wrote a simple, strophic song, with an instrumental interlude between

13. Published in 1860 by Firth, Pond & Co. in New York.

stanzas to allow the company to do their version of a slave dance. A playbill dated Monday, April 4, 1859, from a performance of Bryant's Minstrels in Mechanics Hall in New York lists "Mr. Dan Emmett's new Plantation Song and Dance *Dixie's Land*" as part of the program.

The song reached the South in 1860, when it was sung by Mrs. John Wood in a production of John Brougham's *Pocahontas* in New Orleans, and was published in that city by P. P. Werlein with no mention of Emmett as the composer. Henry Hotze, a Confederate agent in London for most of the war, wrote of its reception in the South:

> It is marvelous with what wild-fire rapidity this tune of "Dixie" has spread over the whole South. Considered as an intolerable nuisance when first the streets reechoed with it from the repertoire of wandering minstrels, it now bids fair to become the musical symbol of a new nationality, and we shall be fortunate if it does not impose its very name on our country.[14]

"Dixie" was played for the inauguration of Jefferson Davis as President of the Confederate States of America in early 1861, and from that time no political rally, band concert, parade of Southern troops, or singing session around campfires was complete without at least one rendition.

Emmett's claim to the authorship of the song did not go unchallenged. The Louisville publisher D. P. Faulds said that two of his clerks, Charles Ward and William Shakespeare Hays, wrote the words in 1857 or 1858, fitting them to a tune widely known among Southern blacks, and it was this version that first reached New Orleans and then the entire South. Other reports identify the song as having been sung by blacks, particularly stevedores on the Mississippi River, and the word *Dixie* does seem to have been used to refer to the South before this song was published. Emmett probably appropriated tunes from oral tradition (such as "Old Dan Tucker") for some of his earlier songs, and it is possible that he did the same for "Dixie." But no published version has been found before Firth & Pond's 1860 edition.

Whatever its origin, there is no denying the critical role this "wild refrain, that brings the faint heart back to life again," as John Hill Hewitt called it, played in rallying, unifying, and sustaining the South during and after the war.

"The Bonnie Blue Flag," the semiofficial national anthem of the Confederacy, was "written" by Harry B. Macarthy in early 1861, in Jackson, Mississippi. Macarthy, born in England in 1834, came to the States in 1849 to pursue a career on the stage, soon billed himself as "the Arkansas Comedian," and found himself in the South when war broke out. As was the case with many British, his sympathies were with the South (or, perhaps more accurately, against the North). His song, detailing the birth and early struggle of the Confederacy, was fitted to a traditional Irish tune ("The Irish Jaunting Car") and was received with

---

14. Richard B. Harwell, *Confederate Music* (Chapel Hill, North Carolina: The University of North Carolina Press, 1950), p. 43.

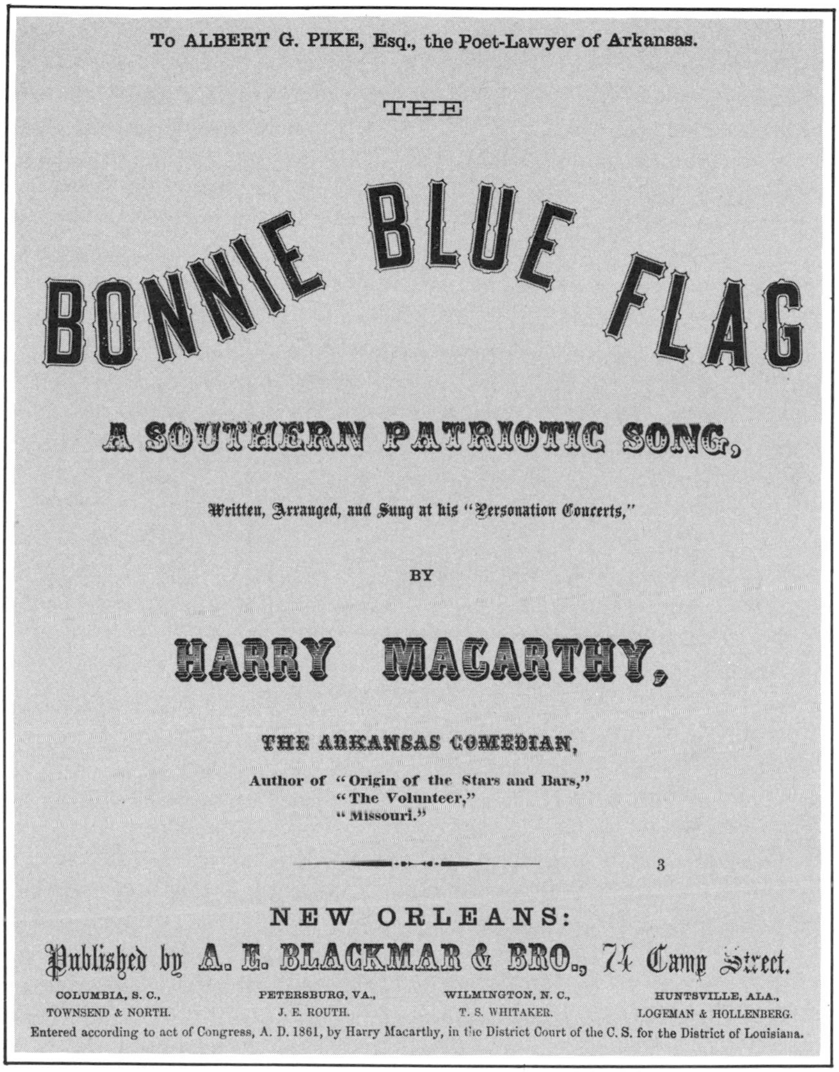

To ALBERT G. PIKE, Esq., the Poet-Lawyer of Arkansas.

THE

BONNIE BLUE FLAG

A SOUTHERN PATRIOTIC SONG,

Written, Arranged, and Sung at his "Personation Concerts,"

BY

HARRY MACARTHY,

THE ARKANSAS COMEDIAN,

Author of "Origin of the Stars and Bars,"
"The Volunteer,"
"Missouri."

3

NEW ORLEANS:

Published by A. E. BLACKMAR & BRO., 74 Camp Street.

| COLUMBIA, S. C., | PETERSBURG, VA., | WILMINGTON, N. C., | HUNTSVILLE, ALA., |
| TOWNSEND & NORTH. | J. E. ROUTH. | T. S. WHITAKER. | LOGEMAN & HOLLENBERG. |

Entered according to act of Congress, A. D. 1861, by Harry Macarthy, in the District Court of the C. S. for the District of Louisiana.

Harry Macarthy's "Bonnie Blue Flag" was published in 1861 under an act of congress of the Confederate States in the District of Louisiana.

great enthusiasm, particularly when he sang it on a program at the New Orleans Academy of Music in September of 1861. It was quickly printed in a number of editions, and soon was familiar in every corner of the Confederacy.

Macarthy sang all over the South in the first years of the war; his programs usually included several of his other songs, such as "Missouri! or, A Voice from the South" and "The Volunteer; or, It Is My Country's Call." When the tide of the war turned against the South, he went to Philadelphia (in 1864), never to return to the region he had furnished with one of its most cherished songs. He died in Oakland, California, in 1888.

Thus the two great patriotic songs of the Confederacy were fashioned from a minstrel walk-around and a traditional Irish tune.

The most talented songwriter to cast his lot with the Confederacy was John Hill Hewitt, discussed earlier as the most successful American songwriter before Stephen Foster. He had spent many years in the South, had lived in Baltimore for the decades before the outbreak of the war, and had repeatedly taken an antiabolitionist stand. Thus, it was quite natural for him to offer his services to the South in 1861.

After a year in Richmond, he went to Augusta, where he wrote and produced pro-Southern stage works. The melodrama *The Scouts; or, The Plains of Manassas* (1861) celebrated the first great Confederate victory of the war; *The Battle of Leesburg* (1862) was another melodrama; *The Exempt; or, Beware of the Conscript Officer* (1863) was a comedy with interpolated music; one of Hewitt's most ambitious works for the musical stage was the "musical burletta" *King Linkum the First* (1863), a vicious satire of Lincoln, his cabinet, and his generals.

But it was as a songwriter that he made his most important mark on the war years. He first fitted new, patriotic words to his most successful song, "The Minstrel's Return from the War":

A nation has sprung into life
   Beneath the bright Cross of the South;
And now a loud call to the strife
   Rings out from the shrill bugle's mouth.

New songs followed: "Dixie, the Land of King Cotton," "The Soldier's Farewell," "The Unknown Dead," "The Young Volunteer," and many others.[15] Eight were published together as *The Musical Olio; or, Favorite Gems of That Popular Southern Composer, John H. Hewitt.*

Particularly popular was "Somebody's Darling," written in 1864 to a text by Marie Revenel De La Coste and quoted with striking effect by Margaret Mitchell in *Gone with the Wind*. It is a classic example of a type of song that became more and more common as the war dragged on, with mounting casualties and no apparent end in sight to the slaughter and sorrow:

Into the ward of the clean, white-wash'd halls
   Where the dead slept and the dying lay;
Wounded by bayonets, sabres and balls,
   Somebody's darling was borne one day.

Somebody's darling, so young and so brave,
   Wearing still on his sweet, yet pale face,
Soon to be hid in the dust of the grave,
   The lingering light of his boyhood's grace.

15. All were published by John C. Schreiner & Son of Macon and Savannah.

Somebody's darling,
Somebody's pride,
Who'll tell his mother
    where her boy died.

Hewitt's greatest triumph, though, one with which he finally matched the artistic and popular success of "The Minstrel's Return'd from the War" of some forty years earlier, was "All Quiet Along the Potomac Tonight," arguably the best song to come out of the war.

On November 30, 1861, an anonymous poem, "The Picket Guard," was published in *Harper's Weekly*; it told the story of a picket who was shot, but since "not an officer [was] lost, only one of the men," the official report read as usual: "All quiet along the Potomac tonight."

Major Lamar Fontaine, a Confederate cavalry leader, claimed that he wrote the poem after he had visited a friend on picket duty; the soldier had stirred the fire to warm them, revealing his position to a Union soldier on the opposite bank who had shot him, and as Fontaine attempted to help his dying friend, his eyes fell on a newspaper with the headline "All Quiet Along the Potomac." This melodramatic story was apparently fictitious, since it now seems certain that the poem was by Mrs. Ethel Lynn Eliot Beers of Goshen, New York, whose only contact with picket lines and the Potomac was through newspaper accounts.[16]

In the North, musical settings of the poem, still titled "The Picket Guard," were made by H. Coyle, W. H. Goodwin, J. Dayton, and David A. Warden. By far the most successful, popular in both South and North, was that by Hewitt. The music, like that of so many effective songs, is deceptively simple. The main melodic phrase, outlining a major triad, hints at a bugle call; harmonic progressions are confined to the fundamental chords of B-flat major; the only obviously expressive melodic device is the appoggiatura on the penultimate note of most of the phrases (in the first stanza on the words "picket," "thicket," "battle," and "rattle"). One is tempted to suggest that the song works so well precisely because the musical means are so limited, allowing the poem to be heard with little interference from the music. That this is not the case can be demonstrated by listening to the other settings of the poem, which use equally limited means but do not make the same impression. Hewitt was a skillful and experienced songwriter who understood, as did Schubert and Stephen Foster, that the best songs have music that allows the verse to be understood with no competition from the music, but the music must intensify the words through its own distinctive character.

There were no large publishing houses in the South before the war comparable to Root & Cady, Oliver Ditson, or Firth, Pond & Company in the North. Sheet music had been published in Charleston and New Orleans, but on a small scale. The war was actually a boon to music publishing in the South. Denied

---

16. James Wood Davidson, the Southern author of *The Living Writers of the South* (New York, 1869), said that even though he would like to claim it for the South, he was convinced that Mrs. Beers had indeed written this poem, which would be appreciated "as long as wars and the memories of wars continue—as long as bloody deaths in distant lands break loving hearts at home."

The evocative and melodramatic illustration for "All Quiet Along the Potomac," from the collection *The World's Best Music* (1904).

access to sheet music from the North for the duration of hostilities, the South spawned a host of publishing houses which sprang up in New Orleans, Macon, Nashville, and Richmond. At least ten other Southern cities also supported music publishers in the later years of the war. It has been estimated that some 700 different items of sheet music were published by the various Confederate presses during the four years of the conflict.[17] But surrender in 1865 and the en-

17. Harwell, pp. 22–23.

suing economic disaster put almost all these firms out of business, and it was not until well into the twentieth century that music publishing in the South was revived on a large scale.

Exhaustive bibliographical work on the output of Southern publishers enables us to reconstruct with some precision the tastes in popular song during the war years.[18] Since the Confederacy did not recognize copyright protection in the North, publishers in the South were free to bring out whatever songs they chose. The most popular songs were those already mentioned, as well as "God Save the South," a competitor for designation as the national anthem of the Confederacy,[19] and "Maryland! My Maryland!" with a text by James Ryder Randall fitted to the tune of the German "Tannenbaum, O Tannenbaum." Otherwise, musical tastes in the South reflected those of the entire country.[20]

Perhaps the most popular nonwar song in the South was "Lorena," written in 1857 by the Reverend H. D. L. Webster and set to music by his brother, Joseph Philbrick Webster. Published first in Chicago by Higgins Brothers, the song unaccountably caught on in the South early in the war and was brought out in at least eight different editions by publishers in various cities. It is found in almost every songster and prompted such comments as "this doleful old ditty started at the start and never stopped until the last musket was stacked and the last camp fire cold."[21] The Reverend Webster supposedly wrote the poem after an unhappy and unsuccessful romance, the appeal to troops and civilians, obviously, was in the sentiment of parted lovers:

A hundred months have passed, Lorena,
　　Since last I held that hand in mine,
And felt the pulse beat fast, Lorena,
　　Though mine beat faster far than thine.

Scarcely less popular was "Aura Lee; or, The Maid with the Golden Hair," written by W. W. Fosdick and George R. Poulton, and first published in Cincinnati in 1861. It is, like "Lorena," a sentimental love song:

18. Marjorie Lyle, *Confederate Imprints; A Check List Based Principally on the Collection of the Boston Athenaeum*, 2 vols. (Boston: The Boston Athenaeum, 1955), 2:561–669; and Richard Harwell, *More Confederate Imprints* (Richmond, Virginia: The Virginia State Library, 1957), pp. 225–32.

19. With words by George H. Miles of Baltimore and music by Charles Wolfgang Amadeus Ellerbrock.

20. Southern presses brought out songs by Stephen Foster ("Come Where My Love Lies Dreaming," "I See Her Still in My Dreams"), songs fashioned from Italian opera ("Hear Me, Norma," "Make Me No Gaudy Chaplet"), favorites from *The Bohemian Girl* ("I Dreamt That I Dwelt," "Then You'll Remember Me"), Irish and Scottish songs ("The Girl I Left Behind Me," " 'Tis the Last Rose of Summer," "Mary of Argyle," "Annie Laurie"), and German songs (Abt's "When the Swallows Homeward Fly"). A particular favorite was "Her Bright Smile Haunts Me Still," by the British composer W. T. Wrighton. Some war songs written and published in the North came out in Southern editions, among them Root's "The Vacant Chair," "When This Cruel War Is Over" by Tucker and Sawyer, and Sawyer's "Who Will Care for Mother Now?"

21. Brander Matthews, *Pen and Ink* (New York: Longmans Green, 1894), p. 156.

> Yet if thy blue eyes I see,
>   Gloom will soon depart;
> For to me, sweet Aura Lee
>   Is sunshine through the heart.

Though only a single Confederate edition has been recovered,[22] it was apparently one of the best selling of all Confederate imprints, and the song has lingered in popular memory for over a century: in its original form; in an adaptation as "Army Blue," a traditional West Point song; and more recently as "Love Me Tender," with new words, popularized by Elvis Presley in 1956.

The years of the Civil War brought no new musical styles to American song. The passions and emotions of the era were expressed in forms and idioms developed in the decades leading up to the conflict.

Most songs are cast in the verse-chorus form discussed in the three previous chapters: the story or incident is narrated in several verses written for solo voice with piano accompaniment, and a three- or four-voice chorus concludes each stanza, often with an echo of the chief melodic material of the verse.[23] The exceptions, such as "All Quiet Along the Potomac" and "Maryland! My Maryland!" are usually settings of texts written for publication as poems, later made into songs.

One remarkable detail of many songs from this period is the persistent use of melodies from the Anglo-Celtic oral tradition, fitted with new, topical texts. This is hardly a new development in popular song: Thomas Moore's *Irish Melodies*, as well as other Irish and Scottish songs published in the late eighteenth or early nineteenth centuries, were arrangements and harmonizations of traditional tunes, and most of the earliest minstrel songs were based on tunes or fragments of tunes drawn from oral tradition. But Stephen Foster and his contemporaries wrote original songs drawing on other traditions, and it had been several decades since popular song had been close to oral-tradition tunes.

For instance, "The Bonnie Blue Flag," the semiofficial national anthem of the Confederacy, was fashioned from the Irish tune "The Irish Jaunting Car." The same tune was used by Septimus Winner for a semicomic song about a young conscript in the Union Army, "He's Gone to the Arms of Abraham":

SEPTIMUS WINNER, "HE'S GONE TO THE ARMS OF ABRAHAM"

Animated

My   true love is   a   sol-dier In the   ar-my now to-day,   It

22. That by Geo. Dunn & Company of Richmond.

23. This feature is obscured in one of the most comprehensive modern collections of Civil War songs: Paul Glass, ed., *The Spirit of the Sixties. A History of the Civil War in Song* (St. Louis: Educational Publishers, 1964). Here the chorus for all songs has been reduced to a single melodic line, giving each song the appearance of a solo song.

was the cru - el war that made him Have to go a - way; He's

gone, He's gone, As meek as an - y lamb, They took him, yes they

took him, to the arms of A - bra - ham.

Another tune fitted with words in both North and South was "The Wearing of the Green," which was used by Patrick S. Gilmore for another version of James Sloane Gibbons's poem "We Are Coming Father Abra'am" and also became "Wearing of the Grey!," published by A. E. Blackmar in New Orleans just after the end of the war:

PATRICK S. GILMORE, "WE ARE COMING FATHER ABRA'AM"

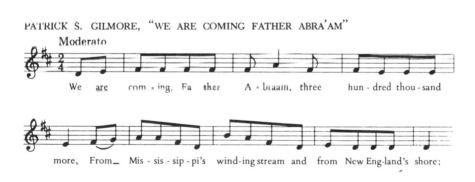

We are com - ing, Fa ther A - braam, three hun - dred thou - sand

more, From— Mis - sis - sip - pi's wind-ing stream and from New Eng-land's shore;

"WEARING OF THE GREY"

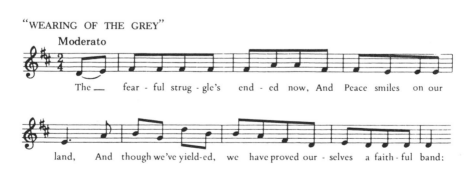

The — fear - ful strug - gle's end - ed now, And Peace smiles on our

land, And though we've yield - ed, we have proved our - selves a faith - ful band;

The tune "The Girl I Left Behind Me" had been known in oral tradition in America since the time of the Revolution and had turned up in Moore's *Irish Melodies* as "As Slow Our Ship Her Foamy Track"; during the Civil War it was published in both North and South with the traditional words beginning "The dames of France are fond and free," and the tune was fitted with at least one set of new words, "I Goes to Fight mit Seigel," a dialect song about German soldiers fighting with the Union Army:

> I've come shust now to tells you how,
> I goes mit regimentals,
> To schlauch dem voes of Liberty,
> Like dem old Continentals.

Though such oral-tradition tunes were sometimes fitted with new words and printed as sheet music in the North, the practice was much more widespread in the South, probably because a higher percentage of the population was descended from English-Irish-Scottish immigrants, and had maintained closer ties with the folk culture brought by these people to America.[24]

However, the many instances of direct borrowings do not convey the impact of Anglo-Celtic oral-tradition melody on Civil War song. One need look no further than "When Johnny Comes Marching Home." Patrick Gilmore claimed authorship in the first edition,[25] and no scholar has yet found a specific model for the melody, though it has all the stylistic earmarks of a traditional tune. The same is true of Bernard Covert's "Can I Go, Dearest Mother?," published by Brainard in Cleveland in 1862:

BERNARD COVERT, "CAN I GO, DEAREST MOTHER?"

I am writ-ing to you Moth-er, know-ing well what you will say. When you

read with tear - ful fond-ness what I write to you to-day.

Other songs were composed in deliberate imitation of Anglo-Celtic idiom. Henry Clay Work's comic "Grafted into the Army" is obviously intended to sound like an Irish dance:

24. In addition to the songs mentioned above, the Southern presses turned out "Where Are You Going, Abe Lincoln" (based on one of the tunes associated with the Child ballad "Lord Lovell"), "The Southern Soldier Boy" (a new text fitted to the tune "Boy with the Auburn Hair"), "Riding a Raid" (a poem praising the Confederate general J. E. B. Stuart, fitted to "The Bonnie Dundee"), and the bitter postwar "O I'm a Good Old Rebel," set to the tune "Joe Bowers."
25. Published in Boston by Henry Tolman in 1863.

HENRY CLAY WORK, "GRAFTED INTO THE ARMY"

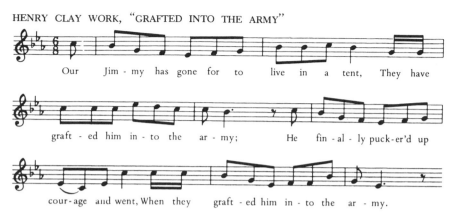

Our Jim - my has gone for to live in a tent, They have graft - ed him in - to the ar - my; He fin - al - ly puck-er'd up cour-age and went, When they graft - ed him in - to the ar - my.

There are also borrowings from minstrel songs. "Ellsworth Avengers" draws its tune from H. S. Thompson's "Annie Lisle," and there were parodies of R. P. Buckley's "Wait for the Wagon" both South and North. Frank Wilder's humorous "The Invalid Corps" has a tune and text that would have been perfectly at home on the minstrel stage:

FRANK WILDER, "THE INVALID CORPS"

Chorus

So, now I'm with the in - va - lids, And can - not go and fight, sir! The doc - tor told me so, you know, Of course it must be right, sir!

Such extensive reliance on music drawn from or related to traditional Anglo-Celtic melody gives much Civil War music a flavor quite different from that of the surrounding decades. All classes of American society were drawn into the conflict; the armies of both sides were heavily dependent on men descended from lower-class, nonliterate immigrants from the British Isles. It was entirely appropriate that so many songs of this period should have something to do with the music most familiar to them and their families.

As for the rest of the songs of the period, the predominant style was the amalgamation of English, Irish, and Italian song epitomized in so many of the songs of Stephen Foster. A single example will suffice: Will S. Hays's "The Drummer Boy of Shiloh" is written in an eclectic style, with echoes of Irish melody and Italian opera giving the song a flavor that by now was characteristically American—and appropriately poignant for the sad tale of the wounded boy who "prayed before he died":

WILL S. HAYS, "THE DRUMMER BOY"

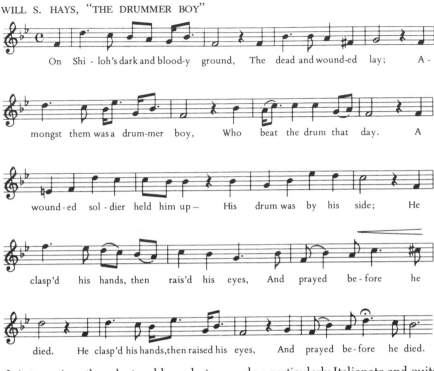

On Shi - loh's dark and blood-y ground, The dead and wound-ed lay; A-
mongst them was a drum-mer boy, Who beat the drum that day. A
wound-ed sol-dier held him up— His drum was by his side; He
clasp'd his hands, then rais'd his eyes, And prayed be-fore he
died. He clasp'd his hands, then raised his eyes, And prayed be-fore he died.

It is tempting, though, to add as a last example a particularly Italianate and quite typical phrase from one of the very most popular songs of the war, as a final reminder of how important Italian flavor continued to be:

HENRY TUCKER, "WEEPING, SAD AND LONELY"

When you vow'd to me and coun - try, Ev - er to be true.

The Civil War was a people's war, drawing into its political and military events a vast majority of the people of the country. Its music likewise was a people's music, written and sung by probably the widest range of Americans ever to be involved with popular song.

TWELVE

"The Old Home Ain't What It Used to Be";

OR.

American Song in the Postwar Years

AMERICA HAD been severely wounded by the Civil War, the aftermath of which dominated the two decades following the collapse and surrender of the Confederacy in the early spring of 1865.

There was scarcely a home untouched by tragedy. It was a rare American who had not had a relative or a friend killed or maimed. The energy and vitality of the country had been wasted on warfare, and there was little left for anything else. But bitterness, tragedy, and recrimination continued. There was the trauma of the assassination of Abraham Lincoln, following hard on the heels of the peace so long hoped for by most Americans. Hatred between North and South was so deeply ingrained that it colored lives for decades to come. Political corruption throughout the country discouraged many who had sturggled so hard to preserve a way of life they believed in.

Culturally—with a few important exceptions—it was a quiet period in America. Such men as Walt Whitman, who had matured in the 1850s and '60s, continued to be productive, but few important new creative artists emerged until the last two decades of the century. Immigration continued, with Germans and Scandinavians particularly numerous, but no new national group brought with it a sturdy and vivid enough culture to affect the course of the arts in America.

Songs written just before and during the Civil War mirrored events and emotions of the time with such precision and passion that if all other records of the war had been lost, it would be possible to reconstruct from these songs an accurate and vivid picture of that period—the military and political events, the heroes and villains, the civilian folk heroes, the patriotic fervor and pride of both sides, the tragedies and heartbreaks of civilians and soldiers alike.

But even though songs continued to be written in profusion after the war, no such picture of the postwar years can be formed from them. They offer no insight into political scandals, the difficult emotional adjustments of widowed women, orphaned children, and crippled ex-soldiers, the tragic plight of the millions of black freedmen in the South, the extraordinary bitterness of so many whites in that region.

The South was effectively out of the mainstream of American life for the rest of that century and well into the twentieth. Almost all of America's songs in the last third of the nineteenth century were written by men and women living in the North, East, and West, who quite understandably had little interest in the problems and struggles of either blacks or whites in the South, and who chose not to write songs dealing with postwar problems in the rest of the country, either. It may have been largely a matter of emotional overload; passions had been at such a fever pitch for so long that there seemed to be little force left. Poets and songwriters were quite content to turn out songs of romantic love and nostalgia, many of them reminiscent of the sentiments so popular in American songs of the 1820s and '30s.

Nostalgia had run its course elsewhere in the Western world by 1865. There were new and more urgent concepts to be wrestled with by artists, philosophers, and historians: a rising tide of nationalism; a new sense of the power man possessed to subdue natural forces and elements to serve his own needs in a new and exciting and scientific and mechanical age; a new openness in dealing with man's sexual needs. American scientists, and some writers, were soon in the forefront of these currents; American songwriters ignored them.

In deliberately turning away from contemporary issues, our songwriters made of popular song something it had never been before—escapism.

Musically, American popular song of the postwar years took on a consistency and character so clear as to allow for a quite precise description. Almost all songs of this time

> begin with a piano (instrumental) introduction of 4 or 8 measures, usually stating the chief melodic material of the song;
> have a verse for a solo voice, of 16 measures subdivided into 4 phrases of 4 measures each, in such melodic patterns as AABC, ABAC, AABA, or ABCB. There is text for 2 to 4 verses, each sung to the same music, unfolding a brief drama or sketching a vignette usually of nostalgic, cautionary, pathetic, or tragic content;
> continue with a refrain, most often arranged for four voices, derived

musically from some part of the verse—sometimes the first phrase or two, but just as often the last phrases. Quite commonly, the last 4 measures of the verse and the chorus are identical melodically, giving the effect of a musical end-rhyme. The text of the chorus is almost always derived from that of the first verse. It functions as a choral commentary on the dramatic situation developed in the successive verses;

conclude with a piano postlude of 4 or 8 measures, derived melodically from the first phrase of the verse, sometimes identical with the introduction.

One need look no further than at any of the several songs that have best survived in popular memory for examples of this structure. "Silver Threads Among the Gold," a setting by H. P. Danks of a poem by Eben Rexford, will serve. The piano has a 4-measure introduction of two phrases, AB; the verse has the melodic pattern of AABA; the chorus is half the length of the verse and melodically repeats the last two phrases of the verse, BA; the piano postlude is identical to the introduction, AB, except for a few notes necessary to define the full cadence at the end. The four verses develop the conceit that the love of the speaker will never fade with age, concluding with "Since I kissed you, mine alone, / You have never older grown." The chorus concludes each verse with:

Darling, I am growing old,
Silver threads among the gold,
Shine upon my brow today;
Life is fading fast away.

The verse-chorus pattern, one of the most distinctive features of these songs, had developed first in songs of the singing families of the 1840s and '50s and in minstrel songs of the same period. By this time it was an almost univeral pattern and was one of the most uniquely American features of this body of song. It was equally appropriate for performance at home, where the better singers could take the solo verses and all others could join in the chorus, and on the minstrel stage, where the entire troupe could echo the verses sung by one of the stars.

Many of the best songs of the period were written by composers who had made their reputations before and during the Civil War. Henry Clay Work, for instance, had published his first song as early as 1853, but had remained virtually unknown until the success of war favorites such as "Grafted into the Army," "Wake Nicodemus," and "Marching Through Georgia." Though he lived until 1884, his productivity dropped off sharply after 1866, and he only rallied his creative forces enough to turn out a song or two on rare occasions. Circumstances of his life stifled his creativity: his wife suffered from severe mental problems, and Work became involved in a futile, one-sided romantic attachment that obsessed him almost until his death. Nevertheless, two of his postwar songs are among his best, and both achieved considerable popularity.

"Come Home, Father" was actually written and published during the war, in 1864, but its popularity dates from later, probably because its text has nothing to do with the conflict. It is a rare example of a song with a social "message" that achieved popularity after the war. One of a large body of temperance songs, it was the only one to achieve wide and lasting popularity in sheet music form among Americans at large. Interpolated into the most famous of all temperance plays, Timothy Arthur's *Ten Nights in a Barroom*, it is the melancholy tale of a young girl sent three times—at one, two, and three o'clock—by her mother to try to persuade the father to leave the bar and come home to his sick and dying son Benny. The tragedy reaches its inevitable climax in the third verse:

Father, dear father, come home with me now!
　　The clock in the steeple strikes three;
The house is so lonely—the hours are so long
　　For poor weeping mother and me.
Yes, we are alone—poor Benny is dead,
　　And gone with the angels of light;
And these were the very last words that he said—
　　"I want to kiss Papa good-night."

And the chorus echoes, as it has after each verse

Hear the sweet voice of the child,
　　Which the nightwinds repeat as they roam!
Oh, who could resist this most pleading of prayers?
　　"Please, father, dear father, come home!"

This is strong stuff, amusing to some today, perhaps, but irresistible in its pathos. It called forth a number of "reply" songs, each seeking to soften the tragedy through some sort of happier sequel, most revolving around the repentant husband's giving up drink and becoming a model parent and husband.

　　Work's other great and enduring song was "Grand-Father's Clock," one of three songs written late in 1875 after a creative hiatus of almost four years. The new spirit of the 1870s hangs over the song; the passion of the war years is gone and the song is affectionate and reflective rather than pathetic or dramatic. There are the sure and telling strokes that characterize his best songs, most notably in the abrupt stop of the pervasive eighth-note pattern in the accompaniment at the precise moment that the text proclaims that the clock "stopped—short—never to run again" at the moment of the old man's death.

　　Work was elated at having composed again, as he wrote to a friend on December 26, 1875:

I have just written three new songs—written them, not because I thought it was time to take up my pen again; that motive has been ineffectually ap-

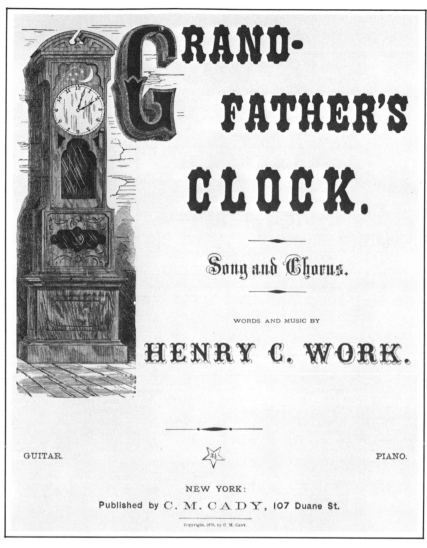

The decorative sheet music cover for Henry Clay Work's "Grand-Father's Clock" (1875).

pealing to me for years; but because, through a combination of circumstances I have heard a voice saying, "Write!" If now, with one tenth part as much emphasis I can say to my friends, "Sing!" my purpose will be accomplished. . . . I have reached, unmistakably, a turning-point in my history. I had supposed that all roads to success were long since past; but a new one opens most unexpectedly. Failure now would prove a final failure.[1]

1. Richard S. Hill, "The Mysterious Chord of Henry Clay Work," *Music Library Association Notes* 10 (1952–53): 381–82.

But inspiration flowed from his pen as slowly as before, and he died in 1884 without writing another notable song. It is a tragedy that the most talented song-writer of the generation after Stephen Foster was prevented—by circumstances of his life and his inability to deal with them—from producing more than a handful of songs in the last twenty years of his life.

Henry Tucker, who had published an arrangement of James N. Sayles's "Star of the Evening" as early as 1855, and whose "Weeping, Sad and Lonely" was among the most popular songs of the war, continued to turn out songs until the early 1880s, almost all of them in the ubiquitous verse-chorus mold of the day. His second great success came with "Sweet Genevieve," written in 1869 to a text by George Cooper, who had furnished Stephen Foster with poems for many of his war songs. "Sweet Genevieve" was published by Wm. A. Pond & Co., the successor to Foster's major publisher. Little need be said about the song beyond the statement that it is a classic example of the introduction-verse-chorus-postlude type of song described above. One musical detail is worth noting, how-ever: the first phrase uses a type of sliding chromaticism rarely encountered in prewar songs; this is expanded somewhat in the chorus in a clear anticipation of the chromatic, "barbershop" harmony of the 1880s and '90s.

HENRY TUCKER, "SWEET GENEVIEVE"

The immediate and immense popularity of the song is difficult to explain in musical terms, since the song closely resembles so many others of the time. It may be that Cooper wrote the text while in the grip of a deeply felt emotion and

somehow managed to capture the sentiment in a direct and quite honest way—
and that Tucker's music merely underlines and intensifies this mood, without
being exceptional in itself.

Tucker remained a prolific composer, turning out hundreds of songs after
"Sweet Genevieve," none of which matched the success of his best-remembered
hit. He was a favorite in Great Britain, where his songs struck English ears as pos-
sessing a distinctly American flavor.

Septimus Winner wrote many songs before, during, and after the Civil
War. He will be discussed here because he was most prolific after the war, and
because several issues raised in examining his songs belong in a discussion of the
postwar era.

Septimus Winner
(1827–1902).

Born in Philadelphia in 1827, his first published song was "How Sweet Are
the Roses" (1850)[2] and in the same year he wrote what was to be his first great
hit, "What Is Home without a Mother," which was not published until 1854. Its
success may be measured in part by the flood of imitations, parodies, and "an-
swers": "What Is Home without a Baby" (Gilmore), "What Is Home without a
Brother" (Haynes), ". . . without a Father" (Rees), ". . . a Husband" (H. C. P.),

2. Brought out by Lee and Walker of his native city.

". . . a Sister" (Haynes, again), ". . . a Wife" (Fiske), and ". . . without the children" (Keller) were only some of them.

Winner was a man of immense energy and ambition, not one to confine himself to a single activity. With only a few months of formal instruction on the violin, he played for five years in the Music Fund Orchestra and was leader of the Philadelphia Band. He taught himself to play the guitar, piano, and organ, then opened a music store in Philadelphia, selling sheet music and musical instruments and offering instruction on a variety of instruments. He was soon publishing his own music, writing his own song texts, and engraving his own songs.

Even this was not enough to keep him busy. He served as music editor for *Peterson's Magazine*, made almost 2,000 arrangements of various tunes and pieces for violin, guitar, and piano, brought out some sixty instruction books for various instruments, served as an officer of the Board of Music Trade, ran a branch music store in the Philadelphia suburb of Germantown, and raised a large family. A reporter visiting him in 1879 described him as:

> . . . quite stout, but tall in proportion, weighing some two hundred and twenty-five pounds; a face beaming with intelligence and good nature, gray hair, mustache (!) and short stiff beard; his manner, frank and affable. Altogether a hale, hearty, cheerful, well-preserved, successful man. . . . He is able to boast that he has never been confined to the house by sickness for longer than a day in his life. Perhaps this fact is owing in a great measure to his regular and strictly temperate habits. . . . He is a genial companion, a good conversationalist, quick at repartee, fond of a joke, and full of anecdote (!) and pleasant reminiscences. Mr. Winner is still writing ballads . . . and words and music seem just as new and fresh and full of sentiment and feeling as in the first years of his career . . .[3]

He poured out songs in a seemingly effortless stream. "Listen to the Mocking Bird" appeared in 1855 under the pen name "Alice Hawthorne"; contemporary with Stephen Foster's most successful minstrel songs, it shares with them at least some of the credit for popularizing and standardizing the verse-chorus form that was to characterize the next four decades of American song. Of his several dozen war songs, none achieved top popularity; his next successful songs were "Down the Quiet Valley" and "Dolly Vardon," postwar plantation songs very much in the style of the later songs by Stephen Foster.

Winner's songs exhibit more variety than those of most of his American contemporaries. He knew and admired the German song repertory and emulated the German style in some of his later songs such as "The Dead Leaves Fall," in which the absence of a chorus is an immediate clue that this is not a typical American song; the presence of a more independent piano part, more chroma-

3. George Birdseye, "America's Song Composers, VI: Septimus Winner," *Potter's American Monthly* 12 (1879): 436.

ticism, and extensive use of melodic sequence bring to mind the songs of Franz Abt and his German contemporaries:

SEPTIMUS WINNER, "THE DEAD LEAVES FALL"

Claribel must have been another of his favorites; "Wherefore," one of his most widely anthologized songs, could easily be mistaken for one of hers. It is a solo song without chorus, with a piano accompaniment and melodic line very much in her style. Even the text of "Only Friends and Nothing More" shows his dependence on her style:

> We met as many have before
>   Nor wish'd nor hoped to meet again;
> Ne'er dreaming of our fate in store
>   With days of pleasure or of pain.
> We met again with right good will
>   Yet paus'd when parting at the door;
> We linger'd with a sigh, but still
>   As only friends and nothing more.

Winner was one of the first composers to make arrangements of traditional black American melodies (his "Heaven's a Great Way Off" is labeled "Slave's Camp Hymn"), and he wrote songs in triple meter anticipating the flood of waltz-songs that were to dominate the market at the turn of the twentieth century:

SEPTIMUS WINNER, "UNDER THE EAVES"

A critic said of his texts, "While not claiming to be of a very high order of poetry, they are always simple, pleasing, and full of feeling and sentiment."[4] The same might be said of his songs. It would be a mistake to claim that he was one of the great American songwriters, but it would be equally wrong to ignore him. The fact that three of his songs, each quite different from the others, have endured for more than a century—"Listen to the Mocking Bird," "Whispering Hope," and "Where, Oh Where Has My Little Dog Gone?"—is an appropriate memorial to his wide-ranging gifts.

The story of "I'll Take You Home Again, Kathleen," written in 1875 by Thomas Paine Westendorf (1848–1923), reminds us that this was the era of Horatio Alger (1834–99), when in fiction and sometimes in fact an American of the humblest origin could achieve fame and fortune. Westendorf was totally unknown when he wrote this song; he was an instructor of music at the Indiana House of Refuge for Juvenile Offenders in Plainfield, Indiana. Destined to be one of the most successful and enduring hits of the era, the song was written "at the foot of a tree that then stood on the slope of the hill near where the drive turns on the way to the upper part of the campus"[5] and was first performed on an organ at the school. Its first public performance was in the Town Hall in Plainfield; it was picked up by a local tenor who sang it at Macaulay's Theatre in Louisville and was first published in March of 1876 in the *Musical Visitor*, a

4. Ibid., p. 435.
5. Richard S. Hill, "Getting Kathleen Home Again," *Music Library Association Notes* 5 (1948): 345.

house journal of the John Church Company of Cincinnati. A modest beginning, but this was a time when "people were unmolested by zealous 'song pluggers' and new compositions were judged in the homes. The art of advertising songs through the various channels was not yet perfected and ballads depended entirely on their intrinsic merit to win popular favor."[6]

Reaction was favorable enough for Church to bring the song out as a sepa-

The decorative and highly literal cover for the sheet music of "I'll Take You Home Again, Kathleen" by Thomas P. Westendorf, published in 1876.

6. James J. Geller, *Famous Songs and Their Stories* (New York: Macaulay, 1931), p. 6.

rate item of sheet music, and sales soared into the tens of thousands. Because of its success, the Church company published twenty-two new songs by Westendorf in 1876–78; more than twenty other publishers brought out other new songs of his in the decade following the appearance of "Kathleen"; and eventually some 300 songs by Westendorf were copyrighted and published. But not one even approached the popularity of his very first song, and only "Kathleen" was thought worth copyright renewal when the original protection expired.

Westendorf continued to teach in reform schools in Illinois, Indiana, and then Washington state, where he served for fifteen years as superintendent of the State Training School for Boys at Chehalis.

The John Church Company, which had bought the song outright for a very small fee, sent Westendorf a check for $50 each month for many years, in gratitude. Thomas Edison, who requested that "Kathleen" be sung at his funeral, once sent him $250 as a spontaneous gesture of admiration. Otherwise, once publishers gave up the notion that he might produce another great success, he realized nothing from his songwriting. One can guess, from what is known of his character, that the appreciation of the millions of Americans who knew and loved the song was the best possible reward for Westendorf.

"Silver Threads Among the Gold," written in 1872 by Hart Pease Danks (1834–1903), was equally successful and popular.

Danks, unlike Westendorf, made a living from his songwriting and can be considered the great pragmatist of the era. His first published song dates from well before the Civil War, and dozens of his pieces were published, some with modest success, before 1865. That year marked the turning point in his career; making essentially the same decision as Stephen Foster, Danks moved to New York and devoted himself completely to writing and selling songs. Refusing to bind himself to any one publisher, he shopped around and gave each song to the publisher who offered him the most money. Various of his songs were brought out by many of the most successful publishers of the day. He also had a contract with a leading London firm. His first widely successful song was "Don't Be Angry with Me, Darling" (1870), which sold tens of thousands of copies in both America and Great Britain. "Silver Threads Among the Gold" sold over 300,000 copies in America and almost as many in England in the first five years; it eventually sold some 2,000,000 copies before the turn of the century, and at least a million more following a revival in 1907. The fact that Danks died in poverty is a reflection of his inability to manage money and should not obscure the fact that he was one of the first American songwriters to make an excellent living from his music.

Musically, his songs conformed to the current styles of parlor and minstrel songs. He was a craftsman, who took popular song as he found it and added hundreds of new pieces to the repertory without changing the mold. In the words of a contemporary writer:

Mr. Danks' life has been one of constant labor and application. He has been indefatigable. There are few of our composers, if any, who can point to a list of between six and seven hundred of their own productions, and so many of superior excellence.[7]

In terms of sheer quantity of output and success in sales, the two most important songwriters of the two decades following the Civil War were William Shakespeare ("Will") Hays and Charles A. White. Though they lived in quite different parts of America—Hays in Louisville and White in Boston—they wrote songs strikingly similar in style, demonstrating the pervasiveness of the postwar verse-chorus type of song. A further (and surprising) point of similarity is that both were best known for their minstrel songs.

Hays, born in 1837, was a staff writer for the *Louisville Courier-Journal*, completely self-taught in music. His first song, "Evangeline," came out in 1862, followed in the same year by his great war hit "The Drummer Boy of Shiloh," the first of a flood of songs depicting the battlefield deaths of young boys serving both sides as drummers, fifers, and standard bearers. A border-state Unionist, Hays managed to have songs published in both North and South during the war. Some are pro-South in sentiment, some pro-North, most neutral. One, "The Unhappy Contraband," concerns an escaped slave who wishes he were back in Louisiana ("I'se a-libin' in de Norf among de strangers, / An' dey ain't a-gwine to gib me work to do . . ."). J. L. Peters (New York) published many of his war-years songs, including "My Southern Sunny Home" (1864), which surprisingly became quite popular in the North.

The peak of his success came after the war. "Write Me a Letter from Home" and "We Parted by the River Side," both of 1866, are sentimental verse-chorus songs of the sort discussed earlier; both are reputed to have sold more than 300,000 copies. "Driven from Home" (1868), "I'll Remember You, Love, in My Prayers" (1869), "Nobody's Darling" (1870), and "Molly Darling" (1871) are in the same mold and enjoyed comparable success. These and others like them are somewhat pallid in comparison to songs of the war years. "We Parted by the River Side," for instance, is a sentimental ballad of separated lovers:

> Tell me that you love me yet,
>   For, oh! the parting gives me pain;
> Say, tell me, that you'll not forget,
>   For we may never meet again:

But others, "Driven from Home," for instance, still echo the intensity of the best songs of 1861–65:

> Out in this cold world, out in the street,
>   Asking a penny of each one I meet,

---

7. George Birdseye, "America's Song Composers, V: H. P. Danks," *Potter's American Monthly* 12 (1879): 335.

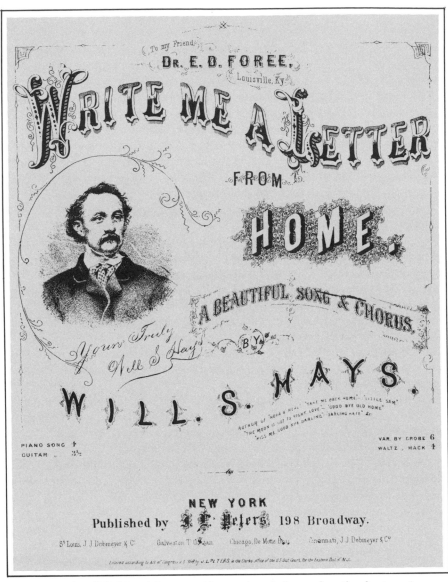

A portrait of Will S. Hays (1837–1907) is prominently featured on the sheet music cover of his very successful song "Write Me a Letter from Home" (1866).

Shoeless I wander about thro' the day,
    Wearing my young life in sorrow away;
No one to help me, no one to love,
    No one to pity me, none to caress,
Fatherless, motherless, sadly I roam,
    A child of misfortune, I'm driven from home.

though the music, a slow waltz in a major key, seems strangely incongruous:

WILL S. HAYS, "DRIVEN FROM HOME"

Charles A. White, born in Boston in 1830, wrote similarly sentimental verse-chorus songs for the home market early in his career. His first song to sell well nationally was "The Widow in the Cottage by the Sea Side," published by Oliver Ditson in 1868. His period of greatest success came shortly afterward, when he established his own publishing house—White, Smith & Petty—and brought out such hits as "Come, Birdie, Come" and "Put Me in My Little Bed," both of 1870.

His reputation as a songwriter was clinched in 1871 with "The Little Church Around the Corner." White seized on a dramatic and widely publicized incident for his text: when the popular actor George Holland died in late 1870, the minister of a large church in New York refused to allow the funeral services to be conducted in his church, on the grounds that the deceased had not been a member of his congregation, and commented that there was a "little church around the corner" that attended to "such things." This church, the Church of the Transfiguration, did indeed perform the service, and within a matter of months the theatrical community of New York had adopted it as its own, and White's song—dedicated to Holland's widow—was selling tens of thousands of copies.

Though White continued to write sentimental verse-chorus parlor songs until his death in 1892, he—like Hays—was most successful in the 1870s as a composer of minstrel songs.

The postwar minstrel show developed into something rather different from what it had been before. Productions still consisted of loosely organized sequences of songs, comic skits, dances, dialogues in dialect, and ensemble numbers involving the entire troupe; but companies under the management of Charles Callender and J. H. Haverly offered productions on a much larger scale, more lavish in costume and stage decoration, more varied in content, and staged in a more polished, professional fashion. Satirical and comic songs often dealt with ethnic groups other than blacks—the Irish, German, American Indian, and Chinese, for instance.

An even more drastic change was that blacks themselves began appearing in minstrel shows. The first successful all-black group was the Georgia Minstrels of Brooker and Clayton, organized in 1865. Callender, a white man, organized a large all-black troupe in 1872 that performed all over America, even going into the South; Haverly purchased the company from him in 1878 and enlarged it to more than a hundred performers, who toured England in 1881 after several successful and profitable seasons in America. Callender's Consolidated Colored Minstrels, his new troupe, was so successful that by 1882 it was split up into three different traveling companies. Charles Hicks, a talented black performer who had been on the minstrel stage since 1865, organized a black company that made a three-year tour through Australia, China, Japan, Java, the Middle East, England, Ireland, Wales, and various countries on the European continent. Individual black performers became famous—Hicks, Billy Kersands, Sam Lucas, James Bland—and when the minstrel show finally died out as a viable professional commodity at the turn of the century, the idea of black professionals in the theatrical world had been firmly established through the minstrel show, and the way had been paved for black entertainers such as Bert Williams and W. C. Handy to participate in burlesque and other forms of stage entertainment in the early twentieth century.

Though a brutal war had just been fought at least in part over the issue of slavery, postwar minstrel shows and the songs performed in them offered essentially the same image of the American black as before the war. Callender advertised that his troupe portrayed "the darky as he is at home, darky life in the cornfield, canebrake, barnyard, and on the levee and flatboat,"[8] and a present-day historian concludes that in the 1870s and '80s, "caricatures of darkies, in their idyllic plantation homes, served minstrels as romantic symbols of stability, simplicity, and order."[9]

Hays's minstrel songs of the 1870s offer familiar attitudes and sentiments:

Dar was a happy time to me,
  'Twas many years ago,
When de darkies used to gather round de door,

8. Robert C. Toll, *Blacking Up: The Minstrel Show in Nineteenth-Century America* (New York: Oxford University Press, 1974), p. 205.
  9. Ibid., p. 168.

When dey used to dance an' sing at night,
    I played de ole banjo.
        —"The Little Old Cabin in the Lane" (1871)

Oh! Sammy, put dat banjo down, O Sam!
You good for nuffen lazy houn', O Sam!
    Drive de dog in, out de rain,
    Milk de cows for Liza Jane;
    Liza's got de hoopin' cough,
    De ole man's drunk in de stable loff.
        —"Oh! Sam" (1872)

and the music of such songs was equally reminiscent of prewar minstrel songs:

WILL S. HAYS, "SUSAN JANE"

Though White lived and worked in Boston, which had been the spiritual center of the abolitionist movement, he wrote similar minstrel songs. "Nancy Till" and "Old Bob Ridley," for instance, exhibit a deliberately simplistic style, an obvious attempt to portray the "stability, simplicity, and order" of life among black Americans. Melodies are diatonic and simplistic, accompaniments cling to the three-chord spectrum of prewar minstrels:

CHARLES WHITE, "NANCY TILL"

Down in the cane-brake close by the mill,

There liv'd a yel-low girl, her name was Nan-cy Till;

White's "The Old Home Ain't What It Used to Be" (1874) epitomizes the sentiments and musical style of the postwar minstrel song. It is dedicated to the black minstrel star Charles B. Hicks and is known to have been sung by him with the Georgia Minstrels. Its text is a lament for the "good old days" of slavery—pure and simple:

> Oh, the old home ain't what it used to be,
>   The banjo and fiddle has gone,
> And no more you hear the darkies singing,
>   Among the sugar cane and corn.
>
> Now the old man would rather lived and died
>   In the home where his children were born,
> But when freedom came to the colored man,
>   He left the cotton field and corn.
>
> *Chorus:*
> No, the old home ain't what it used to be,
>   The change makes me sad and forlorn,
> For no more we hear the darkies singing,
>   Among the sugar cane and corn.

This is not a song by an unrepentant Southerner, wishing the Civil War had turned out differently; it was written by a Republican Yankee from Boston, for

Sheet music cover for C. A. White's "The Old Home ain't what it used to be" (1874).

performance by minstrel troupes in mostly Northern theaters. Further, it is known to have been sung by a black performer, with an all-black company.

It was suggested earlier that there were two stages of the minstrel song before the Civil War, the "nigger song" and the "plantation song." Postwar minstrel songs of the sort just discussed form a third stage of this genre, combing elements of the first two. There was soon a fourth, the minstrel-spiritual.

In 1871, a student choir from Fisk University, the Fisk Jubilee Singers, toured the North giving programs to raise money for their school, established in Nashville in 1866 as the first all-black institution of higher education in America. Under the direction of George White, a white faculty member, they offered spirituals—traditional black religious songs arranged by White in European-style harmony. Widely hailed in America and Europe as genuine American folk music, these spirituals were quickly imitated by other black choirs—and by black and white minstrel companies. From 1875, ensemble numbers featur-

The original Fisk Jubilee Singers, 1873.

ing the entire cast singing pseudoreligious songs regularly opened and closed the performances of many minstrel troupes. Will Hays scored the first success in this genre with his "Angels, Meet Me at the Cross Road" of 1875, a great hit both on the stage and in sheet music. The text, by Hays himself, is a clever imitation of certain of the Jubilee Singers' spirituals:

> Come down, Gabriel, blow your horn,
>   Call me home in de early morn;
> Send de chariot down dis way,
>   Come and haul me home to stay, O!

The chorus—for it is a verse-chorus song—mimics the call-and-response pattern of so many spirituals:

> Angels, meet me at de Cross roads, (. . . meet me!)
> Angels, meet me at de Cross roads, (. . . meet me!)
> Angels, meet me at de Cross roads, (. . . meet me!)
>   Don't charge a sinner any toll.

The simple, scalewise, diatonic melody and the tonal harmony closely resemble similar works by White and other arrangers of spirituals. The rhythmic patterns, though, are—quite simply—those of a polka, as can be heard immediately in the piano introduction!

WILL S. HAYS, "ANGELS, MEET ME AT THE CROSS ROADS"
INTRODUCTION

"Early in de Mornin' " (1877) and "Keep in de Middle ob de Road" (1878) were other popular minstrel-spirituals by Hays. The latter song comes closer to capturing the call-and-response pattern of Afro-American music by having the chorus answer phrases of the solo singer during the verse itself:

> (Solo) I hear dem angels a callin' loud,
> (Chorus) Keep in de middle ob de road.
> (Solo) Dey's a waitin' in a great big crowd,
> (Chorus) Keep in de middle ob de road.

The postwar minstrel show produced the first successful black American songwriter, James Bland (1854–1911). He was born into a middle-class home: his father attended Wilberforce and Oberlin Colleges, held a law degree from Howard University, and moved from Flushing, New York—where James was born—to Washington, D.C., to take a position as an examiner in the United States Patent Office (the first black to be named to such a post). James enrolled at Howard himself, but after seeing the minstrel star George Primrose (white, Canadian-born) perform, he dropped out of school to pursue a career on the minstrel stage. After a few years in and around Washington as a singer-banjoist-songwriter for private parties, weddings, and the like, he starred in and managed the Original Black Diamonds, based in Boston, beginning in 1875. Within a few years he was a star performer for Sprague's Georgia Minstrels, a troupe that included the two greatest black entertainers of the day, Billy Kersands and Sam

Lucas, in its cast. Next Bland joined the Haverly Colored Minstrels, in 1880, going with them to England and remaining in that country to organize his own troupe. He was the favorite minstrel performer of the day there, billed as the "Idol of the Music Hall"; he was also tremendously popular in Germany, where he was reputed to have earned the large (for the day) sum of $10,000 a year. His career went downhill after he returned to America in 1890, and he died a pauper, in Philadelphia.

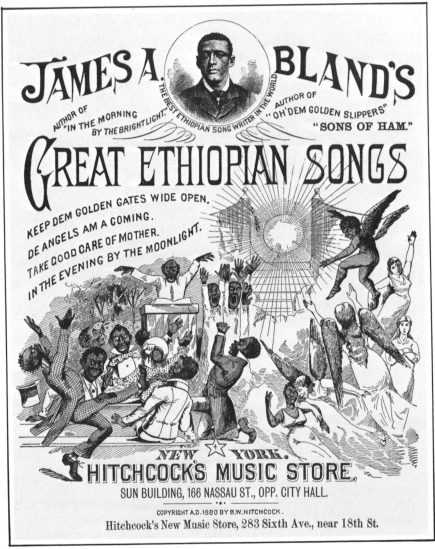

James A. Bland's realistic portrait is prominently displayed on the sheet music cover for a group of his Ethiopian songs. It in no way resembles the caricatured stereotyped "darkies" shown singing, dancing, and praying that were so fashionable in this postwar period.

1. **Carry Me Back to Old Virginny.** (Song & Chorus.) 4

2. **In the Morning** by the **Bright Light.** (End Song.) 4

3 **Oh dem Golden Slippers.** (Song & Chorus.) 4

Words and Music by JAMES BLAND, of Sprague's Georgia Minstrels.

BOSTON:

JOHN F. PERRY & Co., Music Publishers.

Copyright 1879, by JOHN F. PERRY & Co.

The cover for this collection of successful songs by James Bland continues the tradition of grotesque caricatures within a sentimentalized setting.

His success as a songwriter began early: one of his most popular songs, "Carry Me Back to Old Virginny," was probably written in 1875, the year he took to the stage, and published in 1878;[10] "Oh! Dem Golden Slippers" and "In the Morning by the Bright Light" both came out in 1879, as did also "In the Evening by the Moonlight." Bland wrote some 700 songs, most of them minstrel songs or sentimental parlor ballads.

10. By J. F. Perry & Co. of Boston.

Various writers have attempted to trace Bland's style to the folk music of Southern blacks. But the musical environment that shaped his style was the minstrel stage, not the plantation, and Bland's songs are no more indebted to black music than those of such white contemporaries as Hays and White:

JAMES BLAND, "IN THE MORNING BY THE BRIGHT LIGHT"

Black music was to have a profound effect on popular song in America, but at a later date.

The lyrics, written by Bland himself, give no different view of the American black in the late nineteenth century than those just examined. One need only recall lines from one of his most famous songs:

Massa and Missis have long gone before me,
    Soon we will meet on that bright and golden shore,

There we'll be happy and free from all sorrow,
    There's where we'll meet and we'll never part no more.

All dem happy times we used to hab' will ne'er return again,
    Eb'rything was den so merry gay and bright,
And I neber will forget it, when our daily toil was ober,
    How we sang in de ebening by de moonlight.

A present-day observer summarizes the content of Bland's songs:

> His nostalgic Old Darkies expressed great love for their masters and mistresses; his plantation songs were free from antislavery protests and from praise of freedom; his religious songs contained many stereotyped images of flashy dressers and of overindulgent parties; and his Northern Negroes strutted, sang, danced, and had flapping ears, huge feet, and gaping mouths.[11]

Minstrel songs by both white and black composers established and perpetuated a lie about the postwar American black, all over America and in Europe as well. There were, of course, extenuating circumstances for black songwriters: no other image of the black would have been acceptable on the minstrel stage. But certainly the plight of the black in late-nineteenth-century America was obscured and falsified by postwar minstrel songs.

The most talented songwriter in America in the 1870s and '80s was probably David Braham (1838–1905), born in London and trained as a theater musician. Coming to America at age eighteen, he held a series of jobs as a violinist in pit orchestras of New York theaters. His first songs did not appear until the late 1860s, when he was almost thirty. He wrote for assorted singers: minstrel songs; songs for character actors and comedians; songs for Major Tom Thumb when Barnum put the famous midget on display. His method of composing was somewhat eccentric: "He composed most of his songs on the violin, rather than the piano. Sometimes he would cover the wall of a room with music paper, and pace the floor sawing off a new tune, while his son George . . . stood to one side and scribbled down the notes his father fiddled."[12]

His early musical experience had been with English music-hall song, and there are clear differences between his songs and those of his American-born contemporaries. "Adolphus Morning Glory," for instance, a minstrel song written in 1868 to a text by the famous minstrel J. B. Murphy, has no chorus; the three stanzas are sung by a solo voice, with neither a quartet-chorus nor even a refrain line for the soloist at the ends of verses. The piano introduction and conclusion are elaborate and technically difficult, obviously being a piano reduction of music conceived for a theater orchestra. The tune has no suggestion of

11. Toll, p. 251.
12. E. J. Kahn, Jr., *The Merry Partners: The Age and Stage of Harrigan and Hart* (New York: Random House, 1955), pp. 151–52.

pentatonicism; the harmonies go far beyond the three-chord deliberate simplicity of most minstrel songs. The jaunty rhythms, the marchlike tempo, such details as the sustained note at the beginning of the last phrase—these all point to the style of the English music hall.

DAVID BRAHAM, "ADOLPHUS MORNING GLORY"

"Over the Hills to the Poor House," one of Braham's more popular early songs, was "Written and Composed Expressly For and Sung by Mr. James W. McKee, Character and Comic Vocalist." The text sketches the melancholy tale of a man devoted to his children, so much so that he had given them the deed to his property; but now that he is old and feeble, they have "driven him . . . so helpless and old (Oh, God, may their crimes be forgiven), to perish out here in the cold." There is a refrain, to be sung at the end of each of the five verses:

For I'm old, and I'm helpless and feeble,
  The days of my youth have gone by;
Then over the hills to the poor house,
  I wander alone there to die.

Such songs were merely a prelude to Braham's most important and successful activity as a composer, writing the music for the Harrigan and Hart shows that
dominated the New York stage in the 1870s and '80s.

Edward ("Ned") Harrigan (1845–1911) was born in New York's sixth ward;
a census of the neighborhood in which he grew up revealed only 10 native-born
white Americans, as opposed to 812 Irish, 218 Germans, 189 Poles, 186 Italians,
39 blacks, and a "scattering of unclassifiable persons."[13] Harrigan once remarked
that "below Fourteenth Street, after eight o'clock at night, the U.S. language was
a hard find."[14] Tony Hart (Anthony J. Cannon) was born in 1855 in an Irish
slum in Worcester, Massachusetts, the son of immigrants from County Mayo
who had fled the great potato famine of the 1840s. Both had enjoyed moderate
success on the stage before a chance meeting in Chicago in 1871 led to their first
appearance as a comedy and song team at the Winter Garden in that city. The
following year (1872) they signed a contract to appear as a team at the Theatre
Comique, a variety house in New York where the musical director was David
Braham.

Harrigan wrote the material for their sketches and the texts for songs set to
music by Braham. One of Harrigan's Irish sketches, "The Mulligan Guard," met
with such success in 1873 that it was moved to the important final spot on their
act, and repeated many times. The sketch revolved around the members of an
urban, paramilitary, Irish group organized by the fictitious Dan Mulligan. Continued popularity led Harrigan to write a series of sequels, further developing the
character of Mulligan and his family and friends and adding other ethnic types—
German, black, English, Italian. The sketches expanded in length and in
number of characters and songs; "The Mulligan Guard Picnic" (1878) lasted
forty minutes, "The Mulligan Guard Ball" (1879) was almost a full evening's entertainment—and ran for 100 consecutive performances. The string of Mulligan
Guard hits continued until 1885, when Hart left the stage; Harrigan and Braham
continued to turn out successful songs for other shows for another decade.

Harrigan, Hart, and Braham were urban-born and raised, and the three
spent their entire professional lives in large cities, mostly New York. Harrigan
was the first writer in the history of the American stage to deal exclusively and
sympathetically with urban people of diverse ethnic backgrounds. His Irish characters are rough, rowdy, garrulous, quick-tempered, and intemperate; his Germans are a bit slow-witted, pompous, stubborn, and addicted to heavy food and
drink; his blacks love to dress in overly elaborate costumes and use long words in

13. Ibid., p. 58.
14. Ibid., p. 58.

Harrigan (left) and Hart as the officer and the private on the sheet music cover of "The Mulligan Guard" (1873).

imaginative but inaccurate syntax. They are all basically good people, and though there are problems and tensions between ethnic groups, these are resolved without lasting malice or harm.

Harrigan sketched city life with a keen eye for humor, but also with love. His stage works were intended for urban audiences, and the galleries were always filled with "his" people, who responded enthusiastically to the Harrigan-Braham songs in these shows. As one writer put it, "In the seventies and eighties, it would have been a rare experience to stroll past a row of tenement houses on a summer night without hearing one or another of [Braham's] melodies being soothingly intoned within."[15] And Harrigan was very much aware of the role that popular song could play in the lives of the people for whom he wrote:

> The short-lived bits of music, coming and going with the freedom and irresponsibility of wild flowers, helped to lighten the toil of the working people and were, and are now, potent peacemakers at many a gathering where they calm the angry passions of the poor, admitting sunshine into many a darkened life. Virtue, disguised as music, enters the home of poverty, and holds temptation at bay with the gentle weapon called the popular song. Make songs for the poor, and you plant roses among the weeds.[16]

Harrigan and Braham created many dozens of songs that were enormously popular in New York.[17] William A. Pond brought out a collection of ninety-five of the best Harrigan-Braham songs in 1883. But these songs enjoyed little success in other parts of America. They were written for and about the peculiar mix of people populating New York City, and written in a musical style somewhat at odds with the prevailing patterns of American popular song. They represent the beginning of urban popular song, and thus anticipate what song was to become in the following decades.

As at other times in the history of popular song in America, songs from England streamed into the American market.

There were those, first of all, by Arthur Sullivan (1842–1900), perhaps the most talented British composer of the era. He was a musical prodigy—a chorister at the Chapel Royal as a child, a prize-winning student at the Royal Academy of Music in London and the Leipzig Conservatory, a widely acclaimed composer by age twenty, a professor of composition at the Royal Academy when he was only twenty-four. He wrote some ninety songs for voice and piano, of which more than two-thirds date from before the first operetta he wrote with William S. Gilbert, *Trial by Jury* (1875).

The first to be sold widely in America was "Birds in the Night," published

15. Ibid., p. 153.
16. Harrigan, as quoted in ibid., pp. 152–53.
17. "The Skidmore Guard" (1874), "The Babies on our Block" (1879), "Locked Out after Nine" (1880), "I Never Drank behind the Bar" (1882), "My Dad's Dinner Pail" (1883), and "Poverty's Tears Ebb and Flow" (1885) are a handful of the most successful.

first in London in 1869, a setting of a text by Lionel H. Lewin. Also popular here were "Looking Back" (1870, poem by Louisa Gray), "Let Me Dream Again" (1875, poem by B. S. Stevenson), "My Dearest Heart" (1876, to his own text), and the very popular "The Lost Chord" of 1877, written to a poem by Adelaide Proctor. These are quite different from American songs of the time. They are solo songs, with no choral refrain; the technical demands on the voice, in range and flexibility, are great; the piano accompaniments call for a pianist with considerable agility; chromatic chords and frequent modulations give a much richer harmonic color than those of any songs mentioned before in this chapter. No one could possibly mistake a passage such as this for an excerpt from a song by Will Hays, Charles A. White, or H. P. Danks:

ARTHUR SULLIVAN, "LET ME DREAM AGAIN"

Is this a dream? then wak - ing would be pain, Oh! do not wake me, do not wake ___ me, ___ let me dream a - gain.

Today, we can see that Sullivan, a classically trained composer, was writing "art" songs drawing heavily on the German style, while Hays, White, and Danks were writing popular songs. But Sullivan's songs came out in the same format and were sold at the same stores as parlor and minstrel songs by American composers; anthologies from the late nineteenth and early twentieth centuries contain songs by Sullivan next to American songs, as do numerous homebound collections of sheet music. Publishers, audiences, and composers were yet to draw a hard line between classical and popular song; and listeners and home performers enjoyed a wider stylistic range of songs than was to be the case in much of the twentieth century.

Songs from the Gilbert and Sullivan operettas were published as sheet music. Some enjoyed brisk sales, and several—"Farewell, My Own" from *H.M.S. Pinafore* (1878) and "I'm Called Little Buttercup" from *The Mikado* (1885)—sold well enough to rank among the most popular songs of their respective years and to be included in various American song anthologies of the turn of the century. But none became popular enough to affect the course of American song, as had songs from English stage works by Reeve, Shield, and Arnold in the late eighteenth century, and songs from the Italian operas of Bellini and Donizetti half a century later.

These songs by Sullivan, and a few others by Virginia Gabriel ("Ruby" and "Only a Light in the Window"), James A. Butterfield ("When You and I Were Young, Maggie"), and Annie Fortesque Harrison ("In the Gloaming" of 1877) became part of the enduring song tradition of America. But the number of British songs taking root in America in the decades following the Civil War made up a much smaller percentage of the song repertory than had been the case in the first half of the century—not because of any drop in productivity and quality among British songwriters, but because American song was now sturdy enough to supply almost all the needs of the American public.

An observer of this era in America was ambivalent about what he saw and heard:

> With the moral import of our songs no fault is to be found. They breathe a domestic allegiance that is highly commendable. . . . The tenor of their verse is in the direction of strictly permissible reminiscence and affectionate expostulation. . . . These American songs are commendable for sobriety of statement and worthiness of purpose. They whine somewhat, but they do not offend the moral sense, nor do they surprise by their absolute vacuity.[18]

Much in this clumsily worded commentary is accurate and even perceptive. However, it fails to mention the most striking aspect of popular song in the decades following the Civil War—that in moving out of contact with the realities of life in the United States, it began painting an essentially false picture of certain aspects of American society.

18. Henry Frederic Reddall, comp., *Songs That Never Die* (Philadelphia: J. H. Moore, [1894]), p. 267.

THIRTEEN

"After the Ball";
OR.
The Birth of
Tin Pan Alley

*When writing popular songs always bear in mind that
it is to the masses, the untrained musical public, that
you must largely look for support and popularity.
Therefore, do not offer them anything which in subject
matter or melody does not appeal to their ears. To do
so is just so much time thrown away.*

Charles K. Harris[1]

NEW YORK has been the cultural and artistic center of America for much of the
twentieth century, but this was not always the case. In the field of popular song, it
was no more important than several other cities for most of the nineteenth century. Some important composers lived and worked there, and active music publishers had been based there since the late eighteenth century. But Oliver Ditson
of Boston had the largest catalog of any publisher in America for much of the
later nineteenth century; Root and Cady in Chicago built a large and aggressive
sheet music business until the firm was wiped out by fire in 1871; Philadelphia
was a center of songwriting and music publishing throughout the century (Lee &
Walker of that city was one of the leading publishers in the second half of the
nineteenth century); the Willig family of Baltimore was a leading publisher for
many decades; John Church & Co. in Cincinnati became one of the largest and
most active music publishers after the Civil War; and many other cities boasted
important resident songwriters and music publishers.

1. Charles K. Harris, *After the Ball: Forty Years of Melody* (New York: Frank-Maurice,
1926), pp. 60–61.

All this began to change in 1881, however, with the establishment in New York of the T. B. Harms publishing firm, founded by the brothers Alex and Tom Harms. Their first successful published song was "Wait Till the Clouds Roll By" by Charles E. Pratt, who wrote both text (under the pen name J. T. Wood) and music (as H. T. Fulmer). The song was in no way remarkable; it was in the verse-chorus form of so many thousands of songs of the day. But it sold well enough to keep the Harms brothers in business, and it therefore owns the distinction of being the first "Tin Pan Alley" song, since the ensuing commercial success of the Harms company eventually revolutionized the music publishing business and changed the character of American song.

"When the Robins Nest Again" (1883), a sentimental verse-chorus ballad by Frank Howard, was even more successful, and by the time the Harms company brought out Paul Dresser's first hit in 1886, "The Letter That Never Came," their business methods were attracting emulation and competition. The newly established Willis Woodward & Co. had a popular item in 1884 in Banks Winter's "White Wings," followed the same year by Jennie Lindsay's "Always Take Mother's Advice." Woodward lured Paul Dresser away from Harms, and brought out a succession of his songs, including "The Outcast Unknown" (1887) and "The Convict and the Bird" (1888). M. Witmark & Sons began publication in 1886, enjoying moderate success until 1891, when Charles Graham's "The Picture That's Turned to the Wall" sold enough copies to give them a financial basis for further expansion.

A spectacular demonstration of the financial potential of popular songs was witnessed in 1892. Charles K. Harris, angered when sent a royalty check of 85¢ by the Witmarks for his song "When the Sun Has Set," established his own company, and almost immediately struck gold with his song "After the Ball," which quickly reached sales of $25,000 a week, sold more than 2,000,000 copies in only several years, eventually achieving a sale of some five million.

This unprecedented bonanza inspired dozens of other song-publishing firms, all based in New York. Joseph Stern & Co. had its first success in 1894 with "The Little Lost Child," with music by Stern himself to a poem by Edward B. Marks, and an even bigger hit in 1896 with Maud Nugent's "Sweet Rosie O'Grady." Howley, Haviland & Dresser brought out Paul Dresser's later songs, as well as such popular hits as "The Sidewalks of New York" (1894) by Charles B. Lawlor and James W. Blake, and Gussie L. Davis's "In the Baggage Coach Ahead" (1896). Harry Von Tilzer and Charles B. Ward, successful songwriters, established their own publishing firms in the early 1890s. Other important firms established in this decade were Shapiro, Bernstein & Company, Jerome H. Remick & Co., and the Leo Feist Music Publishing Company.

Many of these companies first had their offices in the Union Square section of New York, on East 14th Street, in what was then the heart of the theater district. The Witmarks were the first to move uptown to 28th Street; others followed, and by the late 1890s almost every major music publisher had an office on or near this street, which was dubbed "Tin Pan Alley" by the composer

"After the Ball," published by Charles K. Harris himself in 1892, was one of the legendary successes in the sheet music business.

Monroe H. Rosenfeld. Eventually the nickname of the street came to be used for the popular-song industry centered there and for the style of song brought out by these publishers.

By 1900, control of the popular-song industry by these new publishers was virtually complete, and it was a rare song that achieved mass sales and nationwide popularity after being published elsewhere.

Oliver Ditson & Company of Boston epitomized the traditional, nineteenth-century approach to music publishing. They brought out thousands of songs for voice and piano, but these represented only a fraction of their catalog; they also published piano pieces (dances, transcriptions of vocal works, "characteristic" piano solos), choral music, instruction books and graded pedagogical pieces for a variety of instruments, song collections for school and church, chamber music, and piano-vocal scores of operas and oratorios. All were on sale in their main store in Boston, various items were shipped to other retail stores around the country, any piece would be sent on demand to a store or an individual outside of Boston. Catalogs were published, covers of one piece would carry lists of similar pieces available from Ditson, advertisements were taken out in musical journals.

The Tin Pan Alley publishers, by comparison, brought out only popular songs and marketed these with a wider variety of techniques.

A word, first, about a critical development in the American theater. The Tin Pan Alley era in popular song coincided with the final fading of the minstrel show as the chief form of American stage entertainment and its replacement by the variety show, or vaudeville. There are many similarities between the two: both consisted of a succession of comic sketches, songs, dances, and other entertainment strung together, unencumbered by a plot. But whereas the minstrel show was unified in a way by the presence of the entire troupe on stage from the beginning of the show until the end, with various members performing individual solo and group specialties with punctuating ensemble numbers by the entire company, vaudeville performers were on stage only for their own numbers and were not seen or heard from otherwise. Also, the range of entertainment was much greater in vaudeville, with such acts as acrobats, magicians, ventriloquists, animal acts, and jugglers.

Tony Pastor (1837–1908) was more responsible than any other individual for the establishment and popularization of the variety show. A performer in circuses and minstrel shows from early youth, he opened Tony Pastor's Opera House in the Bowery section of New York in 1865, quickly making it the most popular showplace in the city. In 1881 he opened a new theater on 14th Street, continuing to bring the most famous entertainers of the age to his stage—Harrigan and Hart, Lillian Russell, George M. Cohan, May Irwin, Weber and Fields, and Vesta Victoria, to mention only a few. By this time variety houses had sprung up all over New York and in other cities. Keith and Albee organized a circuit of vaudeville houses all over America, with hundreds of entertainers crisscrossing the country from coast to coast.

Variety shows always presented singers who performed sentimental ballads, dialect songs, or humorous sketches including comic songs. By the 1880s and '90s more Americans were hearing songs in vaudeville than in any other form of live entertainment; thus singers in such shows became prime targets for Tin Pan Alley publishers who understood that having songs heard in public was the best method of persuading potential customers to buy sheet music. In the words of Charles K. Harris,

The real start at popularizing a song is to sell it to the performers. If it strikes their fancy, they will surely sing it for the public. Common sense tells one that the bigger the reputation and ability of the performer whose assistance the author and composer enlists, the more chances of its success in catching the public's favor. . . . A new song must be sung, played, hummed, and drummed into the ears of the public, not in one city alone, but in every city, town, and village, before it ever becomes popular.[2]

An early photograph (1881) of Tony Pastor's Opera House on 14th Street.

The trick, of course, was to persuade singers to include a given song in their act. Persuasion tactics ranged from furnishing singers with free copies of new songs, to performing small or large kindnesses for them, to out-and-out payment by the publisher—a flat fee, or in some cases a promise of a percentage of profits from sales of sheet music. The folklore of Tin Pan Alley identifies the Willis Woodward Company as the first to carry out systematic payments to singers to perform new songs. Charles K. Harris wrote vividly of the attention paid singers:

Daily in Tin Pan Alley, the song pluggers, from early morning until late at night, stood in front of their respective publishing houses waiting for singers to come along, when they would grab them by the arm and hoist them into the music studios. There was no escape. Once the singers entered the block, they left it with a dozen songs crammed into their pockets. . . . It was a common sight any night to see these pluggers, with pockets full of profes-

2. Ibid., pp. 36, 39–40.

sional copies, stop the singers on the street and lead them to the first lamp-post, where the plugger would sing a song from a professional copy. It mattered not how many people were passing at the time. . . . They [the singers] certainly had a good time of it, as the pluggers and the publishers fed them up with cigars, drinks, and food of all kind *gratis*. In order that a firm's song might be heard in different cities, many a singer's board bill was paid and many a new trunk, together with a railroad ticket, was purchased by the particular firm whose song the singer was exploiting. The publishers spent their money freely, their slogan being, "Anything and everything to land a hit."[3]

And in a more distinguished literary style, Theodore Dreiser, American novelist and brother of the songwriter Paul Dresser, gives a view of the inside of the publisher's office:

In Twenty-seventh or Twenty-eighth Street, or anywhere along Broadway from Madison to Greeley Square, are the parlors of a score of publishers. . . . Rugs, divans, imitation palms make this publishing house more bower than office. Three or four pianos give to each chamber a parlor-like appearance. The walls are hung with the photos of celebrities, neatly framed. In the private music-rooms, rocking-chairs. A boy or two waits to bring *professional copies* at a word. A salaried pianist or two wait to run over pieces which the singer may desire to hear. . . . And then those "peerless singers of popular ballads," as their programs announce them, men and women whose pictures you will see upon every song-sheet, their physiognomy underscored with their own "Yours Sincerely" in their own handwriting. Every day they are here, arriving and departing, carrying the latest songs to all parts of the land. These are the individuals who in their own estimation "make" the songs the successes they are. In all justice, they have some claim to the distinction. One such, raising his or her voice nightly in a melodic interpretation of a new ballad, may, if the music be sufficiently catchy, bring it so thoroughly to the public ear as to cause it to begin to sell. . . . In flocks and droves they come, whenever good fortune brings "the company" to New York or the end of the season causes them to return, to tell of their successes and pick new songs for the ensuing season. Also to collect certain pre-arranged bonuses.[4]

A picture comes into focus of a ferociously competitive industry dominated by the publisher, with the singer his most powerful ally. Songwriters seem to have been looked upon, mostly, as a necessary evil; except for exceptional cases, songs were bought outright, the usual fee ranging from 10 to 25 dollars, with the composer relinquishing all further claims to income from the song—even if it were to sell a million copies. The simple reason so many composers became publishers—Harry Von Tilzer, Edward Marks, Kerry Mills, Joseph Stern,

3. Ibid., pp. 212–14.
4. Theodore Dreiser, "Whence the Song," *The Color of a Great City* (New York: Boni and Liveright, 1923), pp. 244–45, 249; originally published in *Harper's Weekly*, December 8, 1900.

Charles Harris, Paul Dresser, among others—was to share in the profits of a song that sold well.

Even lower on the scale was the writer of the lyrics. It was the songwriter's responsibility to locate and pay for his texts; he most often wrote them himself, took them from some source not protected by copyright, or paid an author a sum of perhaps five dollars to write a text for him—the writer having no further claim to his text, financial or otherwise.

Publishers controlled not only what songs were published, but to a large extent the style of these songs. Through the singers who performed their songs, they had a finger on the public's pulse, and a good idea of what type of song would go over well. Many would also spend much of their time in the variety houses, listening to as many songs as possible and observing the public's response to each. Edward Marks describes a typical night in 1897, when in the course of one evening he visited Atlantic Gardens, the National Theatre, Miner's Bowery, the Winter Garden, Tony Pastor's, the Alhambra Music Hall, the Prospect Garden Music Hall, the Haymarket, and finally the Abbey, listening to songs in each place and chatting with singers, managers, and pit musicians.[5]

Publishers concluded that the public wanted familiar songs, and new songs in a familiar style. Tin Pan Alley songwriters soon reached a stylistic plateau, a much more homogeneous style than had ever before been the case in the history of song in America. An experienced songwriter and publisher gave the following advice to neophyte composers:

> Watch your competitors. Note their success and failures; analyze the cause of either and profit thereby. Take note of public demand.
>
> Avoid slang and vulgarisms; they never succeed.
>
> Many-syllabled words and those containing hard consonants, wherever possible, must be avoided.
>
> In writing lyrics be concise; get to your point quickly, and then make the point as strong as possible.
>
> Simplicity in melody is one of the great secrets of success.
>
> Let your melody musically convey the character and sentiment of the lyrics.[6]

The following list of sixteen songs of this era will serve two purposes: to fix more firmly in the reader's mind the song repertory of the 1890s and 1900s; and

5. Edward B. Marks, *They All Sang: From Tony Pastor to Rudy Vallée* (New York: Viking, 1934), pp. 5–21.
6. Harris, pp. 360–61.

to serve as a starting point for a discussion of the musical style of early Tin Pan Alley songs. Each of the sixteen enjoyed outstanding commercial success in the years following first publication—most sold a million or more copies of sheet music—and has retained some degree of popularity and familiarity to the present day.

"The Bowery" (1892) . . . . words, Charles H. Hoyt
music, Percy Gaunt
"After the Ball" (1892) . . . . words and music,
Charles K. Harris
"Daisy Bell" (1892) . . . . words and music, Harry Dacre
"The Sidewalks of New York" . . . . . . words and music,
(1894) Charles B. Lawlor and
James W. Blake
"The Band Played On" (1895) . . . . . words, John E. Palmer
music, Charles B. Ward
"Sweet Rosie O'Grady" (1896) . . . . . words and music, Maud Nugent
"When You Were Sweet Sixteen" . . words and music, James Thornton
(1898)
"My Wild Irish Rose" (1899) . . . . words and music,
Chauncey Olcott
"You Tell Me Your Dream" . . . . words, Seymour Rice and
(1899) Albert H. Brown
music, Charles N. Daniels
"A Bird in a Gilded Cage" . . . . words, Arthur J. Lamb
(1900) music, Harry Von Tilzer
"In the Good Old Summer Time" . . words, Ren Shields
(1902) music, George Evans
"Sweet Adeline" (1903) . . . . words, Richard H. Gerard
music, Harry Armstrong
"Meet Me in St. Louis, Louis" . . . . . words, Andrew B. Sterling
(1904) music, Kerry Mills
"My Gal Sal" (1905) . . . . words and music, Paul Dresser
"Wait 'Til the Sun Shines, ... words, Andrew B. Sterling
Nellie" (1905) music, Harry Von Tilzer
"In the Shade of the Old Apple . . . . words, Harry H. Williams
Tree" (1905) music, Egbert Van Alstyne

Only two were published outside of New York: "You Tell Me Your Dream" was first brought out by Daniels, Russell & Boone in St. Louis, and Charles K. Harris's "After the Ball" was published by the composer himself in Milwaukee, though he soon afterward opened an office in New York.

Musically, all sixteen songs begin with a brief introduction or prelude for the piano, sometimes stating melodic material from the verse or the chorus, sometimes merely setting the key and tempo for the song to follow. All proceed in verse-chorus form, but with an important difference from songs of the previous era: the "chorus" is given to the solo voice, rather than to a quartet of mixed voices. And the relationship between verse and chorus, in length and importance, has changed: in the majority of these songs, verse and chorus are of equal length, and in some the chorus is longer than the verse. More importantly, the chief melodic material is now in the chorus, not the verse. A person knowing any of these songs from memory, upon being asked to play or sing it, will invariably respond with the music of the chorus, not the verse—and may not even be familiar with the latter. Any of the sixteen songs could be used to illustrate this point. Choosing at random, almost anyone upon being asked to sing "My Wild Irish Rose" would begin with the chorus:

CHAUNCEY OLCOTT, "MY WILD IRISH ROSE"

not with the verse:

song,   Of a   flow - er that's   now droped and   dead. _____

Accompanying the increasing melodic importance of the chorus is a steady diminution in the number of verses. The oldest song, "The Bowery," has six verses; the eight songs written between 1892 and 1899 have two or three verses; and each of the seven written after 1900 has only two.

Almost all American popular songs of the nineteenth century are strophic, without chorus until the 1840s and usually with chorus after that. The succeeding strophes or verses unfold a dramatic narrative, or sketch a situation or portrait; the chorus echoes or comments on this drama. Increasingly in the period after about 1885, the drama sketched in the verses becomes simpler, while the chorus becomes more important and self-contained both musically and dramatically. The chorus of, say, Stephen Foster's "Old Folks at Home" does not make enough sense alone to survive without the several verses:

> All de world am sad and dreary
> Ebery-where I roam,
> Oh! darkeys how my heart grows weary,
> Far from de old folks at home.

But the following could stand alone—and often has done just that:

> In the good old summer time,
> In the good old summer time,
> Strolling thro' the shady lanes,
> With your baby mine;
> You hold her hand and she holds yours,
> And that's a very good sign,
> That she's your tootsey wootsey in
> The good old summer time.

The relationship between verse and chorus begins to approach the recitative-aria pattern of opera, with a first section of lesser musical interest sketching a dramatic situation, which is elaborated on in a second section containing the most memorable melodic material.

The disappearance of the quartet-chorus coincides with the progression from minstrel stage to variety show. A singer performed his songs alone on the stage in vaudeville, and took both verses and chorus himself—though if a song became well known, the audience might sing along with the chorus, and many vaudeville singers encouraged the audience to do just that.

All but three of the sixteen songs are waltzes, written in ¾ time and usually labeled "Valse" or "Tempo di Valse." (The three exceptions are "When You Were Sweet Sixteen," "Sweet Adeline," and "Wait 'Til the Sun Shines, Nellie.") The reasons for the popularity of the waltz-song in America at this time are not clear. German songs of the mid-nineteenth century were often in triple time, as were also many of the songs of the popular English woman songwriter Claribel. The great popularity of the operettas of Johann Strauss II in the late nineteenth century might have had more to do with it.

Harmonically, these songs persist in the tradition (now at least half a century old) of simple tonal structures, invariably in a major key, with three basic chords dominating the harmonic support of the voice. In doing so, they diverged even further from the harmonic practice of contemporary classical music. Little more than a half-century earlier, excerpts from operas by Bellini and Donizetti and songs by Schubert had been acceptable, with their original melodies and harmonies, as popular songs, and other songwriters had taken the style of such works as models for their own songs. But in the middle decades of the nineteenth century, American songwriters had simplified harmonic and melodic patterns, in order to have their songs acceptable to an even wider range of listeners and performers, at the very time that classical composers such as Chopin and Wagner were pushing in the other direction, constantly expanding the harmonic limits of tonal music. The first Tin Pan Alley composers were contemporaries of Claude Debussy, Richard Strauss, Gustav Mahler, and Arnold Schoenberg; there was almost no common ground now between popular and classical music, no possibility that a piece of contemporary art music could be fashioned into a popular song.

A harmonic mannerism encountered in the songs of almost all composers of this period is the introduction of the dominant of the dominant chord, just before the final cadence. Carried one step further, to yet another dominant, this mannerism results in a string of chromatic chords leading up to the final cadence:

PAUL DRESSER, "MY GAL SAL"

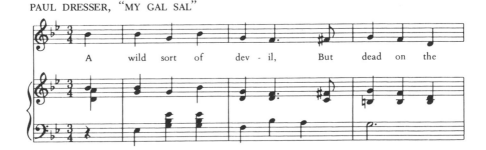

Sheet music cover for "In the Good Old Summer Time" (1902).

Such patterns are the basis for the characteristic harmonic style of "barbershop harmony," so linked in the popular mind today with music of this period.

The popular image today of this era in American history and culture is of the "Gay Nineties," a carefree, innocent time before the problems and pressures of the twentieth century robbed America forever of its youth and innocence, a time when popular song was part of the general exuberance and carefree nature of the day.

Some of the sixteen songs listed above, and others of the period, suggest a carefree, warmhearted world, with their lilting waltz rhythms and their texts: "Sweet Rosie O'Grady" and "In the Good Old Summer Time" speak of childhood joys in rural America, "The Sidewalks of New York" and "The Band Played On" are similar portraits of happy childhood in the city. Others are sentimental reminiscences of young, romantic love. But others are anything but gay, happy songs, once the text of the verses is heard.

"The Bowery," for instance, has a chorus that is indeed a lively, catchy waltz tune. But the six verses recount the adventures of a young man on his first visit to New York. Disregarding advice to stay away from the Bowery section of town, he is—in succeeding verses—bilked at an auction, bounced from a variety hall because he objected to the tone of the entertainment (the singer was offering a "coon" song of the time, "New Coon in Town"), "clipped" in a cheap barbershop, and battered in a scrap in a bar. These misadventures are described in a somewhat comic fashion, yet the familiar refrain "I'll never go there any more" has a rather different ring when heard as a refrain after verses detailing such mishaps.

Even more surprising—to those who know these songs only from their choruses—is that out-and-out tragedy is spelled out in the verses of almost half of the songs on the list above. The chorus of "In the Shade of the Old Apple Tree" is often sung alone, without the two verses, taken as a song of simple nostalgia for childhood days:

> In the shade of the old apple tree,
> Where the love in your eyes I could see,
>   When the voice that I heard,
>   Like the song of a bird,
> Seem'd to whisper sweet music to me;
>
> I could hear the dull buzz of the bee,
> In the blossoms as you said to me,
>   With a heart that is true,
>   I'll be waiting for you,
> In the shade of the old apple tree.

But the second verse outlines events that put the chorus in a very different light, when sung at the conclusion of these lines:

I've really come a long way from the city,
And though my heart is breaking I'll be brave,
I've brought this bunch of flow'rs, I think they're pretty,
To place upon the freshly moulded grave;

If you will show me, father, where she's lying,
Or if it's far just point it out to me,
Said he, "she told us all when she was dying,
To bury her beneath the apple tree."

Similarly tragic tales are told in the verses of "My Gal Sal" ("Gently I pressed her to my breast, Soon she would take her last long rest; She looked at me and murmured 'Pal,' And softly I whispered, 'Goodbye Sal.' "), "After the Ball" ("Long years have passed, child, I've never wed; True to my lost love, though she is dead."), and "You Tell Me Your Dream":

Sadness has entered the household, where happiness once reigned supreme—
The sunshine of life has now vanished, grief has dispelled their bright dream;
For Mary, his kind loving helpmate, had yesterday passed away—
And in sorrow Tom thinks of the morning, when in childhood to her he did say:
(*Chorus*) You had a dream, well, I had one too . . .

The subject matter of "Gay Nineties" songs was much more varied than is generally thought today; some idea of this will emerge in the following sketches of four of the leading composers of the period

Charles K. Harris (1867–1930) epitomizes better than any other songwriter the attitudes and methods of the first generation of Tin Pan Alley composers. His career as a composer spans the entire period; his "After the Ball" was the first spectacular demonstration of the market potential of popular song, and his book with the same title is the best contemporary verbalization of the philosophy of both songwriters and publishers of the time.

Born in Poughkeepsie, New York, Harris spent his childhood in East Saginaw, Michigan, and then in Milwaukee, where, as a teenager, he rented a room and hung out a sign announcing "Banjoist and Song Writer, Songs, Written to Order." He was completely self-taught in music, learning the rudiments of the art from hanging around theaters, talking with performers, and studying the George C. Dobson Banjo Book. He never learned musical notation, as he admits in his book:

The reader will naturally wonder how it was possible for me to write music to a song when even to this day I cannot distinguish one note from another.

Charles K. Harris (1867–1930).

The answer is simple. As soon as a melody occurred to me, I hummed it. Then I would procure the services of a trained musician for the purpose, hum or whistle the melody for him and have him take it down on paper with notes. He would then arrange it for the piano.[7]

His first songs, such efforts as "If I Were the Chief of Police" and "Bake That Matzoth Pie," were written for amateur singers of his acquaintance in

7. Ibid., p. 15.

Milwaukee, for local entertainments. Meanwhile, Harris made a habit of frequenting the theaters and variety halls of Milwaukee, meeting singers who came through town and trying to persuade them to program his songs. The story of the creation and marketing of "After the Ball" sums up his methods—which, on large scale, were the methods of the entire popular-song industry.

The story of the song was suggested by an incident he observed while attending a ball in Chicago; noticing a young man leaving with a woman whom he had not come with, obviously to arouse jealousy in his original date, Harris thought of the line "Many a heart is aching, after the ball." Back in Milwaukee, Harris was asked to write a new song by his tailor, a gentleman by the name of Sam Doctor who was also an aspiring singer. Harris recalled the incident in Chicago, and "in one hour's time [I] wrote the complete lyric and music of *After the Ball.*"[8] He expanded the incident into a pathetic tale, recounted in three verses, of how a misunderstanding at a ball had led to a life of bachelorhood for the hero, who could not forget his first love.

The first performance was a failure when the tailor-minstrel forgot the words to the third verse. Harris next showed the song to May Howard, a singer appearing in Milwaukee, but she and her husband found it ludicrous and advised the young songwriter to destroy it. The ballad singer Dick Jose came through Milwaukee with the Primrose & West Minstrels, and was willing to look at the song, but he advised Harris that one of his earlier songs, "Kiss and Let's Make Up," was much better. Then came Raymond Moore, who was having such success with a song called "Mary and John"—now forgotten—that he wasn't interested in another one.

The next big show in Milwaukee was Hoyt's *A Trip to Chinatown*, one of the most successful stage productions of the decade and already boasting a number of successful songs by Percy Gaunt, including "The Bowery." Harris knew Ben Singer, the manager of the show, and was introduced to J. Aldrich Libby, a member of the cast and one of the most popular ballad singers of the day, who was in a position to interpolate songs of his own choice into the show. The young songwriter not only showed Libby his new song, he also told him that he was a correspondent for the New York *Dramatic News* and could arrange for a glowing write-up for the singer if he sang the song, and—perhaps most to the point—reportedly offered him $500. Libby agreed, Frank Palma (the leader of the orchestra of the touring show) quickly made an orchestration—his fee was one good cigar—and Libby introduced the new song at the first matinee performance. According to Harris, the audience sat in silence for a full minute, rose to its feet and applauded for fully five minutes, then insisted on six encores of the chorus.

Julius Witmark immediately offered Harris $10,000 for rights to the song, but the young songwriter "reasoned that if it was worth $10,000 to Witmark & Sons, it should certainly be worth double that amount to me."[9] In quick succes-

8. Ibid., p. 57.
9. Ibid., p. 73.

sion, Annie Whitney sang the new song in Providence, May Irwin introduced it to New York at Tony Pastor's, and Oliver Ditson & Co. wired Harris an order for 75,000 copies—25,000 to be sent to Boston, 25,000 to New York, and 25,000 to Chicago. The song was not yet in print, and no press in Milwaukee could handle such a volume, but Hack & Anderson in Chicago agreed to run off the 75,000 copies within 10 days. Harris soon had a check for $14,250 from Ditson, and another 100,000 copies of the song were quickly run off and just as quickly sold. After this, Harris never looked back. The continuing success of "After the Ball" and his uncanny ability to judge which songs of his (and other composers) were most likely to sell well quickly made him one of the most successful and powerful publishers of popular song in America, with offices in Milwaukee, Chicago, and New York.

Though none of his later songs sold as well as his first great hit, many of them were among the most popular items of the period. "Break the News to Mother," published in 1897, sold more than a million copies; a pathetic song with a Civil War setting, it seemed oddly out of step with the times, but the outbreak of the Spanish-American War created a sympathetic climate for it. "While the Dance Goes On" was a sequel to "After the Ball," with an obvious reference to Henry Clay Work's still popular "Come Home, Father": the story is of a young mother enjoying herself at a ball while her baby lies dying at home. Famous singers now approached Harris for songs; J. Bernard Dyllyn, one of the most popular male singers of the 1890s, made a great hit with Harris's "Just Behind the Times" (1896), and Lydia Barry featured his "Always in the Way" (1903) for several years. He persisted with his habit of basing songs on incidents he observed or read about. "Hello Central, Give Me Heaven" (1901), his second most successful song, was inspired by a news item:

> I remember one morning at breakfast my wife called my attention to an interesting item in a newspaper. It was the story of a coal dealer in Chicago who had lost his wife, leaving a little daughter, aged seven, to comfort him. As he was reading his evening paper, his little girl, who had been playing with some wooden blocks close by, suddenly threw them aside and climbed on a chair so as to reach a telephone hanging on the wall. Cranking the small handle of the old-fashioned telephone then in use, she said: "Hello, Central, give me heaven, for my mama's there."
>
> When the child's message reached the operator in the telephone exchange, the latter was rendered speechless. She told the other girls to listen in, which they did.
>
> "Gee! I don't know how to answer the kid," said the operator.
>
> One of the girls said: "Just say you're her mother and console her. It will soothe her little heart."
>
> The father then took the little girl upon his knee and kissed her; and, with a smile on her face, the child fell alseep in his arms.[10]

10. Ibid., pp. 167, 171.

The cover of "Break the News to Mother" (1897), with its Civil War vignettes.

Similarly, a scene in the play *Secret Service* was the stimulus for "Break the News to Mother"; a fragment of conversation between two children, overheard in a store during the Christmas shopping season, led to "Always in the Way"; an article in a local newspaper about the forced retirement of an aging minister prompted Harris to write "Just Behind the Times"; a single line in the poem "The End of Our Sinning" by Ella Wheeler Wilcox eventually became the song "Cast Aside"; an oil painting of cows grazing in a field blossomed in his mind into the text for " 'Mid the Green Fields of Virginia." A chance meeting with Booker T. Washington on a train led to a conversation during which the famous black educator asked the composer if he had been born in the South, since he had written "so many Southern songs, with such delightful Southern melodies"; Harris responded:

> All imagination. . . . I had to inquire if there was corn raised in Virginia, and if there were hills in Carolina. This information, was given me by my office superintendent, Mr. Blaise, a native Southerner, and my imagination did the rest.[11]

Harris's approach to songwriting is curiously detached and objective. His stimuli always came from the outside world, never from within himself; his songs never drew on events of his own life. Though his autobiography is shot through with observations of the emotional effect of his songs on performers and audiences, there is no hint that he was himself moved by the pathetic episodes that inspired many of these songs, or by the songs themselves. Harris is not known to have championed any political or social cause, and it seems fair to say that his songs were calculated to inspire listeners to buy copies, not to go from the theater determined to right the injustices of American society.

Harris has not been treated kindly by present-day writers on popular music. A typical evaluation is:

> The career of Charles K. Harris remains a convincing proof of the fact that one can become an enormously popular songwriter without ever writing a really good song. His work was a perfect reflection of the essential naïveté of his period.[12]

But in his approach to songwriting and to the business of selling songs, he did more than any other single person to set the style for several generations of songwriters and publishers.

In an era in which most songwriters turned out catchy, easily memorable tunes set against an accompaniment based on a dance rhythm—the waltz, later ragtime—Paul Dresser (1857–1906) persisted in writing songs dependent for their appeal on the effectiveness of the human dramas sketched in their verses, their invocation of painful nostalgia, grief, and the burden of lost happiness and hope. Dresser's songs, in their expressive content, are squarely in the tradition of Thomas Moore and Stephen Foster. He was the only worthy successor to these two; the songs of the three frame and define the most important strain of nineteenth-century song.

11. Ibid. p. 318.
12. Sigmund Spaeth, A History of Popular Music in America (New York: Random House, 1948), p. 262.

Paul Dresser (1857–1906).

Born in Terre Haute, Indiana, Dresser was the older brother of the novelist Theodore Dreiser (1871–1945). When the latter came to New York in 1894, at the urging of his brother, he found Paul a successful, gregarious person, very much at the center of the popular-song industry of the city:

Admitting, as I freely do, that he was very sensuous (gross, some people might have called him), that he had an intense, possibly an overdue fondness for women, a frivolous, childish, horse-playish sense of humor at times, still he had other qualities which were absolutely adorable. . . . He

Sheet music cover for "My Gal Sal" (1905).

was all life and color, and thousands (I use the word with care) noted and commented on it. . . . He was in his way a public restaurant and hotel favorite, a shining light in the theater managers' offices, hotel bars, and lobbies and wherever those flies of the Tenderloin, those passing lords and celebrities of the sporting, theatrical, newspaper and other worlds, are wont to gather. . . . It was wonderful, the loud clothes, the bright straw hats, the canes, the diamonds, the "hot" socks, the air of security and well-being, so easily assumed by who gain an all too brief hour in this pretty, petty world of make-believe and pleasure and pseudo-fame. Among them my dearest brother was at his best.[13]

13. Theodore Dreiser, "My Brother Paul," *Twelve Men* (New York: Boni and Liveright, 1919), p. 79, and passim.

Paul had run away from his strict, strongly religious family at sixteen, first joining a traveling medicine show as a singer and entertainer, later performing with a
series of minstrel shows, and becoming a noted end-man with the Thatcher,
Primrose, and West Minstrels. Settling in New York, he became a favorite comedian and singer, in both blackface and whiteface, at the leading vaudeville
houses, including Tony Pastor's. His first published song, "Wide Wings"—
inspired by the considerable success of Banks Winter's "White Wings" of
1884—was brought out by a small retail music house in Evansville, Indiana, and
within two years his songs were being published by the most successful early Tin
Pan Alley houses. For two decades he brought out a string of successful songs,
from "The Letter That Never Came" (1886) and "The Outcast Unknown"
(1887) through "Just Tell Them That You Saw Me" (1895) and "On the Banks
of the Wabash" (1897), to "My Gal Sal" (1905), written less than a year before
his death.

His first songs show clear relationships with the various repertories he performed as a minstrel and variety hall star. "The Letter That Never Came" immediately invokes the rich tradition of sentimental plantation ballads, with its diatonic simplicity, its melody hinting at a pentatonic scale, and its characteristic
"Scottish snap":

PAUL DRESSER, "THE LETTER THAT NEVER CAME"

The verse carries the chief melodic material, with the chorus consigned to the role of echo and commentary.

In later songs, though, the melodic interest shifts from verse to chorus (the "tune" of "My Gal Sal" and "On the Banks of the Wabash" is the music of the chorus), the number of verses becomes standardized at two, increasingly chromatic harmonies appear just before cadences, and the quartet-chorus disappears. But his texts continue to deal, poignantly and painfully, with the theme of lost innocence and happiness.

Paul Dresser and Theodore Dreiser were in close contact during the period when the latter wrote his first novel, *Sister Carrie* (1899–1900), the story of a young woman who leaves her rural home for the city, where she is caught up in a whirl of events leading eventually to tragedy.

This was precisely the theme of most of Paul Dresser's songs. Excluding his minstrel and war songs and a handful of others, one can see that the majority of his songs deal with different stages of a single drama, the same drama that runs through *Sister Carrie*. In song after song, Dresser wrote of a young man or woman leaving home,

> She grew kind o' restless and wanted to go,
> Said she'd be back in a few weeks or so,
> She went to the city with a tear in her eye,
>   but she never returned.
>   —"She Went to the City" (1904)

leaving behind a mother, waiting only for the day when her child will return:

> I wonder where she is tonight, what can the matter be,
> I wonder if some guiding angel will bring her back to me,
> I wonder if the angels guard her in the gray twilight,
> I wonder if she says her prayers where e'er she be tonight.
>   —"I Wonder Where She Is Tonight" (1899)

While her child, caught up in a new life in the city, nevertheless longed for the peace and security of home:

> Just again to hear the village choir,
> Just to hear the songs they used to sing,
> Just to see the little church and spire
> Half-hidden by the trees in spring . . .
> —"The Town Where I Was Born" (1905)

Things go badly in the city:

> I long to see them all again, but not just yet, she said,
> 'Tis pride alone that's keeping me away.

Just tell them not to worry, for I'm all right don't you know,
Tell mother I am coming home some day.
            —"Just Tell Them That You Saw Me" (1895)

The tragedy runs its course, and death—resulting from an inability to cope with urban life—comes before the uprooted victim has been able to return home:

'Tis the grave of an outcast who died long ago,
Who has sinned and no mercy was shown;
So one cold winter's day, her soul passed away,
And they buried her there all alone.
            —"The Outcast Unknown" (1897)

Unlike Charles K. Harris, who depended on external stimuli for subject matter for his songs, Paul Dresser drew from inside himself. Certainly the drama sketched in his songs is autobiographical; despite his effusive, gregarious exterior, Dresser felt uprooted and lost in the city, and died alone and lonely. In his life, and in his songs, there runs one of the critical currents in American life at the turn of the century: a shift from a largely rural society to one dominated more and more by urban centers, and the emergence of new problems for individuals and American society in this new city life.

Theodore Dreiser was both fascinated and repelled by the life he saw through his brother, and was moved to write about popular songs, and the people who wrote, sang, and published them, on numerous occasions.[14] He saw his own activities—journalism, the writing of novels and other literary works—as a much higher form of creation than what Paul was engaged in, and often made disparaging remarks about his brother's songs:

And what pale little things they were really, mere bits and scraps of sentiment and melodrama in story form, most asinine sighings over home and mother and lost sweethearts and dead heroes such as never were in real life . . .[15]

At other times, he wrote with more sympathy on the subject, as when he spoke of how his brother worked:

He was always full of music of a tender, sometimes sad, sometimes gay, kind. . . . He was constantly attempting to work them [his songs] out of himself, not quickly but slowly, brooding as it were over the piano wherever he might find one and could have a little solitude, at times on the organ (his favorite instrument), improvising various sad or wistful strains, some of which he jotted down, others of which, having mastered, he strove to fit

14. Dreiser, "Whence the Song"; Dreiser, "My Brother Paul"; Theodore Dreiser, *A Book About Myself* (New York: Boni and Liveright, [c. 1922]); Paul Dresser, *The Songs of Paul Dresser; With an Introduction by His Brother Theodore Dreiser* (New York: Boni and Liveright, 1927).
15. Dreiser, "My Brother Paul," p. 97.

words to. . . . He seemed to have a particular fondness for the twilight hour, and at this time might thrum over one strain or another until over some particular one, a new song usually, he would be in tears![16]

And on occasion he wrote more movingly about popular song than any writer in the history of American literature:

[Popular songs] reach far out over land and water, touching the hearts of the nation. In mansion and hovel, by some blazing furnace of a steel mill, or through the open window of a farmland cottage, is trolled the simple story, written in halting phraseology, tuned as only a popular song is tuned. . . . All have heard the street hands and the organs, the street boys and the street loungers, all expressing a brief melody, snatched from the unknown by some process of the heart.

Yes, here it is, wandering the land over like the sweet breath of summer, making for matings and partings, for happiness and pain. That it may not endure is also meet, going back into the soil, as it does, with those who hear it and those who create.[17]

It was at least a minor American tragedy that Theodore Dreiser was the last serious American writer for at least half a century who tried to come to terms with popular song.

To the extent that quantity is a legitimate criterion for ranking composers of popular song, the most important composer of the first decades of Tin Pan Alley was Harry Von Tilzer (1872–1946), who claimed to have written 8,000 songs. Some 2,000 were published; at least dozen of these sold more than a million copies; and Von Tilzer estimated that several hundreds of millions of copies of his pieces were sold during his lifetime.

His story is similar to that of Charles K. Harris, in most respects. Born in the Midwest, in Detroit, he grew up in Indianapolis. As a child, he haunted theaters and the hotels where vaudeville performers stayed, and at fourteen he went on the road with the Cole Brothers Circus, as a tumbler. Switching to a burlesque touring company, he found ready performers for the songs he was already turning out in profusion. The singer Lottie Gilson sang his "I Love You Both" in Chicago in 1892, and persuaded Willis Woodward to publish it. This encouragement was all Von Tilzer needed to head for New York, where he found a job as a pianist in a saloon, for $15 a week, and had time to turn out dozens of songs each month, selling some to small publishing houses for as little as $2 each. He wrote every possible sort of song—sentimental waltz-songs, minstrel songs, Irish and German dialect pieces.

16. Dreiser, *Twelve Men*, pp. 96–97.
17. Dreiser, "Whence the Song," p. 259.

In 1898 he sold two songs to Orphean Music Co., run by William C. Dunn, for $30. To the astonishment of all concerned, one of them, a sentimental ballad ("My Old New Hampshire Home") quickly sold over a million copies, and the other, a novelty "coon" song ("I'd Leave My Happy Home for You"), did almost as well. Dunn happily sold his business to two ambitious young men, Maurice Shapiro and Louis Bernstein, and retired with a tidy profit; the two new publishers, in turn, immediately hired Von Tilzer as a staff songwriter, paid him $4,000 against the mounting profits from his two songs as a gesture of good will, and soon made him a junior partner in the business. Their faith in his potential paid off almost immediately: one of his very first songs for the new company, "A Bird in a Gilded Cage" (1900), sold 2,000,000 copies in the year following publication, and the firm of Shapiro, Bernstein & Von Tilzer was suddenly one of the giants of Tin Pan Alley.

"A Bird in a Gilded Cage" is squarely in the center of early Tin Pan Alley style, in music and content. It is a graceful waltz, the most conventional musical gesture of the day, particularly appropriate here because the verse immediately sets the scene at a ball:

> The ball-room was filled with fashion's throng,
> It shone with a thousand lights,
> And there was a woman who passed along,
> The fairest of all the sights.

The story unfolded in the two verses is of a young woman married to a wealthy but elderly man; the second verse tells of her death, and the chorus is heard in its proper light, as the soliloquy of an unidentified narrator over her grave:

> 'Tis sad when you think of her wasted life,
>   For youth cannot mate with age,
> And her beauty was sold
> For an old man's gold,
>   She's a bird in a gilded cage.

The form is conventional for the period; an 8-measure introduction, a 32-measure verse, and a 32-measure chorus. The "tune," the melody that comes immediately to the mind of a person who knows the song, is in the chorus, but much of it is anticipated in the verse, which has entire phrases in common with the chorus. Thus both the introduction and the verse prepare us for the chorus, by introducing strains to be heard later. In a broader sense, the music is familiar even before one hears the song for the first time; the style is similar to that of thousands of other songs written before (and after) this particular song. The harmonies and the characteristic sound of the octave doubling in the right hand of the piano part had been heard in innumerable songs:

HARRY VON TILZER, "A BIRD IN A GILDED CAGE"

And her beau - ty was sold, For an old man's gold, She's a bird in a gild - ed cage.

Though Von Tilzer was rewarded handsomely by Shapiro and Bernstein, he followed the lead of Charles K. Harris by establishing his own publishing house, in order to have all the profits from his songs. In 1902 he opened an office on 28th Street, Tin Pan Alley itself, and success was almost immediate—and spectacular. Four songs published in his first year of operation had a combined sale of over 5,000,000 copies: "The Mansion of Aching Hearts," "On a Sunday Afternoon," "Down Where the Wurzburger Flows," and "Please Go 'Way and Let Me Sleep." These four are samples of the most successful types of songs of the first decades of the twentieth century; the first is a melodramatic waltz-song, a sequel to "A Bird in a Gilded Cage"; the second is a cheerful waltz, speaking of good times in New York; the third is a spirited, pseudo-German drinking song; and the last is in "negro" dialect, a last descendant of the minstrel song of the nineteenth century.

Other songs written and published in the first decade of Von Tilzer's own company are samples of still other types: "Where the Morning Glories Twine" (1905) is a final bow to the nineteenth-century nostalgia-for-lost-childhood song:

> Mother dear will come to meet me,
> And a sweetheart's kiss will greet me,
> Where the morning glories twine around the same old door.

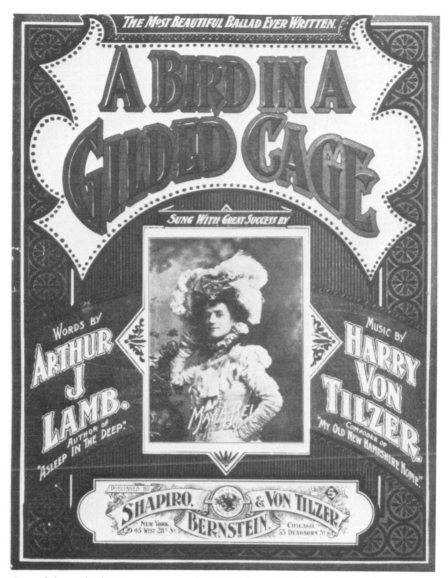

One of the early sheet music covers for "A Bird in a Gilded Cage" (1900).

"A Little Bunch of Shamrocks" (1913) is one of his many Irish songs, and "I Want a Girl—Just Like the Girl That Married Dear Old Dad" (1911) is a classic and still-popular "mother" song.

Von Tilzer wrote into the 1920s, then became an interested observer of a new sort of song he was not able or willing to write.

For George M. Cohan (1878–1942) writing songs was but a single facet of a career that embraced every aspect of the theater—acting, singing, dancing, managing, directing, playwriting, choreographing, casting, and financing. More than any other individual, he shaped the American musical stage into something with a character and vitality all its own, in the first decades of the twentieth century.

The theater was Cohan's entire life, quite literally. Born into a theatrical family, he was on the stage himself from early childhood. He briefly attended school in Providence, Rhode Island; but after the age of nine or ten he had no home other than the stage, and had little contact with American life and culture beyond what he witnessed on the stage and what he observed in traveling from one city to another. With scant interest in his country's past, musical or otherwise, he wrote songs that grew out of the then-present state of the American musical theater and were pure products of the twentieth century.

His father, a minstrel and vaudeville performer, incorporated the various members of his family into his act as they appeared on the scene. Helen Costigan joined him on the stage immediately following their marriage, taking time out only for the birth of their two children, Josie and George. By the time he was nine, George was a member of "The Four Cohans," dancing, doing comic skits, and playing the violin. He was almost completely self-taught in music; violin lessons, started at the age of seven, lasted for two weeks, terminating with a note from his teacher to his father: "Impossible to teach this boy any more. HE KNOWS IT ALL."[18]

His first songs were written in his early teens, when the family was working out of Buffalo. As he told it:

> I turned out no less than half a dozen ballads a week for some little time. The New York music publishers must have grown tired of sending back my manuscripts, because after a while they didn't even bother to do that. One fellow, however, was at least courteous enough to write a letter. It ran as follows: "Dear Sir: Your songs are not publishable. Please do not send any more." Even that didn't stop me. As a matter of fact, it made me fighting mad.[19]

The Cohans decided to try their luck in New York in the early 1890s, accepting a contract for an engagement at Keith's Union Square Theatre. The outcome surprised and shocked the family: daughter Josie was offered a long-term contract at a leading vaudeville house, as a solo act, at the same salary the entire family would have expected. Thus George found himself in New York with plenty of time on his hands, and he decided to concentrate on songwriting:

> I became one of the regular "hangers-on" around several music houses, and was observing and alert enough to keep my eyes open and my ears cocked.

18. George M. Cohan, *Twenty Years on Broadway* (New York: Harper & Brothers, 1924), p. 9.
19. Ibid., pp. 29–30.

My heart was set on being a popular-song writer. I practiced verse writing night and day.

"The words must jingle, the words must jingle," I'd keep repeating over and over again.

I could play four chords on the piano in F sharp. I'd vamp these four chords and hum tunes to myself for hours at a time. I never got any further than the four F sharp chords, by the way. I've used them ever since.

From one music-publishing house to another I traipsed with my song manuscripts week in and week out. I had about exhausted the entire tin-pan-alley circuit. They all said the same thing.

'No market for songs of that kind.'
'I'll write any kind you want,' I'd reply.
'We don't want any right now,' they'd answer.

Inside of six months, during which I worked like a trojan to improve my style of melody and learn how to jingle words in rhyme, no less than half a dozen manuscripts of mine had been accepted for publication.

I played no favorite with the publishers. I'd sell a song wherever I could get the price. The price was from ten to twenty-five dollars, according to the subject and merits of the thing. The paying of so much a copy as royalties was an exceptional arrangement in those days. The average song writer (comparatively few at the time) was usually pressed for ready cash, and couldn't afford to gamble.[20]

His first published song, "Why Did Nellie Leave Home?," was brought out by the Witmark company; the second, "Hot Tamale Avenue," was introduced by the popular May Irwin. By now the "Four Cohans" were back on stage together, suddenly in demand all over the country, asking and getting $1,000 a week. The twenty-year-old George was writing all their material—songs, comic skits, dramatic routines. They became the "Five Cohans" in 1899 when George married the singer Ethel Levey, who had introduced his most successful song to date, "I Guess I'll Have to Telegraph My Baby" (1898).

Cohan's most successful and enduring songs were written for a series of "musical plays" beginning in the early 1900s. These were works planned as a full evening's entertainment, unified by a continuous plot, with newly composed songs interspersed throughout. The first was *The Governor's Son* (1901), which had a modest run of thirty-two performances; none of the dozen songs (which included "Too Many Miles from Broadway" and "The Story of the Wedding March") achieved much popularity. *Running for Office* was next, in 1903; it ran for forty-eight performances and, like its predecessor, starred the five members of the Cohan family.

Little Johnny Jones (1904) had a larger cast, a more lavish production, a more tightly knit plot, and better integration of music into the drama. Some-

20. Ibid., pp. 102–3, 86–87.

George M. Cohan, the "Yankee Doodle Comedian," on the sheet music for "Give My Regards to Broadway" from *Little Johnny Jones* (1904).

times called the first musical comedy, it starred George in the role of an American jockey in England, and was the first collaboration between the Cohans and the producer Sam Lewis. It got a surprisingly lukewarm reception from critics and audiences for a show that looms so large in American theatrical history; but two of Cohan's songs from it, "Give My Regards to Broadway" and "The Yankee Doodle Boy," were his first to achieve great and enduring popularity.

Forty-Five Minutes from Broadway (1906) was a similar but much more successful show, with a strong cast including the great vaudeville star Fay Tem-

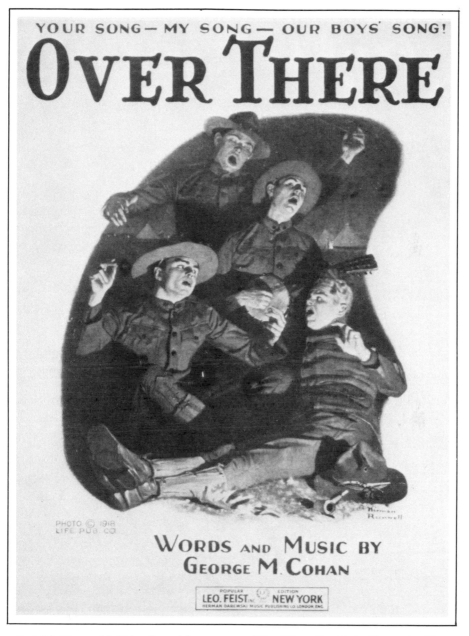

Probably George M. Cohan's most famous song, "Over There," published in 1918, with a Norman Rockwell illustration on the cover.

pleton, and Victor Young in his first major role. The most memorable of its many successful songs was "Mary's a Grand Old Name." Later that year *George Washington, Jr.* introduced the hit song "You're a Grand Old Flag."

There were three major Cohan shows on Broadway in 1907–8, followed by two the following season. Eleven more shows—five musical comedies, five dramas without music, one revival—marked the years 1910–17, and he tried still other theatrical ventures: a minstrel show, silent movies, revues. World War I inspired perhaps his most famous song, "Over There" (1917); after the war he continued to write and direct plays, and to take more dramatic roles himself, in such productions as O'Neill's *Ah! Wilderness* (1933) and the Rodgers and Hart *I'd Rather Be Right* (1937).

In all, he wrote and directed some 40 plays, was involved (as actor, producer, or singer) in almost 150 others, published approximately 500 songs, and made an estimated 4,000 personal appearances. His popularity continued after his death: the movie *Yankee Doodle Dandy* (1942) brought James Cagney an Academy Award for his portrayal of Cohan; and a Broadway musical, *George M!* (1968), had Joel Grey in the title role. Both productions featured many of his songs.

Cohan was in no way a musical innovator. His songs were all written in the introduction/two-verse-solo/chorus form that had become virtually standard by the turn of the century. Some of his earlier hits were waltz-songs:

GEORGE M. COHAN, "FORTY-FIVE MINUTES FROM BROADWAY"

But his most characteristic and successful songs are usually marked "Tempo di Marcia," capturing the spirit of the marches of the John Philip Sousa and Arthur Pryor bands, often with simple syncopations that begin to suggest the flavor of ragtime:

GEORGE M. COHAN, "YOU'RE A GRAND OLD FLAG"

You're a grand old flag tho' you're torn to a rag, And for-ev-er in peace may you wave.

If there is anything new about his songs, it is their verve: brash, noisy, aggressively patriotic, oriented to the present, usually devoid of sentimentality. They are very much in the spirit of certain aspects of life in America, as the country moved into a new century.

The first two decades of Tin Pan Alley coincide with the emergence of ragtime. Most of the history of this genre lies outside the range of the present book, since it is instrumental music, but it enjoyed a period of such intense popularity that some of its elements eventually colored the sound of some popular songs.[21]
Ragtime is syncopated piano music, developing out of a dance known as the cakewalk, which supposedly originated among Southern blacks. It crystallized in the Midwest, mostly in and around St. Louis, and its most famous practitioner was Scott Joplin (1869–1917), a black pianist and composer whose most famous piece was named after the Maple Leaf Club in Sedalia, Missouri, where he performed for some years. The first published ragtime piece was *Mississippi Rag* by a white orchestra leader named William H. Krell, brought out on January 24,

21. See Rudi Blesh and Harriet Janis, *They All Played Ragtime*, 4th ed. (New York: Oak Publications, 1971) for the most complete discussion of this music.

1897, by the S. Brainard company of Chicago. The first published rag by a black was Thomas Turpin's *Harlem Rag,* in December of 1897, and Joplin's first was *Original Rags* of 1899.

The credit for bringing ragtime to New York goes to Benjamin Robertson Harney (1871–1938), who was booked at Tony Pastor's in 1897 as the "Inventor of Ragtime," published a *Rag Time Instructor* the same year, and wrote such songs as "You've Been a Good Old Wagon But You Done Broke Down" (1895) and "Mr. Johnson, Turn Me Loose" (1896), generally accepted as the first "ragtime songs." The problem is that if we take as a definition of ragtime "the application of systematic syncopation to piano playing and composition"[22] with "a syncopated treble melody which operates in opposition to a harmonic and non-syncopated bass line,"[23] neither of these two songs by Harney fits such a definition. "You've Been a Good Old Wagon," in fact, has no more syncopation in its melody than many contemporary minstrel songs, or a typical march or quickstep of the time. The most interesting feature of the tune, stylistically and historically, is its pentatonic character and its close resemblance to a familiar, traditional Anglo-American melody:

It is thus one more tantalizing link between the melodic tradition of traditional Anglo-American music and music produced by black Americans.[24]

The same difficulty persists with the most successful of the early ragtime songs, "Hello! Ma Baby," written in 1899 by Joseph E. Howard. Though it is not identified on the cover or elsewhere as a ragtime song, it came out in a piano version labeled "Rag-Time March," and everyone who has ever written about it has linked it to ragtime. The extent of its relationship to ragtime is evident in the first few measures:

22. Gilbert Chase, *America's Music: From the Pilgrims to the Present,* 2nd rev. ed. (New York: McGraw-Hill, 1966), pp. 434–35.

23. Frank Tirro, *Jazz: A History* (New York: W. W. Norton, 1977), p. 89.

24. Most writers have assumed that Harney, born in Kentucky, was white, but Alec Wilder, *American Popular Song: The Great Innovators, 1900–1950* (New York: Oxford University Press, 1972), p. 9, relies on Eubie Blake's insistence that he was black.

JOE HOWARD, "HELLO! MA BABY"

If the feature that distinguishes ragtime from earlier forms of syncopated piano music is not merely the rhythmic pattern short-long-short (♪ ♩ ♪) but the tying of the last note in this pattern across the barline, with the result that no note in the treble is struck on the first beat of the following measure (short-long-short, short-long-short) (♪ ♩ ♪♪ ♩ ♪),

then "Hello! Ma Baby" and all the other best-known ragtime songs merely *suggest* the rhythmic spirit of ragtime, and there is little or no difference between their rhythmic patterns and those of the spirited, march-inspired songs of George M. Cohan.

For that matter, there is difficulty in separating songs now thought of as rag-

Sheet music cover for one of the greatest ragtime songs—"Bill Bailey, Won't You Please Come Home?" (1902).

time songs from "coon" songs, the last stage of the minstrel song. "Coonville Guards" (1881) and "The Coon Dinner" (1882), both by Jacob J. Sawyer, anticipated the first great hit of this genre, "New Coon in Town" (1883) by J. S. Putnam. Vaudeville star May Irwin became known as the greatest "coon shouter" of the day with her performance of such pieces as "The Bully Song" and the "Frog Song," both by Charles E. Trevathan, and this type of song peaked with Barney Fagan's "My Gal Is a Highborn Lady" (1886)—sung by Ernest Haverly of Haverly's Minstrels—and Ernest Hogan's "All Coons Look Alike to Me" of the same year.

The "coon" song is usually in dialect, with a text somewhat less than complimentary to blacks. Musically, it takes on the verse-solo form of contemporary Tin Pan Alley song, with the chief melodic material in the chorus, and is sung at a lively tempo, usually with some bits of simple syncopation. It is, in fact, nothing more or less than a slightly deviant offspring of Tin Pan Alley song, difficult to distinguish in style from the classics of the ragtime song: Hughie Cannon's "Bill Bailey, Won't You Please Come Home?" (1902); Bob Cole's "Under the Bamboo Tree" (1902); Joe Howard's "Good Bye, My Lady Love" (1904); Irving Berlin's "Alexander's Ragtime Band" (1911); and Lewis F. Muir's "Waiting for the Robert E. Lee" (1912).

Ragtime songs differ from other Tin Pan Alley songs more in spirit than musical style; they are brash, spirited, slightly syncopated, breezy, almost always humorous—characteristics they share with many of the songs of George M. Cohan. And, almost without exception, they were written and performed by whites.

A pattern was established with the ragtime song that was to recur time and again in the twentieth century: white popular music skimmed off superficial stylistic elements of a type of music originating among black musicians, and used these to give a somewhat different, exotic flavor to white music. Though Scott Joplin and a handful of other black ragtime musicians realized a modest profit from their music, the important money went to the white publishers, performers, and composers of ragtime songs.

Mention should be made of one additional type of song from this period, epitomized by Reginald De Koven's "Oh Promise Me" (1889). There is nothing in the song reminiscent of a waltz, a march, or a syncopated piano piece. The piano accompaniment consists of repeated chords in the right hand against a supporting bass, in the style of Robert Schumann or Franz Abt, moving through chromatic changes far beyond the harmonic vocabulary of Charles K. Harris or Paul Dresser; the vocal line rises to small climaxes in each phrase, with the final large climax—the point to which the entire song has been moving—reserved for the end of the last phrase, where the singer has a *fortissimo* high note supported by a thickened accompaniment and a crashing dynamic level:

REGINALD DE KOVEN, "O PROMISE ME"

It is all quite operatic, not surprising in view of De Koven's training (a degree from Oxford in England, followed by extended study of classical music in Vienna, Frankfurt, Stuttgart, and Paris) and his activity as a composer, which included one of the most successful American operas of the nineteenth century, *Robin Hood* (1890). De Koven thought of "Oh Promise Me" as an art song, certainly, but even this late in the century the line between classical and popular music was not yet drawn as distinctly as it would be several decades later, and his song was sung and heard by many people who were also concerned with popular song.

Victor Herbert (1859–1924) was the most successful composer of this sort of song. Born in Dublin, the grandson of songwriter Samuel Lover, he was trained in cello and theory at the Stuttgart Conservatory and came to America at twenty-seven, as a cellist in the pit orchestra of the Metropolitan Opera House, after some years as a member of the famous Johann Strauss Orchestra in Vienna. He composed some forty operettas, successfully adapting the Viennese style to the American stage and in the process turning out such top-selling songs as "Gypsy Love Song" from *Fortune Teller* (1898), "Kiss Me Again" from *Mlle. Modiste* (1905), "Because You're You" and "The Streets of New York" from *The Red Mill* (1906), and "Ah! Sweet Mystery of Life," "I'm Falling in Love with Some-one," and "Italian Street Song," all from his most successful operetta, *Naughty Marietta* (1910). Unlike many classically trained composers, he sought wide public acceptance for his works; his songs were brought out by the Tin Pan Alley firm of M. Witmark & Sons and marketed with the same techniques used for all the other songs in their catalog.

Herbert had the rare gift of writing songs close enough to the popular idiom to be quite acceptable to persons who enjoyed only this type of song, yet at the same time musically interesting enough to appeal to others with a preference for classical music.

Ethelbert Nevin (1862–1901) had a similarly classical training, in Dresden and Berlin, and enjoyed a brief career as a concert pianist. His "The Rosary" (1898) succeeded as a popular parlor song, as a recital piece for operatic and lieder singers, and as an enduring religious song. Carrie Jacobs-Bond (1862–1946) wrote both lyrics and music for her songs, set up her own small publishing firm in Chicago when Tin Pan Alley companies rejected her songs as "too classical," designed and hand-painted her own covers, and plugged her own songs in recitals for friends and potential buyers. Her talent and perseverance eventually paid off; "Just a-Wearyin' for You" (1901) and "I Love You Truly" (1906) outsold all but the most popular Tin Pan Alley products, and "A Perfect Day" (1910) almost matched the success of these two. Ernest R. Ball (1878–1927) managed to combine elements of classical and popular music in his career and his songs. Trained as a pianist at the Cleveland Conservatory, he went on to become a vaudeville pianist and then a staff composer for M. Witmark & Sons, becoming so valuable to the firm that he was signed to a twenty-year con-tract. He wrote—and sang himself in vaudeville—such successful songs as "Will You Love Me in December as You Do in May?" (1905) and "Love Me and the World Is Mine" (1906), and his classical training enabled him to write somewhat more sophisticated songs, popular in recitals and in the parlors of the genteel, including "Mother Machree" (1910), "When Irish Eyes Are Smiling" (1913), and "A Little Bit of Heaven" (1914).

Songs of this sort were attractive to a somewhat different audience from the one frequenting variety houses, and remind us that the song style of the 1890s and the 1900s, despite the strong trend of the time toward homogeneity, was still sprinkled with some variety.

The centralization of the popular music industry in New York and the de-velopment of new marketing techniques revolutionized the business of popular

Sung with Great Success by
GEO. DONALDSON
OF THE SYMPHONY QUARTETTE

YOU'RE THE FLOWER OF MY HEART,

SWEET ADELINE

Ballad & Refrain.

WORDS BY
RICHARD H.
GERARD.

MUSIC BY
HENRY W.
ARMSTRONG.

M. WITMARK & SONS

One of the great products of early Tin Pan Alley, "Sweet Adeline" (1903).

music. Sheet music sold in previously unimaginable quantities, and significant amounts of money could be made by enterprising, imaginative, and aggressive music publishers. These publishers became the most powerful force in the business, determining what songs and even what kinds of songs were to be published. By the first decade of the new century, musical trends in popular song were largely controlled by a relatively small number of men—mostly in New York— who through talent, energy, and business sense had established a virtual monopoly on popular music.

These publishers were city people, many of them first-generation Americans with little contact with American life and culture outside of New York City, and little or no knowledge of the Anglo-American and Afro-American music that was the native musical language of many millions of Americans.

Tin Pan Alley music quickly penetrated to all parts of America and delighted most people who heard it. In time, many of the songs of Tin Pan Alley passed into oral tradition, as songs that people heard, remembered, sang from memory, even taught to other people. "Take Me Out to the Ball Game," written in 1908 by a man (Albert Von Tilzer, brother of Harry) who had no interest in baseball but wrote a song about the game in the hope that it would "catch on," has become a part of American tradition, sung—by memory, by ear—by millions of people each year. Similarly, many Americans know and can sing "Sweet Adeline," "Down by the Old Mill Stream," "When Irish Eyes Are Smiling," "The Sidewalks of New York," and many other products of the first decades of Tin Pan Alley, without knowing who composed them or associating them with any particular era.

Tin Pan Alley did not draw on traditional music—it created traditional music.

FOURTEEN

"It's Only a Paper Moon";
OR.
The Golden Years of Tin Pan Alley

Bread lines seemed less burdensome if one could sing. Somehow, political chaos was less unsettling if you hummed through its storms. And Armageddon couldn't threaten us if we kept whistling Bye Bye Blackbird.[1]

I'd rather have a Paper Doll to call my own,
Than have a fickle-minded real live girl.[2]

Jerome Kern and I were one time contemplating writing a musical version of Donn Byrne's Messer Marco Polo. *Discussing the general problems of adaptation, I confronted Jerry with what I considered to be a serious question about the score. I said, "Here is a story laid in China about an Italian and told by an Irishman. What kind of music are you going to write?" Jerry answered, "It'll be good Jewish music."*[3]

THE ERA marked off roughly by America's involvement in the two great world wars of the twentieth century was one of the peaks of the entire 200-year history

---

1. *100 Best Songs of the '20s and '30s*, with an Introduction by Richard Rodgers (New York: Harmony Books, 1973), p. xiv.
2. Johnny S. Black, "Paper Doll" (1942).
3. Jerome Kern, *The Jerome Kern Song Book*, ed. with an Introduction by Oscar Hammerstein II (New York: Simon and Schuster, 1955), p. 3.

of popular song in America. Scores of talented songwriters and lyricists turned out hundreds of songs that delighted, charmed, and soothed not only their fellow Americans, but much of the rest of the Western world as well. This music penetrated deep into American culture; one need merely mention the names of several American songwriters of the period—George Gershwin, Irving Berlin, Jerome Kern, Cole Porter, Richard Rodgers, Harry Warren—to be reminded of the brilliance of this era and of the role these men and their songs played in the continuing emergence of a uniquely American culture.

Yet this era represents a single chapter in the continually unfolding story of popular song in America, linked at its beginning to the more-than-a-century-old tradition of American song and giving way at its conclusion to yet another musical style. It was neither the beginning nor the end of American popular song, and it will be treated in the present book in the same way all other eras have been—as a single link in the unbroken chain of styles and events that make up the narrative with which this book is concerned.

Most eras of popular song in America have been dominated by one or another of the national or ethnic groups making up the complex web of American society—the English, the Irish, the Italians, the Germans, the Africans. The period with which the present chapter is concerned was no exception; it was dominated by Jewish Americans, and represents one of the first great contributions to American culture by the New York Jewish community, which was to be at the center of so much of America's cultural and artistic life in the twentieth century.

Jews had made up a tiny portion of the American population since shortly after the settling of the land. Coming mostly from Great Britain and the Germanic countries, they settled in urban areas, many of them becoming shopkeepers, merchants, and small-business men. Others were active in the arts, many as performing musicians and teachers of music in various American cities and towns. Though scattered through various parts of the country, they were particularly prominent in New Orleans and in New York City, which had a Jewish population of some 80,000 by the 1880s.

They had been involved in popular song in this country almost from the beginning. John Braham, singer and songwriter of the early nineteenth century, and Henry Russell, the most important songwriter in America before Stephen Foster, were Jews. And they had played a particularly important role in the first decades of Tin Pan Alley: Charles K. Harris, Monroe Rosenfeld, and Edward B. Marks were successful composers in the first years of the era; and Harris, Marks, Lew Bernstein, and Maurice Shapiro were only the most notable of the American Jews who established successful music publishing houses in the formative years of Tin Pan Alley.

The Jewish population of the United States increased dramatically in the decades surrounding the turn of the century, as a result of a series of events set in motion by the assassination of Alexander II, czar of Russia, on March 1, 1881.

The historic oppression of the Russian Jews had been moderated under Alexander, but his successor, Alexander III, did little to curb a rising tide of anti-Semitism sweeping over the land. Jews fled Russia by the millions, seeking refuge elsewhere; American immigration laws permitted several million to come to the States, and by 1910 there were more than a million Jews in New York City alone, making up more than a quarter of the population.

Most of these new immigrants were poorly schooled, and they encountered a certain amount of anti-Semitism even here. Life in New York was often desperate at first; but their native intelligence, aptitudes, skills, and determination enabled many of them to achieve financial and professional success within a decade or two, and soon entire fields—real estate, the clothing industry, entertainment—were dominated and altered by their successful pursuit of a sort of life denied them in Eastern Europe for so many centuries.

Vaudeville and other forms of popular American theater would have been quite different, and much poorer, without such entertainers as Sophie Tucker, Al Jolson, George Jessel, Eddie Cantor, Jack Benny, Ted Lewis, George Burns, Fanny Brice, Milton Berle, and hundreds of others. New York's vaudeville circuit was dominated largely by such ambitious and imaginative men as the Schuberts, Marcus Loewe, and Adolph Zukor. The Hollywood movie industry was built up mostly by the "Moguls," Jewish Americans such as Louis B. Mayer, Samuel Goldwyn, William Fox, the Warner brothers, and the Selznicks, described by a recent historian as

> Often vulgar, crude, and overbearing, they were brilliantly attuned to the needs of their business; they commanded and used to the full a profound instinct for the common denominator of taste; and they left a deep imprint on American popular culture. Trusting their own minds and hearts, shrewd enough not to pay too much attention to the talented or cultivated men they hired, the Moguls knew which appeal to sentiment, which twirl of fantasy, which touch of violence, which innuendo of sexuality, would grasp native American audiences. It was something of a miracle and something of a joke.[4]

As the present chapter will detail, Jewish Americans had dominated another form of entertainment—popular song—for several decades before the Moguls built their movie dynasties, anticipating their astonishing grasp of "the common denominator of taste." Unlike the Moguls, these songwriters worked in a field with a long and successful tradition, which they carefully used as the basis for their own creations. And they were anything but "vulgar, crude, and overbearing."

Various theories have been set forward to explain the astonishing success of Jewish Americans in the various areas of entertainment in the first half of the twentieth century. They were, first of all, talented. Certainly another factor was

4. Irving Howe, *World of Our Fathers* (New York: Harcourt, Brace, Jovanovich, 1976), p. 165.

that Jews already held important posts in the entertainment world, and thus the new immigrants did not encounter the iron wall of anti-Semitism that met them elsewhere.

> Just as blacks would later turn to baseball and basketball knowing that here at least their skin color counted for less than their skills, so in the early 1900's young Jews broke into vaudeville because here too people asked not, who are you? but what can you do? It was a roughneck sort of egalitarianism, with little concern for those who might go under, but at best it gave people a chance to show their gifts.[5]

Even the most cursory biographical survey of the leading songwriters, lyricists, performers, and publishers of popular song in the first half of the twentieth century underlines the domination of Jewish Americans. More important, their cultural and musical heritage colored their products, giving them a flavor quite different from that of earlier popular songs and bringing yet another ethnic strain to the already polygenous style of American song.

If a single songwriter were to be chosen to epitomize the era, it would certainly be Irving Berlin. He wrote songs from the very beginning of the period through to the end (and even into the next era); his songs represent all of the various types that characterized these years; and dozens of his songs were among the most popular products of the Tin Pan Alley years. Furthermore, his career and his music point up the strong links between the first and second generations of Tin Pan Alley, and the emergence of a somewhat different song style in the 1920s and '30s.

Born Israel Baline in Temun, Russia in 1888, he came to America when his father, a cantor, fled the Cossack pogroms in 1892. Settling in New York City's Lower East Side, which was rapidly becoming a haven for Russian Jews, the family lived in desperate poverty at first; Berlin's rise to fame and fortune is one of the great American success stories.

> The tale of Berlin has a lilt to it for those who see it as a microcosm of this nation's history. If we keep green the memory of those gallant adventurers who first wrung a living from this resisting land, if there be a challenge for us still in the coming of the longboat that rescued the desperate settlement at Jamestown or in the gaze of the wondering priests who first sailed down the Mississippi,—well, here is a fresh reminder that the romance of America is an unfinished story. The life of Irving Berlin is a part of the American epic and the epic is still in the making.[6]

He was on the streets of New York by the age of eight, selling newspapers, and by fourteen he had left home for good, making a living as a saloon pianist and sing-

5. Ibid., p. 557.
6. Alexander Woollcott, *The Story of Irving Berlin* (New York: G. P. Putnam's Sons, 1925), p. 222.

ing waiter. If he had formal musical training beyond what he picked up from his father, the fact has escaped his biographers. He had his first steady job on Tin Pan Alley at sixteen, plugging songs for the Harry Von Tilzer publishing firm; his first published song, "Marie from Sunny Italy" (1907), was written in collaboration with Nick Nicholson, pianist at Pelham's Café in Chinatown. Hired as a staff lyricist for the Ted Snyder publishing house in 1909, he collaborated with Snyder on many songs in the ensuing several years.

A photograph taken in 1917 of Irving Berlin in uniform, flanked by Ed Wynn (left) and Sam H. Harris.

Ragtime songs were the craze, and Berlin turned them out by the dozens: "Yiddle on Your Fiddle, Play Some Ragtime" (1909), "That Mesmerizing Mendelssohn Tune" (1909), "Stop That Rag" (1910), "Dat Draggy Rag" (1910), "Oh, That Beautiful Rag" (1910), and "Ragtime Violin" (1911) all enjoyed some degree of success as vaudeville songs and as sheet music published by Ted Snyder. The idiom was ragtime as seen through the eyes of Tin Pan Alley, of course. Berlin probably never heard true ragtime as played by the great black ragtime pianists of the day, but he knew, very well, the popular ragtime songs that skimmed off several superficial elements of the ragtime style and transplanted them into otherwise typical popular songs.

"Alexander's Ragtime Band," written and published in 1911, shot the young songwriter to the top of the struggling heap of aspiring composers. Scholars have long since put the song in its proper stylistic perspective ("It is now an old story that *Alexander's Ragtime Band* not only had nothing to do with the

Sheet music cover of Irving Berlin's incredibly successful "Alexander's Ragtime Band" (1911).

development of ragtime, but is actually a song with hardly a trace of ragtime in it."7), but audiences and critics of the day were swept away by it:

> How much ragtime had been sung and played before, no man may calculate; it had been heard in every minstrel show, and its musical elements were thoroughly familiar. What was needed was a crystallization, was one

7. Sigmund Spaeth, *A History of Popular Music in America* (New York: Random House, 1948), p. 376.

song which should take the whole dash and energy of ragtime and carry it to its apotheosis; with a characteristic turn of mind Berlin accomplished this in a song which had no other topic than ragtime itself. *Alexander's Ragtime Band* appeared with its bow to negro music and its introduction of *Swanee River;* it was simple and passionate and utterly unsentimental and the whole country responded to its masterful cry, *Come on and hear!*[8]

A million and a half copies sold quickly, Berlin's reputation as a songwriter was firmly established, and the remainder of his career has been simply success after success.

The overwhelming success of "Alexander's Ragtime Band" bore two immediate fruits: Ted Snyder made Berlin a partner in his publishing firm, and Berlin was in immediate and great demand as a performer. He had been on the vaudeville stage before, most notably in *Up and Down Broadway* (1910), for which he had written "Oh! That Beautiful Rag" as a featured song for himself. Now he was booked into Oscar Hammerstein's Victoria Theater on Times Square, and given a choice of other engagements. Honored at a dinner at the Friars Club in New York, Berlin was introduced by none other than George M. Cohan, the most powerful figure in the American musical theater of the day, who introduced him as "a Jew boy that had named himself after an English actor and a German city" and went on to praise him in characteristic style:

> Irvy writes a great song. He writes a song with a good lyric, a lyric that rhymes, good music, music you don't have to dress up to listen to, but it is good music. He is a wonderful little fellow, wonderful in lots of ways. He has become famous and wealthy, without wearing a lot of jewelry and falling for funny clothes. He is uptown, but he is there with the old downtown hard sell.[9]

Making his first overseas appearance in London later that year, Berlin arrived to find even the newsboys whistling "Alexander's Ragtime Band," and the English press hailing him as the "father of ragtime." Back in America, he found the demand for new songs and shows more than even he, one of the most prolific composers in the history of American song, could keep up with. The most famous entertainers of the day—Al Jolson, Eddie Cantor, and others—vied for his new songs. He wrote for the glorified vaudeville style of the Ziegfeld Follies and for musical plays that, following Cohan's lead, were held together by at least a thread of a plot. C. B. Dillingham persuaded him to write music for a revue featuring Irene and Vernon Castle, *Watch Your Step* (1914); another revue, *Stop! Look! Listen!* (1916) starred Gaby Deslys, the great French entertainer, and introduced one of Berlin's most perennially popular songs, "The Girl on the Magazine Cover." America's entry into World War I found him a draftee at

8. Gilbert Vivian Seldes, *The Seven Lively Arts* (New York: Harper & Brothers, 1924; repr. New York: Sagamore Press, 1957), p. 71.

9. Quoted in Woollcott, p. 95.

Camp Upton, a mere private undergoing basic training, but at the urging of the commanding general he wrote the book and songs for a show, *Yip, Yip, Yaphank*, that netted some $80,000 for the war effort and also yielded "Oh, How I Hate to Get Up in the Morning," another million-and-a-half-copy seller for the still-young songwriter.

Berlin's most successful songs to this point were mostly fast, rhythmic numbers invoking some semblance of ragtime rhythm, cast in the inevitable song form of Tin Pan Alley: a verse (or maybe two) sketching a situation or a vignette; and a chorus, almost always of 16 or 32 measures, consisting of the most memorable music, the tune that would come to mind if the title of the song were mentioned. Writers still spoke of him as a composer of ragtime, and more and more a new word, jazz, was used in connection with his songs.

As the man who took ragtime when it was little more than a mannerism of the pianists in the rathskellers and bordellos and made it into a custom of the country, there must, of course, be a chapter on Irving Berlin in any history of the new music. For jazz is ragtime gone daffy. [10]

My feeling is simply this,—whether you like it or not, and wherever it eventually leads us, the sensitive student of musical development in this country must surely recognize the fact that our contemporary popular music, inadequately labeled "jazz," is the first spontaneous musical expression of the United States of America and as such deserves attention. . . . To my mind, the importance of Berlin lies not only in the fact that he is pure gold, but also in that he must be regarded as a pioneer (in jazz). [11]

Jazz historians of today wince at such words; their definitions of jazz exclude Berlin and other writers of popular songs, and indeed see such music as exploitive of the black American and his music. But the view from New York, in the 1920s, was quite different.

Despite the phenomenal success of his "ragtime" and "jazz" songs, Berlin was not content to write new songs endlessly in the same mold. "When I Lost You" (1912), written after the death of his first wife Dorothy on their honeymoon trip to Cuba, was a slow, sentimental song quite different in mood—if not in form—from his more popular numbers; and more and more of his songs after World War I were slower in tempo and more lyric in their melodic lines. Eventually such songs came to be called ballads, to distinguish them from faster songs in dance rhythms and tempos. "A Pretty Girl Is Like a Melody" (1919), written for the Ziegfeld Follies of 1919, was his first postwar ballad and one of his greatest all-time hit songs. "All By Myself" (1921), "All Alone" (1924), "What'll I Do" (1924), "Always" (1925), "Blue Skies" (1927), "Where Is the Song of Songs for Me?" (1928), and "How Deep Is the Ocean?" (1932) are only a few of his ballads that helped change the taste of the American public from the rhythmic,

10. Ibid., p. 216.
11. Ibid., p. 212.

dance-oriented songs of the 1910s to the slower, more introspective ballads that formed the core of the popular song repertory between the wars.

Shortly after World War I, Berlin severed his decade-long partnership with Ted Snyder and set up his own publishing firm in partnership with Max Winslow. With Sam H. Harris, a longtime collaborator of George M. Cohan, he opened the Music Box, a theater for the production of his own shows; the first *Music Box Revue* (1921) featured such new songs as "Say It with Music." His publishing firm prospered, both with his own songs—"What'll I Do" was the first of these that he published himself to sell more than a million copies—and with those by other songwriters. Like his successful predecessors, Berlin had a "nose" for songs that would sell well; "Tuck Me to Sleep in My Old 'Tucky Home" (1921) by George M. Meyer, a song now thoroughly forgotten, sold more than 2,000,000 copies in rather short order after Berlin selected it and brought it out as one of his early publications.

The late 1920s saw the emergence of an exciting, wide-open, new medium of entertainment, the sound movie. *The Jazz Singer* (1927) was the first spectacular demonstration of the potential of the "talkie," grossing the unprecedented sum of some three million dollars for its producers, Warner Brothers. Much of the movie was still silent, but sound was introduced at critical points, most memorably when the star, Al Jolson (portraying a cantor's son in New York who becomes a successful singer of "jazz" songs), sang several songs already popularized on the vaudeville stage: "My Mammy," from the show *Sinbad* (1920), with words by Joe Young and Sam Lewis and music by Walter Donaldson; "Toot, Toot, Tootsie," from *Bombo* (1922), by Gus Kahn, Ernie Erdman, and Dan Russo; and the more recent "Blue Skies" (1927) by Berlin. *The Coconuts* (1929), starring the Marx Brothers, was the first movie to feature music by Irving Berlin; it was essentially a filming of the musical of the same name which had run for 377 performances in New York after its opening in December of 1925. Many of Berlin's songs written for the stage version were incorporated into the film, with only "When My Dreams Come True" written specifically for the movie.

Like so many songwriters who had previously composed mostly for vaudeville and musical comedy, Berlin channeled much of his creative energy into film music in the 1930s and '40s. *Mammy* and *Puttin' on the Ritz*, both of 1930, had new songs by Berlin. *Top Hat* (1935), starring Fred Astaire and Ginger Rogers, featured such successful songs as "Cheek to Cheek" and "Top Hat, White Tie and Tails"; *Follow the Fleet* (1936), *On the Avenue* (1937), *Carefree* (1938), and *Second Fiddle* (1939) were major movies, each introducing several songs by Berlin that went on to become perennial favorites. *Holiday Inn* of 1942, starring Bing Crosby and Fred Astaire, introduced "White Christmas," one of the most popular songs of the entire twentieth century, as well as "Be Careful, It's My Heart," "Let's Start the New Year Right," and half a dozen others of exceptional merit. *Easter Parade* (1948), with Fred Astaire and Judy Garland, demonstrated the power of the cinema to popularize even older songs: the title song, first written for the show *As Thousands Cheer* in 1933, enjoyed a second round of success after the movie came out.

Writing songs for movies did not preclude Berlin's continuing his career as one of the most successful writers for the musical stage. Two revues, both with books by Moss Hart, were among the most acclaimed works of the 1930s: *Face the Music* (1932), introducing "Let's Have Another Cup of Coffee" and "How Deep Is the Ocean?"; and *As Thousands Cheer* (1933), featuring Clifton Webb and Ethel Waters, with such songs as "Easter Parade," "Heat Wave," and "Not for All the Rice in China." Berlin's most successful musical comedies came late in his career: *Louisiana Purchase* (1940), with a book by Morrie Ryskind and a cast featuring Victor Moore and Vera Zorina, had an opening run of 444 performances; *This Is the Army* (1942), the World War II successor to *Yip, Yip, Yaphank*, had a cast made up mostly of members of the armed services and a

Bing Crosby singing Irving Berlin's "White Christmas" to Marjorie Reynolds in a scene from the film *Holiday Inn* (1942).

string of excellent songs, including one of the best ballads, "I Left My Heart at the Stage Door Canteen"; *Annie Get Your Gun* (1946), one of the legends of Broadway with its first run of 1147 performances, had one of his most memorable scores, including "They Say It's Wonderful," "The Girl That I Marry," "There's No Business Like Show Business," and "Doin' What Comes Naturally."

When Berlin wrote his first songs, the phonograph industry was in its infancy. Because of technical limitations, most popular music chosen for recording was instrumental rather than vocal—ragtime pieces, marches, a wide variety of dances. But Enrico Caruso demonstrated that vocal music could be commercially successful; between 1906, when he recorded his first operatic aria, and 1921, the year of his death, his discs sold so phenomenally well that he himself earned some two million dollars from his recordings. The sale of discs of popular songs increased steadily through the 1910s, with such singers as Bill Murray, Edna Brown, Henry Burr, and above all Al Jolson enjoying success and profit from their recordings, and with the major recording companies slowly strengthening their popular catalogs. Such success had been made possible by the introduction of the 12-inch, 78-rpm disc in 1902, on which up to four minutes of music could be recorded—enough for the typical popular song of the day. It cost considerably less than the cylinder of earlier times and became even more of a bargain when Victor and Columbia began using both sides of the disc in 1904, thus giving the customer two songs for little more than the price of one.

It was not until 1919 that the potential of the phonograph recording as a mass disseminator of popular song was demonstrated in dramatic fashion: an almost unknown songwriter by the name of George Stoddard persuaded Victor to record his song "Mary," still in manuscript, and to the astonishment of almost everyone the disc sold some 300,000 copies, bringing Stoddard royalty payments of some $15,000. Later that year—on November 20, in New York—a group calling itself Selvin's Novelty Orchestra (after its leader, Ben Selvin, violinist and vocalist) cut a historic disc (Victor 18633) of the song "Dardanella" by Fred Fisher (words) and Felix Barnard and Johnny S. Black (music)—historic because it was the first recording of a popular song to sell in the neighborhood of a million copies. Even this staggering figure was soon topped: Victor 18690, a coupling of "Whispering" (words by Malvin Schonberger, music by John Schonberger) and "The Japanese Sandman" (words by Raymond B. Egan, music by Richard A. Whiting) as recorded by Paul Whiteman and his Ambassador Orchestra in Camden, New Jersey, in August of 1920, sold more than *two* million copies.

Irving Berlin's first top-selling phonograph recording was apparently Eddie Cantor's version of "You'd Be Surprised" from the *Ziegfeld Follies of 1919*, recorded in New York in December of 1919 and released as Emerson 10102. By the mid-1920s, sales of phonograph records of certain songs approached and even surpassed the sale of sheet music. "What'll I Do" (1924) sold more than a million copies of sheet music, and also more than a million discs as recorded by such singers as Henry Burr, Lewis James, and Paul Specht, and by Paul Whiteman's orchestra. Berlin's own figures are dramatic evidence of this new phenomenon:[12]

Song	Sheet Music Sales	Phonograph Discs
"You'd Be Surprised" (1919)	783,982	888,790
"Nobody Knows" (1919)	1,143,690	843,062
"Say It with Music" (1921)	374,408	1,239,050
"All By Myself" (1921)	1,053,493	1,225,083

Two decades later, Berlin's "White Christmas" (1942) was to demonstrate even more the staggering sales potential of the phonograph record. Within five years of publication, more than 3 million copies of sheet music had been sold, and more than 5 million discs. But this was only the beginning of the story: Bing Crosby's recording alone (Decca 18429) eventually sold more than 25 million copies, and by the end of 1976, more than 108 million copies of various recordings of the song had been sold in the United States and Canada, and another 25 million in various other countries.

Berlin's career as a songwriter extended well into the eras of commercial radio and television. From a modest beginning in 1920, with stations only in Pittsburgh (KDKA) and Detroit (WWJ), radio expanded to include some 500 stations in all parts of the country by 1922, and this number was doubled in the following five years. Popular music was programmed on radio from its beginning, with broadcasts of bands from hotel nightclubs and singers from the studios. Many popular performers of the 1920s, such as "Whispering Jack" Smith and Lanny Ross, made their reputations exclusively on radio. "Your Hit Parade," a program featuring the top hit songs of the previous week, came to the networks in 1935 and rapidly established itself as one of the most listened-to shows in the brief history of the medium. Experimental television began in 1930, with commercial stations first licensed in 1941. By 1949, there were some 200,000 TV sets in the United States, most of them concentrated in major cities, and in the following decade the medium spread to almost every corner of the country. Variety shows offered popular music from their inception, and in 1950, "Your Hit Parade" was moved from radio to television.

Thus, Berlin's career spanned the time when several new media for the dissemination of popular song—the sound movie, radio, the phonograph record, television—brought about radical changes in the business of music, the several industries concerned with the reproduction and marketing of the product produced by songwriter and lyricist. By the middle of the twentieth century, the size and wealth of the music industry had swollen to proportions unimaginable to even the most ambitious publishers in the early years of Tin Pan Alley. But these new and sweeping technological developments sparked no new styles or forms of

12. Figures given in Woollcott, p. 147.

popular song. Songs written by Irving Berlin in 1915 are essentially the same as those written thirty years later; continuity of musical style is one of the most striking features of the Tin Pan Alley era. One can hear this with one's own ears, or reflect on the many songs that have remained popular for decades, or were revived after a long hiatus and were indistinguishable from the most recent inventions. For instance:

> *Variety* magazine, reviewing in its issue of December 23, 1953, a newly released album, *The Eddie Cantor Story*, commented that "Cantor's singing style on the 1917 waxing was just about the same as it is today and the songs might easily be current pops."
>
> In 1946, Decca released an LP album, *Al Jolson*, with a song repertory mostly from the late 1910s and the 1920s, which became the best-selling LP according to *Billboard*'s popularity charts, remained in the No. 1 spot for 25 weeks, and was among the 10 most popular albums for 65 consecutive weeks. *Al Jolson—Volume 2* (1947) and *Al Jolson—Volume 3* (1948) also became No. 1 hits, holding the top spot in *Billboard*'s charts for 10 and 14 weeks, respectively.
>
> Irving Berlin's "God Bless America," one of the most popular songs of 1939–40 (and since), was actually written in 1917, in essentially the same form in which it was published more than twenty years later.
>
> "Peg o' My Heart," written by Fred Fisher in 1913, was revived in 1947, became a No. 1 single disc as performed by the Harmonicats, was featured on "Your Hit Parade" for 20 weeks, and for 14 consecutive weeks held the first or second spot on this show.
>
> "You Belong to Me," written by Victor Herbert in 1916 for the opretta *The Century Girl*, became a top-selling single in 1952, as sung by Jo Stafford, appeared on "Your Hit Parade" for 19 consecutive weeks, and was also recorded successfully by Dean Martin and Pattie Page.

These are a mere handful of the examples that could be cited to support the contention that the style of Tin Pan Alley songs was constant throughout the creative lifetime of Irving Berlin and remained constant in the face of the most astounding technological changes yet experienced since popular song became part of American life shortly after the American Revolution. There would seem to be two explanations for this persistence of style at a time when every other aspect of the popular-music industry was fluid and even revolutionary, one political and one musical.

ASCAP (the American Society of Composers, Authors and Publishers) was founded in 1914 in an attempt to force restaurants, theaters, and other establishments featuring live music to pay fees for the public use of music. To that point, copyright protection covered only the purchase and mechanical reproduction of published compositions. Composers, lyricists, and publishers received no compensation from live performances of their music. After a series of legal battles eventually reaching the Supreme Court, the young organization won its case (in a ruling handed down on January 22, 1917), and all hotels, theaters, dance halls, cabarets, and restaurants were required to obtain a license from ASCAP—for a fee—before they could play a piece written by a composer or published by a publishing house belonging to the organization. In time, similar rulings were handed down in cases involving radio stations and motion picture studios. The ASCAP membership increased dramatically in the 1920s, eventually including all important publishing houses and almost all of the leading composers and lyricists of the day, and by the mid-1930s some $10,000,000 in licensing fees were paid annually, most of the money being distributed to the membership according to a complex rating system. The recording industry was already obligated to pay fees to composers and publishers, under the "mechanical reproduction" clause of the copyright law of 1909, which had fixed a fee of 2¢ per disc or cylinder to be paid to the copyright owner.

The net effect of these several developments was that each of the new media—the phonograph record, radio, the sound movie—obtained its music from ASCAP composers and publishers, whose chief concern, quite naturally, was with the type of music already being produced, rather than with new types of music perhaps more appropriate to the several media. Putting matters in the simplest possible terms, the songs performed on radio and in the movies were written in a style born in vaudeville and other forms of musical theater in the late nineteenth and early twentieth centuries. There is no way to tell, from listening to a song by Irving Berlin or any of his contemporaries, whether it was written for vaudeville, musical comedy, the movies, or simply composed for radio play and possibly recording. The exploitation of the characteristic and differing potentials of each of the new media would wait for a later time.

The second reason for the persistence of a single musical style in the popular songs of the Tin Pan Alley era is simply that this style was a vital, viable, successful, somewhat flexible, and relatively new one. Changes in musical style, in popular song as in other forms of music, tend to come about when the prevailing style has been in use for a considerable period of time, when composers and audiences feel that it is beginning to be exhauusted, when it has lost its "cutting edge," as Virgil Thomson once put it. The 1910s, '20s, and '30s saw a large number of extremely talented songwriters exploiting a song style that had not yet grown old, that still seemed to them to be perfectly suitable to express what they wanted to express, that could still be modified in its details enough for each of them to carve out a somewhat distinctive profile.

The first half of the twentieth century thus saw a conflict between two cycles—a musical one, still in its strong and formative stages, and a technological one, just beginning, that made possible, at least in theory, some radically new concepts in song. In this instance, musical impulses proved to be stronger than technology.

Irving Berlin's contribution to American song has been summed up thus:

He represented, in song, every phase of musical fashion for forty-five years or more. . . . This is not to say that he was the best writer in each and every area of popular music. . . . Let it be said that he is the best all-around song writer America has ever had. In this area or that, I will say, and have said, that I believe so-and-so to be the master. But I can speak of only one composer as the master of the entire range of popular song—Irving Berlin.[13]

The range of his songs, in content and mood, if not in form, is enormous, from his early dialect and spirited "ragtime" songs, to his sentimental ballads, to the many songs written at all periods of his career that exploit one type of humor or another. Some take on a bit of the flavor of ragtime, of the blues, of country-western music, Latin-American music, or jazz. In an era that had almost forgotten the waltz, he wrote a succession of excellent, sentimental waltz-songs harking back to the first decades of Tin Pan Alley, including such perennial hits as "What'll I Do?," "Always," and "The Girl That I Marry." Some of his earliest songs represent the final phase in the century-long history of the minstrel song: his ragtime songs and such others as "I Want to Be in Dixie" (1912) and "When It's Night Time in Dixie Land" (1914) were written for Jewish blackface vaudeville performers ("Black became a mask for Jewish expressiveness, with one woe speaking through the voice of another."[14]). But through all of this, Berlin turned out a steady stream of slow, lyric, sentimental songs that have retained their popularity after other types have become dated and forgotten, songs that prompted his most recent biographer[15] to label him "America's Number One Balladeer," and that brought the following comment from a sympathetic contemporary:

It may be the inheritance of his tribe in Irving Berlin that tinges so many of his songs with the mournfulness of solitude and self-pity. But somewhere within him the voice of the publisher also whispers reassuringly that sadness is rather apt to sell better than gayety in the song market.[16]

Though he was one of the few songwriters of the era to write his own lyrics, he has been sparing with words otherwise: he has had absolutely nothing to say about himself, his songs, his working methods, his opinions of the songs of other writers. It is said that he never learned to read music, that he works by ear at the piano, that he has always employed an assistant to write down and perhaps arrange his songs. Almost from the beginning of his songwriting career, there were persistant rumors that his songs were ghostwritten, or were at the least heavily dependent on assistance from musicians with more technical knowledge. Characteristically, he has never acknowledged these rumors or commented on them; but several persons close to him have described his working methods in detail, reaching the conclusion,

13. Alec Wilder, *American Popular Song: The Great Innovators, 1900–1950,* ed. and with an Introduction by James T. Maher (New York: Oxford University Press, 1972), pp. 119–20.
14. Howe, p. 563.
15. Michael Freedland, *Irving Berlin* (New York: Stein & Day, 1974).
16. Woollcott, p. 157.

So, though it is known that he has for years paid a professional musician to harmonize his songs under close supervision, it is very nearly impossible, upon hearing some of these melodies, to believe that every chord was not an integral part of the creation of the tune.[17]

The phenomenal and perennial success of so many of his songs cannot be explained in technical, musical terms, any more than can the similar success of Stephen Foster. The explanation lies in his innate talent and in his "profound instinct for the common denominator of taste."[18] In the words of one of his peers:

> He honestly absorbs the vibrations emanating from the people, manners and life of his time, and in turn, gives these impressions back to the world,—simplified,—clarified,—glorified.[19]

Jerome Kern (1885–1945) was an almost exact contemporary of Berlin's, at least for the period when they were both creative; his songs were written in the same forms and in the same general harmonic and melodic language; many of his songs cannot be distinguished from those of Berlin by a listener who does not already know which of the two had written them. Despite all this, there are subtle and important differences in the careers and the compositions of the two, differences that remind us that even in a period when all songwriters willingly and comfortably filled their compositions in the same molds, there was still room for different personalities and individual tastes to express themselves.

The most obvious differences between the two are that Kern had a sound education in music and that he wrote almost from the beginning of his career for operetta and musical comedy, rather than for vaudeville and revue.

Somewhat of a prodigy, Kern was given early instruction in piano and organ by his mother, then studied at the New York College of Music and briefly in London, where, in 1903, he had his first experience in writing for the musical stage, turning out musical filler material for various shows. Back in New York, he served a lengthy apprenticeship in Tin Pan Alley, working as a shipping clerk for E. B. Marks, as a song plugger, and as a rehearsal pianist for a succession of musical shows. Though his first successful song was published in 1905—"How'd You Like to Spoon With Me?," interpolated into *The Earl and the Girl*—it was another decade before he began writing genuinely successful songs and was recognized as an important songwriter in the musical and dramatic circles of New York City. He wrote his first complete score for a musical play in 1912, *The Red Petticoat*, and his first unqualified hit song came in 1914, with "They Wouldn't Believe Me," sung by Julia Sanders in *The Girl from Utah*.

Nobody Home (1915) marked his first collaboration with Guy Bolton in what became a long string of highly successful musical shows at the Princess

17. Wilder, p. 93.
18. Howe, p. 165.
19. Jerome Kern, quoted in Woollcott, p. 215.

Theatre; others were *Very Good, Eddie* (1916), *Oh, Boy!* (1917)—which ran for 463 performances and saw Kern's first songs with lyrics by P. G. Wodehouse— *Have a Heart* (1917), *Leave It to Jane* (1917), *The Riviera Girl* (1917), *Oh, Lady! Lady!* (1918), *Oh, My Dear!* (1918), *Sally* (1921, 570 performances), and *Sitting Pretty* (1924). *Sally* featured Kern's most popular song to that point, "Look for the Silver Lining," with lyrics by Bud De Sylva. The Princess shows enjoyed such lengthy runs that Kern had time to compose songs for other shows as well.

Jerome Kern with Nancy Kelly on the set of *Caribbean Holiday* (1950).

He was, in fact, so much in demand and so well rewarded for his compositions that he commanded the highest annual income for songwriting alone of any American writer of the day; Edward B. Marks reported that during the period of World War I, Kern had an income of some $3,000 per week from his musical comedy scores alone.[20]

These musical comedies were among the most successful works of the genre in the decade after George M. Cohan had revolutionized the musical stage with his "musical plays," and represent a further step in defining and popularizing the American musical theater style. Their indebtedness to European operetta was still apparent:

20. Edward B. Marks, *They All Sang; From Tony Pastor to Rudy Vallée* (New York: The Viking Press, 1934), p. 191.

Kern . . . had his musical roots in the fertile middle European and English school of operetta writing, and amalgamated it with everything that was fresh in the American scene to give us something wonderfully new and clear in music writing in the world. Actually he was a giant with one foot in Europe and the other in America.[21]

Another immense stride forward came with *Show Boat* (1928), one of the great landmarks in American musical theater. American in theme and plot, its cast of characters included Southern belles, riverboat gamblers, wealthy plantation owners, and even blacks; it was an essentially serious work, leaving behind the gaiety and sophistication of so many earlier American musical comedies. The book and lyrics were by Oscar Hammerstein II, based on Edna Ferber's novel of the same name; Kern and Hammerstein had first worked together in *Sunny* (1925), which had a run of 517 performances and yielded the hit songs "Who?" and "Sunny." The sets and costumes of *Show Boat* were spectacular, the cast superb, the book tight and moving smoothly from large ensemble numbers involving the entire cast to effective dramatic climaxes, and Kern's score is arguably the best ever written for a musical comedy, with such superlative and perennially popular songs as "Why Do I Love You?," "Can't Help Lovin' dat Man," "Bill," "Make Believe," and "Ol' Man River." It opened at the Ziegfeld Theatre in New York on December 27, 1927, ran for 572 performances there, was revived for long and equally successful runs in 1932 and 1946, was made into a movie in 1929 and again in 1936, and has been singled out by critics and historians as pointing the way to a series of the most characteristically American musicals the stage has ever seen, in the ensuing half-century.

Unlike Stephen Foster and several other American songwriters who wrote their best pieces early in their careers, Kern became an even better and more successful composer as the years passed. *Show Boat* was followed by a succession of other successful musical comedies, each with superb songs: *The Cat and the Fiddle* (1931) brought such songs as "The Night Was Made for Love," to lyrics by Otto Harbach; *Music in the Air* (1932) featured songs written in collaboration with Hammerstein again, including "I've Told Ev'ry Little Star" and "The Song Is You"; *Roberta* (1933) introduced three of his very best songs—"Smoke Gets in Your Eyes," "Yesterdays," and "The Touch of Your Hand"—with lyrics by Harbach; and his last stage score, for *Very Warm for May* (1939), included "All the Things You Are."

Like Berlin, Kern wrote for Hollywood sound movies almost from the beginning of the history of this new form of entertainment. *Show Boat* was made into a movie in 1929, and other musical comedies of his were filmed in succeeding years. Beginning with the film *I Dream Too Much* (1935), most of his new songs were written for the movies; almost every film for which he composed brought one or more new hit songs. *Swing Time* (1936), starring Fred Astaire and Ginger Rogers, featured such Kern/Dorothy Fields songs as "The Way You Look

21. Kern, p. xii.

CAN'T HELP LOVIN' DAT MAN

FLORENZ ZIEGFELD

PRESENTS

SHOW BOAT

ADAPTED FROM EDNA FERBER'S NOVEL OF THE SAME NAME

BOOK & LYRICS BY

OSCAR HAMMERSTEIN 2nd

MUSIC BY

JEROME KERN

ENSEMBLES & DANCES BY
SAMMY LEE
SETTINGS BY
JOSEPH URBAN

Make Believe
Can't Help Lovin' Dat
    Man
Ol' Man River
Why Do I Love You?
Bill
You Are Love
SELECTION

T. B. HARMS
COMPANY
NEW YORK

Sheet music cover for one of the great popular songs from Jerome Kern's *Show Boat* (1927), "Can't Help Lovin' Dat Man."

Tonight" and "A Fine Romance." *High, Wide and Handsome* had songs written to lyrics by Hammerstein, including "The Folks Who Live on the Hill"; *Joy of Living* (1938) introduced "You Couldn't Be Cuter"; *Lady Be Good* (1941) brought one of his finest songs, "The Last Time I Saw Paris"; *You Were Never Lovlier* (1942) yielded "Dearly Beloved." *Cover Girl* (1944) had Kern collaborating with Ira Gershwin to produce such songs as "Long Ago and Far Away" (one of the most successful songs in the entire history of "Your Hit Parade," remaining on the show for twenty consecutive weeks), and *Can't Help Singing* (1944) brought yet more new Kern songs, including "More and More." *Centennial Summer* (1946), released after his death, showed that he had retained his skill and talent to the very end, with "All Through the Day."

Almost all of Kern's songs, then, were written for the musical theater and films; he contributed one or more compositions to some 120 of these. Almost without exception, his most successful songs were lyric ballads, drawing as much on the tradition of European operetta as on indigenous American song. The sentimental waltz-song was all the rage when Kern began composing, but few of his songs were of this sort; when the ragtime craze swept over Tin Pan Alley, he mostly disdained it; few of his songs of the 1920s and '30s use the traces of jazz flavoring so popular with many of his peers. He was in this regard a much more limited composer than Berlin, yet by any method of calculation his list of "top hit" songs is fully as long as Berlin's. In assessing the contribution of these two men to American song style, it must be kept in mind that their first songs appeared several decades before those of most of the songwriters to be discussed and mentioned later—Gershwin, Porter, Rodgers, Nacio Herb Brown, Harry Warren—and to the extent that there is a general similarity of style in the songs of all these men, Berlin and Kern wrote the songs that served as models for their somewhat younger contemporaries.

There are technical differences between Kern's songs and those of Irving Berlin. Kern was more a master of pure melody, able to create tunes that progress, move, rise to peaks, and descend from these so naturally and effectively that his technique, mastered over so many years of apprenticeship, passes unnoticed. To the writer who has most thoroughly studied the music of this era,

> Kern does exemplify the pure, uncontrived melodic line more characteristically than any other writer of American theater music. Long before I knew the first thing about music, I knew his melodies. They pleased me, they even haunted me. . . . Even when he did use more elaborate harmony, and I had become involved myself in the excitement of lush harmonic patterns, I didn't need to know or hear his harmony in order to enjoy thoroughly his lovely melodic flights.[22]

An even more obvious contribution to American song style, hinted at in the quotation above, was his use of more complex and sophisticated chords and harmonic changes than had been used by the first generation of Tin Pan Alley songwriters. This point will be developed in a later section of this chapter, dealing with the musical characteristics of songs of this era.

Kern not only had one foot in Europe and the other in America, he also—like Berlin—had a thorough knowledge of, and a respect for, the songs of the American songwriters preceding him. The early songs of these two men were the strongest link connecting the first two generations of Tin Pan Alley.

22. Wilder, pp. 29–30.

Parts of the story of George Gershwin (1898–1937) need not be told in detail here, since they so closely resemble those of so many other songwriters and lyricists of the era: birth, childhood, and early education in New York (Brooklyn, in Gershwin's case); early apprenticeship with a Tin Pan Alley publisher (Gershwin became a song plugger for the Jerome H. Remick Music Company in May of 1914); a thorough, practical knowledge of the song style of the day (Gershwin admired Irving Berlin, and one of his earliest compositions, "Ragging the Traumerei," was an emulation of Berlin's "That Mesmerizing Mendelssohn Tune"). An excellent pianist, Gershwin sometimes accompanied such singers as Louise Dresser and Nora Bayes in his early professional years, and he cut some 125 player-piano rolls in 1915 and the years following. His first published song was "When You Want 'Em, You Can't Get 'Em, When You Got 'Em, You Don't Want 'Em," to a lyric by Murray Roth, brought out by the Harry Von Tilzer house in 1916. His first stage song, "Making of a Girl," was written for *The Passing Show of 1916*, and the following year he was signed to an exclusive contract as house songwriter for the T. B. Harms publishing firm.

Like so many songwriters throughout the entire history of popular song, he was almost unknown until a single song brought him instant fame and fortune. In Gershwin's case, it was "Swanee," written in 1919 to a lyric by Irving Caesar. The latter's account of the early career of the song underlines the role played by top performers in popularizing a new composition:

> Funny thing about "Swanee." It was received with great enthusiasm, but it wasn't a hit right off the bat. The Capitol opening [of *Demitasse Revue*] was tremendous, and it was the largest theater in the world at that time. Sixty girls danced to "Swanee;" they had electric lights in their shoes. Arthur Pryor's band played it. Seventy in the band. Everyone on stage sang it. Everyone applauded. There were thousands of copies in the lobby—but they didn't sell.
>   One day Al Jolson gave a midnight party after a show at the Winter Garden. . . . George was invited up by Buddy De Sylva, with whom he also wrote songs. Buddy was a great friend of Jolson's and asked George to play for Jolson. At that party George played "Swanee," among several other numbers, and Jolson at once adopted it and introduced it within three or four days, and the rest is history. Jolson made "Swanee" a hit, the biggest hit song George has ever had. If Jolson hadn't performed it with that great warmth he had, it probably wouldn't have happened.[23]

The song rather quickly sold some million copies of sheet music for T. B. Harms; it also sold more than two million discs, as recorded by Jolson for Columbia, and by such other entertainers of the day as Yerke's Novelty Five, the All-Star Trio, and the Peerless Quartet. Gershwin was consequently in great demand to write for revues and other works for the musical theater. He wrote

23. Quoted in Robert Kimball and Alfred Simon, *The Gershwins* (New York: Atheneum, 1973), p. 24.

George Gershwin (1898–1937).

songs for *George White's Scandals* for the years 1920–24; one of his all-time hits, "Somebody Loves Me," was introduced in the last of these. 1924 also brought his first collaboration with his brother Ira as lyricist, in the show *Lady Be Good*; their partnership bore such immediate fruits as the title song and "Fascinating Rhythm," and the show—starring Fred and Adele Astaire—ran for 330 performances. *Tip Toes* (1925), *Oh, Kay!* (1926), *Funny Face* (1927), *Rosalie* (1928), *Treasure Girl* (1928), *Show Girl* (1929), *Strike Up the Band* (1930), *Girl Crazy* (1930), *Of Thee I Sing* (1931), *Let 'Em Eat Cake* (1933), and *Pardon My English*

(1933) all had songs by the Gershwin brothers, including such classics as "Someone to Watch Over Me," " 'S Wonderful," "Soon," "I Got Rhythm," "But Not for Me," and "Of Thee I Sing." These shows, in their popularity and the sustained excellence of their songs, may be said to be the 1920s equivalent of the Princess Theatre shows (with their Kern/Wodehouse songs) of a decade earlier.

Al Jolson singing "Swanee" in the movie based on Gershwin's life, *Rhapsody in Blue*.

Like Berlin and Kern, Gershwin turned to writing for Hollywood movies in the 1930s. The film *Delicious* (1931) was the first to feature new songs by him; *A Damsel in Distress* (1937) introduced "A Foggy Day," *Shall We Dance?* included "They Can't Take That Away from Me" among its new songs, and *The Goldwyn Follies*, released in 1938 after his death, brought "Love Walked In."

Thus far, Gershwin's story reads like that of many other songwriters of the Tin Pan Alley era, distinguished only by the magnitude of his success and the quality of his songs. But two things set him apart from his peers: his involvement with classical music and with jazz.

His training and musical activity mixed popular and classical idioms from early in his life. He developed a serious interest in music after hearing a classmate at Public School 25, Maxie Rosenzweig, play Dvořák's *Humoresque* on the violin at a school assembly. His piano teacher, Charles Hambitzer, insisted on a sound classical training and helped him build a reliable technique while exposing him to the music of Bach, Beethoven, Liszt, Chopin, and the moderns of the

Fred and Adele Astaire were starred in Gershwin's *Lady, Be Good!* (1924).

day, Debussy and Ravel. Throughout his career, even during the periods of his greatest success as a writer of popular songs, he insisted that there need not be an irreconcilable gap between popular and serious music, and attempted to write music that would reach listeners of both persuasions. *Blue Monday Blues*, which he thought of as a one-act opera, was written for *George White's Scandals of 1922*. He accompanied the soprano Eva Gauthier for a recital in Aeolian Hall on November 1, 1923, on which she programmed songs by Byrd, Purcell, and

Bellini, others by the contemporary composers Hindemith, Schoenberg, and Milhaud, and still others by Berlin, Kern, and Gershwin himself. His first large instrumental work, *Rhapsody in Blue*, written for "jazz" band and piano and orchestrated by Ferde Grofé, was premiered at Aeolian Hall on February 12, 1924, by Paul Whiteman's orchestra, with Gershwin as piano soloist. His *Concerto in F*, an even more ambitious work, was first done on December 3, 1925, at Carnegie Hall, by the New York Symphony Orchestra conducted by Walter Damrosch. He performed a set of piano preludes on a program given with the contralto Marguerite d'Alvarez in 1926; three of these were published and have been played often by concert pianists. A symphonic work, *An American in Paris*, was premiered on December 13, 1928, again by Damrosch; his *Second Rhapsody*, for piano and orchestra, was first done on January 29, 1932, by the Boston Symphony under Serge Koussevitzky. His most extended work, the full-length opera *Porgy and Bess*—based on a novel by Du Bose Heyward—was introduced at the Alvin Theater in New York on October 10, 1935.

The relevance of these pieces to the present book is that Gershwin, through his involvement with classical music, brought more harmonic innovation and sophistication to his songs than any of his contemporary songwriters, even including Jerome Kern, and his harmonic experimentation helped expand the style of some of his peers, who listened to what he was doing and learned from it.

Equally distinctive in his career was his affinity for the music of blacks. Almost alone of the Tin Pan Alley songwriters, he sought out black musicians, befriended them, listened to their music, played with them. He knew James Reese Europe (1881–1919), who had organized the first bands specializing in syncopated dance music in New York in 1905 and had been an important figure in the early days of the dance craze that brought the fox trot and similar dances to prominance; he was a frequent visitor to "Black Bohemia," the center of fashionable black life in New York, on the West Side of Manhattan; he knew the black ragtime pianists James P. Johnson and Luckey Roberts. He was particularly close to Will Vodery (1885–1951), musical supervisor of Florenz Ziegfeld's productions; it was Vodery who orchestrated Gershwin's *Blue Monday*, his first attempt at a "negro" opera. Carl van Vechten recalled that he and Gershwin went together to parties, concerts, and other events in Harlem in the early 1920s.[24] Another biographer comments:

> George Gershwin was certainly one of the earliest to seek out black music purely from personal interest. He soaked himself in it, and this early enthusiasm would contribute mightily to that special fusion of European and Negro elements that is the Gershwin style.[25]

Du Bose Heyward, author of the novel *Porgy* on which Gershwin's *Porgy and Bess* was based, recounted an incident occurring when Gershwin came South to

24. Edward Jablonski and Lawrence D. Stewart, *The Gershwin Years* (Garden City, New Jersey: Doubleday, 1973), p. 24.
25. Kimball and Simon, p. 18.

discuss the libretto with him and to assimilate some of the flavor of that part of America:

> Under the baking suns of July and August we established ourselves on Folly Island, a small barrier island ten miles from Charleston. James Island with its large population of primitive Gullah Negroes lay adjacent, and furnished us with a laboratory in which to test our theories, as well as an inexhaustible source of folk material. But the most interesting discovery to me, as we sat listening to their spirituals, or watched a group shuffling before a cabin or country store, was that to George it was more like a homecoming than an exploration. . . . The Gullah Negro prides himself on what he calls "shouting." This is a complicated rhythmic pattern beaten out by feet and hands as an accompaniment to the spirituals and is indubitably an African survival. I shall never forget the night when, at a Negro meeting on a remote sea-island, George started "shouting" with them. And eventually to their huge delight stole the show from their champion "shouter." I think he is the only white man in America who could have done it.[26]

It is no easy matter to pinpoint the precise stylistic details in Gershwin's songs that reflect his interest in, and involvement with, the music of black Americans. The matter is made more difficult by the fact that the music accepted by jazz historians today as "true" jazz was almost unknown in New York in the 1910s and '20s. Gershwin had little or no opportunity to hear country blues, or the urban blues developing in Chicago and other cities of the Midwest. New York heard little or no authentic New Orleans jazz in those days, and the territory bands of Kansas City and other such cities remained largely unknown in the East. The term *jazz*, as used by such writers and critics as Gilbert Seldes, John Alden Carpenter, and Alexander Woollcott, referred to the ragtime songs of Irving Berlin and other New York composers, and to the syncopated dance music played by such white bands as those of Paul Whiteman, Isham Jones, and Ben Selvin. Thus in recent years, the research and attitudes of jazz historians have led to such judgments as:

> The *Rhapsody in Blue*, however, is not jazz, not even jazz dolled up. . . . Although he indicated that the *Rhapsody* was scored for "jazz band and piano," even the most cursory examination of the *Rhapsody* reveals it to be a work of symphonic music that owes far more to the influence of Tchaikovsky and Liszt . . . than of Buddy Bolden or King Oliver.[27]

Admitting that this is true—and the same remarks would apply equally to Gershwin's other instrumental works, his operas, and even his songs—there still remains the fact that Gershwin knew and assimilated the music of various black musicians, and that his own music has had an appeal, over the years, to black

26. David Ewen, A Journey to Greatness. The Life and Music of George Gershwin (New York: Henry Holt, 1956), pp. 257–58.
27. Kimball and Simon, p. 36.

musicians (singers and jazz instrumentalists alike)—an appeal not shared by the songs of other Tin Pan Alley composers. Certainly some specific details can be isolated; the syncopated rhythms in many of his songs go far beyond the rather elementary, Western European–bound rhythms of the songs of Berlin and Kern, and he made more frequent and telling use of "blue" notes than did most of his white contemporaries.

But the heart of the matter seems to be a point that cannot be well illustrated by the usual techniques of the music historian. There was something in the music of black Americans that struck a responsive chord somewhere deep in Gershwin, something about their music that he grasped in an instinctive way. In turn, this same indefinable quality found its way into many of his songs, to which black Americans responded in a similarly instinctive way.

Scholars and historians can point to evidence supporting this contention: almost any listing of repertories of black jazz musicians in the 1920s, '30s, and even '40s will include songs by Gershwin, and black singers have favored his songs ever since they were written. One can even suggest reasons for this affinity: both Jews and blacks have a long and sorry history as oppressed minorities (but why did blacks not respond to the songs of other Jewish songwriter such as Berlin and Kern? It is even possible to come full circle and suggest that the increased harmonic sophistication of jazz in the 1920s and '30s owed some small debt the the new chord changes black musicians learned from playing Gershwin tunes.

The present book deals chiefly with the history of popular song and the role such songs have played in American life and culture. Biographies of songwriters of various periods have been included to illustrate what sorts of people turned to songwriting, what their ethnic and cultural backgrounds were, what music they knew in their formative years, what they thought of the role of popular song, and where they fit in the general history of music in America. In other words, their lives have been dealt with only insofar as they help illuminate the central thrust of the book, and not for the sake of biography itself.

Thus there is no reason to detail the lives and careers of other Tin Pan Alley songwriters, since the material presented to this point on Irving Berlin, Jerome Kern, and George Gershwin has served to establish the essential portrait of the era and of the men who wrote its songs. Furthermore, lengthy discussions of a large number of composers of this period would distort the coverage of the age of Tin Pan Alley in comparison with the other periods with which this book is concerned, each of which contributed in its own way to the entire, two-hundred-year, continuing history of popular song.

This approach is not intended to minimize the talents and individual songs of many other songwriters of the 1920s, '30s, and '40s, some of whom were among the most gifted composers in the entire history of American song. Cole Porter (1892–1964), for instance, wrote songs that consistently matched those of Berlin, Kern, and Gershwin, with whom he is ranked by every writer concerned with this era. His career was exceptional for the era: he was born in Peru, Indiana (rather than New York); his musical training came at Yale and Harvard, and at the Schola Cantorum in Paris (rather than as an apprentice on Tin Pan Alley); he lived in Europe for several extended periods and was independently wealthy; success as a songwriter came late for him, not until he was in his middle thirties. Writing mostly for the musical stage and the movies, he eventually produced songs that ranked, in quantity and quality, with those of any songwriter of the

June Knight and Charles Walters dance "Begin the Beguine" in the 1935 production of *Jubilee* by Cole Porter.

age, including the top hits "What Is This Thing Called Love?" (1930), "Night and Day" (1932), "Begin the Beguine" (1935), "Just One of Those Things" (1935), "I've Got You Under My Skin" (1936), "In the Still of the Night" (1937), "At Long Last Love" (1938), "You'd Be So Nice to Come Home To" (1943), "Don't Fence Me In" (1944), "Wunderbar" (1949), and "True Love" (1956), to mention only the most obvious. His lyrics—his own—are the equal of any of the era in cleverness, sophistication, and range of subject matter. Perhaps because of his unconventional background and training, and his independence of mind and spirit, many of his songs extend and even break the usual formal patterns of Tin Pan Alley, and his harmonic vocabulary was as rich and complex as that of Kern or Geshwin.

Richard Rodgers (1902–), in collaboration with a string of the outstanding

Sheet music cover for "People Will Say We're in Love," from Richard Rodgers's most successful musical, *Oklahoma* (1943).

lyricists of the day—Lorenz Hart, Oscar Hammerstein II, Stephen Sondheim—produced a number of the most successful musical comedies of the second quarter of this century, including the landmarks *A Connecticut Yankee* (1927), *On Your Toes* (1936), *Babes in Arms* (1937), *The Boys from Syracuse* (1938), *Oklahoma!* (1943), *Carousel* (1945), *South Pacific* (1949), and *The King and I* (1951). These works are the core of the American musical stage for this period. *Oklahoma!* became the most successful work of its sort—2,212 performances after its opening on March 31, 1943, followed by a fifty-one-week tour to all parts of America; a road company took the show to an estimated 10,000,000 people in the course of a ten-year tour; its London run of three and one-half years was the second longest in the history of the English stage; the show grossed at least forty million dollars. *South Pacific* was scarcely less successful, with its opening run in New York of 1,925 performances, and comparable success on the road and as a movie. *Carousel* ran for a comparatively modest 890 performances, but was acclaimed as one of the most important, innovative stage works of the century, serious in theme, bridging the gap between musical comedy and opera.

The magnitude of Rodgers's talent as a songwriter is apparent from the briefest listing of only the most sensationally successful of his songs, from his first big hit, "The Blue Room" (1926), through "My Heart Stood Still" (1927), "With a Song in My Heart" (1929), "Blue Moon" (1934), to "It's Easy to Remember" (1935). His popularity is easier to chart once "Your Hit Parade" came on the air: the No. 1 song on the very first broadcast, on the night of April 20, 1935, was his "Soon," from the movie *Mississippi*; later songs that were top favorites and featured on the show for many weeks were "This Can't Be Love" (1938), "People Will Say We're in Love" (1943, from *Oklahoma!*, broadcast for thirty consecutive weeks, a record second only to "White Christmas"), "Oh What a Beautiful Morning" (1943), "If I Loved You" (1945), "It Might As Well Be Spring" (1945, from the movie *State Fair*), "Some Enchanted Evening" (1949), "Bali Ha'i" (1949), and "No Other Love" (1953). *Variety's* list of the Golden 100 songs of Tin Pan Alley (see Appendix 6) contains nine by Rodgers, putting him in a tie for first place with Irving Berlin. Alec Wilder, in his extended study of songs of this era, finds "an extraordinary incidence of inventiveness in practically all of Rodgers's songs," and concludes that "of all the writers whose songs are considered and examined in this book, those of Rodgers show the highest degree of consistent excellence, inventiveness, and sophistication."[28] He is, by any method of judgment, one of the two or three most talented and successful songwriters of his age, and is given less attention in the present book than several other composers only because his songs broke no new ground—but are superb examples of a song style established by several of his older contemporaries.

The seven songs by Harold Arlen on *Variety's* Golden 100 list entitle him to rank behind Berlin and Rodgers only. Born in Buffalo in 1905, Arlen gravitated toward black musicians and their music, as had Gershwin. In the early 1930s, he wrote the music for shows at the Cotton Club; many of his songs draw on the expressive content of the blues, if not on their structure. "Stormy Weather" (1933) was written for Cab Calloway and became a vehicle for such black singers as Ethel Waters and Lena Horne; "Blues in the Night" (1941) was featured in a movie of the same name, with a largely black cast; Pearl Bailey's first important stage role came in the Broadway musical *St. Louis Woman* (1944), with music by Arlen.

He was equally gifted in other kinds of songs, as well. His first film song,

28. Wilder, p. 163.

"It's Only a Paper Moon" (1933), has been one of those rarities that retained its popularity into the 1970s. "Over the Rainbow," sung by Judy Garland in the original *Wizard of Oz* (1939), won an Academy Award as the best film song of the year and became one of the most enduring songs in the entire history of "Your Hit Parade." His success continued into the 1940s, with "That Old Black

Harold Arlen (1905–).

Magic" (1942), "Ac-cent-tchu-ate the Positive" (1944), and "Come Rain or Come Shine" (1946), to name but a few. He was surely the most talented and versatile songwriter in the third generation of Tin Pan Alley composers, those born several decades after Berlin and Kern.

The quality of invention scarcely drops off as one continues down the list of other songwriters of this period and their best songs: Harry Warren, matched only by Irving Berlin in the variety of types of songs and the high standard of professionalism he brought to them ("Shuffle Off to Buffalo," 1932; "Lullaby of Broadway," 1935; "Chattanooga Choo Choo," 1941; "You'll Never Know," 1943; "On the Atchison, Topeka & Santa Fe," 1945); Vincent Youmans ("Tea for Two," 1924; "Without a Song," 1929; "Orchids in the Moonlight," 1933); Jimmy McHugh ("I Can't Give You Anything But Love," 1928; "On the Sunny Side of the Street," 1930); Walter Donaldson ("My Blue Heaven," 1927; "Carolina in the Morning," 1922); Hoagy Carmichael ("Stardust," 1929; "Two Sleepy People," 1938; "Ole Buttermilk Sky," 1946); Arthur Schwartz ("Something to Remember You By," 1930; "Dancing in the Dark," 1931; "You and the Night and the Music," 1934; "They're Either Too Young or Too Old," 1943); and Duke Ellington ("Mood Indigo," 1931; "Don't Get Around Much Anymore," 1942).

This is an imposing list, and one that could be expanded further with little or no drop in quality or popular success. But the present book does not pretend to be a catalog of names and works; these men must share the fate of many excellent and successful songwriters of earlier times whose names have not found their way onto these pages.

The era of Tin Pan Alley is the only one for which a detailed study of the musical style of its songs has been written: *American Popular Song. The Great Innovators, 1900–1950*, by Alec Wilder, a successful songwriter. The thesis of the book is stated in the first pages:

Stephen Foster created the first truly native songs. . . . With his death something mysterious happened. The peculiarly native quality that he had brought to American popular song, a quality borrowed from Negro music, disappeared quite as suddenly as it had arrived. And it did not return until the 1880's. . . .

Not until the Negro musicians and song writers were able, late in the century, to perform directly for the white community [did] the message slowly [come] through to white America that the Negro's musical talent was unique, and that something musically remarkable was emerging from the ghetto. . . .

During the thirty-year period between 1885 and World War I, American popular music underwent many fundamental changes. Finally, when these changes—rhythmic, harmonic, melodic—were consolidated, a unique kind of song emerged: American song.[29]

After saying that he considers the period with which he is dealing an age of "professional songwriters," and the period that followed (the era of rock 'n' roll and rock) to be a "flamboyant age in which it is unsurprising to read grotesquely

29. Ibid., pp. 3–7, *passim*.

extravagant tributes to the creations of untutored amateurs,"[30] Wilder proceeds to examine and discuss hundreds of Tin Pan Alley songs, concentrating chiefly on harmonic and rhythmic details, finding "more sophistication, more complex melody writing, much more involved harmonic patterns, shifting song form, greater elegance, and infinitely superior theater song writing"; but he concludes with a final tribute to "the early anonymous Negroes who, in spite of their dreadful, ignominious plight, had managed to create the beginning of an *entirely new music*" (italics mine).[31]

His contention that uniquely American popular song came about only with the second generation of Tin Pan Alley composers is not new: the American composer John Alden Carpenter, for instance, observed in the 1920s, "I am strongly inclined to believe that the musical historians of the year 2000 will find the birthday of American music and that of Irving Berlin to have been the same."[32] But the history of any kind of music can appear quite different when observed from the perspective of several decades, rather than from the present and the immediate past. As I have already posited, I question the role of "negro" music in the formation of the song styles of Stephen Foster and of the first generation of Tin Pan Alley writers. Similarly, I believe that only several quite superficial aspects of "negro" music were skimmed off by songwriters of the 1910s, '20s, and '30s, to add a touch of exotic seasoning to their products—and that emphasis on these details serves to detract attention from the more important fact that the chief stylistic features of the songs of the composers discussed in this chapter came from an earlier generation of American songwriters and from the music of Central and Eastern Europe. It does the history of music by black musicians no lasting good to insist on interpretations that are historically unsound, and it may also obscure the profound effect that black music had on American song in the mid-1950s and afterward.

In considering these points, a convenient place to start is with the shape of Tin Pan Alley songs. With almost no exceptions, they are in verse-chorus form, the verse sketching a dramatic situation or an emotional vignette,

> Time and again I've longed for adventure,
>   Something to make my heart beat the faster.
> What did I long for? I never really knew.
>
> Finding your love I've found my adventure,
>   Touching your hand, my heart beats the faster,
> All that I want in all of this world is you.

and the chorus following as a "set" piece, a more lyric section, elaborating on the situation set out by the verse:

30. Ibid., p. 29.
31. Ibid., p. 28.
32. Woollcott, p. 38.

You are the promised kiss of springtime
That makes the lonely winter seem long.
You are the breathless hush of evening
That trembles on the brink of a lovely song.
You are the angel glow that lights a star,
The dearest things I know are what you are.
Some day my happy arms will hold you,
And some day I'll know that moment divine,
When all the things you are, are mine.
        —"All the Things You Are" (1939), by Jerome
        Kern and Oscar Hammerstein II

Anyone who knows this song will be familiar with the chorus and will recognize it and perhaps even be able to whistle or sing it; few people will know, or even recognize, the verse. As pointed out earlier (p. 293), the verse-chorus form of Tin Pan Alley songs functions in much the same way as the recitative-aria patterns in opera.

A musician in the early 1920s observed:

Previous to 1897 every song had to have six or seven verses and each verse had eight or ten lines. Now there are two verses of a scant four lines each, and even at that, the second verse counts scarcely at all. The whole story must be told in the very first verse and chorus and usually there is very little to it anyway, the music being what matters.[33]

In fact, a single verse became standard in the 1920s, and even this was often omitted in performance away from the stage, perhaps because the dramatic setting of a song was unimportant when it was heard over the radio or from a phonograph recording. And in less than a decade, composers themselves began treating the verse as an optional part of a song: though most songs of the '30s and '40s continued to be written in verse-chorus form, one need look no further than at the most popular songs (by Jerome Kern and Otto Harbach) in *Roberta* (1933)—"Smoke Gets in Your Eyes" and "Yesterdays"—for examples of verseless songs.

To summarize, Tin Pan Alley's verse (optional)-chorus songs represent a final step in a formal evolution that had taken place over a time span of more than a century:

strophic solo songs, with many verses, sometimes with a refrain line or two at the end of each verse: late eighteenth and early nineteenth centuries;
strophic solo songs, with many verses, and a refrain (sometimes sung by a chorus) at the end of each verse; the verse longer than the chorus, and containing the chief melodic material: early and mid-nineteenth century, minstrel songs, songs of the singing families, and the songs of Stephen Foster and his contemporaries;

33. Paul Whiteman and Mary Margaret McBride, *Jazz* (New York: J. H. Sears, 1926), p. 171.

strophic solo songs, with several verses, and with quartet or choral refrain; verse and chorus of approximately equal length, either or both with chief melodic material: post–Civil War songs;

strophic solo songs, with two or three verses, with a chorus after each verse sung by the solo singer; verse and chorus of approximately the same length, with the chief melody in the chorus: late nineteenth and early twentieth centuries, first generation of Tin Pan Alley songwriters;

verse-chorus songs, one or two verses, most important melodic material always in the chorus; the verse optional: 1920–55, second and third generations of Tin Pan Alley writers.

Formally, then, the songs of this era fall squarely into the continuing and evolving patterns of American popular song—and not, it might be added, into the patterns of Afro-American music, which most characteristically is built over harmonic patterns repeated an indeterminate number of times, as in the blues and the emerging jazz style.

Table I: Twenty-Three Representative Tin Pan Alley Songs

Date	Title	Composer	Form of Chorus
1915	"The Girl on the Magazine Cover"	Irving Berlin	$A^8A^8B^8C^8$
1917	" 'Til the Clouds Roll By"	Jerome Kern	$A^8B^8A^8B^8$
1918	"I'm Always Chasing Rainbows"	Harry Carroll	$A^8B^8C^8A^8$
1919	"A Pretty Girl Is Like a Melody"	Irving Berlin	$A^8B^8A^8C^8$
1920	"Avalon"	Al Jolson, Vincent Rose	$A^8A^8B^8A^8$
1921	"April Showers"	Louis Silvers	$A^8B^8A^8C^8$
1921	"I'm Just Wild about Harry"	Noble Sissle, Eubie Blake	$A^8B^8A^8C^{12}$
1922	"Carolina in the Morning"	Walter Donaldson	$A^8B^8A^8C^8$
1924	"The Man I Love"	George Gershwin	$A^8A^8B^8A^8$
1924	"Tea for Two"	Vincent Youmans	$A^8B^8A^8C^8$
1927	"My Blue Heaven"	Walter Donaldson	$A^8A^8A^8B^8$
1927	"My Heart Stood Still"	Richard Rodgers	$A^8A^8B^8A^8$
1930	"Body and Soul"	John W. Green	$A^8A^8B^8A^8$
1930	"Embraceable You"	George Gershwin	$A^8B^8A^8C^8$
1932	"Night and Day"	Cole Porter	$A^{16}A^{16}A'^{16}$
1933	"Smoke Gets in Your Eyes"	Jerome Kern	$A^8A^8B^8A^8$
1934	"Cocktails for Two"	Arthur Johnston, Sam Coslow	$A^8A^8B^8A^8$
1934	"Blue Moon"	Richard Rodgers	$A^8A^8B^8A^8$
1936	"Easy to Love"	Cole Porter	$A^8B^8A^8C^8$
1939	"Over the Rainbow"	Harold Arlen	$A^8A^8B^8A^8(B^8)$
1940	"The Last Time I Saw Paris"	Jerome Kern	$A^8A^8B^8A^{8+2}$
1942	"White Christmas"	Irving Berlin	$A^8B^8A^8C^8$
1943	"That Old Black Magic"	Harold Arlen	$A^{16}A^{16}B^{16}A^{16+8}$

The chorus of Tin Pan Alley songs is almost always cast in four sections of equal length. Table I lays out the formal designs of the choruses of twenty-three representative songs from the period, selected to cover the entire time span covered by this chapter and to represent the most successful songwriters. As can be seen from the table—and from an examination of any other representative group of songs from this period—the chorus is almost always 32 measures in length, the only exceptions coming from a doubling of measures in songs of lively tempos (to 64 measures) or from extensions of the last phrase. The four sections are most often in AABA or ABAC patterns, with occasional variants such as AABC and ABCA.

Thus the skill and genius of Tin Pan Alley composers (and lyricists) was revealed by what could be done within a tightly restricted formal structure, rather than by flights of fancy soaring to new and complex designs. One is reminded of similar restrictions embraced by writers of sonnets, by the Japanese poets of *haiku* verse, and by the great American bluesmen.

With such a limited musical time span, Tin Pan Alley composers had little space for tonal contrast and variety. Many songs—most of them from the early years of the era—stay in the tonic key throughout. But increasingly, through the 1920s and '30s, there is at least some degree of tonal shifting, even within the narrow confines of thirty-two measures. In its simplest form, as in "Blue Moon" (Richard Rodgers, 1934), the B section of the AABA structure begins in the dominant and modulates back to the tonic for the reprise of A. In other songs (more of them as the period moved into and past its midpoint), the B section is written in other keys, some quite remote from the tonic: "My Heart Stood Still" (Richard Rodgers, 1927) is in F major, with the B section in the parallel minor, F minor; George Gershwin's "The Man I Love" (1924) moves to the relative minor, C minor, before returning to the tonic of E flat; Jerome Kern's "Smoke Gets in Your Eyes" (1933) is in E flat, with a B section shifting to the flat sixth degree, C flat (written enharmonically as B); Cole Porter's "Night and Day" is in C, with a section in the middle in E flat; and "Body and Soul" (John W. Green, 1930), with a tonic of C, moves up a half-step to D flat for its B section.

Some of these tonal contrasts necessitate considerable harmonic ingenuity in getting back to the tonic key for the final A section:

JOHN W. GREEN, "BODY AND SOUL" (1930)

Are you pre-tend - ing, it looks like the end - ing Un -

less I could have one more chance to prove, dear,

My life a wreck you're mak - ing,

JEROME KERN, "SMOKE GETS IN YOUR EYES" (1933)

Yet to - day,__ My love has flown a - way,__ I am with -

out my love.

Actually, many songs of the era have a B section which is tonally unstable, moving through a sequence of chromatic chords back to the tonic for the return of A; the character of such a section is often more that of a bridge between the second and the last statements of A than of a separate, contrasting section. The four or eight measures taking on this function are known as the "release," and it is here that the composer had his best chance to engage in tonal adventures:

HARRY CARROLL, "I'M ALWAYS CHASING RAINBOWS" (1918)

Some fel-lows look and find the sun - shine, I al - ways look and find the

rain, Some fel-lows make a win - ning some - time, I

nev - er e - ven make a gain,

JEROME KERN, "I'VE TOLD EV'RY LITTLE STAR" (1932)

Such freer modulations and greater harmonic sophistication in the release were not an isolated phenomenon, but rather part of a general trend toward freer and more varied harmonic usage. Many songs of the late 1910s and early '20s still depended on the chains of three or four sequential dominant harmonies leading to the final cadence for their harmonic variety, showing their indebtedness to such songwriters of the first generation of Tin Pan Alley songwriters as Paul Dresser:

FELIX BARNARD, JOHN S. BLACK, "DARDANELLA" (1919)

like the chil-dren of the O-ri - ent. Oh ____ sweet Dar - da-nel - la, my star of love di - vine. ____

GEORGE GERSHWIN, "NOBODY BUT YOU" (1919)

Hon - ey, tell me who You know it's no - bod-y but you. ____

But by the mid-1920s, such composers as Kern and Gershwin had pushed the harmonic bounds of popular song immeasurably further, with much freer use of chromatic chords anywhere in a song, nondominant seventh and ninth chords, and a willingness to alter almost any note in a chord for richer harmonic color:

JEROME KERN, "LOOK FOR THE SILVER LINING" (1920)

GEORGE GERSHWIN, "THE MAN I LOVE" (1924)

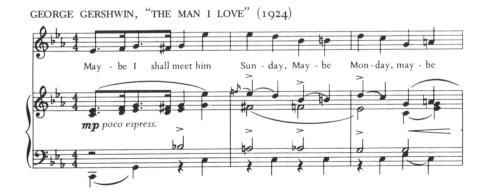

The harmonic language of Tin Pan Alley had been so expanded that almost every chord could have added tones, nonharmonic notes, and chromatically altered notes, alone or in combination:

RICHARD RODGERS, "IT'S EASY TO REMEMBER" (1934)

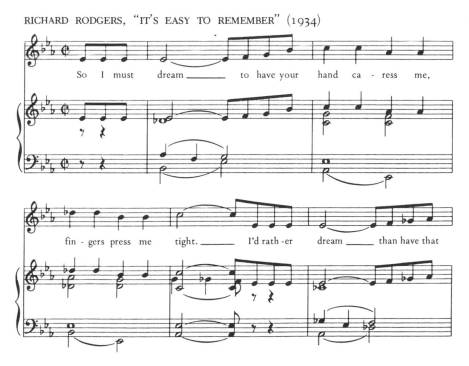

lone - ly feel - ing steal - ing through the night. _____

The source of this new harmonic richness and variety in popular song is hardly a secret. The men who introduced it were Jerome Kern, who was classically trained, and George Gershwin, who also had classical training and continued to be involved in "serious" music throughout his career. Richard Rodgers, slightly younger but also one of the first to expand the harmonic language of Tin Pan Alley, was educated at Columbia University and at the Institute of Musical Art in New York. These men knew the music of classical composers of the eighteenth and nineteenth centuries, particularly that of the great Russian and German composers of the second half of the nineteenth century, and of such early "moderns" as Ravel and Debussy; they enriched the harmonic language of popular song in many of the same ways these men expanded the harmonic and tonal vocabulary of classical music. Gershwin's songs, no less than his intrumental works, show his acquaintance with such writers as Liszt and Tchaikovsky and are equally "akin in spirit and quality to the Russian music [he] heard in his formative years."[34]

Paul Whiteman, a famous band leader of the 1920s and a lively observer of what he called "jazz," may have been the first to call attention to the dependence of popular song of the 1920s on classical music:

> Do you not know that more than half the modern art of composing a popular song comes in knowing what to steal and how to adapt it—also, that at least nine-tenths of modern jazz music turned out by Tin Pan Alley is frankly stolen from the masters? . . .

> Pretty nearly everybody knows now that Handel's Messiah furnished the main theme of the well-known "Yes, We Have No Bananas." Perhaps it is not such general knowledge that most of the "banana" song which wasn't taken from the Messiah came from Balfe's famous "I Dreamt That I Dwelt in Marble Halls." Chopin supplied "Alice Blue Gown" [Harry Tierney, 1919]. "Avalon" [Al Jolson and Vincent Rose, 1920] was Tosca straight.

> Chopin came into the limelight again with "I'm Always Chasing Rainbows" [Harry Carroll, 1918], taken from the beautiful "Fantasie Impromptu Opus 66." The same master furnished the theme for "Irene" [Harry Tierney, 1919]. . . . "Iola" [Charles L. Johnson, 1920] came from "The Blue Dan-

34. Kimball and Simon, p. 36.

ube Waltz." "Every Cloud Has a Silver Lining" [i.e., "Look for the Silver Lining" by Jerome Kern, 1920] more than suggests a Paderewski Minuet. "The Love Nest" [Louis A. Hirsch, 1920] is Tschaikowsky. "Russian Rose" [Hugh Charles and Sonny Miller, c. 1920] is a frank adaption of the "Volga Boat Song."[35]

Had this been written later, the author would have had many more examples to add. The Broadway musical *Blossom Time* (1921) used songs by Franz Schubert, adapted by Sigmund Romberg; one, "Song of Love," became a top-selling item of sheet music. Romberg's "Lover, Come Back to Me," from the musical *New Moon*, used a piano piece by Tchaikovsky for the middle section. "My Moonlight Madonna" (1933) was adapted by William Scotti from the piano piece "Poeme" by the Czech composer Zdenko Fibich. "Moon Love" (1939) was an adaption of the second movement of Tchaikovsky's *Symphony No. 5*, by Mack David, Mack Davis, and André Kostelanetz; "Our Love" (also 1939) was fashioned from the same composer's "Romeo and Juliet"; "Tonight We Love" (1941) came from the first movement of his *Piano Concerto No. 1*. Chopin's career on Tin Pan Alley was continued with "Till the End of Time" (1945), an adaption of his *Polonaise in A-Flat Major* that sold over a million copies of both sheet music and phonograph records. "My Reverie" (1938) was fashioned from Debussy's piano piece "Reverie" by Larry Clinton, and Maurice Ravel's *Pavane pour une enfante défunte* yielded "The Lamp Is Low" (1939).

The successful conversion into popular songs of these and other classical works merely underlines a more general kinship between these two bodies of music. Both have the sense of forward motion through time, a linear progression through space. Phrases are goal-oriented, with melodies and their supporting chords constructed to lead the listener from one point in the piece to the next, until a high point or a climax is reached, with a resting point (cadence) following. Though the listener may not understand what the composer is doing, technically, he senses the forward thrust and momentum and would be frustrated if it stopped short of its goal or cadence. For instance, anyone listening to Jerome Kern's "Smoke Gets in Your Eyes"—even for the first time—senses forward movement through the first two measures to the word "true," and a similar pull in the melodic line to the final word of the section, "denied," after which there is a pause.

JEROME KERN, "SMOKE GETS IN YOUR EYES" (1933)

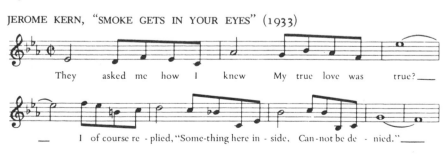

35. Whiteman, pp. 181–82.

This type of momentum is achieved partly by harmonic means—chords arranged in certain patterns so as to give a strong sense of pull, of tension and release, from one to the next (so-called functional harmony), with these tensions increased through chromatically altered or nonharmonic tines—and partly through melodic sequence (melodic patterns repeated at different pitch levels). Melodic sequence, in fact, is the most characteristic device of Tin Pan Alley tunes, occurring in every possible part of a song. The chorus may have two phrases related by sequence:

GEORGE GERSHWIN, "EMBRACEABLE YOU" (1931)

A melody may begin with a longer chain of sequences:

RICHARD RODGERS, "BLUE MOON" (1934)

The sequence may come at the end of a melodic motive, rather than at the beginning:

JAY GORNEY, "BROTHER, CAN YOU SPARE A DIME?" (1932)

And almost invariably the release leads back to the tonic key and the return of the A section of the tune, by way of melodic sequence:

JEROME KERN, "ALL THE THINGS YOU ARE" (1939)

This sense of forward thrust, achieved through the pervasive use of melodic sequence and functional harmony intensified through frequent chromatic alteration, links songs of the second generation of Tin Pan Alley composers with European classical music. Not all music has this sense of movement, intensification, climax, and release. Many folk songs, for instance, consist of a number of phrases following one another in a certain order, an order learned when one hears the song; but there may be no abstract musical logic underlying this order, and as the songs are passed on in oral tradition, the order may become different, or one or more phrases may be replaced by others, with no apparent adverse effect. Other music, such as much African and Afro-American music, is built on insistent repetition of a single melodic or harmonic pattern. And even though almost all nineteenth-century American popular song uses functional harmony of a simple sort, there is no sense of gradual and inevitable intensification and movement toward a musical climax, such as one finds in classical music of the eighteenth and nineteenth centuries and in the best songs of later Tin Pan Alley songwriters.

The earliest American popular songs, of the late eighteenth and early nineteenth centuries, were quite close in style to the instrumental and vocal music of Thomas Arne and his English contemporaries, who drew on Italian and German classical models; the melodic and harmonic style of Rossini, Bellini, and Donizetti was at the core of much popular song in the 1820s, '30s, and '40s; the songs of Schubert and his German contemporaries were fashioned into popular songs in the 1830s and '40s, and some songwriters imitated this style. But after Stephen Foster had forged a uniquely American song style out of several national schools of song, popular song diverged more and more from its contemporary classical music. By the 1890s and 1900s, there were almost no common stylistic features between popular song—as written by Charles K. Harris, Paul Dresser, George M. Cohan, Harry Von Tilzer, and their peers—and the classical music of the immediate past and the present, as written by Brahms, Musorgsky, Mahler, Debussy, and the early Stravinsky and Schoenberg.

Thus the similarity between popular and classical style in the period covered by the present chapter represents a return to a situation that had existed before, but had been lost for some generations. There is a difference, however, One would search in vain for stylistic connections between the songs of Kern, Gershwin, Berlin, and Rodgers, and the serial music of Arnold Schoenberg and Anton Webern, the neoclassical works of Igor Stravinsky, the folk-based pieces of Béla Bartók, or the avant-garde compositions of George Antheil and Edgard Varèse. Tin Pan Alley was keyed to the music of the past generation of classical composers, not the present. And in this, it was a mirror of the classical musical life of America during these decades, when audiences and performers were finding it difficult to come to terms with contemporary music and were taking refuge in repeated performances of the compositions of past ages, whose style was more familiar and accessible.

The mature style of Tin Pan Alley, then, drew its formal structures from earlier generations of popular song writers in America and its harmonic and melodic language from Western European classical music, particularly the German, Russian, and French composers of the second half of the nineteenth century and the very first years of the twentieth.

Despite this, the songs of Berlin, Gershwin, Kern, and their contemporaries struck the ears of both Americans and Europeans as being distinctly and peculiarly American. One reason for this was the frequent use of rhythmic patterns originating in ragtime, in the syncopated dance music played by black bands, and in the music played by early black jazz bands, particularly those popular in Harlem in the 1920s. Syncopated rhythms, displacements of beats, anticipations of rhythmic resolutions at the ends of phrases, and the use of triplet figures in duple time all gave American songs of the 1910s and '20s a piquant flavor unlike that of songs written in Europe:

GEORGE GERSHWIN, "I GOT RHYTHM" (1930)

BEN BERNIE *et al.*, "SWEET GEORGIA BROWN" (1925)

HAROLD ARLEN, "IT'S ONLY A PAPER MOON" (1933)

More difficult to define, but nonetheless real in lending a uniquely American flavor to so many songs of the era, was the combination of rhythmic patterns such as those mentioned above with lyrics that often managed to be sentimental, flippant, and vaguely humorous at the same time—a curious mixture of sentiments poised somewhere between the minstrel show, Gilbert and Sullivan operettas, vaudeville, and older songs of sentiment:

> Ev'ry morning, ev'ry evening, ain't we got fun,
> Not much money, oh, but honey, ain't we got fun.
> The rent's unpaid, dear, we haven't a sou,
> But smiles were made, dear, for me and for you . . .
> —Richard A. Whiting, "Ain't We Got Fun" (1921)

'S wonderful! 'S marvelous! You should care for me!
'S awful nice! 'S paradise! 'S what I love to see!
    —George and Ira Gershwin, " 'S Wonderful!" (1927)

Picture you upon my knee,
    Just tea for two and two for tea,
    Just me for you and you for me . . .
    —Vincent Youmans and Irving Caesar,
            "Tea for Two" (1924)

I'm just wild about Harry, and Harry's wild about me.
The heav'ly blisses of his kisses fill me with ecstasy.
He's sweet just like choc'late candy, and just like honey from the
    bee . . .
    —Noble Sissle and Eubie Blake, "I'm Just Wild about Harry" (1921)

You can bring Pearl, she's a darn nice girl, but don't bring Lulu,
You can bring Rose with her turned up nose, but don't bring Lulu,
    Lulu always wants to do
    What we boys don't want her to;
When she struts her stuff around, London bridge is falling down . . .
    —Ray Henderson, Billy Rose, and Lew Brown, "Don't Bring Lulu" (1925)

Pointing out stylistic links between Tin Pan Alley songs and various other types of music does not make them any less American. An important thread running through most of the present book—and, more importantly, through several hundred years of music in America—is that all music emerging as distinctly American in style has its ancestry in earlier music imported to this country; what is American is the distinctive mix, occurring only here. As one writer has put it succinctly:

> And if anyone, on hearing Kern say that Berlin *IS* American music, is then so fatuous as to object on the grounds that he was born in Russia, it might be pointed out that if the musical interpreter of American civilization came over in the foul hold of a ship, so did American civilization.[36]

At the same time, it must be remembered that millions of people from various parts of the world had been coming to America for many centuries before Irving Berlin arrived, bringing their own sort of music with them and creating new music here. The same arguments used to justify putting the label "American" on the songs of Irving Berlin and other Tin Pan Alley composers can be used for the songs discussed in most of the thirteen preceding chapters of this book. Tin Pan Alley songs were unquestionably American songs—but nothing gives them a unique claim to this designation.

36. Woollcott, p. 218.

The 1920s and '30s were an era of specialization in popular song. There were composers, lyricists, performers, and publishers—and it was rare for a single individual to be involved in more than one of these areas. Irving Berlin was the great exception, a throwback to the multitalented men of the first generation of Tin Pan Alley: he wrote his own lyrics, was a successful singer in the 1910s, and formed his own publishing house. Cole Porter wrote his own lyrics, also. Otherwise, the songwriters of the time depended on other people to furnish them with lyrics, sing their songs once they were written, and publish them.

It was the best era yet for lyricists. Only a generation earlier, the going price for a lyric had been five dollars, with no further claim on a song's earnings. But as Tin Pan Alley moved into a period of unprecedented prosperity, there was greater appreciation of the importance of a good lyric to the success of a song; and with the formation of ASCAP, lyricists were regarded as virtual equals of composers, sharing both publishers' royalties and the annual ASCAP fund accumulating from licensing fees and performance rights.

They came from the same milieu as the songwriters with whom they worked. The best and most successful of them, including Ira Gershwin, Oscar Hammerstein II, Lorenz Hart, E. Y. Harburg, Alan Jay Lerner, Billy Rose, Irving Caesar, Howard Dietz, and Dorothy Fields, were products of New York City; most came from families already involved in entertainment, or served early apprenticeships with Tin Pan Alley firms or on Broadway. Only Johnny Mercer, born in Savannah, Georgia, was an outsider, geographically.

The lyrics they produced dealt, at first, with a wide range of situations and emotions. No lyricist in the entire history of popular song in America produced texts of such variety—comic, sentimental, romantic, dramatic, ethnic, satirical—as did Irving Berlin in the first decade of his career. America's entry into World War I brought a rash of war songs, some of them rivaling the immediacy and intensity of the best songs of the Civil War: "Over There" (George M. Cohan, 1917), "The Rose of No Man's Land" (Joseph A. Brennan and Jack Caddingan, 1918), "Oh! How I Hate to Get Up in the Morning" (Irving Berlin, 1918), "Till We Meet Again" (Richard A. Whiting and Raymond B. Egan, 1918), and "Hello, Central! Give Me No Man's Land" (Jean Schwartz, Sam M. Lewis, and Joe Young) were among the most popular.

But somehow, as America moved into the 1920s and then the '30s, the expressive range of popular song narrowed. Texts began dealing almost exclusively with personal emotions, almost never with events outside of the person. An increasingly large percentage of the most popular songs was concerned with one aspect or another of romantic love. A glance at the titles on any representative list of the most popular songs of the period between 1920 and 1945, such as Variety's Golden 100 Tin Pan Alley songs (see Appendix 6), is enough to verify this generalization. Observers of the time were quite aware of this shift:

The sentimental ballads before 1920 were often about babies, separation, death. The theme of the sentimental song two generations later was the impotence of the male. . . . They celebrated sadly the failure of the man to keep his woman.[37]

And a songwriter of the period suggested that the preoccupation with personal love was a mirror of the times:

> The Twenties sang of carefree nights and the frenetic days that rushed headlong into the nightmare and fantasy of the Thirties. Both had their reality, both voiced it. This was a score of years in which love grew from an idle and pleasant pastime into a vital avocation—romance.[38]

One searches almost in vain for songs touching in any way on the great social and political issues of those years—the continuing desperate plight of the black American in white America; the struggle of working class citizens to combat by unionization and strikes their exploitation by management; the worsening situation of ethnic minorities in Central and Eastern Europe and the inexorable rise to power of totalitarian regimes in many of these countries. A handful, a tiny handful, of popular songs deal with the Great Depression; "Brother, Can You Spare a Dime?" (Jay Gorney and E. Y. Harburg, 1932) stands virtually alone in its serious treatment of poverty. And no war in which America had been involved before produced so few songs as did World War II; such songs as "Praise the Lord and Pass the Ammunition" (Frank Loesser, 1942), "I Left My Heart at the Stage Door Canteen" (Irving Berlin, 1942), "We Did It Before and We Can Do It Again" (Cliff Friend and Charles Tobias, 1941), and "Comin' in on a Wing and a Prayer" (Jimmy McHugh and Harold Adamson, 1943) made up a tiny percentage of the songs written during the war years.

The perspective of history is helpful here, to remind us that other eras of song had similarly been concerned with subjective matters and personal feelings. Thomas Moore's *Irish Melodies* leap to mind as an earlier example of songs dealing with the inner workings of man, rather than with external events. And Tin Pan Alley's pose was a quite deliberate one, tied directly to the most powerful elements of the New York musical stage and the Hollywood sound film, which held that these media were best used to entertain people, to take their minds away from personal and national problems—not to remind them of such things.

The urbanization of American popular song, set in motion by events of the last decades of the nineteenth century, was effectively completed in the 1910s and '20s. Even more than had been the case during the formative years of Tin Pan Alley, the field was dominated by composers and lyricists born and trained in New York, writing songs for publishers who not only had their offices in New York, but were themselves products of the city. The style of the music and of the lyrics had become a New York style, and general attitudes as to what a song should be and where it should fit into American culture were also shaped by the

37. Seldes, p. 58.
38. Rodgers, p. xiv.

climate and taste of New York. There was little effective cultural input from the rest of America into New York in these days, and to the extent that Tin Pan Alley songs reflected American culture in a broader sense, they did so because the rest of the country was willing to accept a uniquely urban, New York product, not because New York was absorbing elements of American culture from west of the Hudson River or south of Atlantic City. Hollywood was not a real exception to this, since it was musically a West Coast extension of New York. The songs of Kern, Gershwin, Porter, and their contemporaries were urban, sophisticated, and stylish, and they were intended for people who could be described by one or more of these adjectives—or aspired to be.

The result of all this was a product accepted all over America, true enough, but accepted by a more narrow range of Americans than had been the case in some earlier periods of popular song. The genre had been limited, before the advent of the phonograph record, radio, and the sound movie, to persons who were musically literate, who could purchase a piece of sheet music and either play or sing it in their homes. But ties to oral traditional music had resulted in dissemination even among people who did not read music. Moore's *Irish Melodies* and other Irish and Scottish songs of the early nineteenth century became known to nonliterate Americans whose own music was close enough in style for them to learn such new songs by ear. Songs from minstrel shows and the songs of Stephen Foster were disseminated both through sheet music and by ear; a Northern-born lady living in the South wrote:

> Although first published in the North, you there know nothing of the power and pathos given them [Negro melodies] here. The whites first learn them—the negroes catch the air and the words from once hearing, after which woods and fields resound with their strains—the whites catch the expression from these sable minstrels—thus Negro Melodies have an effect here not dreamed of at the North.[39]

Ned Harrigan could still write, in the 1880s, of popular song helping to "lighten the toil of the working people" and to "admit sunshine into many a darkened life";[40] and as late as the turn of the century, Theodore Dreiser was witness to the fact that popular songs reached "mansion and hovel . . . the blazing furnace of a steel mill . . . the open window of a farmland cottage."[41] The word *populist* leaps to mind as an appropriate one for song throughout the nineteenth century. But the audience changed considerably during the first quarter of the twentieth century:

> *Progress of a popular song* (from fall in New York to summer throughout the country). Harlem cabarets, other cabarets, Reisenfeld's classical jazz, the Rascoe's private orchestra, the hand organs, the phonographs, the radio, the

39. *Dwight's Journal of Music*, February 26, 1853.
40. Cf. quotation on page 279.
41. Cf. quotation on page 307.

Webster Hall balls, other balls (college proms), men going home late at night whistling it on the street, picked out on Greenwich Village ukeleles, sung in late motor rides by boys and girls, in restaurants—hotel restaurants, Paul Whiteman and Lopez, vaudeville, played Sundays by girls at pianos from sheet music with small photographs on the cover, of both the composer and the person who first sang it—first sung in a popular musical comedy (introduced several times—at the end of the second act pathetically—and played as the audience are leaving the theater)—pervading the country through the movie pianists, danced to in private houses to the music of a phonograph—the Elks fair—thrown on a screen between the acts at the National Winter Garden Burlesque and sung by the male audience—Remey's Dancing Academy (decayed fairies).[42]

It seems fair to generalize that Tin Pan Alley songs were for white, urban, literate, middle- and upper-class Americans. They remained practically unknown to large segments of American society, including most blacks (excepting musicians and a handful of urban blacks aspiring to a life-style approaching that of whites), and the millions of poor, white, rural Americans of English, Irish, and Scottish stock clustered in the South and scattered across the lower Midwest. These two groups had their own distinctive types of music, oral-tradition music that was given a tremendous boost in the 1920s and '30s by the new technology that brought commercial radio and wide dissemination of the phonograph record.

The 1910s saw popular song closely allied with social dancing for the first time. Earlier periods had their own forms of dance, but the music accompanying them was instrumental; the first generation of Tin Pan Alley songwriters wrote mostly waltz-songs, but these invoked the rhythm and flow of this popular dance for expressive purposes and were rarely used to accompany actual dancing. It was not until the 1910s and '20s that popular songs were played and even sung as dance pieces.

Though America was developing an appetite for social dancing before Vernon and Irene Castle began their meteoric rise to stardom in 1913, this couple gave direction to the phenomenon and symbolized the trend. The Castles first appeared at Louis Martin's restaurant, in a series of tea dances: they demonstrated various dance steps, then encouraged the audience to join them in the fox trot, the bunny hug, the grizzly bear, or one of various other dances in 2/4 or 4/4 time. Their first Broadway musical, *The Sunshine Girl*, with a score by Paul Rubens, opened in February of 1913 and featured performances of the turkey trot and the tango; Irving Berlin provided the music for their next show, *Watch Your Step* (1914). They founded the Vernon Castle School of Dancing and were a top attraction in vaudeville and nightclubs, commanding fees of as much as $30,000 a week; by now there were countless emulators of their act, and hundreds of restaurants, nightclubs, and dance palaces were employing dance

42. Edmund Wilson, *The Twenties. From Notebooks and Diaries of the Period* (New York: Bantam Books, 1975), p. 183.

Vernon and Irene Castle in 1915.

bands to provide appropriate music for the couples who flocked to these places to enjoy the amusement and recreation of dancing.

Jim Europe, a black bandleader who had introduced his brand of syncopated dance music to New York at the Clef Club in 1910, was hired as musical director for the Castles in 1913, with his new Society Orchestra. He went on to become the first black bandleader to make recordings, was the first to introduce syncopated band music to France (with his 369th Infantry Band of black enlisted men), and was a familiar and popular enough figure to be greeted by a million people in New York on his return from France. Other black musicians formed "syncopated" bands in the 1910s—Wilbur Sweatman, W. C. Handy, Ford Dabney, among others. But most of the bands furnishing dance music in the 1910s were white. Their names were usually taken from the establishment where they played—the Waldorf-Astoria Dance Orchestra (directed by Joseph M. Knecht), Erdody's Hotel Pennsylvania Orchestra, Abe Lyman's California Ambassador Hotel Orchestra, Vincent Lopez and his Pennsylvania Hotel Orchestra, the Bar Harbor Society Orchestra—and shortly after the end of World War I, as America rapidly grew more prosperous and the dance craze blossomed even more, such orchestras were recorded by all the major recording companies, and their discs became the backbone of many catalogs. Many bands brought out hundreds of

Vincent Lopez and his Pennsylvania Hotel Orchestra, 1922.

records over a time span of several decades: Paul Whiteman, Ben Selvin, Nat Shilkret, Nathan Glantz, Sam Lanin, Vincent Lopez, Lou Gold, Adrian Schubert, and Joe Green were only a few of the bandleaders whose discs made up a major portion of the recorded repertory from 1918 until the mid-1930s.

At first these bands played and recorded lively numbers, appropriate for the energetic and even acrobatic dancing styles of the 1910s and '20s. Their instrumentation was most usually 2 trumpets, 1 trombone, 3 reeds (saxophones and clarinets), 1–2 violins, piano, banjo, and drums; much of their repertory was made up of pieces with some degree of syncopation; their sound was imitative of that of the early black syncopated bands. Standards of the repertory were "Bugle Call Rag" (J. Hubert ["Eubie"] Blake and Carey Morgan, 1916), "Avalon" (Al Jolson and Vincent Rose, 1920), "St. Louis Blues" (W. C. Handy, 1914), "Dardanella" (Felix Bernard, Johnny S. Black, and Fred Fisher, 1919), "The Sheik of Araby" (Ted Snyder, Harry B. Smith, and Francis Wheeler, 1921), "That's a-

Plenty" (Bert A. Williams and Henry Creamer, 1909), and "Whispering" (John and Malvin Schonberger)—a mixture of both vocal and instrumental pieces written by white and black composers. It was this music, together with the ragtime songs of Irving Berlin and contemporaries, that made up what white, urban writers referred to as "jazz."

As the 1920s rolled by and popular taste turned more to slower ballads, bands played this newer repertory for a style of dancing that was now more intimate, smoother, more romantic. All dance bands now used vocalists; Tin Pan Alley songs were performed as a string of several choruses, with the instruments alternately playing alone and then accompanying the singer. Bands became the chief disseminators of popular songs, in live performances for dancing, over the radio, and on phonograph recordings.

Meanwhile, black bands were developing a style of playing somewhat different from their white counterparts, a style accepted by more recent writers as the "true" jazz style. There were the bands featured at such Harlem clubs as the Alhambra Ballroom, the Cotton Club, and the Savoy Club: Bill Brown and his Brownies, Marion Hardy's Alabamians, the Savoy Bearcats. There were regional, "territory" bands in the Midwest and Southwest: the Bennie Moten Band, the Jay McShann Band, Alphonso Trent's Band. And there were bigger, even more famous groups: McKinney's Cotton Pickers, the Luis Russell Band, and above all the band of Fletcher Henderson, with such talented players and arrangers as Don Redman.

A comprehensive history of the bands of the 1920s and '30s has yet to be written; most writers who have dealt with the topic are jazz historians, whose chief interest has been in the black bands and in those white ones, such as those organized by Charlie Barnet and the Dorsey brothers, whose playing style most nearly approaches jazz, as defined by modern scholarship. But for the history of popular song, the Casa Loma Orchestra, founded in 1929, was an important step in the direction of what was to become "swing," the most successful and popular amalgamation of popular and jazz styles before World War II.

An offshoot of the Jean Goldkette band, whose membership had included such talented white players as Jimmy and Tommy Dorsey, the Casa Loma group was slightly larger than earlier bands, with 5 brasses (3 trumpets, 2 trombones), 4 reeds, 4 rhythm (banjo, bass, piano, drums), and several vocalists, and from the beginning they featured an unusually high level of technique and ensemble. "Those guys just rehearsed and rehearsed," grumbled a trumpet player who had a four-day tryout with the band; "after full rehearsals they'd get off by themselves and rehearse."[43] And in the words of a jazz historian:

> With the skill and foresight of such arrangers as Southern-born-and-bred Gene Gifford, the band learned to read harmonized solos and play riffs, the brass and reed sections calling and responding to each other in a variety of

43. Albert McCarthy, *Big Band Jazz* (New York: G. P. Putnam's Sons, 1974), p. 190.

ways. What is more, they learned to roll along together, generating considerable swing as a whole.[44]

From the beginning, their repertory consisted mostly of current Tin Pan Alley songs rather than instrumental pieces. In their first years they played and recorded such hits as "Happy Days Are Here Again" (Milton Ager and Jack Yellen, 1929), "Exactly Like You" (Jimmy McHugh and Dorothy Fields, 1930), "On the Sunny Side of the Street" (McHugh and Fields, 1930), "In the Still of the Night" (Cole Porter, 1937), and "Lazybones" (Hoagy Carmichael and Johnny Mercer, 1933), with vocalists Jack Richmond, Kenny Sargent, and Connie Boswell fronting the band. They were one of the first bands to appeal to college audiences, often playing for campus proms and other dances. They were also the first "jazz" band to be featured on a regular, commercial radio series, broadcast live from summer engagements at Glen Island Casino in 1933 and later years; and in December of 1935 the Casa Lomas were booked into the Paramount Theatre in New York as the feature attraction, the first band to play such an engagement. They set a house record for take, their engagement was extended for several weeks, and they paved the way for other bands to play such engagements.

Various events have been heralded as signaling the beginning of the big-band era. Benny Goodman, who formed his first permanent band in 1934 after a dozen years of playing for other groups, was one of three bands featured on a three-hour broadcast, "Let's Dance," sponsored by the National Biscuit Company; the first program, carried on a nationwide hookup, was on December 1, 1934. After a tremendously successful booking at the Palomar Ballroom in Los Angeles in the summer of 1935, the band was engaged at the Congress Hotel in Chicago for many months and was voted the best swing band of the year by *Metronome* magazine. Engagements at the Manhattan Room of the Hotel Pennsylvania (New York) and the Paramount Theatre followed, then a first-ever swing concert at New York's Carnegie Hall in 1938, and a triumphant appearance as part of a six-hour, 25-band "Carnival of Swing" at Randall's Island in New York that summer. Tommy and Jimmy Dorsey formed a band together in 1934, then split, each to form his own group the following year. Woody Herman debuted with his band at the Roseland in Brooklyn in 1936, Artie Shaw formed a band the same year, Gene Krupa and Harry James soon followed. The Age of Swing was in full flower.

The style of the big bands of the swing era was heavily indebted to the black bands led by Fletcher Henderson, Jimmie Lunceford, Benny Carter, and above all Count Basie. The latter is generally credited with bringing the style of Midwest and Southwest territory bands to New York: a repertory drawing on blues and riff themes, a compromise between arranged and improvised elements, all played with liberal doses of that mysterious element of swing. Benny Goodman

44. Ibid., p. 192.

played arrangements by Fletcher Henderson; Tommy Dorsey hired Sy Oliver, the arranger for Jimmie Lunceford's band. With rare exceptions, though, black musicians did not play in the white big bands. The size of the bands gradually increased, until it was not uncommon to find 8 brasses and 5 reeds, in addition to the 4 members of the rhythm section. The sound could be rich, mellow, over-poweringly loud, driving, sensuous, above all exciting; it captured the mood of a country struggling out of the depths of the Great Depression, toward economic stability and expansion—and, soon, involvement in a war enveloping almost the entire world, an involvement that would lift the country to a peak of military and industrial strength and thrust it to a position of leadership and power.

> The Great Band era was a huge and marvelous musical bazaar—a bub-bling, exciting mixture of places, names, melodies and events. They were immediately and exhilaratingly real, but at the same time they were part of the fabric of dream-world fantasy. . . . It was a time when the late-night air was filled with music—live music. Radio networks began their nightly rounds of "remote" broadcasts at 11 P.M. or even 10, and for four hours you could hear a different band every half hour, coming right into your living room from one after another of America's great dance floors. . . . There were swing bands and there were sweet bands and there were bands that were a bit of both. It was a period when dance music was freshened by crosswinds that brought jazz and popular music together for the first—and only—time. [45]

Some of the music played by the white big bands was indeed jazz, by almost anyone's definition. Their concerts, dance gigs, and radio broadcasts were sprin-kled with instrumental numbers, usually at fast tempos, often featuring solos by such musicians as Benny Goodman himself and other white players who could more than hold their own when playing with black jazz musicians of the day. But the majority of their pieces featured vocalists backed by the band; these were the best singers of the day, including Bob Eberle (with the Jimmy Dorsey Band), Frank Sinatra (with Tommy Dorsey and Harry James), Helen Ward (with Benny Goodman), Edythe Wright (Tommy Dorsey), Helen Forrest (Artie Shaw, Benny Goodman, and Harry James), Jo Stafford (Tommy Dorsey), Ray Eberle (Glenn Miller), and even Bing Crosby (Paul Whiteman, and briefly with the Dorseys) and Billie Holiday (Artie Shaw and Benny Goodman). And the songs performed by these singers fronting big bands were Tin Pan Alley products, typical ones. Just as the song style of this era maintained its distinctive character even when transplanted to the phonograph record, to radio, and to the sound movie, it was still hardy enough to survive and continue to flourish in the environment of big-band jazz. Tin Pan Alley songwriters did not modify their products to conform to the new sounds and playing styles of the big bands; the bands accommodated these songs. Seeing only the sheet music of popular songs of the period 1936–45,

45. John S. Wilson, *The Great Band Era* (1936–1945) (liner notes for RCA Custom Records RD3-25-1-10, made for *Readers' Digest*), pp. 6–7.

one would nave no idea of the changes in band styles that took place then. These songs were written in the same forms, using the same types of chords and similar lyrics (with a few exceptions), as those of the previous two decades.

Two examples will suffice to show how Tin Pan Alley songs were incorporated into big-band jazz. "These Foolish Things Remind Me of You" (Jack Strachey, Harry Link, and Holt Marvell, 1936) was recorded by Benny Goodman and His Orchestra in 1936, with Helen Ward as vocalist; it was one of Goodman's first popular hits with his own band. The song, cast in the usual AABA form, is a sentimental ballad recounting the various objects and incidents that remind an unsuccessful lover of his lost sweetheart. The problem was to incorporate the entire song into an arrangement that also spotlighted the sound of the band, and some of its instrumentalists as soloists. The solution:

introduction	solo clarinet	solo trombone	bridge	vocal solo	coda
(band)	A^1	A^2	(band)	$A^1A^2BA^3$	(band)

Thus a complete vocal chorus is embedded in the performance; the entire band plays alone for the 4-measure introduction and coda, and the bridge in the middle; clarinet (Goodman himself) and trombone soloists are given 4-measure solos in a half-chorus leading into the vocal chorus; there is no trace of a verse.

Tommy Dorsey's version of "I'll Be Seeing You" (Sammy Fain and Irving Kahal, 1938), recorded in 1944 with Frank Sinatra as vocal soloist, proceeds in much the same way. The song, in A^1BA^2C form, is arranged:

introduction	solo trumpet	bridge	vocal solo	bridge	solo clarinet
(band)	A^2C	(band)	A^1BA^2C	(band)	A^2C

The layout is essentially the same, with a complete chorus given to Sinatra in the middle, introductory and bridging sections giving the full band a chance to be heard, and two solo instrumentalists playing half-choruses (the second half is chosen because of the climactic high note at the very end of C). Again there is no verse.

Thus the era of the big bands brought no deviation in the course of popular song, only a change in the sound of the accompanying band and a sharing of the melodic material between singer and instrumental soloists. As had been the case at least twice before in the history of popular song, elements of black music were skimmed off to give a different and exotic flavor to the sound of songs (in this case, rhythms and instrumental timbres from black jazz), but the essential nature of the song itself was untouched and unchanged. And—as had been the case before—black musicians did not share in the immense profits to songwriters and publishers, nor even the more modest fees paid to instrumentalists in the various white bands, when big-band music became the most popular of its day.

The first top-selling record on the then-new *Billboard* weekly charts was "I'll Never Smile Again" (Ruth Lowe, 1939) as recorded by Tommy Dorsey and His Orchestra, with Frank Sinatra as vocalist; it was the No. 1 record on the first chart, published on July 20, 1940, and for eleven weeks following. With few exceptions, these charts were topped by records by the bands of the Dorseys, Glenn Miller, Kay Kyser, Artie Shaw, and Freddie Martin, through 1943. Glenn Miller, for example, had thirty-six records among the Top Ten—including seven No. 1 hits—for the period extending from July of 1940 to the end of 1943, and Jimmy Dorsey had five best-selling records in 1941 alone.

Frank Sinatra with Tommy Dorsey in 1941.

The demise of big-band music was heralded by the success of "Paper Doll" (Johnny S. Black, 1942) in a performance by the Mills Brothers, a black close-harmony group. Recorded in New York on February 18, 1942, but not released until mid-1943, the record could scarcely have been more different in sound from the big bands, with its four smoothly harmonizing voices accompanied only by acoustic guitar, keyboard, and bass. But it became the biggest hit of the entire decade: it was on *Billboard*'s Best Selling Singles charts for 30 consecutive weeks, 12 of these as the No. 1 hit (and this at a time when only ten to fifteen records made up the weekly chart); it appeared on "Your Hit Parade" for 23 weeks, a record topped by only seven other songs; and some 6,000,000 copies of the record were eventually sold. It is a typical Tin Pan Alley song in style, structure, and sentiment, proving the versatility of this product one more time.

The ten-year period following the end of World War II can best be characterized as the era of the "big singer." Even before the release of "Paper Doll," there had been signs that popular song was moving toward dominance by star singers, rather than bands or songwriters. Bing Crosby had sung only briefly with big bands; despite this, he had maintained his popularity, and he alone of the era's vocalists had brought out a string of successful discs under his own name, right through the dominance of the big bands. Dick Haymes had sung with several of the top bands, including those of Harry James and Benny Goodman, before launching his solo career in mid-1943 with the successful "It Can't Be Wrong" (Max Steiner and Kim Gannon, 1942); his version of "You'll Never Know" (Harry Warren and Mack Gordon, 1943) anticipated the success of "Paper Doll" by reaching the top spot on the *Billboard* charts briefly in mid-1943. Dinah Shore left the Xavier Cugat band for a solo career; her first top-selling record came in 1944, with "I'll Walk Alone (Jule Styne and Sammy Cahn). Frank Sinatra's first successful solo record (after he left Tommy Dorsey's band in late 1942) was his version of "You'll Never Know" in mid-1943; Perry Como left the Ted Weems band for a solo career in 1942; Jo Stafford also struck out on her own in late 1942, leaving Tommy Dorsey. A ranking of the top recording artists for the period 1940–55 includes only three bands among the first ten names:[46]

1. Bing Crosby
2. Perry Como
3. Eddie Fisher
4. Sammy Kaye
5. Jo Stafford
6. Patti Page
7. Vaughn Monroe
8. Andrews Sisters
9. Nat "King" Cole
10. Glenn Miller

These were the names known to record buyers, the names that would persuade them to purchase a given recording—not the names of the songwriters.

Irving Berlin, Cole Porter, Richard Rodgers, and Harry Warren were still writing songs in the postwar years, though with the exception of Rodgers, the peak of their quantitative productivity had passed. Though individual songs by younger composers were sometimes fully comparable to the best of those by the great songwriters of the 1910s, '20s, and '30s, no single individual or even small group of writers dominated the third generation of Tin Pan Alley; a survey of the

46. Joel Whitburn, *Top Pop Records, 1940–1955* (Menomonee Falls, Wisconsin: Record Research, 1973), p. 83.

most successful one hundred songs on "Your Hit Parade (1935–58), for instance, reveals that no one songwriter was responsible for more than three of these. In contrast, eight composers—Irving Berlin (9), Richard Rodgers (9), Harold Arlen (7), Cole Porter (6), George Gershwin (6), Jerome Kern (4), Jimmy McHugh (4), and Vincent Youmans (4)—accounted for half (49) of the songs on *Variety's* Golden 100 list of top Tin Pan Alley songs (1918–35) (Appendix 6).

Bing Crosby, the Andrews Sisters, and Irving Berlin looking at a copy of "Freedom Train" (1948).

The song style that had served Tin Pan Alley so well had changed very little, except in details, for almost half a century. It was still serviceable, but there were increasing signs that songwriters and audiences alike were reaching a saturation point and were beginning to cast about for a new type of song. Sentimental ballads still made up the core of the repertory, but other types of songs began to appear with increasing frequency in the decade following the end of World War II. There were more and more "novelty" songs, usually humorous: "Open the Door, Richard" (Jack McVea and Dan Howell, 1947); "Woody Woodpecker," based on the theme from a popular animated cartoon (George Tibbles and

Ramey Idriss, 1947); "The Thing" (Charles R. Grean, 1950); "Come on-a My House" (Ross Bagdasarian and William Saroyan, 1951); "That Doggie in the Window" (Bob Merrill, 1953). There were songs using Latin American rhythms: "Rum and Coca-Cola" (Jeri Sullavan and Paul Baron, 1944); "Mañana" (Peggy Lee and Dave Barbour, 1948); the instrumental "Blue Tango" (Leroy Anderson, 1952). There were songs invoking the American West: "On the Atchison, To-peka and the Santa Fe" (Harry Warren and Johnny Mercer, 1945); "Riders in the Sky" (Stan Jones, 1949); "Mule Train" (Johnny Lange, Hy Heath, and Fred Glickman, 1949); "Don't Fence Me In" (Cole Porter, 1944); "Buttons and Bows" (Jay Livingston and Ray Evans, 1948). This is not a random selection of song titles; each was a top-selling disc on the *Billboard* charts, and each was pro-grammed ten or more times on "Your Hit Parade."

Political events in the music business also played some role in the trend away from the traditional Tin Pan Alley ballad. When a five-year contract be-tween ASCAP and the major radio networks expired in 1940, the former de-manded a new contract at double the $4½-million-a-year fee of the previous agreement. The networks refused; ASCAP held out. The practical result was that radio's backlog of already recorded discs ran out, and there were no new songs to play over the air, since no live or recorded music written by an ASCAP com-poser or published by an ASCAP firm could be broadcast. Radio listeners found themselves listening to pre-ASCAP music (Stephen Foster enjoyed an unex-pected vogue), to folk music of various sorts, and to songs written by composers who were not ASCAP members. A new organization was hastily formed—BMI (Broadcast Music Incorporated)—to produce music for broadcast purposes; its membership was made up of composers and lyricists who had not been invited to join ASCAP, many of them young and others who had been involved with sorts of music not favored by ASCAP songwriters and publishers. A new contract was eventually signed by ASCAP and the networks in 1941, and Tin Pan Alley music was back on the air. But BMI had at least a foot in the door of the popular music industry, and the radio and recording industries continued to use some of their products, including such offbeat songs as "You Are My Sunshine" (copyrighted in 1940 by Jimmie Davis, a country music singer and politician from Louisiana who was to become governor of the state), "Amapola" (a Spanish song written in 1924 by Joseph M. Lacalle, which became a top-selling record in early 1941 in a performance by Jimmy Dorsey), the pseudo-Western song "Deep in the Heart of Texas" (written in 1941 by Don Swander and June Hershey, and successfully recorded by both Bing Crosby and Alvino Rey), and "Pistol Packin' Mama" (Al Dexter, 1943, a No. 1 best-seller as recorded by the composer himself, and also popular in a version that same year by Bing Crosby and the Andrews Sisters). These and other early BMI products were yet another barometer of a changing taste in popular song in the 1940s.

As mid-century passed, New York had been the center of the publication and composition of popular song for some sixty years. An urban song style had grown up in the city, a style combining elements of the previous generations of

American song with fresh harmonic and melodic ideas from nineteenth-century European classical music—and this mixture spiced with rhythmic and instrumental idiosyncracies of the music of black Americans. The resulting product was the vehicle for some of the finest and most successful songs in the history of the genre. But the mood of America was changing, the Tin Pan Alley style had lost its freshness and cutting edge, and it was only a matter of time before another corner would be turned and American song would once again incorporate new elements from the rich and complex musical heritage of the country.

FIFTEEN

"Rock Around the Clock";

OR.

The Rise of Rock 'n' Roll

Nobody likes rock and roll but the public.
—Bill Haley

I came from a family where my people didn't like rhythm and blues. Bing Crosby–"Pennies from Heaven"–Ella Fitzgerald, was all I heard. And I knew there was something that could be louder than that, but I didn't know where to find it. And I found it was me.
—Little Richard (Penniman)

BILLBOARD magazine, the trade journal of the popular music industry, listed "Rock Around the Clock" by Bill Haley and the Comets as the top song for the week of July 9, 1955. The song held the top spot for eight weeks, and at the end of the year *Cash Box* reported that it had been the best-selling phonograph record for the entire year.

These simple statistics confirmed what the music industry already knew— that a revolution of major proportions was sweeping the field of popular music.

At no other point in the two-hundred-year history of popular song in America had there been such a drastic and dramatic change in such a brief period of time. And it was an all-encompassing revolution, affecting not only musical style but also the entire music industry and the audience for such music. Beyond that, this new music was merely the tip of an iceberg, a visible clue that American life and culture were undergoing violent, traumatic changes.

The years immediately preceding the emergence of rock 'n' roll were still dominated by the Tin Pan Alley–Hollywood–Broadway style defined in the preceding chapter.

Tied for first place in record sales for 1953 were "Song from Moulin Rouge" from a movie of that year, with a tune by the French composer Georges Auric, and "Till I Waltz Again with You," as recorded by Teresa Brewer. Next was "April in Portugal," adapted from a song written in 1947 by Raul Ferrão, in the international-popular style. The Broadway musical *Kismet*, with songs adapted from melodies by the nineteenth-century Russian composer Borodin, yielded several hit songs, including "Stranger in Paradise." There were new songs by Cole Porter, from his musical *Can-Can*, and by Rodgers and Hammerstein, from *Me and Juliet*. The year 1954 brought "Hey There," from the Broadway musical *Pajama Game* (by Richard Adler and Jerry Ross), and "Secret Love" by Paul Francis Webster and Sammy Fain, from the movie *Calamity Jane*. The best-selling record was Kitty Kallen's "Little Things Mean a Lot" (Edith Lindeman and Carl Stutz), squarely in the mainstream of Tin Pan Alley musical style.

In addition to these new songs, there was considerable radio play and record sales of older songs. *Variety* magazine for January 13, 1954, listed the "Top Standards" for the year just ended, according to radio and TV exposure:

1. "Tea for Two" — 1924 *w*, Irving Caesar, *m*, Vincent Youmans
2. "White Christmas" — 1942 *w,m*, Irving Berlin
3. "Lover" — 1933 *w*, Lorenz Hart, *m*, Richard Rodgers
4. "By the Light of the Silv'ry Moon" — 1909 *w*, Edward Madden, *m*, Gus Edwards
5. "Tenderly" — 1946 *w*, Jack Lawrence, *m*, Walter Gross
6. "There's No Business Like Show Business" — 1946 *w,m*, Irving Berlin
7. "That Old Black Magic" — 1942 *w*, Johnny Mercer, *m*, Harold Arlen
8. "Easter Parade" — 1933 *w,m*, Irving Berlin
9. "Winter Wonderland" — 1934 *w*, Dick Smith, *m*, Felix Barnard
10. " 'S Wonderful" — 1927 *w*, Ira Gershwin, *m*, George Gershwin

Though music publishers continued to dominate the industry, the sale of discs was increasing with tremendous rapidity; *Variety* reported that recordings had grossed $215,000,000 in 1953; increases were expected in 1954. *Variety* and other music trade journals had recently begun to carry weekly and yearly reports on record sales, including charts listing top sellers. The songs on such lists are virtually identical with the best-selling pieces of sheet music: 34 of the 35 Sheet Music Best Sellers of 1954 listed in *Variety* for January 13, 1954, are also on the Disc Best Sellers of 1954 in the same issue.

The recording industry was controlled by a handful of major companies;

Variety's list of the fifty best-selling discs of 1954, as published in the issue for January 6, 1955, breaks down by company as follows:

Victor	11
Columbia	8
Capitol	8
Decca	8
Mercury	7
Others	8
	50

Popular song, then, seemed to be very much the same as it had been for many decades, with familiar composers still turning out new songs and younger composers writing in the same style; with frequent performances of older songs drawn from a fifty-year period; and with no significant change in musical style since early in the twentieth century.

Only twenty-five years after the fact, the early years of rock 'n' roll are already clouded with mists of nostalgia. Most people who were young then, upon hearing "golden oldies" now, tend to reminisce about a happier and simpler time, when music was uncomplicated, cheerful, and mostly amusing. But in truth this music was taken by most people in 1955 as shocking, exciting, and most of all, extraordinarily different from what had preceded it.

Bill Haley and the Comets (1955).

"Rock Around the Clock" was by no means the first piece of rock 'n' roll. Haley's recording of "Shake, Rattle, and Roll," released in 1954, passed the 1,000,000 mark in record sales in February of 1955, having been among the top five best-selling discs for some twenty weeks. But it was "Rock Around the Clock" that signaled in most dramatic form, by its rise to the top spot in record sales, that this new music was indeed a serious challenge to the long-established traditions of Tin Pan Alley.

Bill Haley and his group brought out seven other discs in 1955 that sold well enough to be listed on the Top Fifty charts of *Billboard* magazine: "Birth of the Boogie," "Burn That Candle," "Dim, Dim the Lights," "Mambo Rock," "Razzle Dazzle," "Rock a Beatin' Boogie," and "Two Hound Dogs." Later that year "Maybellene," sung by Chuck Berry, became the first widely successful piece of rock 'n' roll by a performer other than Bill Haley. Berry was a Southern black (born in St. Louis), as was also the next performer to have a successful rock 'n' roll record: "Tutti-Frutti," recorded by Little Richard (Penniman) of Macon, Georgia, made an appearance on *Billboard*'s Top Fifty charts in December of 1955. Rock 'n' roll was thus established, in its first year, as an interracial music.

The year of fruition for rock 'n' roll was 1956, when any lingering doubts about its continuing commercial potential were laid to rest. Bill Haley continued to flood the market with new discs, some of which enjoyed some success ("R.O.C.K.," "Saints' Rock and Roll," and "See You Later Alligator"), and Little Richard ("Long Tall Sally") and Chuck Berry ("Roll Over Beethoven") continued to record. But the biggest news came from new performers. Elvis Presley, who had recorded several blues and country-western songs for Sun Records in Memphis, brought out his first disc under a new contract with RCA-Victor, "Heartbreak Hotel." Recorded in Nashville on January 10, 1956, it rose to the No. 1 position on the *Billboard* weekly chart of pop music, retaining the top spot for two months. In August another Presley disc, "Hound Dog"/"Don't Be Cruel," rose to the top, staying there for eleven weeks, and was then replaced by still another Presley disc, "Love Me Tender." One or another of his records held the No. 1 position for 25 of the 52 weeks of 1956.

Carl Perkins was doing a radio show in Jackson, Tennessee, when he recorded "Blue Suede Shoes" for Sun Records; the song sold well for many weeks, at one point reaching the No. 4 spot on *Billboard*'s weekly charts. Jerry Lee Lewis was another white Southerner (born in Ferriday, Louisiana) to record early rock 'n' roll. His first disc, "Whole Lotta Shakin' Going On," (Sun Records, 1957) was in *Billboard*'s Top Fifty charts for 29 weeks, rising as high as the No. 3 spot, and his "Great Balls of Fire" later that year was almost as successful.

These six men—Bill Haley, Chuck Berry, Little Richard, Elvis Presley, Carl Perkins, and Jerry Lee Lewis—were at the center of early rock 'n' roll. Their discs sold tens of millions of copies between 1955 and 1958, and this new popular style was perfectly defined in their music.

It differed in almost every possible way from the music that had dominated popular song in America for almost half a century. There was, first of all, the sheer intensity of rock 'n' roll. There are no strings, no lush chords spread through an orchestra, no mellow big-band sounds. Bill Haley recorded with a small group: several guitars, a bass, a coarse-sounding saxophone, and an energetic drummer. Chuck Berry used the same instruments, backed with a larger horn section of saxes, trumpets, and trombones. Little Richard sang with a small band, with piano, guitars, and a sax dominating the sound. Presley recorded with only guitar (which he played himself), bass, piano, and drums, and later with a male quartet; Carl Perkins recorded with guitars, bass, and drums; Jerry Lee Lewis accompanied himself with piano, supported by guitar, bass, and drums. The sound, for each, was driving, spare, percussive, loud; the guitars—the usual six-string acoustic instruments of folk and country-western music—were amplified by a microphone or by an electronic pick-up; and the bass line was heavy and prominent. The instruments were those of country-western and black music. Not a violin was to be heard, nor a flute, cello, or oboe.

Singing styles were those of white and black rural music. Bill Haley's voice was grating, nasal, delivered in a style somewhere between shouting and singing—a voice that would have been ludicrous in a Tin Pan Alley song. Chuck Berry and Little Richard sang in vocal styles derived from black gospel music

A triple shot of Chuck Berry on stage.

and jazz; Jerry Lee Lewis and Carl Perkins sounded like the country-western singers they were. There was no crooning, no sustained high notes reminiscent of the vocal techniques of Western European art music, no legato phrasing. To ears accustomed to European-American classical-popular singing, the early rock 'n' roll stars shouted, screamed, snarled, rasped, whined—did everything, in fact, but sing.

Every early rock 'n' roll song is based on the 12-bar blues form, a widely popular pattern not only in blues but also in much jazz. The structure is simple and repetitious:

	a				b				c			
/	I	I	I	I /	IV	IV	I	I /	V	IV	I	I /

The three phrases are each of 4 measures, with the chord on each measure shown in the diagram above. Melodically, the a and b phrases are similar, giving an overall pattern of AAB. Precisely the same pattern is repeated over and over, with no change whatsoever in the chords, until the piece is over. Thus a piece in this form contains only three chords. There are no chromatic chords, no modulations, none of the harmonic shadings and subtleties taken over by Tin Pan Alley from classical music of the nineteenth and early twentieth centuries. Since each chorus moves through precisely the same harmonies, there is no overall movement of chords toward a final climax near the end of the song. The effect, harmonic and melodic, is of insistence and repetition, rather than movement and contrast.

Even more than its instrumental and vocal sound and its harmonic style, the rhythmic patterns and impulses of this music struck listeners as very different from what they were accustomed to in popular song. Almost all early rock 'n' roll pieces moved along at a fast, driving tempo; there was heavy emphasis on the first beat of every measure, marked by a strong rhythmic accent in all instruments, but particularly in the rhythm section (drums, piano, bass); the second and fourth beats of the measure were given secondary accents. Europeans branded it "big beat" music; and a reporter from *Time* magazine, one of the first "establishment" publications to comment on this new musical phenomenon, wrote:

> Only the obsessive beat pounds through, stimulating the crowd to such rhythmic movements as clapping in tempo and jumping and dancing in the aisles. Sometimes the place vibrates with the beat of music and stamping feet, and not infrequently kids have been moved to charging the stage, rushing ushers and theater guards. There is no denying that rock 'n' roll evokes a physical response from even its most reluctant listeners, for that giant pulse matches the rhythmical operations of the human body, and the performers are all too willing to specify it.[1]

Texts were equally remote from the romantic-love-oriented lyrics so pervasive in Tin Pan Alley songs. "Rocking" and "rolling" were common euphemisms for sexual intercourse among American blacks, and when Bill Haley sang

> Oh when it's eight, nine, ten, and eleven, too,
> I'll be going strong and so will you,
> We're gonna rock around the clock tonight . . .

1. *Time*, June 18, 1956.

there was not a member of his audience, even white middle-class kids in their early teens, who didn't understand. With its driving, pulsing, insistent rhythm and suggestive texts, early rock 'n' roll was a raucous and sometimes crude celebration of sex, intended as such by its composers and performers, understood as such by the audience. The stage deportment of many of the early performers, particularly Elvis Presley, did even more to convey this message to the audience.

> Elvis Presley ripped off Ike Eisenhower by turning our uptight young awakened bodies around. Hard animal rock energy beat/surged hot through us, the driving rhythm arousing repressed passions.[2]

A country singer, Bob Luman, wrote of his first encounter with Presley, when he was still enjoying only local fame:

> This cat came out in red pants and a green coat and a pink shirt and socks, and he had this sneer on his face and he stood behind the mike for five minutes, I'll bet, before he made a move. Then he hit his guitar a lick, and he broke two strings. I'd been playing ten years, and I hadn't broken a *total* of two strings. So there he was, these two strings dangling, and he hadn't done anything yet, and these high school girls were screaming and fainting and running up to the stage, and then he started to move his hips real slow like he had a thing for his guitar.[3]

Newsweek reported in its first account of him that "his bodily movements were embarrassingly specific,"[4] and another critic wrote:

> Without preamble, the three-piece band cuts loose. In the spotlight, the lanky singer flails furious rhythms on his guitar, every now and then breaking a string. In a pivoting stance, his hips swing sensuously from side to side and his entire body takes on a frantic quiver, as if he had swallowed a jackhammer.[5]

This music polarized America almost instantly. On one side were a goodly number of the teenagers of the country, who flocked to rock 'n' roll concerts in unprecedented numbers when a live show was available, and listened to this new music on their phonographs and radios constantly. They made up the almost exclusive audience for this new music, which they were able to enjoy at will with the aid of postwar technological advances and the healthy state of the American economy. Lightweight, battery-operated, inexpensive radios made it possible for them to take rock 'n' roll with them wherever they went; some ten million of

2. Jerry Rubin, *Do It! Scenarios of the Revolution* (New York: Simon and Schuster, 1970), p. 18.

3. Jim Miller, ed., *The Rolling Stone Illustrated History of Rock & Roll* (New York: Rolling Stone Press, 1976), p. 30.

4. *Newsweek*, May 14, 1956.

5. *Time*, May 14, 1956.

Elvis Presley in action at the height of his popularity.

these new portable radios were sold every year during the late 1950s. Phonographic playback equipment was also within their price range now, and the new 45-rpm records introduced in 1948 made discs with one song on each side available for less than a dollar. Their chief allies were disk jockeys—a new breed of radio personality, usually young, mostly sympathetic to this type of music themselves, often ambitious and seeking an identification with rock 'n' roll as a means of furthering their careers. DJs, beginning with Alan Freed, at station WJW in Cleveland, devoted entire programs to rock 'n' roll, rather than spotting pieces here and there on programs made up of various types of music; soon several large city stations were offering rock 'n' roll almost around the clock.

Devotion to this music often bordered on fanaticism. Fans in Fort Worth, Texas, were reported to have carved Elvis Presley's name on their arms with knives when he performed there in the spring of 1956; a melee broke out between fans and policemen during a rock 'n' roll concert in San Jose, California in July of 1956, ending with eleven persons injured and $3,000 damage to the dance hall where the concert was held; Presley was mobbed by frenzied teenagers while playing in Jacksonville, Florida, and almost all his clothes were ripped off; a disk jockey at station KSDA in Redding, California, played Presley's "Hound Dog"/"Don't Be Cruel" record for several hours in defiance, after some listeners phoned in to protest his airing such "obscene and vulgar" music; a San Francisco disk jockey played "Love Me Tender" fourteen times in a row to protest a ban his station, KYA, had placed on the playing of rock 'n' roll between 10 A.M. and 4 P.M.; in Miami, a disk jockey who had refused to play Presley's records on his program had his hairpiece snatched off his head in public by an irate teenager.

But almost everyone else in America, it appeared, had equally strong feelings *against* rock 'n' roll. Religious leaders spoke out quickly and strongly: the Roman Catholic church in Boston urged that rock 'n' roll be banned in that city, and the Rev. Charles Howard Graf, rector of the Protestant Episcopal Church of St. John's in New York, said from his pulpit that teenagers were having a "vicarious fling" that would soon pass, that Elvis Presley made up for lack of musical talent by "innuendo and suggestion, by curl of lip and shake of hip," and that "basically, I don't think youth wants this sort of thing."[6] Juvenile Court Judge Marion Gooding of Jacksonville, Florida, prepared warrants for Presley's arrest on charges of impairing the morals of minors, in anticipation of a Presley concert, declaring that he intended to serve the warrants if things got "out of hand" at the concert. Dr. Francis J. Braceland, psychiatrist-in-chief of the Institute of Living in Hartford, Connecticut, called rock 'n' roll a "communicable disease" and a "cannibalistic and tribalistic" form of music. Piano tuner O. J. Dodd protested to delegates of a National Piano Tuners convention in Kansas City that the playing of rock 'n' roll pianists was a threat to the nation's keyboards. The "responsible" press of America largely ignored rock 'n' roll for several years, then

6. *New York Times*, December 17, 1956.

attacked it; the *New York Times* for September 16, 1956, carried a column by Jack Gould chiding the television industry for its "lack of responsibility" in "exploiting teen-agers," citing a recent appearance by Presley on the Ed Sullivan show during which he "injected movements of the tongue and indulged in wordless singing that were singularly distasteful," and concluding that "selfish exploitation and commercialized overstimulation of youth's physical impulses is certainly a gross national disservice."

Even stronger words came from many musicians. The great Spanish cellist Pablo Casals wrote:

> You want to know what I think of that abomination, rock 'n' roll? I think it is a disgrace. Poison put to sound! When I hear it I feel very sad not only for music but for the people who are addicted to it. I am also sorry for America—that such a great country should have nothing better to pour into the expectant ear of mankind than this raucous distillation of the ugliness of our times. . . . The French have a word *abrutissant*, for anything that brutalizes man and tends to turn him into a beast. That's the word for this terrible, convulsive sound. It is against art, against life. It leads away from the exaltation and elevation of spirit that should spring naturally from all good music.[7]

And the distinguished American composer and educator Howard Hanson wrote that "rock and roll is acoustical pollution. . . . Is this progress? We have lost our sense of values . . ." and voiced his fear that America would "sink in swamps of mediocrity" unless certain trends, musical and otherwise, were reversed.[8]

At least some of the problems surrounding rock 'n' roll stemmed from the fact that it was integrated music. There were racial overtones to many of the disturbances: there were problems in the audience, with the police dispatched to keep order when Fats Domino's band played to an integrated crowd in Houston's City Auditorium; Rear Admiral Ralph D. Earle, Jr., banned rock 'n' roll performances at the enlisted men's club in Newport, Rhode Island, after a disturbance during a show by Fats Domino ("The cause of the melee . . . was the excitement accompanying the fever-pitched 'Rock 'n' Roll' among the audience of white and Negro sailors and marines and their wives and dates" reported the *New York Times* for September 20, 1956); and the same band was involved in another melee, this time in Fayetteville, North Carolina, caused by "the beat and the booze"—police fired tear gas into the crowd, two soldiers from Fort Bragg were stabbed, and four members of the band received minor cuts. Asa E. ("Ace") Carter of the North Alabama Citizens Council, a group formed to resist court-ordered school desegregation, said in an interview (*Newsweek*, April 23, 1956) that jazz and rock 'n' roll were part of a plot by the NAACP to "mongrelize America" by forcing "Negro culture" on the South; he characterized rock 'n'

7. "A Disgrace to Music," *Music Journal*, January 19, 1961, p. 18.
8. Howard Hanson, "Rock and Roll: Is This the Way?," *Clavier* 1/5 (1965), p. 8.

roll as "the basic, heavy-beat music of Negroes. It appeals to the base in man, brings out animalism and vulgarity."

The first protests against this new music, though, had come from the music industry itself. In early 1955, before most of the country was aware of what was happening, *Variety* magazine, the trade journal of the entertainment world, ran a first-page article in its issue of February 9 under the headline "Music Biz Now R&B Punchy."[9] *Variety* chose to attack this new music on "moral" grounds, with frequent articles on disturbances at rock 'n' roll concerts, on protests against this music (particularly if they came from religious or civic leaders), and on such things as the firing of a "brave" disc jockey at radio station KXLW who stood by his principles and refused to play rock 'n' roll. *Variety*'s own position was stated in the issue for February 23, 1955, in an unprecedented editorial, "A Warning to the Music Business," calling on the music industry to police itself before "Governmental and religious lightning" struck:

> The most casual look at the current crop of "lyrics" must tell even the most naive that dirty postcards have been translated into songs. Compared to some of the language that loosely passes for song "lyrics" today, the "pool-table papa" and "jelly-roll" terminology of yesteryear is polite palaver. Only difference is that this sort of lyric then was off in a corner by itself. It was the music underworld—not the mainstream.
>
> Music "leer-ics" are touching new lows and if the fast-buck songsmiths and music-makers are incapable of social responsibility and self-restraint then regulation—policing, if you will—will have to come from more responsible sources. . . .
>
> What are we talking about? We're talking about "rock and roll," about "hug" and "squeeze" and kindred euphemisms which are attempting a total breakdown of all reticences about sex. In the past such material was common enough but restricted to special places and out-and-out barrelhouses. Today "leer-ics" are offered as standard popular music for general consumption by teen-agers.
>
> Some may argue that this is a proposal of "censorship." Not at all. It is a plea to ownership to assume the responsibilities of ownership and eliminate practices which will otherwise invite censorship. In short, chums, do it yourself or have it done for you.

The response was immediate: the next issue of *Variety* carried letters from a number of important men in the music industry. Herman Finkelstein, general legal counsel for ASCAP, applauded *Variety* for taking a stand against those people who "pander to the lowest possible public taste" and recounted an incident at the Riverside Hospital: a nurse had forced teenaged narcotic addicts to stop playing rock 'n' roll during recreational periods because they "played certain records over and over again, danced in a slow, moody manner and came close to

9. The term "rock 'n' roll" was not yet in common use, and this music was often referred to as "rhythm-and-blues," the label for popular music of black Americans.

a state of hypnosis." Martin Levine, general manager of Brandy Theatres, wrote, "I have a couple of growing youngsters of my own. I'd rather they didn't hear the complained of stuff. Neither their mother nor I wants to set up as two house dicks checking on the morality of the music lyrics they hear." Frank B. Walker, president of MGM records, wrote that he was "happy that you have taken up the cudgel in behalf of good music and, particularly, good lyrics."

The popular music industry—the major recording companies, the publishing houses, the ASCAP songwriters and lyricists, the singers and instrumentalists who performed Tin Pan Alley music—had ample reason for alarm.

Victor dropped from 11 discs on the Top 50 Disc Best Sellers in 1954 to 5 in 1955, and Columbia was down from 8 to 3. A new company, Dot, suddenly had 7 discs among the Top 50, and the total number of records by small companies had risen from 8 in 1954 to 19 in 1955. The following year saw even greater erosion of the former near-monopoly by the major companies: Victor-Capitol-Decca-Mercury-Columbia, which had accounted for 42 of the Top 50 as recently as 1954, had only 17 top-selling discs in 1956; no fewer than 25 different recording companies were represented by one or more discs among the Top 50. And there could be no mistaking the cause of this upheaval—among these 25 were a number of "indies" (small, independent record companies) such as Chess Records, Dootone, Sun Records, and Imperial, which recorded only black or country-western performers.

The situation with the major music publishers was even worse. Simply put, the advent of rock 'n' roll caused a precipitous decline in sheet music sales, so dramatic as to threaten the entire industry. Sheet music versions of all the successful rock 'n' roll songs were published—mostly by smaller firms, some not even located in New York—but their sales were only a fraction of the number of discs sold of these songs. Such songs as "Shake, Rattle, and Roll," "Maybellene," "Tutti-Frutti," and "Hound Dog," best-sellers in their recorded versions, did not even show up on Variety's Sheet Music Best Seller lists. Within two years of the advent of rock 'n' roll, according to Variety magazine, "the sales of sheet music [were] dwindling to the point of no return," and

> For the oldtime Tin Pan Alley publishers and songsmiths, the revolution in the music biz is now an irreversible fact. Once the dog that wagged the tail and then reduced to the dog that was wagged by the tail, the publishing phase of the music business is now primarily an appendage to the disk, the all-powerful boss of the music biz which calls the tunes and makes the hits.[10]

At the root of this switch of power from music publishers to recording companies was perhaps the most fundamental change in the entire history of popular song in America—from a music existing in a written tradition to one in oral tradition.

Almost without exception, the early rock 'n' roll performers, both black and

10. *Variety: 42nd Anniversary Issue,* January 1958.

white, were from the South. Despite intense and continuing problems between the races in this section of the country, it was only in the South that there was significant contact and communication between blacks and whites in America. Inevitably, the two races exchanged elements of their cultures, and the South over a period of time had developed its own, distinct variant of American culture, indebted to interracial exchange.

To observe what this means in musical terms, one needs look no further than Elvis Presley. Born into a poor white family in the rural Deep South, his first musical experiences were at the Pentecostal First Assembly of God Church, where an ecstatic singing practice had developed similar to that of many black churches. An avid radio listener from childhood, he was able to tune in to stations playing white, country-western music (Roy Acuff, Eddy Arnold, and the other stars of the *Grand Ole Opry* broadcasts from Nashville, as well as less well known local and regional favorites performing live), to black popular music (Billy Eckstine, the Ink Spots), and to authentic black country-blues singers (Big Bill Broonzy and Big Boy Crudup, for instance). When he moved to Memphis at thirteen, he was in a city with a distinctive blues tradition of its own; Howlin' Wolf, Sonny Boy Williamson, B. B. King, and Rufus Thomas were merely the best known of the many blues singers who could be heard live and on discs, over such Memphis stations as WDIA, the first black-operated radio station in the South. Memphis was also the home of Sun Records, operated by Sam Phillips, a former radio announcer from Florence, Alabama, for "negro artists in the South who wanted to make a record but just had no place to go."[11] In Memphis, as elsewhere in the South, many white kids were picking up slang, clothing styles, and other tastes from blacks.

It was at Sun Records that Presley cut his first commercial disc, on July 5–6, 1954, "That's All Right"—a blues which Presley knew from a recording by Big Boy Crudup. As performed by Presley, backed by Scotty Moore on guitar and Bill Black on bass, it was a successful marriage of black and white Southern music of the time. A straightforward 12-bar blues in form, it bounces along at a lively tempo, with a prominent bass part and some effective use of "blue" notes in the lead guitar, played by Presley. But the rhythm guitar plays the simple strummed chords of country-western music and Presley's singing is mostly on the beat—with little of the rhythmic and melodic elaboration and embellishment heard in black singers—and the sound has more than a trace of the nasal singing style so characteristic of traditional Anglo-American music and its offspring, country-western music. In every detail, the result is a piece of rock 'n' roll, though the term was not yet in use.

Both traditions to which this music is indebted, Afro-American and Anglo-American music, exist in oral tradition, learned and passed on by ear, without benefit of musical notation. Presley and his two backup musicians knew "That's All Right" from having heard it; for their recording, they

11. Miller, p. 32.

worked out, by ear, an arrangement that suited them and reflected their individual and collective styles and talents. All early rock 'n' roll songs were worked out in the same way. If the song was a new one, the person who had "written" it taught it to the other members of the performing group, by ear, and they worked on it together until the results were acceptable. There was no written arrangement; not even the melody was written down; at most, one of the players might jot down the sequence of chords in the piece to jog his memory. Once a piece was recorded, other performers might pick it up for their own use, again by listening to it enough times to get the melody, lyrics, and chord changes in mind, then working it out by ear to fit their own collection of instruments and their own musical style. It is true that there were soon sheet music arrangements of the popular and successful rock 'n' roll songs, but these were made by someone hired by the publisher to get the music down on paper *after* the song had been performed and recorded. And these were skeleton versions, often merely approximations of the melody with a rudimentary piano part that in no way captured the style of the individual performers making up a rock 'n' roll band.

Thus rock 'n' roll threatened the established popular music industry at almost every level. There was no need for arrangers, orchestrators, or conductors; instrumentalists with standard schooling, who could play only by note, could not cope with it; publication of songs as sheet music was incidental and a quite minor part of the process; the singing style appropriate to such music was alien to most of the singers who had made careers as performers of Tin Pan Alley songs.

There were problems for the recording industry also, but of quite a different nature.

Just as Charles K. Harris's "After the Ball" had been the first spectacular demonstration, half a century earlier, of the market and profit potential of sheet music, Elvis Presley's early discs demonstrated that rock 'n' roll had the potential of previously unimagined record sales. "Heartbreak Hotel" sold more than 1,000,000 copies in the several months following its release in early 1956, and "I Want You, I Need You" also quickly topped the million mark. The pairing of "Hound Dog" and "Don't Be Cruel" sold more than 3,000,000 discs in only a year, and sales orders *before release* for "Love Me Tender" were more than a million. In 1956 alone, Presley's discs sold more than 10,000,000 copies. The recording industry had seen nothing like this. Bing Crosby's "White Christmas" and Gene Autry's "Rudolph, the Red-Nosed Reindeer" had sold many millions of copies, and both Patti Page's version of "Tennessee Waltz" and Tennessee Ernie Ford's recording of "16 Tons" approached sales of 3,000,000, but these figures represented the accumulation of sales over a period of many years.

The recording industry had assumed, from the time it began bringing out discs of popular music, that there were three different layers of American society, each with its own music:

white, literate, largely urban, middle- and upper-class	Tin Pan Alley popular song

white, rural, working-class country-western music
black, rural and urban blues, gospel, jazz

Though precise figures on record sales during the 1920s, '30s, and '40s are almost impossible to find, certainly the first group of these three had the most money to spend on recordings, and sales of discs for this market accounted for a major share of the income from popular music. *Billboard* magazine began a

Presley at a recording session in 1956.

weekly chart of Best Selling Singles in its issue of July 29, 1940, ranking the discs that had sold the most copies the previous week; these charts continued until the issue of October 26, 1955, then were replaced by a Top 100 chart beginning with the issue of November 2, 1955, with a change of name to The Hot 100 in August of 1958. Until 1955, these lists chart the final two decades of Tin Pan Alley's domination of popular music; the singers selling the most discs between 1940 and 1955 were Bing Crosby, Perry Como, Eddie Fisher, Sammy Kaye, Jo Stafford, and Patti Page; their repertory consisted almost entirely of songs by the second and third generations of Tin Pan Alley songwriters.

Meanwhile, sales of recordings by black performers intended for black listeners became large enough in the early 1940s for *Billboard* to introduce a weekly chart of the ten best-selling records on the Harlem Hit Parade. This was replaced by a chart of the fifteen top Race Records in the mid-'40s, and on June

17, 1949, *Billboard* changed the title to "Rhythm & Blues," the number of discs charted gradually rising to 50. *Billboard*'s first Best Selling Retail Country & Western Records chart appeared on June 17, 1949, listing the fifteen top discs of this genre; the title became "C & W" on June 20, 1956, and the number of charted records gradually grew to fifty by the mid-1960s.

These three markets were almost completely segregated, each with its own performers, its own radio stations, its own retail outlets. Until the 1950s, it never occurred to anyone that a disc could cross over from one chart to another. There were a few straws in the wind in the early 1950s suggesting that such rigidity might give way: college students, in the South and East, were listening to and buying "race" records, and several white disk jockeys, beginning with Alan Freed at station WJW in Cleveland, were discovering a large and enthusiastic audience among young whites for this music. But it still came as a complete surprise to the recording industry when in the summer of 1955, Bill Haley's "Rock Around the Clock," the top-selling single on the "white" charts, showed up also on the rhythm-and-blues charts, rising as high as the No. 4 position. Even more startling was the fact that Chuck Berry's "Maybellene," the top-selling single on the rhythm-and-blues charts in the early fall of the same year, appeared also on the "white" best-selling singles chart, staying there for 14 weeks and moving as high as the No. 5 spot. Elvis Presley's "Heartbreak Hotel" brought an even greater surprise: it became the top-selling record on both the Top 100 and the country-western charts, and was the No. 5 song on the rhythm-and-blues chart, simultaneously. Presley's "Hound Dog"/"Don't Be Cruel" disc of mid-1956 was even more stunning, rising to the top spot on all three charts.

There had been several earlier examples of crossovers, not so dramatic as those of the first rock 'n' roll years of 1955–56, but in retrospect, clear anticipations of what was to come. Discs by such black performers as the Mills Brothers and the Ink Spots had sold well among whites in the 1940s and '50s; the repertory of these groups was drawn mostly from Tin Pan Alley, their singing was in a style not markedly different from that of white performers, and such discs had enjoyed little sale among blacks, who apparently heard this as "white" music. But "Crying in the Chapel" by the Orioles, a black group clearly descended from the Ink Spots and Mills Brothers, reached the top of the rhythm-and-blues charts in the summer of 1953—and also made the "white" charts for 8 weeks, reaching as high as the No. 11 position. "Gee" by the Crows, another black close-harmony group, showed up on both black and white charts in early 1954, and "Earth Angel" by the Penguins—a similar group—became a top-selling disc on the rhythm-and-blues market in December of 1954 and also rose to No. 8 on *Billboard*'s Best Selling Singles (i.e., "white") chart at the same time.

Table I lists the most important crossover discs of the 1950s. The industry's concept of three different markets was breaking down, and one reason for the phenomenal success of Presley and other early rock 'n' roll performers was that their popularity cut across racial and cultural-ethnic lines.

As always, American popular music was a mirror of the society that created

Table I: Chart Crossovers—Popular / Rhythm-and-Blues / Country-Western

Month and Year	Song and Performers	Pop	R&B	C-W
7/53	"Crying in the Chapel" (Orioles)	11	1	—
3/54	"Gee" (Crows)	17	6	—
12/54	"Earth Angel" (Penguins)	8	1	—
5/55	"Rock Around the Clock" (Bill Haley)	1	4	—
7/55	"Maybellene" (Chuck Berry)	5	1	—
7/55	"Only You" (Platters)	5	1	—
11/55	"The Great Pretender" (Platters)	1	1	—
2/56	"Heartbreak Hotel" (Elvis Presley)	1	5	1
* 7/56	"Don't Be Cruel"/"Hound Dog" (Elvis Presley)	1	1	1
9/56	"Blueberry Hill" (Fats Domino)	4	1	—
10/56	"Love Me Tender" (Elvis Presley)	1	4	3
2/57	"I'm Walking" (Fats Domino)	5	1	—
3/57	"All Shook Up" (Elvis Presley)	1	1	3
5/57	"Bye Bye Love" (Everly Brothers)	2	5	1
* 6/57	"Let Me Be Your Teddy Bear (Elvis Presley)	1	1	1
6/57	"Whole Lotta Shakin' " (Jerry Lee Lewis)	3	1	1
8/57	"That'll Be the Day" (Buddy Holly)	3	2	—
9/57	"Wake Up Little Susie" (Everly Brothers)	1	2	1
* 10/57	"Jailhouse Rock" (Elvis Presley)	1	1	1
11/57	"Great Balls of Fire" (Jerry Lee Lewis)	2	3	1
2/58	"Sweet Little Sixteen" (Chuck Berry)	2	1	—
2/58	"Breathless" (Jerry Lee Lewis)	7	6	4
* 4/58	"All I Have to Do Is Dream" (Everly Brothers)	1	1	1
8/58	"Bird Dog" (Everly Brothers)	2	3	1
5/59	"Battle of New Orleans" (Johnny Horton)	1	3	1
4/60	"Cathy's Clown" (Everly Brothers)	1	1	—
11/60	"Are You Lonesome Tonight?" (Elvis Presley)	1	4	3

* No. 1 on all three charts.

it. World War II had been one of the great watersheds in American history, dislocating traditional geographical and cultural patterns of American society. Tens of millions of Americans had moved from areas where their families had lived for many generations, as a result of induction into the armed forces or relocation to take lucrative jobs in defense plants. Americans from rural areas poured into cities; Southerners—both black and white—came in large numbers to the North, East, and West. Suddenly Americans were thrown into contact, in the service or in their jobs, with other Americans of vastly different geographical, cultural, and ethnic backgrounds. When the war ended, many returned to the lives they had known before, untouched by the experience; but many more stayed in their new environments. America suddenly came much closer to being what it had often claimed to be, a true mixture of many races and ethnic groups. It was no coincidence that a massive push toward integration of black and white

Americans, at many levels, came in the decade after the end of World War II, and that this same period saw the emergence of a form of popular music which grew out of the musical cultures of Americans who had not been part of the mainstream of American life until forced into it by the war.

On several occasions earlier in this book—during discussions of the songs of Stephen Foster and James Bland and ragtime songs—I have offered the opinion that the influence of black music on American popular song has been exaggerated by certain writers, and that it was more a case of white musicians skimming off quite superficial elements of black music to add a faintly exotic touch to their songs, which remained alien to blacks. Rock 'n' roll presents a far different picture. One has only to listen to Willie Mae "Big Mama" Thornton's 1953 recording of "Hound Dog," later a best-seller for Elvis Presley, to hear how much of the style and substance of the early rock 'n' roll style was already present in black rhythm-and-blues music, several years before Bill Haley and Alan Freed brought this style of music to the attention of white audiences.

Thus far, this chapter has dealt exclusively with "hard-core" Southern early rock 'n' roll, a type of music built on the 12-bar blues form; performed at a fast, driving tempo with heavy emphasis on the bass line and the beat, by a singer backed with a small band made up of amplified guitars, bass, drums, and sometimes a piano and/or one or more saxophones; using a text that usually contained thinly veiled sexual innuendos and delivered in such a way as to underline and emphasize this sexual message. This was the type of music performed by the six players discussed at the beginning of this chapter, and the first type of music to be labeled rock 'n' roll. But the term soon was used to cover a much wider range of musical styles.

Rock 'n' roll was so associated in the public mind with the music of American blacks, that any music by black performers enjoying popularity on the white market was labeled rock 'n' roll after 1955. Songs by the Orioles, Crows, Penguins, and several other black close-harmony groups were soon taken under the umbrella of rock 'n' roll, though their music had as much to do with white popular style as with black. The same was true of Antoine ("Fats") Domino, a New Orleans–born black singer, pianist, and bandleader who was far and away the most successful rhythm-and-blues performer of the 1950s and '60s. Between the release of his first disc for Imperial Records ("The Fat Man") in 1950 until he left Imperial for one of the major white recording companies in 1962, he had a succession of No. 1 hits on the rhythm-and-blues charts unmatched by any other performer of the time; more than twenty of these sold a million or more copies each, and the total sale of his records for this thirteen-year span approached 65,000,000! Despite this, he was almost completely unknown to most white listeners until rock 'n' roll broke down the color barrier in popular music. After his initial breakthrough to the Best Selling Singles *Billboard* chart with "Ain't It a Shame" in 1955, he had a long string of discs that sold well enough among whites to be included on the Top 100 charts, including several that were among

"Fats" Domino.

the top ten: "I'm in Love Again" (1956), "Blueberry Hill" (1956), "I'm Walking" (1957), and "Whole Lotta Loving" (1958). Some of his pieces were rhythmic, 12-bar blues songs close in style to "hard-core" rock 'n' roll, but others were more eclectic, jazz-flavored pieces that also borrowed sounds from Tin Pan Alley; his most successful disc, "Blueberry Hill," was his version of a 1940 song by Al Lewis, Larry Stock, and Vincent Rose, first popular as a white, big-band piece.

Other black performers who enjoyed success on the white market in the early days of rock 'n' roll were the Platters (with No. 1 discs in both 1955 and 1956, "The Great Pretender" and "My Prayer"), Clarence "Frog Man" Henry, the Charms, the Dell-Vikings, the Coasters (with a top-selling disc in 1958, "Yakity Yak"), Sam Cooke ("You Send Me" of 1957 rose to the top of the "white" charts), Jackie Wilson, Lloyd Price (with a No. 1 hit in 1958, "Stagger Lee"), Ray Charles, the Diamonds, and the Monotones (with "Book of Love" in 1958). These men performed in a variety of styles, running almost the entire gamut of black popular music of the day, from rhythmic blues to close-harmony songs to jazz-flavored tunes to relics of Tin Pan Alley days (the Platters had No. 1 hits in 1958 with "Twilight Time" and "Smoke Gets in Your Eyes," the latter, of course, Jerome Kern's hit from 1933).

The same was true, to a lesser degree, of country-western music. The Everly Brothers, Don and Phil, the children of a moderately successful husband-and-wife country-music team, brought out their version of "Bye Bye Love" by Nashville songwriter Boudleaux Bryant in 1957; the song not only rose to the top

The Everly Brothers.

of the country-western chart, it reached the No. 2 position on the "pop" charts as well, and quickly sold over a million copies for Cadence Records. "Wake Up Little Susie," recorded later the same year, enjoyed even more remarkable success, topping both the Top 100 and the country-western charts and rising as high as No. 2 on the rhythm-and-blues charts. "All I Have to Do Is Dream" of early 1958 was the only disc by someone other than Elvis Presley to become the top disc on all three charts—popular, rhythm-and-blues, and country-western. And though these and other hits by the Everly Brothers have as much to do with country-western music and with Tin Pan Alley (particularly their later songs) as with black music, they were welcomed as additions to the rock 'n' roll repertory.

Then there were the "covers"—versions by white popular singers of songs first recorded by rhythm-and-blues and country-western performers. Table II, a list of the best-selling white covers for the period 1951–56, shows that the practice began in the early 1950s, when record producers were looking for fresh material and were at the same time fearful that the success of such country-western stars as Hank Williams would spill over to the "pop" market. They recorded a number of country-western songs with the greatest potential appeal to "pop" audiences, using established popular singers backed by Tin Pan Alley arrangements. This tactic was so successful that it was repeated, this time with covers of black music, when rock 'n' roll threatened the white market in 1955.

Table II: Some Important Covers of Rhythm and Blues and Country-Western Songs (1950–56)

Song	Cover	Original
"Tennessee Waltz"	Patti Page (Mercury, 1950)	Short Brothers (1948)
"Cold, Cold Heart"	Tony Bennett (Columbia, 1951)	Hank Williams (MGM, 1951)
"Hey, Good Lookin' "	Jo Stafford & Frankie Laine (Columbia, 1951)	Hank Williams (MGM, 1951)
"Jambalaya"	Jo Stafford (Columbia, 1952)	Hank Williams (MGM, 1952)
"Half As Much"	Rosemary Clooney (Columbia, 1952)	Hank Williams (MGM, 1952)
"Your Cheatin' Heart"	Joni James (MGM, 1953)	Hank Williams (MGM, 1953)
"Crying in the Chapel"	June Valli (RCA-Victor, 1953)	Orioles (Jubilee, 1953)
"Sh-Boom"	Crew-Cuts (Mercury, 1954)	Chords (Cat, 1954)
"Shake, Rattle and Roll"	Bill Haley (Decca, 1954)	Joe Turner (Atlantic, 1954)
"Hearts of Stone"	Fontane Sisters (Dot, 1954)	Charms (DeLuxe, 1954)
"Sixteen Tons"	Tennessee Ernie Ford (Capitol, 1955)	Merle Travis (1946)
"Earth Angel"	Crew-Cuts (Mercury, 1955)	Penguins (Dootone, 1954)
"Ko Ko Mo"	Perry Como (RCA-Victor, 1955) / Crew-Cuts (Mercury, 1955)	Gene & Eunice (Combo, 1955)
"Dance With Me Henry"/ "Work With Me Annie"	Georgia Gibbs (Mercury, 1955)	Midnighters (Federal, 1954)
"Ain't It a Shame"	Pat Boone (Dot, 1955)	Fats Domino (Imperial, 1955)

Song	Cover	Original
"At My Front Door"	Pat Boone (Dot, 1955)	El Dorados (Vee Jay, 1955)
"Only You"	Hilltoppers (Dot, 1955)	Platters (Mercury, 1955)
"Tweedle Dee"	Georgia Gibbs (Mercury, 1955)	Lavern Baker (Atlantic, 1955)
"Hound Dog"	Elvis Presley (RCA-Victor, 1956)	Willie Mae Thornton (Peacock, 1953)
"Long Tall Sally"	Pat Boone (Dot, 1956)	Little Richard (Specialty, 1956)
"Tutti-Frutti"	Pat Boone (Dot, 1956)	Little Richard (Specialty, 1956)
"I'll Be Home"	Pat Boone (Dot, 1956)	Flamingoes (Checker, 1956)
"I Almost Lost My Mind"	Pat Boone (Dot, 1956)	Ivory Joe Hunter (MGM, 1950)
"Chains of Love"	Pat Boone (Dot, 1956)	Joe Turner (Atlantic, 1951)

In 1955 and 1956, the years in which the major recording companies were losing their virtual monopoly on the popular market, the most successful of the new companies was Dot Records, which had seven best-selling discs in the annual survey of 1955 and six in 1956. The information in Table II demonstrates their successful way of coping with the new situation facing the recording industry; rather than fighting or ignoring rock 'n' roll, they dealt with it on their own terms—by taking over much of the new repertory, but recording it with singers and instrumental backing reminiscent of Tin Pan Alley style. Thus what many people, particularly adults, had found so objectionable about rock 'n' roll—its volume, the rasping and raucous singing styles, the percussive and relentless instrumental sound—was removed. And, not incidentally, Dot's performers were all white.

Pat Boone was accepted by white audiences as a rock 'n' roll performer, though country-western and rhythm-and-blues audiences had little interest in his recordings. After the success of his early covers, he sang mostly other repertory. "Friendly Persuasion" (1956) was from the Hollywood film of the same name, with music by veteran Hollywood composer Dmitri Tiomkin; the song was runner-up for the Academy Award for best film song of the year. Boone's great hit of 1957 was "Love Letters in the Sand," the No. 1 song on *Billboard's* weekly charts for more than a month and the second top-seller for the entire year. The song had absolutely nothing to do with rock 'n' roll, and was in fact a Tin Pan Alley product, written in 1931 by J. Fred Coots, published by Irving Berlin, Inc., and recorded by such performers of the day as Ruth Etting and Les Baxter. "April Love," also of 1957, was a similar song, written for a Hollywood film by Sammy Fain, a veteran Tin Pan Alley songwriter who had been turning out such successful songs as "I'll Be Seeing You," "That Old Feeling," and "Secret Love" since 1925.

Pat Boone's success set a precedent for the hard-pressed popular music industry. By making a token bow to rock 'n' roll, then singing songs in a more traditional style, he demonstrated how the threat of rock 'n' roll could be contained and even utilized.

ABC-Paramount quickly followed Boone's success with their own "teen idol," as these white, clean-cut, Northern, urban "rock 'n' roll" singers were soon called—Paul Anka, whose first disc, "Diana" (1957), quickly rose to the No. 2 spot on the *Billboard* weekly charts. Even more successful songs followed, including "Lonely Boy" and "Put Your Head on My Shoulder" (both of 1959) and "Puppy Love" (1960). His songs were mostly sentimental ballads, heavily orchestrated, written in the conventional song forms of Tin Pan Alley music. The only musical link to early rock 'n' roll was the use of one or more amplified guitars and a rhythm section (bass, piano, drums) much more prominent than had been customary in the 1930s and '40s.

Frankie Avalon was cast in the same mold. His publicity pictures projected the image of a nice, white, upper-middle-class lad who might be voted Most

Frankie Avalon.

Likely to Succeed by his high school class. His first discs were released by Chancellor Records in 1958; his first No. 1 hits came the next year, with "Venus" and "Why." The latter will serve as an example of what his music was all about. The ear first hears a smooth, rich musical texture of soft, shimmering amplified guitars and a humming chorus, discreetly backed by piano and bass, and other instruments too much in the background to be distinguished. The text is a child's parody of Tin Pan Alley:

> I'll never let you go,
>   Why? because I love you;
> I'll always love you so,
>   Why? because you love me.

Avalon sings with the voice of a high school student—basically sweet, untrained, tentative, incapable of sustaining a musical line. Its appeal is in its simplicity, its innocence, perhaps its very mediocrity.

Others followed—Bobby Darin, Danny and the Juniors, Bobby Rydell, Brenda Lee. And even at the height of popularity of early rock 'n' roll, music in the established Tin Pan Alley style was by no means exterminated. Though Elvis Presley dominated 1956, Doris Day's recording of "Whatever Will Be, Will Be" by Jay Livingston and Ray Evans, from the film *The Man Who Knew Too Much*, was the fifth best-selling disc of the entire year, and was voted an Academy Award as best film song of the year; Dean Martin's version of "Memories Are Made of This" was No. 1 on the "pop" charts for five weeks early in the year; Frank Sinatra's "Hey, Jealous Lover," by veteran Tin Pan Alley composer Sammy Cahn, sold well; Nelson Riddle's lush arrangement of "Lisbon Antigua" was the top-selling disc for four weeks; Vic Damone had a hit with "On the Street Where You Live" from the Broadway musical *My Fair Lady* by Alan Jay Lerner and Frederick Loewe; and Perry Como had four successful records. All these pieces, and many others, were in Tin Pan Alley style, untouched by the revolution or rock 'n' roll.

A similar pattern emerged in 1957. Elvis Presley's "All Shook Up" and "Jailhouse Rock," Chuck Berry's "School Days," Jerry Lee Lewis's "Whole Lotta Shakin'," "Searchin' " by the Coasters, "Silhouettes" by the Rays, and Fats Domino's "I'm Walkin' " were the rock 'n' roll songs that attracted the most attention and notoriety. But the best-selling disc for the entire year, selling even more copies than any single record by Presley, was Debbie Reynolds's "Tammy," written for the film *Tammy and the Bachelor* by Jay Livingston and Ray Evans; both film and song were pitched at young, white, middle-class audiences, and the disc enjoyed minimal sale on the country-western and rhythm-and-blues markets. The second best-seller for the year was Pat Boone's "Love Letters in the Sand"; Johnny Mathis's "It's Not for Me to Say" and Tab Hunter's "Young Love" were other successful songs written and sung in a pre–rock 'n' roll style.

Thus while rock 'n' roll found a place in popular song, it did not sweep away the type of song that had preceded it, but rather coexisted with it.

Curiously, there was a softening of style even among the performers who had brought the first wave of rock 'n' roll. The first discs by the Everly Brothers had much in common with the rock 'n' roll styles of Presley, Carl Perkins, and Jerry Lee Lewis. But beginning in 1958 with "All I Have to Do Is Dream," they released a series of discs gentler in sound, with less rhythmic propulsion; others were "Devoted to You" (1958) and " 'Til I Kissed You." Exactly the same progression can be observed in the music of Ricky Nelson, who launched his career in 1957 with "Stood Up" and "Be-Bop Baby," establishing him as the only non-Southerner to approach the hard-core style of early rock 'n' roll. But with "Poor Little Fool" in 1958, he switched to a more lyrical, ballad style, using a larger and richer instrumental group for backing. He became one of the "teen idols," with such success that more than 8,000,000 copies of his various discs had been sold by 1963.

For that matter, precisely the same evolution took place in the music of Elvis Presley. His first discs, for Sun Records in Memphis, were cut with only guitar and bass backing his singing and playing. His first national hits, after he signed with RCA-Victor, were recorded in Nashville, with piano, drums, and a male quartet (the Jordanaires) added to the backing group, resulting in a larger and richer sound. Most of his early discs were of fast, driving, 12-bar blues–structured songs, but "Love Me Tender" (1956) established early that he was interested in—and capable of—other types of songs; an adaptation of the Civil War ballad "Aura Lee," the song has three strophes, in AABB form. The first two phrases are accompanied only by strummed chords on the acoustic guitar; a male quartet supports the last two phrases, with rich, chromatic chords reminiscent of the barbershop harmonies of the late 1890s and early 1900s. Nothing about the song has to do with the style of rock 'n' roll as defined at the beginning of this chapter; not unexpectedly, it sold better in sheet music form than any other of his early hits.

Other lyrical, slow-paced ballads were interspersed among his faster, driving, rhythm-and-blues-based discs—"Any Way You Want Me" (1956), "That's When Your Heartaches Begin" (1957), "Loving You" (1957), "Are You Lonesome Tonight?" (1960).

"Can't Help Falling in Love" (1961) is a sample of a piece even further removed from the type of song he first recorded. Written by George Weiss, Hugo Peretti, and Luigi Creatore—all alien to the world of rock 'n' roll—it was featured in one of Presley's most successful movies, *Blue Hawaii*. The introductory measures—arpeggiated chords on the piano, supported by bass and chimes, reminiscent of the first measures of a song by Beethoven or Schubert—alert the listener that we are in a musical world far removed from that of Chuck Berry or Little Richard. The song, lyric and sentimental, is crooned against a rich backdrop of humming chorus, piano, guitars, bass, and discreet percussion. Cast in the venerable Tin Pan Alley form of AABA, the melody is strongly reminiscent, in its first measures, of the nineteenth-century French song "Plaisir d'amour."

Presley's following among the three audiences, as defined by *Billboard*'s charts, reflects perfectly the subtle change in his musical style. Through 1956 and 1957, his discs consistently were at or very near the top of the country-western charts, but after "Hard-Headed Woman" of 1958, no disc of his was in the Top Ten, and many of his best-sellers on the "white" charts do not even appear on the country-western charts. "Are You Lonesome Tonight" (1960), one of his most successful "pop" hits, made only a brief appearance on the country-western charts, rising no higher than No. 22. The rhythms-and-blues charts tell a similar story; his last No. 1 song was "Jailhouse Rock" (1957), a scattering of his discs shows up between 1958 and 1963, and after that his name is totally absent.

Similar polarization took place with the other early rock 'n' roll performers who once were popular with all three audiences. The Everly Brothers almost disappeared from the country-western and rhythm-and-blues charts after 1958, though they continued with some success on the "pop" market for another five years. Jerry Lee Lewis, on the other hand, had thirteen Top Ten hits on the country-western charts between 1958 and 1971, but he completely disappeared from the rhythm-and-blues charts after 1958, and the highest weekly position of any of his songs on the "pop" charts after 1958 was the No. 40 ranking of his version of "Me and Bobby McGee" in 1971.

By 1960, the early rock 'n' roll style (as defined at the beginning of this chapter) had virtually dropped out of sight. There were contributing external events: Presley went into the army, Little Richard turned to religion, Jerry Lee Lewis was boycotted by record companies and impresarios because of adverse publicity attending his marriage to his thirteen-year-old cousin, Chuck Berry was in prison for an alleged violation of the Mann Act, Buddy Holly was killed in a plane crash, Alan Freed was under indictment for taking bribes. And the established popular music industry had learned to cope with this threat by absorbing some of its surface elements into a kind of music it could handle on its own terms. The rock 'n' roll scene was now epitomized not by riotous live concerts with scandalous behavior by performers and audience, but by "American Bandstand," a TV show from Philadelphia hosted by Dick Clark, carried across the nation by ABC, with urban, mostly white, middle-class teenagers dancing to the music of the popular performers of the day.

There were occasional throwbacks to early rock 'n' roll style. Johnny Horton, a white Southerner (born in Tyler, Texas), recorded a series of hits, beginning with "The Battle of New Orleans" in 1959, that were the last discs to sell well to all three audiences; his career was ended by an automobile accident in November of 1960. Chubby Checker had a No. 1 hit in the summer of 1960 with "The Twist," a song written by Hank Ballard; solidly in the rhythmic 12-bar blues style of early rock 'n' roll, it was popularized partly by means of the dance named after the song, which became a national craze in the early '60s. "Twist" songs that followed, by Checker and others, sometimes approached the form and rhythm of early Little Richard and Chuck Berry, and sold well to both whites and blacks—though not among country-music audiences.

But the most striking feature of popular music in America in the early 1960s was the diversity of musical styles, the coexistence of wildly different songs. If rock 'n' roll had not conquered the world of popular music, as it had once threatened to do, it had been the agent for the fragmentation of the field, opening it to a wide and sometimes bewildering variety of songs. The confusion and chaos of musical style is epitomized by the list of the eight best-selling discs of 1961, as compiled by *Cash Box*. No. 1 for the entire year was "Exodus"—not even a song, but the theme music from the movie of the same name, written by Ernest Gold and recorded by Ferrante and Teicher; it is a typical Hollywood pseudo-classical piece, "easy listening" music. Astonishingly, the second best-selling disc of the year was Lawrence Welk's recording of "Calcutta," a German song written in 1958 by one Heino Gaze, fitted with English words and performed by the band whose "champagne music" had been entertaining Middle America on an ABC network TV show since 1953. It was, incidentally, Welk's first and last appearance on the Top Ten.

"Will You Love Me Tomorrow" by the Shirelles was third. It was the first top-selling record by this black female group; the song, a classic Tin Pan Alley product in form and content, was written by Carole King, one of a group of songwriters working out of the Brill Building in New York (others were Barry Mann, Neil Sedaka, Jerry Leiber, and Mike Stoller). "Tossin' and Turnin'," No. 4, was sung by Bobby Lewis, a black disc jockey; it comes as close in style to early rock 'n' roll as any of these ten songs, with its driving, heavily accented rhythm section and its energetic singing backed by jazz combo.

Bert Kaempfert's "Wonderland by Night," No. 5, is pure Tin Pan Alley "pop"; No. 6, Elvis Presley's "Are You Lonesome Tonight?," had much more to do with Tin Pan Alley than with rock 'n' roll; No. 7, Ricky Nelson's "Travellin' Man," falls somewhere between his early rock 'n' roll and his later "pop" styles.

There was no stylistic focus and no apparent direction to popular song that year. No major new talent emerged, and not one of the songs was to enjoy continuing popularity.[12] Rock 'n' roll had shaken the very foundations of popular song, but had not succeeded in bringing about a new stability once the old patterns were broken.

The situation was reminiscent of one almost a century earlier, during the three decades preceding the Civil War, when English songs, songs fashioned from Italian opera, Irish songs, German songs, songs of American family singing groups, and minstrel songs coexisted. That era had culminated in the songs of Stephen Foster, a genius who had woven stylistic threads from all these types of songs into his own style, which became a model for American songwriters for some decades.

Something similar happened in the early 1960s, when a British group called

12. The only exception was "Will You Love Me Tomorrow?," which was to be included on a top-selling LP album by Carole King herself, a decade later.

the Beatles gave direction and vitality to what had become a confused situation.

The week of April 4, 1964, was a historic one in the history of popular song in America: the top five songs on the *Billboard* Top 100 chart were all by the Beatles, who had been almost unknown in America only three months earlier:

1. "Can't Buy Me Love"
2. "Twist and Shout"
3. "She Loves You"
4. "I Want To Hold Your Hand"
5. "Please Please Me"

The Beatles at one of their earliest recording sessions for EMI in 1962.

Seven other songs by the Beatles were on the Top 100 chart, and both the first and second best-selling LP[13] albums were also theirs—*Meet the Beatles* and *Introducing the Beatles*. Nothing approaching such domination of popular music had ever been seen before.

In 1956, John Lennon (then 15) and Paul McCartney (only 13), both from working-class families in Liverpool, England, began playing with the Quarrymen, a group influenced almost entirely by American rock 'n' roll. George Harrison, a 15-year-old guitar player, joined them in 1958; the group became

---

13. The 33-⅓-rpm LP (long playing) record had been introduced by RCA Victor as far back as 1931, but was not financially successful until the 1950s, when more reliable and less expensive playback equipment was perfected. Capable of playing up to twenty-five minutes of music on each side of a disc, its repertory at first was chiefly classical, aimed at well-to-do and older listeners. But it had great and obvious advantages for popular music—a single LP disc could hold ten or more songs—and as the following chapter will detail, it became a decisive factor in popular music dissemination as the 1960s progressed.

the Moondogs, then the Silver Beatles. Stu Sutcliffe, electric bass, joined them in 1959, followed by the drummer, Pete Best, the next year. In 1960 they played outside Liverpool for the first time, in Hamburg, Germany—like Liverpool, a hotbed of small clubs featuring live performances of rock 'n' roll. Under the title of "Tony Sheridan and the Beat Brothers," they brought out their first disc in 1961, a coupling of "My Bonnie Lies Over the Ocean" and "When the Saints Go Marching In." Late in 1961 they acquired a manager—Brian Epstein, who owned a record store in Liverpool—and Ringo Starr became the drummer of what was now a quartet.

Each of the four Beatles has spoken or written, at one time or another, of the critical and almost exclusive role played by American rock 'n' roll in the formation of their own early style. Even had they remained silent on this point, the same conclusion could have been reached from the evidence of the music they played and recorded during their formative years. The following are songs they are known to have performed, grouped under the name of the performer who popularized them:[14]

Chuck Berry: ★"Rock and Roll Music" / ★"Roll Over Beethoven" / "Carol" / "I'm Talking About You" / "Johnny B. Goode" / "Little Queenie" / "Memphis, Tennessee."

Little Richard: ★"Hey-Hey-Hey-Hey" / ★"Kansas City" / ★"Long Tall Sally" / "Good Golly, Miss Molly" / "Lucille"

Elvis Presley: "Hound Dog" / "I Forgot to Remember to Forget"

Carl Perkins: ★"Everybody's Trying to Be My Baby" / ★"Honey Don't" / ★"Matchbox" / "Sure To Fall in Love With You"

Buddy Holly: ★"Words of Love" / "Crying, Waiting, Hoping"

various rhythm-and-blues: ★"Twist and Shout" (The Isley Brothers) / ★"Baby, It's You" (Shirelles) / ★"Please Mr. Postman" (Marvellettes) / ★"Chains" (Cookies) / ★"You Really Got a Hold on Me" (Smokey Robinson and the Miracles) / ★"Boys" (Shirelles) / "Lawdy Miss Clawdy" (Lloyd Price) / "I Got a Woman" (Ray Charles) / "Be My Baby" (Ronettes) / "Three Cool Cats" (Coasters)

country-western: ★"Act Naturally" (Buck Owens) / ★"Nobody's Child" (Hank Snow) / "You Win Again" (Hank Williams)

While the style of early rock 'n' roll had almost disappeared from American popular music by the end of the 1950s, it was kept alive in England—and elsewhere in Europe—through cover performances by the Beatles and similar groups. And when these groups began fashioning their own music, it grew out of rock 'n' roll and other music by rhythm-and-blues and country-western performers.

The Beatles did not achieve their immense, unprecedented popularity in

14. Asterisks identify recorded songs.

Europe and America through these covers, but with their own songs, most of them written by John Lennon and/or Paul McCartney. "Love Me Do" (1957) was their first song to attract attention outside of their immediate circles in Liverpool and Hamburg, and their first to appear on the British record charts, in December of 1962. "Please Please Me" and "From Me to You" followed in early 1963, rising to the No. 2 and the No. 1 spots, respectively.

Their first LP album, *Please Please Me*—containing eight of their own songs and six covers of American songs—was released in Britain on March 22, 1963, and by May 4 had reached the top position among albums, remaining there for 30 weeks and maintaining a spot in the Top Ten until June 27, 1964, an incredible 65 weeks. The record industry had never seen anything remotely approaching the success of this album, which revolutionized the thinking about record production by demonstrating that an album could sell as many copies as a single disc, if not more. The success of their second album, *With the Beatles*, was scarcely less astonishing—it was the top-selling LP in its first week on the British charts (December 30, 1963) and maintained this spot for 22 weeks, to be replaced by yet another album by the Beatles, *A Hard Day's Night*.

Their first four successful singles will serve as a fair sample of what their music was like when they became the most popular performers in England in late 1962 and in 1963. In all four, the rhythm section is in the foreground of the sound—Ringo on drums and Paul on electric bass[15] playing the hard-driving, heavily accented patterns of "big beat" music—with a persistent, insistent accent on the first beat of each measure and secondary accents on the second and fourth beats. The percussive, amplified guitars of John and George overlay this, filling out the driving, hard sound of the group without cluttering it. There are no other instruments in the background, no strings to mellow the sound. But the four manage a compact but full and resounding texture, not unlike that achieved in Elvis Presley's first recordings by only three players.

John and Paul do most of the singing, usually together, beginning in unison and moving to two-part harmonies, with George often joining them at ends of phrases to fill out three-part chords. The sound of the voices is almost nondescript on the first discs, being in neither "pop" style nor yet quite that of black or country-western music; but in "From Me to You" and "She Loves You" something different begins to creep in—singing above the normal range of the male voice, often drifting into falsetto. This is a sound unknown to white popular music, but common in music of American blacks, both in groups (which often feature an unusually high male voice taking the lead) and in solos. Smokey Robinson, Clyde McPhatter, and Dee Clark were among the chief proponents of this sound in the 1960s.

Other aspects of the Beatles' early music differ from the style of early Ameri-

15. The solid-body electric guitar in both six-string and bass models—pioneered by Les Paul in the 1950s—gradually replaced amplified acoustic instruments, though exploitation of its unique sound potential was not to come for several years.

can rock 'n' roll. Though many of the American pieces they performed in their early days were in 12-bar blues form, their own songs were not. "Love Me Do" is cast in the classic AABA form of Tin Pan Alley and European popular song (though the A section is an odd 13 measures in length), and the other three are variations of the same form. Harmonies are rather more complex than the three-chord patterns of most rock 'n' roll; though they were not yet using many chromatically altered chords or chords out of the tonic key, Lennon and McCartney had a way, even in their earliest songs, of using a common chord in an unusual context. "From Me to You" contains a typical example—the harmonic transition from the A section to the B prepared the ear for a certain chord, but the B section begins rather with a quite different one. And the very last chord of the piece is, quite unexpectedly, a chord other than the expected tonic—a minor chord, as a matter of fact. Equally unexpected is the final chord of the first section of "She Loves You," a dissonant three-part chord that simply hangs, without resolving.

Their lyrics usually have more to do with romantic love than sex:

You think you've lost your love,
Well I saw her yesterday,
It's you she's thinking of,
And she told me what to say .

The verse is almost doggerel, yet—as has been the case with the lyrics of so many popular songs over the years—its simplicity is a critical element in its effectiveness: despite the fast tempo and rather loud level of the song, every word comes through to the listener, and the song is perceived as a wedding of words and music. And though the sentiments of many of the early Beatles songs approach those of Tin Pan Alley, the driving, often hard quality of the music prevents them from being cloying.

•   "I Want to Hold Your Hand" was the first of their songs to become a hit in America. Released here on January 13, 1964, by Capitol Records, it quickly rose to the top of the charts, remaining there for seven weeks. "She Loves You" and "Please Please Me" followed as American releases, then "Can't Buy Me Love," which became their second top-selling disc, in early April. Three other top hits followed: "A Hard Day's Night," "I Feel Fine," and "Eight Days a Week." For the 60-week period beginning February 1, 1964, and extending to March 20, 1965, one or another of the Beatles' songs was at the top of the singles chart for 23 weeks—a string reminiscent of Elvis Presley's success in 1956.

Even more remarkable, for the 91-week period from February 15, 1964 to November 6, 1965, an album by the Beatles was the best-selling LP album for 54 weeks, and for 22 weeks the second top album was also one of theirs. This phenomenon began with *Meet the Beatles*, released by Capitol on January 20, 1964, and continued with *Beatles' Second Album, A Hard Day's Night, Beatles*

'65, *Beatles* VI, and *Help!* As had been the case in England a year earlier, their success in America demonstrated that LP albums could sell as many as or more copies than single discs.

Capitol spent over $50,000 to publicize the Beatles' first American hit, "I Want to Hold Your Hand"; their presence in America, including a nationwide concert tour and a sensational appearance on Ed Sullivan's television show, brought them a tremendous amount of public exposure just at the time their first American singles and albums were being released; their first movie, *A Hard Day's Night*, was released during this same year, 1964. But in the end, it was their music, and their music alone, that brought them their unparalleled popularity in England, America, and elsewhere.

Their five top-selling singles in America in the first year and a half of their success here—"I Want to Hold Your Hand," "A Hard Day's Night," "I Feel Fine," "Eight Days a Week," and "Can't Buy Me Love"—define their style of this period, when they were beginning to mature as performers. Though their music was still firmly rooted in American rock 'n' roll, it was clearly moving in other directions.

These songs, like their earliest ones, take the venerable AABA form as a starting point, though the structure begins to loosen, with freer and more frequent alternation of the A and the B sections. "Can't Buy Me Love," for instance, becomes almost a rondo, with an ABBABBABBA shape. B sections are invariably in new and often unexpected keys. Sections are of different lengths in the various songs: "Eight Days a Week" has both A and B sections in the conven-

The Beatles performing in concert, 1964.

tional 8 measures; but "I Want to Hold Your Hand" has 12-measure phrases, "I Feel Fine" has 10, "Can't Buy Me Love" alternates between 8 and 12.

More striking than such structural details is the gradual change in the sheer sound of the group. John and George are now playing electric guitars, rather than amplified acoustic ones; combined with the electric bass of Paul, and Ringo's crisper drumming, they give an even harder and more driving sound than heard on their first discs. And they begin to exploit the unique sound potential of the electric guitar: "A Hard Day's Night" begins with a crashing, clanging, dissonant, electric chord, quite unlike anything heard in early rock 'n' roll; a 12-measure instrumental break in "Can't Buy Me Love" opens with a scream from one of the singers, harsh electric chords, and then a frantic, piercing electric guitar solo that has little to do with the guitar style of Chuck Berry or Elvis Presley; the strummed electric guitar introduction to "Eight Days a Week" is like nothing heard before in rock 'n' roll; and "I Feel Fine" starts with an innovative, sustained note on an electric guitar that moves into feedback, sheer electric sound, setting a new kind of mood for the song to follow.

The success of the Beatles in America sparked an invasion—through disc and personal appearance—by other British groups. The Dave Clark Five was first; like the Beatles, they came to America in 1964, pushing sales of their records by live concert and television appearances. Their most successful albums in America were released in 1964, *Session with Dave Clark Five* and *Glad All Over*, and a top single, "Over and Over" (1965). Next came the Searchers, and Gerry and the Pacemakers, the latter another Liverpool band. The Animals, featuring Eric Burdon—who mastered the techniques of American black singers better than did any of his countrymen—had a top-selling single with "The House of the Rising Sun" (1964) and a successful album, *Animals* (1964) Herman's Hermits had top-selling singles ("Mrs. Brown, You've Got a Lovely Daughter" and "I'm Henry VIII, I Am") and two LP albums that rose to the No. 2 position. And another group, the Rolling Stones, was first heard from in 1964, with an album (*Rolling Stones*) and only after that with a single, "Time Is on My Side."

Like the Beatles, these and other British groups took American rock 'n' roll of the mid-1950s as the basis of their own style. Their music can be heard as a continuation of what had begun in America in 1955–58—the only continuation, since American music in 1959–64 had moved in quite different directions.

For the second time in less than a decade, the American music industry had misread the situation. In the first quarter of 1964, some 60 percent of all recordings sold in America—both singles and LP albums—were by the Beatles, and the other British groups began enjoying a substantial percentage of sales here later that year. Part of this had to do with the fact that the Beatles were, quite simply, among the most talented songwriters and performers in the entire history of popular song, and their popularity pulled similar English groups along with it. But another side of the coin was that American recording companies had made a mistake in assuming that in containing the onslaught of early rock 'n' roll and offering in its place a bastardized, hybrid product, they were satisfying the needs of the American record-buying public. The Beatles proved otherwise.

The music of the Beatles—like that of the American rock 'n' roll, rhythm-and-blues, and country-western music that they admired and emulated—was in oral tradition, in that they created songs and worked out arrangements by ear, without resorting to musical notation. Sheet music versions of their songs came after the fact, and were the work of other people. Their music was conceived orally, disseminated orally—through live performances and recordings—and in this way conformed to the traditions of the music that had initially inspired them.

In this sense, the Beatles continued what had been the most radical aspect in the emergence of rock 'n' roll as popular song—the change from an almost two-centuries tradition of notated song to a new practice of non-notated music.

SIXTEEN

"Sympathy for the Devil";

OR,

The Age of Rock

"Lose your dreams and you'll lose your mind . . ."
The Rolling Stones, "Ruby Tuesday"

THE *Berkeley Barb*, one of the first "underground" newspapers of the 1960s, reported the death of rock 'n' roll in its issue of March 11, 1966, and left no question as to who had been the murderer:

> "The kids ain't buying singles no more" is the word in Frisco's portion of the nationwide rock industry.
>
> Today's Top 40 singles, it is explained, have sales figures which wouldn't have gotten them on the Top 100 a year or two ago, because the high school kids, rock's major market for the past several years, have quit buying records. . . .
>
> Rock died as significant music years ago, and as a marketable product in 1964. . . .
>
> Ultimately the death was caused by the exploitation of rock by the worst elements in the music industry, a fairly disgusting industry at best. They never understood the music they were selling and their contempt for the music, its performers, and its audience has swept the nation rooting out any hopes for a serious or sustained audience. The crisis has been evident for years in the pattern of rock sales, for the market has been getting younger and younger. Increasing numbers of older kids have dropped rock in favor of television when they got married, or jazz or folk if they went on to college, and to compensate for this process the Top 40 sell has gotten harder and harder as it became directed towards younger kids.

The terms *rock* and *rock 'n' roll* are used interchangeably in this obituary. While it may have been true that rock 'n' roll was dead, at least in America, a rather different style of popular song, soon to be designated "rock," was beginning to struggle to life at just this time.

One must go back a bit to pick up the beginnings of this new story, to what is usually called the "folk-music revival," and to the emergence of California as a new focus of American culture.

As far back as the late 1920s, a handful of people found traditional Anglo-American music an attractive alternative to Tin Pan Alley songs. John Jacob Niles, for instance, born in Louisville, Kentucky, in 1892, collected, sang, published, and recorded traditional songs from his native state. His first audiences were college students and urban Easterners; RCA Victor brought out his first album in 1939, *Early American Ballads,* others followed in the 1940s and '50s, and his following became such that he was able to attract capacity crowds to New York's Town Hall, where he gave a memorable recital in 1946.

Burl Ives (born in Jaspar County, Illinois, in 1909) was even more successful. A multitalented performer, he combined singing with a career as an actor and writer. After attracting attention at such spots as the Village Vanguard in New York, he was given his own radio show on CBS in 1940 (called "The Wayfarin' Stranger," after one of his most popular songs), and Columbia Records brought out a set of four records of his versions of such songs as "On Top of Old Smoky" and "Sweet Betsy from Pike." He reached a wider audience than Niles, perhaps partly because of his fame as an actor and movie performer, and a handful of his discs, both singles and albums, began appearing on *Billboard*'s charts.

In a way, Niles and Ives did just what Thomas Moore had done 150 years earlier with his *Irish Melodies*—take tunes from oral tradition, smooth off the rough edges, and fit them with a harmonic accompaniment. Urban audiences found the tunes and texts—which often dealt with such forbidden Tin Pan Alley topics as death, alcohol, rape, murder, sex—a refreshing change of pace from the usual popular songs of the day, but they were not yet ready for the sound of the music as done by traditional performers: the thin, nasal, "high country" style of singing, the brittle and rasping sound of banjos and fiddles. Niles and Ives had voices that reflected their years of vocal training, and they accompanied themselves on mellow-sounding acoustical guitars and similar instruments.

At just the same time, others were attempting to put this same traditional music to a quite different use. Marxist theorists had long dreamed of a "people's music" that would strengthen their movement in America by carrying it to the "masses"—the working class, which had remained largely indifferent to their overtures. The "proletariat renaissance" of the late 1930s and the '40s finally succeeded in bringing elements of the intellectual-radical community together with a handful of musicians from the lower classes. On March 13, 1940, Will Geer organized a benefit program for migrant workers, featuring Leadbelly (Huddie Ledbetter, an itinerant black blues singer and song writer), Aunt Molly Jackson

Burl Ives in the early 1940s, when he was known primarily as a folk singer.

("poetess laureate of the Kentucky miners"), Peter Seeger (Harvard-educated, who had left college to "look for America"), Burl Ives, Alan Lomax (folk-song collector and cofounder of the Archive of American Folksong at the Library of Congress in Washington), his wife Bess, and Woody Guthrie ("folk poet of the Dust Bowl"). This group was the nucleus of the first "hootenanny," held as part of a Democratic fund-raising drive in Seattle, and also of the Almanac Singers, who embarked on a cross-country trip in 1941, singing for union meetings and gatherings of radical-intellectual groups, and who brought out an album, *Talking Union.*

Most of the songs of this circle were fashioned from traditional tunes, fitted with new and usually political texts. But they had little or no circulation among the Americans who were their target, partly because most rural and working-class Americans were in no mood for radical political change, even in the dreary days of the Great Depression, and partly because these people were much more interested in the new country-western music of the Carter Family, Jimmie Rodgers, Eddy Arnold, and the like, than in reworkings of traditional tunes.

Several members of the Almanac Singers regrouped after World War II to form the Weavers, debuting in 1949 at the Village Vanguard. The following year Decca Records, sensing a restlessness among popular music audiences, signed the Weavers to a contract. Singing with Gorden Jenkins and his orchestra, they brought out several discs of nonpolitical traditional songs that sold well on the popular market, including "On Top of Old Smoky" and "Goodnight, Irene," which held the No. 1 spot on the *Billboard* weekly charts for thirteen consecutive weeks in the summer of 1950. But the new political climate of the Cold War put an abrupt end to their commercial success, and it was ten years before any members of the group were able to appear publicly again.[1]

Harry Belafonte, second only to Elvis Presley as the most popular singer of the 1950s, built much of his career around traditional music of another sort. Born in New York in 1927, son of an immigrant couple from the Caribbean, he studied traditional West Indian music in the Archive of American Folk Music in Washington and based much of his early repertory on his own adaptations of this material. Several successful dramatic roles in the early 1950s brought him national recognition as an actor and singer, as did also several appearances on the Ed Sullivan Show—a stepping stone to fame for so many performers of the time. Signed by RCA Victor, he brought out two LP albums in 1956, *Belafonte* and *Calypso*, both of which rose to the top of *Billboard*'s LP album charts, the second staying among the best-selling albums for an astonishing 99 weeks. Even this was surpassed by *Belafonte at Carnegie Hall* (1959), which remained on the charts for an unprecedented 168 weeks.

Belafonte was a trained singer, and his material—which ranged from calypso and other songs of the West Indies, to Negro spirituals, to folk songs of other countries, to newly composed popular songs—was always smoothly and professionally arranged, bringing the sound of whatever he was doing into the sound spectrum of late Tin Pan Alley style. He reached a quite different audience from that of the early rock 'n' roll performers; only a handful of his songs were released as single discs, and of these only "Banana Boat" (1957) enjoyed much success. Twenty-four of his LP albums released between 1956 and 1970

1. This story is told in detail in R. Serge Denisoff, *Great Day Coming* (Urbana: University of Illinois Press, 1971).

Harry Belafonte during a recording session for RCA Victor

sold well enough to be charted in *Billboard*, however, with nine of these becoming Top Ten sellers. He was the first singer to achieve such popularity through LP albums rather than singles; his singing style and choice of material were of more interest to older people than to the teenagers who made up the largest part of the rock 'n' roll audience—and older persons could better afford to buy LPs. The mere titles of the best-selling LPs in the first decade after their introduction in 1948 by Columbia Records give a profile of a conservative product for an older audience; LPs holding the No. 1 position in the sales for the most weeks were:

Album, Performer, Date	No. of Weeks
South Pacific (original cast), 1949	69
Al Jolson Album, Vol. 1, 1947	25
With a Song in My Heart (Jane Froman), 1952	23
The Student Prince (Mario Lanza), 1954	18
Showboat (movie soundtrack), 1951	18
Music for Lovers Only (Jackie Gleason), 1953	17
Hans Christian Andersen (Danny Kaye), 1953	17
An American in Paris (movie soundtrack), 1952	16

Belafonte, who is black, enjoyed almost no success with black audiences. Only two of his discs turned up on *Billboard*'s rhythm-and-blues charts, each for several weeks only. His relationship to the black market was analogous to that of Burl Ives and the Weavers to country-western audiences—even though the musical material was drawn from traditional music, it is arranged and presented in a way that gives it an alien sound.

The Kingston Trio took a similar approach to traditional music. These three college students—Bob Shane, Dave Guard, and Nick Reynolds—had no direct ties to Anglo-American oral-tradition music and learned their "folk" songs from records and live performances of other musicians and from printed collections. After a brief career on the club and campus circuit, they released their version of the traditional murder ballad "Tom Dooley" for Capitol Records in 1958 and saw it rise straight to the top, remaining on the charts for twenty-one weeks. Their greatest success came with their LP albums, however. Their first, *The Kingston Trio* (1958), became the best-selling LP by November and remained on the *Billboard* charts for a staggering 195 weeks, or almost 4 *years*. Four of their next five albums became best-sellers, the other rose to the No. 2 spot—just behind one of the others. Fourteen of their first seventeen LPs were among the

The Kingston Trio.

Top Ten albums for one or more weeks; *The Best of the Kingston Trio*, released in 1962, was on the charts for 105 weeks.

The point made by these statistics is that many millions of Americans were buying and listening to albums by the Kingston Trio for almost a decade. What they heard were smoothly harmonized arrangements of a wide range of folk songs, accompanied by acoustic guitars. The relationship to traditional oral-tradition music was the same as with Niles, Ives, the Weavers, and Belafonte—the tunes were the same, but everything else (singing style, harmonization, accompaniment) was different, aimed at a different audience. No disc by the Kingston Trio ever appeared on the *Billboard* country-western charts.

The most successful of the ensuing hundreds of "folk" groups was Peter (Yarrow), Paul (Stookey), and Mary (Travers), brought together and managed by Albert Grossman, organizer of the Newport Folk Festival and interested observer of the financial success of the Kingstons. Launched at the Bitter End, a new "folk" club in Greenwich Village, their rise to fame and success was as meteoric as that of the Kingston Trio: their first album, *Peter, Paul & Mary* (1962) rose to the top of the charts, and remained on them for 185 weeks; two singles, "Lemon Tree" and Pete Seeger's "If I Had a Hammer," also sold well. Their first five LPs all reached the Top Ten. Their style was even more polished than that of the Kingstons—and their music held equally little interest for country-western audiences.

The same holds true for the next star of the folk-music revival, Joan Baez. A student at Boston University in the late 1950s, she began listening to other urban folk musicians and singing in small clubs. After a sensational debut at the Newport Folk Festival in 1959, she was engaged at the Gate of Horn in Chicago; performances on college campuses and at top clubs in San Francisco and New York led to a recording contract with Vanguard. Though she never studied voice formally, her vocal sound and production were solidly in the tradition of "cultured" Western music, and it was the sound of this voice that captivated her urban audiences:

> Her voice is as clear as air in autumn, a vibrant, strong, untrained, and thrilling soprano. . . . The purity of her voice suggests purity of approach.⁎ She is only 21 and palpably nubile. But there is little sex in that clear flow of sound. It is haunted and plaintive, a mother's voice, and it has in it distant reminders of black women wailing in the night, of detached madrigal singers performing calmly at court, and of saddened gypsies trying to charm death into leaving their Spanish caves.[2]

Though vocal production, harmonizations, and accompaniments of these and other stars of the folk-music revival drew largely on Western art music and contemporary popular song, several elements of these songs represented depar-

2. *Time*, June 1, 1962, pp. 39–40.

tures from Tin Pan Alley style. Like real folk songs, they are mostly strophic and narrative, with a tale or a drama unfolded in successive stanzas sung to the same music, and are thus quite different in structure and content from the (verse)-chorus pattern of popular song. And the tales offered in many of these songs had to do with topics almost never encountered in Tin Pan Alley—death, religion, sex, murder, children, tragedy of various sorts. Though many listeners were drawn to the music of the folk revival because the sounds of harmonizing voices and soft guitars fell gently on their ears, as seductive in their own way as the lush strings and rich chords of the Indian summer of Tin Pan Alley, many others were attracted by the novelty of songs that told stories and dealt with subjects skirted by the popular songs of recent memory.

A further step was taken by Bob Dylan, born Robert Zimmerman in Duluth, Minnesota, in 1941. His story resembles that of the Kingston Trio and Joan Baez, to a point. While enrolled at the University of Minnesota, he developed a

© 1965 Daniel Kramer

Bob Dylan and Joan Baez in 1965.

fixation on Woody Guthrie, eventually traveling to New York to visit his idol, who was ailing and hospitalized. He began singing at important folk-music clubs there, places like the Gaslight and Gerde's Folk City, and was signed to a contract by John Hammond, Sr., of Columbia Records. His first album, *Bob Dylan*, was released in March of 1962. More club and concert gigs followed, then his highly acclaimed appearances at the Monterey and Newport Folk Festivals and a recital at New York's Town Hall on April 12, 1963. Two more albums came out that year, *Freewheelin' Bob Dylan* and *The Times They Are a-Changin'*, making him the most publicized and controversial figure of the folk-song revival, acclaimed by some as the most original figure yet to appear, criticized by others for not conforming to the style practiced by other members of the movement.

Like his peers discussed above, his success as a recording artist came chiefly through LP albums: ten were released in the 1960s, of which seven reached the Top Ten in sales. By contrast, only four of his singles reached the Top Ten, the first not until "Like a Rolling Stone" in 1965.

Two critical points set him apart from his predecessors. His singing style was nasal, rasping, declamatory, patterned after that of Woodie Guthrie and various black and country-western performers, in no way calculated to fall easily on ears conditioned by Bing Crosby, Frank Sinatra, Burl Ives, or Joan Baez. He accompanied himself on the guitar, with ringing, percussive, harsh chords of little harmonic sophistication; sometimes he treated his guitar as a drone instrument, at other times his chord changes seemed simply wrong—to ears trained by Western harmonic music. He also played the harmonica, strapped around his neck, to introduce songs and bridge stanzas with unpolished and piercing lines.

The other difference is that he wrote most of the songs he performed. His first album had included the traditional Scottish "Pretty Peggy-O," the Southern "mountain song" "Man of Constant Sorrow," the 12-bar blues "See That My Grave Is Kept Clean" (learned from a recording by Blind Lemon Jefferson), and "House of the Rising Sun," learned from Dave Von Ronk, a member of the New York folk circle. But almost all the songs on his second album were his own, including the stunningly original "Blowin' in the Wind," "Masters of War," "A Hard Rain's a-Gonna Fall," and "Don't Think Twice, It's All Right."

And it was not just that these songs were original; much of their impact came from their concern with political and social issues, or with intensely personal experiences. "Oxford Town" deals with the drama of the court-enforced admission to the University of Mississippi of James Meredith, the first black ever to attend that school; Dylan was quoted as saying about "Blowin' in the Wind" that "I'm only 21 years old and I know that there's been too many wars. . . . You people over 21 should know better."[3] "A Hard Rain's a-Gonna Fall" was "a desperate kind of song," written during the Cuban missile crisis of late 1962 when the spectre of atomic holocaust first loomed.

From this time on, Dylan was no longer a folk singer in the sense of using traditional materials, though the term continued to be applied to him and other singers who sang strophic songs to the accompaniment of a guitar or banjo.

It had become quite rare during the Tin Pan Alley period for a composer of popular songs to be a public performer as well. There were a handful of exceptions, early in the twentieth century: George M. Cohan appeared in many of his own musical plays, and Irving Berlin sang his own material on rare occasions.

---

3. Nat Hentoff, liner notes for *The Freewheelin' Bob Dylan*, Columbia KCS 8786 (1964).

But even in these cases, it was a matter of a songwriter *also* singing, as an activity secondary to his chief business: writing songs. Tin Pan Alley developed such a high degree of specialization that one takes it for granted that there are no songs *by* Bing Crosby, Margaret Whiting, Frank Sinatra, or Fred Astaire.

But Bob Dylan changed this. Folk groups like Peter, Paul, and Mary, who had only sung arrangements of traditional tunes, began writing their own material: "Puff, the Magic Dragon," released in early 1963, was not only their most successful single to that point, it was also their first successful original song (written by Peter, with Leonard Lipton). Within a year of the appearance of Dylan's second album, it was almost unthinkable for a "folk" performer to sing a traditional song, and the country was flooded with paradoxical hybrids: "original folk songs."

At precisely the same time, the Beatles were having their first impact on British audiences, performing much American rock 'n' roll, but also their own songs. And a new American group, the Beach Boys, brought out their first album featuring songs they had written themselves. The credit for establishing the primacy of new songs, written by the performer—so basic to the early history of rock—should not go to Dylan alone; it was more a matter of something being in the wind and happening spontaneously to different musicians.

But there can be no denying Bob Dylan the credit for transforming the folk-revival movement from one preoccupied with new arrangements of traditional tunes to one concerned with original songs dealing with social and political issues, songs of an intensely personal and controversial nature.

Just as the rural South had been the geographical and spiritual home of rock 'n' roll, so California was the climate in which rock sprouted and first ran rampant.

California was a very different place from the South. Admitted to the Union as a Free State in 1850, it had a long and complex cultural and political history; but most of the pople who lived there in the mid-twentieth century were recent arrivals, with no ties with its earlier history. There were 92,000 inhabitants when it became a state; the population reached the one million mark in the 1880s, then doubled again in the next two decades; by 1940 there were some 7,000,000 Californians, and this number doubled again in less than two decades. By the late 1960s, the population of the two largest urban areas alone—Los Angeles and San Francisco—was over 10,000,000.

Thus half of its residents in the 1960s had been born elsewhere, and another quarter of them had been Californians for only a single generation. In addition, few Europeans emigrated to California; its foreign-born population was chiefly from Mexico and the Orient. These factors gave it a character quite different from any other part of America; most of its inhabitants had quite recently left family and geographical roots behind and were devoid of a clear or compelling communal tradition. So they created one on the spot—the California image, the American dream come true:

California—it was the one place west of the Mississippi where everyone wanted to be. Rich and fast, cars, women, one suburban plot for everyone: a sea of happy humanity sandwiched between frosty mountains and toasty beaches, all an easy drive down the freeway.[4]

This was the image projected by the Beach Boys, California's first distinctive contribution to popular song, in their first discs of 1961–62. They were a local group, all from Hawthorne (California), and mostly from one family—Brian Wilson, his younger brothers Dennis and Carl, their cousin Mike Love, the only nonrelative being Alan Jardine. Their songs dealt with the "good life" in California—surfing (their first disc, "Surfin'," "Surfin' Safari," and their first national hit disc, "Surfin' U.S.A.") cars ("Little Deuce Coupe," "Fun, Fun, Fun"), women ("Barbara Ann," "California Girls"). They performed their own songs to the virtual exclusion of other repertory, except for an occasional nod to a favorite such as Chuck Berry. They featured close, clean, four- and five-part vocalizing, against a rhythmic background of guitars and drums that had much of the propulsion of early rock 'n' roll, but with no trace of the ethnic sound of either rhythm-and-blues or country-western music. They made the most imaginative use of rock 'n' roll materials of any Americans in the early 1960s, and they quickly rose up the ladder of popular acceptance and commercial success with a series of top-selling singles, beginning with "I Get Around" (1964).

The early 1960s were marked by a plurality of style in popular music. There were remnants of early rock 'n' roll, watered down and "whitewashed" ("Take Good Care of My Baby" by Bobby Vee, 1961; and "Roses Are Red" by Bobby Vinton, 1962); music of the folk revival was just beginning to move from the college campus and urban folk clubs to the Top Forty charts and radio stations (*Peter, Paul, and Mary*, 1962); there was a sudden and overwhelming invasion by the Beatles and other British groups, with music based on American rock 'n' roll but beginning to move in quite different directions; and the style of Tin Pan Alley was stubbornly refusing to die out ("Breaking Up Is Hard to Do" by Neil Sedaka, 1962; and "Everybody Loves Somebody" by Dean Martin, 1964).

There was a coming together of purpose, a political unity among a large number of people, rather than a distinct musical style, that led to the next clearly defined period of American song, the Age of Rock—as differentiated from rock 'n' roll.

This purpose began taking shape when various members of the folk-revival movement allied themselves with the struggle for equal rights in the South by attending rallies and marches and singing for assembled crowds. Pete Seeger and Tom Paxton ventured south with the Freedom Riders in 1962, and Seeger organized and performed at a large and well-publicized concert rally at Carnegie

4. Jim Miller, "The Beach Boys," in *The Rolling Stone Illustrated History of Rock & Roll* (New York: Random House, 1976), pp. 159–60.

Hall on June 8, 1963.[5] By the time the March on Washington took place, culminating with a rally of a quarter-million people, performers like Bob Dylan, Joan Baez, and Peter, Paul, and Mary were publicly supporting the Civil Rights movement, singing at rallies and releasing discs consisting largely of protest songs.

This protest was directed against certain traditional, discriminatory patterns of American life and those people who perpetuated them, but the next act in the drama of political activism of the 1960s took a different turn, with a new setting—California—and a new villain, the American government itself.

The Bay Area, embracing San Francisco, Berkeley, and encircling suburbs, emerged as the cradle of the dissident student movement of the 1960s and of the music associated with it. The University of California at Berkeley was the scene of the first large-scale involvement of American students in protest movements, first the Free Speech Movement, headed by Mario Savio, then protests against American involvement in Vietnam, headed by the Vietnam Day Committee. Dissatisfied by what they saw as the University's lack of concern with these matters, a group of students (and nonstudents) occupied the administration building, refused to leave, and were eventually arrested, some 800 of them, affording America its first view—on television—of young Americans defying authority and being subjected to police action as a result. And music, in the form of Joan Baez and other members of the folk revival, was part of this scene from the beginning.

It was at just this time that another group from California, the Byrds, flashed on the stage of popular song. They were very different from the Beach Boys in background, musical style, and political orientation. Roger McGuinn, guitarist and lead vocalist, had come to California from Chicago and from New York's Greenwich Village, where he had been part of the folk-revival scene; other members of the group had similar backgrounds in "folk" music, and they all shared an almost fanatical admiration of the Beatles.

Their first single, "Mr. Tambourine Man," rose to the No. 1 position on the *Billboard* charts in the summer of 1965, and their first LP, released at the same time, sold quite well, even against the competition of the Beatles. Other singles, including "Turn! Turn! Turn!," and another album followed before the end of the year. Part of their appeal was in their sound and texture, quite unlike that of any previous group. They used folk instruments—McGuinn played a 12-string guitar, and the autoharp and tambourine can also be heard—but heavily amplified, giving a unique brittle, twanging, percussive texture. Their vocal style was likewise new, with chords built on fourths and fifths—and sometimes more dissonant intervals—resulting in something vaguely reminiscent of medieval music, but derived in fact from the vocal harmonizing of country-western music, a descendant of traditional shape-note singing of the rural South. Like Bob Dylan, the Byrds produced a sound closer to that of traditional music than did the King-

5. Portions of this concert were recorded and released by Columbia Records as Stereo CS 8901.

ston Trio, Peter, Paul, and Mary, and Joan Baez; but their use of electric instruments and amplification was something quite new.

Their alliance with the protest movement was clear from the beginning;
their first hit was their version of a Bob Dylan song ("Mr. Tambourine Man"),
and their second a song by Pete Seeger ("Turn! Turn! Turn!"). Their third LP,
Fifth Dimension (summer, 1966), linked them unmistakably with certain trends
coming into focus in the Bay Area, with such songs as "Eight Miles High."

The Byrds.

San Francisco and Berkeley had become a magnet for many people, mostly
young, from all over America, drawn by a developing new culture loosely unified by an interest in perception-altering drugs, Eastern philosophies and
religions, and a disdain for traditional American values. These people, soon
labeled "hippies," were most strongly concentrated in the Haight-Ashbury district of San Francisco, which

> had long been a favorite residential area for persons of liberal disposition in
> many occupations, in business, labor, the arts, the professions, and aca-
> demic life. It had been equally hospitable to avant-garde expression, to
> racial diversity, and to the Okies and Arkies who came after World War II.
> Its polyglot population, estimated at 30,000, was predominantly white, but

it included Negroes and Orientals in sizable numbers, and immigrants of many nations. Here William Saroyan and Erskine Caldwell had lived.[6]

This was the setting for what soon came to be known as America's "counterculture" of the 1960s, described by a contemporary observer:[7]

It was easier to see than understand: the visual came first, and the visual was so discordant that tourists drove with their cars locked and an alarmed citizenry beseeched the police to clean it out.

It was easy to see that the young men who were hippies on Haight Street wore beards and long hair and sometimes earrings and weird-o granny eye-glasses, that they were barefoot or in sandals, and that they were generally dirty. A great many of the young men, by design or by accident, resembled Jesus Christ, whose name came up on campaign pins or lavatory walls or posters or bumper stickers. *Are You Bombing With Me, Baby Jesus. Jesus is God's Atom Bomb.* . . . It was easy to see that the young women who were hippies were draped, not dressed; that they, too, were dirty from toe to head; that they looked unwell, pale, sallow, hair hung down in strings unwashed. Or they wore jeans, men's T-shirts over brassieres. When shoes were shoes the laces were missing or trailing, gowns were sacks, and sacks were gowns. *If You Can't Eat It Wear It.* . . .

The shops of the "hip" merchants were colorful and cordial. The "straight" merchants of Height Street sold necessities, but the hip shops smelled of incense, the walls were hung with posters and paintings, and the counters were laden with thousands of items of nonutilitarian nonsense— metal jewelry, glass beads, dirty pictures, "underground" magazines, photographs of old-time movie stars, colored chalk, dirty combs, kazoos, Halloween masks, fancy matchboxes, odd bits of stained glass, and single shoes. . . .

Once the visual scene was ignored, almost the first point of interest about the hippies was that they were middle-class American children to the bone. To citizens inclined to alarm this was the thing most maddening, that these were not Negroes disaffected by color or immigrants by strangeness but boys and girls with white skins from the right side of the economy in all-American cities and towns from Honolulu to Baltimore. After regular educations, if only they'd want them, they could commute to fine jobs from the suburbs, and own nice houses with bathrooms, where they could shave and wash up.

Anybody who was anybody among hippies had been arested for something, or so he said—for "possession" (of drugs), for "contributing" (to the delinquency of a minor), for panhandling, for obstructing the sidewalk, and if for nothing else, for "resisting" (arrest). The principal cause of their conflict with the police was their smoking marijuana, probably harmless but definitely illegal. Such clear proof of the failure of the law to meet the

6. Mark Harris, "The Flowering of the Hippies," in *The Atlantic Monthly*, 220 (1976): 66.
7. Ibid., pp. 63–65.

knowledge of the age presented itself to the querulous minds of hippies as sufficient grounds to condemn the law completely. . . .

The music everywhere was rock 'n' roll out of Beatles, folk, African drums, American pop, jazz, swing, and martial.

Music was indeed everythwere, not merely part of the hippie scene, but absolutely fundamental to it. As one observer put it, "Rock was the organized religion of the sixties—the nexus not only of music and language but also of dance, sex, and dope, which all came together into a single ritual of self-expression and spiritual tripping."[8]

The first band to be a regular part of this Haight-Ashbury scene was the Charlatans, which had played briefly at the Red Dog Saloon in Virginia City in the summer of 1965 before settling in as the house band at Longshoremen's Hall in San Francisco, where many of the first community dances were held. Their music was patently derivative, mixing country-western elements with echoes of the folk revival and rock 'n' roll, with an occasional dash of Spanish-American flavoring. What mattered most was the band's successful integration into the total environment, the way it was received by the people who had come together to share an experience of sound and sight, with perceptions altered by drugs.

The success of these dances in the fall of 1965 was so great that two "rock palaces" opened, with music, dancing, and "tripping" almost every night: the Avalon, run by Chet Helms, and Fillmore Auditorium, managed by Bill Graham. Bands were needed to fill these halls with sound, and dozens and then hundreds sprang up in the Bay Area or came there from elsewhere. They were mostly cast in the image of the Charlatans—heavily amplified and electric, dressed in outlandish costumes, mixing elements of rock 'n' roll and country-western music. All understood that their audience was heavily "into" drugs and expected "head" music, making more sense to someone stoned or tripping than to a "straight" listener. None of these bands was known outside the Bay Area in 1965 and 1966. The outside world knew of this music only from occasional articles and criticisms, such as Ralph J. Gleason's column in the San Francisco *Chronicle* for September 13, 1965, in which he suggests that "something is going on here in the popular music field which bears watching" and goes on to label this music "contemporary-popular-music-folk-rock . . . we have no less cumbersome phrase to use so far. They sing everything from Bob Dylan to the blues, from Burl Ives to Miriam Makeba, from Lightning Hopkins and Jimmy Reed to 'Midnight Hour.' " America at large first heard of it through an article in *Newsweek* on December 19, 1966:

Every weekend in such immense halls as the Fillmore and the Avalon Ballroom, and college auditoriums like the Pauley Ballroom at Berkeley, the music assaults the ears; strobe lights, pulsating to the beat, blind the eyes

8. Morris Dickstein, *Gates of Eden. American Culture in the 60s* (New York: Basic Books, 1977), pp. 185–86.

and sear the nerves. Psychedelic projections slither across the walls in pro-
toplasmic blobs, restlessly changing shape, color and size. Two or three
thousand young people jam the floor, many in "ecstatic" dress—men with
shoulder-length locks and one earring, cowboy outfits, frock coats, high
hats; women in deliberately tatty evening gowns, rescued from some attic,
embellished by a tiara and sneakers. Arab kaftans are worn by both sexes,
who also affect bead necklaces, the high sign of LSD initiation.

Some of the crowd crouch close to the bandstand where the sound is most
ear-splitting, listening as raptly as if Horowitz were playing Mozart. . . .

Among the most popular of these bands were Quicksilver Messenger Service, Big Brother and the Holding Company (the house band at the Avalon),
Great Society (featuring the singer Grace Slick), Country Joe and the Fish (built
around Joe McDonald, who had been a "folk" singer in and around Berkeley),
and Moby Grape. But it was the Grateful Dead which soon emerged as the quin-
tessential early San Francisco rock band.

They were folkies (plus one avant-garde electronic music dropout); a former
bluegrass banjoist, a blues organist and some others. . . . Shortly after getting into electrified rock, they'd fallen in with the big action of the Stanford
psychedelic scene: the Acid Test LSD parties being put on by the novelist
Ken Kesey and his Merry Pranksters. With this background and the early
patronage of Owsley Stanley, the famous LSD chemist, the Dead became
the most notable acid *existencialistas* on the scene, making decisions and
managing their affairs as a huge, extended family, without regard for status
or conventional chains of command. They had a considerable reputation
for playing while stoned, and for taking half an hour to tune up and decide
on the next song.[9]

Jefferson Airplane, a popular group at the Fillmore, brought this music to
the rest of the country, and to the world. They were the first to sign a contract
with a recording company (RCA Victor), the first to bring out a successful album
(*Jefferson Airplane Takes Off*, August 1966), the first to receive nationwide media coverage, the first to perform in New York (in early 1967), and the first to convert the San Francisco sound-light concert into a traveling show, with the aid of
Glenn McKay's Headlights. They were also the first to carry San Francisco rock
to *Billboard*'s pop charts; their second album, *Surrealistic Pillow*—cut after
Grace Slick had joined them as lead singer—was on the *Billboard* LP album
charts for fifty-six weeks, rising as high as No. 3, and two singles from the album,
"Somebody to Love" and "White Rabbit," made the Top Ten in the singles
charts.
Their success prompted other recording companies to bring out San Fran-

9. Charles Perry, "The Sound of San Francisco," in *The Rolling Stones Illustrated History of
Rock & Roll*, pp. 246–48.

Jefferson Airplane recording for RCA Victor.

cisco rock. Warner Brothers signed the Grateful Dead and brought out their first album in the summer of 1967; Country Joe and the Fish signed with Vanguard, Moby Grape with Columbia, Big Brother and the Holding Company with Mainstream. Bill Graham brought the rock environment to New York by opening Fillmore East in 1967; the bands became top-drawing attractions on college campuses and large city auditoriums; *Cheap Thrills*, featuring Janis Joplin with Big Brother and the Holding Company, became a No. 1 LP album in 1968; Jimi Hendrix and others took rock to Europe that same year; and suddenly this new music was no longer the exclusive property of the San Francisco community, but was listened to throughout the world.

Rock was important not only because of the success of these California-based bands, but for the impact it had on other performers. To understand this, it will help to define the rock style more precisely, to isolate the elements that made it very different from rock 'n' roll:

Rock is electric. It was not just a matter of amplifying instruments to make louder sounds, but of exploring and exploiting new sound resources: distortion of live sound through feedback, electronic filtering, mixing, and other means; the use of electric instruments other than the guitar (electric organ and piano, and soon various sorts of synthesizers); manipulation of recorded sound in the studio, through splicing, overdubbing, laying of multiple tracks, collaging tapes of both musical and natural sounds.

Rock drew from some of the same sources as rock 'n' roll—rhythm-and-blues and country-western—but added non-Western music of several sorts, classical music, folk music of sorts other than those that fed into rock 'n' roll, and contemporary avant-garde music.

Formal structures of rock were much more varied than the 12-bar blues and Tin Pan Alley patterns that dominated rock 'n' roll. Rock songs sometimes used these also, but more often the forms of this new music were either simpler or more complex. They were often improvisatory and apparently formless, not restricted to the 3–4 minute limitation imposed on rock 'n' roll by the necessity of fitting each song onto a single 45-rpm disc. Rock songs were conceived with either a live audience or an LP album in mind and could be of any duration.

Most rock 'n' roll was limited harmonically to the 12-bar-blues patterns of only three chords, repeated over and over. Rock, drawing on a wider range of models, ran the gamut from a complete absence of Western harmony (in pieces based on Indian music), to simple rock 'n' roll chords, to sophisticated progression borrowed from classical music, to the atonal sound of avant-garde music.

Some rock pieces incorporated the big beat of rock 'n' roll, others were much slower—sometimes with a free flow that appeared to have no beat—and some were even faster. Rock was dance music just as much as rock 'n' roll had been, but rock dancing could take any form and proceed at any tempo, being largely improvisational.

Rock lyrics tended to be political, in the sense of making a statement about something. Some made clear reference to the war in Vietnam and other political and social issues of the day; most made more oblique statements by presenting an attitude at variance with those dominating American life. Some lyrics were overtly philosophical or religious, or at least attempted to be.

The ways in which rock altered the music of performers who were not part of the San Francisco scene is reflected in the music of the Beatles in the several years following their initial success in America and their unprecedented dominance of the American charts. Their tours in this country not only served to bring their brand of rock 'n' roll to this country, but also to bring them into contact with the music of Bob Dylan, various black performers, and the San Francisco rock groups. They were also in touch with the new moods of young America: the growing impatience with the powerful, militaristic pose of the country, the fascination with alternate religions and philosophies, the experimentation with "mind-freeing" drugs. And like so many great musicians, they continued to listen and learn even after becoming successful and famous.

The album *Help!* (1965), containing mostly songs from their movie of the same name, was their last pure rock 'n' roll effort. *Rubber Soul*, released in December of 1965, is the first fruit of their contact with the California counterculture; "Norwegian Wood," never brought out as a single, is the best example of new directions in their music. The drive and propulsion of rock 'n' roll is gone, replaced by a gentle, almost static mood, enhanced by the sound of a sitar (an Indian instrument) played by George Harrison, giving a shimmering, gently metallic quality to the sound, much more suggestive of the Byrds than of Chuck Berry. John Lennon's text is rather enigmatic:

And when I awoke I was alone,
    this bird had flown,
    so I lit a fire,
    isn't it good?
Norwegian wood.

It has been taken by some as the first "head song" (i.e., making reference to drugs) by the Beatles.

"Yesterday," released as a single in September of 1965, is remarkable for its use of a string quartet to accompany Paul McCartney's solo, resulting in a sound never before heard in popular song. *Revolver*, a collection of songs recorded between early April and mid-June of 1966, contained many surprises. There was "Eleanor Rigby," a fragmentary vignette of the life of a parish priest, Father McKenzie, and a member of his flock, Eleanor Rigby; 4 violins, 2 violas, and 2 cellos make up the accompanying group, and the text concludes with a sentiment alien to both Tin Pan Alley and early rock 'n' roll:

All the lonely people, where do they all come from?
All the lonely people, where do they all belong?

"Love You Too," by George, features an Indian tabla player, Anil Bhagwat; "Yellow Submarine" has lyrics with special meaning for those initiated into the new drug culture, plus sound effects of bubbles and swirling water; and John Lennon's "Tomorrow Never Knows" has background sound effects and electronics, arranged by Paul.

In August of 1966, the Beatles abruptly ended their latest concert tour— their last appearance was, fittingly, in San Francisco—and returned to England to work on a new album, soon rumored to be startlingly different from anything they had done before. They were never to perform in public again.

The long-awaited album was almost a year in coming: *Sgt. Pepper's Lonely Hearts Club Band*, released at midnight on June 1, 1967, was a stunning achievement, drawing together dozens of stylistic threads into a whole that was somehow unified, summing up much of what the 1960s had been about— musically and otherwise—and casting a shadow over the entire next decade.

The eleven songs were in a variety of styles. "She's Leaving Home," by Paul McCartney, is a narrative ballad descended from "Eleanor Rigby," with a harp added to the string accompaniment. George Harrison's "Within You Without You" showed his continuing preoccupation with Indian music; his vocal solo is backed by a group of Indian musicians, with no participation from the other three Beatles. In John Lennon's "Lucy in the Sky with Diamonds," the electric guitars almost take on the sound of a sitar, and Paul's bass sounds amazingly like a tabla; the voices have a ghostly, thin, almost electronic timbre, through filtering of the tape in the studio. Paul McCartney's "When I'm Sixty-Four" is reminiscent of a turn-of-the-century British music-hall number, backed by a small wind band. The title cut begins with indistinct crowd noises, and there are brass instruments joining the Beatles and their usual instruments as the song progresses. The last song, "A Day in the Life," enlists what sounds like a full symphony orchestra.

The Beatles, costumed for their album *Sgt. Pepper's Lonely Hearts Club Band* (1967).

The range of instrumental and vocal sound was unprecedented in popular song. George Martin, the producer, had worked with dozens of studio musicians, with tapes of natural and musical sounds, and with the most sophisticated electronic equipment ever assembled for music of this sort. He taped, filtered, laid track over track, spliced—at times working with his sound sources almost in the way a painter works with colors. Each of the songs is the result of repeated tapings and dozens of hours of work with the resources of the new electronic technology; the album was reputed to have taken 700 hours of studio time to produce. And it *is* a studio album, using devices and techniques possible only in a studio. Even if the Beatles had continued to perform, they would not have been able to reproduce the sound of the album in live performance.

It was also the first widely popular LP album conceived as a whole, rather than as a collection of unrelated songs.[10] *Sgt. Pepper* is put together in somewhat the same way as James Joyce's *Dubliners*, as a collection of portraits of people at different stages of life and in different situations, the unity coming from the fact that they are all part of the contemporary world, and they are all seen through the eyes of the Beatles. As with the Joyce book, separate episodes may be enjoyed alone, but the work makes much more sense taken as a whole.

The cast of characters may be British, but the view of them is from California. Many of the songs have drug references, from "I Get High with a Little Help from My Friends" through "Lucy in the Sky with Diamonds" (which, despite denials from the Beatles, was widely perceived as an "LSD song"), to the very end ("Found my way upstairs and had a smoke, somebody spoke and I went into a dream").[11] "She's Leaving Home" deals with a classic theme of the mid-1960s, a child running away from home to escape a life in which "something inside me . . . was always denied, for so many years." "Good Morning, Good Morning" offers the view of the life of "ordinary" people as being empty and meaningless ("Nothing to do but save his life . . . Nothing to say but it's O.K.").

The album, which became the best-selling LP in America the week after its release and stayed on the *Billboard* charts for 113 weeks, attracted a far wider range of listeners and buyers than was usually the case with popular song, and the range of critical response was unprecedented; newspapers and journals not usually concerned with "pop" music wrote about it and reviewed it; musicians whose preoccupation had been with classical music listened to it and even tried to analyze it.

The Rolling Stones, like the Beatles, moved from an early rock 'n' roll style based largely on the music of American performers of the 1950s to a more complex and sophisticated style in the mid-1960s. They admired Chuck Berry and Elmore James, and among their first recordings were covers of songs by Muddy Waters, Otis Redding, and Sam Cooke. Their first successful single in the U.K. came in 1963, their first No. 1 hit in both England and America was "(I Can't Get No) Satisfaction," released in the summer of 1965. Their stage act was patterned after those of the sexually suggestive Americans of the mid-1950s:

No one had ever seen a white man move on stage the way Jagger moved. . . . He was to become the prototype for stage sexuality, the most imitated singer in rock. . . . His lips and no-hips drove every relevant point home;

10. For a discussion of some of the early "concept" LP albums, see Dale Cockrell, *Sergeant Pepper's Lonely Hearts Club Band and Abbey Road, Side Two: Unity in the Rock Recording*, master's thesis, The University of Illinois at Urbana-Champaign, 1971.
11. The Beatles made no secret of their use of marijuana at this time.

most of the girls who watched had never before had the word put to them quite so explicitly. It was heady stuff for fourteen-year-old virgins, and others besides.[12]

But soon elements foreign to early rock 'n' roll began to creep into the Stones' songs. "Play with Fire" (1965) suggests Bob Dylan and other folk-revival singers, with its modal melody accompanied mostly by arpeggiated guitar chords. "As Tears Go By" (late 1965) was their response to the Beatles' "Yesterday" and "Eleanor Rigby," with its backing by a small string group. "Satisfaction" starts off

Mick Jagger (behind the mike) and the Rolling Stones.

with an aggressive, snarling ostinato on the electric guitar that continues throughout the song, almost hypnotic (and quite non-Western) in its insistence on this sound from beginning to end. "Paint It Black" (1966) begins with the sound of a sitar, the first vocal phrase is accompanied only by sitar and tabla, and the timbre is dominated by the nasal, twanging sound of sitar and electric guitar. "Ruby Tuesday" (1966) has a soft, gentle texture dominated by piano, sustained notes on the bass, and two recorders. "Sympathy for the Devil," from the album *Beggars Banquet* (1968), was one of their most popular songs in the late 1960s despite the fact it was never released as a single, since it was much too long to fit on a 45-rpm record. *Their Satanic Majesties Request* (late 1967) was their "psychedelic" response to *Sgt. Pepper*. The point is not that the Stones were unusually imitative—they were not—but that certain elements were becoming common property among rock groups of the day.

12. Lillian Roxon, *Rock Encyclopedia* (New York: Grosset & Dunlap, 1971), p. 423.

Bob Dylan, the rock star.

Their lyrics and their public posture and behavior also mirror common attitudes of the time: they sang of sexual freedom ("Let's Spend the Night Together" and many others), drugs ("Something Happened to Me"), and a general pose of anger, defiance, and rowdiness ("Street Fighting Man"). In the fall and winter of 1967, three members of the group were arrested and convicted of drug usage; though their sentences were eventually suspended and they were able to continue recording without serious interruption, they were refused entry into the United States for several years.

Other performers began assimilating elements of rock into their music. Bob Dylan, for instance, used electronic instruments on the album *Bringing It All Back Home* in 1965 and antagonized many members of the "folk" scene by playing a set with electric guitar at the Newport Folk Festival on July 25 of that year. He followed with *Highway 61 Revisited*, using a band of eight—most playing electric instruments—as a back-up group. Both these albums sold well enough to be in the Top Ten on the *Billboard* charts—his first albums to achieve such general popularity—and he also became, for the first time, a success on Top Forty radio, with such songs as "Subterranean Homesick Blues," "Like a Rolling Stone," and "Rainy Day Women #12 & 35." Dylan the "folkie" had become Dylan the rock star.

Peter, Paul, and Mary discovered electricity in 1967, with their *Album 1700*. Back-up musicians playing electric guitar, bass, and organ accompany them on such songs as "Weep for Jamie" and "I Dig Rock and Roll Music," which have more complex textures than any heard before in folk-revival music; "I'm in Love with a Big Blue Frog" has natural sounds overlaid in the studio; "Whatshername" has complex harmonies, in the style of progressive jazz; and "The House Song" is an out-and-out "head" song, with multiple overlaid tracks giving a dense, rich texture of swirling strings and humming voices, an interlude between stanzas that is purely electronic, and a text that makes more sense if the listener is stoned.

Paul Simon and Art Garfunkel followed a similar path from folk revival to rock. Their earliest hits were sung in an urban "folk" style, with smooth harmonies accompanied by acoustic guitars; their first successes came with the singles "Homeward Bound" and "I Am a Rock" and the albums *Sounds of Silence* and *Parsley, Sage, Rosemary and Thyme*, all of 1966. *Bookends*, released in April of 1968, was suddenly a rock album: "Save the Life of the Child" has a full, rich texture, with electric guitars and electric bass, and with multiple tracking that superimposes a ghostly chorus against the two singers; drums, an electric organ, and a clarinet support the guitars in "America"; "Voices of Old People" is a tape collage of conversations recorded in an old people's home, without a note of music; "Old Friends" is backed by a string orchestra that builds to a dissonant, symphonic climax. The first side of the album is not a random collection of songs, but rather a song cycle, moving through the various stages of life—adolescence, young adulthood, middle age, old age—framed by the "bookends" of common musical material at beginning and end.

Other performers beginning their careers in the mid-1960s never went through a first stage of rock 'n' roll or folk music. The Who, for instance, had their first hit in late 1965 with "My Generation," already in full-blown rock style, featuring a ringing, throbbing, electric sound. There were only four musicians, but with a style based on electronic modification, amplification, and distortion at a thunderous volume, they made more than enough sound to fill whatever space they played in. Their stage antics matched the frantic, frenzied, overpowering sound: Peter Townshend attacked his guitar as though to rip it

Simon and Garfunkel early in their career.

apart with each full-arc stroke, singer Roger Daltrey was second only to Mick Jagger in his posturing and prancing, Keith Moon was a frenzied drummer; and from early on they ended their shows with a scene of complete pandemonium, with Townshend smashing and destroying his guitar in a frenzy of ear-splitting electronic feedback.

They fitted into the rock scene in every way. "My Generation," was such a put-down of the older generation that it "became the national anthem of the under-twenty-fives in England."[13] They gave public support to Mick Jagger and

13. Ibid., p. 527.

Keith Richard when the two members of the Rolling Stones were jailed on drug charges. Townshend became a disciple of Meher Baba, an Indian guru who allegedly went forty-four years without speaking. Their songs were long and complex, designed for live performance and for the LP album rather than being restricted by the 45-rpm single; "A Quick One While He's Away" and "Rael" were called "miniature rock operas" by Townshend and were sketches for *Tommy*, a full-blown "rock opera" released in 1969. A thread of a plot holds this 75-minute work together (a deaf, dumb, and blind boy becomes a pinball wizard

Peter Townsend of The Who (right) and Eric Clapton in a scene from Ken Russell's film of the rock opera *Tommy*.

and then a religious leader); despite the price of the two-disc album, it was on the *Billboard* charts of LP albums for 110 weeks and was eventually performed at the Metropolitan Opera House in New York, marking a high point in the acceptance of rock by the "establishment."

Jimi Hendrix was a left-handed guitar player from Seattle who worked for years as a back-up performer for such stars as Little Richard and Wilson Pickett before emerging in 1967 with his own act, the Jimi Hendrix Experience, tried out and polished in Europe before their first American appearance at the Monterey Pop Festival of 1967. The amplification and electronic manipulation of live sound went beyond anything heard to that point, and Hendrix's stage deportment shocked even other rock performers:

> . . . black hair flying from his head in electric fright, doing things to his guitar so passionate, so concentrated and so intense that anyone with half-way decent manners had to look away. And that was the way the act began, not ended. By the time it was over he had lapped and nuzzled his guitar with his lips and tongue, caressed it with his inner thighs, jabbed at it with a series of powerful pelvic thrusts. . . . What Mick Jagger and the early rockers had so saucily promised and hinted at, Jimi Hendrix delivered.[14]

The act ended with Hendrix dousing his guitar with lighter fluid and burning it on stage, with the insane sounds of its death throes mightily amplified.

In immediate demand at rock palaces, festivals, and antiwar rallies, he also brought out five LP albums (*Are You Experienced*, *Axis: Bold as Love*, *Electric Ladyland*, *Smash Hits*, *The Cry of Love*) that were all among the five best-selling albums, before and after his death in 1970.

Then there was Jim Morrison, who formed a group called The Doors in California in 1966. Originally a favorite group of the radical underground community of Los Angeles, projecting an image of sexuality, rebellion, and neuroticism, they astonishingly achieved great national success with their first album, *The Doors*, in early 1967. Included on the album were such cuts as "The End," an 11½-minute mini-drama ending as the protagonist kills his own father, and "Light My Fire," an erotic "love" song that became a top-selling single. Morrison was an intense, sullen, totally nonconformist performer; two of his concerts ended in well-publicized arrests—in New Haven, police allegedly used the chemical mace on him and a young fan in his dressing room before the concert, so he harangued the audience from the stage about police "brutality"; and in Miami, on March 2, 1969, he was arrested again for exposing himself during a performance. It is a measure of the mood of the times that such defiant songs and behavior only served to enhance his popularity among rock audiences.

Janis Joplin was another bright, brief star of the late 1960s. A frenetic blues singer, probably the only white female singer to capture the essence of the blues, she recorded and performed first with Big Brother and the Holding Company

14. Ibid., pp. 228–29.

The late Janis Joplin.

(the album *Cheap Thrills* of 1968 was a No. 1 seller, featuring Joplin's most stunning recorded performance, a lengthy version of "Ball and Chain"), and later brought out three equally successful albums of her own, as well as a top-selling single "Me and Bobby McGee" in 1971. She was as compelling a stage presence as Morrison, matching her vocal pyrotechnics with appropriate stage deportment, drinking and talking with the audience while on stage, sometimes launching long, rambling monologues about the futility of war and the necessity for love and brotherhood.

The common thread among these and other rock musicians was not so much stylistic as ideological.

The Oracle, an underground San Francisco paper, laid out a credo for rock in its issue of February 1967:

SOME PRINCIPLES

—That rock is essentially head (or even psychedelic) music.

—That rock is a legitimate avant garde art form, with deep roots in the music of the past (especially the baroque and before), great vitality, and vast potential for growth and development, adaptation, experiment, etcetera.

—That rock is an intensely participational and nontypographical art form, forerunner of something much like McLuhan's covertly projected spherical society.

—That far from being degenerate or decadent, rock is a regenerative and revolutionary art, offering us our first real hope for the future (indeed, for the present) since August 6, 1945;[15] and that its effects on the younger population, especially those effects most deplored by typeheads, have all been essentially good and healthy so far.

—That rock principles are not limited to music, and that much of the shape of the future can be seen in its aspirations today (these being mainly total freedom, total experience, total love, peace and mutual affection).

—That rock seems to have synthesized most of the intellectual and artistic movements of our time and culture, cross-fertilizing them and forcing them rapidly toward fruition and function.

—That group participation, total experience and complete involvement are rock's minimal desiderata and those as well of a world that has too many people.

—That rock is creating the social rituals of the future.

15. The date of the explosion of the atomic bomb over Hiroshima, Japan.

—That the medium is indeed the message, and rock knows what that means.

By the late 1960s, rock was solidly and openly at the center of the protest movements that characterized this decade. No antiwar rally was complete without rock; student protests and demonstrations against policies of American colleges and universitites marched and surged to rock bands; police and national guard troops, confronting students and other young Americans over a variety of issues, found themselves also confronting rock music and often some of its musicians; practically every rock musician advocated the use of drugs, and a goodly number of the most popular rock songs of the late 1960s made direct or veiled reference to drug usage. Rock music was heard by many of its followers not as sound but as propaganda; musicians were welcomed into the "movement" and their music became part of the rock scene if their sympathies and politics were acceptable, whatever the sound of their music. Ravi Shankar played at rock concerts and his albums sold widely to the same audience buying albums by Jimi Hendrix, the Who, and the Rolling Stones. Joan Baez was considered a member of the rock scene, even when she was singing "Swing Low, Sweet Chariot" without accompaniment. B. B. King, a traditional black blues singer, was welcomed and listened to, as were the Incredible String Band (several Irish "folkies"

On August 16, 1969, over 300,000 fans gathered on a 600-acre farm near Woodstock, New York, to listen to rock music for four days. Sullivan County reeled from the massive dose of music, marijuana, and mud.

playing a variety of traditional and new instruments), Virgil Fox (playing works of Bach on the organ), the Staple Singers (a black gospel group), and such veterans of the folk revival as Pete Seeger. Politics and sympathies counted, not musical style. For several giddy years in the late 1960s, millions of mostly young Americans were convinced that traditional patterns of American life and culture were changing, that the new counterculture would dominate, that the United States would become a land of peace, love, and drugs—and that rock music would be one of the chief agents of this change.

Just as the musical style of rock had some of its most important roots in early rock 'n' roll, the tide of social and political protest that swept through the 1960s was seen by some as growing out of the ripple of protest accompanying the emergence of the new musical style of the mid-1950s. Little Richard, for one, had difficulty in separating the two periods:

> Like I don't like the word "hippie." I call it the "real people." Because they are saying "hippie." I was the first one, 'cause I've been wearing the long hair and fancy clothes, I've been doing it all my life, so I was the first hippie, yeah, in Macon, Georgia. And everyone would call me silly and stupid, my father would put me outdoors, he said, "The man has gone crazy." So I like to say the "real people," they are willing, they've got guts enough to admit they're doing their thing, what they want to do and expressing their rights and don't care what society thinks, because what is society? . . . What I think society is mad about is they're getting old and very soon they'll be gone, and they are wondering what these young people are gonna do with this world, and they're mad because they can't do what they used to do and they can't dance because they've got arthritis and rheumatism, they can't jump up in the air. It's jealousy against the young race . . .[16]

There is disagreement today as to the lasting effect on American life resulting from the postures and actions of the '60s, and some critics now question the methods and even the motives of the leaders of the "movement." Historically, though, there can be no denying the fact that millions of Americans honestly and openly questioned the motives and methods of their own government, on moral and philosophical grounds, and that popular music—in the form of rock—was a central and critical part of this process. Not since the decades before the Civil War, the era of the Huchinson Family, had popular song played such an active role in political and social dialogue and action.

The recording industry had learned its lesson in the mid-1950s, and it was not caught napping this time. Rather than ignoring new musical trends or attempting to pass moral judgment on what was happening in the 1960s, the major companies snapped up the top stars of the folk revival and of rock:

16. David Dalton, "Little Richard," in *The Rolling Stones Interviews* (New York: Paperback Library, 1971), pp. 368–69.

Columbia	Bob Dylan, Byrds, Moby Grape, Simon and Garfunkel, Janis Joplin
Capitol	Kingston Trio, Beach Boys, Quicksilver Messenger Service, Beatles
Warner Brothers	Peter, Paul, and Mary; Grateful Dead
Vanguard	Joan Baez, Country Joe and the Fish
RCA Victor	Jefferson Airplane
Decca	The Who
London	Rolling Stones

Thus the very companies that a decade earlier had taken a stand against the "immorality" of early rock 'n' roll were now releasing and promoting music that spoke openly of illegal drug usage and sex, that opposed the foreign and domestic policies of the American government, that even opposed the philosophies and practices of capitalism—the system at the very heart of the recording industry itself.

By supporting rock, these companies were also helping kill off the music that had been the core of their popular catalog for so many years, the music of Tin Pan Alley. For some years after 1955, many people had persisted in the belief that rock 'n' roll and its associated styles would die out, and the musical style that had dominated popular song in America for almost the entire century would reassert itself. Indeed, as pointed out in the previous chapter, songs in Tin Pan Alley style had coexisted with the newer styles, never disappearing, never changing; and by the end of the 1950s and the beginning of the '60s, such performers as Frank Sinatra and Johnny Mathis—who had continued to perform an older repertory, and never became part of the rock 'n' roll scene—enjoyed a new surge of popularity. Table I lists ten performers of the 1950s and '60s whose repertory and style were largely retrospective, with the number of their LP albums charted by *Billboard* in the top ten weekly sellers for each year between 1958 and 1970. A peak is reached in 1960 and 1961; only about half as many such albums sold for the period 1962–66; and beginning with 1967, albums of this sort practically disappear from the list of top-selling albums. It was not that these performers suddenly stopped bringing out discs; to the contrary, Frank Sinatra, Johnny Mathis, Lawrence Welk, and their peers continued to bring out their two to four albums each year through this entire time span.

Table II lists ten leading rock and folk-revival groups and performers for these same years. These two tables complement one another perfectly; the plummeting market for Tin Pan Alley products coincided precisely with the rising market for folk-revival music and rock.

It was rock 'n' roll that first challenged the long-time supremacy of Tin Pan Alley style, but it was "folk" music and rock that finally replaced it.

There was talk of the "silent majority" in the late 1960s and early '70s, talk that even though the protests and demonstrations of the mostly college-age political activists were receiving so much media attention, the majority of Americans

Table I: Top Ten LP Albums by Tin Pan Alley–Oriented Performers

	1958	1959	1960	1961	1962	1963	1964	1965	1966	1967	1968	1969	1970
Frank Sinatra	3	3	1	6	1	3	1	3	3	—	—	—	—
Johnny Mathis	3	3	3	1	—	1	—	—	1	—	—	—	—
Mantovani	2	1	2	1	1	1	—	—	—	—	—	—	—
Mitch Miller	2	3	3	4	—	—	—	—	—	—	—	—	—
Lawrence Welk	—	—	1	2	3	—	—	—	—	—	—	—	—
Percy Faith	—	—	2	1	—	—	—	—	—	—	—	—	—
Ray Conniff	2	1	3	1	2	—	—	—	—	—	—	—	—
Henry Mancini	—	2	1	1	1	2	1	—	—	—	—	—	—
Barbra Streisand	—	—	—	—	—	2	2	2	2	—	—	—	—
Andy Williams	—	—	—	—	1	1	3	1	1	2	1	1	—
	12	13	16	17	9	10	7	6	7	2	1	1	0

Table II: Top Ten LP Albums by Folk Revival and Rock Performers

	1961	1962	1963	1964	1965	1966	1967	1968	1969	1970
Beatles	—	—	—	4	4	2	2	1	2	2
Rolling Stones	—	—	—	1	3	3	3	1	2	1
Bob Dylan	—	—	—	—	2	1	1	1	1	2
Beach Boys	—	—	3	2	3	2	1	—	—	—
The Doors	—	—	—	—	—	—	2	1	1	2
Jimi Hendrix	—	—	—	—	—	—	—	2	1	1
Jefferson Airplane	—	—	—	—	—	—	1	2	1	1
Janis Joplin	—	—	—	—	—	—	—	1	—	1
Monkees	—	—	—	—	—	1	3	1	—	—
Steppenwolf	—	—	—	—	—	—	—	2	1	1
	0	0	3	7	12	9	13	11	9	10

were conservative, supportive of their government, and quite content with American life and culture as it had existed in their lifetimes. This may have been true; the elections of Richard Nixon to the presidency in 1968 and 1972 seemed to support this notion. But the picture was quite different in popular music: Frank Sinatra and Lawrence Welk were far outvoted by Bob Dylan and the Beatles, not only in sales of singles—considered to be the barometer of youthful taste since 1955—but equally so in LP album sales, the traditional medium for older, more conservative taste.

This book, from its first chapter, has concerned itself with those songs which were demonstrably most popular, in terms of sales of sheet music and phonograph recordings. The present chapter has been devoted mostly to folk revival and rock songs, not because of any bias on my part, but because this music was listened to and bought by the largest number of Americans. Perhaps this merely reflects a changing economy, with LP albums now in the price range of high school and college youth. But is also suggests that disillusionment with many aspects of American life was more widespread than many writers and politicians supposed, among a "silent majority" of Americans—many of them not yet of voting age—who were drawn to music that became a symbol of discontent.

Rock was the music of white, urban, middle- and upper-class Americans, the children of the people who had been the audience for Tin Pan Alley songs. Black Americans and the rural whites who made up the traditional country-western audience were not turned on by the Beatles, or Bob Dylan, or the Beach Boys, or Jefferson Airplane, or the Rolling Stones, or the Who. *Billboard*'s charts of phonograph record sales to those segments of the population, through the 1960s and into the early 1970s, were devoid of a single listing of a disc or album by any of them. "Folk" and rock performers were almost all white, mostly urban, mostly from the East, North, or California. Even the rare black rock musician, Jimi Hendrix, for example, never appeared on *Billboard*'s "soul" charts, as they were now called.

Blacks continued to listen to the music that had been at the core of their popular song since the rise of recorded black music in the 1920s and '30s: blues, more rhythmic pieces combining elements of jazz with blues, some gospel music. These styles had all originated in the South and among Southern blacks who had emigrated to the North, and most of the leading rhythm-and-blues performers of the 1950s and early '60s had been born in the South, pursued their professional careers mostly in the North, and developed their personal styles out of some distinctive blend of jazz, blues, gospel, and pop elements. The most successful were Ray Charles (born in Albany, Georgia), B. B. King (Indianola, Mississippi), James Brown (Augusta, Georgia), Aretha Franklin (Memphis, Tennessee), and Otis Redding (Macon, Georgia); only Sam Cooke, from Chicago, was born north of the Mason-Dixon line. These were the singers who dominated the *Billboard* rhythm-and-blues charts through the 1950s and into the early '60s; there were also enough white listeners drawn to this music to enable Charles to

Ray Charles.

have eleven Top Ten singles on the *Billboard* popular charts from 1959 to 1965, and for Brown to appear almost as frequently on the same charts in the late 1960s.

The 1960s also saw the rise of the first urban, black, Northern popular song, originating in Detroit and quite different in style from earlier black popular song. Known as the "Detroit sound," or the "Motown sound" (after the recording company that was at the center of this development), this new but hybrid strain of American popular song was the brainchild of Berry Gordy, a black songwriter and record producer. His first disc was "Come to Me," (1959) one of his own songs performed by Marv Johnson in a style that became characteristic of black popular song of the 1960s: "simple lyrics set to a stock rock chord progression . . . [with] a churchy female chorus for some call-and-response trades, and a bubbling male bassman . . . anchored by a persistent baritone sax and tambourine, with a flute break in the middle. The result was a clean R&B record that sounded as white as it did black."[17]

The first indication of the market potential of this new mix came with "Shop Around," recorded in late 1960 by the Miracles, headed by Smokey Robinson, songwriter and lead singer. The disc sold more than a million copies, quickly rising to the No. 1 position on the *Billboard* rhythm-and-blues charts, and selling equally well among whites (it rose as high as the No. 2 position on the "white pop" charts). The Miracles retained their popularity for the entire decade of the 1960s: they had no fewer than twenty Top Ten hits on the rhythm-and-blues charts between 1960 and 1970; six of these discs also scored in the Top Ten on the "white" charts; and this decade of success was climaxed by "The Tears of a Clown" (1970), which was top-seller among both white and black audiences.

"Please Mr. Postman" (1961) by the Marvelettes, a female trio, was the second million-seller produced by Gordy, becoming the No. 1 hit on both "black" and "white" charts. Mary Wells and Marvin Gaye were also successful singers in the early years, and "Heat Wave" by Martha and the Vandellas (1963) was another landmark, marking the first success of the songwriting-arranging team of Lamont Dozier, Brian Holland, and Eddie Holland, who were to refine and standardize the Motown sound into one of the most characteristic nonrock styles of the 1960s.

The peak of commercial success of urban black popular song came between 1963 and 1970. Diana Ross and the Supremes had a dozen No. 1 hits on *Billboard* "pop" charts, a record bettered only by the Beatles (with twenty) and Elvis Presley (fourteen). The Temptations and the Four Tops did almost as well, and with other performers such as Stevie Wonder and Marvin Gaye also appearing on the Motown label, the company sold some twelve million discs each year in the middle and late '60s. It had become one of the largest black-owned corporations in the country, and nothing could better typify the growing black presence in America than the Motown story.

The singing style of Motown artists had a great deal to do with black gospel music, itself a product of the urban North; this is hardly surprising, since most of the Motown singers had begun singing in black churches. The vocal style was rich, full-voiced, highly melismatic and filled with melodic ornamentation. The rhythmic underpinning was also firmly and obviously rooted in rhythm-and-blues and gospel music, with a solid bass and rhythm section giving the foundation for rhythmically flexible solo lines, and for the offbeat rhythmic punctuation on the second and fourth beats common in black popular song.

17. Joe McEwen and Jim Miller, "Motown," in *The Rolling Stone Illustrated History of Rock & Roll*, p. 222.

Diana Ross and the Supremes, backed by the Temptations.

Smokey Robinson.

Marvin Gaye.

In other ways, though, the Motown style was modeled on white popular song of the Tin Pan Alley era. There was, first of all, the sound of the accompanying orchestra. The Holland-Dozier-Holland team perfected a rich texture using the full range of orchestral instruments; strings dominated, but there was also a full complement of brass and wind instruments, and even such symphonic instruments as the harp. The sound is that of a slightly scaled-down symphony orchestra, very close to the arranging style of such latter-day Tin Pan Alley arrangers as Nelson Riddle. The expressive range is narrower than earlier rhythm-and-blues: almost as much as Tin Pan Alley songs of the 1920s, '30s, and '40s, Motown songs are concerned with romantic love, as is evident from mere titles: "The Tracks of My Tears," "My Girl Has Gone," and "The Tears of a Clown" (Miracles); "It's the Same Old Song," "Reach Out, I'll Be There," and "Standing in the Shadows of Love" (Four Tops); "Back in My Arms Again," "Stop! In the Name of Love," and "Someday We'll Be Together" (Supremes); and "Since I Lost My Baby," "Ain't Too Proud to Beg," and "I Know I'm Losing You" (Temptations).

The 12-bar blues form, a foundation of so much black music, is conspicuously absent from Motown music, replaced by the song forms of white popular music. And, almost as if to acknowledge this new kinship, Motown artists frequently performed and recorded Tin Pan Alley songs, past and present: Smokey Robinson and the Miracles did George Gershwin's "Embraceable You" and Cole Porter's "I've Got You Under My Skin"; the Four Tops recorded "On the Street Where You Live" (Lerner and Loewe, from *My Fair Lady*) and the Rodgers and Hammerstein "The Sound of Music"; Diana Ross and the Supremes did Vincent Youman's "Without a Song" (1929), Rodgers and Hart's "With a Song in My Heart" from the same year, and an entire album entitled *Supremes Sing Rodgers and Hart*, released in 1967; Stevie Wonder sang a wide spectrum of Tin Pan Alley songs, from the Jimmy McHugh/Dorothy Fields "On the Sunny Side of the Street" of 1930 to "When You Wish Upon a Star" (Leigh Harline/Ned Washington) from Walt Disney's *Pinocchio*; Marvin Gaye went back to 1933 for Harold Arlen's "It's Only a Paper Moon" and to 1943 for an old Mills Brothers' hit, Alec Wilder's "I'll Be Around."

Motown music appealed to many Americans who were attracted to black culture as an alternative to their way of life; but certainly there were others who turned to Motown music because of its kinship with the style, substance, and even repertory of an older and declining body of white popular song.

Folk-revival music and rock were no more popular among the audiences that had traditionally listened to country-western music than they were among blacks. One searches the *Billboard* country-western charts of the 1960s in vain for a single disc by Peter, Paul, and Mary, Bob Dylan, the Beach Boys, the Byrds, Jefferson Airplane, or even Janis Joplin. Likewise, the Hot 100 charts, reflecting white, urban musical taste, are almost completely devoid of discs by the most successful country-western singers of the 1960s—Eddy Arnold, Webb Pierce, Sonny James, Ray Price, Buck Owens, Jim Reeves, George Jones, Marty

Robbins, Merle Haggard, and others from the South and West. These men continued a decades-old tradition of song, in a style that changed but little during the turbulent era of the late 1950s and the '60s: strophic, mostly narrative songs dealing with a wide range of emotions and situations; accompaniments still heavily dependent on guitars (both acoustic and electric), fiddles, dobros or steel guitars, and bass (both acoustic and electric); a vocal style still reminiscent of the nasal, declamatory singing of traditional Anglo-American ballads and songs. Performers and audiences of this music held to their traditional views of American society, in the face of sweeping challenges and changes. Both the musical style and the politics of the folk and rock movements were alien to them; Merle Haggard's "Okie from Muskogee" (1969) may have been written as a tongue-in-cheek indictment of the counterculture, but it was taken by its audience as an anthem of defiance and rejection of the "insanity" that was sweeping so much of the country.

The 1960s, then, saw a new era of polarization, political and musical, of the three audiences that had been briefly brought together by early rock 'n' roll in the mid-1950s.

There may be those who will disagree with the shape of the present chapter on the basis of personal taste or from conviction that folk revival and rock were not the main currents of popular song in the 1960s. But all available statistical evidence insists that this was indeed the case. There is no way to compare the sales of single discs of folk and rock songs during the '60s with those of black music and country-western songs; only scattered data are available, since recording companies released sales figures only when they were exceptional, as when a given disc sold more than a million copies. Thus it is impossible to compare sales of Top Ten recordings on the *Billboard* "white pop" charts with the best-selling ten discs of soul and country-western music.

It is possible, however, to compare sales of LP albums of the various types of popular song. *Billboard*'s weekly chart of best-selling albums, compiled since 1955, does not separate recordings into the three repertories of the singles charts—Hot 100 (white, pop), soul, and country-western. Rather, all data are fed into a single chart; albums sold in both urban and rural areas, in the North and the South, in record shops in black urban areas and those in all-white suburbs, in Nashville and Los Angeles and Detroit and Atlanta and Des Moines—all are raw data for the chart. Table III (on p. 464) summarizes the top ten LP albums for the periods 1960–65 and 1966–71, by categories: performers associated with an older style of Tin Pan Alley song; rock performers; black performers; and country-western. The table supports the chief thesis of this chapter: the first years of the decade saw a resurgence of the pre-1955 style, the second half was dominated by folk-revival and rock music; music by black performers intended primarily for black listeners made up a strong minority of the market (some 15–20 percent) throughout the decade; and country-western music made up an insignificant portion of total LP album sales.

Table III: Top Ten LP Albums for 1960–71 *

	1960–65	1966–71
Tin Pan Alley–oriented	65 (5)	22 (1)
Folk Revival and Rock	22 (8)	57 (16)
Rhythm-and-Blues and Soul	13 (2)	20 (2)
Country-Western	2 (0)	2 (1)
	105 (15)	111 (20)

* The numbers in parentheses give the No. 1 albums in each category.

Folk and rock music were indeed the core of the popular song repertory in the middle and late 1960s.

EPILOGUE

The Seventies and Beyond

THE 1970s had just begun when I took the first steps toward writing the present book. As it is completed, the decade, too, has almost ended, and a general picture of popular song since 1955 has come much more sharply into focus.

Rock 'n' roll was superseded by music of the folk revival and by the style of rock characteristic of the late 1960s and early '70s. From the perspective of today, however, all this music—and that of the 1970s—can be seen as different dialects of a single musical language that has persisted for almost three decades. The distinction between rock 'n' roll and rock has become blurred, and the latter has become the generic term embracing all popular music in America from 1955 to the present.

Audiences and performers of today instinctively perceive a continuity stretching back to 1955. Radio stations devoted to popular music often play pieces from as far back as the early days of rock 'n' roll, and even though vintage Chuck Berry, Elvis Presley, and Jerry Lee Lewis may sound somewhat quaint to ears coming of age today, they are still speaking in a contemporary language. The Beatles are almost as familiar to teenagers now as they were during the years of their greatest triumphs. *The Buddy Holly Story* and *Hot Wax*, two movies of the late 1970s dealing with popular music of the mid-1950s, attracted large and sympathetic audiences in their teens and early twenties, as well as the over-35s.

And though rock performers continue to feature original pieces, many of them also play and sing "standards" chosen from the past twenty-five years; such pieces seem perfectly at home in today's environment.

The songs of Irving Berlin, Cole Porter, and George Gershwin, on the other hand, are ancient history to most Americans under the age of 30; they are relics of a world that may once have existed, but has long since faded into the mists of the past. One can listen to endless hours of DJ programs without hearing a single song written before 1955, and songs considered by older Americans to be part of the national heritage draw uncomprehending stares from their children and grandchildren. Frank Sinatra is known to younger Americans as a movie actor and a "personality," but he has not issued a disc that placed in the top twenty-five since 1966.

As Paul Simon once put it, "Joltin' Joe has left and gone away." For sure.

Popular song has been in a period of stylistic continuity for almost a quarter-century. This does not imply that the music of the 1970s is inferior to its predecessors, nor that the new performers are less talented than those of the early days of rock. To the contrary, technical facility and sheer professionalism among popular musicians have risen to new peaks in the 1970s, and the decade has probably seen as many talented songwriters and arrangers as any earlier period of popular song in this country.

It does mean, though, that no radically new ground has been broken, no striking new trends or techniques have appeared, no new directions have revolutionized the industry or the audience.

It means that future historians will look back to the 1970s as comparable to the several decades following the Civil War, or the period between 1945 and 1955—a time marked by continuity and consolidation, a period of reworking existing forms of popular song, of marking time until the inevitable lightning of some new stylistic breakthrough strikes.

Many performers of the 1960s have been active through the present decade, continuing to perform much the same sort of music. The Rolling Stones, for instance, have brought out a continuous string of successful singles and albums, with no change in personnel or basic style, and made their most successful American tours ever in 1972 and 1975. Paul Simon has continued to write and sing the sensitive and imaginative songs that have made him one of the great songwriters of the twentieth century; the '70s gave us new works like "Mother and Child Reunion" (1971), "Kodachrome" (1973), "50 Ways to Leave Your Lover" (1975), and "Slip-Sliding Away" (1976). Stevie Wonder's special brand of pop-soul, with its strong roots in the Motown style of the 1960s, brought him even greater success and acclaim in the new decade; his two-disc LP, *Music in the Key of Life* (1976), was one of the top achievements of the decade. One of the most successful recent LP albums was *Rumours*, by Fleetwood Mac, a group who were popular in England as far back as the late '60s. Many other names familiar from the previous decade turn up time and again on *Billboard*'s charts of the 1970s: Neil Diamond, Bob Dylan, the Staple Singers, Elvis Presley, the Four

Neil Diamond in concert,
1972.

Tops, John Lennon, Gladys Knight, the renamed Jefferson Starship. And when the charts were dominated for several months in 1978 in a way not seen since the early days of Presley and the Beatles, it was not by a new band bursting on the scene with a blaze, but rather by the Bee Gees, the three Gibbs brothers from Australia, who had been frequent visitors to Top Forty radio and *Billboard* since 1967.

There were new performers, many of them with outstanding talent. The '70s welcomed a steady procession of new bands playing their own variations on the mainstream rock style: the group America, debuting in 1972 with a No. 1 hit, "A Horse with No Name"; the Eagles, from California, also first heard from in 1972 but reaching a peak of popularity in the mid- and late 1970s with such successes as "Best of My Love," "One of These Nights," "Lyin' Eyes," "Take It to the Limit," and "Hotel California"; the Doobie Brothers, whose first No. 1 disc was "Black Water" (1974); several Southern bands, including the Allman Brothers and the Marshall Tucker Band, who brought a somewhat different dialect and a reminder that the important roots of rock lay in the South; and two highly successful bands of the late '70s, Kansas and Boston.

The 1970s has swung more strongly in the direction of solo singing than did the '60s, with its predominance of groups. Elton John raised the curtain on solo popular song of the decade with "Your Song" in 1970 and followed with literally dozens of successful numbers; James Taylor was close behind with "Fire and Rain" (1970) and "You've Got a Friend" (1971), the latter his first No. 1 hit. Jim

Elton John and friend.

James Taylor.

Billy Joel.

Bruce Springsteen.

Croce, Peter Frampton, Bruce Springsteen, Billy Joel, and Jackson Browne are only a few of the male singers who rose to prominence with unique styles and repertories. The decade has also been somehow more sympathetic to female singers than the early years of rock. Carole King, a successful songwriter through the 1960s, turned to performing her own songs, and in the process dominated the early years of the decade with her albums *Tapestry* and *Music*. Carly Simon, Helen Reddy, and Tennille followed, and Olivia Newton-John and Linda Ronstadt became two of rock's brightest stars in the second half of the decade. But here too, it cannot be said that the '70s brought innovation; each of these singers, as well as many others, brought distinctive voices and styles to the world of popular song—without breaking in any serious way with the established tradition of singing in the age of rock.

Other bands, most of them English, emulated the "heavy metal" style of Iron Butterfly and Led Zeppelin by stressing heavy, propulsive, highly amplified textures—Deep Purple, Grand Funk Railroad, Black Sabbath. The Moody Blues pointed the direction toward "fusion" music, drawing elements from jazz, popular music, and the classics, and making extensive use of electronic amplification, mixing, distortion, and sound production. Some of the sounds produced by Emerson, Lake and Palmer, King Crimson, Pink Floyd, and Tangerine Dream rival and even surpass those of an augmented symphony orchestra, in variety, richness, and especially volume. The harmonic, melodic, and textual vocabulary of such groups draws heavily on classical music of the late nineteenth and early twentieth centuries; sometimes even their repertory draws on the classical repertory, as in Emerson, Lake, and Palmer's versions of Musorgsky's *Pictures at an Exhibition*, Aaron Copland's *Rodeo*, and several works by J. S. Bach. Some of this recent music moves away from song completely; Mike Oldfield's *Tubular Bells* (1973), for instance, was created entirely in an electronic studio, of natural and electronic sounds spliced, altered, mixed, and overlaid.

Other patterns of post-1955 popular song have continued into the 1970s; the present decade has seen a steady succession of "crossovers" between mainstream popular music and the country-western repertory, for instance. Glen Campbell has remained successfully poised somewhere between the two ever since his "Wichita Lineman" of 1968 attracted both audiences; his "Rhinestone Cowboy" was a No. 1 hit on both the "pop" and country-western charts in the summer of 1975, for instance. The same year, John Denver's "Thank God I'm a Country Boy" and "I'm Sorry" both achieved the same double success. The Eagles enjoyed their first successes on Top Forty radio, but such later songs as "Lyin' Eyes" (1975) have sold well among country-western audiences as well; Crystal Gale's "Don't It Make My Brown Eyes Blue" (1975) and Freddy Fender's "Before the Next Teardrop Falls" (1975) were such successful blends of country-western and popular styles that they reached the top position on both charts; Olivia Newton-John, born in England and raised in Australia, enjoyed equal success on the two charts with songs like "Let Me Be There" (1973), "If You Love Me" (1974), and "Have You Never Been Mellow" (1975); she was voted top female vocalist of 1974 by the Country Music Association, despite the fact that her songs have little to do with traditional country-western style and are sung to lush accompaniments, with strings and the other trappings of neo–Tin Pan Alley style. Dolly Parton, whose roots are solidly in country-western music, has become equally successful among pop audiences in the late 1970s with such songs as "Two Doors Down" and "He'll Come Again." With these last-named singers, stylistic differences between the two bodies of music have almost completely broken down and what has emerged can best be labeled "country pop."

The 1970s also saw continuing interaction between black and white popular music. Some black singers were almost equally popular with both audiences: Roberta Flack's "The First Time Ever I Saw Your Face" (1972), "Killing Me Softly with His Song" (1973), and "Feel Like Makin' Love" (1974) all reached

One of the country star "crossovers," Willie Nelson.

the No. 1 position on both charts; Gladys Knight and the Pips, Billy Preston, Stevie Wonder, and many other black singers had a substantial following among whites. The center of black popular music shifted from Detroit, the home of Motown, to Philadelphia, carrying with it a refinement of style which featured a lighter, more shimmering, and sensuous sound, achieved by the use of strings in combination with vibraphone and marimba, crisp but light drumming supported by a solid and flexible electric bass, and extensive use of male falsetto singing. Music by black performers began to make up an even larger percentage of record sales to white audiences. Among the more successful of the new black performers were Harold Melvin and the Blue Notes ("If You Don't Know Me By Now," 1973), the O'Jays ("Love Train," 1973; "I Love Music," 1975), the Delphonics

Stevie Wonder.

Members of the group Earth, Wind, and Fire, without instruments.

("Didn't I Blow Your Mind This Time," 1970), and the Stylistics ("Break Up to Make Up," 1973; "You Make Me Feel Brand New," 1974).

Discotheques—clubs featuring dancing to recorded music, presided over by a live disc jockey—had enjoyed some popularity in the 1960s, but their peak came in the second half of the '70s. The Philadelphia sound—light, intensely rhythmic, sensual—was just right for the style of dancing favored by "disco" patrons, and the demand for disco music mushroomed as the fad spread across America. Florida became second only to Philadelphia in supplying this demand, with studios such as TK turning out a succession of pieces like Betty Wright's "Clean Up Woman," Timmy Thomas's "Why Can't We Live Together," and "Get Down Tonight" by KC and the Sunshine Band. Somewhat more raucous and rowdy music, by bands like Funkadelic and Earth, Wind and Fire, also proved suitable for disco dancing, and as the craze continued, new performers appeared (Donna Summer and Gloria Gaynor, for instance) who were associated with this style from the beginning of their careers. There were even such novelties as "Disco Duck" by Ricky Dee's Cast of Idiots and disco versions of classical music (Walter Murphy's "A Fifth of Beethoven").

When disco music reached its commercial peak, though, the cast was largely white. One of the most successful movies of 1977, *Saturday Night Fever*, was set in a discotheque in Brooklyn, patronized mostly by whites; much of the music of the soundtrack was recorded by the Bee Gees, who had begun their career a decade earlier as one of the most successful "Beatle sound-alike" groups, but who had managed to accommodate their style to the current sounds and rhythms. The original sound track album from the movie, and several singles extracted from it (including "Stayin' Alive" and "How Deep Is Your Love"), dominated record sales and *Billboard* charts in a way not seen since the days of the Beatles.

Thus a persistent pattern in popular song in America, of white performers skimming stylistic elements off of black music and reaping financial rewards far beyond those possible for black musicians, was repeated once more.

Though the song repertory of Tin Pan Alley days has continued to remain off bounds in the 1970s, certain singers and songwriters have favored styles differing very little from those of the 1930s and '40s. Barbra Streisand, whose singing style owes much to earlier stars like Judy Garland, has had considerable success with her recordings of songs that in style and structure would not have been out of place in the decade following 1945. She even had a No. 1 single in 1973, "The Way We Were." Barry Manilow, very much a neo–Tin Pan Alley songwriter, first showed up on *Billboard*'s Hot 100 charts in 1974 with a No. 1 single, "Mandy," and has repeated that success several times ("I Write the Songs," 1975, and "Copacabana," 1978). For that matter, many of the most successful discs by the most popular female singers of the late 1970s (Olivia Newton-John, Roberta Flack, Crystal Gale, Linda Ronstadt, even late Dolly Parton) feature songs that have more in common with the repertory of the 1940s and early '50s

Barbra Streisand.

than with any form of rock; back-up by string-dominated bands heightens the impression that this music harks back to prerock days.

Musical comedy—once a chief arena for the launching and popularization of hit tunes—has been mostly out of step with recent popular song styles of America. Its audience today is predominantly urban, sophisticated, and upper class; its songs seem to have little to say to teenage and college audiences who comprise the bulk of the market for popular song. Even the extraordinarily talented Stephen Sondheim, widely regarded as the most gifted writer of lyrics and music for the musical theater of the past two decades, remains largely unknown to the mass rock audience. The original cast album of his finest show to date, *A Little Night Music* (1973), sold primarily to older listeners and those in touch with the culture and tastes of New York City, and at its peak, placed no higher than ninety-fifth on *Billboard*'s chart of best-selling LPs. The only song from the show to enjoy even modest circulation among the rock audience was "Send in the Clowns," as recorded by Judy Collins in 1975.

Despite all these points of similarity between today's popular music and that of the earlier days of rock, the 1970s has taken on a certain character of its own. The idealism of the late 1960s, which had peaked with the gigantic Woodstock Festival of August, 1969, and its days of "peace, love, and brotherhood," seemed to slip away suddenly in the first years of the new decade. The rock world was troubled by the drug-related deaths of some of its brightest stars—Jimi Hendrix, Janis Joplin, Jim Morrison, Brian Jones—and by scenes of violence, and even murder, at such subsequent rock festivals as the one at Altamont, California. Coinciding with the end of the war in Vietnam, songs with texts of social and political protest virtually disappeared, and those of the '70s began dealing again with purely personal experiences and emotions. This is not to say there has been a return to the pervasive escapism of Tin Pan Alley. The view of life offered by songs of the '70s is often a hard one; what has disappeared is the suggestion that political or social action should follow the recognition that life is often hard and unfair.

Though the appearance, attire, and antics of many performers are still outlandish by the standards of mainstream American life, rock has become an important member of the once-scorned "establishment," with evidence of its new respectability and power on every hand. At the simple level of affluence, income from rock music in the '70s has shot far beyond anything imaginable even fifteen years ago. Carole King's *Tapestry* ushered in the decade with stunning sales figures that ultimately approached 14,000,000; multimillion sales of LP albums have become almost commonplace, with Don McLean's *American Pie*, several of Elton John's releases, *Peter Frampton Comes Alive*, *Saturday Night Fever*, the first album by Boston, and others. The journal *Rolling Stone*, almost a bible of the dissident 1960s, is now filled with news of increasingly wealthy rock performers and producers, has a much larger and more varied readership (including professionals, financial experts, educators, even politicians), can be found among current periodicals in the libraries at even the most conservative universities, has become a corporation itself (branching out to other publication ventures), and is taken so seriously by politicians that a cabinet member of the Ford administration was forced to resign following the publication of a damaging interview in this formerly parochial paper. All major newspapers now review popular and rock performances and recordings; lectures and academic courses concerned with this music have become commonplace in American and British colleges and universities; theses and dissertations on the Beatles and their peers have been written. Jimmy Carter often wore an Allman Brothers tee-shirt while campaigning for the presidency, Southern rock bands played at his political rallies, and rock music was heard at the White House during his Inaugural Ball.

As for the future of popular song in America, a safe guess is that it will both change and stay the same.

The chief thread running through this book has been that American song, throughout its two-hundred-year history, has drawn on a succession of national and ethnic song styles—English, Irish, Scotch, Italian, German, African, Eastern European, and others. Whenever popular song has remained on a stylistic plateau long enough to begin to lose its vitality, appeal, and cutting edge, there has eventually been an infusion from a different quarter, bringing with it new vigor and excitement.

American popular song has been on such a stylistic plateau for several decades, as this is written. There are rumblings, hints of restlessness, tentative gropings for a new direction. History suggests that soon, perhaps in the next decade, there will be another stylistic shift. If the pattern of the past is followed, the catalyst for such a change will come from the music of an ethnic or racial minority. Prophecy is risky; but within a few years the Latin-American population of the United States will become its largest minority, outnumbering American blacks. Popular song of the past and present has occasionally reflected elements of the rich, vigorous, and varied music of these people (the *bossa nova* and the *reggae*). They appear to be a quite possible source of inspiration for the next chapter of American popular song.

Yet no matter how the musical details of popular song have changed over the years, no matter which national school of song has been the source of the popular music of one age or another, certain things have remained the same. One is tempted to paraphrase Gertrude Stein, and say that a song is a song is a song. There has always been a place and a need in American life for songs with texts touching on some aspect of the human condition, sung by one singer or a small group of vocalists to music that enhances the words and their meaning. Whenever the stream of musical fashion has led in directions that threaten to overwhelm the human voice and its texts, popular song has quickly swung back to a style that allows the voice and its messages of nostalgia, despair, hope, frustration, defiance, escape—and most of all love—to sound once again over and through the music.

There is no reason to think this will change.

Appendices

ONE

The Most Popular Songs in America Printed before 1800*

1. "The Galley Slave" (from *The Purse*) — William Reeve
2. "Lullaby" (from *The Pirates*) — Stephen Storace
3. "Henry's Cottage Maid" — Ignaz Pleyel
4. "Life Let Us Cherish" ("Freut euch des Lebens") — Hans George Nägeli
5. "Since Then I'm Doom'd" (from *The Spoil'd Child*) — anon.
†6. "The Little Sailor Boy" — Benjamin Carr
7. "Within a Mile of Edinburgh" — James Hook
8. "Lucy, or Selim's Complaint" — James Hook
9. "The Silver Moon" — James Hook
†10. "I Have a Silent Sorrow Here" — Alexander Reinagle (arranger)
11. "Mary's Dream, or Sandy's Ghost" — John Relfe
12. "The Cheering Rosary" (from *The Midnight Wanderers*) — William Shield
13. "Owen, a Favorite Welch Air" — anon.
14. "The Soldier's Adieu" (from *The Wags*) — Charles Dibdin
15. "Ellen, the Richmond Primrose Girl" — Reginald Spofforth

* Compiled from information given in A *Bibliography of Early Secular American Music* by Oscar George Theodore Sonneck, revised and enlarged by William Treat Upton, augmented with information from *Secular Music in America, 1801–1825* by Richard J. Wolfe.

† Written by a composer living in America.

16.	"The Wedding"	James Hook
17.	"The Tear"	James Hook
18.	"Pauvre Madelon" (from *Surrender of Calais*)	Samuel Arnold
19.	"The Request"	Gerard Vogler
20.	"Rise Cynthia Rise"	James Hook
21.	"Alone by the Light of the Moon"	James Hook
22.	"The Heaving of the Lead" (from *The Hartford Bridge*)	William Shield
23.	"Crazy Jane"	John Davy
24.	"The Nightingale"	James Hook
25.	"Bright Phoebus Has Mounted"	James Hook
26.	"The Streamlet" (from *The Woodman*)	William Shield
27.	"The Wood Robin"	Reginald Spofforth
†28.	"The Wounded Hussar"	James Hewitt
29.	"The Blue Bell of Scotland"	anon.
30.	"When Pensive I Thought" (from *Blue Beard*)	Michael Kelly
31.	"The Way Worn Traveller" (from *The Mountaineer*)	Samuel Arnold
†32.	"The Primrose Girl"	James Hewitt
33.	"Amidst the Illusions" (from *The Mountaineer*)	William Shield
34.	"The Caledonian Laddy"	James Hook
†35.	"One Kind Kiss"	George Jackson
36.	"Hark the Goddess Diana"	Reginald Spofforth
37.	"A Prey to Tender Anguish"	Franz Joseph Haydn
38.	"Ere Around the Huge Oak" (from *The Farmer*)	William Shield
39.	"When a Little Merry He" (from *The Purse*)	William Reeve
40.	"Here a Sheer Bulk; or, Poor Tom Bowling" (from *The Oddities*)	Charles Dibdin

TWO

The Most Popular Songs
in America, 1801–1825[*]

1. "Home! Sweet Home" (1823; from   Henry Bishop
   Clari or The Maid of the Mill)
2. "Come Rest in This Bosom"   Thomas Moore/Jean-Joseph-Benoît Pollet
   (Fleuve du Tag) (1820)
3. "Life Let Us Cherish" (1796)   Hans Georg Nägeli
4. "The Blue Bell of Scotland" (c. 1800) Dorothea Bland Jordan
5. "A Canadian Boat Song" (1805)   Thomas Moore
6. "The Knight Errant" (1818)   Hortencia, Queen of Holland
7. "Jessie the Flow'r o' Dumblane"   Robert Archibald Smith
   (1811)
8. "The Minute Gun at Sea" (1812)   Matthew Peter King
9. "Strike the Cymbal" (1811)   Vincenzo Puccitta
10. "Blue Eyed Mary" (1817)   anon.
11. "Away with Melancholy" (1801; from Wolfgang Amadeus Mozart
    Die Zauberflöte)
12. "I Have Lov'd Thee; Dearly Lov'd   James Hook
    Thee" (1812)
13. "All's Well" (1803–4; from *The   John Braham
    English Fleet in 1342*)
14. "See from Ocean Rising" (1804; from Joseph Mazzinghi
    Paul and Virginia)
15. "Hope Told a Flatt'ring Tale" (1804) Giovanni Paisiello
16. "Tho' Love Is Warm Awhile" (1812;   John Braham
    from *The Devil's Bridge*)

[*] Compiled from information given in *Secular Music in America, 1801–1825*, by Richard J. Wolfe.

17. "Roy's Wife of Aldivalloch" (1801)   traditional—Scotch
18. "Sweet Is the Vale" (1807)   Georgiana Spencer Cavendish
19. "Believe Me If All Those Endearing   Thomas Moore/John Andrew Stevenson
    Young Charms" (1809)
20. "Is There a Heart That Never Lov'd"   John Braham
    (1812)
21. "Bruce's Address to His Army" (1812)   traditional—Scotch
22. "Oh! Say Not Woman's Heart" (1820)   John Whitaker
23. "Robin Adair" (1812)   William Reeve (arranger)
24. "The Garland of Love" (1808; from   James Hook
    Tekeli)
25. "The Wood Robin" (1801)   Reginald Spofforth
26. "Wilt Thou Say Farewell Love" (1810)   Thomas Moore
27. "Eveleen's Bower" (1809)   Thomas Moore/John Andrew Stevenson
28. "The Light House" (1814)   Thomas Moore/Charles Willson
29. "I Knew by the Smoak [sic] that So   Charles Willson
    Gracefully Curl'd" (1807)
30. "The Song of Fitz-Eustace" (1811)   John Clarke
31. "Ah! What Is the Bosom's   Michael Kelly
    Commotion" (1807; from *The Forty
    Thieves*)
32. "The Maid of Lodi" (1803)   William Shield
33. "Will You Come to the Bow'r" (1807)   Thomas Moore
34. "Flow On Thou Shining River" (1818)   Thomas Moore/John Andrew Stevenson
35. "I Won't Be a Nun!" (1820)   anon.
36. "The Soldier's Bride" (1817)   anon.
37. "Sandy and Jenny" (1803)   James Sanderson
38. "Love Sounds the Trumpet of Joy"   William Reeve
    (1806)
39. "Drink to Me Only with Thine Eyes"   traditional—English
    (1801)
40. "Beautiful Maid" (1802; from *The   John Braham
    Cabinet*)
41. "Love's Young Dream" (1811)   Thomas Moore/John Andrew Stevenson
42. "Love Has Eyes" (1814; from *The   Henry Bishop
    Farmer's Wife*)
43. "To Sigh Yet Feel No Pain" (1819)   Thomas Moore/Franz Joseph Haydn
44. "Now at Moonlight's Fairy Hour"   Thomas H. Thompson
    (1808)

THREE

Stephen Foster's List of Royalties Received for Various of His Songs, to 1857[*]

Song	Royalty Payment
1. Old Folks	$1647.46
2. Kentucky Home	1372.06
3. Dog Tray	1080.25
4. Massa's in, &c	906.76
5. Ellen Bayne	642.34
6. Nelly Bly	564.37
7. Farewell Lilly	551.12
8. Willie we have missed	497.77
9. Oh Boys	394.70
10. Hard Times	283.84
11. Maggie by my side	278.01
12. Jeanie with light &c	217.80
13. Eulalie	203.14
14. Camptown Races	101.25
15. Oh Lemuel	100.00
16. Willie my brave	91.15
17. I would not die in Springtime	78.12
18. Old Memories	62.52
19. Some folks	59.91
20. Come where my love lies dreaming	59.88
21. Come with thy sweet voice	54.33
22. Little Ella	50.72

[*] Compiled from information given in *Stephen Foster, America's Troubador*, by John Tasker Howard.

23.	Way down in Cairo	44.72
24.	Crystal Schottisch	44.06
25.	Gentle Annie	39.08
26.	Village Maiden	36.08
27.	Ring de banjo	35.24
28.	Dolly Day	33.75
29.	Molly Do You Love Me	32.50
30.	Farewell Old Cottage	30.58
31.	My hopes have departed	25.04
32.	Melinda May	24.37
33.	Wilt thou be gone love	22.20
34.	Dolcy Jones	21.46
35.	Annie my own love	19.12
36.	Lilly Ray	18.08
37.	Voice of bygone days	17.54
38.	Holiday Schottisch	17.37
39.	I cannot sing tonight	16.98
40.	Angelina Baker	16.87
41.	The hour for thee and me	14.30
42.	Laura Lee	13.12
43.	I would not die in Summer time	11.26
44.	Village Bells Polka	10.00
45.	Mary loves the flowers	8.98
46.	Ah! may the red rose live alway	8.12
47.	Once I Loved thee Mary	8.00
48.	Give the stranger happy cheer	7.50
49.	Turn Not Away	7.50
50.	Mother thou'rt faithful to me	6.87
51.	Sweetly She Sleeps	5.62
52.	Spirit of my Song	5.00

FOUR

The Top-Selling Foreign Songs in America in 1870*

"Annie Laurie" w, m, Lady John Douglas Scott (née Alicia Ann Spottiswood)

"Kathleen Mavourneen" w, Mrs. Annie Barry Crawford; m, Frederick William Nicholls Crouch

"Home! Sweet Home" (*from Clari or The Maid of the Mill*) w, John Howard Payne; m, Henry Bishop

"Her Bright Smile Haunts Me Still" w, m, W. T. Wrighton, J. E. Carpenter

"Juanita" w, Caroline Norton; Spanish melody

"Five O'Clock in the Morning" w, m, Claribel (Mrs. Charlotte Alington Barnard)

"I Cannot Sing the Old Songs" w, m, Claribel (Mrs. Charlotte Alington Barnard)

"Mary of Argyle" w, C. H. Jefferys; m, Sydney Nelson

"La Serenade" w, W. W. S.; m, Franz Schubert

"Comin' Thro' the Rye" w, Robert Burns; m, (Julius?) Benedict

"Thou Art So Near, and Yet So Far" w, John Oxenford; m, Alexander B. Reichardt

"The Last Rose of Summer" w, m, Thomas Moore

"Angels Ever Bright and Fair" (from *Theodora*) w, Thomas Morell; m, George Frederick Handel

"The Brook" w, Alfred Lord Tennyson; m, Dolores

"Heart Bowed Down" (from *The Bohemian Girl*) w, Alfred Bunn; m, William Michael Balfe

*Compiled from information given in **Stephen Foster, America's Troubador**, by John Tasker Howard.

"I Dreamt That I Dwelt in Marble Halls" (from *The Bohemian Girl*) — w, Alfred Bunn; m, William Michael Balfe

"I'll Pray for Thee" (from *Lucia di Lammermoor*) — w, W. Ball; m, Gaetano Donizetti

"Ingle Side" — w, Hew Ainslée; m, T. F. Weisenthal

"It Is Better to Laugh than be Sighing" (from *Lucrezia Borgia*) — w, G. Linley; m, Gaetano Donizetti

"Not for Joseph" — m, Arthur Lloyd

"Oft in the Stilly Night" — w, m (arr.), Thomas Moore

"Sing, Birdie, Sing" — w, Zeila; m, Wilhelm Ganz

"Too Late" — w, Alfred Lord Tennyson; m, Miss M. Linday (Mrs. M. Bliss)

"We Met by Chance" — Eng. w, W. Bartholomew; m, Friedrich Wilhelm Kücken

"What Are the Wild Waves Saying?" — w, J. E. Carpenter; m, Stephen Ralph Glover

"Where Are the Friends of My Youth?" — w, Lt. Col. Addison; m, George Arthur Barker

"By the Sad Sea Waves" (from *The Brides of Venice*) — w, Alfred Lord Tennyson; m, Sir Julius Benedict

"Captain Jinks of the Horse Marines" — w, William Horace Lingard; m, T. Maclagan

"Do They Think of Me at Home?" — w, J. E. Carpenter; m, Charles W. Glover

"Good-night, Farewell" — m, Friedrich Wilhelm Kücken

"Hear Me, Norma" (from *Norma*) — w, C. Jefferys; m, Vincenzo Bellini

"Long, Long Ago" — w, m, Thomas Haynes Bayly

"The Marseilles Hymn" — w, m, Claude Joseph Rouget de Lisle

"My Mother Dear" — w, m, Samuel Lover

"O Ye Tears! O Ye Tears!" — w, Dr. Charles Mackay; m, Franz Abt

"Shells of the Ocean" — w, J. W. Lake; m, John William Cherry

"Take Back the Heart that Thou Gavest" — w, m, Claribel (Mrs. Charlotte Alington Barnard)

"Valley of Chamouni" — w, F. Enoch; m, Stephen Ralph Glover

Top Forty: The Most Often Recorded Songs in America, 1900–1950*

1. "St. Louis Blues" (1914)   w, m, W. C. Handy
2. "Tea for Two" (1924; from No, No,   w, Irving Caesar; m, Vincent Youmans
   Nanette)
3. "Body and Soul" (1930; from Three's a   w, Edward Heyman, Robert Sour, Frank
   Crowd)   Eyton; m, John W. Green
4. "After You've Gone" (1918)   w, m, Henry Creamer, Turner Layton
   "How High the Moon" (1940; from   w, Nancy Hamilton; m, Morgan Lewis
   Two for the Show)
6. "Blue Skies" (1927; from Betsy)   w, m, Irving Berlin
7. "Dinah" (1925; from Plantation   w, Sam M. Lewis, Joe Young; m, Harry
   Revue)   Akst
8. "Ain't Misbehavin' " (1929; from   w, Andy Razaf; m, Thomas Waller, Harry
   Connie's Hot Chocolates)   Brooks
   "Honeysuckle Rose" (1929; from Load   w, Andy Razaf; m, Thomas Waller
   of Coal)
10. "Star Dust" (1929)   w, Mitchell Parish; m, Hoagy Carmichael
11. "Sweet Georgia Brown" (1925)   w, m, Ben Bernie, Maceo Pinkard,
                                                    Kenneth Casey
12. "Sugar" ("That Sugar Baby o' Mine")   w, Edna Alexander, Sidney Mitchell; m,
    (1926)   Maceo Pinkard
13. "That's a-Plenty" (1909)   w, Henry Creamer; m, Bert A. Williams
    "Darktown Strutters' Ball" (1917)   w, m, Shelton Brooks

* Compiled from information given in *The Complete Encyclopedia of Popular Music and Jazz,
1900–1950*, by Roger D. Kinkle.

"I Can't Give You Anything But Love" (1928; from *Lew Leslie's Blackbirds of 1928*) — w, Dorothy Fields; m, Jimmy McHugh

"I Surrender Dear" (1931) — w, Gordon Clifford; m, Harry Barris

"The Man I Love" (1924; from *Lady Be Good!*) — w, Ira Gershwin; m, George Gershwin

"Someday Sweetheart" (1919) — w, m, John C. and Benjamin Spikes

19. "Farewell Blues" (1923) — w, m, Elmer Schoebel, Paul Mares, Leon Rappolo

20. "Sweet Sue—Just You" (1928) — w, Will J. Harris; m, Victor Young

"The Sheik of Araby" (1921; from *Make It Happy*) — w, Harry B. Smith, Francis Wheeler; m, Ted Snyder

"Somebody Loves Me" (1924; from *George White's Scandals of 1924*) — w, B. G. De Sylva, Ballard Macdonald; m, George Gershwin

23. "Indiana" (1917) — w, Ballard Macdonald; m, James F. Hanley

"I Got Rhythm" (1930; from *Girl Crazy*) — w, Ira Gershwin; m, George Gershwin

"Sweet Lorraine" (1928) — w, Mitchell Parrish; m, Cliff Burwell

"On the Sunny Side of the Street" (1930; from *Lew Leslie's International Review*) — w, Dorothy Fields; m, Jimmy McHugh

"Rose Room" (1918) — w, m, Harry Williams(?)

28. "China Boy" (1922) — w, m, Dick Winfree, Phil Boutelje

29. "Night and Day" (1932; from *Gay Divorce*) — w, m, Cole Porter

"Ghost of a Chance" (1933) — w, m, Victor Young

31. "My Melancholy Baby" (1912) — w, George A. Norton; m, Ernie Burnett

"I've Found a New Baby" (1926) — w, m, Jack Palmer, Spencer Williams

33. "Beale St. Blues" (1916) — w, m, W. C. Handy

"I Know That You Know" (1926; from *Oh, Please!*) — w, Anne Caldwell; m, Vincent Youmans

35. "Nobody's Sweetheart" (1924; from *The Passing Show of 1923*) — w, m, Elmer Schoebel, Ernie Erdman, Gus Kahn, Billy Meyers

"Liza" ("All the Clouds'll Roll Away") (1929; from *Show Girl*) — w, Ira Gershwin, Gus Kahn; m, George Gershwin

37. "Blue Moon" (1934) — w, Lorenz Hart; m, Richard Rodgers

"Coquette" (1928) — w, Gus Kahn; m, Carmen Lombardo, John Green

39. "Stars Fell on Alabama" (1934) — w, Mitchell Parrish; m, Frank Perkins

40. "All the Things You Are" (1939; from *Very Warm for May*) — w, Oscar Hammerstein II; m, Jerome Kern

"Oh Lady, Be Good" (1924; from *Lady, Be Good!*) — w, Ira Gershwin; m, George Gershwin

SIX

Variety Magazine's Golden 100 Tin Pan Alley Songs, 1918–1935

Song	Date	Lyricist/Composer
"After You've Gone"	1918	w, m, Henry Creamer, Turner Layton
"Ah, Sweet Mystery of Life"	1910	w, Rida Johnson Young; m, Victor Herbert
"Alexander's Ragtime Band"	1911	w, m, Irving Berlin
"All Alone"	1924	w, m, Irving Berlin
"All the Things You Are"	1939	w, Oscar Hammerstein II; m, Jerome Kern
"Always"	1925	w, m, Irving Berlin
"A Pretty Girl is Like a Melody"	1919	w, m, Irving Berlin
"April in Paris"	1932	w, E. Y. Harburg; m, Vernon Duke
"April Showers"	1921	w, Bud G. De Sylva; m, Louis Silvers
"As Time Goes By"	1931	w, m, Herman Hupfeld
"Ballin' the Jack"	1913	w, Jim [James Henry] Burris; m, Chris Smith
"Begin the Beguine"	1935	w, m, Cole Porter
"Bewitched, Bothered and Bewildered"	1941	w, Lorenz Hart; m, Richard Rodgers
"Blue Moon"	1934	w, Lorenz Hart; m, Richard Rodgers
"Blues in the Night"	1941	w, Johnny Mercer; m, Harold Arlen
"Body and Soul"	1930	w, Edward Heyman, Robert Sour, Frank Eyton; m, John W. Green
"Chicago"	1922	w, m, Fred Fisher
"Come Rain or Come Shine"	1946	w, Johnny Mercer; m, Harold Arlen
"Dancing in the Dark"	1931	w, Howard Dietz; m, Arthur Schwartz

"Darktown Strutters' Ball"	1917	w, m, Shelton Brooks
"Dinah"	1925	w, Sam M. Lewis, Joe Young; m, Harry Akst
"Easter Parade"	1933	w, m, Irving Berlin
"Exactly Like You"	1930	w, Dorothy Fields; m, Jimmy McHugh
"For Me and My Gal"	1917	w, Edgar Leslie, E. Ray Goetz; m, George W. Meyer
"Get Happy"	1930	w, Ted Koehler; m, Harold Arlen
"God Bless America"	1939	w, m, Irving Berlin
"Goodnight Sweetheart"	1931	w, m, Ray Noble, James Campbell, Reg. Connelly; Am. ver. by Rudy Vallee
"Great Day"	1929	w, William Rose, Edward Eliscu; m, Vincent Youmans
"Happy Days Are Here Again"	1929	w, Jack Yellen; m, Milton Ager
"Heartaches"	1931	w, John Klenner; m, Al Hoffman
"How Deep is the Ocean?"	1932	w, m, Irving Berlin
"How High the Moon"	1940	w, Nancy Hamilton; m, Morgan Lewis
"I Believe"	1953	w, m, Erwin Drake, Irvin Graham, Jimmy Shirl, Al Stillman
"I Can't Give You Anything But Love"	1928	w, Dorothy Fields; m, Jimmy McHugh
"I Could Have Danced All Night"	1956	w, Alan Jay Lerner; m, Frederick Loewe
"I Get a Kick Out of You"	1934	w, m, Cole Porter
"I Got Rhythm"	1930	w, Ira Gershwin; m, George Gershwin
"I'll Be Seeing You"	1938	w, Irving Kahal; m, Sammy Fain
"I'll See You in My Dreams"	1924	w, Gus Kahn; m, Isham Jones
"I'm in the Mood for Love"	1935	w, Dorothy Fields; m, Jimmy McHugh
"It Might as Well Be Spring"	1945	w, Oscar Hammerstein II; m, Richard Rodgers
"I've Got the World on a String"	1933	w, Ted Koehler; m, Harold Arlen
"I've Got You Under My Skin"	1936	w, m, Cole Porter
"I Wonder Who's Kissing Her Now"	1909	w, Will M. Hough, Frank R. Adams; m, Joseph E. Howard [, Harold Orlob]
"Just One of Those Things"	1935	w, m, Cole Porter
"Kiss Me Again"	1905	w, Henry Blossom; m, Victor Herbert
"La Vie en Rose"	1946	w, (Eng.) Mack David, (Fr.) Edith Piaf; m, Louiguy
"Let Me Call You Sweetheart"	1910	w, m, Beth Slater Whitson, Leo Friedman
"Love Me or Leave Me"	1928	w, Gus Kahn; m, Walter Donaldson
"Lover"	1933	w, Lorenz Hart; m, Richard Rodgers
"Lover Come Back to Me"	1928	w, Oscar Hammerstein II; m, Sigmund Romberg
"Marie"	1928	w, m, Irving Berlin
"My Blue Heaven"	1927	w, George Whiting; m, Walter Donaldson

"My Funny Valentine"	1937	w, Lorenz Hart; m, Richard Rodgers
"My Heart Stood Still"	1927	w, Lorenz Hart; m, Richard Rodgers
"My Melancholy Baby"	1912	w, George A. Norton; m, Ernie Burnett
"Night and Day"	1932	w, m, Cole Porter
"Old Black Magic"	1942	w, Johnny Mercer; m, Harold Arlen
"Ol' Man River"	1927	w, Oscar Hammerstein II; m, Jerome Kern
"On the Sunny Side of the Street"	1930	w, Dorothy Fields; m, Jimmy McHugh
"Over the Rainbow"	1939	w, E. Y. Harburg; m, Harold Arlen
"Peg o' My Heart"	1913	w, Alfred Bryan; m, Fred Fisher
"Pennies from Heaven"	1936	w, John Burke; m, Arthur Johnston
"Poor Butterfly"	1916	w, John L. Golden; m, Raymond Hubbell
"Rudolph, the Rednosed Reindeer"	1949	w, m, Johnny Marks
"School Days"	1907	w, Will D. Cobb; m, Gus Edwards
"September Song"	1938	w, Maxwell Anderson; m, Kurt Weill
"Shine on Harvest Moon"	1908	w, Jack Norworth; m, Nora Bayes, Jack Norworth
"Smoke Gets in Your Eyes"	1933	w, Otto Harbach; m, Jerome Kern
"Somebody Loves Me"	1924	w, Ballard MacDonald, B. G. De Sylva; m, George Gershwin
"Some Enchanted Evening"	1949	w, Oscar Hammerstein II; m, Richard Rodgers
"Some of These Days"	1910	w, m, Shelton Brooks
"Sometimes I'm Happy"	1927	w, Irving Caesar; m, Vincent Youmans
"Stardust"	1929	w, Mitchell Parish; m, Hoagy Carmichael
"St. Louis Blues"	1914	w, m, W. C. Handy
"Stormy Weather"	1933	w, Ted Koehler; m, Harold Arlen
"Summertime"	1935	w, Du Bose Heyward; m, George Gershwin
"Swanee"	1919	w, Irving Caesar; m, George Gershwin
"Sweet Sue"	1928	w, Will J. Harris; m, Victor Young
" 'S Wonderful"	1927	w, Ira Gershwin; m, George Gershwin
"Take Me Out to the Ball Game"	1908	w, Jack Norworth; m, Albert Von Tilzer
"Tea for Two"	1924	w, Irving Caesar; m, Vincent Youmans
"Tenderly"	1946	w, Jack Lawrence; m, Walter Gross
"The Birth of the Blues"	1926	w, B. G. De Sylva, Lew Brown; m, Ray Henderson
"The Man I Love"	1924	w, Ira Gershwin; m, George Gershwin
"The Nearness of You"	1940	w, Ned Washington; m, Hoagy Carmichael
"These Foolish Things"	1935	w, Holt Marvell; m, Jack Strachey, Harry Link
"Tiger Rag"	1917	m, Original Dixieland Jazz Band
"Wait 'Til the Sun Shines Nellie"	1905	w, Andrew B. Sterling; m, Harry Von Tilzer
"Waiting for the Robert E. Lee"	1912	w, L. Wolfe Gilbert; m, Lewis F. Muir

"What a Difference a Day Makes"   1934   *w*, (Eng.) Stanley Adams, (Span.)
Maria Grever; *m*, Maria Grever

"What is This Thing Called Love?"   1930   *w*, *m*, Cole Porter

"White Christmas"   1942   *w*, *m*, Irving Berlin

"Who?"   1925   *w*, Otto Harbach, Oscar Hammerstein
II; *m*, Jerome Kern

"With a Song in My Heart"   1929   *w*, Lorenz Hart; *m*, Richard Rodgers

"Without a Song"   1929   *w*, William Rose, Edward Eliscu; *m*,
Vincent Youmans

"You Go to My Head"   1938   *w*, Haven Gillespie; *m*, J. Fred Coots

"You'll Never Walk Alone"   1945   *w*, Oscar Hammerstein II; *m*, Richard
Rodgers

"You Made Me Love You"   1913   *w*, Joe McCarthy; *m*, James V. Monaco

"Zing Went the Strings of My Heart"   1935   *w*, *m*, James F. Hanley

SEVEN

The Top Songs on "Your Hit Parade," 1935–1958 *

Song	Composer	Year of Appearance on "Your Hit Parade"
1. "Too Young" (1951)	Sid Lippman	1951
2. "White Christmas" (1942)	Irving Berlin	1942
3. "Because of You" (1940)	Arthur Hammerstein, Dudley Wilkinson	1951
4. "You'll Never Know" (1943)	Harry Warren	1943
"I'll Be Seeing You" (1938)	Sammy Fain	1944
6. "Now Is the Hour" (Maori Farewell Song) (1946)	Dorothy Stewart, Clement Scott	1948
7. "Peg O' My Heart" (1913)	Fred Fisher	1947
"People Will Say We're in Love" (1943)	Richard Rodgers	1943
"A Tree in the Meadow" (1948)	Billy Reid	1948
10. "Some Enchanted Evening" (1949)	Richard Rodgers	1949
11. "Buttons and Bows" (1948)	Jay Livingston, Ray Evans	1948
"The Gypsy" (1945)	Billy Reid	1946
13. "If" (1934)	Tolchard Evans	1951
"Hey There" (1954)	Richard Adler, Jerry Ross	1954
15. "I'll Walk Alone" (1944)	Jule Styne	1944
"The Song from The Moulin Rouge" (1953)	Georges Auric	1953

* Compiled from information given in *This Was "Your Hit Parade,"* by John R. Williams.

Song	Composer	Year of Appearance on "Your Hit Parade"
17. "My Heart Tells Me (Should I Believe My Heart?)" (1943)	Harry Warren	1943
"My Foolish Heart" (1949)	Victor Young	1950
19. "You Belong to Me" (1952)	Pee Wee King, Redd Stewart, Chilton Price	1952
20. "Don't Let the Stars Get in Your Eyes" (1953)	Slim Willet, Cactus Pryor, Barbara Trammel	1952
"Melody of Love" (1954)	H. Engelmann	1955
"Mister Sandman" (1954)	Pat Ballard	1954
23. "I Hear a Rhapsody" (1940)	George Fragos, Jack Baker, Dick Gasparre	1941
"Unchained Melody" (1955)	Alex North	1955
25. "They Say It's Wonderful" (1946)	Irving Berlin	1946
"Vaya con Dios" ("May God be with You") (1953)	Larry Russell, Inez James, Buddy Pepper	1953
"Long Ago (And Far Away)" (1944)	Jerome Kern	1944
"Symphony" (1945)	Alex Alstone	1945
"Till the End of Time" (1945)	Buddy Kaye, Ted Mossman	1945
"The Ballad of Davy Crockett" (1955)	George Bruns	1955
"Don't Fence Me In" (1944)	Cole Porter	1944
"Mona Lisa" (1949)	Jay Livingston, Ray Evans	1950
33. "To Each His Own" (1946)	Jay Livingston, Ray Evans	1946
"Autumn Leaves" (1947, 1950)	Joseph Kosma	1955
"Slow Poke" (1951)	Pee Wee King, Redd Stewart, Chilton Price	1951
36. "Paper Doll" (1930)	Johnny Black	1943
"Dream" (1944)	Johnny Mercer	1945
"Tammy" (1957)	Jay Livingston, Ray Evans	1957

Bibliography

The American Musical Miscellany: A Collection of the Newest and Most Approved Songs, Set to Music. Northampton, Mass.: Andrew Wright, 1798. Facs. ed., with a new introduction by H. Wiley Hitchcock. Earlier American Music, 9. New York: Da Capo Press, 1972.

Anderson, Bruce W. *Popular American Music: Changes in the Consumption of Sound Recordings, 1940–1955*. Unpublished thesis, University of Pennsylvania, 1974.

Appelbaum, Stanley, ed. *Show Songs from "The Black Crook" to "The Red Mill." Original Sheet Music for 60 Songs from 50 Shows, 1866–1906*. New York: Dover Publications, 1974.

Armitage, Merle. *George Gershwin, Man and Legend*. New York: Duell, Sloan and Pearce, 1958.

Austin, William W. *Susanna, Jeanie, and The Old Folks at Home: The Songs of Stephen C. Foster from His Time to Ours*. New York: Macmillan Publishing Co., 1975.

Barney, William. *Flawed Victory; a New Perspective on the Civil War*. Preface by James P. Shenton. New York: Praeger, 1975.

Belz, Carl. *The Story of Rock*. New York: Oxford University Press, 1969.

Birdseye, George. "America's Song Composers, V.–H. P. Danks," in *Potter's American Monthly* 12 (1879): 333–35.

———. "Septimus Winner. America's Song Composers, VI," in *Potter's American Monthly* 12 (1879): 433–36.

Blesh, Rudi, and Harriet Janis. *They All Played Ragtime*. 4th ed. New York: Oak Publications, 1971. (Originally published by Alfred A. Knopf, 1950.)

Brink, Carol. *Harps in the Wind. The Story of the Singing Hutchinsons*. New York: The Macmillan Co., 1947.

Burney, Charles. *A General History of Music from the Earliest Ages to the Present Period*. Repr., with critical and historical notes by Frank Mercer. New York: Dover Publications, 1957. (Originally published in London, by the author, 1782–89, 2 vols.)

Burton, Jack. *The Blue Book of Broadway Musicals*. Watkins Glen, N.Y.: Century House, 1952.

―――. *The Blue Book of Hollywood Musicals*. Watkins Glen, N.Y.: Century House, 1953.

―――. *The Blue Book of Tin Pan Alley*. Rev. ed. Watkins Glen, N.Y.: Century House, 1965.

Castleman, Harry, and Walter J. Podrazik. *All Together Now. The First Complete Beatles Discography, 1961–1975*. New York: Ballantine Books, 1975.

Chappell, William. *The Ballad Literature and Popular Music of the Olden Times; a History of the Ancient Songs, Ballads and of the Dance Tunes of England, with Numerous Anecdotes and Entire Ballads; also a Short Account of the Minstrels*. London: [n.p.], 1859. Repr. with a new introduction by Frederick W. Sternfeld, 2 vols., New York: Dover Publications, 1965.

Chapple, Joe Mitchell, ed. *Heart Songs*. Boston: The Chapple Publishing Co., 1909.

Chase, Gilbert. *America's Music: From the Pilgrims to the Present*. Rev. ed. New York: McGraw-Hill, 1966.

Claghorn, Charles Eugene. *The Mocking Bird: The Life and Diary of Its Author, Septimus Winner*. Philadelphia: Magee Press, 1937.

Cohan, George M. *Twenty Years on Broadway*. New York and London: Harper & Brothers, Publishers, 1924.

Crandall, Marjorie Lyle. *Confederate Imprints: A Check List Based Principally on the Collectin of the Boston Athenaeum*. 2 vols. Boston: The Boston Athenaeum, 1955.

Crawford, Richard, ed. *The Civil War Songbook. Complete Original Sheet Music for 37 Songs*. New York: Dover Publications, 1977.

Damon, S. Foster. *Series of Old American Songs, Reproduced in Facsimile*. Providence: Brown University Library, 1936.

Da Ponte, Lorenzo. *Memoirs of Lorenzo Da Ponte, Mozart's Librettist*. Translated, with an Introduction and Notes by L. A. Sheppard. Boston: Houghton Mifflin Co., 1929.

David, Phillip. *Immigration and Americanization. Selected Readings*. Boston: Ginn and Co. 1920.

Denisoff, Serge. *Great Day Coming. Folk Music and the American Left*. Urbana: University of Illinois Press, 1971.

Denison, Frederic, Albert A. Stanley, and Edward K. Glegen, eds. *Memorial of Oliver Shaw. Prepared and Published under the Auspices of the Rhode Island Veteran Citizens' Historical Association*. Providence: J. A. & R. A. Reid, 1884.

Dibdin, Charles. *A Complete History of the English Stage*. 5 vols. London: C. Dibdin, [1800].

Dichter, Harry. *Baseball in Music & Song: A Series in Facsimile of Scarce Sheet Music*. Philadelphia: Musical Americana, 1954.

Dichter, Harry, and Elliott Shapiro. *Early American Sheet Music: Its Lure and Its Lore.* New York: R. R. Bowker Co., 1941.

Dick, James C. *The Songs of Robert Burns (Now Printed with the Melodies for Which They Were Written): A Study in Tone-Poetry.* London: Henry Frowde, 1903.

Dickstein, Morris. *Gates of Eden. American Culture in the Sixties.* New York: Basic Books, 1977.

Disher, Maurice Willson. *Victorian Song, from Dive to Drawing Room.* London: Phoenix House, 1955.

Dreiser, Theodore. *A Book About Myself.* New York: Boni and Liveright, c. 1922.

———. "My Brother Paul," in *Twelve Men,* pp. 76–109. New York: Boni and Liveright, 1919.

———. "Whence the Song," in *The Color of a Great City,* pp. 246–63. New York: Boni and Liveright, 1923. (Originally published in *Harper's Weekly,* December 8, 1900, 1165 ff.)

Dresser, Paul. *The Songs of Paul Dresser. With an Introduction by His Brother Theodore Dreiser.* New York: Boni and Liveright, 1927.

Dunlap, William. *A History of the American Theatre.* New York: J. & J. Harper, 1832.

Eisen, Jonathan, ed. *The Age of Rock. Sounds of the American Cultural Revolution. A Reader.* New York: Random House, 1969.

Epstein, Dena J. *Music Publishing in Chicago Before 1871: The Firm of Root & Cady, 1858–1871.* Detroit Studies in Music Bibliography, 14. Detroit: Information Coordinators, 1969.

———, ed. *Complete Catalogue of Sheet Music and Musical Works, 1870.* New York: Da Capo Press, 1973. (Originally published by the Board of Music Trade of the United States of America in 1871.)

Ewen, David. *All the Years of American Popular Music.* Englewood Cliffs, N.J.: Prentice-Hall, 1977.

———. *American Popular Songs From the Revolutionary War to the Present.* New York: Random House, 1966.

———. *Great Men of American Popular Song.* Rev. and enl. ed. Englewood Cliffs, N.J.: Prentice-Hall, 1972.

———. *The Life and Death of Tin Pan Alley: The Golden Age of American Popular Music.* New York: Funk and Wagnalls Co., 1964.

Faner, Robert D. *Walt Whitman and Opera.* Carbondale, Ill.: Southern Illinois University Press, 1972.

Fisher, William Arms. *Notes on Music in Old Boston.* Boston: Oliver Ditson Co., 1918.

Flattery, Paul. *The Illustrated History of British Pop.* New York, London: Drake Publishers, 1975.

Foster, Morrison. *My Brother Stephen.* Indianapolis: The Hollenbeck Press, 1932. (A reprint of the biographical foreword of Morrison Foster's *Biography, Songs and Musical Compositions of Stephen C. Foster,* published in Pittsburgh by the Percy F. Smith Printing and Lithographing Co., 1896.)

Franklin Square Song Collection, No. 2. New York: Harper & Brothers, 1884.

Freedland, Michael. *Irving Berlin.* New York: Stein & Day, 1974.

Fuld, James J. *American Popular Music (Reference Book), 1875–1950.* Philadelphia: Musical Americana, 1955.

Gagey, Edmond McAdoo. *Ballad Opera*. New York: Columbia University Press, 1937.

Gardiner, William. *Music and Friends; or, Pleasant Recollections of a Dilettante*. 2 vols. London: Longman, Orme, Brown, and Longman, 1838.

Geller, James J. *Famous Songs and Their Stories*. New York: The Macaulay Co., 1931.

Gershwin, George. *George Gershwin's Song-Book*. New York: Simon and Schuster, 1932.

Gillett, Charlie. *Making Tracks: Atlantic Records and the Growth of a Multi-Billion Dollar Industry*. London: Sunrise Books, 1974.

————. *The Sound of the City. The Rise of Rock 'n' Roll*. New York: Bell Publishing Co., 1972.

Glass, Paul, ed. *The Spirit of the Sixties. A History of the Civil War in Song*. St. Louis: Educational Publishers, 1964.

Glass, Paul, and Louis C. Singer. *Singing Soldiers: A History of the Civil War in Song*. St. Louis: Educational Publishers, 1964.

Goldberg, Isaac. *George Gershwin, A Study in American Music*. New York: Simon and Schuster, 1931.

Grossman, Lloyd. *A Social History of Rock Music*. New York: David McKay Co., 1976.

Grove's Dictionary of Music and Musicians. 5th ed. Ed. Eric Blom. New York: St. Martin's Press, 1955.

Grove's Dictionary of Music and Musicians. American Supplement, Being the 6th Volume of the Complete Work. Ed. Waldo Selden Pratt. New York: The Macmillan Co., 1944.

Hall, Harry H. *A Johnny Reb Band from Salem: The Pride of Tarheelia*. Raleigh, N.C.: The North Carolina Confederate Centennial Commission, 1963.

Hamm, Charles. *An Evening with Henry Russell*. Liner notes for Nonesuch Record H-71338 (stereo), 1977.

————. *Songs of the Civil War*. Liner notes for New World Records NW 202 (stereo), 1976.

————, Bruno Nettl, and Ronald Byrnside. *Contemporary Music and Music Cultures*. Englewood Cliffs, N.J.: Prentice-Hall, 1975.

Hansen, Marcus Lee. *The Atlantic Migration, 1607–1860: A History of the Continuing Settlement of the United States*. Cambridge: Harvard University Press, 1940.

Harris, Charles K. *After the Ball. Forty Years of Melody*. New York: Frank-Maurice, 1926.

Harris, Mark. "The Flowering of the Hippies," in *The Atlantic Monthly*, 220 (September 1967): 63–72.

Harwell, Richard B. *Confederate Music*. Chapel Hill: The University of North Carolina Press, 1950.

————. *More Confederate Imprints*. Richmond, Va.: The Virginia State Library, 1957.

Haywood, Charles, ed. *The James A. Bland Album of Outstanding Songs*. New York: Edward B. Marks Music Corp., 1946.

Heaps, Willard A. and Porter W. *The Singing Sixties. The Spirit of Civil War Days Drawn from the Music of the Times*. Norman: University of Oklahoma Press, 1960.

Herbage, Julian. "The Vocal Style of Thomas Augustine Arne," in *Proceedings of the Royal Musical Association* 78 (1950–52), 83–96.

Hesbacher, Peter. "Contemporary Popular Music: Suggested Directions for Further Research," in *Popular Music and Society* 2 (1973): 297–310.

Hewitt, James. *Music of Erin*. New York: [n.p.], 1807.

Hewitt, John Hill. *Shadows on the Wall; or, Glimpses of the Past*. Baltimore: Turnbull Brothers, 1877.

Hill, Richard S. "Getting Kathleen Home Again," in *Music Library Association Notes* 5/3 (1948): 338–53.

———. "The Mysterious Chord of Henry Clay Work," in *Music Library Association Notes* 10 (1952–53): 211–25, 367–90.

Hitchcock, H. Wiley. *Music in the United States: A Historical Introduction*. Englewood Cliffs, N.J.: Prentice-Hall, 1969.

Hopkins, Jerry. *Elvis. A Biography*. New York: Simon and Schuster, 1971.

Howard, John Tasker. *Our American Music. Three Hundred Years of It*. New York: Thomas Y. Crowell Co., 1929.

———. *Stephen Foster, America's Troubador*. New York: Thomas Y. Crowell Co., 1934.

Howe, Irving. *World of Our Fathers*. New York and London: Harcourt Brace Jovanovich, 1976.

Hubbard, W. L., ed. *History of American Music*, one volume of *The American History and Encyclopedia of Music*. 12 vols. Toledo, New York, Chicago: Irving Squire, 1908.

Hutchinson, A. E. *The Granite Songster: Comprising the Songs of the Hutchinson Family*. Boston and New York: Charles Holt, Jr., 1847.

Hutchinson, John Wallace. *Story of the Hutchinsons (Tribe of Jesse)*. 2 vols. Boston: Lee and Shepard, 1896.

[Hutchinson], Joshua. *A Brief Narrative of the Hutchinson Family. Sixteen Sons and Daughters of the "Tribe of Jesse."* Boston: Lee and Shepard, 1874.

Jablonski, Edward, and Lawrence D. Stewart. *The Gershwin Years*. Rev. ed. Garden City (New York): Doubleday & Co., 1973.

Jackson, Richard, ed. *Popular Songs of Nineteenth-Century America*. New York: Dover Publications, 1976.

Jefferson, Thomas. *The Writings of Thomas Jefferson*. 20 vols. Ed. Andrew A. Lipscomb. Washington, D.C.: Thomas Jefferson Memorial Association of the United States, 1903–4.

Johnson, H. Earle. "The Germania Musical Society." in *The Musical Quarterly* 39 (1953): 75–93.

———. *Musical Interludes in Boston, 1795–1830*. New York: Columbia University Press, 1943.

Jones, Howard Mumford. *The Harp That Once—A Chronicle of the Life of Thomas Moore*. New York: Henry Holt and Co., 1937.

Jordan, Philip D. *Singin' Yankees*. Minneapolis: The University of Minnesota Press, 1946.

———, and Lillian Kessler. *Songs of Yesterday*. New York: Doubleday, Doran and Co., 1941.

Kahn, E. J., Jr. *The Merry Partners: The Age and Stage of Harrigan and Hart*. New York: Random House, 1955.

Kimball, Robert, and Alfred Simon. *The Gershwins*. New York: Athenaeum, 1973.

Kimball, Robert, ed. *Music and Lyrics by Cole Porter. A Treasury of Cole Porter*. New York: Random House and Chappell & Co., n.d.

Kingsley, George. *The Social Choir. Designed for a Class Book, or the Domestic Circle.* 12th ed. 2 vols. Boston: Crocker & Bresster, 1855.

Kinkle, Roger D. *The Complete Encyclopedia of Popular Music and Jazz, 1900–1950.* 4 vols. New Rochelle, N.Y.: Arlington House Publishers, 1974.

Krohn, Ernst C. *Music Publishing in the Middle Western States Before the Civil War.* Detroit Studies in Music Bibliography, 23. Detroit: Information Coordinators, 1972.

———. "Nelson Kneass: Minstrel Singer and Composer," in *Yearbook for Inter-American Musical Research* 7 (1971): 17–41.

Lahee, Henry C. *Annals of Music in America.* Boston: Marshall Jones Co., 1922.

Laws, G. Malcolm, Jr. *American Balladry from British Broadsides.* Philadelphia: The American Folklore Society, 1957.

———. *Native American Balladry.* Philadelphia: The American Folklore Society, 1964.

Leibovitz, Annie, ed. *Shooting Stars. The Rolling Stone Book of Portraits.* San Francisco: Straight Arrow Books, 1973.

Levant, Oscar. *A Smattering of Ignorance.* New York: Doubleday, Doran & Co., 1940.

Levy, Lester S. *Grace Notes in American History: Popular Sheet Music from 1820 to 1900.* Norman, Ok.: University of Oklahoma Press, 1967.

———. *Picture the Songs. Lithographs from the Sheet Music of Nineteenth-Century America.* Baltimore and London: The Johns Hopkins University Press, 1976.

Lowens, Irving. *A Bibliography of Songsters Printed in America Before 1821.* Worcester, Mass.: American Antiquarian Society, 1976.

———. *Music and Musicians in Early America.* New York: W. W. Norton & Co., 1964.

McCarthy, Albert. *Big Band Jazz.* New York: G. P. Putnam's Sons, 1974.

Marks, Edward B. *They All Had Glamour: From the Swedish Nightingale to the Naked Lady.* New York: Julian Messner, 1944.

———. *They All Sang: From Tony Pastor to Rudy Vallee.* New York: The Viking Press, 1934.

Mathews, Mrs. Anne (Jackson). *Memoirs of Charles Mathews.* London: R. Bentley, 1838–39.

Mathews, Charles. *The London Mathews Containing an Account of This Celebrated Comedian's Trip to America.* Philadelphia: Morgan & Yeager, 1824.

Mathews, W. S. B., ed. *A Hundred Years of Music in America.* Chicago: G. L. Howe, 1889.

Mattfeld, Julius. *A Handbook of American Operatic Premieres, 1731–1962.* Detroit Studies in Music Bibliography, 5. Detroit: Information Coordinators, 1963.

———. *A Hundred Years of Grand Opera in New York, 1825–1925.* New York: The New York Public Library, 1927.

———. *Variety Music Cavalcade: Musical-Historical Review, 1620–1969.* 3rd ed. Englewood Cliffs, N.J.: Prentice-Hall, 1971.

Matthews, Brander. *Pen and Ink.* New York: Longmans Green, 1894.

Meyer, Hazel. *The Gold in Tin Pan Alley.* Philadelphia and New York: J. B. Lippincott Co., 1958.

Miller, Jim, ed. *The Rolling Stone Illustrated History of Rock & Roll.* New York: Rolling Stone Press (Random Press), 1976.

Minstrel Songs Old and New. Boston: Oliver Ditson, 1882.

Moers, Ellen. *Two Dreisers*. New York: The Viking Press, 1969.

Mooney, H. F. "Popular Music Since the 1920's: The Significance of Shifting Taste," in *American Quarterly*, 20/1 (Spring, 1968): 67–85.

Moore, Thomas. *Irish Melodies, with the Original Prefatory Letter on Music: and a Supplement Containing a Selection from His Poetical Works.* 3rd complete American ed., from the 13th London ed. New York: R. P. Bixby & Co., 1843.

————. *Letters*. 2 vols. Ed. Wilfred S. Dowden. Oxford: Clarendon Press, 1964.

————. *Melodies, Songs, Sacred Songs, and National Airs. Containing Several Never Before Published in America.* Exeter: J. & B. Williams, 1836.

————. *Notes from the Letters of Thomas Moore to His Music Publisher, James Power, (the Publication of which were Suppressed in London). With an Introductory Letter from Thomas Crofton Croker.* New York: Redfield, [1854].

Morneweck, Evelyn Foster. *Chronicles of Stephen Foster's Family*. 2 vols. Pittsburgh: University of Pittsburgh Press, 1944.

Moss, Harold Gene. "Popular Music and the Ballad Opera," in *Journal of the American Musicological Society* 26 (1973): 365–82.

Muir, Percy H. "Thomas Moore's Irish Melodies, 1808–1834," in *The Colophon*, September, 1933.

Myers, Robert Manson. *The Children of Pride: A True Story of Georgia and the Civil War*. New Haven, Conn.: Yale University Press, 1972.

Nathan, Hans. "The Career of a Revival Hymn," in *Southern Folklore Quarterly* 7/2 (1943): 89–100.

————. *Dan Emmett and the Rise of Early Negro Minstrelsy*. Norman, Ok.: University of Oklahoma Press, 1962.

Nevin, Robert P. "Stephen C. Foster and Negro Minstrelsy," in *Atlantic Monthly* 20 (November, 1867): 608–16.

Newsom, Jon. *Who Shall Rule This American Nation? Songs of the Civil War Era by Henry Clay Work*. Liner notes for Nonesuch Record H-71317 (stereo), 1975.

Nugent, Stephen, and Charlie Gillett. *Rock Almanac. Top Twenty American and British Singles and Albums of the '50's, '60's, and '70's.* Garden City, N.Y.: Anchor Press/Doubleday, 1978.

Odell, George Clinton Densmore. *Annals of the New York Stage*, 15 vols. New York: Columbia University Press, 1927–49.

Oppenheimer, George. *The Vintage Irving Berlin*. Liner notes for New World Records NW 238 (mono), 1977.

Parke, W. T. *Musical Memoirs; Comprising An Account of the General State of Music in England, from the First Commemoration of Handel, in 1784, to the Year 1830.* 2 vols. London: Henry Colburn and Richard Bentley, 1830.

Parkinson, John A. *An Index to the Vocal Works of Thomas Augustine Arne and Michael Arne*. Detroit Studies in Music Bibliography, 21. Detroit: Information Coordinators, 1972.

Paskman, Daily, and Sigmund Spaeth. *"Gentlemen, Be Seated!" A Parade of the Old-Time Minstrels*. New York: Doubleday, Doran & Co., 1928.

Pearsall, Ronald. *Popular Music of the Twenties*. London: David & Charles, 1976.

Reddall, Henry Frederic, comp. *Songs That Never Die*. Philadelphia: J. H. Moore Co., [1893].

Redway, Virginia Larkin. "The Carrs, American Music Publishers," in *The Musical Quarterly* 18 (1932): 150–77.

Rice, Edw. Le Roy. *Monarchs of Minstrelsy, from "Daddy" Rice to Date*. New York: Kenny Publishing Co., 1911.

Ritter, Frédéric Louis. *Music in America*. New York: Charles Scribner's Sons, 1883.

Roche, James Jeffrey, ed. *Rory O'More. A National Romance by Samuel Lover*. New York: The Athenaeum Society, 1901.

Rodgers, Richard, intro. *100 Best Songs of the 20's and 30's*. New York: Harmony Books, 1973.

The Rolling Stone Interviews. New York: Paperback Library, 1971.

Rollins, Hyder E. "The Black-Letter Broadside Ballad," in *Proceedings of the Modern Language Association* 34 (1919): 258–339.

Root, Deane Leslie. *American Popular Stage Music, 1860–80*. Ph.D. dissertation, The University of Illinois at Urbana-Champaign, 1977.

Root, George F. *The Story of a Musical Life*. Cincinnati: John Church Co., 1891.

Roxon, Lillian. *Lillian Roxon's Rock Encyclopedia*. New York: Grosset & Dunlap, 1971.

Rubin, Jerry. *Do It! Scenarios of the Revolution*. New York: Simon and Schuster, 1970.

Russell, Henry. *Cheer! Boys, Cheer! Memories of Men and Music*. London: J. Macqueen, 1895.

Sainsbury, John S. *A Dictionary of Musicians from the Earliest Times*. London: Sainsbury and Co., 1825. Repr. with an introduction by Henry George Farmer, 2 vols., New York: Da Capo Press, 1966.

Schwartz, Charles. *George Gershwin. A Selective Bibliography and Discography*. Bibliographies in American Music, 1. Detroit: Information Coordinators, 1974.

Seldes, Gilbert Vivian. *The 7 Lively Arts*. New York: Sagamore Press, 1957. (First published, New York: Harper & Brothers, 1924.)

Shapiro, Nat. *Popular Music. An Annotated Index of American Popular Song*. New York, 1964.

Shemel, Sidney, and M. William Krasilovsky. *This Business of Music*. New York: The Billboard Publishing Co., 1964.

Simpson, Claude M. *The British Broadside and Its Music*. New Brunswick, N.J.: Rutgers University Press, 1966.

Smith, Cecil Michener. *Musical Comedy in America*. New York: Theatre Arts Books, 1950.

Smith, Gregg, ed. *America's Bicentennial Songs from The Great Sentimental Age, 1850–1900*. New York and London: G. Schirmer, 1975.

Sonneck, Oscar George Theodore. *A Bibliography of Early Secular American Music (18th Century)*. Rev. and enl. William Treat Upton. Washington: The Library of Congress, 1945.

———. *Early Concert-Life in America (1731–1800)*. Leipzig: Breitkopf & Härtel, 1907.

———. *Early Opera in America*. New York: G. Schirmer, 1915.

Southern, Eileen. *The Music of Black Americans: A History*. New York: W. W. Norton & Co., 1971.

Spaeth, Sigmund. *A History of Popular Music in America*. New York: Random House, 1948.

———. *Read 'Em and Weep. The Songs You Forgot to Remember*. New York: Doubleday, Page & Co., 1926.

————. *Weep Some More, My Lady.* New York: Doubleday, Page & Co., 1927.

Stambler, Irwin: *Encyclopedia of Popular Music.* New York: St. Martin's Press, 1965.

————, and Grelun Landon. *Encyclopedia of Folk, Country, and Western Music.* New York: St. Martin's Press, 1969.

Stephens, John Anthony. *Henry Russell in America: Chutzpah and Huzzah.* DMA thesis, The University of Illinois at Urbana-Champaign, 1975.

Thornton, Robert D. *The Tuneful Flame. Songs of Robert Burns as He Sang Them. Edited and Transcribed with an Introduction.* Lawrence, Ka.: University of Kansas Press, 1957.

Tirro, Frank. *Jazz: A History.* New York: W. W. Norton & Co., 1977.

Toll, Robert C. *Blacking Up: The Minstrel Show in Nineteenth-Century America.* New York: Oxford University Press, 1974.

Upton, William Treat. *Art-Song in America: A Study in the Development of American Music.* Boston: Oliver Ditson Co., 1930.

Waldo, Terry. *This Is Ragtime.* New York: Hawthorn Books, 1976.

Whitburn, Joel. *Top Pop Records (1940–1955); Top Pop Records (1955–1972); Top LPs (1945–1972); Top Country and Western Records (1949–1971); Top Rhythm and Blues Records (1949–1971); Top Easy Listening Records (1961–1974).* With yearly supplements. Menomonee Falls, Wisc.: Record Research, 1973–present.

Whitcomb, Ian. *After the Ball: Pop Music from Rag to Rock.* New York: Simon and Schuster, 1973.

————. *Tin Pan Alley. A Pictorial History (1919–1939).* New York: Two Continents Publishing Group, 1975.

Whiteman, Paul, and Mary Margaret McBride. *Jazz.* New York: J. H. Sears & Co., 1926.

Wilder, Alec. *American Popular Song: The Great Innovators, 1900–1950.* Ed. and intro. James T. Maher. New York: Oxford University Press, 1972.

Williams, John R. *This Was "Your Hit Parade."* Rockland, Maine: Courier-Gazette, 1973.

Williams, Thomas. *A Discourse on the Life and Death of Oliver Shaw.* Boston: Charles C. P. Moody, 1851.

Wilson, Edmund. *The Twenties. From Notebooks and Diaries of the Period.* New York: Bantam Books, 1975.

Wilson, John S. Liner notes for *The Great Band Era (1936–1945).* RCA Custom Records RD3-25-1-10, made for Readers Digest.

Witmark, Isidore, and Isaac Goldberg. *The Story of the House of Witmark: From Ragtime to Swingtime.* New York: L. Furman, 1939.

Wittke, Carl. *Tambo and Bones, a History of the American Minstrel Stage.* Durham, N.C.: Duke University Press, 1930.

Wolfe, Richard J. *Secular Music in America, 1801–1825: A Bibliography.* 3 vols. New York: The New York Public Library, 1964.

Woollcott, Alexander. *The Story of Irving Berlin.* New York & London: G. P. Putnam's Sons, 1925.

Wroth, Warwick. *The London Pleasure Gardens of the Eighteenth Century.* London: Macmillan and Co., 1896.

Yerbury, Grace D. *Song in America (from Early Times to About 1850).* Metuchen, N.J.: The Scarecrow Press, 1971.

Copyright Acknowledgments

"Ain't We Got Fun"—lyric by Gus Kahn and Raymond B. Egan; music by Richard A. Whitting. © 1921 WARNER BROS. INC. Copyright Renewed. All Rights Reserved. Used by permission.

"All the Things You Are"—lyric by Oscar Hammerstein II; music by Jerome Kern. © Copyright 1939 by T. B. Harms Company. Copyright Renewed. All Rights Reserved. Used by permission.

"Blue Moon"—lyric by Lorenz Hart; music by Richard Rogers. © 1934 renewed 1961 METRO-GOLDWYN-MAYER, INC. Rights controlled by Robbins Music Corporation. Used by permission.

"Body and Soul"—lyric by Edward Heyman, Robert Sour and Frank Eyton; music by John Green. © 1933 WARNER BROS. INC. Copyright Renewed. All Rights Reserved. Used by permission.

"Brother Can You Spare A Dime?"—lyric by E. Y. Harburg; music by Jay Gorney. © 1932 WARNER BROS. INC. Copyright Renewed. All Rights Reserved. Used by permission.

"Don't Bring Lulu"—lyric by Billy Rose and Lou Brown; music by Ray Henderson. © 1925 WARNER BROS. INC. Copyright Renewed. All Rights Reserved. Used by permission.

"Eleanor Rigby" by John Lennon and Paul McCartney. Copyright © 1966 Northern Songs Limited. All rights for the U.S.A. and Mexico controlled by Maclen Music, Inc. c/o ATV Music Corp. Used by permission. All rights reserved.

"Embraceable You"—lyric by Ira Gershwin; music by George Gershwin. © 1930 WARNER BROS. INC. Copyright Renewed. All Rights Reserved. Used by permission.

"I Got Rhythm"—lyric by Ira Gershwin; music by George Gershwin. © 1930 WARNER BROS. INC. Copyright Renewed. All Rights Reserved. Used by permission.

"I'm Always Chasing Rainbows"—lyric by Joseph McCarthy; music by Harry Carroll. © 1918, renewed 1946 ROBBINS MUSIC CORPORATION. Used by permission.

"I'm Just Wild About Harry"—words and music by Noble Sissle and Eubie Blake. © 1921 WARNER BROS. INC. Copyright renewed. All Rights Reserved. Used by permission.

"It's Easy to Remember"—lyric by Lorenz Hart; music by Richard Rogers. Copyright © 1934 and 1935 by Famous Music Corporation. Copyright renewed 1961 and 1962 by Famous Music Corporation. Used by permission.

"It's Only a Paper Moon"—lyric by Billy Rose and F. Y. Harburg; music by Harold Arlen. © 1933 by WARNER BROS. INC. Copyright Renewed. All Rights Reserved. Used by permission.

"I've Told Ev'ry Little Star"—lyric by Oscar Hammerstein II; music by Jerome Kern. © Copyright 1932 by T. B. Harms Company, New York, N.Y. Copyright Renewed. All Rights Reserved. Used by permission.

"Look For the Silver Lining"—lyric by Bud De Sylva; music by Jerome Kern. Copyright © 1920 by T. B. Harms Company. Copyright Renewed. All Rights Reserved. Used by permission.

"The Man I Love"—lyric by Ira Gershwin; music by George Gershwin. © 1924 WARNER BROS. Copyright Renewed. All Rights Reserved. Used by permission.

"Nobody But You"—lyric by Arthur J. Jackson and B. G. De Sylva; music by George Gershwin. ©
1919 WARNER BROS. INC. Copyright Renewed. All Rights Reserved. Used by permission.

"Norwegian Wood" by John Lennon and Paul McCartney. Copyright © 1965 Northern Songs
Limited. All rights for the U.S.A. and Mexico controlled by Maclen Music, Inc. c/o ATV Music
Corp. Used by permission. All rights reserved.

"Rock Around the Clock" by Max C. Freedman and Jimmy DeKnight (ASCAP) © 1953 by Myers
Music, Inc. New York, New York.

"She Loves You" by John Lennon and Paul McCartney. Copyright © 1963 Northern Songs Ltd.
Lyrics used by permission of Gil Music Corp., 1650 Broadway, New York, N.Y.

"Smoke Gets In Your Eyes"—lyric by Otto Harbach; music by Jerome Kern. Copyright © 1933 by
T. B. Harms Company. Copyright Renewed. All Rights Reserved. Used by permission.

"Sweet Georgia Brown"—words and music by Ben Bernie, Maceo Pinkard and Kenneth Casey. ©
1925 WARNER BROS. INC. Copyright Renewed. All Rights Reserved. Used by permission.

" 'S Wonderful"—lyric by Ira Gershwin; music by George Gershwin. © 1927 WARNER BROS.
INC. Copyright Renewed. All Rights Reserved. Used by permission.

"Tea For Two"—lyric by Irving Ceasar; music by Vincent Youmans. © 1924 WARNER BROS.
INC. Copyright Renewed. All Rights Reserved. Used by permission.

"Why" by DeAngelis and Marcucci. © 1959 Debmar Music Publishing Co., Inc. Used by permission.

Photographs reproduced in this volume have been supplied by the following, whose courtesy is
gratefully acknowledged:

ABC-Paramount Records, 409
Atlantic Records, 446, 459
American Antiquarian Society, 97
Capitol Records, 422
CBS Records, 447, 452, 468 (top right, bottom left, bottom right), 470, 473
CBS Records/Dan Hunstein, 356
CBS Records/Bruce W. Tabman, 471
Neil Diamond, 467
Doubleday, Page & Co., 344
EMI Records, 418
Harvard Theatre Collection, 4, 7, 28, 65, 105, 119, 174, 177
Life Publishing Co. © 1918, 315
B. Uzzle/Magnum, 454
Motown Records, 361, 471
Music Division, Performing Arts Research Center, The New York Public Library at Lincoln Center,
    Astor, Lenox and Tilden Foundations, 15, 31, 67, 163, 166, 191, 237, 259, 271, 275, 280, 286,
    331, 347, 395, 427
Theatre Collection, Performing Arts Research Center, The New York Public Library at Lincoln
    Center, Astor, Lenox and Tilden Foundations, 22, 288, 295, 298, 303, 342, 348, 353 (Van
    Damm Photos)
White Studio Photos, Performing Arts Research Center, The New York Public Library at Lincoln
    Center, Astor, Lenox and Tilden Foundations, 349
Terry O'Neill, 468 (top left)

COPYRIGHT ACKNOWLEDGMENTS / 506

Michael Ochs Archive, 393, 398, 413, 430, 437, 449
Courtesy Polydor, 450
RCA Records, 405, 429, 441
Warner Brothers Records, 410
Copyright © 1943 by Williamson Music, Inc. Copyright Renewed. International Copyright Secured. ALL RIGHTS RESERVED. Used by permission, 354

Index

Italic numerals indicate photographic illustrations.

Abbey Theatre (New York), 290
ABC-Paramount Records, 413
Abel, Karl Friedrich, 8, 23
Abner (trumpeter), 191
Abt, Franz, 195–98, *196*, 200, 222, 261, 321
Academy of Music (New York), 68
Academy Vocalist, The, 82
"Ac-cent-tchu-ate the Positive" (Arlen), 356
Acis and Galatea (Handel), 5
"Act Naturally" (Owens), 419
Acuff, Roy, 403
"Address to a Tuft of Violets" (Shaw), 97
"Adelaide" (Beethoven), 195
Adelphi Theatre (London), 128
"Adieu! 'Tis Love's Last Greeting" (von Weyrauch), 192–94
"Adolphus Morning Glory" (D. Braham), 277–78
Aeolian, The . . . six popular airs arranged for the Piano Forte, 82
Aeolian Hall (New York), 349, 350
Aeolian Vocalists, 142, *143*, 145, *147*
  see also Hutchinson Family
African Grove, 114
African Melodists, 132
Afro-American music, as forerunner of rock 'n' roll, 403

"After the Ball" (Harris), 285, *286*, 291, 297, 299, 404
"Ah! che la morte" (Verdi), 87
"Ah! Fondly I Remember" (John H. Hewitt), 105
"Ah How Hapless is the Maiden" (Carr), 29
"Ah! I Have Sighed to Rest Me," *see* "Ah! che la morte"
"Ah! May the Red Rose Live Alway" (Foster), 205–6
"Ah perdona alprimo affetto," 72
"Ah Seek to Know" (J. C. Bach), 37
"Ah! Sweet Mystery of Life" (Herbert), 323
Ah! Wilderness (O'Neill), 316
"Ain't It a Shame," 408, 411
"Ain't Too Proud to Beg" (Temptations), 462
"Ain't We Got Fun" (Whiting), 374
Albert Hall (London), 167
Albion Theatre (New York), 85
Alboni, Madame, 71
Albrecht, H. F., 191
Album 1700 (Peter, Paul, and Mary), 448
"Alexander's Ragtime Band" (Berlin), 321, 330, 331
Alger, Horatio, 262
Alhambra Music Hall (New York), 290
"Alice Blue Gown" (Tierney), 368
Al Jolson, 338
Al Jolson Album, Vol. 1, 429
"All Alone" (Berlin), 333
"All By Myself" (Berlin), 333, 337

"All Coons Look Alike to Me" (Hogan), 321
Alleghenians, the, 153
"Allen-A-Dale" (Gilfert), 100, 101
"All I Have to Do Is Dream" (Everly Brothers), 407, 410, 415
"All is Over" (von Weber), 187
Allman Brothers, 467, 474
"All Quiet Along the Potomac Tonight" (John H. Hewitt), 108, 245, 246, 248
"All Shook Up" (Presley), 407, 414
All-Star Trio, 346
"All's Well," 164
"All the Things You Are" (Kern), 343, 359, 371
"All Things Bright and Fair Are Thine" (Shaw), 96
"All Through the Day" (Kern), 345
Almanac Singers, see Weavers, the
"Alone by the Light of the Moon" (Dibdin), 25
"Alpine Horn, The" (John H. Hewitt), 106
Alvarez, Marguerite d', 350
"Always" (Berlin), 333, 340
"Always in the Way" (Harris), 300, 301
"Always Take Mother's Advice" (Lindsay), 285
amante astuto, L' (Garcia), 65
"Amapola" (Lacalle), 389
America (band), 467
"America" (Simon and Garfunkel), 448
"American Bandstand," 416
"American Flag, The," 82
"American Hymn," 190
American in Paris, An (Gershwin), 350, 429
American Musical Miscellany, The, 35, 44, 56, 59, 95
American Society of Composers, Authors and Publishers (ASCAP), see ASCAP
American Songster, The, 44
American Standard, 150
American Theatre (New York), 121
"Amidst the Illusions" (Shield), 23
"Amid this Greenwood Smiling" (Thalberg), 187
"Amyntor, A Pastoral Song" (Taylor), 40
Anderson, Leroy, 389
Andrews Sisters, 387, 388, 389
"Angelina Baker" (Foster), 137, 209
"Angels, Meet Me at the Cross Road" (Hays), 272–73
"Angel's Whisper, The" (Lover), 174, 175, 176
Angrisani, Felix, 64
Animals, the, 423
Anka, Paul, 413
Annie Get Your Gun (Berlin), 336
"Annie Laurie" (Moore), 56, 231, 247n
"Annie Lisle" (Thompson), 139, 251
"Annie, My Own Love" (Foster), 224
Antheil, George, 372
Anthony, Susan B., 154
"Any Way You Want Me," 415
"April in Portugal" (Ferrão), 392
"April Love" (Fain), 412
"April Showers" (Silvers), 360
Arban, Jean-Baptiste-Laurent, 82
Archers, The, or The Mountaineers of Switzerland (Carr), 29, 41
Are You Experienced (Hendrix), 451
"Are You Lonesome Tonight?," 407, 415, 416, 417
Arlen, Harold, 355–56, 356, 360, 388, 392
Armstrong, Harry, 291
"Army Blue," 248
Arne, Cecilia, 4, 11

Arne, Thomas, 4–16, 7, 19, 41, 51, 63, 90, 92, 95, 142, 169, 372
  musical style of, 9–12
  types of songs, 5–8
Arnold, Eddy, 403, 428, 462
Arnold, Samuel, 5, 19n, 27, 29, 37, 39, 63, 169, 170, 283
Arnold, Mrs. (singer), 23
Artaxerxes, 165
Arthur, Timothy, 256
"As a Beam o'er the face of the Waters May Glow," 55
ASCAP (American Society of Composers, Authors and Publishers), 338, 339, 376, 389, 401, 402
"As I View These Scenes So Charming" (Bellini), 74
"Ask Me Not Why," see "Child of the Regiment, The"
"As Slow Our Ship Her Foamy Track" (Moore), 250
Astaire, Fred and Adele, 334, 343, 347, 349, 434
"As Tears Go By" (Rolling Stones), 446
As Thousands Cheer, 335
Astor Place Opera House (New York), 68, 70
Athenaeum Collection, The, 236
Atlantic Gardens (New York), 290
Atlantic Monthly, 118, 236
Atlantic Records, 411
"At Long Last Love" (Porter), 353
"At My Front Door," 412
"Auld Lang Syne," 29, 61, 231
"Auld Robin Gray" (Reinagle), 37
"Aunt Harriet Becha Stow" (John H. Hewitt), 140
"Aura Lee; or, the Maid with the Golden Hair" (Poulton), 139, 247–48, 415
Auric, Georges, 392
Austin, Mrs., 71
Autry, Gene, 404
"Avalon" (Jolson), 360, 368, 381
Avalon, Frankie, 413
Avalon, the (San Francisco), 439, 440
"Ave Maria" (Schubert), 187, 194n
"Away Down South" (Foster), 207, 210
"Away to My Mountain Home Away" (John H. Hewitt), 106
"Away with Melancholy," 72
Axis: Bold as Love (Hendrix), 451

Babes In Arms (Rodgers), 354
"Babies on Our Block, The" (D. Braham), 281n
"Baby, It's You" (Shirelles), 419
Bach, Carl Phillip Emanuel, 36
Bach, Johann Christian, 8, 63
Bach, Johann Sebastian, 348, 455, 469
"Back in My Arms Again" (Supremes), 462
Bacon, R. M., 76
Baez, Joan, 431, 432, 433, 436, 437, 454, 456
Bagdasarian, Ross, 389
Bagiloli, Signor, 67
Bailey, Pearl, 355
"Bake That Matzoth Pie" (Harris), 298
Balfe, Michael William, 84–87, 132, 173, 178, 368
  influence of Italian opera on, 85–87
"Bali Ha'i" (Rodgers), 355
"Balinamore Ora," 44n
Ball, Ernest R., 323
ballad opera, 17–19
  in America, 21–23
"Ball and Chain" (J. Joplin), 453
Ballard, Hank, 416

"Balm of Gilead," 135
Baltimore Clipper, 105
Baltimore Musical Miscellany, The, 32
"Banana Boat" (Belafonte), 428
"Band Played On, The" (Ward), 291, 296
"Barbara Ann" (Beach Boys), 435
Barber of Seville, The, see barbiere di Siviglia, Il
barbiere di Siviglia, Il (Paisiello), 63
barbiere di Siviglia, Il (Rossini), 63, 65, 67, 74, 84
   English adaptation of, 70
   first American performance of, 64–65
Barbieri (singer), 64
Bardin, Edward, 21
Barnard, Charlotte Alington, *see* Claribel
Barnard, Felix, 336, 364, 392
Barnes (singer), 70
Barnet, Charlie, 382
Barney, William, 229n
Barnum, P. T., 126, 277
Barry, Lydia, 300
Bartók, Béla, 372
Basie, Count, 383
"Battle Cry of Freedom, The" (Root), 230, 232, 234,
   236, 241
"Battle Hymn of the Republic" (Howe), 230, 236, 241
Battle of Leesburg, The, 244
"Battle of New Orleans" (Horton), 417, 462
Bayley, Thomas, 205
Beach Boys, the, 434–35, 436, 456, 458, 462
Beadle's Dime Songs for the War, 231
Beard, Charles, 5
Beatles, the, 418–24, 418, 422, 436, 444, 456, 457,
   458, 460, 465, 467
   early style of, 420
   formation of, 418–19
   influence of American rock 'n' roll on, 419
   last album of, 443–45
   later styles of, 422–23, 442–44
   success of first recordings, 420–22
Beatles' Second Album, 421
Beatles VI, 422
Beatles '65, 422
Beatrice di Tenda (Bellini), 82
"Beautiful Child of Song" (Foster), 222
"Beautiful Dreamer" (Foster), 222
"Beautiful Maid" (J. Braham), 164
"Be-Bop Baby," 415
"Be Careful, It's My Heart" (Berlin), 334
"Because You're You" (Herbert), 323
Beecher, Reverend Lyman, 150
Bee Gees, the, 467, 472
Beethoven, Ludwig van, 98, 99, 184, 189, 190, 191,
   195, 204, 348, 415
"Before the Next Teardrop Falls" (Fender), 469
Beggar's Banquet (Rolling Stones), 446
Beggar's Opera, The (Gay), 17–19, 21, 22, 63
"Begin the Beguine" (Porter), 353
Belafonte, 428
Belafonte, Harry, 428, 429, 430, 431
Belafonte at Carnegie Hall, 428
bel canto, 87
"Believe Me, If All Those Endearing Young Charms,"
   46
Bellini, Vincenzo, 66, 67, 68, 70, 74–82, 83, 87, 88,
   105, 132, 133, 142, 176, 178, 182, 194, 219, 283,
   294, 349, 372

"Be My Baby," 419
Bennett, Tony, 411
Benny, Jack, 328
"Bereaved Slave Mother, The" (Hutchinson), 150
Bergmann, Carl, 191
Berkenhead, Dr., 96
Berle, Milton, 328
Berlin, Irving, 321, 327, 329–41, 330, 345, 346, 348,
   350, 351, 355, 356, 360, 372, 375, 376, 377, 382,
   387, 388, 392, 433, 466
   early success of, 331–33
   first jazz songs of, 333
   as ragtime composer, 330–33
Bernie, Ben, 373
Berry, Chuck, 394, 395, 406, 407, 414, 415, 416, 417,
   419, 423, 435, 443, 445, 465
Best, Pete, 419
"Best of My Loves" (Eagles), 467
Best of the Kingston Trio, The, 431
Big Brother and the Holding Company, 440, 441, 451
"Bill" (Kern), 343
"Bill Bailey, Won't You Please Come Home?"
   (Cannon), 320, 321
Billboard magazine, 385, 386, 389, 391, 394, 405, 406,
   408, 412, 416, 418, 426, 428, 429, 430, 431, 436,
   440, 445, 448, 451, 457, 458, 459, 460, 462, 463,
   467
Billings, William, 1
"Bird Dog," 407
"Bird in a Gilded Cage, A" (Von Tilzer), 291, 309–10,
   311
"Birds in the Night" (Sullivan), 281
"Birks of Invernay, The," 44n
Birmingham (England) Journal, 158
"Birth of the Boogie" (Haley), 394
Biscaccianti, Eliza O., 219
Bishop, Sir Henry, 13, 44, 47, 48, 70, 76, 105, 142,
   165, 170, 194, 204, 205, 206
   as adaptor of Italian opera, 70, 78
   composer of "Home Sweet Home," 166
   style of, as songwriter, 171–72
Bishop, Madame, 132
Bitter End (New York), 431
Black, John S., 336, 364, 386
blackface entertainments
   early history of, 116–28
   proliferation of, 132–33
Black Sabbath, 469
black songwriters and musicians, 273–77, 318, 357–58,
   381–82, 394–96, 408–10, 416, 428–30, 458–62,
   469–72
"Black Water" (Doobie Brothers), 467
Blake, James W., 285, 291
Blake, J. Hubert ("Eubie"), 360, 375, 381
Bland, James, 268, 273–77, 274
   influence of minstrel songs on, 276, 408
Bland, Mrs. (singer), 13
"Blink oer the burn my Laddie dear" (Hook), 15
"Bloom Is on the Rye, The" (Bishop), 172
Blossom Time (Romberg), 369
"Blowin' in the Wind" (Dylan), 433
Blue Beard (Kelly), 37
"Blue Bell of Scotland, The," 60
"Blueberry Hill," 407, 409
"Blue Danube Waltz, The," 368
Blue Hawaii, 415

Blue Monday Blues (Gershwin), 349, 350
"Blue Moon" (Rodgers), 355, 360, 361, 370
"Blue Room, The" (Rodgers), 355
"Blues in the Night" (Arlen), 355
"Blue Skies" (Berlin), 333, 334
"Blue Suede Shoes" (Perkins), 394
"Blue Tango" (Anderson), 389
"Boatman Dance," 128
Bob Dylan, 432
"Body and Soul" (Green), 360, 361
Bohemian Girl, The (Balfe), 84–86, 132
Bolden, Buddy, 351
Bombo, 334
"Bonja Song, a Favorite Negro Air" (anon.), 116
"Bonnie Blue Flag, The" (Macarthy), 230, 242, 243, 248
"Bonnie Laddie, Highland Laddie" (Burns), 61
Bononcini, M. A., 62
Bookends (Simon and Garfunkel), 448
"Book of Love," 410
Boone, Pat, 411, 412, 413, 414
Bordogni, Luigia, 66, 67, 84
Boston (band), 467, 474
Boston Daily Journal, 239
Boston Evening Post, 94
Boston Handel and Haydn Society, 95, 98, 99, 189, 191
Boston Handel and Haydn Society Collection of Church Music, 38, 159
Boston Harmoneons, 137
Boston Magazine, The, 2
Boston Musical Miscellany, The, 32, 46
Boston Philharmonic, 191
Boston Symphony, 350
Boswell, Connie, 387
"Bowery, The" (Gaunt), 291, 296, 299
Bowery Amphitheatre, 126, 127
Bowery Theatre (New York), 85, 100, 118, 123
Boyce, William, 5, 90
"Boys" (Shirelles), 419
Boys from Syracuse, The (Rodgers), 354
Bradbury, William R., 159
Brag Is a Good Dog, But Holdfast Is Better, 126
Braham, David, 277–81
   urban songs of, 279–81
Braham, John, 76, 147, 162–65, 163, 327
Brahms, Johannes, 199, 372
Brandt, 191
"Breaking Up is Hard to Do" (Sedaka), 435
"Break the News to Mother" (Harris), 300, 301
"Break Up to Make Up" (Stylistics), 472
"Breathless," 407
Brent, Miss (singer), 4, 5
Brett, Miss (singer), 21
Brewer, Teresa, 392
Brice, Fanny, 328
"Bridal Chorus" (R. Wagner), 199
"Bridge of Sighs, The" (Hutchison), 159
"Bright Glowing Iris," 82
"Bright Phebus" (Hook), 37
Bringing It All Back Home (Dylan), 448
British music
   of Arthur Sullivan, 281–83
   decline of, in late-19th-century America, 283
   dominance of, in 18th-century America, 1–25,
      26–41, 91–94, 95–96, 100–103, 105
   influence of, on Stephen Foster, 204–6

Italianate style in songs of, 14–16
   popularity of, in 19th century, 162–86, 277–81
   see also Beatles, the
Broadcast Music Inc. (BMI), 389
Broadhurst, Miss (singer), 22, 29
Broadway Journal, 69
Broadway Tabernacle (New York), 152, 153, 165
Broadway Theatre (New York), 72
Broonzy, Big Bill, 403
"Brother, Can You Spare a Dime?" (Gorney), 370–71, 377
"Brother, Tell Me of the Battle" (Root), 232
Brough, Mr. (singer), 179
Brougham, John, 242
Brower, Frank, 126, 127, 128
Brown, Albert H., 291
Brown, Bill, 382
Brown, Edna, 336
Brown, James, 458, 459
Brown, John, 236
Brown, Nacio Herb, 345
Browne, Jackson, 468
"Brudder Gum" (Foster), 209
Bryant, Boudleaux, 410
Bryant, H. T., 135
Bryant, William Cullen, 239
Bryant's Minstrels, 72, 128, 241, 242
Buchheister, William, 191
Buckley, R. P., 250
Buckley's Serenaders, 72
Buddy Holly Story, The, 465
"Bugle Call Rag" (Blake), 381
Bull, Ole, 191
"Bully Song, The" (Trevathan), 321
Bundes der Norddeutschen Liedertafeln, 195
Bunn, Alfred, 84
Bunting, Edward, 46, 47, 54, 55
buona figliola, La (Piccini), 63
Burney, Charles, 9n, 10, 63
Burns, George, 328
Burns, Robert, 60, 61
"Burn That Candle" (Haley), 394
Burr, Henry, 336, 337
"But Not for Me" (Gershwin), 348
Butterfield, James A., 283
"Buttons and Bows" (Livingston), 389
"Bye Bye Love," 407, 410
Byrd, William, 349
Byrds, the, 436–37, 437, 443, 456, 462
"By the Light of the Silv'ry Moon" (Edwards), 392

Cabinet, The, 164, 165
Cadence Records, 410
Caesar, Irving, 346, 374, 376, 392
Cagney, James, 316
Cahn, Sammy, 387, 414
Calamity Jane, 392
"Calcutta," (Gaze), 417
"Caledonian Laddy, The" (Hook), 59
"California Girls" (Beach Boys), 435
Callender, Charles, 268
Callender's Consolidated Colored Minstrels, 268
Calloway, Cab, 355
Calvé, Mademoiselle, 82
Calypso (Belafonte), 428
Campbell, Glenn, 469

Camp Fire Songster, The, 231
"Canadian Boat Song, A," 47
Can-Can (Porter), 392
"Can I Go, Dearest Mother?" (Covert), 250
Cannon, Anthony J., *see* Hart, Tony
Cannon, Hughie, 320, 321
"Can't Buy Me Love" (Beatles), 418, 421, 422, 423
"Can't Help Falling in Love," 415
"Can't Help Lovin' Dat Man" (Kern), 343, 349
Can't Help Singing (Kern), 345
Cantor, Eddie, 328, 332, 337
Capitol Records, 393, 402, 411, 421, 422, 430, 457
Carefree, 334
Caribbean Holiday (Kern), 342
Carmichael, Hoagy, 357
Carnegie Hall (New York), 350, 383, 435
"Carol," 419
Carolan (O'Carolan), Turlogh, 55
"Carolina in the Morning" (Donaldson), 357, 360
Carousel (Rodgers), 354, 355
Carpenter, John Alden, 351, 358
Carr, Benjamin, 27–32, 28, 39, 40, 41, 59
Carr, Joseph, 27
Carroll, Harry, 360, 363, 368
"Carry Me Back to Old Virginny" (Bland), 275
Carter, Benny, 383
Carter Family, the, 428
Caruso, Enrico, 336
Casa Loma Orchestra, 382, 383
Casals, Pablo, 400
Cash Box Magazine, 391, 417
"Casta diva" (Bellini), 78, 82
"Cast Aside" (Harris), 301
Castle, Irene and Vernon, 332, 379–80, 380
Castle of Andalusia, The (Arnold), 37
Catalani, Angelica, 76
Cat and the Fiddle, The (Kern), 343
Catharine of Cleves, 126
"Cathy's Clown," 407
Catley, Nan (Anne), 5
Cavendish, Georgiana Spencer, *see* Devonshire, Duchess of
"Celebrated Echo Song, The" (Bishop), 170
Celebrated Negro Melodies, as Sung by the Virginia Minstrels, 128
Cenerentola, La (Rossini), 63, 67
    see also Cinderella
Centennial Summer (Kern), 345
Century Girl, The (Herbert), 338
"Chains," 419
"Chains of Love," 412
Chains of the Heart, 164
Chambers, Mr., 20
Charlatans, the, 439
Charles, Ray, 410, 419, 458, 459
Charleston Theatre (Charleston), 100
"Charlie Is My Darling" (Cavendish), 37n
Charms, the, 410, 411
Chatham Gardens (New York), 114
"Chattanooga Choo Choo" (Warren), 357
Cheap Thrills, 441, 453
Checker, Chubby, 416
"Cheek to Cheek" (Berlin), 334
Cheer, Boys, Cheer! (Russell), 178
"Cherry Ripe" (Horn), 184
Chess Records, 402

Chestnut Street Theatre (Philadelphia), 78
Chicago Musical College, 192
"Child of the Regiment, The" (Donizetti), 83, 87
Children in the Wood, The (Arnold), 27, 29
Chopin, Frédéric, 88, 294, 348, 368–69
chorus, in popular songs, 254–56, 258, 291–94, 306, 360–61
Christy, E. P., 130, 209, 210, 215
Christy, George, 130
Christy's Minstrels, 130, 131, 132, 207, 212, 213, 214, 234, 236
Cimarosa, Domenico, 63, 67
Cincinnati Conservatory of Music, 192
Cinderella (Rossini), 71, 72, 73, 74, 87
    New York success of, 71
    parody versions of, 72
    performances of, in cities other than New York, 72–75
Cinderella in Black, 72
Circassian Bride, The (Bishop), 169
Civil War songs, 228–52, 265
    British and Irish melodies in, 248–52
    of the Confederacy, 241–45
    patriotic types of, 231–40
    sentimental types of, 240
    in songsters, 231
    Southern publishers of, 245–48
"Clar de Kitchen" (Rice), 123
Clari; or, The Maid of Milan (Bishop), 165, 167
Claribel (pseud. for Charlotte Alington Barnard), 37n, 184–86, 261, 294
Clark, Dick, 416
Clarke, Stephen, 61
Clark's School Visitor, 226
classical music, influence on popular song, 8–9, 14–16, 87–88, 98–100, 184, 194–95, 198–99, 294, 321–23, 341, 348–50, 366–68, 368–72
    see also opera, British; opera, Italian
Clay, Henry, 178, 179
"Clean Up Woman" (Wright), 472
clemenza di Tito, La (Mozart), 63
Clinton, Larry, 369
Clooney, Rosemary, 411
"Coal Black Rose" (Dixon), 117, 126, 207
Coasters, the, 410, 414, 419
"Cocktails for Two" (Johnston-Coslow), 360
Coconuts, The, 334
Cohan, George M., 287, 311–17, 314, 320, 321, 332, 334, 342, 372, 433
"Cold, Cold Heart," 411
Cole, Bob, 321
Cole, Nat "King," 387
Collection of Favorite Songs, Arranged for the voice and pianoforte, A, 2, 37
Collection of New English Songs, A (Hook), 12
Collection of Songs Sung at Vauxhall and Marylebone Gardens (Hook), 12
Collins, Judy, 474
Columbia Garden (New York), 21
Columbia Records, 393, 402, 411, 426, 429, 432, 441, 457
"Come Back to Erin" (Claribel), 185
"Come, Birdie, Come" (White), 267
"Come Home, Father" (Work), 256, 300
"Come on-a My House" (Bagdasarian), 389
"Come Rain or Come Shine" (Arlen), 356

"Come Rest in This Bosom" (Moore), 46, 60, 215, 216
"Come to Me" (Gordy), 460
"Come Where My Love Lies Dreaming" (Foster), 222, 247n
"Come with Thy Sweet Voice Again" (Foster), 222
"Coming Home; or, The Cruel War is Over," 240
"Comin' In On a Wing and a Prayer" (McHugh), 377
"Comin' Thro the Rye" (Burns), 61
Commercial Advertiser (New York), 183
Como, Perry, 387, 405, 411, 414
Complete Celebrated Method for the Trumpet, 82
"Comrades, Fill No Glass for Me" (Foster), 217
Concerto in F (Gershwin), 350
Confederate Veteran, The, 241
Congo Melodists, the, 132
Congo Minstrels, the, 132
Connecticut Yankee, A (Rodgers), 354
Conniff, Ray, 457
"Convict and the Bird, The" (Dresser), 285
Cook, Eliza, 180
Cooke, Sam, 410, 445, 458
"Coolun," 44
"Coon Dinner, The" (Sawyer), 321
"coon" songs
  related to ragtime songs, 321
  see also plantation songs
"Coonville Guards" (Sawyer), 321
Cooper, George, 258
"Copacabana" (Manilow), 472
Copland, Aaron, 469
Coquet, The (Storace), 5
Cornucopia (New York), 127
"Corporal Schnapps" (Work), 231
Corre, Joseph, 21
Cosi fan tutte (Mozart), 66
Coslow, Sam, 360
"Cot Where We Were Born, The" (Heath), 145
Country Joe and the Fish, 440, 441, 456
country-western songs, 389, 410–12, 469
  performed by the Beatles, 419
  style of, in the 1960s, 462–63
  top hits of, in *Billboard,* 406
Covent Garden (London), 22, 70, 71, 147, 164, 165, 169, 170
Cover Girl (Kern), 344
Covert, Bernard, 145, 158, 250
"Cows in a Cornfield" (Hutchinson), 145
Coyle, H., 245
Creation, The (Haydn), 95
Crew-Cuts, the, 411
Crivelli, Giovanni, 64
Croce, Jim, 468
Crosby, Bing, 334, 335, 337, 384, 387, 388, 389, 391, 404, 405, 433, 434
Crosby, L. V. H., 137
Crows, the, 406, 407, 408
Crudup, Big Bill, 403
"Crying in the Chapel," 406, 407, 411
"Crying, Waiting, Hoping," 419
Cry of Love, The (Hendrix), 451
Cugat, Xavier, 387
Cultivation of the Voice Without a Master, The, 82
"Cypress Wreath, The" (Gilfert), 100

Dacre, Harry, 291
"Daisy Bell" (Dacre), 291

Daltry, Roger, 449
Damone, Vic, 414
Damrosch, Walter, 350
Damsel in Distress, A, 348
"Dance With Me, Henry," 411
"Dancing in the Dark" (Schwartz), 357
"Dandy Broadway Swell," 209
"Dandy Jim from Caroline" (Emmett), 128, 129
Danks, Hart Pease, 255, 264–65, 282, 283
Danny and the Juniors, 414
Da Ponte, Lorenzo, 66–68
"Dardanella" (Barnard-Black), 336, 364–65, 381
Darin, Bobby, 414
Darley, J., 13, 29
"Darling Nelly Gray" (Hanby), 137–38, 139
"Dat Draggy Rag" (Berlin), 330
Dave Clark Five, 423
Davis, Gussie L., 285
Davis, Jefferson, 242
Davis, Jimmie, 389
Day, Doris, 414
"Day in the Life, A" (Beatles), 444
Dayton, J., 245
"Dead Leaves Fall, The" (Winner), 260–61
"Dearest Mae," 109, 137
"Dearly Beloved" (Kern), 344
"Death of Nelson, The" (Braham), 164
Debussy, Claude, 294, 349, 368, 369, 372
Decca Records, 393, 402, 428, 457
"Deep in the Heart of Texas" (Swander), 389
Deep Purple (band), 469
De Koven, Reginald, 321–22
De La Coste, Marie Revenel, 244
Delacroix, Joseph, 21
Delicious, 348
"Dell'aura tua profetica," 82
Dell-Vikings, the, 410
Delphonics, the, 470
Denver, John, 469
"Derry Down," 44n
Deserter, The (Dibdin), 27
Deslys, Gaby, 332
"Desponding Negro, The" (Reeve), 111
De Sylva, Buddy, 342, 346
Deutscher Liederkranz (New York), 190
Deux Quadrilles de Contredanses pour le Piano Forte, Composés et Arrangés sur des Motifs de l'Opera de Bellini La Sonnambula, 77
Devil's Bridge, The, 164, 165
Devonshire, Duchess of (Georgiana Spencer Cavendish), 37
"Devoted to You," 415
Dexter, Al, 389
Diamond, Neil, 466, 467
Diamonds, the, 410
"Diana," 413
Dibdin, Charles, 5, 17, 18, 19, 20, 22, 24, 27, 29, 37, 63, 92, 94, 110, 111, 162, 169
Dibdin, Charles (son), 170
Dickens, Charles, 109, 146
"Didn't I Blow Your Mind This Time" (Delphonics), 472
Dietz, Howard, 376
Dignum, Charles, 13
dilettante, Il (Hook), 5
"Dim, Dim the Lights" (Haley), 394
"Dirge for General Washington" (Jackson), 38

"Disco Duck" (Dee), 472
Disco music, 472
"Di tanti palpiti" (Rossini), 66, 72, 73
Divorce, The (Hook), 5
"Dixie" (Emmett), 128, 230, 241
"Dixie, the Land of King Cotton" (John H. Hewitt), 244
Dixon, George Washington, 117–18, 123, 134, 207, 209
"Doin' What Comes Naturally" (Berlin), 336
"Dolly Day," 209
"Dolly Vardon" (Winner), 260
Domino, Fats, 400, 407, 408, 409, 411, 414
Donaldson, Walter, 334, 357, 360
Don Giovanni (Mozart), 63, 66, 72
  in America as The Libertine, 70
Donizetti, Gaetano, 63, 68, 70, 82, 87, 88, 178, 184, 219, 283, 294, 372
  popularity of, in America, 82–84
Don John; or, a Ghost on a High Horse, 72
donna del lago, La (Rossini), 67
"donna è mobile, La" (Verdi), 87
"Don't Be Angry with Me, Darling" (Danks), 264
"Don't Be Cruel" (Presley), 394, 399, 404, 406, 407
"Don't Bring Lulu" (Henderson et al.), 375
"Don't Fence Me In" (Porter), 353, 389
"Don't Get Around Much Anymore" (Ellington), 357
"Don't It Make My Brown Eyes Blue" (Gale), 469
"Don't Think Twice, It's All Right" (Dylan), 433
Doobie Brothers, 467
Doors, the, 451, 456
Dootone Records, 402
Dorsey, Jimmy and Tommy, 382, 383, 384, 385, 386, 387, 389
Dot Records, 402, 411, 412
Douglass, Frederick, 146, 149
"Down by the Old Mill Stream," 325
"Down the Burn, Davy" (Carr), 29
"Down the Quiet Valley" (Winner), 260
"Down Where the Wurzburger Flows" (Von Tilzer), 310
Dozier, Lamont, 460, 462
"Dream of the Reveller, The" (Russell), 179n
Dreiser, Theodore, 289, 303, 306, 307, 308, 378
Dresser, Paul, 285, 289, 290, 291, 294, 302–7, 303, 321, 372
  song themes of, 306–7
"Drimendoo," 44
"Driven from Home" (Hays), 265, 267
"Drummer Boy of Shiloh, The" (Hays), 251, 252, 265
Drury, Robert, 18
Drury Lane Theatre (London), 22, 84, 164, 169, 178
Dublin Theatre Royal, 87
Duenna, The, 19n, 44
Dunlap, William, 29
Dunn, William C., 309
Durand, Lansing, 130
Dvořák, Antonín, 348
Dwight's Journal of Music, 109, 183
Dyhrenfurth, Julius, 190
"Dying Child, The" (Heath), 145
Dylan, Bob, 432–34, 432, 436, 437, 439, 442, 446, 447, 456, 457, 458, 462, 466
  as rock singer, 448
Dyllyn, J. Bernard, 300

Eagles, the, 467, 469
Earl and the Girl, The, 341

Early American Ballads, 426
"Early in de Mornin' " (Hays), 273
"Earth Angel," 406, 407, 411
Earth, Wind and Fire, 471, 472
Easter Parade, 334, 392
"Easter Parade" (Berlin), 335
Eastman, Charles G., 216
"Easy to Love" (Porter), 360
Eberle, Bob, 384
Eberle, Ray, 384
"Echoing Horn, The" (Arne), 19
Eckstine, Billy, 403
Eddie Cantor Story, The, 338
Edison, Thomas, 264
Eduardo e Cristina (Rossini), 67
Edwards, Gus, 392
"Eight Days a Week" (Beatles), 421, 422, 423
"Eight Miles High" (Byrds), 437
El Dorados, the, 412
"Eleanor Rigby" (Beatles), 443, 446
Electric Ladyland (Hendrix), 451
electronics and popular song, 395, 423, 441–42, 444–45, 448–51, 469
Elegant Extracts for the German Flute or Violin, 35, 39
Elijah (Mendelssohn), 189, 195
Elisa e Claudio (Mercadante), 67
"Ella Ree" (Porter), 137, 139
"Ellen Bayne" (Foster), 215
"Ellen, the Richmond Primrose Girl" (Spofforth), 35
Ellerbrock, Charles W. A., 247n
Ellington, Duke, 357
Elliston, Robert W., 178
"Ellsworth Avengers," 251
"Embraceable You" (Gershwin), 360, 370, 462
Emerson, Lake and Palmer, 469
Emerson, Luther O., 239
Emigrant's Dream, The; or, the Land of Promise (Lover), 174
EMI Records, 418
Emmett, Daniel Decatur, 126, 128, 130, 134, 209, 241–42
Empire Minstrels, 212
"End, The" (Doors), 451
English Fleet in 1342, The (Braham), 19, 162, 164
"Enraptur'd I Gaze" (Hopkinson), 92
Epstein, Brian, 419
Ethiopian Band, 132
Ethopian Harmonists, 132
Ethiopian Melodists, 132
Ethiopian Minstrels, 132
Ethiopian Mountain Singers, 132
Ethiopian Operatic Brothers and Sable Sisters, 132
Ethiopian Serenaders, 132, 136
Ethiopian Troupe, 132
"Eulalie," 223
Europe, James Reese (Jim), 350, 380
"Evangeline" (Hays), 265
Evans, George, 291
Evans, Ray, 414
"Eveleen's Bower" (Moore), 114
Evening Brush, The (Reeve), 111
"Evening Song" (Abt), 198
Everly Brothers, 407, 410, 415, 416
"Everybody Loves Somebody" (Martin), 435
"Everybody's Trying to Be My Baby," 419
"Exactly Like You" (McHugh), 383

Exempt, The; or, Beware of the Conscript Officer, 244
"Exodus," 417

Face the Music, 335
Fagan, Barney, 321
Fain, Sammy, 385, 413
"Fairies, The" (Jackson), 39
Faith, Percy, 457
"Fall of the Oak" (John H. Hewitt), 106
Family Quarrels, 164
"Fantasie-Impromptu" (Chopin), 368
"Farewell, My Lilly Dear" (Foster), 214
"Farewell, My Own" (Sullivan), 283
"Farewell, Old Cottage" (Foster), 183, 220
"Farewell, Since We Must Part" (John H. Hewitt), 105
Farmer's Daughter, The, 170
Farrell, Bob, 118, 123
"Fascinating Rhythm," 347
"Fat Man, The," 408
Favourite Selection of Music, A (Shaw), 97
Federal Overture (Carr), 28
"Feel Like Makin' Love" (Flack), 469
Fender, Freddy, 469
Ferber, Edna, 343
Fibich, Zdenko, 369
Fielding, Henry, 18
Fields, Dorothy, 343, 376, 383, 462
Fifth Dimension (Byrds), 437
"Fifth of Beethoven, A" (Murphy), 472
"50 Ways to Leave Your Lover" (Simon), 466
figlia dell'aria, La (Garcia), 66
Fille du régiment, La (Donizetti), 82
Fillmore Auditorium (San Francisco), 439, 440
Fillmore East (New York), 441
films and popular song, 334–35, 343–45, 348
"Fine Old Colored Gemman" (Emmett), 128
"Fine Old English Gentleman" (Russell), 128
"Fine Romance, A" (Kern), 344
"Fire and Rain" (Taylor), 467
"First Time Ever I Saw Your Face, The" (Flack), 469
Fisher, Eddie, 387, 405
"Fisher Maiden" (Schubert), 194n
Fisk Jubilee Singers, 271, 272
Fitzball, Edward, 87, 172
Fitzgerald, Ella, 391
"Five O'Clock in the Morning" (Claribel), 185
Flack, Roberta, 469, 472
"Flag of Fort Sumter, The," 231
Flawed Victory: A New Perspective on the Civil War (Shenton), 228
Fleetwood Mac, 466
Flint, Timothy, 99
"Flooded Hut of the Mississippi, The" (Lover), 176
Flora; or, Hob in the Well, 21
"Flow On, Thou Shining River" (Moore), 216
Flucht nach der Schweiz, Die (Kücken), 198
"Foggy Day, A" (Gershwin), 348
Folk City (New York), 432
folk revival
    oral tradition of, in 1950s, 426–33
    origins of, in California, 434–40
    popularity of, in 1950s, 426–28
    popularity of, in 1960s, 448, 463–65
    in social protest, 433–39
"Folks Who Live on the Hill, The" (Kern), 344
Follow the Fleet, 334

Fontaine, Major Lamar, 245
Fontane Sisters, 411
Forbes, Mrs. (singer), 5
Ford, Tennessee Ernie, 404, 411
Forrest, Helen, 384
Fortune Teller (Herbert), 323
"Forty-Five Minutes from Broadway," 314, 316
Fosdick, W. W., 247
Foster, Charlotte Susanna, 203, 204, 215
Foster, Dunning, 225
Foster, Henrietta Angelica, 203
Foster, Morrison, 203, 206, 207, 225
Foster, Stephen Collins, 44, 56–57, 76, 82, 95, 102, 106, 117n, 131, 132, 137, 139, 158, 172, 176, 177, 180, 182, 183, 194, 198, 202, 203–27, 231, 234, 239, 244, 245, 248, 251, 258, 258, 260, 264, 293, 302, 327, 341, 343, 357, 358, 359, 389, 408, 417
    as composer of minstrel music, 206–15
    early musical education of, 203
    first songs of, 204–6
    influence of English song on, 204–6
    influence of Italian and German music on, 219–22
    influence of Moore on, 215–19
    Irish-Italian elements of, in songs, 223–24
    and publishers, 224–26
    "white minstrel songs" of, 223
Foster, William, 225
Four Cohans, The, 312, 313
Four Tops, the, 460, 462, 466
Fox, Virgil, 455
Fox, William, 328
Frampton, Peter, 468
Francis, Sanuel, 21
Franklin, Aretha, 458
Freed, Alan, 399, 406, 408, 416
Freedom Ho!, 101
Freewheelin' Bob Dylan, 433
Freischütz, Der (von Weber), 84, 102, 165
Friend, Cliff, 377
"Friendly Persuasion," 412
"Frog Song" (Trevathan), 321
Froman, Jane, 429
"From Me to You" (Beatles), 420, 421
Fry, Joseph Reese, 78
Fry, William Henry, 78
Fuller, Metta Victoria, 216
Fulmer, H. T. (pseud.), *see* Pratt, Charles E.
"Fun, Fun, Fun" (Beach Boys), 435
Funkadelic, 472
Funny Face, 347

Gade, Nils, 191
"Gaily Through Life I Wander," *see* "Libiamo"
Gale, Crystal, 469, 472
"Galley Slave, The" (Reeve), 23
"Gal with the Blue Dress On, The," 132
"Gambler's Wife, The" (Russell), 144, 150, 179n
Gannon, Kim, 387
Garcia, Joaquina Sitchès, 64
Garcia, Manuel, 64, 65, 66, 70
Garcia, Manuel (son), 64
Garfunkel, Art, 448, 449, 456
Garland, Judy, 334, 356
"Garland, The" (Hopkinson), 91
Garrison, William Lloyd, 149, 161, 239

Gaslight (New York), 432
Gaunt, Percy, 291, 299
Gauthier, Eve, 349
Gay, John, 17, 18
Gaye, Marvin, 460, 461, 462
"Gay Nineties"
    subject matter of songs in, 296–97
    waltzes in, 294
Gaynor, Gloria, 472
gazza ladra, La (Rossini), 63, 67
"Gee," 406, 407
"Gems of German Song; From the Most Ad-
    mired Compositions . . . Adapted to English
    Words . . . ," 187, 190, 192, 194n
Gene & Eunice, 411
General Collection of the Ancient Irish Music, A, 46
"General Wolfe," 1
"Gentle Annie" (Foster), 139, 217
"Gentle Goddess," see "Casta diva"
George M!, 316
George Washington, Jr., 315
George White's Scandals, 347, 349
Georgia Minstrels of Brooker & Clayton, 268, 270
Gerard, Richard H., 291
Germania Musical Society, 190, 191
German music
    influence of, on Stephen Foster, 222
    in 19th century America, 187–200, 260–61
Germon, Francis, 136
Gerry and the Pacemakers, 423
Gershwin, George, 327, 345, 346–62, 347, 353, 360,
    361, 365, 366, 367, 370, 372, 373, 375, 378, 388,
    392, 462, 466
    early success of, 346–48
    fusion of European and Negro music in songs of,
        350–52
    influence of classical music on, 348–50, 368
    movie songs of, 348
Gershwin, Ira, 344, 347, 376, 392
"Get Down Tonight" (KC and Sunshine Band), 472
"Get Off the Track" (Hutchinson), 150, 151, 152
Gibbons, James Sloan, 239, 249
Gibbs, Georgia, 411, 412
Gilbert, William S., 281, 283
Gilbert and Sullivan, 84, 283, 374
Gilfert, Charles, 100–102
Gilmore, Patrick, 195, 239, 249, 250, 259
Gilson, Lottie, 308
Girl Crazy, 347
Girl from Utah, The (Kern), 341
"Girl I Left Behind Me, The," 247n, 250
"Girl on the Magazine Cover, The" (Berlin), 332, 360
"Girls Beware" (John H. Hewitt), 105
"Girl That I Marry, The" (Berlin), 336, 340
"Give My Regards to Broadway" (Cohan), 314
Glad All Over (Dave Clark Five), 423
Glantz, Nathan, 381
"Glendy Burk, The" (Foster), 215
Glover, C. W., 83, 205
Gluck, Christoph Willibald, 95
"Go and Ask My Mother" (John H. Hewitt), 106
"God Bless America" (Berlin), 338
"Goin Ober de Mountain," 128
Gold, Ernest, 417
Gold, Lou, 381
Golden Harp, 226

Goldkette, Jean, 382
Goldwyn, Samuel, 328
Goldwyn Follies, The, 348
Gone with the Wind, 244
"Goober Peas," 231
"Good Bye, My Lady Love" (Howard), 321
"Good Golly, Miss Molly," 419
Goodman, Benny, 383, 384, 385, 387
"Good Morning, Good Morning" (Beatles), 445
"Good Night, Farewell" (Küchen), 199
"Goodnight, Irene," 428
"Good Old Days of Yore, The" (Hutchinson), 159
Goodwin, W. H., 245
Gordon, Mack, 387
Gordy, Berry, 459, 460
Gorney, Jay, 370, 377
Gough, Daniel, 5
Governor's Son, The, 313
"Grafted into the Army" (Work), 231, 232, 250–51, 255
Graham, Charles, 285
Gram, Hans, 94
"Gramachree," 44n
"Grand-Father's Clock" (Work), 256–57, 257
Grand Funk Railroad, 469
Granger, F., 95
Grania Uaile (Lover), 173
Grateful Dead, 440, 441, 456
Graupner, Gottlieb, 97
"Grave Digger" (Kalliwoda), 187
"Grave of Bonaparte, The" (Heath), 145
Gray, Louisa, 282
Grean, Charles R., 389
"Great Balls of Fire" (Lewis), 394, 407
"Great Pretenders, The," 407, 409
Great Society, 440
Greeley, Horace, 156
Green, Joe, 381
Green, John W., 360, 361
"Gretchen am Spinnrade" (Schubert), 160
Grey, Joel, 316
Grigg's Southern and Western Songster, 32
Grisi, 132
Grofé, Ferde, 350
Gross, Walter, 392
"Groves of Blarney, The," 46
Guglielmi, 63
Guitar at Home, The, 82
Gumbert, 199
Gumbo Family, the, 132
Gung'l, Joseph, 222
Guthrie, Woody, 427, 432, 433
"Gwine to Run All Night," 209
"Gypsy Love Song" (Herbert), 323

"Had I a Heart" (Linley), 43
Haggard, Merle, 463
Haley, Bill, 391, 393, 394, 395, 396, 406, 407, 408,
    411
"Half As Much," 411
Hallam, Miss, 21
Hallam, Mr., 21
Hallam's London Company of Comedians, 22
Hambitzer, Charles, 348
Hammerstein, Oscar, 332, 359
Hammerstein, Oscar II, 343, 344, 354, 376, 392, 462
Hammond, John, 432

Hanby, B. R., 137
Handel, George Friderik, 5, 8, 36, 62, 63, 90, 95, 98, 99, 165, 171, 368
Handy, W. C., 268, 380, 381
"Hannah's at the Window Binding Shoes" (Hutchinson), 154
Hanover Square Rooms (London), 183
Hans Christian Anderson, 429
Hanson, Howard, 400
"Happy Days Are Here Again" (Ager), 383
Harbach, Otto, 343, 359
Harburg, E. Y. ("Yip"), 376, 377
Hard Day's Night, A (Beatles), 420, 421, 422
"Hard Day's Night, A" (Beatles), 421, 422, 423
"Hard-Headed Woman," 416
"Hard Rain's a-Gonna Fall, A," 433
"Hard Times Come No More" (Foster), 223
Hardy, Marion, 382
"Hark Eccho Sweet Eccho," 14
"Harlem Rag" (Turpin), 318
Harline, Leigh, 462
Harney, Benjamin Robertson, 318
Harper, Edward, 125
Harper's Weekly, 245
"Harp That Once Through Tara's Halls, The," 46
Harrigan, Edward ("Ned"), 279–81, 280, 287, 378
Harris, Charles K., 285, 286, 287, 288, 290, 291, 297–302, 298, 307, 308, 310, 321, 327, 372, 404
and success of "After the Ball," 299–300
and themes of his songs, 300–301
Harris, Sam H., 330, 334
Harrison, Annie Fortescue, 283
Harrison, George, 418, 420, 423, 442, 443
Hart, Lorenz, 354, 376, 392, 462
Hart, Tony (pseud. for Anthony J. Cannon), 279–81, 280, 287
Harvard Musical Association, 191
"Has Sorrow Thy Young Days Shaded" (Moore), 216
Hastins, Thomas, 99, 159
Hatton, Ann Julie, 32
Haunted Tower, The (Storace), 19n
Havana Opera Company, 68
Have a Heart (Kern), 342
Haverly, J. H., 268
Haverly Colored Minstrels, 274, 321
"Have You Never Been Mellow" (Newton-John), 469
Hawthorne, Alicia (pseud.), see Winner, Septimus
Haydn, Joseph, 9, 23, 95, 98, 99, 171, 190
Haymarket Theatre (New York), 290
Haymes, Dick, 387
Hays, William Shakespeare ("Will"), 139, 251, 265–69, 266, 272–73, 282, 283
minstrel songs of, 268–69
Hayward, J. Harry, 231
"Hazel Dell, The" (Root), 139, 234
"Hear Me, Norma," 78, 82, 247n
"Heartbreak Hotel" (Presley), 394, 404, 406, 407
"Hearts of Stone," 411
Heart Songs, 46, 230–32
Heath, Lyman, 145, 158
"Heat Wave" (Berlin), 335, 460
"Heaven's a Great Way Off" (Winner), 261
"Heaving of the Lead, The" (Shield), 23
"He'll Come Again" (Parton), 469
"Hello Central, Give Me Heaven" (Harris), 300
"Hello, Central! Give Me No Man's Land" (Schwartz, et al.), 376

"Hello! Ma Baby" (Howard), 318, 320
Help! (Beatles), 422, 442
Henderson, Fletcher, 382, 383, 384
Hendrix, Jimi, 441, 451, 454, 456, 458, 474
Henry, Clarence ("Frog Man"), 409
"Henry's Cottage Maid" (Pleyel), 23, 24
"Her Absence Will Not Alter Me" (Moore), 56
Herald of Freedom, 149, 150, 158
Herbert, Victor, 322–23, 338
"Her Bright Smile Haunts Me Still" (Wrighton), 247n
Herman, Woody, 383
Herman's Hermits, 423
"He's Gone to the Arms of Abraham" (Winner), 248–49
"He Stole My Heart Away," 60
Hewitt, James, 21, 27, 32–36, 33, 41, 44, 50, 51, 102, 103, 219
Hewitt, James Lang, 102
Hewitt, John Hill, 32, 102–8, 105, 139, 183, 225, 242
Italian influence on, 105–6
musical style of, 105–8
reminiscences of, 107–8
as songwriter for the Confederacy, 244–45
"Hey, Good Lookin'," 411
"Hey-Hey-Hey-Hey," 419
"Hey, Jealous Lover," 414
"Hey There" (Adler), 392
Heyward, Du Bose, 350
Hicks, Charles B., 268, 270
Higginson, Thomas W., 76
Highway 61 Revisited (Dylan), 448
High, Wide and Handsome (Kern), 344
"Hill Tops, The," 1
Hindemith, Paul, 350
"Hindoo Girl hath Decked her Shell," see "Dell'aura tua profetica"
H.M.S. Pinafore (Gilbert and Sullivan), 283
Hodgkinson, Mr. and Mrs., 21, 29, 39
"Ho! For a Rover's Life" (John H. Hewitt), 106, 183
Hogan, Ernest, 321
Holiday, Billie, 384
Holiday Inn, 334
Holland, Brian and Eddie, 460, 462
Holland, George, 267
Holly, Buddy, 407, 416, 419
Holman, Agnes (Mrs. Charles Gilfert), 100
Holyoke, Samuel, 94
"Home of My Soul" (Shaw), 98
"Home of Youth, The," 82
"Home, Sweet Home" (Bishop), 53, 76, 158, 165, 166, 167, 169, 170, 172, 206, 231
"Homeward Bound" (Simon and Garfunkel), 448
Hone, Philip, 69
"Honey Don't," 419
Hood, Thomas, 150
Hook, James, 3, 5, 12–17, 24, 51, 59, 74, 92, 94, 95, 97, 103, 170
musical style of, 14–16
Hooley, R. M., 130
Hopkins, Lightning, 439
Hopkins' New Orleans 5 Cent Song-Book, 231
Hopkinson, Francis, 2, 89–94, 90, 95
as first American songwriter, 89–94
Horn, Charles Edward, 184, 204
Horne, Lena, 355
"Horn of Chace, The" (Gilfert), 101
Horowitz, Vladimir, 440
"Horse With No Name, A" (America), 467

Horton, Johnny, 407, 416
"Hotel California" (Eagles), 467
"Hot Tamale Avenue" (Cohan), 313
Hot Wax, 465
"Hound Dog" (Presley), 394, 399, 402, 404, 406, 407, 408, 412, 419
"House of the Rising Sun, The" (Animals), 423, 433
"House Song, The" (Peter, Paul, and Mary), 448
Howard, Frank, 285
Howard, Joseph E., 318, 321
"How Can I Forget" (Shield), 23
"How Deep Is the Ocean?" (Berlin), 333, 335
"How Deep Is Your Love" (Bee Gees), 472
"How'd You Like to Spoon with Me?" (Kern), 341
Howe, Julia Ward, 230, 236
"How Happy Was My Humble Lot" (James Hewitt), 36
Howlin' Wolf, 403
"How Sweet Are the Roses" (Winner), 259
Hummel, Johann Nepomuk, 189
Hunchback, The, 126
Hungarian Ethiopian Minstrels, 132
Hunter, Tab, 414
Huntley, Miss, 40
Hutchinson, Abby, 142, 144, 153, 156, 157
Hutchinson, Asa, 142, 143, 144, 153, 154, 156, 157
Hutchinson, Elisha, 141
Hutchinson, Jesse, 141, 142, 146, 147, 231
    and antislavery movement, 149–53
Hutchinson, John, 142, 143, 144, 146, 149, 153, 154, 156, 157, 183, 237
    memoirs of, 157–58
Hutchinson, Joshua, 142, 156, 161
Hutchinson, Judson, 142 43, 144, 145, 147, 153, 155, 157, 158
Hutchinson, Kate, 155, 156
Hutchinson, Richard, 141
Hutchinson Family, 76, 117n, 137, 141–61, 183, 239, 455
    see also Aeolian Vocalists
Hutchinson Family Quartet, 76, 137, 141–61, 152
    and abolition movement, 147–54
    controversy over, 152–53
    disbandment of, 154
    English tour of, 146
    first tour of, 145–46
    formation of, 145
    musical style of, 159–61
    political importance of, 156–58
    and temperance movement, 147–48
Hutchinson's Republican Songster for 1860, 156

"I Almost Lost My Mind," 412
"I Am a Rock" (Simon and Garfunkel), 448
"I Cannot Sing the Old Songs" (Claribel), 185–86
"I Cannot Sing Tonight" (Foster), 223–24
"(I Can't Get No) Satisfaction" (Rolling Stones), 445
"I Can't Give You Anything But Love" (McHugh), 357
"I'd Be a Butterfly" (Bayley), 205
"I Dig Rock and Roll Music" (Peter, Paul, and Mary), 448
"I'd Leave My Happy Home for You" (Von Tilzer), 309
"I'd Mourn the Hopes That Leave Me," 55
"I'd Rather Be Right" (Rodgers), 316
"I Dreamed My Boy Was Home Again" (Sawyer), 240
"I Dream of Jeanie" (Foster), 217–19
"I Dreamt I Dwelt in Kitchen Halls," 132

"I Dreamt That I Dwelt in Marble Halls" (Balfe), 85, 247n, 368
I Dreamt Too Much (Kern), 343
"I Feel Fine" (Beatles), 421, 422
"If I Had a Hammer" (Seeger), 431
"If I Loved You" (Rodgers), 355
"If I Were a Voice" (Hutchinson), 157, 161
"If I Were the Chief of Police" (Harris), 298
"I Forgot to Remember to Forget," 419
"If You Don't Know Me By Now" (Melvin), 470
"If You Love Me" (Newton-John), 469
"I Get Around" (Beach Boys), 435
"I Get High with a Little Help from My Friends" (Beatles), 445
"I Goes to Fight mit Seigel," 250
"I Got a Woman," 419
"I Got Rhythm" (Gershwin), 348, 373
"I Guess I'll Have to Telegraph My Baby" (Cohan), 313
"I Have a Silent Sorrow Here" (Reinagle), 37
"I Know I'm Losing You" (Temptations), 462
"I Left My Heart at the Stage Door Canteen" (Berlin), 336, 377
Iliff, Mrs., 37
"I'll Be Around" (Wilder), 462
"I'll Be Home," 412
"I'll Be Seeing You" (Fain), 385, 413
"I'll Meet Thee, Love" (John H. Hewitt), 105
"I'll Never Smile Again" (R. Lowe), 385
"I'll Pray for Thee," 83
"I'll Remember You, Love, in My Prayers" (Hays), 265
"I'll Take You Home Again, Kathleen" (Westendorf), 262–64, 263
"I'll Walk Alone" (Styne), 387
"I Love Music" (O'Jays), 470
"I Love You Both" (Von Tilzer), 308
"I Love You Truly" (Jacobs-Bond), 323
"I'm Always Chasing Rainbows" (Carroll), 360, 363, 368
"I'm Called Little Buttercup" (Sullivan), 283
"I'm Falling In Love with Someone" (Herbert), 323
"I'm Henry VIII, I Am" (Herman's Hermits), 423
"I'm in Love Again," 409
"I'm in Love with a Big Blue Frog" (Peter, Paul, and Mary), 448
"I'm Just Wild About Harry" (Sissle-Blake), 360, 375
Imperial Records, 402, 408
"I'm Sorry" (Denver), 469
"I'm Talking About You," 419
"I'm Walking," 407, 409, 414
Incledon, Charles, 13, 164
Incredible String Band, 454
"I Never Drank behind the Bar" (Braham), 281n
"In Happy Moments" (Wallace), 87
Inkle and Yarico (Arnold), 19n
Ink Spots, the, 403, 406
"In the Baggage Coach Ahead" (Davis), 285
"In the Evening by the Moonlight" (Bland), 275
"In the Eye Abides the Heart" (Abt), 222
"In the Gloaming" (Harrison), 283
"In the Good Old Summer Time" (Evans), 291, 295, 296
"In the Morning by the Bright Light" (Bland), 275, 276
"In the Shade of the Old Apple Tree" (Van Alstyne), 291, 296
"In the Still of the Night" (Porter), 353, 383
Introducing the Beatles, 418
"Invalid Corps, The," 251

"Iola" (Johnson), 368
"Irene" (Tierney), 368
"Irish air of Grammachree," 44
"Irish Jaunting Car, The," 242, 248
Irish Melodies (Thomas Moore), 42, 44–59, 60, 61 96,
    114, 142, 158, 172, 214, 217, 248, 250, 377, 378,
    426
    American editions of, 46
    influence of, on American song, 54–57
    pentatonic scale in, 55–57
    popularity of, 44, 57–59
Irish song
    in Civil War songs, 248–52
    influence of, in America, 42–60, 171, 242–43, 311
    influence of, on Samuel Lover, 172–76
    influence of, on Stephen Foster, 215–19, 223
    see also Moore, Thomas; *Irish Melodies*
Iron Butterfly, 469
Irwin, May, 287, 300, 313, 321
"I See Her Still in My Dreams" (Foster), 217, 226, 247n
Isherwood, B., 21
Isley Brothers, 419
Israel in Egypt (Handel), 95
"Is There a Heart That Never Lov'd" (Braham), 164,
    165
italiana in Algeri, L', 63, 67
Italian Monk, The (Arnold), 29
Italian opera
    in "Englished" versions, 70–72, 74
    first performed in America, 64
    influence of, on Stephen Foster, 219–22
    in song publications, 74–78
Italian Opera House (New York), 67, 69, 70
"Italian Street Song" (Herbert), 323
"It Can't Be Wrong" (Steiner), 387
"It Is Better to Laugh Than be Sighing," 83
"It Might As Well Be Spring" (Rodgers), 355
"It's Easy to Remember" (Rodgers), 355, 367–68
"It's Only a Paper Moon" (Arlen), 356, 374, 462
"It's the Same Old Song" (Four Tops), 462
"I've Been Roaming" (Horn), 184
"I've Got You Under My Skin" (Porter), 353, 462
Ives, Burl, 426, 427, 430, 431, 433, 439
"I've Told Ev'ry Little Star" (Kern), 343, 364
"I Want a Girl Just Like the Girl That Married Dear Old
    Dad" (Von Tilzer), 311
"I Want to Be in Dixie" (Berlin), 340
"I Want to Hold Your Hand" (Beatles), 418, 421, 422,
    423
"I Want You, I Need You," 404
"I Will Be True to Thee" (Foster), 205
"I Wish I Was in Dixie's Land," *see* "Dixie"
"I Wonder Where She Is Tonight" (Dresser), 306
"I Would Not Die At All" (John H. Hewitt), 106
"I Would Not Die in Spring Time" (Foster), 106
"I Would That My Love" (Mendelssohn), 195
"I Write the Songs" (Manilow), 472

Jackson, Aunt Molly, 426
Jackson, George K., 38, 39
Jacobs-Bond, Carrie, 323
Jagger, Mick, 445, 446, 449, 451
"Jailhouse Rock," 407, 414, 416
"Jambalaya," 411
James, Elmore, 445
James, Harry, 383, 384, 387

James, Henry, 109
James, Joni, 411
James, Lewis, 337
James, Sonny, 462
"Jamie's on the Stormy Sea" (Covert), 145
"Japanese Sandman, The" (Whiting), 336
Jardine, Alan, 435
jazz and popular song, 333, 350–52, 355–56, 372–74,
    380–87
Jazz Singer, The, 334
Jefferson, Thomas, 93
Jefferson Airplane, 440–41, 441, 456, 457, 458, 462
Jefferson Airplane Takes Off, 440
Jefferson Starship, 467
Jeffreys, Charles, 78, 83
"Jem of Aberdeen" (Hook), 59
"Jenny's Coming O'er the Green" (Foster), 205
Jessel, George, 328
Jewish-American contributions to popular song,
    327–29
"Jim Along Josey" (Harper), 125
"Jim Crack Corn" (anon.), 135
"Jim Crow" (Rice), 120–21, 123, 126, 206
Joel, Billy, 468
John, Elton, 467, 468, 474
"John Anderson Is My Jo," 61
"John Brown's Body" (Steffe), 156, 230, 235, 236
"Johnny B. Goode," 419
Johnson, Francis, 77
Johnson, James, 60
Johnson, James P., 350
Johnson, Marv, 460
Johnson, Miss, 167
Johnston, Arthur, 360
Jolson, Al, 328, 332, 334, 336, 346, 348, 360, 381
Jones, Brian, 474
Jones, George, 462
Jones, Isham, 351
Jones, John, 20, 71
Jones, Stan, 389
Joplin, Janis, 441, 451–52, 452, 456, 457, 462, 474
Joplin, Scott, 317, 318, 321
Jordan, Mrs. Dorothy Bland, 60
"Jordan Is a Hard Road To Travel" (Emmett), 128
Jose, Dick, 299
Joyce, James, 445
Joy of Living (Kern), 344
Jubilee (Porter), 353
Jubilee, The (Bradbury), 159
"Just A-Wearyin' for You" (Jacobs-Bond), 323
"Just Before the Battle, Mother" (Root), 232
"Just Behind the Times" (Harris), 300, 301
"Just One of Those Things" (Porter), 353
"Just Tell Them That You Saw Me" (Dresser), 305, 307
Juvenile Ethiopian Minstrel Company, 132

Kahn, Gus, 334
Kallen, Kitty, 392
Kalliwoda, Johann, 187, 191
Kansas (band), 467
"Kansas City," 419
"Kathleen Mavourneen," 77
"Katy Darling," 82
Kavanaugh, F. H., 133, 134
Kaye, Danny, 429
Kaye, Sammy, 387, 405

KC and the Sunshine Band, 472
Kean, Edmund, 178
"Keep in de Middle ob de Road" (Hays), 273
Keith and Albee, 287
Keith's Union Square Theatre (New York), 312
Keller, Matthias, 190
Kelly, Nancy, 342
Kentucky Minstrels, 132
Kern, Jerome, 327, 341–45, 342, 348, 350, 352, 353, 356, 359, 360, 361, 362, 364, 366, 368, 369, 371, 372, 375, 378, 388
  as composer of movie scores, 343–45
  influence of classical music on, 368
  musical style of, 345
  success of, in musical shows, 341–43
Kersands, Billy, 268, 274
"Killing Me Softly with His Song" (Flack), 469
"Kindness and a Graceful Air Preferred to Beauty" (Arne), 9
King, B. B., 403, 454, 458
King, Carole, 417, 468, 474
"King Alcohol" (Ditson), 145, 147, 148
King and I, The, 354
King Crimson, 469
"Kingdom Coming" (Work), 230, 232, 236
King Linkum the First, 244
King's Arm Garden (New York), 21
Kingsley, George, 142
King's Theatre (London), 64
Kingston Trio, the, 430, 431, 432, 436, 456
Kingston Trio, The, 430
Kismet, 392
"Kiss and Let's Make Up" (Harris), 299
"Kiss Me Again" (Herbert), 323
Kittredge, Walter, 156, 236, 239
"Kitty Tyrrell," 56
Kleber, Henry, 204, 222
Kneass, Nelson, 132
Knecht, Joseph M., 381
Knickerbocker Magazine, 85
Knight, Gladys, and the Pips, 467, 470
Knight of Snowdoun, The (Bishop), 169
Knowles, Sheridan, 126
"Kodachrome" (Simon), 466
"Ko Ko Mo," 411
Koussevitsky, Serge, 350
Krell, William H., 317
Krupa, Gene, 383
Kücken, Friedrich Wilhelm, 198–99, 200
Kunkel's Nightingale Opera Troupe, 108, 139
Kyser, Kay, 386

Lacalle, Joseph, 389
Lacey, Dr., 204
"La ci darem la mano" (Mozart), 72
Lacy, Rophino, 71, 74, 78
Lad of the Hills, The (O'Keefe), 50
"Lady Be Good" (Gershwin), 347
Lady Be Good, 344, 349
Lady of the Lake, The (Scott), 169
"Lammas Night, A" (Burns), 61
Lampe, Mrs. (Isabella), 5
"Lamp Is Low, The," 369
Langdon, Chauncey, 94
Lange, Johnny, 389
Lanin, Sam, 381

Lanza, Mario, 429
La Scala (Milan, Italy), 78
"Lasses of Dublin, The," 44, 115
"Lass of the Cot, The" (Taylor), 41
"Last Greeting" (Schubert), 187
Last Judgement, The (Spohr), 189
"Last Time I Saw Paris, The" (Kern), 344, 360
"Laura Lee" (Foster), 223
"Lawdy Miss Clawdy," 419
Lawlor, Charles B., 285, 291
Lawrence, Jack, 392
"Lazybones" (Carmichael), 383
Leadbelly (Huddie Ledbetter), 426
Leave It to Jane (Kern), 342
Led Zeppelin, 469
Lee, Brenda, 414
Lee, Peggy, 389
Lee, Robert E., 231
Leesugg, Miss, 70
Le Fanu, Alicia Sheridan, 43
Legends and Stories of Ireland (Lover), 173
Leiber, Jerry, 417
"Lemon Tree" (Kingston Trio), 431
"Lemuel" (Foster), 210
Lennon, John, 418, 420, 421, 423, 443, 467
Lenschow, Carl, 191
Leonard, Mr., 20
Leonora (Fry), 132
Lerner, Alan Jay, 376, 414, 462
Let 'Em Eat Cake, 347
"Let Me Be There" (Newton-John), 469
"Let Me Be Your Teddy Bear," 407
"Let Me Dream Again" (Sullivan), 282
"Let's Have Another Cup of Coffee" (Berlin), 335
"Let's Spend the Night Together" (Rolling Stones), 447
"Let's Start the New Year Right" (Berlin), 334
"Letter That Never Came, The" (Dresser), 285, 305
Levey, Ethel (Mrs. George M. Cohan), 313
Lewin, Lionel H., 282
Lewis, Bobby, 417
Lewis, Jerry Lee, 394, 395, 407, 414, 415, 416, 465
Lewis, Monk, 179
Lewis, Ted, 328
Libby, J. Aldrich, 299
Liberator, 153
Libertine, The, see Don Giovanni
"Libiamo" (Verdi), 87
"Life Let Us Cherish," 60
"Life on the Ocean Wave, A" (Russell), 182
"Light My Fire" (Doors), 451
"Light of Other Days Is Faded, The" (Balfe), 84
"Like a Rolling Stone" (Dylan), 433, 448
"Like the Gloom of Night Retiring" (Bishop), 170
"Lilly Dale" (Thompson), 139
"Lily Ray" (Foster), 223
Lincoln, Abraham, 234, 239, 253
"Lincoln and Liberty" (Jesse Hutchinson), 231
Lind, Jenny, 71, 76, 132, 167, 191
Lindblad, Adolf, 199
Lindsay, Jennie, 285
"Linger in Blissful Repose" (Foster), 222
Link, Harry, 385
Linley, Thomas, 19n, 44, 132, 205
"Lip Hung Down, The," 132
"Lisbon Antigua," 414
"Listen, listen to the voice of love" (Hook), 16, 20, 23

"Listen to the Mocking Bird" (Winner), 139, 260, 262
Liszt, Franz, 348, 351, 368
Literary Gazette (Dublin), 173
"Little Ballad Girl, The," 205
"Little Bit of Heaven, A" (Ball), 323
"Little Bunch of Shamrocks, A" (Von Tilzer), 311
"Little Church Around the Corner, The" (White), 267
"Little Deuce Coupe" (Beach Boys), 435
"Little Ella" (Foster), 217
Little Johnny Jones, 313, 314, 315
"Little Lost Child, The" (Stern), 285
"Little Nell," 81
Little Night Music, A (Sondheim), 474
"Little Queenie," 419
Little Richard (Penniman), 394, 395, 415, 416, 417, 419, 451, 455
"Little Sailor Boy, The" (Carr), 29–32, 31, 41
"Little Things Mean a Lot" (Lindeman), 392
Livingston, Jay, 389, 414
"Locked Out After Nine" (Braham), 281n
Loesser, Frank, 377
Loewe, Frederick, 414, 462
Loewe, Karl, 195
Loewe, Marcus, 328
Lohengrin (R. Wagner), 87, 199
Lomax, Alan, 427
London Times, The, 128
"Long Ago and Far Away" (Kern), 344
Longfellow, Henry Wadsworth, 146
"Long Tail Blue" (Dixon), 117, 118, 207
"Long Tall Sally" (Little Richard), 394, 412, 419
"Long Time Ago" (Rice), 123
"Look For the Silver Lining" (Kern), 342, 366, 369
"Looking Back" (Sullivan), 282
"Loose Were her Tresses" (Giordani), 20
Lopez, Vincent, 381
"Lorena" (Webster), 247
"Lost Chord, The" (Sullivan), 282
"Louisiana Belle" (Foster), 132, 207
Louisiana Purchase, 335
Louisville Courier-Journal, 265
"Love Has Eyes" (Bishop), 170
Love in a Cloud, 118
Love in a Village (Arne), 22, 27, 71n
"Love Letters in the Sand" (Coots), 412, 414
"Lovely Boy," 413
"Lovely Lass, The" (Selby), 95
"Lovely Nan" (Dibdin), 20
"Love Me and the World Is Mine" (Ball), 323
"Love Me Do" (Beatles), 420, 421
"Love Me Tender" (Presley), 248, 394, 399, 404, 407, 415
Love, Mike, 435
Lover, Samuel, 172–76, 174, 205
"Lover" (Rodgers), 392
"Lover, Come Back to Me" (Romberg), 369
"Love's Young Dream," 46, 53
"Love Thee Dearest!" (Gilfert), 102
"Love Train" (O'Jays), 470
"Love Walked In" (Gershwin), 348
"Love You Too" (Harrison), 443
"Loving You," 415
"Low-Back'd Car, The" (Lover), 176
Lowe, Ruth, 385
Lowe, Thomas, 4, 5
Luca Brothers, 155

Lucas, Sam, 268, 274
Lucia di Lammermoor (Donizetti), 83, 87
"Lucille," 419
Lucky Escape, The (Dibdin), 37
Lucrezia Borgia (Donizetti), 83
"Lucy in the Sky with Diamonds" (Lennon), 443, 445
"Lucy Long," 128, 132
"Lucy Neal," 109, 209
"Lucy, or Selim's Complaint" (Hook), 24
"Lula Is Gone" (Foster), 223
"Lullaby" (Dibdin), 25
"Lullaby of Broadway" (Warren), 357
Lunceford, Jimmie, 383, 384
"Lyin' Eyes" (Eagles), 467, 469
Lyman, Abe, 381
Lyric Harmony, 4n
lyrics of popular songs, 5–8, 14, 16, 23–25, 32–35, 52–54, 116–17, 144–45, 182, 184–85, 204–5, 210–14, 230–31, 247–48, 254, 262, 265–66, 276–77, 290, 296–97, 300–2, 306–8, 340, 374–75, 376–77, 396–97, 401, 421, 431–32, 445, 447, 474

Macarthy, Harry, 230, 242, 243
McCartney, Paul, 418, 420, 421, 423, 443
McCauley's Theatre (Louisville), 262
McGuinn, Roger, 436
McHugh, Jimmy, 357, 377, 383, 388, 462
MacKay, Charles, 179, 197
McKee, James W., 278
McKinney's Cotton Pickers, 382
McPhatter, Clyde, 420
"McPherson's Farewell" (Burns), 61
McShann, Jay, 382
McVea, Jack, 388
Madden, Edward, 392
"Mad Girl's Song, The" (Russell), 179n
"Maggie is by My Side" (Foster), 217
"Maggie Lawder," 44n
"Maggie's Secret" (Claribel), 185
Magic Flute, The (Mozart), 63, 72
Mahler, Gustav, 294, 372
Mahmoud, or the Prince of Persia, 164
Maid of Artois, The (Balfe), 84
Maid of the Mill, The (Arnold), 19n
Mainstream Records, 441
"Main Track, The; or, A Leap for Life" (Russell), 179n
Makeba, Miriam, 439
"Make Believe" (Kern), 343
"Make Me No Gaudy Chaplet," 83, 247n
"Making of a Girl" (Gershwin), 346
Malibran Maria (Garcia), 64, 66, 84, 167
"Mambo Rock" (Haley), 394
Mammy, 334
"Mañana" (Lee), 389
Mancini, Henry, 457
"Mandy" (Manilow), 472
"Maniac, The" (Russell), 144, 179, 183
"Man I Love, The" (Gershwin), 360, 361, 366–67
Manilow, Barry, 472
Mann, Barry, 417
Mann, Elias, 94
"Man of Constant Sorrow" (Dylan), 433
"Mansion of Aching Hearts, The" (Von Tilzer), 310
Mantovani, 457
Man Who Knew Too Much, The, 414

Manzoli, Giovanni, 63
"Marching Through Georgia" (Work), 231, 237, 255
"March of the Archers" (Carr), 29
Maretzek, Max, 72
"Marie from Sunny Italy" (Berlin), 330
Maritana (Wallace), 87
"Market Lass, The," 23
Marks, Edward B., 285, 289, 290, 327
Marshall, Mr. and Mrs., 20
Marshall Tucker Band, 467
Martha and the Vandellas, 460
Martin, Dean, 338, 414, 435
Martin, Freddie, 386
Marvelettes, the, 460
Marvell, Holt, 385
Marx Brothers, 334
"Mary" (Stoddard), 336
"Mary Blane," 132, 136
"Mary I Believe Thee True," 47
"Maryland! My Maryland," 247, 248
Marylebone Gardens (London), 5, 12, 13
"Mary Loves the Flowers" (Foster), 205
"Mary, Now the Seas Divide Us" (John H. Hewitt),
    106, 107
"Mary of Argyle," 247n
"Mary's a Grand Old Name" (Cohan), 315
"Mary's Dream, or Sandy's Ghost" (Relfe), 23, 24
"Mary's Tears" (Shaw), 95–96, 97, 98
Masaniello (Auber), 165
Mason, Lowell, 38, 98, 159, 232
Masonic Temple (Boston), 127
Masque of Alfred the Great, The (Arne), 90
Massachusetts Magazine, The, 94
"Massa's in de Cold Ground" (Foster), 213, 214, 215,
    225
"Masters of War" (Dylan), 433
"Matchbox," 419
Mathews, Charles, 112–16, 102
    impersonation of Negroes by, 115–16
Mathis, Johnny, 414, 456, 457
Matilde de Shabran (Rossini), 67
"Matrimonial Sweets" (Hutchinson), 145
matrimonio segreto, Il (Cimarosa), 63
"Maybellene" (Berry), 394, 402, 406, 407
Mayer, Louis B., 328
"Me and Bobby McGee" (J. Joplin), 416, 453
Me and Juliet (Rodgers), 392
Mechanic's Hall (New York), 131, 242
"Meet Me in St. Louis, Louis" (Mills), 291
Meet the Beatles, 418, 421
"Melinda May" (Foster), 137, 212
Melvin, Harold, and the Blue Notes, 470
"Memories Are Made of This," 414
"Memphis, Tennessee," 419
Mendelssohn, Felix, 189, 191, 199
Mendelssohn Quintette Club, 190
Mercadante, Giuseppi, 67
Mercer, Johnny, 376, 383, 389, 392
Mercury Records, 393, 402, 411, 412
Merrill, Bob, 389
"Merrily Danc'd the Quaker," 44n
Metronome Magazine, 383
Metropolitan Minstrels, 132
Metropolitan Opera House (New York), 451
Meyer, George M., 334
MGM Records, 402, 411

Midnighters, the, 411
"Mid the Green Fields of Virginia" (Harris), 301
"Mignon Song" (Schubert), 194
Mikado, The (Gilbert and Sullivan), 283
Milhaud, Darius, 350
Miller, Glenn, 384, 386, 387
Miller, Mitch, 457
Mills, Kerry, 289, 291
Mills Brothers, 386, 406, 462
Miner's Bowery Theatre, 290
Minerva and Saturday Post, 105
Minstrel, The, 46
"Minstrel Boy, The," 46
minstrel music, 108, 109–40, 241–42, 321
    decline of, 287
    European styles in, 122–23, 134–35
    as minstrel-spirituals, 272–73
    "plantation songs" in, 137–39
    in post–Civil War period, 265–78
    of Stephen Foster, 206–15, 223–24, 225
"Minstrel's Return'd from the War, The" (John H.
    Hewitt), 102–4, 105, 245
Miracles, the, 460, 462
"Mira, O Norma" (Bellini), see "Hear Me, Norma"
Mississippi, 355
"Mississippi Rag" (Krell), 317
"Miss Lucy Long," 125
"Miss Lucy Neal" (Sanford), 136–37
"Missouri! or, A Voice from the South" (Macarthy), 243
Mitchell, Margaret, 244
Mitchell, William, 77
Mlle. Modiste (Herbert), 323
Moby Grape, 440, 441, 456
Moller, J. C., 21, 72
"Molly Darling" (Hays), 265
"Molly, Do You Love Me?" (Foster), 205
Monkees, the, 456
Monotones, the, 410
Monroe, James, 95
Monroe, Vaughn, 387
Monsieur Tonson (Moncrieff), 113
Montresor, Giovanni, 66, 67, 70
"Mood Indigo" (Ellington), 357
Moody Blues, the, 469
Moondogs, see Beatles, the
"Moon Love" (David-Davis-Kostelanetz), 369
Moore, Raymond, 299
Moore, Thomas, 42, 44–59, 48, 60, 61, 74, 76, 96,
    102, 114, 142, 158, 170, 172, 173, 175, 176, 182,
    194, 205, 214, 248, 250, 302, 377, 378, 426
    American visit of, 58–59
    influence of, on American song, 57–58
    influence of, on Stephen Foster, 214–19
    poetic themes of, 51–54
    as song composer, 47–49
    see also Irish Melodies
Moore, Victor, 335
"More and More" (Kern), 345
"Moreen, The," 46
Morris, George P., 145, 181, 204
Morrison, Jim, 451, 453, 474
Moscheles, Ignaz, 199
Moten, Bennie, 382
"Mother and Child Reunion" (Simon), 466
"Mother Machree" (Ball), 323
"Mother, Thou'rt Faithful to Me" (Foster), 217

"Mother Would Comfort Me," 240, 247n
Motown songs, 459, 460, 460–62
"Mountain Bugle, The" (John H. Hewitt), 105
Mountaineers, The (Arnold), 37
Mount Vernon Garden (New York), 21
Mozart, W. A., 5, 8, 63, 66, 69, 70, 76, 84, 87, 98, 99, 142, 189, 190, 204, 440
"Mr. Johnson, Turn Me Loose" (Harney), 318
"Mrs. Brown, You've Got a Lovely Daughter" (Herman's Hermits), 423
"Mrs. Lofty and I" (Hutchinson), 159–60
"Mr. Tambourine Man" (Dylan), 436, 437
Muir, Lewis F., 321
"Mule Train" (Lange), 389
Muller, 187
"Mulligan Guard, The," 279, 280
"Munster Man, The" (Moore), 54
Murphy, J. B., 135, 207, 277
Murray, Bill, 336
Music (C. King), 468
musical comedy, 313–16, 341–42, 346–48, 353–55, 472–73
Musical Fund Society of Boston, 189
Musical Journal, The, 27
Musical Magazine, The, 183
Musical Olio; or, Favorite Gems of That Popular Southern Composer, John H. Hewitt, 244
Musical Repertory, The, 59
Musical Repository (Providence), 98
Musical Review, The, 76
Musical Visitor, 262
Musical World and New York Musical Times, 225
Musica Sacra (Hastings), 159
Music Box Revue (Berlin), 334
Music for Lovers Only, 429
Music in the Air (Kern), 343
Music in the Key of Life (Wonder), 466
Music of Erin, The, 44, 50
"Music of the Great Southern Sable Harmonists," 207–8
music publishers, *see* publishers, music; publishing, sheet music
Musikverein (Milwaukee), 190
Musorgsky, Modest, 372, 469
"My Blue Heaven" (Donaldson), 357, 360
"My Bonnie Lies Over the Ocean," 419
"My Dad's Dinner Pail" (Braham), 281n
"My Days Have Been So Wondrous Free" (Hopkinson), 91
"My Dearest Heart" (Sullivan), 282
My Fair Lady, 414, 462
"My Gal Is a Highborn Lady" (Fagan), 321
"My Gal Sal" (Dresser), 291, 294, 297, 304, 305, 306
"My Generation" (Who), 448, 449
"My Girl Has Gone" (Miracles), 462
"My Heart Stood Still" (Rodgers), 355, 360, 361
"My Jesus Says There's Room Enough," 156
"My Lodging is on the Cold Ground," 46
"My Mammy" (Donaldson), 334
"My Moonlight Madonna" (Scotti), 369
"My Mother's Bible" (Morris-Russell), 145, 183
"My Old Kentucky Home, Goodnight" (Foster), 213, 214, 215, 223, 225
"My Old New Hampshire Home" (Von Tilzer), 309
"My Own Native Mountains" (John H. Hewitt), 106
"My Prayer," 409

"My Pretty Jane," *see* "Bloom Is on the Rye, The"
"My Reverie" (Clinton), 369
"My Southern Sunny Home" (Hays), 265
"My Wild Irish Rose" (Olcott), 291, 292

"Nancy Till" (White), 137, 269–70
Nasolini, 63
National Advocate, 114
National Airs (Moore), 48, 53, 170
National Theatre (New York), 77, 290
Naughty Marietta (Herbert), 323
"Negro and His Banja, The" (Dibdin), 110
"Nelly Was a Lady" (Foster), 137, 211
Nelson, Ricky, 415, 417
Nevin, Ethelbert, 323
New and Select Collection of the Best English, Scots and Irish songs, catches, duets, and cantatas, A, 44
"New Coon in Town" (Putnam), 321
"New Langolee," 52
New Minstrel, The, 44
New Moon (Romberg), 369
New Orleans Academy of Music, 243
New Orleans Serenaders, 132, 212
Newport Folk Festival, 431, 432, 448
Newton-John, Olivia, 468, 469, 472
New York American, The, 64, 69, 164
New York Clipper, The, 126
New York Daily Tribune, 236
New York Dramatic News, 299
New York Evening Post, 65, 239
New York Herald, 165
New York Literary Gazette and Phi Beta Kappa Repository, 68
New York Mercury, 20
New York Minstrels, 132
New York Mirror, 167
New York Mirror and Ladies' Literary Gazette, 69
New York Philharmonic Society, 189, 191
New York Symphony Orchestra, 350
Niblo's Garden (New York), 72, 82, 152
Nichols, George, 118, 123
Nicholson, Nick, 330
"Nicodemus Johnson," 135
"Night and Day" (Porter), 353, 360, 361
Nightingale, The, 32, 39
Nightingale Opera Troupe, 132
"Night Was Made for Love, The," 343
Niles, John Jacob, 426, 431
Nixon, Richard, 458
"Nobody But You" (Gershwin), 365
Nobody Home (Kern), 341
"Nobody Knows" (Berlin), 337
"Nobody's Child," 419
"Nobody's Darling" (Hays), 265
"None Shall Weep a Tear for Me" (Foster), 217
non-Western music and popular song, 443, 446
"Noon" (Hook), 14
"No Other Love" (Rodgers), 355
"Nora O'Neal" (Hays), 139
Norma (Bellini), 72, 78, 87, 132
  American premier of, 78
  arrangements of, 82
  English translations of, 78, 81
  first opera score published in America, 81
"Norwegian Wood" (Beatles), 442
No Song, No Supper (Storace), 19n, 165

"Not for All the Rice in China" (Berlin), 335
nozze di Figaro, Le (Mozart), 63
Nugent, Maud, 285, 291

"Of Thee I Sing" (Gershwin), 348
Of Thee I Sing, 347
"Oft in the Stilly Night," 48, 53
"Oh! Blame Not the Bard," 56
Oh, Boy! (Kern), 342
"Oh! Boys Carry Me 'Long" (Foster), 210, 212
"Oh Come to Mason Borough's Grove" (Hopkinson), 91
"Oh! Dem Golden Slippers" (Bland), 275
"Oh How I Hate to Get Up in the Morning" (Berlin), 333, 376
"O I'm a Good Old Rebel," 250n
Oh, Kay!, 347
Oh, Lady! Lady! (Kern), 342
"Oh! Lemuel," 209
"Oh! Mr. Coon," 209
Oh, My Dear! (Kern), 342
"Oh No! We Never Mention Her" (Bishop), 171
"Oh Promise Me" (De Koven), 321, 322
"Oh Susanna" (Foster), 208, 209, 210, 225
"Oh, That Beautiful Rag" (Berlin), 330, 332
"Oh What a Beautiful Morning" (Rodgers), 355
O'Jays, the, 470
"Okie from Muskogee" (Haggard), 463
Oklahoma! (Rodgers), 354, 355
Olcott, Chauncey, 291, 292
Old American Company, 22, 27, 28, 29
"Old Arm Chair, The" (Russell), 180
"Old Bob Ridley" (White), 269
"Old Church Yard, The," 146
Old Dan Emmett's Original Banjo Melodies, 128
"Old Dan Tucker," 128, 150, 242
"Old Dog Tray" (Foster), 213, 214, 225
Oldfield, Mike, 469
"Old Folks at Home" (Foster), 57, 213, 214, 215, 225, 293
"Old Friends" (Simon and Garfunkel), 448
"Old Granite State, The" (Hutchinson), 146, 150, 152
"Old Home Ain't What It Used to Be, The" (White), 270–71, 271
Oldmixon, Miss, 22, 29
"Old Tare River" (Sweeney), 125, 128
"Old Uncle Ned" (Foster), 132, 207, 208, 211, 212
"Old Woman, The," 46, 53
"Ole Buttermilk Sky" (Carmichael), 357
Oliver, King, 351
Oliver, Sy, 384
"Ol' Man River" (Kern), 343
"On a Sunday Afternoon" (Von Tilzer), 310
"Once a King There Chanced to Be," *see* "Una voce poco fa"
"Once I Loved Thee, Mary Dear" (Foster), 205
One Kind Kiss" (Jackson), 39
"One of These Nights" (Eagles), 467
"Only a Light in the Window" (Gabriel), 283
"Only Friends and Nothing More" (Winner), 261
"Only You," 407, 412
"On the Atchison, Topeka & Santa Fe" (Warren), 357, 389
On the Avenue, 334
"On the Banks of the Wabash" (Dresser), 305, 306
"On the Street Where You Live" (Lerner), 414, 462

"On the Sunny Side of the Street" (McHugh), 357, 383, 462
"On Top of Old Smoky" (Ives), 426, 428
On Your Toes (Rodgers), 354
"Open the Door, Richard" (McVea), 388
"Open Thy Lattice, Love" (Foster), 204, 205
opera, British, songs from, 17–20, 21–23, 37, 110–12, 162–72
opera, Italian
    American opposition to, 68–70
    decline of as popular music, 87
    English language versions of, 70–88
    first production of, in America, 64
    influence on American song style, 106, 171–72, 179–82, 212, 219–22, 224, 251–52
    and minstrel show, 72, 132–34
    popularity of, in America, 62–88
    in popular song repertory, 76–88
"Opossum Up a Gum-Tree," 115
Oracle, The (San Francisco), 453
oral-tradition music, relationship to popular song, 9–10, 29, 43–44, 46–48, 50–51, 54–57, 107, 114–15, 123–24, 130, 134–35, 171, 175, 197, 209, 248–51, 304, 389, 395–96, 402–4, 408, 426–34
"Orchids in the Moonlight" (Youmans), 357
Ordway, Dr. John P., 133
Ordways Aeolians, 132
Original Black Diamonds, 274
Original Rags (Joplin), 318
Original Virginia Serenaders, 134, 136
Orioles, the, 406, 407, 408, 411
Orphean Music Company, 309
"O! Soon Return" (John H. Hewitt), 105
Oswald, 90
Otello (Rossini), 65, 66
"Our Love," 369
"Outcast Unknown, The" (Dresser), 285, 305, 307
"Outlaws and Exiles of Erin" (Lover), 174
"Outlaw's Death, The" (Muller), 187
"Over and Over" (Dave Clark Five), 423
"Over the Hills to the Poor House" (D. Braham), 278–79
"Over the Rainbow" (Arlen), 356, 360
"Over There" (Cohan), 315, 316, 376
"Over the Summer Sea," *see* "donna è mobile, La"
Overture in Nine Movements, Expressive of a Battle (Hewitt), 32
Owens, Buck, 462
"Oxford Town" (Dylan), 433
"O Ye Tears!" (Abt)

"Paddy by Land and Sea" (Lover), 174
"Paddy's Portfolio" (Lover), 174
Paddy's Resource, 44n
Paddy Whack in Italia, Il (Lover), 173
Paderewski, Ignace, 369
Padlock, The (Dibdin), 19n, 22, 110
Paer, Ferdinando, 63
Paganini, Niccolò, 173
Page, Patti, 338, 387, 404, 405, 411
"Paint It Black" (Rolling Stones), 446
Paisiello, Giovanni, 63
Pajama Game (Adler), 392
Palma, Silvestro, 90
Palmer, John W., 231

Palmo's Burlesque Opera Company, 133
Palmo's Opera House (New York), 68, 77, 83, 130, 152
"Paper Doll" (Black), 386, 387
Paramount Theatre (New York), 383
Pardon My English, 347
Parepa-Rosa, Madame, 184
Park Theatre (New York), 64, 69, 70, 74, 78, 83, 84, 102, 112, 113, 118, 126, 127, 165, 166, 167, 170
Parnell, Thomas, 91
Parsley, Sage, Rosemary and Thyme, 448
"Parthenia to Ingomar" (Foster), 205
Parton, Dolly, 469, 472
"Passing Bell" (Schubert), 187
Passing Show of 1916, The, 346
Pastor, Tony, 287–88
   see also Tony Pastor's Opera House
"Pastoral" (Hook), 14
"Pat Murphy of the Irish Brigade" (anon.), 231
Paton, Mary Ann, see Wood, Mrs.
Patriot, The, or Liberty Asserted (Hewitt), 32, 41
Patriot, The, or Liberty Obtained (Carr), 29, 41
patriotic songs
   in the Civil War, 230–46
   of George M. Cohan, 315–17
   in World War I, 376
   in World War II, 377
Patti, Adelina, 167, 191
"Paul and Virginia" (Reeve), 111
Pavane pour une enfante défunte (Ravel), 369
Paxton, Tom, 435
Payne, John Howard, 165, 167–69, 168
Pearce, William, 35
Pedrotti, Signora, 66
Peerless Quartet, 346
"Peg o' My Heart" (Fisher), 338
Pelham, Dick, 126, 127
Penguins, the, 406, 407, 408, 411
Penniman, Little Richard, see Little Richard
Pennsylvania Packet, 93
"Pensive Shepherd, The" (Holyoke), 95
"People Will Say We're In Love" (Rodgers), 354, 355
Pepys, Samuel, 3
"Perfect Day, A" (Jacobs-Bond), 323
Pergolesi, Giovanni, 90
Perkins, Carl, 394, 395, 415, 419
Peter Frampton Comes Alive, 474
Peter, Paul, and Mary, 431, 434, 436, 437, 448, 456, 462
Peter, Paul, and Mary, 435
Peterson's Magazine, 260
"Phantom Chorus, from Sonnambula," 209
Philadelphia Band, 260
Philadelphia Courier, 152
Philadelphia Musical Society, 146
Philharmonic Society (Boston), 95
Phillips, Adelaide, 77
Phillips, T., 70, 147
Phillips, Wendell, 149
"Philosophy No Remedy for Love" (Arne), 10
phonograph records, see recording industry
"Piccayune Butler," 135
Piccini, Niccolò, 63
"Picket Guard, The," 245
Pickett, Wilson, 451
Pictures at an Exhibition (Musorgsky), 496
"Picture That's Turned to the Wall, The" (Graham), 285

Pierce, Webb, 462
"Pilgrim's Address to the Diety, The" (Russell), 179n
Pink Floyd, 469
Pinocchio, 462
Pinto, Thomas, 5
pirata, Il (Bellini), 66, 67
"Pistol Packin' Mama" (Dexter), 389
Placide, Mrs., 20
"Plaisir d'amour," 415
"Plankxty Connor," 44n
"Plantation Melodies," 209, 211
"plantation" songs
   in minstrel repertory, 136–39, 260, 271
   of Stephen Foster, 209, 210–15
Platters, the, 407, 409, 412
Playford, John, 18
"Play with Fire" (Rolling Stones), 446
"Please Go 'Way and Let Me Sleep" (Von Tilzer), 310
"Please Mr. Postman," 419, 460
Please Please Me (Beatles), 420
"Please Please Me" (Beatles), 418, 420, 421
pleasure gardens, American, 20–23
pleasure gardens, English, 3–20
   song types of, 5–11
   see also Ranelagh Gardens; Vauxhall Gardens
Pleyel, Ignaz, 23
Pocohontas (Brougham), 242
Poe, Edgar Allen, 105
political songs
   in Civil War period, 149–61
   fewness of, during Depression years, 376–77
   in folk music, 433–39
   in rock music, 454–55
   see also social and political commentary
Polly (Gay), 17
"Poor Black Boy" (Storace), 110, 112, 115
"Poor Little Fool," 415
"Poor Mary" (Carr), 29
"Poor Richard" (Carr), 27
Poor Soldier, The (Shield), 19n
"Poor Tom Bowling" (Dibdin), 24
"Pop Goes the Weasel," 231
popular song
   allied to social dancing, 379–80
   American nature of, 23–25, 41, 89, 107–8, 157–60, 178–79, 234, 357–58, 372–75
   amplified instruments in, 448, 451, 469; see also electronics
   in Civil War, 228–52
   coexistent with rock 'n' roll, 414–15
   continuity of style in, 338–39
   crossovers of, with country-western, 469
   of the counterculture, 437–41
   definition of, xvii
   diverse styles of, in 1960s, 417
   diversity of, in the Beatles, 442–45
   early recordings of, 336–37
   English influence on, 20–23, 162; see also opera, English
   and films, 334–35, 343–45, 348
   in folk revival, 426–34
   influence of classical music on, 8–9, 14–16, 87–88, 98–100, 184, 194–95, 198–99, 294, 321–23, 341, 348–50, 366–68, 368–72
   Italian style of, 176–84; see also opera, Italian
   as means of social protest, 152–58, 435–38, 454; see also social and political commentary

and name singers, 387–88
origins of, in Negro music, 357–58
played by the big bands, 380–86
and solo singers in the 1970s, 467–69
style of, in the "Gay Nineties," 291–97
urbanization of, 377–79
urban themes in, 279–81, 377–78
in variety shows, 287
Porgy and Bess (Gershwin), 350
Porter, Cole, 327, 345, 352–53, 360, 361, 376, 378, 387, 388, 389, 392, 462, 466
Porter, James W., 137
Porter, W., 130
Portsmouth Weekly Magazine, 117
Poulton, George R., 139, 247
"Poverty's Tears Ebb and Flow" (Braham), 281n
Power, Tyrone, 173
Pownall, Mrs., 35
"Praise the Lord and Pass the Ammunition" (Loesser), 277
Prätendent, Der (Kücken), 198
Pratt, Charles E., 285
"President Monroe's March" (Granger), 95
Presley, Elvis, 248, 394, 395, 397–400, 398, 403, 404, 405, 406, 407, 410, 415, 416, 417, 419, 420, 421, 423, 428, 460, 465, 466, 467
Preston, Billy, 470
"Pretty Girl Is Like a Melody, A" (Berlin), 333, 360
"Pretty Peggy-O" (Dylan), 433
Price, Lloyd, 410
Price, Ray, 462
Primrose, George, 273
Primrose & West Minstrels, 299
"Primrose Girl, The" (Hewitt), 35
Princess Theatre (New York), 342–43
Princess Theatre (London), 173
Prize, The (Storace), 110
Proctor, Adelaide, 282
Prospect Garden Music Hall (New York), 290
Pryor, Arthur, 316, 346
Psallonian Society, 98
publishers, music
    Aitken, J., 37
    American Opera Publishing Company of Philadelphia, 81
    Atwill, 122
    Bacon, George, 166
    Benteen, F. D., 225, 226
    Billings, E. W., 242
    Blackmar, A. E., 249
    Blake, G. E., 45n, 72, 73, 100n
    Blake, W. P., 3n
    Bourne, 74
    Brainard, 250
    Brainard, S., 318
    Buckingham, J. T., 46
    Cady, C. M., 257
    Carey, M., 46
    Carr, B., 3n, 27, 59
    Carr, J., 3n, 27, 44
    Chapple Publishing Co., 46, 230
    Church, John, 232, 263, 264, 284
    Crocker & Brewster, 142n
    Daniels, Russell and Boone, 291
    Ditson, Oliver, 53, 78, 81, 82, 98n, 103n, 128, 133, 139n, 145, 147, 188n, 232, 236, 237, 239, 245, 267, 284, 286, 287, 300
    Dobson, J., 3n, 91
    Dunlap & Claypoole, 3n
    Dunn, Geo. & Co., 22n
    Faulds, D. P., 103n
    Feist, Leo, 285
    Fiot, Meignen & Co., 77
    Firth & Hall, 179n, 181, 188n
    Firth, Hall & Pond, 146
    Firth, Pond & Co., 209, 213, 219, 222, 225, 226, 232, 241, 245
    Geib, J. A. & W., 100n, 116n
    Gihon, J. H., 81
    Gilfert, G., 3n
    Gould, J. F., 232
    Hack & Anderson, 300
    Hagen, P. A. von, 3n, 60
    Hall, Wm. & Son, 234
    Harms, T. B., 285, 346
    Harris, Charles K., 285, 286, 289
    Hewitt, J., 3n, 44, 102, 124
    Higgins Brothers, 247
    Holt, C., Jr., 131, 207n
    Howley, Haviland and Dresser, 285
    Lee & Walker, 100, 103n, 259n, 284
    Lucas, P., 46
    Marks, Edward B., 289, 341, 342
    Meignen, L., 81
    Millet, W. F., 207n
    Mills, F. A., 314
    Paff, J. and M., 3n
    Perry, John F., 275
    Peters, J. L., 265
    Peters, W. C., 207n
    Planche, J. R., 81
    Pond, Wm. A. & Co., 103n, 258, 280, 281
    Power, J. and W. and Co., 44, 47, 49
    Reed, George P., 187, 188, 189, 190, 192
    Remick, Jerome H. & Co., 285, 346
    Rivington, James, 44
    Root & Cady, 232, 233, 236, 245, 284
    Russell & Richardson, 234
    Shapiro, Bernstein, 285, 309, 310, 327
    Shapiro, Bernstein, & Von Tilzer, 309, 311, 346
    Shaw, R., 3n
    Sherman, W. F., 232
    Snyder, Ted, 330, 332
    Stern, Joseph & Co., 285, 289
    Thomas, Isaiah, 3n
    Thomas and Andres, 3n
    Tolman, Henry & Co., 188n
    Von Tilzer, Harry, 285
    Ward, Charles B., 285
    Warner and Hanna, 44n
    Werlein, P. P., 249
    White, Smith & Petty, 267
    Willig, G., 3n, 100n, 103n, 284
    Wilson, A., 44n
    Witmark, M. & Sons, 285, 299, 313, 323
    Woodward, Willis & Co., 285, 288
publishing, sheet music, xx–xxi, 2–3
    centered in New York, 284–87, 389
    commercial success of, in "Gay Nineties," 290–91, 323–25
    decline in rock 'n' roll, 402
    during Civil War, 232–39
    of opera airs, 72–77, 82
    of pleasure garden songs, 11–12, 23

publishing, sheet music (*continued*)
  and recording sales, 336–37, 392–93
  of Southern firms, 245–48
  of Stephen Foster's songs, 225–27
  of Tin Pan Alley, 289–90, 312–13
"Puff, The Magic Dragon" (Peter, Paul, and Mary), 434
"Puppy Love," 413
Purcell, Henry, 8, 62, 90, 169, 349
puritani, I (Bellini), 82
Purse, The: or, The Benevolent Tar (Reeve), 23
"Put Me in My Little Bed" (White), 267
Putnam, J. S., 321
"Puttin' On the Ritz," 334
"Put Your Head on My Shoulder," 413

Quaker, The (Dibdin), 19n
"Qual cor tradisti," *see* "Little Nell"
Quarrymen the, *see* Beatles, the
"Quick One While He's Away, A" (Who), 450
Quicksilver Messenger Service, 440, 456
Quincy, Edmund, 149

Radicati, 63
radio and popular song, xxi, 337, 339, 383–84, 397–99, 406
"Rael" (Who), 450
"Ragging the Traumerei" (Gershwin), 346
ragtime, 316–21
  in Irving Berlin songs, 330–33
Rag Time Instructor (Harney), 318
"Rag-Time March" (Howard), 318
"Ragtime Violin" (Berlin), 330
Rainer Family, 142
"Rainy Day Women #12 & 35" (Dylan), 448
Randall, James Ryder, 247
Ranelagh Gardens (London), 5, 13, 20, 92
Ranelagh Gardens (New York), 20, 21
Ravel, Maurice, 349, 368, 369
Raynor, J. W., 136
Rays, the, 414
"Razzle Dazzle" (Haley), 394
RCA-Victor Records, 393, 394, 402, 415, 426, 440, 457
"Reach Out, I'll Be There" (Four Tops), 462
recording industry, xxi–xxii
  and advent of long-playing records, 418n
  best sellers of, in 1950s, 392–93, 402, 428–30
  crossover sales in, 406–12
  early commercial success in, 336–37
  and folk-music albums, 428–31
  and rock albums, 440–41, 444–45, 455–58
  and rock 'n' roll, 404–8, 412–13, 418–23
  and sales of Beatles albums, 421–22
  top LP sellers, by category, 463–64
Redding, Otis, 445, 458
Reddy, Helen, 468
Redman, Don, 382
Red Mill, The (Herbert), 323
Red Petticoat, The (Kern), 341
"Red, Red Rose, A" (Burns), 61
Reed, Jimmy, 439
Reeve, William, 19n, 94, 100, 111, 283
Reeves, Jim, 462
Reichardt, A., 199
Reinagle, Alexander, 2, 22, 36–38, 36, 39

Reinhold, Frederick Charles, 4
Revolver (Beatles), 443
Rexford, Eben, 255
Rey, Alvino, 389
Reynolds, Debbie, 414
Reynolds, Marjorie, 335
Rhapsody in Blue (Gershwin), 350
"Rhinestone Cowboy" (Campbell), 469
rhythm-and-blues, 406
  in music of Fats Domino, 408–9
  origins of, in South, 458
  songs performed by the Beatles, 419
  top hits of, in *Billboard*, 406
Rice, Seymour, 291
Rice, Thomas Dartmouth ("Daddy"), 118–23, 119, 126, 134, 206, 209
  success of, in "Jim Crow," 119–21
Richard, Keith, 450
Richard III (Shakespeare), 114, 126
Richings English Opera Company, 72
Richmond, Jack, 383
Richmond Hill Theatre (New York), 67
Ricky Dee's Cast of Idiots, 472
Riddle, Nelson, 414, 462
"Riders in the Sky" (Jones), 389
"Riding a Raid," 250n
Rifle, The, 126
Rigoletto (Verdi), 87, 88
Rinaldo, 62
"Ring de Banjo" (Foster), 212
rivali di se stessi, I (Balfe), 84
Riviera Girl, The (Kern), 342
Rivington's New York Gazette, 2n
Robbins, Marty, 460
Roberta (Kern), 343, 359
Roberts, Lucky, 353
Robin Hood (De Koven), 322
Robin Hood (Shield), 37
Robinson, Smokey, 419, 420, 460, 461, 462
Rochester Academy of Music, 178, 179
"R.O.C.K." (Haley), 394
"Rock a Beatin' Boogie" (Haley), 394
"Rock and Roll Music," 419
"Rock Around the Clock" (Haley), 391, 394, 406, 407
rock music
  in bands of the '70s, 469–70
  influence of, on folk music, 448
  popularity of, in 1960s 463–64
  in the protest movements, 453–55
  roots of, in rock 'n' roll, 439–41
  style of, in bands, 441–42
rock 'n' roll
  in British rock groups, 423
  coexistence of, with popular songs, 414–15
  controversy over, 397–402
  and decline in sheet music sales, 402
  decline of, 416
  earliest hits of, 394
  interracial nature of, 394, 400, 406–8
  and oral tradition, 403–4
  recording sales of, 404–6
  in songs of the Beatles, 419–23
  structure of songs of, 396
  sung by name white singers, 411
Rodeo, 469
Rodgers, Jimmie, 428

Rodgers, Richard, 327, 345, 353–55, 360, 361, 367, 368, 370, 372, 387, 388, 392, 462
Rogers, Ginger, 334, 343
Rogers, N. P., 150
Rokeby Castle (Reeve), 150
Rolling Stone Magazine, 474
Rolling Stones, the, 423, 445–47, 446, 450, 454, 456, 457, 458, 466
"Roll Over Beethoven" (Berry), 394, 419
Romberg, Sigmund, 369
Romeo (Bellini), 82
Romeo and Juliet, 220
Ronstadt, Linda, 469, 472
"Roof Scrambler, The," *see sonnambula, La*
Root, George F., 139, 230, 232–34, 236, 247n
"Rory O'More" (Lover), 173, 175, 176
Rory O'More, a National Romance (Lover), 173
Rosalie, 347
"Rosalie, the Prairie Flower" (Root), 234
"Rosary, The" (Nevin), 323
Rose, Billy, 375, 376
Rose, Vincent, 360, 381
Rosenfeld, Monroe H., 286, 327
"Rose of No Man's Land, The" (Brennan-Caddington), 376
"Roses Are Red" (Vinton), 435
Rosich, Paolo, 64
Rosina (Shield), 19n
Ross, Diana, 460, 461, 462
Ross, Lanny, 337
Rossini, Giacomo, 63, 65, 66, 67, 69–74, 87, 88, 105, 134, 142, 178, 184, 189, 222, 372
    popularity of, in America, 64–68
    publication of his operas in America, 72
Roth, Murray, 346
"Round the Wreaken" (Shaw), 98
Rowson, Mrs., 29
Royal Academy of Music (London), 281
Royal American Magazine, The (Boston), 1
Rubber Soul (Beatles), 442–43
Rubens, Paul, 379
"Ruby" (Gabriel), 283
"Ruby Tuesday" (Rolling Stones), 446
"Rudolph, the Red-Nosed Reindeer," 404
"Rum and Coca-Cola" (Sullavan), 389
Rumours (Fleetwood Mac), 446
Running for Office, 313
Russell, Henry, 76, 106, 128, 137, 144, 147, 154, 158, 161, 172, 176n, 177, 177–84
    emigration of, to America, 178
    ethnic mixture of, 177, 184
    musical style of, 180–84
    popularity of, in America, 179–83
    and Stephen Foster, 219, 220, 225, 327
Russell, Lillian, 287
Russell, Luis, 382
"Russian Rose" (Charles-Miller), 369
Rydell, Bobby, 414
Ryskind, Morrie, 335

Sable Brothers, 132
Sable Harmonists, 207
Sable Minstrels, 132
Sable Serenaders, 132
Sable Sisters and Ethiopian Minstrels, 132
Sacchini, Antonio, 63

Sacred Melodies (Moore), 215
Sacred Melodies (Shaw), 99
Sacred Music Society of New York City, 189
Sacred Songs (Moore), 48
"Sadly to Mine Heart Appealing" (Foster), 223
"Saint Louis Blues" (Handy), 381
Saint Louis Woman, 355
Saint Paul (Mendelssohn), 189
"Saints' Rock and Roll" (Haley), 394
Sally (Kern), 342
Salvioni, Carlo, 67
San Francisco Chronicle, 439
Sängerfest (Cincinnati), 190
Sans Souci Theatre, 110
Sargent Kenny, 383
"Satisfaction," *see* "(I Can't Get No) Satisfaction"
Saturday Night Fever, 472, 474
"Save the Life of the Child" (Simon and Garfunkel), 448
"Savourna Deilish," 44n
Sawyer, Charles Carroll, 240
Sawyer, Jacob J., 321
"Say, Brothers, Will You Meet Us?," 236
"Say It With Music" (Berlin), 334, 337
Sayles, James N., 258
"Scenes That Are the Brightest" (Wallace), 87
Schoenberg, Arnold, 294, 350, 372
Schonberger, John and Malvin, 382
schöne Müllerin, Die (Schubert), 194
Schoolcraft, Luke, 135
"School Days," 414
Schubert, Adrian, 381
Schubert, Franz, 160, 187, 192, 193, 194, 199, 200, 222, 245, 294, 369, 372, 415
Schubert Brothers, 328
Schultze, Wilhelm H., 191
Schumann, Robert, 189, 190, 191, 195, 198, 321
Schwanengesang (Schubert), 194
Schwartz, Arthur, 357
Scotch songs, 59–61
Scots Musical Museum, 60, 61
"Scots What Hae wi' Wallace Bled" (Burns), 61
Scott, Sir Walter, 169
"Scottish snap," 10, 60, 112, 305
"Scottish" style, 9–10, 14–15, 59–61, 112, 134, 304
    in songs of Arne, 9, 10
Scouts, The; or, The Plains of Manassas, 244
Searchers, the, 423
"Searchin'," 414
Second Collection of Songs, A (Hook), 15
Second Fiddle, 334
Second Rhapsody (Gershwin), 350
"Secret Love" (Fain), 413
"Secret Love" (Webster), 392
Sedaka, Neil, 417, 435
Seeger, Pete, 427, 431, 435, 437, 455
"See That My Grave Is Kept Clean" (Dylan), 433
"See You Later Alligator" (Haley), 394
Seguin, Mr. and Mrs., 84
Selby, William, 94
Seldes, Gilbert, 351
Select Airs from the celebrated Operas composed by Mozart, 72
Selection from the Vocal Compositions of Mozart, A, 72
Selection of the Most Favorite Scots Tunes (Reinagle), 36
Selvin, Ben, 336, 351, 381

Selvin's Novelty Orchestra, 336
Selznick, David, 328
"Send in the Clowns" (Sondheim), 474
Sentz, 191
"Serenade" (Schubert), 194, 222
serva padrona, La (Pergolesi), 5
Session with Dave Clark Five, 423
Seven Songs for the Harpsichord, 2, 89, 91
Sgt. Pepper's Lonely Hearts Club Band (Beatles), 443, 445, 446
Shadows on the Wall (John H. Hewitt), 108, 183
"Shake, Rattle, and Roll" (Haley), 394, 402, 411
Shall We Dance?, 348
Shankar, Ravi, 454
Shaw, Artie, 383, 384, 386
Shaw, Oliver, 96–100
"Sh-Boom," 411
sheet music publishing, see publishing, sheet music
"Sheik of Araby, The," 381
"She Loves You" (Beatles), 418, 420, 421
Shenton, James P., 228
Sheridan, Tony and the Beat Brothers, see Beatles, the
"She's Leaving Home" (McCartney), 443, 445
"She Sung of Love" (Moore), 54
"She Went to the City" (Dresser), 306
Shields, Ren, 291
Shield, William, 19n, 37, 50, 51, 63, 94, 95, 97, 103, 283
Shilkret, Nathan, 381
"Shine On," 135
"Ship on Fire, The" (Russell), 145, 179n
Shirelles, the, 417, 419
"Shop Around," 460
Shore, Dinah, 387
Short Brothers, 411
Show Boat (Kern), 343, 344, 429
Show Girl, 347
"Shuffle Off to Buffalo" (Warren), 357
"Sich a Getting Up Stairs," 119
"Sidewalks of New York, The" (Lawlor-Blake), 285, 291, 296, 325
Siege of Belgrade, The, 165
Siege of Rochelle, The (Balfe), 84
"Sigh No More, Ladies," 20
"Silhouettes," 414
Silver Beatles, see Beatles, the
"Silver Moon, The" (Hook), 14
Silvers, Louis, 360
"Silver Threads Among the Gold" (Danks), 255, 264
Simon, Carly, 468
Simon, Paul, 448, 449, 456, 466
Sinatra, Frank, 384, 385, 386, 387, 414, 433, 434, 456, 457, 458, 466
"Since I Lost My Baby" (Temptations), 462
"Since Then I'm Doom'd" (Dibdin), 25
Sinclair, John, 170
Sissle, Noble, 360, 374
Sister Carrie (Dreiser), 306
Sitting Pretty (Kern), 342
"Sixteen Tons," 404, 411
"Skidmore Guard, The" (Braham), 281n
Slick, Grace, 440
"Slip-Sliding Away" (Simon), 466
Smash Hits (Hendrix), 451
Smith, J. C., 90
Smith, "Whispering Jack," 337

"Smoke Gets In Your Eyes" (Kern), 343, 359, 360, 361, 362, 369, 410
"Snow Storm, The" (Heath), 145
Snyder, Ted, 381
social and political commentary, in popular song, 35, 116–18, 137, 140–41, 147–54, 156–57, 161, 230, 234–44, 256, 397–401, 435–37, 439–40
Social Choir, The, 142
Social Orchestra, The (Foster), 82, 205, 219, 222
Soldier Boy's Songster, The, 231
"Soldier's Adieu, The" (Dibdin), 24
"Soldier's Farewell, The" (John H. Hewitt), 105, 244
"Soldier Tir'd, The" (Arne), 37
"Somebody Loves Me" (Gershwin), 347
"Somebody's Darling" (John H. Hewitt), 244
"Somebody to Love" (Jefferson Airplane), 440
"Someday We'll Be Together Again" (Supremes), 462
"Some Enchanted Evening" (Rodgers), 355
"Someone to Watch Over Me" (Gershwin), 348
"Something Happened to Me" (Rolling Stones), 447
"Something to Remember You By" (Schwartz), 357
Sondheim, Stephen, 354, 473–74
"Song from Moulin Rouge" (Auric), 392
"Song Is You, The" (Kern), 343
"Song of Love" (Romberg), 369
"Song of Sorrow," 52
"Song of the Shirt" (Hood), 150, 155, 160
songsters, 1, 2
    in Civil War, 231
    early American, 1–3
Songs That Never Die, 46
"Song to the Evening Star" (R. Wagner), 87
sonnambula, La (Bellini), 72, 74, 132
    American popularity of, 74–78
    arrangements of, 77–78
    as dance music, 77
    parodies of, 77–78
Sons of Erin; or, Modern Sentiment, 43
"Soon" (Gershwin), 348
"Soon" (Rodgers), 355
Sound of Music, The (Rodgers), 462
Sounds of Silence (Simon and Garfunkel), 448
Sousa, John Philip, 313
South Carolina Gazette, 20
Southern Singers, 132
South Pacific (Rodgers), 354, 429
Spanish Barber, The (Arnold), 29
Spanish Patriots, The, 101
Specht, Paul, 337
Spectator, The (London), 62
Spiller, 70
"Spirit of My Song, The" (Foster), 216
Spirit of the Times, 77
Spirituals, Negro, 261, 271–73
Spofforth, Reginald, 35
Spohr, Louis, 189, 191, 195
Sprague's Georgia Minstrels, 274, 275
Spring Gardens (England), 3
Springsteen, Bruce, 468
Stafford, Jo, 338, 384, 387, 405, 411
"Stagger Lee," 410
Stamitz, Karl, 50
"Standing in the Shadows of Love" (Four Tops), 462
Staple Singers, 455, 466
"Stardust" (Carmichael), 357

"Star of the Evening" (Tucker), 258
Starr, Ringo, 419, 420, 423
"Star-Spangled Banner, The," 190
State Fair, 355
"Stayin' Alive" (Bee Gees), 472
"Stay, Summer Breath" (Foster), 205
Steele, Silas S., 134, 135
"Steersman's Song, The" (Gilfert), 102
Steffe, William, 230, 236
Stein, Charles, 191
Steppenwolf, 456
Sterling, Andrew B., 291
Stern, Joseph, 285, 289
Stevenson, B. S., 282
Stevenson, Miss, 4
Stevenson, Sir John, 44, 47, 48
Stoddard, George, 336
Stoller, Mike, 417
Stone, Lucy, 154
Stonewall Jackson Song Book, The, 231
"Stonewall Jackson's Way" (Palmer), 231
"Stood Up," 415
"Stop! In the Name of Love" (Supremes), 462
Stop! Look! Listen! (Berlin), 332
"Stop That Knocking" (Winnemore), 132
"Stop That Rag" (Berlin), 330
Storace, Stephen (Stefano), 5, 19n, 63, 110, 112, 165
"Stormy Weather" (Arlen), 355
"Story of the Wedding March, The" (Cohan), 313
Strakosch, Maurice, 191
Stranger, The (Sheridan), 37
"Stranger in Paradise," 392
straniera, La (Bellini), 67, 82
Strauss, Johann II, 294, 323
Strauss, Richard, 294
Stravinsky, Igor, 372
"Streamlet, The" (Shield), 37
"Street Fighting Man" (Rolling Stones), 447
"Streets of New York, The" (Herbert), 323
Streisand, Barbra, 457, 472, 473
Strike Up the Band, 347
Student Prince, The, 429
Stylistics, the, 472
Styne, Jule, 387
"Subterranean Homesick Blues" (Dylan), 448
Sullavan, Jeri, 389
Sullivan, Arthur, 281-83
Sullivan, Ed, 422, 428
Sullivan, Thomas D., 231
Sully, Miss, 20
Summer, Donna, 472
"Sunbeam of Summer," 82
"Sunny" (Kern), 343
Sunny, 343
Sun Records, 394, 402, 403, 415
Sunshine Girl, The (Rubens), 379
Supremes, the, 460, 461, 462
Supremes Sing Rodgers and Hart, 462
"Sure to Fall in Love With You," 419
"Surfin' " (Beach Boys), 435
"Surfin' Safari" (Beach Boys), 435
"Surfin' U.S.A." (Beach Boys), 435
Surrealistic Pillow (Jefferson Airplane), 440
"Susan Jane" (Hays), 269
Sutcliffe, Stu, 419
"Swanee" (Gershwin), 346, 348

Sweatman, Wilbur, 380
Sweeney, J. W., 118, 125
"Sweet Adeline" (Armstrong), 291, 294, 324, 325
"Sweet Betsy from Pike," 426
"Sweet Echo" (Arne), 23
"Sweet Genevieve" (Tucker), 258, 259
"Sweet Georgia Brown" (Bernie), 373-74
"Sweet Is the Vale" (Cavendish), 37n
"Sweet Lillies of the Valley" (Hook), 23
"Sweet Little Sixteen," 407
"Sweetly She Sleeps, My Alice Fair" (Foster), 216
"Sweet Rosie O'Grady" (Nugent), 285, 291, 296
"Swing Low, Sweet Chariot," 454
Swing Time (Kern), 343
" 'S Wonderful" (Gershwin), 348, 375, 392
"Sympathy for the Devil" (Rolling Stones), 446

"Take Back the Heart" (Claribel), 185
"Take Good Care of My Baby" (Vee), 435
"Take It to the Limit" (Eagles), 467
"Take Me Out to the Ball Game" (A. Von Tilzer), 325
Talking Union, 428
Tammany, or, The Indian Chief (Hewitt), 32
"Tammy," 414
Tancredi (Rossini), 63, 66, 72
Tangerine Dream, 469
"Tannenbaum, O Tannenbaum," 247
Tannhaüser (R. Wagner), 87, 191, 199
"Tantivy Hark Forward Huzza" (Reinagle), 37
Tapestry (C. King), 468, 474
Taunt, James F., 212
Taylor, James, 463, 468
Taylor, Raynor, 36, 39 41
Tchaikovsky, Peter Ilyich, 351, 368, 369
"Tea for Two" (Youmans), 357, 360, 375, 392
"Tear, The" (Hook), 16, 37
"Tears of a Clown, The" (Miracles), 462
"Tell Me, My Heart" (Bishop), 171-72
Templeton, Fay, 315
Temptations, the, 460
"Tenderly" (Gross), 392
"Tennessee Waltz," 404, 411
Ten Nights in a Barroom, 256
Tennille, 468
"Tenting on the Old Camp Ground" (Kittredge),
    236-37
Thalberg, Sigismond, 187
"Thank God I'm a Country Boy" (Denver), 469
Thatcher, Primrose and West Minstrels, 305
"That Doggie In the Window" (Merrill), 389
"That'll Be the Day," 407
"That Mesmerizing Mendelssohn Tune" (Berlin), 330,
    346
"That Old Black Magic" (Arlen), 356, 360, 392
"That Old Feeling" (Fain), 413
"That's All Right" (Presley), 403
"That's a-Plenty" (Williams), 382
"That's When Your Heartache Begins," 415
Theatre Comique (New York), 279
Theatre Royal (Dublin), 164, 173
Their Satanic Majesties Request (Rolling Stones), 446
"Then You'll Remember Me" (Balfe), 85, 86, 247n
"There Is a Fountain Filled with Blood," 231
"There Lived in Altdorf City Fair" (Carr), 29
"There's No Business Like Show Business" (Berlin),
    336, 392

"There's Nothing True But Heaven" (Shaw), 98
"These Foolish Things Remind Me of You" (Strachey), 385
"They Can't Take That Away from Me" (Gershwin), 348
"They're Either Too Young or Too Old" (Schwartz), 357
"They Say It's Wonderful" (Berlin), 336
"They Told Me to Shun Him" (John H. Hewitt), 105
"They Wouldn't Believe Me" (Kern), 341
"Thing, The" (Grean), 389
"This Can't Be Love" (Rodgers), 355
This Is the Army (Berlin), 335
"Tho' Love is Warm Awhile" (Braham), 164
Thomas, Rufus, 403
Thomas and Sally (Arne), 19n, 23
Thompson, George, 153
Thompson, H. S., 139, 251
Thomson, Virgil, 339
Thornton, James, 291
Thornton, Willie Mae ("Big Mama"), 408
"Tho 'Tis but a Dream" (Bishop), 170
"Thou Art Gone from My Gaze," 132
"Thou Dear Seducer of my Heart," 44
"Three Cool Cats," 419
Tibbles, George, 388
Tierney, Harry, 368
" 'Til I Kissed You," 415
"Till I Waltz Again with You," 392
" 'Til the Clouds Roll By" (Kern), 360
" 'Til the End of Time," 369
" 'Til We Meet Again" (Whiting-Egan), 371
"Time Is on My Side" (Rolling Stones), 423
Times They Are a-Changin', The, 433
Tin Pan Alley
    earliest publishers of, 285–90
    origin of name of, 285–86
    second generation of composers in, 326–79
    third generation of composers in, 383–90
Tin Pan Alley songs
    harmonic styles in, 361–71
    lyricists of, 376
    played by big bands, 385–87
    rhythmic style in, 372–74
    standardization of form in, 358–61
Tiomkin, Dmitri, 412
Tip Toes, 347
" 'Tis the Last Rose of Summer," 46, 56, 76, 205, 247n
Tobias, Charles, 377
"Tom-Big-Bee River," 134, 135
"Tom Dooley" (Kingston Trio), 430
Tommy (Who), 450
"Tomorrow Never Knows" (Lennon), 443
"Tonight We Love," 369
Tony Pastor's Opera House, 287–88, 290, 300, 305, 318
"Too Many Miles from Broadway" (Cohan), 313
"Toot, Toot, Tootsie," 334
Top Hat, 334
"Top Hat, White Tie and Tails" (Berlin), 334
Tosca (Puccini), 368
"Tossin' and Turnin'," 417
"To the Evening Star" (R. Wagner), 199
"To the Moon" (Gilfert), 100
"Touch of Your Hand, The" (Kern), 343
Town Hall (New York), 426, 433

Townshend, Peter, 448, 449, 450
"Town Where I Was Born, The" (Dresser), 306
"Tracks of My Tears, The" (Miracles), 462
"Tramp, Tramp, Tramp" (Root), 232, 233
"Travellin' Man," 417
traviata, La (Verdi), 87
Travis, Merle, 411
Treasure Girl, 347
"Treasury Rats" (anon.), 231
Tree, M., 166
Trent, Alphonso, 382
Trevathan, Charles E., 321
Trial by Jury (Gilbert and Sullivan), 281
Tribe of Asa, The, 155
    see also Hutchinson Family
Trip to Chinatown, A, 299
trovatore, Il (Verdi), 87
"True Love" (Porter), 353
"True Love Can Ne'er Forget" (Lover), 176
Tryon, George W., 81
Tubular Bells (Oldfield), 469
Tucker, Henry, 240, 252, 258–59
Tucker, Sophie, 328
"Tuck Me to Sleep in My Old 'Tucky Home" (Meyer), 334
turco in Italia, Il (Rossini), 63, 66
"Turkey in the Straw," 124
Turner, Joe, 411
"Turn! Turn! Turn!" (Seeger), 436
Turpin, Thomas, 318
"Tutti-Frutti" (Little Richard), 394, 402, 412
"Tweedle Dee," 412
"Twilight Time," 410
"Twinkling Stars Are Laughing, Love," 133
"Twist, The," 416
"Twist and Shout" (Beatles), 418, 419
"Two Doors Down" (Parton), 469
"Two Hound Dogs" (Haley), 394
"Two Sleepy People" (Carmichael), 357
Tyrolean Lyre: a Glee Book, The, 82
Tyrolean Minstrels, see Rainer Family

"Una voce poco fa" (Rossini), 74
"Uncle Gabriel," 128
"Uncle Ned" (Foster), 109, 207
Uncle Tom's Cabin, 140, 215
"Under the Bamboo Tree" (Cole), 321
"Under the Eaves" (Winner), 262
"Unhappy Contraband, The" (Hays), 265
United States Ethiopian Minstrels of Brooklyn, 132
"Unknown Dead, The," 244
Up and Down Broadway, 332

"Vacant Chair" (Root), 232, 247n
Valli, June, 411
Van Alstyne, Egbert, 291
Vanguard Records, 431, 441, 457
Van Vechten, Carl, 350
Varèse, Edgard, 372
Variety Magazine, 355, 376, 388, 392, 401, 402
vaudeville, 277–81, 287–91, 299
Vaughn, Tom, 130
Vaux Hall Gardens (Charleston), 20
Vauxhall Gardens (London), 4, 5, 10, 11, 12, 13, 20, 90, 92, 205

Vauxhall Gardens (New York), 21, 114
Vauxhall Gardens (Philadelphia), 40
Vee, Bobby, 435
Vee Jay Records, 412
"Venus," 414
Verdi, Giuseppe, 87
Vernon, Joseph, 11, 13
verse-chorus form, 210, 223–24, 248, 254–56, 260, 267, 272, 291–93, 306, 316, 321, 358–61
Very Good, Eddie (Kern), 342
Very Warm for May (Kern), 343
Victoria, Vesta, 287
"Village Maiden, The" (Foster), 205
Vincent, Mrs., 4, 5
Vinci, 90
Vinton, Bobby, 435
"Virgin Goddess," *see* "Casta diva"
"Virginia Girl, The," 132
Virginia Harmonists, the, 132
Virginia Minstrels, the, 126–28, 130, 131, 132
"Virginia Rose Bud, The," 133, 134
Virginia Serenaders, the, 132
Virgin of the Sun, The, 101
Vivandiere; or the Daughter of the Regiment, see Fille du régiment, La
Vodery, Will, 350
"Voice of By-Gone Days, The," 219–20
"Voices of Old People" (Simon and Garfunkel), 448
"Voices That Are Gone, The" (Foster), 198
"Volga Boat Song," 369
"Volunteer, The; or, It Is My Country's Call," 243
Von Ronk, Dave, 433
Von Tilzer, Harry, 285, 289, 291, 308–11, 330, 372
"Vulture of the Alps, The," 145

Wagner, Richard, 87, 191, 199, 294
Wags, or the Camp of Pleasure, The (Dibdin), 110
Wainwright, Miss, 20
"Wait For the Wagon" (Buckley), 251
"Waiting for the Robert E. Lee" (Muir), 321
"Wait Till the Clouds Roll By" (Pratt), 285
"Wait 'Til the Sun Shines, Nellie," 291, 294
"Wake Nicodemus" (Work), 232, 255
"Wake Up Little Susie," 407, 410
Wallace, William Vincent, 87
waltzes
  in early Tin Pan Alley songs, 379–81
  in German songs, 198–99
  popularity of, in "Gay Nineties," 294
"Wanderer, The" (Schubert), 194n
Ward, Charles B., 285
Ward, Helen, 384, 385
Warden, David A., 245
Warner Brothers, 328
Warner Brothers Records, 441, 453
Warren, Harry, 327, 345, 356–57, 387, 389
War Songs for Freedom, 231
Washington, Booker T., 301
Watch Your Step (Berlin), 332, 379
Waters, Ethel, 335, 355
Waters, Muddy, 445
"Way Down in Ca-i-ro" (Foster), 212
"Wayfarin' Stranger, The" (Ives), 426
"Way We Were, The," 472
"Way Worn Traveller, The" (Dibdin), 25

"Way You Look Tonight, The" (Kern), 343
"We Are All Washingtonians," 147
"We Are Coming, Father Abra'am" (Emerson), 239, 249
"Wearing of the Green, The," 249
"Wearing of the Grey!," 249
"Weary Lot is Thine Fair Maid, A" (Gilfert), 100
Weavers, the, 428, 430, 431
Webb, Clifton, 335
Webb, George, 98, 159
Weber, Carl Maria von, 102, 187, 189, 195, 204
Weber and Fields, 287
Webern, Anton, 372
Webster, Daniel, 146
Webster, Joseph Philbrick, 247
Webster, Reverend H. D. L., 247
"We Did It Before and We Can Do It Again" (Friend), 377
Weems, Ted, 387
"Weep for Jamie" (Peter, Paul, and Mary), 448
"Weeping, Sad and Lonely; or, When This Cruel War is Over" (Tucker), 240, 247n, 252, 258
"Wegweiser, Der" (Schubert), 193
Weichsell, Mrs., 13
Welk, Lawrence, 417, 456, 457, 458
Wells, Mary, 460
"Wenn die Schwalben heimwärts zieh'n," *see* "When the Swallows Homeward Fly"
"We Parted by the River Side" (Hays), 265
"We're Coming, Sister Mary" (Work), 236
Wesley, Charles, 27
Westendorf, Thomas Paine, 262–64
Wetzel, Karl Friedrich Gottlob, 194
"Whatever Will Be, Will Be," 414
"What Is Home Without a Mother" (Winner), 259
  parody versions of, 259–60
"What Is This Thing Called Love?" (Porter), 353
"What'll I Do?" (Berlin), 333, 334, 336, 340
"What Must a Fairy's Dream Be?" (Foster), 205
"Whatshername" (Peter, Paul, and Mary), 448
"What Will You Do, Love?" (Lover), 176
"When E'er I See Those Smiling Eyes" (Gilfert), 102
"When I Lost You" (Berlin), 333
"When I'm Sixty-Four" (McCartney), 444
"When Irish Eyes Are Smiling" (Ball), 323, 325
"When It's Night Time in Dixieland" (Berlin), 340
"When Johnny Comes Marching Home," 250
"When My Dreams Come True" (Berlin), 334
"When Nights Were Cold" (Carr), 29
"When Pensive I Thought" (Dibdin), 25
"When the Robins Nest Again" (Howard), 285
"When the Saints Go Marching In," 419
"When the Sun Has Set" (Harris), 285
"When the Swallows Homeward Fly" (Abt), 197, 222, 247n
"When You and I Were Young, Maggie" (Butterfield), 283
"When You Want 'Em, You Can't Get 'Em, When You Got 'Em, You Don't Want 'Em" (Gershwin), 346
"When You Were Sweet Sixteen" (Thornton), 291, 294
"When You Wish Upon a Star" (Harline), 462
"Where Are Now the Hopes I Cherished," 78
"Where Are You Going, Abe Lincoln," 250n
"Wherefore" (Winner), 261

"Where Is the Song of Songs for Me?" (Berlin), 333
"Where Is the Spot That We Were Born On?," 132
"Where, Oh Where Has My Little Dog Gone?" (Winner), 262
"Where the Morning Glories Twine" (Von Tilzer), 310
"Where the Sweet Magnolia Grows" (John H. Hewitt), 139
"While the Dance Goes On" (Harris), 300
"Whispering" (Schonberger), 336, 382
"Whispering Hope" (Winner), 262
White, Charles, 128
White, Charles A., 265, 267–72, 282, 283
   minstrel songs of, 269
   minstrel-spirituals of, 272–73
White, George, 272
"White Christmas" (Berlin), 334, 337, 355, 360, 392, 404
Whiteman, Paul, 336, 337, 350, 351, 368, 379, 381, 384
"White Rabbit" (Jefferson Airplane), 440
White's Serenaders, 137
"White Wings" (Winter), 285, 305
Whitlock, William M. (Billy), 125, 126–28, 132
Whitman, Walt, 69, 253
"Who?" (Kern), 343
Who, the, 448–50, 454, 456, 458
"Whole Lotta Loving," 409
"Whole Lotta Shakin' Going On" (Lewis), 394, 407, 414
"Who Will Care for Mother Now?" (Sawyer), 240
"Why," 414
"Why Can't We Live Together" (Thomas), 472
"Why Did Nellie Leave Home?" (Cohan), 313
"Why Do I Love You?" (Kern), 343
"Why, Huntress, Why" (Carr), 29
"Wichita Lineman" (Campbell), 469
"Wide Wings" (Dresser), 305
"Widow in the Cottage by the Sea Side, The" (White), 267
Wignell, Thomas, 22, 37
Wilder, Alec, 355, 357, 462
Wilder, Frank, 251
Williams, Andy, 457
Williams, Bert, 268, 382
Williams, Hank, 411, 419
Williams, Harry H., 291
Williamson, Mr., 29
Wiiliamson, Sonny Boy, 403
"Willie My Brave" (Foster), 205
"Willie, We Have Missed You" (Foster), 217
"Will You Love Me in December as You Do in May?" (Ball), 323
"Will You Love Me Tomorrow?" (Shirelles), 417
Wilson, Brian, 435
Wilson, Dennis and Carl, 435
Wilson, Jackie, 410
"Wilt Thou Be Gone, Love?" (Foster), 220–21
"Wilt Thou Think of Me?" (John H. Hewitt), 105, 106
"Wind of the Winter's Night, Whence Comest Thou?" (Russell), 178–79
Winnemore, A. F., 132, 134
Winner, Septimus, 139, 248–49, 259, 259–62
Winter, Banks, 305
Winter Garden (Chicago), 279
Winter Garden (New York), 290, 346
Winterreise (Schubert), 193

"Winter's Evening, A" (Jackson), 39
"Winter Wonderland" (Bernard), 392
"Wish, The" (Hewitt), 23
Wit and Mirth: or Pills to Purge Melancholy, 18
"With a Song in My Heart" (Rodgers), 355, 429, 462
"Within a Mile of Edinburgh Town" (Hook), 23, 59
"Within You, Without You" (McCartney), 443
"Without a Song" (Youmans), 357, 462
"With Pleasure I Have Past My Days" (Hopkinson), 91
With the Beatles, 420
Witmark, Julius, 299
Wizard of Oz, The, 356
Wodehouse, P. G., 342, 348
Wolf, Hugo, 199
Wonder, Stevie, 460, 462, 466, 471
"Wonderland by Night," 417
"Won't You Tell Me Why, Robin" (Claribel), 185
Wood, J. T. (pseud.), see Pratt, Charles E.
Wood, Mrs. (Mary Ann Paton), 71, 74
Wood, Mrs. John, 242
Woodbury, Isaac B., 82
Woodman, The (Shield), 19n
"Woodman, Spare That Tree" (Russell), 106, 181–82
Woodstock (New York) Festival, 454, 474
Woodward, Willis, 308
"Woody Woodpecker" (Tibbles), 388
Woollcott, Alexander, 351
Wools, Mr., 20, 21
"Words of Love," 419
Worgan, J., 90
Work, Henry Clay, 230, 231, 232, 236, 250, 255–58, 300
"Work With Me, Annie," 411
"Wounded Hussar, The" (Hewitt), 32–35, 41, 102
"Wreath You Wove, The," 102
Wright, Edythe, 384
Wrighton, Mrs., 13
Wrighton, W. T., 247n
"Write Me a Letter from Home" (Hays), 265, 266
"Wunderbar" (Porter), 353
Wurzel, G. Friederich (pseud.), see Root, George F.
Wynn, Ed, 330

"Yakity-Yak," 140
"Yankee Doodle" (Carr), 28, 231
"Yankee Doodle Boy, The" (Cohan), 314
Yankee Doodle Dandy, 316
"Yanko Dear" (Dibdin), 111
"Ye Faded Flowers" (Schubert), 194
"Yellow Submarine" (Beatles), 443
Yerke's Novelty Five, 346
"Yesterday" (Beatles), 443, 446
"Yesterday" (Kern), 343, 359
"Yes, We Have No Bananas," 368
"Yiddle on Your Fiddle, Play Some Ragtime" (Berlin), 230
Yip, Yip, Yaphank (Berlin), 333, 335
"You and the Night and the Music" (Schwartz), 357
"You Are My Sunshine" (Davis), 389
"You Belong to Me" (Herbert), 338
"You Couldn't Be Cuter" (Kern), 344
"You'd Be Surprised" (Berlin), 336, 337
"You'd Be So Nice to Come Home To" (Porter), 353
"You'll Never Know" (Warren), 357, 387
"You Make Me Feel Brand New" (Stylistics), 472
Youmans, Vincent, 357, 360, 375, 388, 392, 462

Young, Charles, 4
Young, Victor, 315
Young Folk's Glee Book, The, 82
"Young Love," 414
"Young Nun" (Schubert), 194
"Young Volunteer, The," 244
"Your Cheatin' Heart," 411
"You're a Grand Old Flag" (Cohan), 315, 317
"You Really Got a Hold on Me," 419
"Your Hit Parade," 337, 338, 344, 355, 356, 386, 388, 389
"Your Song" (John), 467
"You Send Me," 410

"You Tell Me Your Dream" (Daniels), 291, 297
"You've Been a Good Old Wagon But You Done Broke Down" (Harney), 318
"You've Got a Friend" (Taylor), 467
You Were Never Lovelier (Kern), 344
"You Win Again," 419

Zerrahn, Carl, 191
Ziegfeld, Florenz, 350
Ziegfeld Follies, 332, 333, 336
"Zip Coon," 123, 124, 125, 206
Zorina, Vera, 335
Zukor, Adolph, 328